CITIZENSHIP, INFILTRATION AND NRC

About the Author

For more than three decades, Sarajit Kumar Chatterjee, a former member of the Indian Police Service, has been consistently engaged in in-depth studies of policies that continue to have an impact on all Indians. His earlier books include *Communalism and Constitution, Disintegration and Constitution, Panchayati Raj and views of the Founding Fathers, Governor's Role in Indian Constitution, The Scheduled Castes in India, Educational Development of Scheduled Castes:Looking Ahead, North-East India: Disintegration and Discontent, SCs, STs and OBCs in the Indian Polity and Communalism from Indian Perspective.*

CITIZENSHIP, INFILTRATION AND NRC

Sarajit Kumar Chatterjee

CONCEPT PUBLISHING COMPANY PVT. LTD.
NEW DELHI - 110 059

ISBN: 978-93-5594-642-3

First Published 2023

Published and Printed by

Since 1974

Concept Publishing Company Pvt. Ltd.
A/15-16, Commercial Block, Mohan Garden
New Delhi-110059 (India)
T : +91-11-41101460
E: publishing@conceptpub.com, *W*: www.conceptpub.com

Cataloging in Publication--Courtesy: D.K. Agencies (P) Ltd. <docinfo@dkagencies.com>

Chatterjee, S.K. (Sarajit Kumar), author.
Citizenship, infiltration and NRC / Sarajit Kumar Chatterjee.
pages cm
Includes bibliographical references and index.
ISBN 9789355946423

1. Citizenship--India. 2. Noncitizens--India. 3. Illegal immigration--India. 4. India--Population--Registers. 5. Bangladesh--Emigration and immigration. 6. India. Citizenship Amendment Act, 2019. I. Title.

LCC KNS2140.C43 2023 | DDC 323.60954 23

Dedicated to
my daughter and son-in-law
Anuradha and Kalyan
With love and affection

Preface

Human beings started moving out of their habitats tens of thousands of years ago and are still moving in one form or the other. They traversed through mountain passes, valleys, deserts and marshy lands, crossed rivers, rivulets and even oceans, faced hostile climates and endured all sorts of physical discomforts. In the process, the colour of their skin and even the colour of their hair, their physical features, languages and cultures changed. New civilizations grew and perished. But they never gave up their journey. It is still continuing.

In course of time, large human settlements developed where humans lived in groups. These settlements were called cities. This development took place when city-states were the order of the day. The residents of the cities were called citizens, identified by the city where they lived. When the cities were merged to form a larger settlement, the settlement became known as a country or a state, but its residents were still called citizens, now identified as part of a particular country or state. Their identity is linked up with the country they live in—Indian, Chinese, Japanese and so on and so forth. Their area of habitation increased from a city to a state but they continued to be known as citizen, not otherwise. Citizenship now encapsulates the habitants of earmarked territories called country/state, big or small.

A person is a citizen of a well-defined geographical entity called a nation-state and continues to be so till he relinquishes it or is deprived of it. A migrant is a citizen of the country of origin and continues to be so till he gets the citizenship of the country of destination and relinquishes the earlier one. A refugee is also a citizen of the country of origin and retains it till he is not recognized as such by the country of origin. In that case, he becomes a stateless person – a person who is not a citizen of any country. The ten lakh Rohingya refugees from Myanmar now accommodated in Bangladesh camps will be stateless persons if Myanmar refuses to take them back. There were as many as 10 million stateless persons in the whole world as in June 2018.

A citizen is entitled to have certain rights and privileges, generally enshrined in the country's constitution, and is obliged to perform certain duties. The most important right is to elect a person of his choice or get elected in the country's elections.

All countries frame rules for the acquisition and termination of citizenship. India is no exception. On attaining independence, the Constituent Assembly devoted much of its time and energy over the issue of citizenship. It decided to give unfettered power to the Indian Parliament to enact laws for the acquisition and termination of citizenship and all other matters relating to citizenship. Indian Parliament is the supreme body in this regard.

But independence was not an unmixed blessing. It brought vivisection of the country into two, nay three, parts, more or less on the basis of religion though our national leaders refused to accept it. The exchange of population in the western sector was effected by the people themselves. No such exchange of population in the eastern sector was thought of but it did not stand in the way of people, especially of the minority communities, to cross over to the Indian side for safety and security. This movement continued for a very long time so much so that East Pakistan, now Bangladesh, is almost denuded of minority population. These people, without any organised help from the government, poured in and they are now pejoratively called infiltrators or illegal immigrants.

If the policy that was pursued in the western sector was followed in the eastern sector – Muhammad Ali Jinnah had called for such an exchange of population – the menace of infiltration/illegal immigration would not have assumed such a gigantic proportion. And to cap it, not only the minority communities from Bangladesh crossed over, the majority community from that country also saw a fertile ground in this side of the border for eking out a living.

Most of the people from East Bengal after crossing over settled down in Assam, Tripura and West Bengal. The animosity against the Bengali-speaking people in Assam gave birth to movements to drive them away from Assam but the parties who came to power riding on the anti-Bengali sentiments did precious little to stop infiltration from across the border. So the menace of infiltration not only of Bengali-speaking Hindus but also of Bengali-speaking Muslims continued. Given the anti-Bengali mentality in Assam, the infiltrators spread over to other parts of India—even to Delhi, Bengaluru, Mumbai and other corners of India.

The Supreme Court-monitored exercise of preparation of National Registrar of Citizens (NRC) in Assam did produce lists of NRC-included and NRC-excluded persons but these lists are so much 'flawed' that almost all the political parties and organisations are demanding revision of the lists so as to make them as much error-free as possible. In the meantime, the BJP has conferred citizenship on all religious minorities of the three Muslim majority countries of Pakistan, Afghanistan and Bangladesh by amending the Citizenship Act, 1955.

BJP's efforts have drawn flak from the North-eastern States. These states are now proposing to insulate them from the so-called 'outsiders' either by further strengthening the anti-immigration measures like the Inner Line Permit (ILP) or by resorting to their own version of the NRC. BJP sought to buy peace by amending the Citizenship Amendment Bill to accommodate the North-eastern states. Sub-nationalism is in full flow in these States.

In the rest of the country, the protests against the CAA was mounted highlighting its divisive nature. In thc meantime, the Central Government unfolded its commitment to cover the entire country with the NRC. As a prelude to the preparation of the NRC, it readied itself to prepare the NPR along with the Census of 2020-21. Such an attempt spawned an anti-CAA-NPR-NRC movement throughout the length and breadth of the country. The anti-CAA-NPR-NCR movement is the third Pan-India stir in post-colonial India. The first was the JP movement launched by Jaya Prakash Narayan against the autocratic rule of Indira Gandhi in 1975-77 and the second was the Jan Lokpal movement of 2011 led by Anna Hazare against endemic corruption. But unlike the first two, the third mass movement has no leaders. It is a spontaneous uprising of the student community, the youth of the nation and the women against the CAA, later encompassing the NPR and the NRC as well. Once the combo is implemented, the nation could witness the largest 'statelessness' crisis the world has ever witnessed.

In view of this, some other method of counting the citizens and segregating them from the non-citizens should be devised so that the objective of killing the snake without breaking the rod is achieved. After all, it cannot be the policy of any elected government to prepare an NRC with a preconceived target of exclusions thus degenerating it into an instrument of violations of human rights, endless misery, sufferings, harassment, family disruptions, pauperization and even causing NRC-panic deaths.

February 6, 2023 **Sarajit Kumar Chatterjee**

Contents

1
Citizenship Issue in the Constituent Assembly

Open economics, free trade, easy movement of capital—even those who share this vision of the world want to maintain sovereign boundaries when it comes to matters of immigration. Indeed, most governments cannot conceive of the idea of statehood and sovereignty without notions for citizenship and exclusion, distinction between those who belong and those who do not. The attempt to erode this distinction among states within the European Community represents one of the great contemporary triumphs, but even here there has been a dissenting voice in the U.K. who deserted the European Union on the question of unbridled immigration from the rest of the EU countries.[1]

As "British" India was at that time under the Crown, its people were British subjects and their national status and rights of citizenship were governed by the British Nationality Acts passed by the Parliament of the United Kingdom from time to time. The fundamental principle governing the laws of British nationality was that every person born within any part of British territory became at and from birth a British subject. The Indian States did not form part of British territory, and their subjects were not "British subjects". These States had no international personality and under international law their subjects enjoyed the status of British protected persons.

The British Nationality and Status of Aliens Act, first enacted in 1914 and subsequently elaborated in 1918, 1922, 1933 and 1943, did not prevent differential treatment being accorded to different classes of British subjects as to immigration or otherwise; and local nationality could be conferred by the authority of the Legislature of the British possession concerned. Thus, the Immigration into India Act, 1924, as well as its repealing Act, the Reciprocity Act, 1943, empowered the Government of India to regulate on the basis of reciprocity the entry and residence of British subjects domiciled in other British possessions. Local naturalization was regulated by the Indian Naturalization Act, 1926 which provided for the grant of naturalization to persons not being subjects of any State in Europe or America or of any State of which an Indian British subject was prevented by law from becoming a national by naturalization. Nevertheless, the basic concept underlying the 1914 Act was that of a common British nationality for all subjects of the Crown throughout the Empire and the Commonwealth.

The concept had grown out of and crystallized the common law doctrine of allegiance to the King. Separate nationality statutes—accepting and usually incorporating the United Kingdom legislation—were enacted by the Dominions of Canada, Australia, New Zealand and South Africa. So far as India was concerned, Section 110 of the Government of India Act, 1935, placed it beyond the competence of the Legislatures in India to make any law affecting the law of British Nationality. This position remained unchanged at the time of independence.

The concept of Indian citizenship did not exist prior to November 26, 1949, when the Constituent Assembly adopted the Constitution of India, bringing into force at once the provisions relating to citizenship. Citizenship as a concept is not the contribution of modernity. Aristotle wrote about it and so did many others later on. But, the earlier concepts suffered from certain limitations, which are sought to be done away in present times. First, the earlier concept of citizenship had much more to do with duties of individuals towards the monarch or the state rather than rights of individuals *vis-à-vis* the state. Second, even when they spoke of rights, it was a highly restrictive citizenry, which did not include slaves, women, uneducated persons and other non-propertied classes. Third, the concept dealt with just a few civic and political rights rather than the breadth of rights now recognised, while socio-economic rights were invariably excluded. Essentially, the people were subjects rather than rights-bearing citizens. Citizenship in present times becomes crucial for enforcement of rights or even access to welfare schemes.

Presently, loosely speaking, citizenship means individuals who are treated equally before the law within a confined territory and who have civil, political, social and economic rights. In India, rights-bearing citizenship crystallised only from the time of the enactment of the Constitution. Some kind of rudimentary form of citizenship did develop even earlier. Since the beginning of the 20th century, a limited franchise was available. Under the Government of India Act, 1919, this was partially extended. This was further extended under the Government of India Act,

1935. But, even the extended franchise had educational, income and property ownership conditionalities, and not more than one-sixth of the adult population could vote. The powers given to these legislative bodies were very limited, and there was no concept of rights—fundamental or otherwise—under these acts.

Most of the colonialists believed that India was not even potentially a nation, since according to them, such a society, divided on caste, linguistic and religious lines could not yield a conception of citizenship as citizenship was an individual concept while in Indian society, individuals were always mediated through families, castes, clans, tribes, communities, etc.

Even when they spoke of citizenship in the context of India, it was mainly in terms of obedience to the British rule and the justification for this. Territoriality is a precondition for citizenship, and once India was to be independent and decided to go in for the republican form of government, it became essential for the Constitution to deal with citizenship.

The subject of citizenship was one of the first matters to engage the attention of the Constituent Assembly. The citizenship provisions took an exceptionally long time—nearly two years—to reach the stage of finality. A number of drafts were considered by several committees and sub-committees. As the Chairman of the Drafting Committee observed later, no other article in the Draft Constitution except one gave "such a headache" as the provision on citizenship. "I do not know", said Ambedkar, "how many drafts were prepared and how many were destroyed as being inadequate to cover all the cases which it was thought necessary and desirable to cover."[2]

Of the several bodies that deliberated on the question of citizenship in the initial stages, the Sub-Committee on Fundamental Rights was the first. The drafts on fundamental rights submitted to the sub-committee by K.M.Munshi and B.N.Rau contained provisions relating to citizenship. These were examined by the sub-committee on 24 March, 1947, and it was decided to adopt B.N.Rau's draft in the following modified form:

> Every person born or naturalized in the Union and subject to the jurisdiction thereof shall be a citizen of the Union. Further provisions governing the accrual, acquisition and termination of Union citizenship may be made by the law of the Union.[3]

The sub-committee incorporated this provision in its draft report of 3 April, 1947.[4] In his explanatory notes, B.N.Rau, the Constitutional Adviser, pointed out that while the first part of the clause had been adopted from Article XIV, Sec 1, of the U.S. Constitution, the second part was intended to cover the naturalization laws which might be passed by the Union or which might be adopted by the Constitution. He added that citizenship or nationality being part of the subject of foreign affairs, and as such an exclusively Union subject, there could be no provincial citizenship as distinct from the citizenship of the Union.[5]

In his comments on the Draft Report, K.T.Shah observed that the words "the accrual, acquisition and termination of Union citizenship" used in the clause would not necessarily cover the retention of citizenship and might not, therefore, include the case of a woman who, originally a citizen of the Union, married a non-citizen but desired to retain her citizenship of birth.[6]

Reconsidering the clause on 14 April, the sub-committee decided to omit references to "accrual, acquisition and termination of"[7] and, with this change, include the provision in its report submitted on 16 April, to the Advisory Committee on Fundamental Rights, Minorities and Tribal and Excluded Areas.[8]

The clause came up for discussion before the Advisory Committee on 21 April. The discussion centred mainly round the question whether the units in the proposed Union should be entitled to provide for separate citizenship rights. Towards the end of an animated discussion, Alladi Krishnaswamy Ayyar clinched the issue by affirming that while certain qualifications might be added to citizenship within a particular unit, there could be only one citizenship for the whole of the Indian Union. Redrafted on a suggestion by C. Rajagopalachari, the clause was amended by the Committee to read:

> Every person born in the Union or naturalized in the Union according to its laws and subject to the jurisdiction thereof shall be a citizen of the Union.[9]

This short and simple definition of citizenship was incorporated as clause 3 in the interim report of the Advisory Committee submitted to the Constituent Assembly on 23 April.[10]

But when the citizenship clause, as recommended by the Advisory Committee, was moved by Sardar Vallabhbhai Patel in the Assembly on 29 April, 1947, he added another para to this clause which read as follows:

> Further provision governing Union citizenship may be made by the laws of the Union.

He said that the Advisory Committee had originally passed this clause in that form but in printing it was omitted. On his suggestion, K.M.Munshi moved a proposal to add the above words at the end of this clause.[11]

Alladi Krishnaswamy Ayyar explained that there were two different theories on which citizenship laws in various countries were based. In some of the European countries citizenship was determined by blood and race (*lex sanguinis*), regardless of the place of birth while under the Anglo-American system citizenship was determined mainly on grounds of birth (*lex soli*). The Assembly had to make up its mind whether to follow the racial principle or the birth principle. The Advisory Committee had obviously chosen the latter inasmuch as the main idea underlying the existing clause was that a person born in India must get Indian citizenship even if his parents were foreigners. Both Alladi Krihshnaswamy Ayyar and K.M.Munshi emphasized that the clause intended merely to lay down the indispensable conditions for citizenship, as it was difficult to exhaust by enumeration in a Constitution Act the many exceptional cases that might arise: they could be taken care of by a separate Nationality Act to be enacted by the Union Parliament.

The clause generally provoked some opposition and several members including President Rajendra Prasad had misgivings about its appropriateness. The apprehension was expressed that it was too widely worded and might confer citizenship on every person born in India, whether his parents were Indian citizens or not. As a citizen he would be entitled to all the rights and privileges of citizenship: at the same time, he might maintain the nationality of his parents and enjoy the privileges of that nationality. Under the clauses on fundamental rights he might acquire and hold property and the right of following any trade or profession in the country. All this, it was felt, would naturally conflict with the interests of the true citizens of India who had no other nationality. Finally, on a suggestion from Alladi Krishnaswamy Ayyar, it was decided to refer the matter to a small committee of distinguished jurists for further examination and advice.[12]

On 30 April, the President appointed an *ad hoc* committee on citizenship consisting of S.Varadachariar (a former judge of the Federal Court) as chairman and Bakshi Tek Chand, B.L. Mitter, Alladi Krishnaswamy Ayyar, K.N. Katju, K.M. Munshi and B.R. Ambedkar as members. Reporting on the following day, the committee submitted a redrafted clause:

> Every person born in the Union and subject to its jurisdiction; every person either of whose parents was, at the time of such person's birth, a citizen of the Union; and every person naturalized in the Union shall be a citizen of the Union.

Further provision regarding the acquisition and termination of Union citizenship may be made by the law of the Union.

Recommending the draft for adoption by the Assembly, the *ad hoc* committee observed:

> The inclusion in the clause of children born in the Union even of non-citizens, provided they are subject to Union jurisdiction, is a well-marked feature of Anglo-American public law. This principle has been accepted in the Indian Naturalization Act, 1926. There is some authority for the view that the children of visiting foreigners are on the same footing as the children of foreign ambassadors and would as such be regarded as non-citizens even if born in the Union, because of the qualifying phrase "and subject to its jurisdiction." In any event, such cases are likely to be so few and far between that it is unnecessary in our opinion to make a special exception to exclude them from citizenship. As regards the possibility of double nationality, this is a well-known phenomenon, but it can be provided against by appropriate provisions in the Union Naturalization Law calling upon the person concerned to choose one or the other. For this purpose, the clause makes express provision for supplementary legislation terminating citizenship.[13]

When the clause, as redrafted by the *ad hoc* committee was moved for consideration in the Assembly on 2 May, K. Santhanam proposed an amendment seeking to provide that persons born or naturalized in India before the commencement of the Union and subject to its jurisdiction would be citizens of the Union. The redraft, as proposed by the *ad hoc* committee, he pointed out, covered only persons born after the Union came into being; it did not cover those who were born earlier and would already be within the jurisdiction of the Union at the time it came into existence.[14] Santhanam's amendment received support from Rajagopalachari, Sidhva and Ambedkar. But Vallabhbahi Patel, K.M. Munshi and Alladi Krishnaswamy Ayyar considered it unnecessary at that stage to consider the question raised by Santhanam as it was still uncertain what would be the shape of the Union of India in the matter of territories and whether any part of India was going to be separated from the rest. When finality was reached in regard to these matters, the necessary adjustments between the parts—if there were to be parts—could be considered. Alladi Krishnaswamy Ayyar conceded that the question raised by Santhanam had not been considered by the *ad hoc* committee and required careful examination. Finally, the clause was held over for further consideration by the Advisory Committee.[15]

While formulating, towards the end of May, the memorandum on the Union Constitution for the use of the members of the Union Constitution Committee, the Constitutional Adviser removed the citizenship provisions from the list of fundamental rights and placed them in a separate Part—Part II of the memorandum—under the heading "Citizenship." This Part contained three clauses—clauses 1 to 3—which read as follows:

> 1. At the commencement of this Constitution, every person domiciled in the territories included within the Union and subject to its jurisdiction—
>   (a) who has been ordinarily resident in those territories for not less than five years immediately preceding that date, or
>   (b) who, or whose parents, or either of whose parents, was or were born in India
>
>   shall be a citizen of the Union:
>
>   Provided that any such person being a citizen of any other State may, in accordance with Union law, elect not to accept the citizenship hereby conferred.
> 2. After the commencement of this Constitution—
>   (a) every person who is born in the territories included within the Union and subject to its jurisdiction,
>   (b) every person who is naturalized in accordance with Union law, and
>   (c) every person, either of whose parents was, at the time of such a person's birth a citizen of the Union
>
>   shall be a citizen of the Union.
> 3. Further provisions governing the acquisition and termination of Union citizenship may be made by Union law.[16]

B.N. Rau explained that clause 1 was largely based on article 3 of the 1922 Constitution of the Irish Free State, while clauses 2 and 3 followed the provisions suggested by the *ad hoc* committee on Citizenship. He suggested that clause 2 would not be absolutely necessary if the Union Constitution Committee could agree to leave the matter to be regulated by Union law under clause 3. The suggestion meant in effect that the Constitution might confine itself to specifying who would be citizens at the commencement of the Constitution, the rest being left to Union law.[17]

With the decision to partition India as a result of the British government's announcement of 3 June, 1947, a series of consequential changes and adjustments became necessary, both inside and outside the Constituent Assembly. A joint sub-committee of the Union and Provincial Constitution Committees decided on 8 June that the question of citizenship should be re-examined by the *ad hoc* committee as an inevitable sequel to the announcement.[18]

Some representations from individuals received by the Secretariat of the Assembly during the last week of June and suggesting the formulation of certain provisions in the light of the changed conditions that would follow the partition of the country were also referred to the *ad hoc* committee.

Among those who had sent such representations, the Government Solicitor, Dhiren Mitra, stressed the need for considering the important question of nationality in so far as it had a bearing on a man's employment in public service and his status abroad. A member of the Constituent Assembly, and later also a member of the Constitution Drafting Committee, D.P.Khaitan, suggested that the definition of citizenship should cover the case of a woman who, on being married to a citizen of India, would automatically become an Indian citizen. A large number of marriages were likely to take place between the citizens of India and those of Pakistan, as also between the citizens of India and those of the Indian States. In the absence of such a provision, therefore, India would be "full of what would legally be foreign women." A member of the Legislative Assembly of Sind, Ghanashyam J. Shivdasani, pleaded for adequate provision being made for people of the seceding areas who desired to continue their Indian citizenship.[19]

When the Constitutional Adviser's memorandum came up before the Union Constitution Committee on 30 June, consideration of the clauses relating to the citizenship was deferred until after the *ad hoc* committee had made its recommendations.[20] In the report submitted to the Assembly on 4 July, the Union Constitution Committee incorporated the citizenship provisions contained in the memorandum without any change, except that the word "Union" was replaced by the word "Federation" and explanations were added for the words "domicile" and "federal law". The clauses appeared in the report as follows:

1. At the date of commencement of this Constitution, every person domiciled in the territories subject to the jurisdiction of the Federation—

(a) who has been ordinarily resident in those territories for not less than five years immediately preceding that date, or

(b) who, or whose parents, or either of whose parents, was or were born in India

shall be a citizen of the Federation:

Provided that any such person being a citizen of any other State may, in accordance with Federal law, elect not to accept the citizenship hereby conferred.

Explanation—For the purposes of this clause—

"Domicile" has the same meaning as in the Indian Succession Act, 1925.

2. After the commencement of this Constitution—

(a) every person who is born in the territories subject to the jurisdiction of the Federation;

(b) every person who is naturalized in accordance with Federal law, and

(c) every person, either of whose parents was, at the time of such a person's birth, a citizen of the Federation,

shall be a citizen of the Federation.

3. Further provisions governing the acquisition and termination of Federal citizenship may be made by Federal law.

Explanation—In this Constitution, unless otherwise requires, "Federal law" includes any existing law as in force within the territories subject to the jurisdiction of the Federation.[21]

The Union Constitution Committee observed that the draft was meant merely as a basis for discussion and was subject to the decisions of the *ad hoc* committee. Nevertheless, it recognised the inappropriateness of inserting a rigid provision about citizenship and agreed with B.N.Rau's view that the Constitution should confine itself to specifying citizenship at the commencement of the Constitution under clause 1; that clause 2 could be omitted; and that the question of citizenship after the commencement of the Constitution, should be left to be regulated by law under clause 3. In this connection, the Committee quoted with approval the views of a law journal, the Calcutta Weekly Notes:

> It is not possible to define exhaustively the conditions of nationality, whether by birth or naturalization, by the Constitution. If certain conditions are laid down by the Constitution, difficulties may arise regarding the interpretation of future legislation which may appear to be contrary to or

> to depart in any way from them...It would, in our opinion, therefore, be better to specify who would be citizens of the Indian Union at the date when the Constitution comes into force as in the Constitution of the Irish Free State and leave the law regarding nationality to be provided for by legislation by the Indian Union in accordance with the accepted principles of private international law.[22]

Meeting on 12 July, the *ad hoc* committee decided that for being a citizen at the commencement of the Constitution it should not be necessary to have resided in the Union territory for a period of five years. Clause 1 of the memorandum was accordingly redrafted.[23] The redraft came up at a joint meeting of the Union and Provincial Constitution Committees on 18 July. Its consideration was postponed till before the October session of the Assembly, presumably because this redraft was also found to be inadequate in certain respects and it was referred back to the *ad hoc* committee for further scrutiny.[24]

While moving thc report of the Union Constitution Committee for consideration in the Assembly on 21 July, 1947, Nehru observed that the subject of citizenship was still under examination by the *ad hoc* committee. There was consequently no discussion in the Assembly at that stage on the citizenship clauses of the report.[25]

In the draft prepared by the Constitutional Adviser in October, 1947, there was provision, in addition to the incorporation of all the citizenship clauses as earlier recommended by the *ad hoc* committee, for the large number of displaced persons who had come or were still coming to India from Pakistan as a result of partition. In Part II, as many as five clauses, viz., clauses 4, 5, 6, 6A and 7 were devoted to the subject of citizenship. These were as follows:[26]

4. In this Part, unless the context otherwise requires, the expression "Federal law" includes any existing law as in force for the time being.
5. At the date of commencement of this Constitution, every person—
   (a) who, or either of whose parents, or any of whose grand-parents was born in the territories included on that date within the Federation, or
   (b) who on that date has his domicile in those territories,
   shall be a citizen of the Federation:
   Provided that where any such person is a citizen of another State, he may, in accordance with the provisions made in that behalf by

any Federal law, elect not to accept the citizenship conferred by this section.

Explanation: A person shall, for the purposes of this section, be deemed to have his domicile in any territory if he has a domicile therein within the meaning of Part II of the Indian Succession Act, 1925:

Provided that notwithstanding anything contained in Section 11 of the said Act, a person shall, for the purposes of this section, be deemed to have acquired a domicile in the territories included within the Federation if—

(a) before the date of commencement of this Constitution he has made and deposited in some office within those territories appointed for the purpose by the provincial Government a declaration in writing under his hand of his desire to acquire such domicile; and

(b) he has been resident within those territories for a period of not less than one month immediately preceding the time of his making such declaration.

6. After the commencement of this Constitution—

(a) any person who is born in the territories of the Federation not being the child of an alien having diplomatic immunity therein or otherwise not subject of its jurisdiction;

(b) any person either of whose parents at the time of that person's birth a citizen of the Federation and who fulfils any of the following conditions, namely:

(i) such parent was born within the territories of the federation; or

(ii) such parent had become a citizen of the Federation by naturalization or by reason of inclusion of new territory; or

(iii) such parent was at the time of such person's birth in the service of the Federation; or

(iv) such person's birth was registered in accordance with the provisions of any Federal law;

(c) any person who is naturalized in accordance with the provisions of any Federal law;

(d) any person born on board a ship of the Federation, whether in foreign territorial waters or not

shall be a citizen of the Federation.

6A. Any person who is under any acknowledgment of allegiance or adherence to a foreign power or is a subject or citizen or entitled to the rights and privileges of a subject or a citizen of a foreign power shall be disqualified for being chosen as and for being a member of either House of the Parliament of the Federation or of the Legislature of any unit.

7. Further provision may be made by Federal law for regulating the acquisition and termination of citizenship of the Federation and in particular for avoiding double citizenship and the provisions of sections 5, 6 and 6A shall have effect subject to the provisions of any such law.

In a Note dated 7 October, 1947, the Constitutional Adviser explained the rationale behind the incorporations of these provisions thus:

> Clauses 4 to 7 deal with citizenship. Clause 5 deals with persons born before the date of commencement of the Constitution and clause 6 with those born afterwards.
>
> Clause 5 has been drafted in very wide terms so as to make provision not only for ordinary cases but also for the special case of the refugees that have been pouring into India. Sub-clause (a) confers citizenship upon every person who, or either of whose parents, or any of whose grand-parents, was born in the territories initially included within the Federation. Although the laws of some States confer nationality upon descendants of their nationals without any limit as to the number of generations, the best authorities consider that there should be a limit and that it would be reasonable to stop at the second generation. The draft sub-clause does not therefore go beyond the grandchildren of persons born in India.
>
> We have, however, to cover the case of those persons who and whose parents and grand-parents may have been born in Pakistan and who have now been compelled by circumstances beyond their control to migrate to India. Such persons are not covered by sub-clause (a). Sub-clause (b) accordingly provides that every person who, at the date of commencement of the new constitution, has his domicile in India will be a citizen of the Federation. The proviso to the explanation under clause 5 prescribes a specially easy mode of acquiring a domicile in India for the purposes of the clause without any prejudice to any other mode. All that the immigrant has to do is to reside in

> India for a month and then to make and deposit in a prescribed office a written declaration of his desire to acquire domicile in India. These steps should be taken before the commencement of the new constitution. To make it quiet clear that this special mode of acquiring domicile is without prejudice to any other mode, we might insert the words "and without prejudice to any other mode of acquiring a domicile" after the words "said Act" in the proviso to the explanation. In order to discourage double citizenship and prevent divided loyalties, clause 6A has been inserted. The effect of this clause is that any person who is under any acknowledgment of allegiance or adherence to a foreign power or is a subject or citizen of a foreign power is disqualified for membership of any legislature in India whether Central or Provincial. The provision is on the lines of section 44(i) of the Commonwealth of Australia Act.
>
> Clause 6 deals with persons who may be born after the commencement of the new Constitution. This clause is on the lines of the corresponding provision in the British Nationality and Status of Aliens Act, 1914.
>
> Clause 7 emphasizes the unqualified power of the Federal Parliament to make further provision for regulating citizenship so that, if either clause 5 or clause 6 is regarded as going too far, it will be open to the Federal Parliament to narrow the circle of citizenship within any desired limits. The Federal Parliament will also have unrestricted power to make provision for avoiding or terminating double citizenship.[27]

The citizenship provisions as outlined in the Constitutional Adviser's Draft Constitution were discussed by the Drafting Committee on 30 October, 1947[28], 19 January, 1948[29], and 4[30], 5[31], and 6[32] February, 1948. When the Drafting Committee was considering the Constitutional Adviser's draft, S.Dutt, a senior official of the Ministry of External Affairs and Commonwealth Relations, emphatically urged in his letter of 5 December, 1947 that "the unfortunate brothers and sisters" who had to leave their homes in Eastern and Western Pakistan should not be refused citizenship simply because they were born in Pakistan. "The framers of the Constitution", he said, "should look into the matter graciously, at the same time cautiously". The Drafting Committee gave anxious and prolonged consideration to the question of devising a suitable draft. Noting that the point raised by Dutt had already been anticipated by the Constitutional

Adviser, the Committee accepted the basic principles contained in clauses 5 and 7 of the Constitutional Adviser's Draft and decided (i) to omit clauses 4 and 6—the former defining federal law and the latter providing for citizenship after the commencement of the Constitution; and (ii) to transfer clause 6A relating to the disqualification of foreign nationals for membership of the Legislature to the relevant Part dealing with the Legislature. Clauses 5 and 7 were redrafted and included as articles 5 and 6 in the Draft Constitution prepared and submitted to the President of the Constituent Assembly on 21 February, 1948 by the Drafting Committee. These read as follows[33]:

5. At the date of commencement of this Constitution—
    (a) every person who or either of whose parents or any of whose grand-parents was born in the territory of India as defined in this Constitution and who has not made his permanent abode in any foreign State after the first day of April, 1947; and
    (b) every person who or either of whose parents or any of whose grand-parents was born in India as defined in the Government of India Act, 1935 (as originally enacted), or in Burma, Ceylon or Malaya, and who has his domicile in the territory of India as defined in this Constitution;
    (c) shall be a citizen of India, provided that he has not acquired the citizenship of any foreign State before the date of commencement of this Constitution.

    Explanation: For the purpose of clause (b) of this article, a person shall be deemed to have his domicile in the territory of India—
    (i) if he would have had his domicile in such territory under Part II of the Indian Succession Act, 1925, had the provisions of that Part been applicable to him, or
    (ii) if he has, before the date of commencement of this Constitution, deposited in the office of the District Magistrate a declaration in writing of his desire to acquire such domicile and has resided in the territory of India for at least one month before the date of the declaration.
6. Parliament may, by law, make further provision regarding the acquisition and termination of citizenship and all other matters relating thereto.

The Drafting Committee in its forwarding letter to the President of the Constituent Assembly noted that it had given anxious and prolonged consideration to the question of citizenship of the Union. The committee had thought it necessary that, in order to be a citizen of the Union at its inception, a person must have some kind of territorial connection with the Union, whether by birth, or descent, or domicile. The committee doubted whether it would be wise to admit as citizens who, without any such connection with the territory of India, may be prepared to swear allegiance to the Union; for if other States were to copy such a provision, we might have within the Union a large number of persons who, though born and permanently resident therein, would owe allegiance to a foreign State. The committee however, kept in view the requirements of the large number of displaced persons who have had to migrate to India within recent months, and had provided for them specially easy mode of acquiring domicile and, thereby, citizenship. What they had to do (assuming that they or either of their parents or any of their grand-parents were born in India or Pakistan) was—

(a) to declare before a District Magistrate in India that they desire to acquire a domicile in India, and
(b) to reside in India for at least a month before the declaration.[34]

When the Draft Constitution was published and circulated for eliciting opinion, a number of comments and suggestions for amendment of draft articles 5 and 6 were received from members and others. From among the members, B. Pattabhi Sitaramayya, Shrimati G. Durgabai, Thakurdas Bhargava, B.V.Keskar, T.T.Krishnamachari, M. Ananthasayanam Ayyangar and K.Santhanam proposed two amendments to article 5. The first sought to replace the words "permanent abode" in clause (a) by the word "domicile" and to change the date, "first day of April 1947" to "fifteenth day of February 1947". The second proposed the removal of all restrictions like the depositing a declaration in the office of the District Magistrate envisaged in clause (ii) of the Explanation, and the entitlement to Indian domicile of every displaced person from Pakistan who migrated after the first day of April 1947.

Commenting on these amendments, B.N.Rau pointed out that the term "permanent abode" had been used because the term "domicile" was vague and a foreign State might give it an artificial definition. The date, 1 April, 1947, was chosen as the crucial date because, according to information available, the exodus from what later became Pakistan did not begin before that date. Dealing with the suggestion that every displaced person from Pakistan who migrated to India after April 1947 should automatically be entitled to Indian citizenship, he also pointed out that this proposal would allow every temporary migrant the right of citizenship. This would be unwise.[35]

A member of the Madras Legislative Assembly, K.Bhashyam, proposed that in the matter of citizenship rights under clause 5(a), there should be a positive enactment to the effect that a citizen should have either a permanent abode in India or the intention to reside permanently in India. B.N.Rau pointed out that the sponsor of the proposal obviously wanted to impose domiciliary qualification as a condition precedent to the acquisition of citizenship in every case and his intention seemed to be to exclude those persons who, or either of whose parents or any of whose grand-parents, were born in India, but who had made their permanent abode in any country outside India. If such a proposal was accepted *in toto*, he observed, those persons who, or either of whose parents, or any of whose grand-parents, were born in India and who were staying in any country outside India but had not acquired the citizenship of such country, would be left out.[36]

The West Bengal Legislative Assembly proposed (1) the omission of reference to the Indian Succession Act in clause (i) of the Explanation and its substitution by the actual definition of domicile, viz. 'fixed habitation'; and (2) the replacing of the reference to the District Magistrate in clause (ii) of the Explanation by a reference to an officer appointed in that behalf by the provincial government.

Commenting on these suggestions, B.N.Rau pointed out that the object of referring to the Indian Succession Act was to apply all the provisions of Part II of the Act to the determination of the domicile of a person without reproducing them *in extenso*. As for the second suggestion, the purpose of which presumably was that the District Magistrate might not be easily approachable for depositing the declaration of domicile, he felt that the object of the amendment would be met if in clause (ii) of the Explanation, after the words "District Magistrate", the words "or such officer as may be authorized in writing in that behalf by the District Magistrate" were inserted.[37]

The editor of the *Indian Law Review* and some members of the Calcutta Bar criticized the definition of citizenship in draft article 5 as narrow. The definition, they considered, did not include persons who were born or had a fixed habitation in Pakistan but had spent their life in India in the pursuit of their profession, calling or vocation, because domicile as defined in the Indian Succession Act excluded such persons. Commenting on this criticism, B.N.Rau pointed out that the Drafting Committee was definitely of the opinion that persons who were born or had a fixed habitation in Pakistan could be treated as citizens of the Union of India at its inception only if they had some kind of territorial connection with the Union. If there was any doubt as to whether such persons had made their fixed habitation in India and thereby acquired a domicile under the Indian Succession Act, they could avail themselves of the easy mode of acquiring a domicile under clause (ii) of the Explanation by making and depositing in the office of the District Magistrate a declaration of their desire to acquire such domicile.[38]

Captain R.V.Brockman. Private Secretary to Mountbatten, enquired how the provision in the citizenship clause would square up with the principles of the British Commonwealth. Replying to the point, B.N.Rau admitted that the citizenship provisions had been "drafted without any reference to any British Commonwealth law of citizenship": article 5 was not intended to be the entire law on Indian citizenship and further provisions under draft article 6 would have to be made by the Indian Parliament "as early as possible."[39]

Justice Meredith of the Patna High Court commented that draft article 5 left uncertain the position of Europeans in regard to the acquisition of Indian citizenship. Suggesting the insertion of some provision for naturalization, he contended that under the existing articles there was no constitutional protection for non-citizens permanently resident or having their domicile in the country: citizenship appeared to have been made an essential qualification for practically every appointment under the Union of India.

The Constitutional Adviser noted that the point raised by Justice Meredith was considered at a meeting of the Drafting Committee. As a result of the discussion, it was decided to amend article 5 in the following manner:

> 5. At the date of commencement of this Constitution—
>   (a) every person who or either of whose parents or any of whose grand-parents was born in the territory of India, and
>   (b) every person who has his domicile in the territory of India, shall be a citizen of India, provided that he has not voluntarily acquired the citizenship of any foreign country.
>
> *Explanation:* For the purpose of clause (b) of this article, a person shall be deemed to have his domicile in the territory of India if he would have had his domicile in such territory under Part II of the Indian Succession Act, 1925, had the provisions of that Part been applicable to him.[40]

The All-Burma Indian Congress urged that every Indian resident in Burma who was an Indian before 1 April, 1937, when that State was separated, should have the unqualified option of choosing the citizenship either of India or Pakistan; and that this right should also be extended to those overseas Indians who were born in what subsequently became Pakistan territory. The Congress further desired that an easier process of reacquisition of citizenship might be prescribed for Indians resident in Burma who had taken Burmese citizenship but later wanted to reacquire Indian citizenship.

The Constitutional Adviser noted that the comments of the All-Burma Indian Congress were made on 20 February, 1948, and could not therefore have been directed against the provision in the present Draft which was published on 26 February, 1948. Actually the Draft in the present form met them to a large extent.[41]

A memorandum on the draft Constitution submitted by V.T. Krishnamachari, B.H. Zaidi, Sardar Singhji of Khetri and Sardar Jaidev Singh, representatives of the Indian States, pleaded strongly for a separate citizenship of a State in addition to federal citizenship. It suggested a proviso to be added to draft article 6 to preserve the right of the Legislature of a constituent State to deal with the question of citizenship for the local purposes of the State.[42]

Disagreeing with this view, Alladi Krishnaswamy Ayyar explained the position:

> The Indian States had never a nationality law and it was merely a domicile law. In foreign countries in British territories, Indian State subjects came under the category of British protected persons and the protection was afforded by reason of the fact that the States had no voice in the conduct of foreign affairs. Now, since foreign affairs is ceded by all acceding States, they have to be protected abroad by the Indian Government. Since they have conceded the right to the Indian Legislature to pass laws extending to their territory, there is nothing incongruous in there being a unified citizenship. Moreover, any modification in this regard would affect the chapters relating to fundamental rights which have been passed with the assent of everyone. Hence, this objection should not be considered at all.[43]

B.N. Rau observed that Article 5 as in the Draft Constitution was open to the following criticisms:

1. Clause (b) of this article leaves out persons who were born in Pondicherry, Goa, Chandranagore or other foreign territory in India or were born in South Africa, Fiji or other countries outside

India, but were domiciled in the territory of India as defined in the Constitution. There is no good reason why such persons should be less favourably treated than those born in Pakistan or Burma. The words "who or either of whose parents or any of whose grand-parents was born in India as defined in the Government of India Act, 1935 (as originally enacted), or in Burma, Ceylon or Malaya, and" may therefore be omitted from clause (b).

2. "Acquired" is slightly ambiguous. For avoiding doubt we say "voluntarily acquired" instead of "acquired".[44]

S. Dutt, Additional Secretary, Ministry of External Affairs had raised some points in a letter to B.N.Rau in regard to citizenship rights for Indians who had migrated to Malaya. B.N. Rau replied to all these points. The first point was whether those Indians who had resided for a number of years and cultivated land in Malaya would be regarded as having made their permanent abode in Malaya. The answer really turned on their *intention*; if their intention was always to return to India ultimately, the courts would probably hold that they had not made their permanent abode in Malaya. Of course, intention can only be proved by some overt act; if in a particular case, the only fact proved are residence and cultivation for a long period of time in Malaya and there is no other poof of intention, the courts may well infer an intention to make Malaya the permanent abode. The test is always of intention.

Dutt's second point was whether acceptance of Malayan citizenship would be regarded as acquisition of citizenship of a foreign State. B.N. Rau's reply was that an amendment substituting the word "acquired" in article 5(b) by the words "voluntarily acquired" was already being considered; that would remove all ambiguity in the matter. If a person who was an Indian citizen by birth under article 5(a) became a citizen of the Malayan Federation by the automatic operation of Malayan law or became a British subject under the British nationality law, he would not be considered for the purposes of article 5(b) to have voluntarily acquired Malayan citizenship or British nationality. Besides, B.N. Rau said, it was also proposed to exclude Malaya and similar States from the definition of a "foreign State."

Lastly, Dutt had asked whether Government of India would undertake legislation before the commencement of the Constitution to enable persons residing in Malaya to acquire Indian citizenship by declaring their intention in writing before India's representative in Malaya. The intention of the citizenship provisions, B.N. Rau observed, was clearly that no person should at the inception of the new Constitution be a citizen of India unless he was connected with the territory of India by birth, descent or domicile. It was not the intention that persons unconnected with the territory of India in one of these ways should by merely making a statement before some authority outside India qualify for citizenship. If a person was not born in India and was not born of parents or grand-parents born in India, it would be necessary that he should stay in India for at least a month and make a declaration of his intention to acquire Indian domicile.

B.N.Rau suggested a redraft of article 5 incorporating the results of his scrutiny of the various comments and suggestions that had been received:

> At the date of commencement of this Constitution—
> (a) every person who or either of whose parents or any of whose grand-parents was born in the territory of India and who has not made his permanent abode in any foreign country, and
> (b) every person who has his domicile in the territory of India, shall be a citizen of India, provided that he has not voluntarily acquired the citizenship of any foreign country.[45]

The Drafting Committee accepted the redraft proposed by the Constitutional Adviser.[46]

The Special Committee (a body consisting mostly of certain members of the Union Constitution Committee, the Union Powers Committee and the Provincial Constitution Committee) meeting on 10 April, 1948 was of the opinion that article 5 should be divided into two parts: one dealing with cases of general application and the other dealing with persons who had left India with the intention of acquiring a fixed habitation in other countries or who had migrated to India from other countries for acquiring such habitation in India. It was accordingly decided that in the redraft of article 5 of Part I of the list of amendments circulated to the members, the words "who had not made his permanent abode in any foreign country after the first day of April 1947" should be omitted from clause (a), and clause (ii) of the existing Explanation to this article be also omitted, and that a separate provision dealing with persons who have left India with the intention of acquiring a fixed habitation outside India, or who have migrated to India and have taken up such habitation here should be made.[47]

The recommendations of the special committee found favour with the Drafting Committee.

All the comments and suggestions for amendment were carefully considered, along with B.N. Rau's notes thereon, by the Drafting Committee. The Committee decided that the following be substituted for article 5[48]:

5. (1) At the date of commencement of this Constitution—
   (a) every person who or either of whose parents or any of whose grand-parents was born in the territory of India, and
   (b) every person who has his domicile in the territory of India,
   (b) shall be a citizen of India, provided that he has not voluntarily acquired the citizenship of any foreign State.

   Explanation: A person shall be deemed to have his domicile in the territory of India if he would have had his domicilc in such territory under Part II of the Indian Succession Act, 1925, had the provisions of that Part been applicable to him.

   (2) For the purposes of clause (1) of this article—
   (a) a person shall not be deemed to be a citizen of India if he has taken up his fixed habitation after the first day of April,1947, in any territory outside India as defined in this Constitution;
   (b) a person who has migrated to India as so defined from any other territory shall, notwithstanding anything contained in section 11 of the Indian Succession Act,1925, be deemed to have acquired a domicile in the territory of India if he has, before the date of commencement of this Constitution deposited in the office of the District Magistrate a declaration in writing of his desire to acquire such domicile and has resided in the territory of India for at least one month before the date of the declaration.
6. Parliament may, by law, make further provision regarding the acquisition and termination of citizenship and all other matters relating thereto.

Accordingly, the October 1948 reprint of the Draft Constitution contained a fresh redraft of article 5 on these lines.[49]

II

The citizenship provisions came up for discussion in the Assembly on 18 November, 1948, but consideration was deferred as a large number of amendments had been tabled and it was considered desirable to give opportunity to the proposers to exchange views with the members of the Drafting Committee and arrive, if possible, at a consensus.[50]

Meanwhile, the Secretariat of the Constituent Assembly received a memorandum from the Ceylon Indian Congress dated 11 November, 1948, on behalf of Indian nationals in Ceylon. Radhakrishnan Ramani, a well-known Advocate of Kuala Lumpur, Malaya also submitted memoranda—

one on 18 April, 1949 and another on 25 April, 1949—on the problems of the large number of Indians who resided and carried on diverse occupations in Malaya. He apprehended that if the federal citizenship provisions of the new Malayan Constitution came into force earlier than the Indian Constitution, under article 5(b) of the latter, many Indians resident in Malaya would automatically be disqualified for Indian citizenship.[51] But as S.Dutt, Additional Secretary, Ministry of External Affairs pointed out in a note of 16 June, 1949 on citizenship, these fears were based on the assumption that Malayan citizenship would be regarded as citizenship of a foreign State. Actually, so long as India remained in the Commonwealth, there was no question of Malaya being a foreign State. Persons of Indian origin by living abroad in a Commonwealth country would acquire the citizenship of India under article 5(a) even if they had already accepted the citizenship of their country of residence. Thus, a person resident in Malaya but having his origin in the territory of the Union of India would acquire Indian citizenship even if in the meantime he had become a federal citizen of Malaya. The difficulty in the case of persons originating in what later became Pakistan territory and accepting Malayan citizenship could also, if necessary, be obviated by adding a proviso to article 5(b) to cover such cases. In a comprehensive note, Dutt also examined in detail the general question of articles 5 and 6 of the Draft Constitution being adequate or otherwise for meeting the requirements of all persons originating in Indian territories before 15 August, 1947, and living abroad on the date of the inception of the Constitution but anxious to acquire Indian citizenship. Dutt pointed out that most of such people would automatically become Indian citizens under article 5(a), for at least one of their parents or grand-parents must have been born in India. Regarding Indians in Fiji and Guyana (former British Guiana) whose connection with India was as remote as going back to great grand-parents, it was, after discussions with B.N.Rau, considered inadvisable to have any provision in the Constitution.

The next and more difficult question concerned persons originating in territories included in Pakistan but living abroad, who had no intention of returning to Pakistan and who wanted to make their permanent homes in India—persons, for example, who originated in West Punjab, who were subsequently living in Burma, Egypt, Indonesia etc., and whose homes in West Punjab had been destroyed and whose relations had moved to India. Under draft clause 5 as it stood, any such person had to return to India, submit a declaration of his intention to acquire Indian domicile and reside there for at least a month before the date of declaration. This requirement would have placed these persons in a difficult position. Dutt, who raised this issue, pointed out that it would not be fair to compel these thousands of persons, who had no home left in Pakistan, to return to India immediately, leaving their business concerns behind, merely to qualify for Indian citizenship. This matter was taken up by Prime Minister Nehru with the Constitutional Adviser and with Ambedkar, the Chairman of the Drafting Committee. The latter thought that it would not be impossible to allay the apprehensions of Indians by making appropriate changes in the clauses regarding naturalization in the Bill on Indian citizenship which was to be promoted in the near future. The Ministry of External Affairs was apparently not satisfied with this solution; the Ministry wanted special provision in the Constitution which would enable this class of Indians to qualify for citizenship at the commencement of the Constitution.[52]

Consideration of the citizenship provisions was taken up in the Assembly on 10 August, 1949. President Rajendra Prasad suggested that in view of the large number of amendments, about 140, a number of them emanating from the Drafting Committee, it would be better if the Chairman of the Drafting Committee moved the articles in the form in which he had finally framed them. Thereupon, Ambedkar moved a consolidated amendment combining all the amendments proposed by the Drafting Committee. The consolidated amendment sought to replace articles 5 and 6 of the February 1948 Draft Constitution, by six new articles, viz., articles 5, 5A, 5AA, 5B, 5C and 6, as follows:

Citizenship at the date of commencement of the Constitution.

5. At the date of commencement of this Constitution, every person who has his domicile in the territory of India and:
   (a) who was born in the territory of India; or,
   (b) either of whose parents was born in the territory of India; or,
   (c) who has been ordinarily resident in the territory of India for not less than five years immediately preceding the date of such commencement shall be a citizen of India, provided that he has not voluntarily acquired the citizenship of any foreign State.

Rights of citizenship of certain persons who have migrated to India from Pakistan

5-A. Notwithstanding anything contained in article 5 of this Constitution a person who has migrated to the territory of India from the territory now included in Pakistan shall be deemed to be a citizen of India at the date of commencement of this Constitution if—
   (a) he or either of his parents or any of his grand-parents was born in India as defined in the Government of India Act, 1935 (as originally enacted) ; and

(b) (i) in the case where such person so migrated before the nineteenth day of July, 1948, he has ordinarily resided within the territory of India since the date of his migration, and

(ii) in the case where such person has so migrated on or after the nineteenth day of July, 1948, he has been registered as a citizen of India by an officer appointed in this behalf by the Government of the Dominion of India on an application made by him therefor to such officer before the date of commencement of this Constitution in the form prescribed for the purpose by that Government. Provided that no such registration shall be made unless the person making the application has resided in the territory of India for at least six months before the date of his application.

Rights of citizenship of certain migrants to Pakistan

5-AA. Notwithstanding anything contained in articles 5 and 5-A of this Constitution, a person who has after the first day of March 1947, migrated from the territory of India to the territory now included in Pakistan shall not be deemed to be a citizen of India;
Provided that nothing in this article shall apply to a person who, after having so migrated to the territory now included in Pakistan has returned to the territory of India under a permit for resettlement or permanent return issued by or under the authority of any law and every such person shall for the purpose of clause (b) of article 5-A of this Constitution be deemed to have migrated to the territory of India after the nineteenth day of July 1948.

Rights of citizenship of certain persons of Indian origin residing outside India

5B. Notwithstanding anything contained in articles 5 and 5-A of this Constitution, any person who or either of whose parents or any of whose grand-parents was born in India as defined in the Government of India Act, 1935 (as originally enacted) and who is originally residing in any territory outside India as so defined shall be deemed to be a citizen of India if he has been registered as a citizen of India by the diplomatic or consular representative of India in the country where he is for the time being residing on an application made by him therefor to such diplomatic or consular representative, whether before or after the commencement of this Constitution, in the form prescribed for the purpose by the Government of the Dominion of India or the Government of India.

Continuance of the Rights of citizenship

5 C. Every person who is a citizen of India under any of the foregoing provisions of this Part shall, subject to the provisions of any law that may be made by Parliament, continue to be such citizen.

Parliament to regulate the right of citizenship by law

6. Nothing in the foregoing provisions of this Part shall derogate from the power of Parliament to make any provision with respect to the acquisition and termination of citizenship and all other matters relating to citizenship.

Introducing new articles Ambedkar explained the new articles conferred citizenship of the Union on five different categories of persons. They are:

(1) Persons domiciled and born in India—these forming the bulk of the population of the Union of India;[Articles 5(a) & 5(b)]
(2) Persons who are domiciled in India but who are not born in India but have resided in India e.g., persons who were subjects of French or Portuguese settlements in India like Chandranagore, Pondicherry, Goa, etc., or Iranians who had come from Persia and resided in India for a long time and undoubtedly had the intention of becoming citizens of India;[Article 5(c)]
(3) Persons who are residents in India but have migrated to Pakistan;[Article-5AA]
(4) Persons resident in Pakistan but who have migrated to India; [Article-5-A]
(5) Persons who or whose parents are born in India but are residing outside India.[Article-5-B]

The provisions proposed were necessarily somewhat complicated since they had to cover a number of classes of persons, and a situation resulting from a great upheaval in which a large scale exodus of population between India and Pakistan had taken place. The clauses were lucidly explained by Ambedkar. The first category of persons were those who were domiciled in India and who or whose parents were born in the territory of India. They automatically became Indian citizens.

The second category included persons who had resided in India, though they were not born in India. The condition imposed on these persons was that they should have resided in India for a period of not less than five years.

Then there were two categories of persons, those who were resident in India and had migrated to Pakistan, and those who were resident in Pakistan and had migrated to India. The latter category was divided into two classes, those who had come to India before 19 July, 1948, and those who had come after that date (on this day an ordinance had been issued that no one could come in unless he had a permit; and there were three kinds of permits—temporary, permanent, and those for resettlement). Those who came before July 19, 1948, would automatically become citizens of India, but those who came later could acquire citizenship only on following a procedure. They had to make an application to an officer appointed by the Government of India and had to be registered by such officer on an application so made.

As regards persons who had migrated to Pakistan but had returned to India, the position was that if a person who had migrated to Pakistan had, after going there, returned to India on the basis of a permit given to him, not merely to enter India but also to resettle, such person would become a citizen of India on the commencement of the Constitution.

The last category of persons provided for in these articles were those residing abroad but who or whose parents were born in India. These were the persons for whom the Ministry of External Affairs had entered a strong plea. In their case, the only limitation proposed was that they should make an application before the commencement of the Constitution to the Consular Officer or the Diplomatic Reprehensive of the Government of India in the country in which they were staying, and get themselves registered as citizens. This, Ambedkar explained, would be a simple matter.[53]

While commending the new articles for adoption by the Assembly, Ambedkar explained that these articles referred to citizenship not in any general sense but to citizenship on the date of commencement of the Constitution. It was not the object of these articles to lay down a permanent law of citizenship for this country. "This business of laying down a permanent law of citizenship has been left to Parliament, and as Members will see from the wording of article 6 as I have moved, the entire matter regarding citizenship has been left to Parliament to determine by any law that it may deem fit.......The effect of article 6 is this ... the provisions that we are making for citizenship on the date of commencement of this Constitution are not going to be permanent or unalterable. All that we are doing is to decide *ad hoc* for the time being ... The Drafting Committee has provided for five different classes of people ... who can ... become citizens on the date on which the Constitution commences", Ambedkar said.[54]

Discussions on these articles took place on 11 and 12 August when as many as 41 amendments were moved—the largest numbers were moved by Naziruddin Ahmed (10), closely followed by Thakur Das Bhargava (9), P.S. Deshmukh (7) and K.T. Shah (5). Jaspat Roy Kapoor moved three amendments, B.P. Jhunjhunwala two and Krishna Chandra Sharma, Shibban Lal Saxsena, R.K. Sidhva, S.Nagappa and Bhopinder Singh Mann moved one amendment each.

The largest numbers of amendments—as many as 16— were on Article 5. Article 5A also attracted a number of amendmens—14. Six amendments were moved on Article 5B and another 3 on Article 5AA. Only one amendment was submitted on Article 6.

Of these provisions, Articles 5A & 5AA attracted severe criticism from the Members. Article 5AA came under the heaviest fire and evoked keen controversy because it provided for conferment of citizenship rights to those who after having migrated to Pakistan have returned to the territory of India under a permit for resettlement or permanent return. It is better to follow the discussions in the Assembly Article-wise.

(A) Article 5A was criticised on the ground that it would enable everybody to cross over from Pakistan and become Indian citizen without any check.

Jaspat Roy Kapoor wanted that only those persons who were migrating to India from Pakistan 'on account of civil disturbances or the fear of such disturbance'[55] should be given citizenship, because according to the Evacuee Property Ordinance an evacuee has been defined as one who has left a territory because of civil disturbances or because of fear of such disturbances[56]. ... Only those persons who "found it difficult to stay in the place of their original domicile"[57] would be made citizens.

Pandit Thakur Das Bhargava moved amendments to article 5A. One such amendment was that he or she who migrated "on account of civil disturbances or the fear of such disturbances" should be given citizenship. He wanted that all refugees should be treated as Indian nationals. "By the mere fact of partition they have not ceased to be citizens of India, provided that they have come here and want to settle permanently in this country. They have every right to citizenship",[58] he argued. But he was against any large-scale migration of Muslims from Pakistan. He said, "after partition as many as three times the Hindu refugees from East Bengal, Muslims have migrated to Assam. If a Muslim comes to India and bears allegiance to India and loved India as we love her, I have nothing but love for that man. But even after the Partition for reasons best known to themselves many

Mussalmans have come to Assam with a view to make a Muslim Majority in that province for election purposes and not to live in Assam as citizens of India. My humble submission is that those persons have come here for a purpose which is certainly not very justifiable. Those who have come here on account of disturbances in Pakistan or fear of disturbances there, certainly they must get an asylum in India. If any nationalist Mussalman who is afraid of the Muslims of East Pakistan or West Pakistan comes to India he certainly should be welcomed. It is our duty to see that he is protected. We will treat him as our brother and a *bona fide* national of India. In regard to those others who have not come here on account of disturbances, we should not allow them to become citizens of India, if we can help it. Therefore, I have added these words:

'Notwithstanding anything contained in Article 5 of this Constitution a person who on account of civil disturbances or the fear of such disturbances...'

"I would rather insist that that man should not come here and become a citizen just to bolster up a Muslim majority in one of the provinces of India. Therefore, the first condition of migration would be that he comes here on account of disturbance. For those who want to stay here on account of disturbances the doors of India would be open. But to those who come from sinister motives, from motives of occupying lands and usurping the rightful owners by terrorising them and becoming a majority in this country, it is up to us to say that no asylum would be offered here. They are not migrating with a view to live permanently here. Their object is only to create trouble here. But to achieve our object I would request everyone to agree with me that this innovation should be made in article 5A."[59]

B.P. Jhunjhunwala also moved an amendment on the same line. He also contended that "persons other than those who have been refugees or who have been displaced or have come from Pakistan on account of civil disturbances or the fear of such disturbances"[60] should be treated like a foreigner. "The only thing we want to know is the real intention of the person who has come to India and is residing here, and we shall know it better during the period of five years. I have been told that from Eastern Pakistan people are infiltrating into Assam for some sinister motive, i.e. to increase their population. It is not my first-hand knowledge, but responsible reliable persons have told me like this. This has led me to move this amendment. They are going to Assam, not because they are inconvenienced in Pakistan, but simply with a view to remain in Assam and increase their population there. It is to avoid giving right to such persons that I am moving this amendment."[61]

Sardar Bhopinder Singh Man demanded that "any person, who because of communal riots in Pakistan has come over to India, should automatically be considered as a citizen of India and should on no account be made to go to a registering authority and plead before him and establish a qualification of six months domicile to claim rights of citizenship. There may be victims of communal frenzy in our neighbouring State hereafter; it is not only a possibility but a great probability in the present circumstances. Any failure of the evacuee property talks may lead to a flare-up against Hindus and Sikhs in Pakistan, and we must have a clause that these people will in no case be debarred from coming over and becoming citizens of this Union."[62]

Pandit Hirday Nath Kunzru however did not "personally agree with the critics" of Article 5A which "has been criticised on the ground that its provisions are undesirably wide and that it throws open the door of citizenship to people who have no moral right to be regarded as Indian citizens."[63] Criticising Bhargava's amendment he said: "how will it be possible for a person to prove that he left his home on account of the particular cause (on account of civil disturbances or the fear of such disturbances) referred to above? And how would the registering officers be in a position to decide whether the claim was valid or not? ... The amendment that he has proposed will raise many difficulties that he has not thought of. It will probably raise difficulties with regard to the position of the people who have migrated from East Bengal to West Bengal. It will be very difficult for these people to prove that they have left their homes in Eastern Pakistan because of civil disturbances or fear of such disturbances. There are millions of non-Muslims still living in Eastern Pakistan. How will these people then be able to prove that there was any justification for their fears that civil disturbances might break out. The House will thus see that Pandit Thakur Das Bhargava's amendment, instead of removing any real difficulty, will create many more difficulties of a more serious character. I do not think, therefore, that it can be accepted."[64]

Rohini Kumar Choudhury was for extending all support to Pandit Bhargava's amendment. "The same amendment was also tabled by my honourable friend Mr. Jhunjhunwala and was tabled by me who is supposed to represent the Assamese Hindus, by my honourable friend Mr. Basu Matari who represents the tribal people in Assam and by my friend Mr. Laskar, who represents the Bengal Scheduled Castes of Assam. These are the three different groups of persons who have supported Pandit Bhargava. ...By this amendment, I want citizenship rights for those persons—I am particularly concerned with Assam—who had come from East Bengal because they found things impossible for them there. It may be argued in a narrow way that everyone who has come from East Bengal was not really actuated by fear of disturbance or actually living in a place where disturbance had taken place. Can anyone imagine for a moment that there is no fear of disturbance in the minds of these East Bengal People who had come over to West Bengal or Assam? Was there any sense of security in their minds? Has that sense of security, now after a period of two years, been enhanced by the fact that Pakistan has been converted into a theocratic State? I should say in answer to the criticism of Pandit Kunzru, that you need not insist in such cases that the man should be actuated by fear of disturbances or that disturbance should have taken place. The fear is latent in the mind of everybody. The moment any Hindu or a person of any minority community raises a protest against any action which is taken there, disturbances would immediately follow. Is there any doubt about that?

"Therefore, Sir, in answer to Pandit Kunzru's criticism I would say that this condition of fear of disturbance should not at all be insisted in the case of a person coming from Pakistan over to West Bengal or Assam or any other place in India. ...

"I want to make it perfectly clear that I want citizenship rights for those people of East Bengal who has gone over to West Bengal or Assam out of fear of disturbances in the future or from a sense of insecurity and also for those people who have come over from Sylhet, who at the time of coming had no fear of disturbance or anything of that kind, but who, on account of fear of disturbances now have decided to live here.

"At the same time I also have the temerity to say in this House that I would exclude those persons who came only three years ago, who set up the civil disobedience movement, forcibly occupied land which was not meant for them and forced the benevolent and benign Government to have recourse to the military to keep peace in the province. I should be the last person to say ... that that class of persons should by any means be granted citizenship rights in the province. I also make it quite plain that I desire to exclude those persons who surreptitiously introduced themselves into my province and who now having mixed themselves with their own brethern now desire to have citizenship rights, not out of any sense of insecurity on their part, in their own provinces but with a desire to exploit more from that province of Assam. I desire to exclude these people because they had not long ago set up the struggle for Pakistan, they had not long before taken an active part in compelling the politicians of India to agree for Partition; they have their own property and are living peacefully on their own property; not only that, they have brought about such a state of things that they have been able to purchase property for mere nothing, property which belongs to the minority who had come out of fear. ... The Government of Assam have requested the Government of India to give them the authority to issue permits to restrict such entries but they have been denied ... (It was published in newspapers) that in a meeting of the Muslim League at Dacca it was said with some regret—I hope it was with some real regret—that about three lakhs of Muslims had migrated from East Bengal on account of some economic difficulty. Now, you imagine, if three lakhs is the figure which is given by the Muslim League in East Bengal, what must have been the real figure of people who have been infiltrating like this. Every province would like to be prosperous but it should not be at the cost of other persons. If you wish to govern a province properly, you should always try to see that the balance of the population is not so much disturbed and you should see that you do not give citizenship to persons whose presence in the province would be undesirable and prejudicial to the interests of the Dominion of India."[65]

Exhorting the Members to lend support to Pandit Bhargava's amendment he continued: "if they support Pandit Thakur Das Bhargava, not only will the welfare of my province be safeguarded, not only will the interest of East Bengal refugees be safeguarded and also ultimately it will be to the general welfare of India. You will have a province which will be absolutely loyal, which will be absolutely faithful to the government of the Province and which will be unanimously faithful to the Dominion of India. If you do not accept Pandit Thakur Das Bhargava's amendment, and if you do not bring in any other amendment to the same effect, you will expose your frontier, you will expose that province and that province will become a source of great danger to you. Already I have been to Cachar and I have seen in that district, from which crossing the Barak river you come into India, there is trouble; and if this amendment of Dr. Ambedkar is accepted, this district of Cachar will be entirely one district of Pakistan, and who will be responsible for giving one district which should have been kept in our province and which was retained after a good deal of fight but which will be sent to Pakistan? It will be this amendment moved by Dr. Ambedkar."[66]

N. Gopalswami Ayangar admitted the peculiar situation prevailing in Assam and advocated for "devising other measure of solution". "It is no doubt a fact that a substantial number of Muslims do go from East Bengal to Assam. But this kind of migration ...... is nothing new. The numbers vary a bit perhaps; but the question that is put to us is that under this particular provision in the draft we shall open the door for a very large number of Muslims who will come over to India from Pakistan and who will apply for registration and get registered, much to the detriment of the economy of Assam. ... Assam wanted a permit system to be applied as between East Bengal and Assam ... The Assam Government and the Government of India have discussed the matter between themselves. They have held more than one conference for the purpose of arriving at a solution of this trouble. ... At the last conference ... the general consensus of opinion amongst both representatives of the Government of India and the representatives of Assam was that it was not wise to introduce anything like a permit system between East Bengal and Assam on the same lines as obtain between West Pakistan and India. There are complications which perhaps it is unnecessary for me to go into in detail. One very big complication is the repercussion it will have as regards the movement of persons between East and West Bengal. Now, by permitting the extension of the permit system as it works between West Pakistan and India to the area between East Bengal and Assam, we shall be inviting Pakistan to introduce such a system as between East and West Bengal and I only mention this to people who are acquainted with both West Bengal and Assam for them to realise all the enormous complications on the economy of West Bengal which it will entail. The last conference merely came to the conclusion that we should seek and apply other method for preventing or mitigating the influx of a large number of Muslims from East Bengal to Assam and this matter is being investigated, and for my own part, I think it will be possible to devise some kind of legislation which will enable Assam to stem the tide very substantially. ... But we should not altogether ignore the possibility that conditions being what they are in Assam, this kind of thing might be applied by over-zealous officials of the Assam government so as to be prejudicial to, say, the Bengalis who have migrated from East Bengal to Assam and perhaps even from West Bengal to Assam. We have got to take into consideration all these things. Now, I would earnestly request the House that we should not complicate the solution of this problem of citizenship by bringing in this particular trouble between East Bengal and Assam for which we are devising other measures of solution."[67]

Dr. B.R. Ambedkar however took a different stand. "It is only with regard to those who have entered Assam before 19th July, 1948, that they have been declared, automatically so to say, citizens of Assam if they have resided within the territory of India. But with regard to those who have entered Assam, whether they are Hindu Bengalees or whether they are Muslims after the 19th July, 1948, he will find that citizenship is not an automatic business at all. There are three conditions laid down for persons who have entered Assam after the 19th July, 1948. The first condition is that such a person must make an application for citizenship. He must prove that he has resided in Assam for six months and, thirdly, he must be registered by an officer appointed by the Government of the Dominion of India. I would like to state very categorically that this registration power is a plenary power. The mere fact that a man has made an application, the mere fact that he has resided in Assam for six months, would not involve any responsibility or duty or obligation on the registering officer to register him. ... The officer would be entitled to examine on such material as he may have before him, the purport for which he has come, such as whether he has come with a *bona fide* motive of becoming a permanent citizen of India or whether he has come with any other purpose." He contended that if "these three limiting conditions" are strictly adhered to the fear of Mr. Choudhury that "the flood-gates will be opened to swamp the Assamese people either by Bengalees or by Muslims, seems to me to be utterly unfounded."[68]

There was no further discussion on this clause and the same was adopted in the Constituent Assembly on 12 August, 1949.

During the third reading of the Constitution, Kuladhar Chaliha (Assam: General) pointed out that "in the definition of citizen, of course it has been conceived in the best of spirits, but there is a subtle loophole where we may run around ourselves. If a man comes six months before the 19th July and is registered by the officers appointed by the Government of India, he can be a citizen. But when you apply this to a province like Assam, you will find great difficulty. You would be heading towards disintegration. Therefore, when this is applied, we have to be very careful and we should see that we are not led away by the high principles which have been laid down in this Constitution. Therefore, in spite of the fact that the definition of citizenship has been very well framed, yet, there is a little danger in its application, if you want to apply it in the way we would have it here. We have been receiving telegrams from Assam that we are heading towards ruin. Probably every member here has received them from Assam, saying that we would apply this principle with a little reservation, that this definition of citizenship should be applied with a little reservation in Assam, and that this Constitution should take note of this".[69]

III

(B) Now, let us see what were the views of the Members of the Constituent Assembly on Article 5AA. The proviso to Article 5AA was mainly criticised for its Pro-Pak bias, foisting Pakistanis on Indians and asking the Constituent Assembly to uphold the policy and decisions of the Government.

Jaspat Roy Kapoor was against granting this facility to those who had gone to Pakistan but came back from Pakistan. "Those persons who went away to Pakistan went definitely with the intention of settling down there permanently. They gave up their loyalty to this country and they gave their allegiance to the new country of Pakistan. ... The Muslim Leaguers wanted division of the country and exchange of population, and that the number of persons belonging to the Muslim League was tremendously large. To our misfortune, only a handful of nationalist Muslims are opposed to the idea of Pakistan. ... Some of them or quite a good number of them went to Pakistan ... because of the disturbances here. ... Now if they want to come back to India to settle down here permanently ... they must be treated on the same footing as any other foreigner."[70] He also referred to the financial implications. Their properties so long considered as evacuee property would not be available to the refugees who have come from Pakistan. "While it is good to be generous, generosity loses much of its virtue when it is at the cost of others, because this generosity will be at the cost of nobody else but ultimately perhaps at the cost of our refugee brethern",[71] he asserted.

Prof. Shibban Lai Saksena also supported the contention of Jaspat Roy Kapoor. The proviso to 5AA "will allow the executive authority to give anybody a permit and he shall become a citizen of India, so that it will be something changing and it may have repercussions which we do not like. ... A person who has migrated from India will be treated as a foreigner and when he comes back he will have to acquire citizenship by residence of five years and so on",[72] he said.

Pandit Thakur Das Bhargava was also of the same view. He wanted that they should be treated like any other foreigner and that they should come under the Naturalisation Act. His view was, "those who are desirous to become the citizens of Pakistan on the 15th August, 1947 or who left this country to become citizens of Pakistan with open eyes and with the song on their lips :

> 'Hanske liya Pakistan
> Ladke lenge Hindustan'

should not be made the citizens of India. Those persons have now forfeited their right to become citizens of this country."[73] "If the Government of India in their wisdom have seen fit to allow thousands of people to come back from Western or Eastern Pakistan and allowed them permits for resettlement, they are themselves responsible for it. Perhaps you are not conscious as to what difficult question of property and propriety are agitating the minds of the refugees in this connection. Now we all know that Pakistan has refused to give compensation for the properties which it originally agreed to give so far as movable property is concerned. With regard to other properties we know the attitude of Pakistan and how it is behaving. The properties of persons who are living in Pakistan have been declared evacuee property and taken possession of. I do not know how the return of these thousands of Muslims to India will affect the rights of evacuee property here."[74]

He even accused the Government of converting the temporary permit to permanent permits. He said: "At a Conference recently held some responsible persons stated that some people came here with temporary permits obtained from the High Commissioner or Deputy High Commissioner in Pakistan and were taken by Muslim dignitaries and ministers to our high placed ministers and leaders and recommended for permanent permits. This may or may not be so. But even if there was a single instance of this nature, this must give rise to agitation in minds of refugees who are driven from pillar to post and not rehabilitated properly."[75] That there was an effort on the part of temporary permit holders either to prolong their stay or mingle with the population was partly admitted when Moulana Mohd. Hifzur Rahman alleged that "not hundreds but thousands of people ... who had come here with one, two, or three months permit for the purpose of acquiring permanent citizenship ... (and) applied to the local officials for their permanent residence in Indian Union, and cancellation of their permit under the notification of the Government of India, were not made permanent residents and their permits were not cancelled within the fixed period. ... Instead of granting or rejecting their request, they were asked to go back at once. ... The result of this was that many persons in U.P., East Punjab and other Provinces were arrested on the ground that they were not going back after expiry of the fixed period."[76]

Pandit Bhargava even alleged that "the majority of them come with sinister motives, with a view to making money, with a view to dispose of their property and for other purposes. ... They get all the advantage here and all the advantages there. Now, Sir, those especially in Western Pakistan have got much more facilities, much more comfort than we enjoy in East Punjab. There is no reason why they should come here at all. ... Where is the guarantee that he will not go back after he has disposed of his property? My submission is that there is no reason why the Government of India or we should have a soft corner for those people, who come in in order to take advantage of our weakness or leniency towards them."[77]

Sardar Bhopinder Singh Mann was also against this proviso and more or less argued on similar lines. "The purpose of the clause will be completely nullified, because we, who are refugees, due to this exchange of population which necessarily involves exchange of property, will be put to serious trouble. This securing of permit from the Deputy High Commissioner's Office, I can assure you, is a cheap affair in its actual working. ... The securing of a chance permit from the Deputy High Commissioner's Office or any other authority should not carry with it such a prize thing as citizenship of India. ... Apart from that this will adversely affect evacuee property. ... On the one hand, we are sort of property and on the other hand, concessions are being given to them. This is secularism no doubt, but a very one-sided and undesirable type of secularism which goes invariably against and to the prejudice of Sikh and Hindu refugees. I do not want to give rights of citizenship to those who so flagrantly dishonoured the integrity of India not so long ago",[78] he asserted. He had however no objection if "a certain strip of Pakistan territory to India in lieu of this increase of population and release of property is assured."[79]

Mahboob Ali Baig Sahib wished that "this explanation or this 5AA is deleted altogether. I do not want that our dealing with the subject of displaced persons must be undignified. It is enough if we have stated what qualifications persons should have, who have been displaced. That has been dealt with in 5A. That is enough. I do not see any reason why we should make mention of displaced persons from India to Pakistan who might return. The other qualifications are there. ...[80] When partition took place, when the June 3rd agreement was entered into by both parties, it was expected that the minorities would remain where they are in the two Dominions and safeguards would be given to them. That was the honest expectation, that was the honest undertaking, but what happened was that after the transfer of power there was a holocaust, there were disturbances, there were tragedies which compelled persons to migrate. Now, Sir, when these were the circumstances, is there any justification for us to draw any distinction. I would go to the length of saying discrimination between those persons who migrated to India and those who migrated to Pakistan under the same circumstances? Let us not forget what during his life-time Mahatma Gandhi was preaching. What did he say? He invited the persons who had gone to Pakistan to return to their homeland. So, Sir, let us look at this matter calmly. ... So to say those people coming to India might become traitors and therefore they should not be allowed to come back, that is no reason at all. ... That kind of psychology should be shunned, must be got rid of. Moreover, we are only legislating for the present. Parliament may in its discretion, if it thinks it to be necessary, deprive any person of his citizenship and expel him. Parliament is supreme in this matter. Therefore, I do not see any reason why you should make a distinction between persons who go from here to Pakistan and persons who came from Pakistan."[81]

This charge of leniency towards Pakistan was answered by Pandit Jawaharlal Nehru in an emotional speech when he said, "I want the House to examine the word carefully and it is that this Government goes in for a policy of appeasement, appeasement of Pakistan, appeasement of Muslims, appeasement of this and that. I want to know clearly what that word means. Do the Honourable Members who talk of appeasement think that some kind of rule should be applied when dealing with these people which has nothing to do with justice or equity? I want a clear answer to that. If so, I would only plead for appeasement. This Government will not go by a hair's breadth to the right or to the left from what they consider to be right way of dealing with the situation, justice to the individual or the group."[82]

Brajeswar Prasad was for making the proviso more wide. His contention was, "I wish all the people of Pakistan should be invited to come and stay in this country. ... Hindus and Muslims in this country were one. ... We are blood-brothers. May I know if after partition, these blood-brothers have become strangers and aliens ? Sir, it has been an artificial partition. I think that the mischief of partition should not be allowed to spread beyond the legal fact of partition. ... It has also been asserted that it was the fact of partition that was responsible for mass migration. I do not agree with that proposition. The late lamented Mr. Jinnah stood for the principle of exchange of population. We disagreed. The implication of our rejection of that demand was that the fact of partition would have no bearing on the question of loyalty of Muslims of this country. Partition or no partition, the Mohammadans will remain loyal to this country. That was the meaning of the rejection of the demand of Mr. Jinnah. And how can we say that the fact of partition was responsible for mass migration? It must be realised that it was the riots and the disturbances in certain parts of the country which were responsible for mass migration."[83]

Nehru had earlier stated that the difficulties in drafting these articles relating to citizenship "have arisen from two factors. One was of course the partition of the country. ... Now I find that most of the arguments have taken place in regard to people who are the victims in some way or other of partition. I do not think it is possible for you to draft anything, whatever meticulous care you might exercise which could fit in with a very difficult and complicated situation that has arisen, namely the partition."[84]

That this proviso should be included to uphold the policy of the government was admitted by Pandit Nehru himself when he said, "I appeal to the House to consider that whether you pass this amendment of Mr. Gopalswami Ayyangar or not, the fact remains that this policy of the Government has to be pursued and there is no way out without upsetting every assurance and every obligation on the part of the Government, every permit that has been issued after due enquiry."[85] Pandit Bhargava appealed to the Government not to issue any further permit. "When the Act relating to these permits was placed in the House, we did not know that they would acquire this force. Now, since we find that attempts are being made to make citizens of people who have got these permits, I would beg and humbly beg to the Ministry concerned not to issue any further permits. What is the meaning of taking people from Pakistan and foisting them on us when our own people are suffering? My submission is that any further issue of these permits would not be just and would not be conducive to the solidarity of this country",[86] he said.

Alladi Krishnaswami Ayyar also admitted that "the proviso safeguards the dignity, the honour and the plighted word of the Government of India by saying that such a person will be entitled to the benefits of citizenship. ... It is our duty to respect the plighted word of the Government of India."[87]

Pandit Hirday Nath Kunzru also held the same view. "It was open to the Government of India not to allow these people to return and it was also open to the Government of India not to allow them to settle permanently in this country; but permission having been given to them to return and settle down here by our Government, I do not think it will be honourable on our part now to go behind this permission and say that these people should be treated as strangers now. Besides their number is limited",[88] he argued.

N. Gopalswami Ayyanger took shelter of the same argument viz. "solemn word of the Government of India"[89] for their return and permanent resettlement.

Dr. B.R. Ambedkar also harped on "Government undertaking." Since "the class of people covered by this category ... is very small, something between two to three thousand ... the House will (not) be acting rightly or in accordance with what I call public conscience if it says that these people who ... are so small, who have come on the assurance of our own government to make their home here, should be denied the right of citizenship",[90] he commented.

Moulana Mohd. Hifzur Rahman was against holding of any further enquiry by the local officers prior to registering the applicant as a citizen.

His contention was that "the local authorities give a permit only when they are completely satisfied and in no way before it. ...[91] By giving them permanent permits you have allowed them to come and live here. But in this Constitution which you are framing here, you are forcing them to apply for registration. On these applications local officials would make enquiry and after that they would tell them whether they are fit to be registered as citizens or not. ...[92] Local officials should in no case be vested with powers to cancel the citizenship rights of those, who through these permits have been accepted as citizens of India. I would regard that as against all cannons of justice."[93]

Against this view of Moulana Hifzur Rahman Pandit Hirday Nath Kunzur's argument was: "We all know the circumstances in which certain people, or to be more explicit, a certain number of Muslims left India and migrated to Pakistan and not all of them left India because of civil disturbances. A good many left India in order to settle down in Pakistan because they had supported the idea of the establishment of Pakistan when it was put forward and because they thought that they would be able to lead a fuller life in a Muslim country. Can we justifiably be asked to allow these people to come back without complying with any conditions? When they were in India they were against the maintenance of integrity of India and they left India at the earliest opportunity that they could get in order to live in the country of their choice. They have no moral right in these circumstances to demand that they should be allowed to return unconditionally to this country."[94] N. Gopalswami Ayyangar also countered the stand of Moulana Hifzur Rahman. He observed: "They say that there were cases of a considerable number of people who, on account of statements made by certain persons or supposed notifications issued by people under some authority or other, have returned to this country without obtaining permits ... so far as people who migrated to Pakistan from India are concerned, there is this definite fact that their first act was one of giving up their allegiance to India and owing their allegiance to a different State. Before we take them back into India and give them rights of citizenship we must have some definite method by which their intention to return to India is unequivocally expressed. Also we must have definite evidence of the fact that they come back in this country with the imprimatur of the Government of this country. And that is why in this article 5AA we have restricted this eligibility for citizenship to persons who have come back to India on permits issued under the authority of law issued by us and by our officers."[95]

Ambedkar explained that the provision under which Muslims could return to India under a permit and acquire citizenship rights was based on an undertaking given by the Government of India. It would look very invidious, it would look a breach of faith if we now said that we should not allow these people whom our own government, whether rightly or wrongly, allowed to come way from Pakistan for the purpose of permanent residents here, to have this privilege. However, there is nothing to bar the Assembly from bringing in a Bill to prevent the Government from continuing the permit system hereafter, except that the Assembly would perhaps not be acting rightly or in accordance with the public conscience if it decided to deny citizenship rights to the few people who came on the assurance of the Government to make their home in India."[96]

There were no further discussions on this provision namely Article 5AA and the same was adopted on 12 August, 1949.

(C) Another school of thought was to make all Hindus and Sikhs the citizens of India. This was suggested by Dr. P.S. Deshmukh, when he moved the following amendment:— 5(ii) "Every person who is a Hindu or a Sikh by religion and is not a citizen of any other State, wherever he resides, shall be entitled to be a citizen of India." He wanted "to make a provision that every person who is a Hindu or a Sikh and is not a citizen of any other State shall be entitled to be a citizen of India. We have seen the formation and establishment of Pakistan. Why was it established? It was established because the Muslims claimed that they must have a home of their own and a country of their own. Here we are an entire nation with a history of thousands of years and we are going to discard it, in spite of the fact that neither the Hindu nor the Sikh has any other place in the wide world to go to. By the mere fact that he is a Hindu or a Sikh, he should get Indian citizenship because it is this one circumstance that makes him disliked by others. But we are a secular State and do not want to recognise the fact that every Hindu or Sikh in any part of the world should have a home of his own. If the Muslims want an exclusive place for themselves called Pakistan, why should not Hindus and Sikhs have India as their home? We are not debarring others from getting citizenship here. We merely say that we have no other country to look to for acquiring citizenship rights and therefore we the Hindus and the Sikhs, so long as we follow the respective religions, should have the right of citizenship in India and should be entitled to retain such citizenship so long as we acquire no other. I do not think this claim is in any way non-secular or sectarian or communal. If anybody says so, he is, to say the least, mistaken."[97]

Prof. Shibban Lal Saksena supported this stand of Dr. Deshmukh. He said, "Dr. Deshmukh's amendment is quite correct, for the Hindus and Sikhs have no other home but India and I do not see how we can include everyone in this category unless we say it bluntly in this form. We should not be ashamed in saying that every person who is a Hindu or a Sikh by religion and is not a citizen of another State shall be entitled to citizenship of India. That will cover every class whom we want to cover and will be comprehensive. The phrase 'secular' should not frighten us in saying what is a fact and reality must be faced."[98]

Algu Rai Shastri also supported this stand of Dr. Deshmukh. He argued: "People who have migrated from Pakistan to India before a particular date shall be the citizens of India. The fact is, Sir, that we should have said plainly that the Hindus and the Sikhs who may not have acquired voluntarily the citizenship of a foreign state would not have been the right of acquisition of citizenship as is contained in the provision relating to a particular date on which persons could become citizens of India. As against of those who had left this country after partition but who have returned for reasons which may not be known to this country again but I find that in that matter that strictness has not been observed. Naturally those of us who have been ruled so long as by patriotic sentiments do not feel satisfied in regard to this matter."[99]

R.K. Sidhwa wanted to include the Parsis along with the Hindus and the Sikhs. "There are 12,000 Parsis who are professing the same faith as we are here, but their grand-fathers are born in Iran and several of them come to Bombay and to other parts of India; they would like sometimes to make India their home. It is a far-fetched point that I am making, but if at all it is going to be considered, then my point is this that we need not mention necessarily 'any community'; if we do so it would look as if we are ignoring other communities which do require attention and therefore, I place this viewpoint before the House, if they at all want to take this amendment into consideration", he told the Assembly.[100]

Sardar Bhupinder Singh Mann also supported this demand. "Our demand is that any person, who because of communal riots in Pakistan has come over to India and stays here at the commencement of the Constitution, should automatically be considered as a citizen of India and should on no account be made to go to a registering authority and plead before him and establish a qualification of six months domicile to claim rights of citizenship. There may be victims of communal frenzy in our neighbouring State hereafter; it is not only a possibility but a great probability in the present circumstances. Any failure of the evacuee property talks may lead to a flare-up against Hindus and Sikhs in Pakistan, and we must have a clause that these people will in no case be debarred from coming over and becoming citizens of his Union", he said.[101]

Mahboob Ali Baig Sahib however characterised this 'conception' as 'ridiculous'.[102]

Alladi Krishnaswami Ayyar made a passing reference to this suggestion when he said, "we are plighted to the principles of a secular State. We may make a distinction between people who have voluntarily and deliberately chosen another country as their home and those who want to retain their connection with this country. But we cannot on any racial or religious or other grounds make a distinction between one kind of persons and another, or one sect of persons and another sect of persons, having regard to our commitments and the formulation of our policy on various occasions."[103]

During the third reading of the Constitution not many members harped on the citizenship provisions, Only R.K. Sidhva, Kuladhar Chaliha, Pandit Thakur Das Bhargava, Rev. J.J.M. Nichols Roy, Brajeswar Prasad. Algu Rai Shastri, Ajit Prasad Jain, Ari Bahadur Gurung and Shri Alladi Krishnaswami Ayyar spoke about it in passing. Alladi Krishnaswami Ayyar, however, reminded the House of the single citizenship for the whole of India. He said: "In regard to citizenship, the Constitution deliberately adopts the principle of single citizenship for the whole of India and departs from a dual citizenship, a common feature of many Federations. In this respect, the Indian Constitution is in advance of some of the Federal Constitutions. It is hoped that that will lead to the consolidation of the Indian Union. The Constitution does not purport to enact a detailed law as to citizenship, but leaves it for the future Parliament of India to frame such a law."[104]

At the revision stage, the proviso to Article 5, disqualifying a person for Indian citizenship if he had voluntarily acquired the citizenship of a foreign state, was separated and made into an independent article-present article 9—and the existing articles 5, 5A, 5AA, 5B, 5C and 6 were respectively renumbered as 5, 6, 7, 8, 10 and 11. With a few other modifications of a verbal nature, they were finally incorporated in the Constitution adopted on November 26, 1949. Of these, articles 5 to 9 came into force on the adoption of the Constitution on November 26, 1949.[105]

Article 5 allows every person who was born in India or who had been resident in India for not less than five years immediately before the commencement of the Constitution to become a citizen of India.

Article 6 lays down that a person who had migrated to India from the territory now included in Pakistan would be deemed to be a citizen of India. However, according to Article 7, a person who after 1 March, 1947 migrated from India to Pakistan shall not become a citizen of India. But, if he/she returned on or after 19 July, 1948, he or she would be granted citizenship under certain conditions. Under Article 8, Indian citizenship can be granted to certain persons of Indian origin residing outside India

Article 9 disqualifies a person for Indian citizenship if he had voluntarily acquired the citizenship of a foreign state. Article 10 stipulates continuance of the rights of citizenship once acquired subject to any law to be made by the Parliament and Article 11 empowers the Parliament to make any provision with regard to the acquisition and termination of citizenship and all other matters relating to citizenship after the commencement of the Constitution

Niraja Gopal Jayal points out that Article 5 was a preliminary foundational statement of *jus soli* citizenship, albeit one that applied only to persons already living rather than to future persons born after the commencement of the Constitution. It was chosen as a form of 'enlightened, modern civilised' and democratic citizenship, over the rival principle of *jus sanguinis* described by the constitution makers as 'an idea of racial citizenship'. If Article 5 was an enunciation of citizenship for ordinary times, Articles 6 and 7 were articulations of citizenship for extraordinary times. Article 6 provides for citizenship for persons who migrated to India from the territory now included in Pakistan if either of their parents or grand-parents was born in India. If such a person migrated to India before 19 July, 1948, he should have been resident in India since the date of his migration; and if he migrated after that date, he should have been registered as a citizen of India by a designated government official. If Article 6 was intended to accord rights of citizenship to those people who migrated from Pakistan to India around the time of the Partition, Article 7 was correspondingly designed to exclude from cittzenship those persons who migrated from India to Pakistan after 1 March, 1947. However, it provided for rights of citizenship for those who had so migrated from India to Pakistan but returned to India with a 'permit of resettlement or permanent return' issued by an authorised government official, after the same date and by a process similar to that provided for in Article 6. As we have seen Article 7 was a hugely embattled provision in the Constituent Assembly.

Article 9 states that individuals who voluntarily acquired the citizenship of a foreign state cannot be citizens of India. Article 10 provides for the continuance of the rights of citizenship for anyone deemed to be a citizen under the earlier provisions 'subject to the provisions of any law that may be made by Parliament', and Article 11 gives Parliament complete power to 'make any provision with respect to the acquisition and termination of citizenship and all other matters relating to citizenship'. The last two Articles underscore unambiguously the stopgap and *ad hoc* nature of the constitutional provisions on citizenship, which are intended to provide for the specific situation of the extraordinary event of the Partition while a conception of citizenship for normal times awaits the attention of an elected Parliament.[106]

IV

From the trend of discussions it appears that the criticism against the articles rivetted mainly on two points:

(i) It would open the flood-gates of infiltration of Muslims from East Pakistan, and
(ii) It would give a fillip to the Pro-Pak elements to come back again mainly from West Pakistan.

Many members pointed out very forcefully the inherent lacunae in the Draft Article to prevent infiltration of Muslims from East Pakistan. Rohini Chowdhury, as the mouthpiece of Assamese people, projected the dimension of the problem of continuous and unabated infiltration from East Pakistan. He warned about the danger that would befall on the country if the infiltration was allowed to continue. He even predicted a 'great danger' if 'the balance of the population' was thus allowed to be disturbed. But it did not cut any ice. N. Gopalswami Ayyangar pointed out the difficulties in introducing a permit system. Even if the permit system was introduced would it have been effective? Effectiveness of the permit system could only be ensured if the persons coming from the other side did it legally. But what about those who were coming surreptitiously, those coming illegally and then got mingled with their own 'brethren'? Ayyangar assured of 'devising other measures of solution.' And there it rested. Dr. Ambedkar even went to the extent of terming the apprehension of Sri Choudhury as 'unfounded.' He however found panacea in the 'plenary power' of the Registering Authority. But the Registering Authority was supposed to act within the four walls of the legal framework. His 'discretion' cannot 'over ride' constitutional safeguards. The Registering Authority cannot be above the law of the country.

But the Drafting Committee decided to keep their eyes shut to the problem and did not like to take any concrete and meaningful step to solve this problem. They mainly took shelter under Article 11 which empowered the Parliament to enact a citizenship law later for acquisition and termination of citizenship. The philosophy of living for to-day and sidetracking the vexed and unpleasant questions was very much pronounced in the debate. When the members of the Constituent Assembly themselves felt hesitant or were rather unwilling to codify certain safeguards in the Constitution for preventing influx from across the border, how could they expect that the future Parliament at the time of enacting a comprehensive Citizenship Act would take into consideration all the points raised during discussion in the Constituent Assembly and plug the loopholes, especially when the Drafting Committee scotched at those suggestions and apprehensions even at that stage when they had the scope and power to act? It is not feasible to undo the wrong done earlier. It is not possible to take back what was given earlier. This attitude of passing on the buck to somebody else or to shelve it for the time being, which is very much evident in the Constitution, has had its effect on the destiny of the country. The menace of infiltration which started from pre-partition days went on unabated and ultimately assumed such a gigantic proportion that the placid situation in Assam was highly disturbed. The entire region was engulfed in turmoil for a considerable period and the neighbouring States also had to bear the brunt of its consequences. A massive movement continued in Assam since 1979 and many precious lives were lost in the violent incidents that went on with the movement. An agreement popularly known as Assam Accord was signed in August 1985 between the protagonists of the movement and the Central Government. After the Assembly elections in 1985, a change of government took place in Assam. As a follow-up of Assam Accord some steps have been taken or are being taken to try a solution of this problem. Even then, it is doubtful if the problem would be solved altogether and whether this problem in one form or the other will not manifest itself in other states like West Bengal, Meghalaya and Bihar. Already an attempt is being made in some states to start a movement on the pattern of Assam Movement to identify and drive out the so-called 'foreigners.' Some sort of feelings have crept in the minds of a section of people that the legitimate demands of the people won't be heard by the Government unless a strong movement something like 'Assam-type movement' is launched. If this type of movement or rather the philosophy behind the movement, spreads to other areas one can very well imagine its likely impact on the integrity of the country as such. Unwillingness to deal with a problem at the very initial stage has led the country to bigger and challenging problems.

Another casualty of Assam movement is the Bengalee Hindus, a large number of whom are living with an uncertain future. Ayyangar also visualised the 'over-zealous officials of the Assam Government' treating 'the Bengalis (Hindu?) who have migrated from East Bengal to Assam and perhaps even from West Bengal to Assam' in a manner which would be 'prejudicial to their interest.' This shows that the Central Government was aware of such a trend even then. But what constitutional safeguards were provided for them? The problem which was germane even then was not sorted out. Dr. Deshmukh had perhaps this problem in mind when he suggested that the citizenship right be given to all Hindus and Sikhs. This suggestion of Dr. Deshmukh was passed over and none from those who mattered even thought it proper to explain why the suggestion was not acceptable to them. If the suggestion of Dr. Deshmukh was acted upon with requisite variations, the Hindus, especially the Bengalee Hindus of N.E. Region would not have faced the present situation. Regionalism could have been contained to a great extent. The member from Assam, at least in his speech, did not show any bias against Bengali Hindus. It was quite evident even then that the Hindus would not be able to stay in East Pakistan for long, especially after the migration of the leaders, intellectuals and prosperous class of Hindus. No exchange of population took place as was done in Punjab. No constitutional safeguards were provided for those Hindus of East Pakistan who were forced to face the situation not on their own volition. Curiously enough, none from West Bengal raised this issue at the time of the debate. In politics the result is not always discernible at the time of formulation of a policy. A wrong step often leads the country to a greater catastrophe later. A little foresightedness on the part of our elder statesmen would have changed the entire complexion.

Now regarding the persons who migrated to Pakistan in the wake of partition but came back for resettlement in India, mainly Muslims, the saner elements, especially those who were themselves victims of partition, warned the Government of its policy of bringing back all who wanted to come back to India under certain conditions. When no cogent point could be marshalled, all of them including the members of the Drafting Committee more or less pleaded for honouring 'the Government assurance and Government decision.' Constituent Assembly was reduced to a mere rubber stamp of the Government. Pros and cons were not considered, its effects on the economic, political, social, religious and communal situation were not considered and recourse was taken to high-sounding jargons. The proposal of Jinnah for exchange of population was not accepted. As a matter of fact, the Congress could never reconcile itself to the fact of partition. They thought that it was a passing phase and in course of time both the Dominions would merge. The political fact of partition was never accepted by them. If the coming events or the chain of likely events consequent to the formulation of a certain policy could not be assessed in proper perspectives, the country naturally has to suffer for it. In the words of Jaspat Roy Kapoor, "while it is good to be generous, generosity loses much of its virtue when it is at the cost of others." The leaders forgot this concept and helped the country plunge into the present day crisis. Can we blame the Muslim League leaders for this when their proposal for exchange of population was not acted upon? The partition of the country on the basis of two nation theory was agreed upon but objection was raised to the exchange of population, a logical extension of the two nation theory. Did it help anybody? It cannot be gainsaid that it devolves on those who guide the destiny of the nation to always keep the larger interest of the country in view while formulating a policy.

One thing is very surprising. None of the members demanded introduction of Citizens' Identity Card.[107] If that system was introduced from the very inception, from the date of commencement of the Constitution and made obligatory on the part of each and every citizen to possess an Identity Card, as soon as one is born, much of the present day ills would have been kept at bay. The problem of infiltration could have been tackled very effectively and meaningfully, the claims and counter-claims of citizenship could have been sorted out without any trouble, and with proper planning and foresight the menace of 'rigging in election' and of 'the black money' could have been checked. Perhaps the Framers of the Constitution did not see that far.

NOTES

1. Weiner, Myron, "Rejected Peoples and Unwanted Migrants in South Asia", *Economic and Political Weekly,* August 21, 1993, p. 1737.
2. *Constituent Assembly Debates* (henceforth *CAD*), Vol. IX, dated 10-8-49, p. 347.
3. Rao, B. Shiva (ed). *The Framing of India's Constitution*, Select Documents, Volume II, 1967, New Delhi, The Indian Institute of Public Administration, p. 116.
4. *Ibid.*, p. 136.
5. *Ibid.*, pp. 147-148.
6. *Ibid.*, p. 154.
7. *Ibid.*, p. 163.
8. *Ibid.*, p. 171.
9. *Ibid.*, p. 216.
10. *CAD,* Vol. III, p. 440.
11. *Ibid.*, dated 29-4-47, p. 418.
12. *Ibid.*, dated 29-4-47, pp. 417-425.
13. Rao, B. Shiva (ed), Volume II, *Op. Cit.*, p. 678.

14. *CAD*, Vol. III, dated 2-5-47, p. 526.
15. *Ibid.,* pp. 526-31.
16. Rao, *Op. Cit*., Vol. II, pp. 472-73.
17. *Ibid*., p. 473.
18. *Ibid*., p. 616.
19. *Ibid*., pp. 678-682.
20. *Ibid*., pp. 561-562.
21. *Ibid*., pp. 576-577.
22. *Ibid*., pp. 577-578.
23. *Ibid*., pp. 682-683.
24. *Ibid*., p. 613.
25. *CAD*, Vol. IV, dated 21-7-47, p. 711.
26. Rao, *Op. Cit*., Vol. III, pp. 5-6.
27. *Ibid*., pp. 197-198.
28. *Ibid*., p. 325.
29. *Ibid*., pp. 406-7.
30. *Ibid*., pp. 470-72.
31. *Ibid*., pp. 474-75.
32. *Ibid.,* pp. 480-82.
33. *Ibid*., pp. 519-20.
34. *Ibid*., p. 511.
35. Rao, *Ibid*., Vol. IV, pp. 15-16.
36. *Ibid*., pp. 16-17.
37. *Ibid*., pp. 17-18.
38. *Ibid*., pp. 18-20.
39. *Ibid*., p. 21.
40. *Ibid*., pp. 21-22.
41. *Ibid*., pp. 22-23.
42. *Ibid*., p. 222.
43. Rao, *Ibid*., Vol. V, pp. 160-161.
44. Rao, *Ibid*., Vol. IV, p. 23.
45. *Ibid*., p. 24.
46. *Ibid.*
47. *Ibid*., p. 409.
48. *Ibid*., p. 23.
49. *Ibid*., p. 416.
50. *CAD*, Vol. VII, dated 18-11-48, pp. 470-471.
51. Rao, *Op. Cit*., Vol. IV, pp. 520-526.
52. *Ibid*., Vol. V, pp. 163-164.
53. *CAD,* Vol. IX dated 10-8-49, pp. 347-349.
54. *Ibid*., p. 347.
55. *Ibid*., p. 365.
56. *Ibid.*
57. *Ibid.*
58. *Ibid*., dated 11-8-49, p. 381.

59. *Ibid.*, p. 382.
60. *Ibid.*, p. 390.
61. *Ibid.*
62. *Ibid.*, dated 12-8-49, p. 393.
63. *Ibid.*, p. 410.
64. *Ibid.*, p. 417.
65. *Ibid.*, pp. 413-416.
66. *Ibid.*, pp. 411-412.
67. *Ibid.*, pp. 419-420.
68. *Ibid.*, p. 423.
69. *CAD,* Vol. XI, dated 18-11-49, p. 643.
70. *CAD,* Vol. IX, dated 11-8-49, p. 366.
71. *Ibid.*, p. 367.
72. *Ibid.*, p. 377.
73. *Ibid.*, pp. 380-81.
74. *Ibid.*, p. 383.
75. *Ibid.*, p. 384.
76. *Ibid.*, dated 12-8-49, p. 407.
77. *Ibid.*, dated 11-8-49, pp. 384-85.
78. *Ibid.*, dated 12-8-49, pp. 393-94.
79. *Ibid.*, p. 394.
80. *Ibid.*, p. 395.
81. *Ibid.*, pp. 397-398.
82. *Ibid.*, pp. 400-401.
83. *Ibid.*, pp. 404-405.
84. *Ibid.*, p. 398.
85. *Ibid.*, p. 401.
86. *Ibid.*, p. 386.
87. *Ibid.*, p. 403.
88. *Ibid.*, p. 412.
89. *Ibid.*, p. 418.
90. *Ibid.*, p. 424.
91. *Ibid.*, p. 406.
92. *Ibid.*, p. 407.
93. *Ibid.*, p. 409.
94. *Ibid.*, p. 413.
95. *Ibid.*, p. 419.
96. *Ibid.*, p. 424.
97. *Ibid.*, pp. 355-356.
98. *Ibid.*, p. 376.
99. *CAD*, Vol. XI, dated 21-12-49, p. 764.
100. *CAD,* Vol. IX, dated 11-8-49, p. 387.
101. *Ibid.*, dated 12-8-49, p. 393.
102. *CAD*, Vol. XI, dated 21-12-49, p. 396.
103. *Ibid.*, p. 404.

104. *CAD*, Vol. XI, dated 23-11-49, p. 836.
105. Rao, *Ibid.*, Vol. IV, p. 167.
106. Jayal, Niraja Gopal, "Citizenship", In Sujit Choudhury, Madhav Khosla and Pratap Bhanu Mehta (eds.), *The Oxford Handbook of the Indian Constitution*, 2016, Oxford University Press, pp. 166-167.
107. Chatterjee, S.K., Identity Issue in the Indian Context, *Journal of Human & Environmental Sciences,* Vol. 1, No. 1, Spring 1996, pp. 32-40.

2
The Citizenship Act, 1955 and Its Amendments

Constitutions do not ordinarily define citizenship. Despite its invocation in the Declaration of the Rights of Mao (1789), its vesting of national sovereignty in the French people and its canonically inclusive conception of citizenship, the Constitution of the Fifth Republic in France does not actually define this concept. In the American Constitution, citizenship remained undefined until after the adoption of the Fourteenth Amendment in the aftermath of the Civil War and as a reaction to the Supreme Court's decision in *Dred Scott* v. *Sanford* (1857). Even the famously progressive Brazilian Constitution of 1988, which privileges the value of citizenship as a founding principle of the republic, and defines expansively the social and economic rights of the people, does not actually indicate what the source and basis of citizenship will be.[1]

When Indian Constituent Assembly began its deliberations in December 1946, there was no thought of a separate chapter on the topic of citizenship. By the time the Constitution was adopted, the Partition had intervened and citizenship had become the subject of Part II of the Constitution, following the first part on the Union and its Territories.

The chapter on citizenship in the Indian Constitution has two distinctive qualities. First, more than any other set of provisions in the Constitution, the Articles on citizenship have a pronounced quality of immediacy of belonging only to the moment of their enactment. This is unusual because constitutions generally reflect a quality of timelessness in their phrasing, a sense of being enacted in perpetuity rather than speaking to a presumptively fleeting moment in time. The avowedly momentary character is accentuated, secondly, by the self-limiting provision that a more permanent and enduring law on citizenship will be enacted by Parliament in due course. While recommending to the Constituent

Assembly the adoption of these Articles, Dr. Ambedkar clearly stated that these provisions were not intended to lay down a permanent or unalterable law of Indian citizenship but "all that we are doing is to decide *ad hoc* for the time being the question as to who would be citizens on the date of the commencement of the Constitution." Every other matter relating to citizenship would be determined by Parliament. The phrasing of Article 11 reaffirms the transience and self-limiting character of these constitutional provisions.[2]

After a lapse of about six years of the commencement of the Indian Constitution, in 1955, a comprehensive Act for the acquisition and termination of Indian Citizenship was enacted by the Indian Parliament which became the Citizenship Act of 1955 (Act LVII of 1955). Two provisions of this Act namely conferment of citizenship right to migrants from Pakistan and commonwealth citizenship attracted strong criticism from the Members of the Lok Sabha. Members like N.C. Chatterjee[3], H.N. Mukherjee[4], Barman[5], Pandit Thakur Das Bhargava[6], B.K. Das[7], Sadhan Gupta[8], M.S. Gurupadaswamy[9], Gidwani[10], asked the Government to make special provisions for the refugees from Pakistan. They were of the view that those migrants to India from Pakistan etc. when they come to India should not be asked to get themselves registered; they should automatically be considered as Indian citizens.[11] They were not in favour of the provisions of section 5 of the Act which provides for going through the process of registration and taking oath of allegiance. They wanted that the persons who were migrating to India from Pakistan on account of communal disturbances or fear of such disturbance should be considered as citizens of India either by descent under section 4 or by birth under section 3. Sadhan Gupta even brought amendments to sections 3 and 4 to that effect. His amendments to sections 3 and 4 were as follows:

(A) Page 2—after line 37, add:

"(3) Every person who is a citizen of India by virtue of article of the Constitution or is deemed to be such citizen by virtue of article 6 thereof or who, since the commencement of the Constitution has migrated or may migrate to India from Pakistan by reason of communal disturbance or oppression, shall be deemed to be a citizen of India by birth."

(B) Page 3—after line 20 add:

"(4) Notwithstanding anything contained in this section, every person who is a citizen of India by virtue of clause (c) of article 5 of the constitution or who, since the commencement of the constitution has migrated or may migrate to India from Pakistan by reason of communal disturbance or from fear of communal disturbance or oppression, shall be deemed to be a citizen of India, by descent."[12]

B.K. Das thought that "they should have been put in a separate category and a process evolved for their acquiring citizenship."[13]

These arguments however did not cut much ice and the provisions of the Act were not amended.

Another objection raised by them was against the Commonwealth citizenship. Pandit Thakur Das Bhargava thought that there would be influx in Assam due to such persons coming to Assam and seeking registration under section 12 of the Act. He even brought an amendment for insertion of the following new sub-clause to sub-section 1 of section 5:

"(f) The Central Government may in its discretion refuse registration to any person on account of any emergency or in case of large influx in India of such persons as are mentioned in section 5A, for reasons of security or maintenance of the economy of India or any part of it."[14]

Giving reasons for moving this amendment Pandit Bhargava said: "We had the sad experience in Assam. We had to make a law in regard to the immigrants from Pakistan for their expulsion. That did not materialise on account of the Nehru-Liakat Ali Pact. All the same, a similar situation may again arise in Assam or in any other part of the country. Many persons may come in and a sort of emergency may arise. In conditions like this, for reasons of security and the maintenance of the economy of India, as well as in any threatened emergency, Government should refuse registration. It is not only discretionary. I am of opinion that they should refuse registration and they should not allow persons to come into India and endanger the economy of this country."[15]

Mulchand Dube wanted to substitute the words 'ordinarily resident' and 'so resident' occurring in section 5(I)(a) by the word 'domiciled.' His argument was: "The highest courts of the country have distinguished between residence and domicile. ... Domicile in fact implies an intention to make the country one's own. So long as a person has not intended to make Indian territory his home any length of residence should not enable him to get himself registered. I would also draw attention to the Explanation at page-4, which reads:

"For the purposes of this sub-section, a person shall be deemed to be of Indian origin if he or either of his parents or any of his grand-parents, was born in undivided India."

The result of this will be that every person in Pakistan would be entitled to be registered as a citizen of India if only he resides here for six months. Having regard to the disputes and differences that we are having with Pakistan, this kind of thing would not be safe at all. ... The condition of domicile is present in Article 5 of the Constitution."[16]

Pandit Bhargava also wanted that "domicile plus birth should both be applied for the right of citizenship to every person who is born in India."[17]

These amendments were, however, not accepted and the Act was passed in spite of strong opposition from these Members. The Act, as enacted, does not provide any safeguard against infiltration from across the border. The Act does not discriminate between refugees from Pakistan who are coming over being unable to stay in Pakistan (and now Bangladesh also) on account of communal disturbance or fear of such disturbance and those coming for other purposes not being a victim of such disturbances. We have seen that in the Constituent Assembly there was a proposal by Dr. P.S.Deshmukh of making all Hindus and Sikhs the citizens of India, provided they were not citizens of any other country, because they had no other place in the wide world to go to. They should have the right of citizenship in India and should be entitled to retain such citizenship so long as they did not acquire any other.[18] Prof. Shibban Lal Saksena[19], Algu Rai Shastri[20] and Sardar Bhupinder Singh Mann[21] supported Deshmukh while R.K.Sidhwa wanted to include the Parsis along with the Hindus and the Sikhs.[22] The Citizenship Act does not take cognizance of these points raised during the debates on citizenship in the Constituent Assembly.

II

The Constitution of India only laid down the law in regard to citizenship at the commencement of the Constitution. The conferment of a person as a citizen of India is governed by Articles 5 to 11 in Part II of the Constitution of India. According to Article 5, every person who has his domicile in India at the commencement of the Constitution and people born in India or either of whose parents was born in the territory of India or who has been ordinarily resident in the territory of India for not less than five years immediately preceding such commencement shall be a citizen of India. It did not provide for the acquisition and termination of Indian citizenship. Article 11 left it to Parliament to regulate the right of citizenship by law.

The Indian legislation related to this matter is The Citizenship Act, 1955. The Act consisted of nineteen sections and three schedules—sections 3 to 7 for acquisition and sections 8 to10 for termination. The Act was amended in 1957 (Act 65 of 1957 which became effective from 27 December, 1957), 1960 (Act 58 of 1960 which became effective from 26 October, 1960), 1985 (Act 65 of 1985 which became effective from 7-12-85), 1986 (Act 4 of 1986 which came into force with effect from1-7-87), 1992 (Act 39 of 1992 effective from 10-12-92), 2003 (Act 6 of 2004 which became operative from 3-12-2004), 2005 (Act 32 of 2005 which came into force from 28-6-2005), 2015 (Act 1 of 2015 which came into force w.e.f. 6-1-2015) and lastly in 2019 (The Act was assented to on 10 January, 2020).

In the 1980s, major changes were brought about by the Congress government in the Citizenship Act, 1955 concerning citizenship by birth. One of them was the insertion of Section 6A to the Citizenship Act in 1985 to give effect to the Assam Accord [Act 65 of 1985 (effective from 7-12-85)] and the other was the amendment in 1986 [Act 4 of 1986 (effective from 1-7-87)]. As per the amendments, it is no longer adequate to be born in India to be granted Indian citizenship. At the time of birth either one of the parents has to be an Indian citizen for the person to become a citizen of India. Moreover, prior to the coming into force of the Citizenship (Amendment) Act, 1986, i.e., 1st July, 1987, the period of residency immediately before making an application for registration was six months. Now the period is five years. None of these two amendments did make any religion-based distinction.

As per the Assam Accord (placed as Annexure A), 1st January, 1966 was determined to be the precise date based on which the detection and deletion of illegal immigrants from Assam is to take place. It allowed citizenship for all persons coming to Assam from "Specified Territory" before the cut-off date. It further specifies that all persons who came to Assam prior to 1st January, 1966 (inclusive) and up to 24th March, 1971 (midnight) shall be detected in accordance with the provisions of the Foreigners Act, 1946 and the Foreigners (Tribunals) Order, 1939. Names of foreigners so detected will be deleted from the Electoral Rolls in force. Such persons will be required to register themselves before the Registration Officers of the respective districts in accordance with the provisions of the Registration of Foreigners Act, 1939 and the Registration of Foreigners Rules, 1939. On the expiry of the period of ten years following the date of detection, the name of all such persons which have been deleted from the electoral rolls shall be restored. Foreigners who came to Assam on or after 25th March, 1971 shall continue to be detected, deleted and expelled in accordance with law.

To give effect to the Assam Accord, Section 6A was inserted in the Citizenship Act in 1985. The constitutional validity of this Section of the Citizenship Act was challenged in the Supreme Court. A Bench of the

Supreme Court consisting of Justices Ranjan Gogoi and Fali S. Nariman delivered its judgment on 17 December, 2014 in Writ Petition No. 562 of 2012 of Assam Sanmilita Mahasangha & others, as also in Petition (Civil) No. 274 of 2009 of Assam Public Works, and Petition (Civil) No. 876 of 2014 of All Assam Ahom Association and others. The Bench raised a number of points for decision by a Constitution Bench with a minimum of 5 Judges. The following questions were raised by the Bench:

33 (i) Whether Articles 10 and 11 of the Constitution of India permit the enactment of Section 6A of the Citizenship Act in as much as Section 6A, in prescribing a cut-off date different from the cut-off date prescribed in Article 6, can do so without a "variation" of Article 6 itself; regard, in particular, being had to the phraseology of Article 4 (2) read with Article 368 (1)?

(ii) Whether Section 6A violates Articles 325 and 326 of the Constitution of India in that it has diluted the political rights of the citizens of the State of Assam?

(iii) What is the scope of the fundamental right contained in Article 29(1)? Is the fundamental right absolute in its terms? In particular, what is the meaning of the expression "culture" and the expression "conserve"? Whether Section 6A violates Article 29(1)?

(iv) Whether Section 6A violates Article 355? What is the true interpretation of Article 355 of the Constitution? Would an influx of illegal migrants into a State of India constitute "external aggression" and/or "internal disturbance"? Does the expression "State" occurring in this Article refer only to a territorial region or does it also include the people living in the State, which would include their culture and identity?

(v) Whether Section 6A violates Article 14 in that, it singles out Assam from other border States (which comprise a distinct class) and discriminates against it. Also whether there is no rational basis for having a separate cut-off date for regularizing illegal migrants who enter Assam as opposed to the rest of the country?

(vi) Whether Section 6A violates Article 21 in that the lives and personal liberty of the citizens of Assam have been affected adversely by the massive influx of illegal migrants from Bangladesh?

(vii) Whether delay is a factor that can be taken into account in moulding relief under a petition filed under Article 32 of the Constitution?

(viii) Whether, after a large number of migrants from East Pakistan have enjoyed rights as Citizens of India for over 40 years, any relief can be given in the petitions filed in the present cases?

(ix) Whether section 6A violates the basic premise of the Constitution and the Citizenship Act in that it permits Citizens who have allegedly not lost their Citizenship of East Pakistan to become deemed Citizens of India, thereby conferring dual Citizenship to such persons?

(x) Whether section 6A violates the fundamental basis of section 5(1) proviso and section 5(2) of the Citizenship Act (as it stood in 1985) in that it permits a class of migrants to become deemed Citizens of India without any reciprocity from Bangladesh and without taking the oath of allegiance to the Indian Constitution?

(xi) Whether the Immigrants (Expulsion from Assam) Act, 1950 being a special enactment qua immigrants into Assam, alone can apply to migrants from East Pakistan/Bangladesh to the exclusion of the general Foreigners Act and the Foreigners (Tribunals) Order, 1964 made thereunder?

(xii) Whether Section 6A violates the Rule of Law in that it gives way to political expediency and not to Government according to law?

(xiii) Whether Section 6A violates fundamental rights in that no mechanism is provided to determine which persons are ordinarily resident in Assam since the dates of their entry into Assam, thus granting deemed citizenship to such persons arbitrarily?

The Bench, however, gave its order on the Writ petitions on the "footing that Section 6A of the Citizenship Act is valid" till a verdict is given to the contrary by a larger Bench. Amongst other directions, the Bench fixed a time schedule to govern the work of updating of the NRC in Assam so that the entire updated NRC was published by the end of January, 2016. (para 48)

A five-judge Bench consisting of Justices Madan B. Lokur, R.K. Agarwal, P.C. Pant, D.Y. Chandrachud and Ashok Bhushan was constituted to hear this case. The Bench wanted to complete the hearing by 19 May, 2017 but could not as several advocates said it would be difficult to conclude the argument by 19 May. The Bench decided to put off the hearing to the second week of July and referred the matter to the Chief Justice to fix a fresh date.[23]

The retirement of Justice P.C. Pant, one of the Justices, necessitated the constitution of a fresh Bench. Chief Justice Dipak Mishra hinted on 5 February, 2018 that another Constitution Bench would be formed soon.[24] A decision on the constitutional validity of insertion of Section 6A in the Citizenship Act is pending till now.

The next amendment to the Citizenship Act was effected in 1992.The Citizenship Amendment Act of 1992 amends Section 4 of the Citizenship Act providing that a person born outside India on or after January 26, 1950 but before the commencement of the Act (10-12-92) shall be a citizen of India by descent if the father is a citizen of India at the time of his birth; or on or after the commencement of the Act, the person shall be a citizen of India by descent if either of the parents is a citizen of India at the time of his birth. It also replaces references to "male persons" with "persons".

The next major change happened in 2003-04 during the National Democratic Alliance (NDA) regime with the enactment of the Citizenship (Amendment) Act, 2003 [Act 6 of 2004 (coming into force from 3-12-2004)]. For those who were born in India after 30 December, 2004 citizenship would be granted only if one of the parents was an Indian citizen at the time of the child's birth (as it was already prescribed under the 1986 amendment), and the second parent must not be an illegal immigrant. This means that if a child is born to an Indian father who marries a Bangladeshi woman who has illegally entered India, such a child would not be entitled to Indian citizenship. A child born after 30 December, 2004 in India will thus have to prove not only that they are born in India but also that one of their parents is an Indian citizen and that the other parent is not an illegal immigrant.

Sub-section (b) of Section 2 of this amendment defined an "illegal migrant" as a person who entered India without proper travel documents or entered India with proper travel documents but overstayed without permission. Ordinarily, such an illegal migrant could have applied for citizenship by registration or naturalisation by staying for certain number of years in India. But, the 2003 amendment also provided that such an illegal migrant cannot apply at all for Indian citizenship either by registration or naturalisation. Thus if a Bangladeshi crossed the border and came into India, they will not be entitled to Indian citizenship ever even if they get married here to an Indian citizen, stay for 60 years and have children in India. Even such children would not ever be entitled to Indian citizenship. This is totally contrary to the Child Rights Convention which India ratified in 1992 which requires a child to acquire nationality right from birth.

With a view to engaging Persons of Indian Origin (PIOs) with the land of their ancestors in a mutually beneficial relationship, the High Powered Committee on Indian Diaspora, constituted by the Central Government, *inter alia*, recommended the amendment of the Citizenship Act to provide for grant of dual citizenship to persons of Indian origin belonging to certain specified countries. Accordingly, the Citizenship (Amendment) Act, 2003

(6 of 2004) introduces several provisions for overseas citizens regarding their registration, rights in India, etc. The OCI Scheme is operated by the Ministry of Home Affairs. The Scheme provides for registration as Overseas Citizens of India (OCI) of all Persons of Indian Origin (PIOs) who were citizens of India on or after 26 January, 1950 or were eligible to become citizens of India on 26 January, 1950 and who are citizens of 16 specified countries other than Pakistan and Bangladesh.[25]

The 2003 amendment also mandated the Government of India to construct a National Register of Citizens and to issue national identity card to the Citizens.

The next amendment of 2005 [Act 32 of 2005 (operative with effect from 28-6-2005] was an extension of Act 6 of 2004 in respect of Overseas Citizens of India. The Prime Minister in the Pravasi Bhartiya Divas, 2005 made a statement on OCI scheme that the Government has decided to grant OCI to all overseas Indians who migrated from India after 26th January, 1950 as long as their home countries allow dual citizenship under their local laws. In order to implement the Government's decision, an Ordinance called the Citizenship (Amendment) Ordinance, 2005 was promulgated on 28th June, 2005 to extend the scope of OCI for PIOs of all countries except Pakistan and Bangladesh as long as their countries allow dual citizenship. The said Ordinance was replaced by this Act by amending the provisions of the Citizenship Act, 1955 so as to—

(i) expand the scope of grant of Overseas Citizenship of India to Persons of Indian Origin of all countries except Pakistan and Bangladesh; and
(ii) reduce the period of residence in India from two years to one year for the persons registered as Overseas Citizens of India to acquire Indian citizenship.

In early 2011, the then Prime Minister of India, Manmohan Singh, announced that the Person of Indian Origin card will be merged with the Overseas Citizen of India card. This new card proposed to be called the Overseas Indian Card. Following an assurance by Prime Minister Narendra Modi of merger of the PIO and OCI schemes, the Home Ministry notified on 9 January, 2015 that all existing PIO cardholders shall be deemed to be OCI card-holders and that there would be only one OCI card with enhanced benefits. This merger was facilitated by the promulgation of an ordinance on 9 January, 2015 amending the Citizenship Act, 1955, which became an Act following the adoption of the Citizenship (Amendment) Bill 2015 by the Lok Sabha on 1 March, 2015. (Act 1 of 2015 effective from 6-1-2015). Apart from seeking parity between cardholders of PIO and OCI, the Amendment Act provides, among other things, for registration of overseas citizen of India cardholder and deeming the persons of Indian origin cardholders to be overseas citizen of India cardholders. It also provides for conferment of rights on overseas citizen of India cardholders, renunciation of the card and cancellation of registration of the cardholders. It provides certain other relaxations to OCI cardholders like allowing breaks not exceeding 30 days in the one-year continuous stay required before applying for Indian citizenship and registration as an OCI by a minor born to Indian parents or by the spouse of an Indian citizen or OCI after two years of marriage. The Act provides PIOs benefits like life-long visa and exemption from appearing before the local police station on every visit.[26]

In 2015 and 2016, the Central Government issued two notifications exempting certain groups of illegal migrants from provisions of the Foreigners Act, 1946 and the Passport (Entry into India) Act, 1920. These groups are Hindus, Sikhs, Buddhists, Jains, Parsis and Christians from Afghanistan, Bangladesh and Pakistan, who arrived in India on or before December 31, 2014.This implies that these groups of illegal migrants will not be deported or imprisoned for being in India without valid documents.

The Citizenship (Amendment) Act, 2019 provides an easier path to citizenship for these persecuted selected minorities by adding a proviso to the 2003 definition of "illegal migrants". It says that any person belonging to Hindu, Sikh, Buddhist, Jain, Parsi or Christian community from Afghanistan, Bangladesh or Pakistan, who entered into India on or before the 31st day of December, 2014 and who has been exempted by the Central Government by or under clause (c) of sub-section (2) of section 3 of the Passport (Entry into India) Act, 1920 or from the application of the provisions of the Foreigners Act, 1946 or any rule or order made thereunder, shall not be treated as illegal migrant for the purposes of this Act. They will, however, have to fulfill two criteria—firstly they have entered into India before 31st December, 2014 and on an application they are exempted by the Central Government under the Passport (Entry into India) Act, 1920 or Foreigners Act, 1946. Therefore by virtue of this amendment, these persons shall not become automatically a citizen of India but first of all before coming out of the category of illegal migrants they have to prove that they entered into India before 31 December, 2014 and they have taken permission from Central Government.

III

The 1986 amendment restricted citizenship by birth to require that at least one parent had to be an Indian citizen. The 2003 amendment further restricted that aspect by requiring that a parent could not be an illegal immigrant. The 1992 amendment stipulates conditions of nationality of father or either of the parents of a person born outside India to be a citizen of India by descent. The 2019 amendment provided an easier path to citizenship for persecuted selected minorities, i.e., Hindus, Sikhs, Buddhists, Jains, Parsis and Christians from the neighbouring Muslim-majority countries of Bangladesh, Pakistan, and Afghanistan who entered India before 31 December, 2014.

In some of the European countries citizenship was determined by blood and race (*jus sanguinis*), regardless of the place of birth, while under the Anglo-American system citizenship was determined mainly on the place of birth (*jus soli*). The Indian Constitution thought it necessary that, in order to be a citizen of the Union at its inception, a person must have some kind of territorial connection with the Union, whether by birth, or descent, or domicile.[27] There has been a gradual and subtle shift towards a *jus sanguinis* conception since the mid-1980s. "While *jus soli* remains the governing principle of citizenship in India, citizenship law and jurisprudence have come to be manifestly inflected by elements of *jus sanguinis*. Whether it is the issue of 'illegal immigrants' from Bangladesh on the eastern border of India, or that of 'minority Hindus with Pakistani citizenship' on the western border, the law and rules have tended to view these very differently, seeing the latter (but not the former) as people with a rightful claim on Indian citizenship. The accenting of Indian citizenship with *jus sanguinis* is reflected also in the expansive approach latterly adopted towards the Indian diaspora", observes Jayal.[28]

The Citizenship Act 1955, as amended, (Annexure B) provides five methods of acquiring citizenship.

1. Citizenship by birth

Every person born in India on or after the 26th day of January, 1950, but before the 1st day of July, 1987 is a citizen of India by birth. A person born in India on or after the 1st day of July, 1987, but before 3 December, 2004 is a citizen of India if one of the parents is a citizen of India at the time of his birth. Those born in India on or after 3 December, 2004 are considered citizens of India only if both of their parents are citizens of India or if one parent is a citizen of India and the other is not an illegal migrant at the time of their birth. (Section 3 of the Citizenship Act, 1955)

2. Citizenship by descent

Persons born outside India on or after 26 January, 1950 but before 10

December, 1992 are citizens of India by descent if their father was a citizen of India at the time of their birth.

Persons born outside India on or after 10 December 1992 are considered citizens of India if either of their parents is a citizen of India at the time of their birth.

From 3 December, 2004 onwards, persons born outside of India shall not be considered citizens of India unless their birth is registered at an Indian diplomatic mission within one year of the date of birth. In certain circumstances, it is possible to register after one year with the permission of the Central Government. The application for registration of the birth of a child must be made to an Indian diplomatic mission and must be accompanied by an undertaking in writing from the parents of the child that he or she does not hold the passport of another country.

Any person born outside undivided India who was, or was deemed to be, a citizen of India at the commencement of the Constitution shall be deemed to be a citizen of India by descent only. (Section 4 of the Citizenship Act, 1955)

3. Citizenship by registration

The Central Government may, on an application, register as a citizen of India under section 5 of the Citizenship Act, 1955 any person (not being an illegal migrant) if s/he belongs to any of the following categories:

- a person of Indian origin who is ordinarily resident in India for seven years before making application under Section 5(1)(a) (throughout the period of twelve months immediately before making application and for six years in the aggregate in the eight years preceding the 12 months).
- a person of Indian origin who is ordinarily resident in any country or place outside undivided India;
- a person who is married to a citizen of India and is ordinarily resident in India for seven years before making an application for registration;
- minor children of persons who are citizens of India;
- a person of full age and capacity whose parents are registered as citizens of India.
- a person of full age and capacity who, or either of his parents, was earlier citizen of independent India, and has been residing in India for one year immediately before making an application for registration;

- a person of full age and capacity who has been registered as an overseas citizen of India for five years, and who has been residing in India for one year before making an application for registration. (Section 5 of the Citizenship Act, 1955).

4. Citizenship by naturalisation

Any person who does not come under any of the aforesaid categories can acquire citizenship by naturalisation if his application has been granted by the Government of India. Of course, there are some pre-conditions—

(i) He must not be a citizen of a country which prohibits Indians becoming a citizen of that country;

(ii) He must have renounced the citizenship of the country to which he so long belonged;

(iii) He must have resided in India or has been in the service of Government of India for at least one year;

(iv) He must have during seven years preceding the above mentioned one year, have resided in India;

(v) He must have a good moral character;

(vi) He must have sufficient knowledge of a recognised language of India;

(vii) He must inform that he would reside in India and continue his service under Government of India; and

(viii) He must take an oath of allegiance to the Constitution of India.

If in the opinion of the Central Government, the applicant is a person who has rendered distinguished service to the cause of science, philosophy, art, literature, world peace or human progress generally, it may waive all or any of the conditions mentioned above. (Section 6 of the Citizenship Act, 1955)

5. Citizenship by incorporation of territory

If any territory becomes a part of India, the Central Government may, by order notified in the Official Gazette, specify the persons who shall be citizens of India by reason of their connection with that territory; and those persons shall be citizens of India as from the date to be specified in the order. (Section 7 of the Citizenship Act, 1955)

In response to persistent demands for dual citizenship, particularly from the diaspora in North America and other developed countries, the Overseas Citizenship of India (OCI) scheme was introduced by amending The Citizenship Act, 1955 in August 2005. The scheme was launched during the Pravasi Bharatiya Divas convention in Hyderabad in 2006. (Sections 7A, 7B, 7C and 7D of the Citizenship Act, 1955)

Provisions for renunciation of citizenship and termination of citizenship have been made in Sections 8 and 9 of the Citizenship Act. The Act has mentioned the following conditions under which a citizen may lose his citizenship. First, he can declare in prescribed manner his intention to relinquish his citizenship. Secondly, if he voluntarily acquires citizenship of another country, his citizenship of India will terminate. Also, according to The Passports Act, a person has to surrender his/her Indian passport and voter card, and other Indian ID cards must not be used after another country's citizenship is obtained. It is a punishable offence if the person fails to surrender the passport.

Thirdly, his citizenship by naturalisation will be cancelled if he has acquired a title of a foreign country without permission or has shown his disrespect to the Indian Constitution or has favoured an enemy country. Fourthly, a minor who is a citizen of India by virtue of this section and is also a citizen of any other country shall cease to be a citizen of India if he does not renounce the citizenship or nationality of another country within six months of attaining full age. Lastly, a person shall not be a citizen of India by virtue of Section 3 of the Citizenship Act if at the time of his birth— (a) either his father or mother possesses such immunity from suits and legal process as is accorded to an envoy of a foreign sovereign power accredited to the President of India and he or she, as the case may be, is not a citizen of India; or (b) his father or mother is an enemy alien and the birth occurs in a place then under occupation by the enemy.

A person acquiring Indian citizenship by the process of naturalisation or registration may be deprived of his citizenship by an order of the Central Government under section 10

But the provisions regarding renunciation and termination of Indian Citizenship as provided in sections 8 and 9 of the Act are such that it is difficult to prove that those who had gone over to Pakistan for the purpose of settlement but are now coming back to India clandestinely and re-settling themselves here had renounced their citizenship or that their Indian Citizenship had been terminated earlier. As a result, trans-border illegal travel goes on unabated. The influx, illegal resettlement or illegal infiltration, whatever it is called, could not be tackled under this Act. Had it been so, the problem would not have assumed such a dimension.

IV

A case has been made out to allow overseas Indians to have citizenship and political rights. It has been argued that OCIs will bring new and better ideas for governance to improve delivery of public services and reduce corruption. And they will bring all the passion and energy that has allowed them to be successful overseas.[29]

In fact, even as early as 1991several of India's envoys, particularly in Western countries, have been lobbying with the external affairs ministry to speed up the formalities of according dual citizenship facilities to the non-resident Indians (NRIs) as NRIs could get an operating base in India. The dual citizenship move was mainly intended to woo NRI investment and most NRIs with the ability to ply money back left after independence.[30]

With a large number of poor people, India is one of the world's biggest sources of illegal immigrants. Developed countries are not going to give the Indian passport easy access into their airports anytime soon, no matter how much of a world 'power' anyone thinks India has become.

It is for this reason that talented and wealthy Indians who travel frequently and live abroad tend to take foreign citizenship. The act of taking foreign citizenship, for most Indians, is not 'anti-national' but a matter of convenience. Anyone who has filled up a US or UK visa form will empathise.

The Constitution of India does not allow holding Indian citizenship and citizenship of a foreign country simultaneously. A high-level Committee on the Indian Diaspora was set up in 2000 under the chairmanship of Dr L.M. Singhvi to prepare a comprehensive Report on the Indian Diaspora and to recommend measures for a constructive relationship with it. The Report of the Committee was submitted to Prime Minister Vajpayee in January 2002. It recommended that dual citizenship should be permitted and that Sections 9, 10 and 12 of the Citizenship Act, 1955 should be suitably amended. The Report further recommended that persons of Indian origin, who are nationals of any of the 16 countries (including Portugal) mentioned in the Schedule, should be eligible for dual citizenship. The Report also recommended that those who acquire dual citizenship should not be entitled to exercise electoral franchise and should not be inducted into the civil services or the defence or paramilitary forces except by a special order of the Central Government. The Government of India accepted these recommendations. In December, 2003, Parliament enacted the Citizenship (Amendment) Act, 2003 and Rules giving effect to the Act were notified in March 2004.

The Government of India formulated the Person of Indian Origin (PIO) Scheme and the Overseas Citizen of India (OCI) Scheme for the benefit of persons of Indian origin who hold foreign nationality. The PIO card was issued to Indians who have been staying abroad for a couple of generations while the OCI card was granted to more recent emigrants. The validity of the PIO card was fifteen years whilst the OCI card is for life. In 2011, Prime Minister Dr Manmohan Singh announced that the OCI and PIO cards would be merged to create the "Overseas Indian Cardholder Scheme". The Overseas Indian Cardholder is granted a lifelong visa to India, exemption from registration at the FRO for any length of time of stay in India and parity with resident Indians in financial, economic and educational matters except those relating to acquisition of agricultural property. As of 9 January, 2015, the PIO card scheme has been discontinued and applicants are to apply for OCI card only. All PIO Cardholders were advised, from time to time, to convert PIO Card to OCI Card.

Indian authorities have interpreted the law to mean a person cannot have a second country's passport simultaneously with an Indian one — even in the case of a child who is claimed by another country as a citizen of that country, and who may be required by the laws of the other country to use one of its passports for foreign travel (such as a child born in the United States or in Australia to Indian parents), and the Indian courts have given the executive branch wide discretion over this matter. Therefore, Overseas Citizenship of India is not an actual citizenship of India and thus, does not amount to dual citizenship or dual nationality or anyone no longer to use Indian IDs after OCI. Moreover, the OCI card is not a substitute for an Indian visa and therefore, the passport which displays the lifetime visa must be carried by OCI holders while travelling to India. OCI Cards are now being printed without the lifelong "U" Visa Sticker (which is normally pasted on the applicant's passport). The proof of lifelong visa will be just the OCI Card which will have "Life Time Visa" printed on it. The OCI Card will be valid with any Valid Passport. However, countries may consider the OCI as dual citizenship: for example, the UK government considers that, for purposes of the British Nationality Act 1981, "OCI is considered to be citizenship of another State".

Though the Overseas Citizenship of India (OCI) scheme is commonly known as 'dual citizenship' it is generally difficult to have dual citizenship of India and another country, due to the provisions for loss of Indian nationality when an Indian national naturalizes in another country, and the requirement to renounce one's existing citizenships when naturalizing in India. India does offer something called the "Overseas Citizen of India" card. Yet, these "overseas citizens" are not citizens because India doesn't have the option of dual nationality. The OCI status amounts to partial citizenship. It removes all barriers to entering, exiting, living and working in India. What it doesn't allow is the right to vote.

Even as the debate over the new citizenship law continues, over 12.50 lakh Indians gave up their citizenship between January 2014 and December 2022, preferring to be nationals elsewhere. The maximum cases came from the US, followed by Australia and Canada.

Foreign ministry data shows that more than 5.8 lakh Indians gave up citizenship between January 2015 and October 2019; the first 10 months of 2019 saw more than 1.1 lakh people surrendering their passports. The highest number was reported in 2016, when 1.3 lakh people gave up citizenship. All other years in the said period also saw more than a lakh people returning their Indian passports in favour of citizenships of other countries. The MEA data is a compilation of applications filed and granted in Indian missions across the world.

US accounted for 44 per cent of the requests, with 2.5 lakh Indians choosing to be American citizens instead. More than 1 lakh Indians gave up citizenship in Australia, followed by 94,874 in Canada. Australia and Canada together accounted for 33 per cent, leaving just another 1.3 lakh people spread across the remaining countries where Indians have migrated. While several countries like Pakistan and Syria did not see any request, Indian missions in the UK reported 35,986 requests.[31]

More than 1.3 crore Indian citizens have settled abroad as of January 2020; another 35.4 lakh have been granted OCI cards.[32] As foreign countries offer easy citizenship in exchange for cash and investments, the trend is only set to grow. Eighty-five countries in the world offer dual citizenship. [33] The countries that allow dual citizenship belong to both the developed and the developing world. They do so because they realise it is the wise choice in a globalised world of easy travel.

Antigua and Barbuda, the 'land of 365 beaches' allows dual citizenship to any foreigner if he/she invests in the National Development Fund (NDF), purchases government approved real estate or invests in pre-approved business. Since 2014, 28 Indians had applied for citizenship of Antigua and seven of them were granted Antiguan nationality between 1 January and 30 June, 2017, upon investment of $2,00,000. Indians, however, accounted for 2.50 per cent of citizenship requests out of 1,121 foreign nationals who sought refuge there since the inception of this programme. An Antiguan passport allows visa-free access to 132 countries and freedom from extradition.[34]

Many countries have found a way around the technical issues involved. Bangladesh requires its citizens to obtain a "dual nationality certificate" so that it can control who gets to take dual citizenship and under what circumstances. Brazilians can acquire another country's passport but they must enter and exit Brazil only on the Brazilian passport. Canada actually encourages dual citizenship; the US discourages but allows it.[35]

Some of our neighbouring countries, such as Pakistan, Bangladesh and Sri Lanka, allow some kind of dual citizenship. Pakistan permits dual citizenship to citizens from 13 Western countries as well as from Egypt, Jordan and Syria. Pakistanis with dual nationality are forbidden to run for public office, contest elections or join the military. On 20 September, 2012, the Supreme Court of Pakistan disqualified 11 lawmakers, including Interior Minister Rahman Malik, for failing to disclose their dual nationality. Bangladesh permits dual citizenship to persons of Bangladeshi origin who are citizens of the USA, UK, Australia, Canada and countries of the European Union. According to the Constitution of the People's Republic of Bangladesh, "A person shall be disqualified for election, or for being a Member of Parliament if he acquires the citizenship of, or affirms or acknowledges allegiance to a foreign State." Sri Lanka is the only Asian country that permits full dual citizenship. The persons with dual citizenship of Sri Lankan origin have the same rights as the other Sri Lankan citizens.[36] Signing dual citizenship agreements with other countries helps prevent its misuse.

The Indian Passport dropped two places in the Henley Passport Index 2020, which ranks countries according to the travel freedom of their citizens, at 84 with a score of 58. It means 58 countries allow entry to Indian passport holders without a prior visa. [37] The Indian Passport ranked 86 as of 2019, down from 77 in 2010.[38]

There are still some ways in which a person may have dual citizenship of India and another country. On 31 December, 1974, India and Portugal restored diplomatic relations and signed a Treaty to recognise India's sovereignty over Goa, Daman and Diu, Dadra and Nagar Haveli. As per this Treaty, Portugal recognised with retrospective effect the sovereignty of India over the territories which had constituted the Portuguese "Estado da India" from the date of their integration into the Union of India. The Portuguese Nationality Law of 1975 provides that Gaons, born before December 20, 1961 up to the third generation, are entitled to Portuguese citizenship, if they opt for it. This provision did not evoke much interest in Goa until 1986 when Portugal joined the European Union. Then, many Gaons seeking employment abroad found that a Portuguese passport would provide them easy access to the more affluent European countries.[39]

Thousands of Gaons have used the opportunity to migrate to Portugal and subsequently to the UK, thanks to the easy access across countries in the European Union. A significant number of expat Gaons have also availed of the 'Bilhete de Identidade', the Portuguese national identity card, which takes the applicant a step closer towards obtaining the Portuguese passport.

A 'Bilhete de Identidade' (bill of identity) not only allows them to travel to Portugal and other European Union (EU) countries without a visa, it also entitles them to invest in properties and obtain passport of any other EU nation, an official explained.[40] Rough estimates suggest that up to 30,000 Gaons are living in the UK, using the Portuguese citizenship route.[41]

This situation, according to officials has given rise to serious problems relating to nationality and citizenship such as non-surrender of Indian passport on acquisition of Portuguese nationality, illegal stay in India, violations of Foreigners' Act, or registration by a third party without the consent or knowledge of the concerned person.

The issue first came to light in 2012 when a case was filed in the HC of Bombay's Goa bench against Goa Vikas Party MLA Caetano de Silva seeking his disqualification on the grounds that he had registered his birth in Portugal and thus ceases to be Indian national.[42]

A verification by the Centre in 2015 had revealed that several politicians, police officers, and bureaucrats who hold Portuguese citizenship however claimed that it has been done without their knowledge.

The police have been reluctantly registering First Information Reports (FIRs) based on complaints filed by local activist Kashinath Shetye, claiming several politicians, legislators, police officers, bureaucrats, lawyers and thousands of Gaons, have over the years applied and availed themselves of the Portuguese identity card, Bilhete. Police initially refused to register FIRs, but later did so on the directions of a local trial court. Many politicians have also used this as a weapon by filing cases against their rivals.

The FIR registered on Shetye's complaints says people who have Bilhetes should surrender their Indian passports, and such government officers and politicians should resign. The names of many Gaons were deleted from electoral rolls after it became clear that they had obtained Portugese passports.[43]

The issue became contentious for the BJP government, with two legislators, Glen Ticlo (BJP) and Caitu Silva (alliance party member), being accused of having Portuguese passports and having processed their Bilhetes after registering their birth in Portugal. Both have maintained in court that their documentation in Portugal was processed by agents without their knowledge. While Silva lost the election on 4 February, 2017, Ticlo continues as BJP MLA. Silva is facing a petition filed by his political rival in the Bombay High Court at Goa. The BJP coalition government had maintained that the Bilhete alone is not proof of Portuguese identity and the individual continues to be an Indian citizen.[44]

Centre has empowered two district magistrates in Goa to examine the issue of Indian and Portuguese citizenship in the State. The collectors from North and South Goa will be responsible for scrutinising each application in terms of the Indian Citizenship Act, 1955 and Citizenship Rules of 2009, and submit the findings and reports on each case to the Centre, according to home ministry's notification. The notification will be valid for two years, the home ministry said.[45]

The exercise is likely to impact more than 2 lakh citizens of Goa who were issued a 'Bill of identity' by the Portuguese authority.[46]

Not only Goa but Kerala also faces similar problem of dual citizenship. There are several persons in Kerala who have acquired Pakistani citizenship in order to work in Pakistan and are now facing problems like those faced by some Gaons who acquired Portuguese nationality.[47] Several Kerala women—mostly maids—who migrated to the Gulf for jobs are struggling to get Indian citizenship for their children, born to partners in their host countries. More than 500 such cases have been reported from various Gulf countries. Most of the women are from Malabar in the north of Kerala. There are at least 20 such mothers within the Kozhikode Corporation's limits alone. As most of the mothers are poor, with little education and not much freedom of movement within the host countries, they failed to register the births of their children with an Indian embassy. The Kerala State Women's Commission is expected to seek government's support to carry out a detailed survey of the women. Investigation has bought out the fact that several expatriate women did not have certificates proving they were married to their foreign partners—some of them were duped and fell prey to sexual exploitation.[48]

V

Meanwhile, the Supreme Court on 25 July, 2013 sought response of the Centre and 18 States on a PIL demanding a safe haven for religious minorities — Hindus, Sikhs and Christians who escaped into the country from Bangladesh due to religious persecution.

The PIL by NGO *Swajan* stated that the minorities fleeing out of Bangladesh were victims of religious persecution in the neighbouring country and should be entitled to the protection provided to victims of persecution in Bangladesh under Section 2 of Immigrants (Expulsion from Assam) Act, 1950.

With the problem not just limited to Assam but spread across north India, the Bench of Chief Justice P. Sathasivam and Justice Ranjan Gogoi issued notice on the PIL to 18 States, besides Centre, while excluding Jammu & Kashmir and southern States. The petition stated although relief was granted to similarly placed persons from Pakistan and Bangladesh who were displaced during the 1965 and 1971 wars, the religious minorities from Bangladesh were considered illegal migrants and pushed into a no man's land along the border.[49] The BJP government of Madhya Pradesh informed the Supreme Court on 30 July, 2014 that "All 5,464 Bangladeshi immigrants residing in Madhya Pradesh as on June 2014 have been rehabilitated. They have been provided with citizenship, ration cards, shelters and most people have been employed in various projects of the state or are running independent business, apart from being agriculturists."[50]

In the 2014 Lok Sabha elections held in May, the BJP in its election manifesto under heading Foreign Relations—Nation First, Universal Brotherhood says:

> India shall remain a natural home for persecuted Hindus and they shall be welcome to seek refuge here.

So what the BJP government of Madhya Pradesh did was in consonance with the party's stand on this issue. The BJP is perhaps the only political party which from the very beginning made a distinction between migrants from Pakistan, now Bangladesh, who are perceived to be legitimate refugees and those the party regards as foreign "infiltrators". This distinction is made purely on ethnic-religious grounds, with the BJP representing all Hindu migrants from Bangladesh as refugees from an oppressive and intolerant Islamic regime with a natural right to Indian citizenship because of religious persecution. A recurring theme within BJP rhetoric has been to describe the sufferings of all Hindus in Bangladesh in terms of violent atrocities inflicted by Muslim "fanatics", restriction of religious observance, and official policies of discrimination and communalism. Although, in some instances, the BJP has pointed to general religious and/or political persecution as the criterion for granting refugee status, the distinction between "refugee" and "infiltrator", the oppressed Hindu and the encroaching Muslim, regardless of individual circumstances, has been explicit within the BJPs discourse on Bangladeshi migration. As outlined in the RSS weekly *Organiser,* the West Bengal BJP concluded a press conference, held in the wake of the 1991 Lok Sabha elections, in the following manner:

> Thus, with all justification, the BJP in West Bengal will go on harping on this issue of infiltration which is plaguing the State's economy, and press for a public debate on it on all public fora, so as to make the people realise the gravity of the situation. Shri Vishnu Kant Shastri also pointed out that the issue of infiltrators cannot be dealt with at par with the unfortunate Hindu refugees who are being driven out of their homeland in a continual process.
>
> The Hindu refugees had to seek shelter. They have already declared themselves as refugees, whereas the infiltrators are illegally trespassing our national borders, maintaining dual citizenships and creating havoc to the State's economy. The question of dealing with the refugees should be one of sympathy and consideration, whereas the governments should be particularly firm in dealing with the question of illegal infiltrators.[51]

There has been a continual tension and flux within Bangladesh politics between secularist conceptions of the state and polity and the deployment of "Islamic" themes and political mobilizations by various regimes since its formation. In this way, the Hindu minority in Bangladesh has often been caught between these conflicting political compulsions and, especially at moments of systemic crisis such as in 1971, or in the enactment of "Islamic' political strategies and state policies, has suffered direct persecution and dispossession.[52]

In contrast, BJP views Muslim migrants from Bangladesh in totality as "infiltrators" with no right to refugee status in India, regardless of the particular economic or political circumstances that have led to their decision to migrate. In some cases, the BJP has rejected the notion that Muslim migrants have been forced to enter India because of poverty or population pressures. Instead, it has claimed that these migrants form part of an "undeclared" policy of Bangladeshi colonization and invasion of selected districts in order to establish Muslim majorities and facilitate another partition of the country. "Infiltration" has therefore often been projected by Hindu nationalist organisations as a sinister Islamic/ Bangladeshi conspiracy that threatens to drive Hindus from border regions in states such as West Bengal and, indeed, to undermine India's territorial integrity and the demographic basis of a Hindu *Rashtra*. In this vein, the West Bengal unit of the BJP in the RSS weekly stated that there was a deliberate policy to:

> ...convert the border areas into Muslim-dominated areas, so that they can finally raise a plea for their annexation to Bangladesh or to increase the Muslim population in India so that in due course they will be demanding more and more rights for the Muslims in a planned and organised way.[53]

Ever since the Modi government assumed charge in May 2014, nearly 19,000 refugees have been given long-tem visas in Madhya Pradesh. Around 11,000 such visas were given in Rajasthan and 4,000 in Gujarat. There are about 400 Pakistani Hindu refugee settlements in cities like Jodhpur, Jaisalmer, Bikaner and Jaipur in Rajasthan. Many Sikh refugees live in Delhi, Punjab, Haryana and Uttar Pradesh. They are demanding Indian citizenship and even organize demonstrations in New Delhi in favour of their demand.[54]

BJP-ruled Madhya Pradesh granted citizenship rights to over 20,000 Hindu migrants from Pakistan. Special camps were organized in February 2015 in Indore, home to the largest number of such people in the state, and in Bhopal where senior officials from the Union home and external affairs ministries worked with local authorities to help such migrants get such rights.[55]

The Modi government's decision to grant long-term multiple entry tourist visa to aged Bangladeshis above 65 years of age valid for five years[56] led the Congress government in Assam to approve a proposal on16 July, 2014 to grant Indian citizenship to lakhs of refugees from Bangladesh who had fled religious persecution and discrimination in Bangladesh and entered Assam after 25 March, 1971, the cutoff date for determining illegal migrant as per the Assam Accord. The proposal was lying with the state government for the past two years and was likely to benefit about 85 lakh of people staying in the state for the past 45 years.[57]

The Central Government announced on13 November, 2015, a number of concessions for Hindu and Sikh refugees from Pakistan and Afghanistan as part of which it also introduced relaxations in the procedure for granting them Indian citizenship like manual acceptance of applications for granting of Indian citizenship to them.[58]

The BJP assured a rally in Assam on 27 April, 2015 that the BJP would give citizenship to all the Hindus who had come from Bangladesh due to religious disturbances once it came to power in Assam in 2016.[59]

The Passport (Entry into India) Rules provide that anyone who enters into India without proper travel documents can be prosecuted and expelled from India. Foreigners Order, 1948 (which was passed under the Foreigners Act, 1946) also provides for similar consequences. On

7 September, 2015, the Ministry of Home Affairs declared that Pakistanis and Bangladeshis belonging to the minority communities of the two countries and who entered India on or before 31 December, 2014 would be exempt from several provisions, rules and orders made under the Passport (Entry into India) Act, 1920 and the Foreigners Act, 1946 .[60]

A new fee regime was introduced by the Narendra Modi government for foreigners seeking Indian citizenship. The home ministry, in rules notified on 23 December, 2016, declared that Hindus, Jains, Buddhists, Parsis and Christians from Pakistan, Bangladesh and Afghanistan eligible for Indian citizenship will need to pay Rs. 100 with their application. Other applicants will need to pay Rs. 10,000 if they apply in India and Rs. 15,000 if they apply through Indian embassy abroad. Till 23 December, 2016, all applicants to naturalized citizenship—independent of their country, region or community—needed to pay Rs. 15,000. The new fee rules represented a challenge to the concept of a country uniformly welcoming refugees and immigrants, said experts.[61]

The amendments carried out in 2015 and 2016 to the Passport (Entry into India) Rules, 1950 and Foreigners Order, 1948 are the precursor to Citizenship Amendment Bill introduced in 2016. We propose to discuss the fallout and ramifications of the Citizenship Amendment Bill, 2016 and the Citizenship Amendment Act, 2020 in details in Chapter 5.

It may be recalled that the legacy of Partition haunted the Framers of the Constitution. The holocaust that visited the country in the wake of partition, the flow of refugees from this side or that side of the border, the misery of the uprooted families were fresh in their memories. "Echoes of the communally charged atmosphere of the Partition resounded in the assembly as it debated what eventually got enacted as Article 7. Though the markers of religious difference were not openly displayed they are easily recognizable in the debates on Articles 6 and 7 of the Constitution. Article 6 was obviously unexceptionable as it guaranteed rights of citizenship for what were largely Hindu migrants from Pakistan, commonly described in the discourse of the time as refugees. Article 7, however, implicitly referred to those Muslims who had fled India for Pakistan in the wake of the partition-related violence, but later returned to reclaim their livelihood and property. This Article was necessitated by the fact that the numbers of such people were considerable, the High Commission claiming that it received one thousand applications from Muslim refugees on a daily basis. These people were euphemistically described as 'migrants' and this was the most intensely contested Article on citizenship in the Constituent Assembly. It is important to note that though the Constitution does not use the terms refugee and migrant, these words occurred frequently in the speeches made in the Constituent Assembly, and subtly encoded religious identity in a shared universe of meaning."[62]

This "subtly encoded religious identity" was however, jettisoned in the 2004 amendments to the Citizenship Rules 1956 in respect of its application to the States of Gujarat and Rajasthan. These were enacted to address the claims to citizenship of Hindu migrants from Pakistan migrating across the western border into the States of Rajasthan and Gujarat. This region has experienced several waves of such immigration: from the wars between India and Pakistan in 1965 and 1971, and most recently after the demolition of the Babri Masjid in Ayodhya in December 1992. Following this event, the insecurity of members of the Muslim minority in India found parallels in the insecurity of the Hindu minority in Pakistan, approximately17,000 of whom migrated to India. Most of these people, being Pakistani passport holders, travelled on Indian visas that they simply overstayed. They then became applicants for citizenship. The Union government had already, in response to the widespread allegations about the manipulation of citizenship certification in Assam, withdrawn to itself the powers of district collectors all across India to confer citizenship in accordance with the law. To enable the grant of citizenship by District Collectors in Rajasthan and Gujarat, the Union government had to make an exception to this withdrawal of powers and this was accomplished in 2004 through an amendment to the Citizenship Rules 1956, for a specified and limited period and within a limited jurisdiction. This made it possible for District Collectors in these specified States to hold 'Citizenship Camps' to process the applications for citizenship of these migrants from Pakistan. There still remain a few thousand people who are awaiting the legalisation of their citizenship status. The most significant feature of this amendment is its open declaration of the religious identity of the migrants. Until this point, and to the present as far as the main Act is concerned, the religious identity of the migrants (illegal or otherwise) was overtly indicated, but never explicitly indicated. The 2004 amendment to the Rules dispenses with such signaling. It even avoids the description of these people as migrants, much less illegal migrants, the coded 'dog-whistle' label used to indicate immigrants from Bangladesh.[63]

Rule 8A of the amended Citizenship Rules 1956 introduced in 2004 reads:

> In respect of *minority Hindus and Sikhs with Pakistani citizenship* who have migrated to India more than five years back *with the intention of permanently settling down in India* and have applied for Indian citizenship, the authority to

register a person as a citizen of India shall be the concerned Collector of the district where the applicant is normally resident.

The amendment to the Citizenship Rules 1956 does not hesitate to assume and name the religious identity of the recent migrants from Pakistan who are explicitly referred to as 'minority Hindus and Sikhs with Pakistani citizenship.' One wonders whether the CAA 2019 enacted by the NDA III were not germane in the 2004 amendment of the Citizenship Rules 1956 effected by the NDA I government.

NOTES

1. Jayal, Niraja Gopal, "Citizenship" In The Oxford Handbook of The Indian Constitution, *Op. Cit.*, pp. 164-165.
2. *Ibid.*, p. 163.
3. *Lok Sabha Debates* (Henceforth *LSD*), Vol. IX (21st November to 5th December, 1955), dated 2-12-55, pp. 1056-59.
4. *Ibid.*, p. 1089 and p. 1160.
5. *Ibid.*, dated 3-12-55, pp. 1164-65.
6. *Ibid.*, p. 1228.
7. *Ibid.*
8. *Ibid.*, pp. 1245-1248.
9. *Ibid.*, p. 1274.
10. *Ibid.*, dated 5-12-55, pp. 1294-1295.
11. *Ibid.*, dated 2-12-55, p. 1052.
12. *Ibid.*, dated 5-12-55, p. 1340.
13. *Ibid.*, dated 3-12-55, p. 1228.
14. *Ibid.*, date 6-12-55, p. 1458.
15. *Ibid.*, p. 1464.
16. *Ibid.*, pp. 1465-1466.
17. *Ibid.*, dated 3-12-55, p. 1185.
18. *CAD*, Vol. IX dated 11-8-49, pp. 355-356.
19. *Ibid.*, p. 376.
20. *CAD*, Vol. XI, dated 21-12-49, p. 764.
21. *Ibid.*, dated 12-8-49, p. 393.
22. *Ibid.*, dated 11-8-49, p. 387.
23. *The Telegraph,* May 9, 2017, p. 5.
24. *Ibid.*, February 6, 2018, p. 6.
25. *Annual Report 2012-13*, Government of India, Ministry of Overseas Indian Affairs, p. 14.
26. *The Statesman*, March 3, 2015, p. 3.
27. Rao, *Op. Cit.*, Vol. III, p. 511.

28. Jayal, Niraja Gopal, "Citizenship" In The Oxford Handbook of The Indian Constitution, *Op. Cit.*, p. 179.
29. Chaudhuri, Rajiv J., "Let us unite the Great Indian Family: Allow overseas Indians to have citizenship and political rights", *The Times of India*, January 24, 2019, p. 20.
30. *The Telegraph*, March 10, 1992, p. 4.
31. *Ibid.*
32. *Ibid.*
33. It's time for India to adopt dual citizenship – The Print *theprint.in* Opinion.
34. *The Times of India*, July 27, 2018, p. 14.
35. It's time for India to adopt dual citizenship – The Print *theprint.in* Opinion.
36. Faleiro, Eduardo, Dual citizenship, *Herald,* December 3, 2019.
37. Kumar, Chethan, In 5 years 5 lakh Indians gave up Citizenship, *The Times of India*, March 12, 2020, http://timesofindia.indiatimes.comfile:///C:/Users/
38. It's time for India to adopt dual citizenship – The Print *theprint.in* Opinion.
39. Faleiro, Eduardo, Dual citizenship, *Herald,* December 3, 2019.
40. *The Economic Times*, May 30, 2019.
41. Citizenship Law Won't Impact Gaons With Portuguese Passports, www.ndtv.com All India.
42. Over 2 lakh Gaons, enjoying dual citizenship, will have to make a choice between India and Portugal economictimes.indiatimes.com ...Politics and Nation.
43. *The Hindu*, June 24, 2017, p. 4.
44. *Ibid.*, May 6, 2017, p. 4.
45. *Ibid.*, June 24, 2017, p. 4.
46. Over 2 lakh Gaons, enjoying dual citizenship, will have to make a choice between India and Portugal economictimes.indiatimes.com ... Politics and Nation.
47. Faleiro, Eduardo, Dual citizenship, *Herald,* December 3, 2019.
48. *The Statesman*, January 31, 2012, p. 4.
49. *Ibid.*, July 26, 2013, p. 8.
50. *The Times of India*, July 31, 2014, p. 11.
51. *Organiser*, July 21, 1991.
52. Gillan, Michael, "Refugees or Infiltrators? The Bharatiya Janata Party and 'Illegal' Migration from Bangladesh", *Asian Studies Association of Australia,* 2002, p. 85.
53. *Organiser*, July 21, 1991.
54. *The Hindu*, June 15, 2015, p. 1.
55. *The Telegraph*, February 13, 2015, p. 6.
56. *The Times of India*, June 24, 2014, p. 1.
57. *Ibid.*, July 17, 2014, p. 10.

58. *The Statesman*, November 14, 2014, p. 3.
59. *The Hindu*, May 11, 2015, p. 1.
60. Sarker, Suvo Prosun, "How humanitarian is this?" *The Statesman,* October 6, 2015, p. 16.
61. *The Telegraph*, December 28, 2016, p. 4.
62. Jayal, Niraja Gopal, "Citizenhip", In The Oxford Handbook on The Indian Constitution, *Op. Cit.*, p. 167.
63. *Ibid.*, pp. 175-176.

3
Infiltration into India from Bangladesh

Since the Second World War continual obstructions have appeared in the free movement of people; ironically these have coincided in a period of increasing globalisation and closer interdependence between nations. Although the numbers of people moving internationally remain quite small, 11.4 million as against 400 million in the 2011 census so far as India is concerned[1], nations are becoming increasingly protectionist in the name of defence or to safeguard 'national' identity and, therefore, adopting policies to regulate and restrict cross-border migration. An unintended consequence of such migration governance is a steep increase in irregular migrants—a point stressed by several international organizations engaged with labour migration like International Labour Organization (ILO) and International Organization for Migration (IOM). The 'illegal' migration or 'infiltration' into the country/countries of one's choice has become a world phenomenon, afflicting a number of countries, including India. In India, Assam attracted international attention for the movement started from 8 June, 1979 against the infiltrators or illegal migrants.

Assam as the frontier of India during the pre-Partition period attracted millions of settlers from other regions of the subcontinent. The policy of the British government towards the development of the region accelerated the movement of people from outside since the British needed essential human resources including administrators, businessmen and labourers. In this way, the demographic composition of Assam became much diversified and the share of migrants in the total population increased continuously. Among the various migrant communities, it was the Bengali Muslims who became conspicuous targets as 'migrants.' The major influx of Bengali Muslims into the lands along the Brahmaputra valley began in the early 20th century.

The important event in the history of migration in Assam, as observed by C.S. Mullan, Superintendent of Census Operations in Assam in 1931 was "the invasion of a vast horde of land hungry Bengali immigrants mostly Muslims from the districts of Eastern Bengal and in particular from Mymensing." He further remarked that "this invasion began some time before 1911 and the census report of that year was the first report which makes mention of the advancing host."[2] In 1911, few cultivators from Eastern Bengal had gone beyond Goalpara, those censused in other districts of the Assam Valley number a few thousands and being mostly clerks, traders and professional men. In the decade of 1911-21, the movement was extended far up the Valley and the colonialists by 1931 formed an appreciable element in the population of all the four lower and central districts of Goalpara, Kamrup, Darrang and Nowgong. The upper districts, Sibsagar and Lakhimpur, of course, were scarcely touched as yet.[3]

Mullan further wrote:

> The invasion is by no means complete. There are still large areas of waste land in Assam particularly in the North Lakhimpur subdivision and Kamrup. In spite of the large number of immigrants which it has absorbed during the last ten years is capable of holding many more. It is sad but no means improbable that in another thirty years Sibsagar district will be the part of Assam in which an Assamese will find himself at home. [4]

Mullan pointed out that the percentage of persons of foreign extraction in Assam according to his estimate was 23.5 per cent which corresponded closely with the estimate made in 1921.[5]

Nevertheless, it should be noted that from the beginning, the presence of migrants was not always unwelcome. Amalendu Guha states with some emphasis that in the 19th century, the enlightened section of the Assamese middle class welcomed large-scale immigration because their productive labour and skills were indispensable for economic progress under the underpopulated conditions prevailing in those days.[6]

Assam Government's "White Paper on Foreigners' Issue" also mentions about the beneficial effect of migration of Bengali Muslims into Assam. It states:

> It is important to note some positive and beneficial effects of migration of the peasants from East Bengal. The *Goalpara Zamindars* and other landlords had in fact initially encouraged these hardy peasants to settle down in Assam. The peasant migrants from the erstwhile East Bengal brought with them superior cultivation techniques including multiple cropping

> and introduced poultry farming. Because of the agricultural practices of the hardworking immigrants and their contribution to the agricultural economy, rice production increased significantly. A number of vegetables and crops including jute hitherto unknown in the state were also introduced by the migrants.[7]

Muslims migrated from the densely populated East Bengal to land-abundant Assam in search of land of their own. Initially, the newcomers settled in Assam's waterlogged, jungle-infested, riverine belt. However, once they began to move out into the rest of the province, open clashes of interest began between the immigrants and the locals.

The continuous immigration of increasing numbers generated apprehensions among the local Assamese community of being culturally swamped or demographically outnumbered by people with different social, economic, linguistic and religious backgrounds. They began to oppose unrestricted immigration and demanded administrative measures from the government for curbing it. In order to protect the interests of the 'locals', the idea of the "Line System" was mooted by the deputy commissioner of Nowgong, a district in which there was at the time a strong influx of migrants, in 1916 and was adopted in 1920. Under this scheme, a line was drawn in 1920 in the districts under immigratory pressure, whereby immigrants were allowed to settle only in specified segregated areas away from the Assamese.[8] Subsequently, the line system became a bone of contention between Assamese Hindu and Assamese Muslim politicians. Whereas the former called for the imposition of a more rigid policy towards the migrants, the latter demanded the abolition of the line system arguing that it was preventing the assimilation of the immigrants into Assamese society.[9]

As this scheme failed to achieve its objective, Assamese public opinion began to clamour for restrictions again. In 1928, an All Party Committee, with W. Bothan as chairman, enquired into the problem. The Committee consisted of four European and five Indian members including S.M. Saddulla and N.C. Bordoloi. A colonization policy, approved by both Saddulla and Bordoloi, was evolved. A colonization scheme was started first in Nowgang in 1928 and later in Barpeta and Mangaldai. The scheme provided for 20 bighas of land for a small family. By 1936, about 37 per cent of the area in Nowgong was under occupation of immigrants while the rest was in the hands of the local people.[10]

The Muslim migrants from Eastern Bengal continued to pour into Assam. The immigratory inflow, however, required more lands. The immigrant leaders and the Muslim League urged the government to abolish the Line System and adopt a liberal policy towards immigration. The provincial ministers of Assam never had an easy time on immigration issue. A Committee was formed under the chairmanship of F.W. Hockenhull on the working of the Line System. In its report submitted in 1938, it advocated the continuance of the Line System. Chief Minister Saddulla held an All Party Conference on 31 May and 1 June, 1940 to discuss the Line System. The government advocated a development scheme as envisaged in the Hockenhull Report with certain modifications. A Government Resolution of 21 June followed. It banned settlement on waste lands by immigrants entering Assam after 1 January, 1938 and decided to go ahead with a Land Development Scheme for providing land to the landless local people and eligible immigrants in that order of priority. But before the scheme could be put into effect, the Saddulla ministry collapsed. When the Governor took over the administration, by the resolution of 6 March, 1942, he scrapped the Development Scheme since it was harming the interests of the local people and the settled immigrants. As soon as Saddulla returned to power on 25 August, 1942, a new resolution on the land settlement under the slogan "grow more food" was announced. It was widely regarded as a Muslim League ploy to allow more Muslims to settle in Assam.[11]

Grazing and forest reserve lands were opened to migrants. Hasty occupation of lands by the migrants followed. The Assamese Hindus, the Assam Jatiya Mahasabha, Sibsagar Ahom Sabha, Assam Provincial Hindu Sabha, All Assam Kachari Association and Assam Mauzadar Association protested against these actions. Protest Days were observed.[12] Viceroy Wavell visited Assam in December 1943. He observed :

> The chief political problem is the desire of the Muslim Ministers to increase immigration into the uncultivated government lands under the slogan 'Grow More Food'; but what they aim really after is 'Grow More Muslims.'[13]

The Muslim League leader Chowdhury Khaliquzzaman praised the Assam Premier for helping increase the Muslim population in Assam. He claimed that the Muslims in Assam had increased substantially and within the next few years they would emerge as the majority community in Assam.[14] The sinister design of the Muslim League behind this state-sponsored migration became evident as later on it demanded for the inclusion of the entire province of Assam into Pakistan.[15]

The large-scale migration led to a shift in the demographic balance in favour of the Muslims with abnormal rise in their proportion from 9 per cent in 1921 to 19 per cent in 1931 and 23 per cent in 1941. In Barpeta sub-division alone, the proportion of Muslims shot up from 0.15 per cent in 1911 to 49 per cent in 1941.[16]

The trend of influx of East Bengal immigrants continued as in earlier years till 1950. During the years 1945 to 1950 about 33 thousand labourers migrated to Sibsagar district alone from other provinces to work in various capacities. On the other hand, many Santhal and Bodo families of Goalpara district migrated to other districts of the Assam Valley. Moreover, many tribal people, namely, Hajongs, Koches, Dalus, and Garos from Mymensing and Rongpur districts of erstwhile East Pakistan migrated to the Hills of the Garo Hills district.[17]

The enormous success of jute cultivation in East Bengal and its feasibltiy in Assam induced the zamindars to bring hardy peasants—mostly Muslims—from the adjoining Bengal districts. They were officially termed 'immigrant Muslims.' Later they spread to Kamprup, Nowgong and Darrang districts under the land consolidation schemes of the Assam government that changed the religious demography of the state and enabled the immigrants to emerge as a political force under the Muslim League.

After partition, they naturally joined the Congress and formed one of the planks of power structure that represented the interests of the three major ethnic groups—Assamese Hindu, tea labour community and the Muslim peasantry—that enabled the Congress, led by the Assamese upper caste, to rule Assam till 1977 without a break.

The Registrar General of Census in his report on the 1961 census assessed that 2,20,691 infiltrants had entered Assam. In the light of this report of Census 1961 coupled with intelligence reports about entry of infiltrants, police launched a drive in 1962-1964 to detect and deport such infiltrants. By mid-1964, the State Government had also set up 4 tribunals through an executive order to cover those cases of suspected infiltrants who claimed to be Indian. These tribunals were headed by special officers with judicial background who were appointed to scrutinize cases of infiltrants before issuing Quit India notices.

During the period 1961-1966, approximately 1,78,952 infiltrants were either deported or had voluntarily left the country but an estimated 40,000 infiltrants did not leave India. The police drive, which commenced in mid-1962 against infiltrators continued but invited criticism from some leaders of Assam. Pakistan also threatened to drag the issue of deportation to the United Nations. A Conference of Home Ministers of India and Pakistan was held in New Delhi on 7 –11 April 1964 to discuss primarily the deportation issue and the need to maintain communal harmony in the sub-continent including minority protection, but the conference did not yield any substantial result. The issue of eviction of infiltrants was deliberated by the cabinet several times during 1964-66 and there was a general consensus till early part of 1964 that any stoppage of deportation would seriously affect the internal situation in Assam.

It was decided by the Central Government that before eviction every individual case should be examined by judicial authority even though this may result in delay, by introducing a judicial element in the procedure for the eviction of Pakistani infiltrators to stand the test of scrutiny before the international forum. All this culminated in the issue of a statutory order called the Foreigners (Tribunal) Order on 23 September, 1964 and the creation of Foreigners Tribunals under clause 2 of the order, thereby making it mandatory for the appointment of a Member with judicial background. This was done in the context of representations made by various organizations about harassments being caused to *bona fide* Indian persons while 'Quit Notices' were served on infiltrants as also adverse publicity on this issue over the international media. Under the aforesaid statutory order, 4 Foreigners Tribunals were set up in 1964 and as many as 35,080 persons were referred to these Tribunals till the end of August 1965. Apparently, most of the cases were disposed of in 10 months' time. The procedure of detection was relaxed so as to give the suspected infiltrant adequate opportunity to contest the police case, should he desire to do so. In doing so, the Government was also attempting to counter criticisms that procedure followed was arbitrary and unfair. By 1968, there were 9 Foreigners Tribunals with headquarters at Tezpur, Gauhati, Nowgong (2), Sibsagar, Goalpara, Dhubri, Barpeta and Jorhat.

In 1969, Government decided that only the following three categories of foreigners were to be summarily deported: (1) Pakistani nationals who held Pakistani passports, (2) Re-infiltrants who were once deported. (3) Fresh infiltrants caught at the border. Further, the Superintendents of Police were directed not to detain persons being checked at railway stations leading to their missing train connections as a consequence of such checking and detention. If a person was suspected to be a Pakistani, he was to be questioned and followed or information sent to where he was proceeding so that a track is kept on him and future inquiries can be pursued, but he should not be detained at the station itself. The Superintendents of Police were further instructed that there should be no wholesale checking of villages and houses. Only when there were specific suspicious circumstances surrounding the cases, which need to be further gone into, would such a probe be made. The Superintendents of Police were also advised that, as far as possible, the investigation should be done under the supervision of a responsible officer.[18]

In the general elections of 1977, the Congress was routed at the hustings and the Janata Party, formed at the initiative of Jaya Prakash Narayan, came to power at the centre. A ministry under the premiership of Morarji Desai took office. This change of power at the Centre saw a spurt in communal riots all over India including Assam, Meghalaya and Manipur. Coinciding with the change of leadership at the centre, movement for the deletion of names of 'foreigners' from the voters' list and deportation of the 'infiltrators' was started in Assam under the leadership of the All Assam Students Union (AASU) and the All Assam Gana Sangram Parishad (AAGSP).

The death of Hiralal Patwari, sitting Member of Parliament for Lok Sabha representing the Mangaldai LS Constituency on 28 March, 1979 necessitated the holding of by-elections, which set in motion the events leading up to the Assam movement. The Assam agitation was born when it was alleged that a large number of names of suspect nationality was included in the voters' lists in the Mangaldai LS constituency. The All Assam Students' Union (AASU) on 8 June, 1979 sponsored a 12-hour general strike demanding 'detection, disenfranchisement and deportation' of foreigners. This turned out to be the first of such state-wide protests against infiltration. The Assam Agitation (1979-1985) was a mass movement against illegal immigrants in Assam led by the All Assam Students' Union (AASU) and All Assam Gana Sangram Parishad (AAGSP) to compel the Government to identify and expel illegal immigrants.[19] The All Assam Gana Sangram Parishad (AAGSP), formed on 27 August, 1979 emerged as the common platform for the indigenous people of Assam for launching the historic Assam Movement.

In spite of the professed path of Gandhian 'satyagraha' by the agitators, sporadic and organized violence, arson, intimidation and assaults, and destruction of private and public properties were experienced in Assam, Manipur, Meghalaya and Tripura. A few hundred lives were lost and several hundred thousand persons rendered homeless. The State and Central Government offices, all educational institutions and the revenue earnings of national undertakings like the Posts and Telegraphs, Railways and Indian Airlines were paralyzed. Sustained economic boycott of the rest of India was enforced by preventing the supply of crude oil and its products, timber and bamboo etc. The students suffered the loss of two academic sessions and the process of development in the entire region was brought almost to a halt. For the first time in India a general election had to be conducted without the participation of a large number of people. The nearest thing to it that happened was also in the North East India when the Naga National Council organised a total boycott of the first general election in the Naga Hills district of Assam. The Government of India in 1980 did not have the strength to hold the Seventh Lok Sabha elections in all the constituencies in this region. Twelve constituencies in Assam and one in Meghalaya remained unrepresented in the Seventh Lok Sabha, elections to which were held in January 1980. Only two MPs from Cachar district, a Bengali majority district, and one MP from the Garo Hills of Meghalaya got elected. The census operations could not be conducted in Assam in 1981. Social relations in the region were the worst casualty. The affected minorities reacted through formation of their own organizations to save their existence. The All Assam Minority Students Union (AAMSU) was thus formed. The AAMSU launched a protest movement on 26 May, 1980.[20]

In 1980 when the Congress party led by Mrs. Indira Gandhi came to power at the centre, AASU wrote to Prime Minister Mrs. Indira Gandhi on 18 January, 1980 drawing her attention to the problem of infiltration. They submitted some broad proposals for the purpose of detecting and deleting the names of foreigners from the electoral rolls based on the NRC of 1951 and thereafter deporting them. The broad proposals for undertaking such an exercise are briefly summarized below: (1) Updating of NRC of 1951, (2) Cross checking of electoral rolls with the updated NRC, (3) Demarcation of the Indo-Bangladesh border and creation of a free uninhabited belt, (4) Issuing of identity cards throughout the North-east region, (5) Strict maintenance of Birth and Death Registers at all Block and Village levels, (6) Raising of additional armed Police battalions and a River Police Force with a view to checking infiltration. Following AASU's letter to the Prime Minister, the student leaders were invited for discussions and negotiations with the Central Government. The AASU delegation met Prime Minister Indira Gandhi on 2 February, 1980 which signalled the beginning of protracted negotiations between the movement leaders and the Central Government headed by Mrs Gandhi. The AASU delegation also submitted a detailed memorandum to the Prime Minister. The Government of India insisted that 25 March, 1971 be the cut-off date for identifying foreigners, which the AASU rejected and insisted on 1951 being the cut-off year for identifying and deporting foreigners. In April 1980, the Governor of Assam held discussions with AASU during which the Governor suggested that 1967 should be the base year for detection and deletion of foreigners and 1971 for deportation of foreigners. This offer was rejected by AASU vide their General Secretary's letter of 5 April, 1980, which was, however, subsequently accepted by them in 1985. The Prime Minister Mrs. Indira

Gandhi herself came to Assam and held discussions with the AASU leaders on 12 April, 1980 but there was no progress in the negotiation as AASU stuck to their stated position. In September 1980, AASU announced that it would agree to a negotiated settlement for allowing immigrants who came to Assam after 1951 till 1961 provided the Government agreed to shift the immigrants of 1961-1971 stream to other states, which was not agreed to by the Government. It appears that between 1980 and 1982 there were as many as 23 rounds of negotiations, which, however, did not yield any positive outcome.[21]

By one account, representatives of government and the agitation met on as many as 114 days in the calendar years 1980, 1981 and 1982. Various compromises were discussed: one, suggested by the Gandhi Peace Foundation, recommended that those who entered Assam between 1951 and 1961 be conferred rights of residence and voting (in effect citizenship), those who came between 1961 and 1971 be dispersed to other States of India, and those who came after March 25, 1971 (the date on which Bangladesh declared itself a sovereign State) be deported.[22]

In February 1983, in spite of the explosive atmosphere, the ruling Congress Party at the Centre entered the state legislature election (February 14-21, 1983) intent on winning the contest with the support of the migrants. The native organizations called for a boycott and resisted the balloting. Congress won an easy majority and formed the government in Assam, but the price was frightening. The violence between the native Assamese and migrant Bangladeshis cost more than 3,000 lives. A few days before the election, more than 8,000 native Hindu Assamese surrounded a village called Neillie and systematically killed the Bangladeshi Muslim migrants. The toll of that five-hour rampage was more than 1,700.[23]

On becoming the Prime Minister of India in October 1984, Rajiv Gandhi made an earnest effort to bring a peaceful solution of the Assam problem. A Memorandum of Settlement, popularly known as the Assam Accord, was signed on 15 August, 1985 by the president and general secretary of the All Assam Students Union and the Convener of the All Assam Gana Sangram Parishad on the one hand and the Home Secretary, Government of India and the Chief Secretary, Government of Assam on the other, in the presence of Rajiv Gandhi, the then Prime Minister of India. This agreement contains some important clauses relating to the foreigners issue, border fencing, construction of border roads, setting up of border out posts etc. After the signing of this Accord (Annexure A), the 6-year long Assam agitation from 1979 to 1985 was called off.

It has been revealed that the Assam Movement would not have lingered till 1985 if the proposal of Indira Gandhi offered through Zail Singh, the then Union Home Minister in April 1980 was accepted. According to this proposal, either the 31 December, 1966 or 1 January, 1967 was offered as the cut-off date. But the prominent student leaders once again refused to abandon 1951 as the cut-off date. Then it was not evident that these student leaders were entertaining very high political ambition and therefore, they had a secret agenda unknown to the other members of the AAGSP. As the Movement gathered momentum, these student leaders gradually developed the ambition of capturing political power on their own. But constitutionally they were not eligible to contest the election unless they had attained the age of 25 years. The way out was to lengthen the Movement so that these student leaders became constitutionally eligible for contesting in the next elections. Once they had attained the constitutionally fixed age of twenty-five years, the same set of student leaders made a turn of 180 degrees and accepted 25 March, 1971 as the cut-off date while signing the Assam Accord on the night of 14 August, 1985.

> "Still more mysterious and intriguing was the fact that non-student leaders and the executive committee of the AAGSP were not taken into confidence, while secretly preparing the draft of the Assam Accord, with the help of some officials of the MHA. Subsequently, it was learnt that Hiteswar Saikia, who had taken over as the Chief Minister on the basis of the results of the elections held in 1983, was behind the entire exercise and he had agreed to resign once the agreement was signed, so that fresh elections could be held in the State. Executive members of the AAGSP were flown to New Delhi only on the morning of 14 August, but the AASU leaders had gone few days earlier. The executive members of the AAGSP had played no role in drafting the Accord. In fact, some of them refused to attend the Accord-signing ceremony and the party thrown by the Prime Minister, Rajiv Gandhi in celebration of inking the Accord. They left New Delhi by the next available flight. It also subsequently transpired that the student leaders in their haste to capture power were holding secret parleys with few MHA officials and the Cabinet Secretary for quite a while, keeping the executive members of AAGSP in the dark. Needless to mention, the student leaders were no match to the talents of these officers. In this background, it should not be difficult to understand why the talks so far held in New Delhi, particularly during Mrs. Gandhi's regime did not succeed. On the other hand, because of such selfish and obdurate stance

> of a handful of student leaders, the people of Assam had to undergo untold sufferings and inhuman atrocities for six long years. 855 participants of the Movement had to sacrifice their lives during the period."[24]

It is, therefore no wonder that once they captured power, the issue of infiltration was dropped like a hot potato.

Exactly two months after the signing of the Accord, the Movement leaders formed a political party, known as Asom Gana Parishad (AGP), to contest the next election.[25] Bangladeshi Muslim migrants, feeling betrayed by the Congress Party and seeking to resist the onslaught of AGP, formed a political organisation under the banner of United Minorities Front (UMF) to fight the state election in December 1985. The withdrawal of support for Congress led to the defeat of the Congress Party and AGP captured the power in Assam. However, due to inefficiency and factionalism, AGP could not fulfill its election pledge of identifying the foreign nationals in the state. The non-cooperation of the Congress government at the Centre in its effort to win back the Muslim migrants to its fold was another reason for AGP's failure.

The Assam Movement was essentially a strong protest campaign against Central Government for allowing "foreigners" to settle and to illegally take advantage of political and economic opportunities. Despite its vigour and the extent of its influence over state politics as well as its relationship with Central Government, the Assam Movement remained a domestic problem of India, though it instigated the rise of other homeland movements in Assam and elsewhere.[26] It did not affect India's bilateral relationship with Bangladesh, which was identified as the source of the immigrants, mainly because the Central Government as well as part of the State Government was reluctant to implement the identification and deportation of "foreigners."[27]

II

At the time of framing the provisions relating to citizenship at the commencement of the Constitution (Part II of the Constitution) by the Constituent Assembly in August 1949, Rohini Choudhuri did raise the issue of influx of people, especially of the Muslim community to Assam from East Bengal[28], but the credit for bringing the "infiltration" issue on the national plane in India must go to the All Assam Students Union (AASU) and the Assam Gana Sangram Parishad (AGSP) who spearheaded the Assam movement. The fundamental ideological plane of the Assam movement was that the Assamiya as a nationality was facing a crisis of identity in the face of continuous "illegal" immigration to Assam from across the border. The major issues highlighted by the Assam movement were (1) illegal migration of foreign nationals, (2) participation of illegal immigrants in the electoral process, (3) deportation of illegal foreigners, and (4) protection of distinct identity of the Assamiyas from the threat of foreign nationals. For the first time an agitation was launched in North East India on a strictly legal ground which caught the government in an embarrassing position. For, here is a perfectly valid constitutional ground for demanding the disenfranchisement of the non-citizens. Further, the fundamental right to "reside and settle in any part of the territory of India" [Article 19 (e)] is open only to the citizens of India.

On the other hand, it is not within the rights of any citizen or organization, or even a State Government to regulate "admission into, and emigration and expulsion from, India" which is within the exclusive power of the Union Government (Paragraph 19, List I, Seventh Schedule). The States may probably regulate the "right in or over land" (Paragraph 18, List II, Seventh Schedule) in respect of the non-citizens if they do not attract the secular guarantee of "equality before the law or the equal protection of the laws" to all persons. (Article 14)

The 'anti-foreigner' movement also spread to the other North-eastern States. In 1980 and 1994, the All Manipur Students' Union launched a movement against foreigners and later signed an accord with the state government. It undertook to identify and deport those staying illegally but this remained only on paper. The Union has clarified that it is not against outsiders coming to do business and trade but it will not allow them permanent settlement. The latest drive in Manipur is against those who came recently. Till 2014, only 60 of them have reportedly been identified.[29]

While the three states of Assam, Tripura and West Bengal received the bulk of illegal migrants from East Pakistan (later Bangladesh) in the initial decades of independence, in the later years, the other states of the North-East also started registering their presence. For example, Nagaland recorded the highest rate of population growth in India, from 56.08 per cent in 1981–91 to 64.41 per cent in 1991–2001, with Dimapur bordering Assam recording an exceptionally high rate of population growth. This rise in population has been attributed to the illegal influx of Bangladeshi migrants into the state. Likewise, Arunachal Pradesh, Meghalaya and Mizoram also registered substantial population growth rates in the past three decades, which was above the national average. If an increase in the Muslim populations is to be taken as an indicator for illegal migration from Bangladesh, in almost all the north-eastern states of India, barring few exceptions such as Manipur, Muslim population has shown a substantial growth. For instance, in Mizoram, between 1981 and 1991, the Muslim population grew by 105.8 per cent as compared to 42.89 per cent for the Christians. Similarly, Muslim population registered a growth of 135.01 per cent during the same decade in Arunachal Pradesh. In the subsequent decade, Muslim population grew by 122.54 per cent in Mizoram and 73.40 per cent in Arunachal Pradesh. Meghalaya also registered 61.35 per cent growth in its Muslim population compared to 42.31 per cent for Christians.[30]

Bangladeshi nationals have sneaked into some of the remotest parts of Arunachal Pradesh, the Inner Line Permit System notwithstanding. As pointed out by T.V. Rajeswar, a former Director of the Intelligence Bureau and a former Governor of West Bengal:

> The Bangladeshis have managed to seep through to offer their services for cultivating forest lands cleared by the local tribals. The tribals find that without adequate help from cheap labour from outside they are not in a position to cultivate their land in their difficult environment.
>
> The Arunachal tribals would rather prefer the Bangladeshi farm labour than the Chakma tribals from the Tripura-Bangladesh border, some of whom have been settled there, for the simple reason that while the Chakmas have come to stay, the Bangladeshis can always be sent away by invoking the Inner Line restrictions.[31]

Most of the labourers in Meghalaya's coalmines are from Bangladesh or Nepal. They come across because they see opportunities. No indigenous tribal would want to work inside those dark dungeons called coalmines. Rat-hole mining, which the coalmine owners feel is the most economically viable method, requires huge numbers of such desperate souls to go down under a great risk to their lives. Moreover, no construction work will be possible in the hill states unless they import labour.

T.V. Rajeswar pointed out way back in 1990:

> The Bangladeshis have been spread out all over India. In Punjab and Haryana, they are indispensable as farm labour during the harvest season. They are used as expendable couriers both by the Punjab terrorists and the Pakistani Rangers. There is a Bangladeshi colony in the Trans-

> Jamuna area in Delhi. Indeed, next to the Nepalese it is the Bangladeshis you will come across all over India.
>
> However, it is the neighbouring States of Assam, Tripura, West Bengal and Bihar that the impact of Bangladeshi immigration is overwhelming. In Tripura, the demographic picture has undergone a total change after partition, with a predominantly tribal territory being overwhelmed by the influx of plainsmen. In Bihar, some of the north-western tracts adjoining West Bengal, particularly the Purnea district, has a sizeable presence of Bangladeshis.
>
> The narrow neck of Indian territory in the Kishanganj sector is a favourite infiltration route for Bangladeshis via West Dinajpur, especially for the non-Bengali speaking infiltrants.
>
> It would not be an exaggeration to say that the problem of Bangladeshi influx in West Bengal is indeed very serious.[32]

Rajeswar Rao in the two-part article in *The Statesman* on 6 and 7 April, 1990 had warned about the danger emanating from the influx from across the border.

West Bengal Chief Minister, Jyoti Basu, issued a statement on 6 April, 1990 saying that the former Governor of West Bengal had based his conclusions on "wrong and unwarranted assumptions."[33] While applauding this statement of the West Bengal Chief Minister, Syed Shahabuddin, a Muslim leader, suggested (a) to immediately introduce identity cards in the border zone of, say, 25 km so that at least all subsequent infiltrators can be identified; (b) to regularly publish community-wise statistics of infiltrators apprehended by the BSF or the State police so as to set public apprehension at rest about complexion of infiltration; (c) to consider the establishment, under a bilateral agreement, of a zone of free movement across the border as in the case of India and Burma on the basis of identity cards to legitimize trans-border movement which arises out of human and economic compulsion and which, in any case, cannot be eliminated.[34] While these suggestions, especially the one about the issuance of identity cards, are laudable, these suggestions can only be implemented by the Central Government and not by the State Government. So in the fitness of things he should have taken up this matter with the Central Government.

Jyoti Basu, in fact, even before the publication of this article, had sent a letter on irregular migration to the Prime Minister Rajiv Gandhi in February, 1989.[35] In this official communication he appealed to the

Central Government to focus its attention on the relentless inflow of unauthorized immigrants from across the border. It was alluded that the state government had notified the centre several times of the acutely large number of Bangladeshi Muslims entering India through its borders.[36] The defeat of the Congress in the Lok Sabha polI led to the formation of the National Front Government at the Centre in 1989 with the backing of the Bharatiya Janata Party and the Left parties. The NF Government publicly proclaimed that it was going to take stern action against undocumented Bangladeshis in West Bengal. The Minister and Deputy Minister for Home Affairs visited Calcutta for in-depth consultations on various methods to curb illegal flows. It is believed that the decision to issue photo-identity documents to Indian residents in border districts was given prominence. Attention was now directed towards stronger border controls to block such migrations.[37]

Ultimately, it was the Narashima Rao Government which came to power in 1991 that started the harshest measures against undocumented immigrants. Home Minister Shankar Rao Chavan had candidly conceded in Parliament on 2 December, 1991 that the exceedingly generous attitude rife among provincial-level authorities towards undocumented immigrants had mostly contributed to the vast increase in foreign nationals migrating to India.[38] The desperate circumstances in India due to these immigrants, he avowed, had prompted the Central Government to forthwith grant provincial bureaucracies the legal authority to initiate stern proceedings directed at them.[39]

But a report published out of Indore in Madhya Pradesh disputed the veracity of the Minister's articulations. It says:

> It is widely believed that following these directives, the Uttar Pradesh government had identified 10,000 Bangladeshis in different locations and arrested them for allegedly entering the country without passports. It is also broadly accepted that despite repeatedly inviting input from the Central Government on how to deal with these 'uninvited guests', a prolonged silence from this quarter had forced Uttar Pradesh eventually to release the detainees after they had furnished personal bonds.[40]

Prime Minister Narasimha Rao's announcement[41] at a public meeting at Guwahati on 3 July, 1992 that the existing legislation would be amended to help facilitate deportation of illegal immigrants who were 'snatching the bread and butter' of local people and his support to the agitations launched by students' organizations in the past against infiltrators might be construed as indicative of the stand of the Central Government on illegal migration from Bangladesh.

The Delhi police rounded up on 9 September, 1992, a group of 132 persons, 87 men, 23 women and 22 children from a large resettlement colony called New Seemapuri in East Delhi and pushed them back to Bangladesh through the Haridaspur check post of West Bengal on 10 September, 1992. But the unfortunate deportees had their heads shaven and their meagre belongings burnt in front of them before being cast out of the Indian territory. This inhuman treatment attracted media attention. Nikhil Chakravarty wrote:

> "As a part of Operation Pushback or perhaps a prelude to it, the government demonstrated its irresponsible impetuosity by forcibly deporting 132 migrants whose heads were tonsured on the birthday of Prophet Mohammed."[42]

But the most strongly worded critique came from Hiranmay Karlekar. Without mincing his words, he described this process of 'dispatching Bangladeshis' as the 'wanton brutality (that) bares the warts on India's face.'[43]

As with pointed tirades, a highly surprised twist came from the CPIM-led government of West Bengal. Chief Minister Jyoti Basu openly expressed displeasure with the action of the BSF and the Central Government by unexpectedly requesting that future expatriations of Bangladeshis be conducted through border areas outside West Bengal as his government's humanitarian reputation had been sullied by roughly tonsuring the hapless deportees.[44]

The Chief Minister's inflexible judgment appeared quite contrary to a resolution formally taken by his party in mid-September when it had backed the Central Government sponsored new action plan to check clandestine migration.[45] Like CPIM, the protracted inconsistency of many major Indian political parties towards unauthorized Bangladeshis would render the process and its outcome even more chaotic, particularly in succeeding deportation campaigns like 'Operation Flush Out' and 'Operation Find and Evict.'[46]

The 'tonsuring' incident became handy for the Bangladesh Government, which has consistently denied that any large-scale migration has taken place, to resist any deportation of Bangladeshi migrants. In fact, it responded in October 1992 by attempting to deport 92 alleged Indian citizens. These people were then refused entry by the BSF on the grounds that they were Bangladeshi citizens who had already been deported from India.[47] Consequently, in the wake of mounting international and internal pressure, and self-seeking intervention by senior Congress politicians who feared that the issue would harm support for the party among Muslim voters, the organized deportation of Bangladeshi migrants, code-named 'Operation Pushback' was suspended in early November, 1992 as abruptly as it had been inaugurated.[48]

According to official sources, H.K.L.Bhagat, a senior leader of the Congress(I) had exerted tremendous pressure on the Home Ministry and succeeded in putting a stop to further repatriation of Bangladeshis living in the trans-Jamuna areas of Delhi.[49]

Sporadic deportations, however, continued thereafter, for instance, through 'Operation Flush Out' and 'Operation Find and Evict', organized in later years.

Three weeks after the 'tonsuring incident', Union Home Minister S.B.Chavan convened on 28 September, 1992, the Chief Ministers' special conference on 'illegal' migration from Bangladesh. Ministers of nearly all the provinces in close proximity to the eastern boundary participated in this crucial meeting which unanimously adopted a resolution calling for firm action against unauthorized immigrants by the Centre and the States and to adopt time-bound action programme for the same. In his opening remarks, Chavan observed that massive immigration by Bangladeshis, beginning in Assam, then affecting West Bengal, Bihar, and other north-eastern states and lately the capital city, had led to a number of interrelated social, cultural, economic and political problems.[50] While confirming that a realistic estimate of 'illegal' migration was not available, the minister underscored that this 'problem' had acquired very serious severe dimensions.[51] "Whatever may be the compelling motive or cause for the migration", he added, "the continuous flow is a matter of serious concern for all of us."[52]

M.M.Jacob, Minister of State for Home Affairs, proposed the establishment of monitoring groups that would periodically review the activities undertaken by provinces and government bodies to check illegal migration. He also wanted the States to provide land for setting up fencing on the border and construction of roads in the area.[53] Finally, the Chief Ministers endorsed a scheme for issuing identity cards to Indian citizens living in the border districts, provided that it was implemented through approved legislation.[54] But the government failed to execute it.

Earlier P.K.Dave, the Lieutenant Governor of Delhi had disclosed in an article that owners of factories, business and heads of households would be asked to furnish detailed information to the police about the people employed by them. This was to include the employees' native place, duration of employment and their photographs.[55] Finally, he had advised city residents to cooperate with the police in their drive to identify 'illegal' Bangladeshis.[56]

It is unclear why this strategy was not legalized. An analyst thinks that it is very likely that the real prospect of opposition by other political parties to the intended policy dissuaded the Congress-led government. It is equally probable that the continuous accretion of Bangladeshis into the informal sector of this city's economy, together with the unending desire for cheap immigrant servants and casual labourers by well-to-do urban dwellers, may have had some bearing.[57] But the real reason might be what an unidentifiable though obviously disgruntled individual highly-placed in government circles said: "No one wanted to rock the boat."[58]

Since virtually all the political parties in this country have vested interests in the continued infiltration, the problem of infiltration never goes away. On the other hand, as an editorial in *The Hindu* puts it in 1994:

> The problem of illegal infiltration from Bangladesh into the north-eastern States is becoming more and more complex with the State Governments not being able to tackle it in a convincing manner. Reports have it that the influx in Assam, for instance, has created a situation far more explosive than was the case with the anti-foreigner agitation which rocked the State for several years in the early eighties. Some of the Bangladeshis have settled down in Delhi from where they are migrating to States like Rajasthan in search of employment. In the capital, the infiltrators have merged with the local population as had happened in some other cities and they were included in the electoral rolls and provided with ration cards. And, at one time, when the Government wanted to adopt tough methods to secure their deportations there were protests from certain political parties.[59]

III

A study reveals that a host of political and economic factors, such as political upheaval, religious persecution, social insecurity, economic stagnation and absence of job opportunities demographic pressures and environmental crises, have pushed Bangladeshi nationals to leave their homes and migrate to India. At the same time, availability of land, better economic opportunities, education and health facilities and a similar cultural landscape have attracted these migrants to settle in India.[60] Moreover, porous international border and political interest at place of destination are also dominant factors and stable life in West Bengal makes the process more dynamic. Residential setup at the new place is quite viable due to relatives, kin, job opportunities[61], and support from local political party in getting ration card, voting rights within six months to one year after migration.

Besides riots and war, discriminatory land laws were another manifestation of the state repression against the religious minorities. A series of property laws enacted since 1947, such as the East Bengal Requisition of Property Act of 1948, the East Bengal Evacuees (Administration of Immovable Property) Act of 1951 and the East Pakistan Disturbed Persons Rehabilitation Ordinance of 1964, created ways for the state to intervene, manage and even transfer property of persons displaced by communal riots. These laws were further manipulated by vested interest groups and corrupt administrators to dispossess and alienate the Hindus from their own land and property.[62]

The emergence of Bangladesh in 1971 as an independent country, with secularism as one of the pillars of the constitution, did not change the fate of the Hindus in that country. In fact, with each succeeding year, the Bangladeshi political regime was growing more hostile to the minority communities. To begin with, immediately after the liberation of Bangladesh, the government promulgated the Bangladesh Vesting of Property and Assets Order in March 1972, which stated that the property left by the Pakistanis and other displaced people should be considered as one segment. In 1976, the government repealed the previous Act only to consolidate it even more by taking over all rights to administer, manage, dispose and transfer such properties.[63] These laws paved four ways by which a person was dispossessed from his property and forced to migrate: first, forced occupation; second, leasing out of the said property by the government to the third party; third, nominal occupation but legal alienation; and fourth, extreme feeling of insecurity regarding loss of property.[64] According to one estimate, between 1965 and 2006, approximately 1.2 million Hindu households or 6 million Hindus were directly and severely affected by the Enemy/Vested Property Act and lost 2.6 million acres of their land.[65]

Initially, the Bangladesh government's sincere attempts to ensure security of the minority community had raised some signs of hope. Yet there is something seriously amiss somewhere as atrocities on Hindus continue to be a major irritant in governance with Hasina at the helm.

Why India is germane because excesses perpetrated on Hindus instill fear and they tend to migrate to this country for safety and security. As recently as 17 March, 2021, hundreds of followers of hardline Islamist group Hefazat-e-Islam's leader Maminul Haque attacked a Hindu village in Sunamganj district in the country's north-east Sylhet division with sticks and locally made weapons after a Hindu youth allegedly criticized Haque in a Facebook post over a speech he made at a recent event. Several Hindus fled their houses and the mob ransacked and looted as many as 70 to 80 houses. The police arrested 22 suspects and filed criminal cases against 700 more. Meanwhile, human rights groups and Hindu leaders said the minorities had been targeted in a planned way with the aim to drive them away. "This country belongs to everyone...We want harmony", Hindu Parishad leader Sujan Kumar Mishra said at a rally in Dhaka.[66]

"Terror is unleashed on Hindus who live in a state of fear. They stay awake at nights to guard their property lest it get usurped. Those who cannot protect their property are forced to sell at low prices and cross over to India for safety and greener pastures. There are also reports of large-scale forging of documents and fake mutations to manipulate ownership of Hindu propertics", alleged an analyst.[67] It devolves on the Awami League-led government with Hasina at its helm to create an atmosphere conducive for the Hindus, whose number has already dwindled to less than 9.5 per cent of the country's population, not to leave the country out of desperation and communal conflict. It is high time that the elected government of the country act not only positively but also decisively along with forward-looking civil rights groups and personalities who have been active crusaders to save the onslaught on Hindus by a handful of fanatics and anti-India forces to uphold the international image of Bangladesh as a secular country.

The unabated infiltration from Bangladesh has a severe impact on the ethnic, linguistic, religious, economic and ecological fabric of north-eastern States, West Bengal and other States where the 'infiltrators' have settled. Apart from creating economic pressure on India, the main danger of infiltration is mounting social tension and contrived electoral verdict. But any attempt to deport them from the areas they have settled in is foiled by legal and logistical wrangles, apart from vote-bank politics.

The illegal migrants take up jobs as Indian citizens, occupy public land, strain civic amenities and welfare services and cause social tension and environmental degradation. In rural border areas of Assam and West Bengal, Bangladeshi migrants provide a cheap source of rural labour to rich peasantry. In Assam, they have sustained themselves through small holding cultivation of unoccupied lands. In Kolkata and its suburbs, many migrants have found employment as construction workers, street hawkers and domestic help. It has also been estimated that one-third of the women working in the main prostitution locality of the city are Bangladeshi migrants.[68] Similarly in other cities such as Mumbai and New Delhi, Bangladeshi migrants have found work as day labourers, rag pickers, cycle rickshaw pullers and domestic labourers.[69]

Despite the often marginal nature of the employment found by Bangladeshi migrants and their inherent vulnerability to exploitation, migration have become a necessary survival strategy as a result of prevailing conditions of poverty, political and ethnic/religious marginalization, and environmental pressures in Bangladesh. They have been driven out of Bangladesh by a shortage of food, land and employment[70] as well as environmental factors such as floods, river silting and soil erosion.[71] They have been attracted to India by a perception of income and wage differentials between Bangladesh and India.[72]

The process of immigration often takes place by means of a system of migration agents (dalals) who facilitate travel to the border, organise crossing points, transport, accommodation and bribes for border officials where necessary and even establish a connection with a *dalal* in India to receive migrants on the other side of the border. Upon entry, migrants are often able to rely on support from family members or fellow local community members from Bangladesh who have already succeeded in settling in India. At the same time, long-term security is sought by attempting to gain ration cards and register on electoral rolls in order to gain a degree of leverage with officials and politicians within the Indian political process[73], and at the time of elections they cast their votes in favour of the party who protect them.

The pattern of infiltration, however, remains the same. Given the relatively less hostile terrain West Bengal, Assam, Tripura and Meghalaya are the favourite entry points. The infiltrators slip into India and, after walking a few kilometers, hop on to a bus that takes them into the hinterland. A woman in the family crossing ostensibly to deliver her child at a hospital is another tactic for gaining entry. The father follows soon. Armed with birth certificate, man and wife make their way on to the voters' list.

The unfenced portion of 4096 km-long Indo-Bangladesh border apart, long stretches of riverine areas provide ideal infiltration routes. Once the border is crossed by land or water, immigrants are helped by political parties from across the ideological spectrum—from red and green with patches of saffron thrown in for good measure. Ration cards are provided, children are admitted in schools and the infiltration process culminates in enlistment in the voters' list. They generally have documents with an address in any of the bordering States. Mostly, it is a West Bengal address.

In West Bengal, the ruling CPIM party was blamed for extending all facilities to the Bangladeshi infiltrators. Organizing racket of fake Voter Cards and false ration cards throughout the State was laid at its door[74], which was alleged to be only a tip of the iceberg of corruption during the Left Front regime.[75] The disclosure in a press conference on 7 January, 2006 by the CPIM West Bengal State Secretary, Anil Biswas, that about 6 lakh fake ration Cards could be identified throughout the State in special drives in the districts in the last 11 days[76], only gave credibility to the above charges. The Food ministry of the Central Government has weeded out nearly 4.4 crore bogus ration cards in 2013-2020 and of them 68.62 lakh were in West Bengal.[77]

There were even allegations that the Bangladeshis had infiltrated into party apparatus and occupied other elective posts like Panchayat Upa Sabhapati, Municipal councillors. One Kamal Saha of the CPIM and Up-Savapathui of Satbakura Gram Panchayat under Garbeta Police Station, District Midnapore and two of his nephews were arrested by police on 3 March, 2006 under the Foreigners Act on question of their citizenship.[78] Ramendra Nath Halder, Councillor of Ward No. 29 of North Dum Dum Municipality and many others, all belonging to the CPIM, were alleged to be infiltrators from Bangladesh.[79] One of their MPs, Alokesh Das, submitted documentary proof of his Indian nationality to the Election Commission on 17 March, 2006.[80] Administrative enquiry was started against Nripen Choudhury, Murshidabad Disitrict Secretary of CPIM, on the question of his Indian nationality.[81]

Curiously enough, L.K.Advani, accused the Central Government on 8 April, 2006 for having surrendered to the infiltrators[82], but in the same breadth expressed his satisfaction for the role of the CM of West Bengal, Buddhadeb Bhattahcarjee, in preventing infiltration from across the border.[83] Everything is possible in politics![84]

Saturation point having been reached in West Bengal, the unfavorable socio-political climate in Assam has diverted the migration route of Bangladeshi Muslims towards northern and western parts of India even to Delhi, Bengaluru and Mumbai. Some Bangladeshis have moved on to Nainital, Terai and many other parts of India. In selected rural areas they have been attracted by the availability of low-cost marginal lands, which they have made fertile again through hard work. This has often aroused the resentment of local people. Others seek rural land because of the difficulty in adjusting to urban life and daily employment. Being of rural origin they are most at home cultivating the land.[85]

As early as in 1995, Rajasthan government was embroiled with the problem of Bangaldeshi migrants. While the Joint Director of Census, R.P.Tomar pointed out that there were nearly 12,000 Bangladeshis residing in Rajasthan, the actual figure might be even higher.[86] The Mumbai Police, in 1998, tried to deport illegal Bangladeshi migrants, but met with resistance in Kolkata.[87]

The trend of movement of Bangladeshi migrants to the rest of India, which was increasingly noticed in late 1980s, has increased in the last two decades. Himachal Pradesh was keeping a strict vigil on migrant labourers following tip-offs from Army and other intelligence agencies in March 2006 about possible infiltration of activists into the state.[88] The Gujarat Police identified and deported 440 Bangladeshis who were illegally staying in Ahmedabad since 2009.[89]According to the media quoting Uttar Pradesh officials, in 2010, approximately 8,500 Bangladeshis were illegally staying in the state, of which 6,000 were living in Meerut, 1,800 in Lucknow and 350 in NOIDA.[90] Katihar, Kishanganj and Purnea districts of Bihar have also recorded illegal presence of Bangladeshis. In July 2013, 6,000 persons were accused of being Bangladeshis in the state and were handed over notices to prove their Indian citizenship or leave India.[91] In the same year, the Odisha government identified nearly 4,000 Bangladeshis in the state.[92] These were allegedly staying in the districts of Kendrapara, Jagatsinghpur, Malkangiri and Bhadrak. Presence of Bangladeshis has also been observed in coastal states of the country such as Gujarat, Karnataka, Tamil Nadu and Kerala.

The Tamil Nadu state BJP complained on 6 February, 2006 that there were as many as 30,000 illegal immigrants from Bangladesh in Tamil Nadu.[93] The Jharkhand state BJP executive committee passed a resolution on 20 June, 2016 to take up the issue of Bangladeshi infiltrators in Sahibganj and Pakur districts with the Centre.[94] A chance arrest of 16 Bangladeshi immigrants from a rice mill at Pneugonda in West Godavari district of Andhra Pradesh on 21 November, 2014[95] shows that they are infiltrating far off places after crossing the border. Bhaskar Rao, Bengaluru city police commissioner claimed on 29 January, 2020 that there were around 3 lakh Bangladeshis across the state and around 3000 of them had left the city following the recent crackdown.[96] Only in June 2014, as many as 200 people from Bangladesh's hills belonging to Chakma and Tripuri tribes entered Dhalai district of Tripura to escape sectarian violence and group clashes in Bangladesh.[97]

However, this 'influx unbound'[98] of Bangladeshi nationals has reached such an alarming proportion that it is turning the demographic profile and socio-economic fabric of the five border States on the Indian side upside down. Rampant and recurring are arms-drug-salt-cycle-cow smuggling, pilferage of domestic animals and sneaking in of fake Indian currency. More destabilizing is the increasing incidence of infiltration of fundamentalists, *jehadis* and secessionists who slip into India after receiving training, resources and implicit support from our neighbours.

The George C. Francis Committee, comprising five officials from security agencies, has in fact mentioned the "demographic invasion" in the light of the vulnerability of the Bangladeshi illegal immigrants in terms of being utilized by the ISI to continue its "Operation Pin Code" launched in 2004. Talking about "demographic invasion", the report says the concentration of Bangladeshi illegal migrants from the 24 Parganas district of West Bengal to Barpeta in Assam is more than half the local population which could influence as many as 25 Lok Sabha seats in the region.[99]

'Demographic invasion' as a process is akin to 'expulsion of surplus inhabitants', a phenomenon described by Beltran to explain the colonization process in Mestizo America.[100] As the new migrants increase their number through infiltration, they gradually achieve the capacity for self-defense as a group and do not seek affiliation with the local people. Rather they remain apart as a differentiated group, through the years strengthening their characteristics as a separate entity. This process is more visible in territories contiguous to their original habitation.

To make matters worse, most of the migrants who were deported from Assam in the 1960s re-entered the country. This trend was reflected in the census figures of 1971 for Assam, which revealed an increase of 8,20,000 Muslims–4,24,000 more than that could be accounted through natural increase.[101]

The steady rise of Muslim population in the state of Assam from 24.68 per cent in 1951 to 28.43 per cent in 1991 to 34.2 per cent in 2011 is also taken as an indication of large-scale migration from Bangladesh[102]; an assertion further reinforced by the increase of Muslim population in the bordering districts of Goalpara, Nowgong and Cachar, from 42.94 per cent, 34.18 per cent and 38.49 per cent in 1951 to 51.31 per cent, 38.42 per cent and 45.47 per cent respectively in 2001.[103]

Since the 1960s, the population of the Hindus in West Bengal has been steadily declining. The proportion of Muslims, on the other hand, registered an increase of 0.46 per cent in 1971, which grew further to 5 per cent in 2001. Between 1991 and 2001, North 24 Parganas, Murshidabad and Malda, bordering Bangladesh, registered a population rise of 22.64 per cent, 23.70 per cent and 24.77 per cent respectively—a growth rate which was higher than the state's average of 17.84 per cent. On the whole, between 1951 and 2001, while the growth rate of Hindus was 198.54 per cent, the Muslims recorded a growth rate of 310.93 per cent. This significant upswing in population growth of the Muslims in the state is attributed to illegal migration from Bangladesh.[104]

The inclusion of tens of thousands of undocumented Bangladeshi immigrants on voter rolls and ration card lists, as well as their competition for menial jobs, has engendered resentment by legal residents in Tripura, Maharashtra, Bihar, Jharkhand, Uttar Pradesh, Gujarat and other States of India. It has been only a matter of time before the psychological stresses of the accelerating socio-economic transition would prompt communal elements to seize the opportunity to use the issue for their selfish political ends, warns Lin and Paul.[105]

The political patronage extended to illegal migrants helped successive streams of migrants to cross the border easily, find shelter and jobs in India, and finally settle down permanently. One of the fallouts of large-scale illegal migration of Bangladeshis has been that the border areas, especially in West Bengal and Assam, which earlier had a mixed composition of population, that is, both Hindus and Muslims cohabited, are giving way to new settlements based on exclusive religious identities.[106] In fact, the peopling of the border belt by Bangladeshi illegal migrants has led to the Hindu inhabitants migrating further into the interior of the state and the Muslims migrants gradually filling up the vacant space. In a number of cases, it has been observed that much of the migration is forced as Muslim migrants, who have become demographically preponderant in the border region, use force and intimidation to evict the Hindus.[107] Thus, a wide section of border is inhabited by a people having identical ethnic, linguistic, cultural and religious background.[108]

Another outcome of the large-scale settlement of illegal migrants is that a number of mosques and madrasas have come up to cater to the needs of the migrant population in these areas. Madrasas, mosques, *dargahs* form almost a dotted line along the border of which some are new, some brought back to life, but all of them often act as a network of linkages offering social and temporary economic protection and religious and community solidarity to the Muslim migrant.[109] The construction of mosques and madrasas demonstrates the cultural and religious assertion by the illegal migrants who are overwhelmingly Muslims. The locals, especially the Hindus, believe that these mosques and madrasas, funded by money from Saudi Arabia, Kuwait, Bangladesh, etc., propagate anti-Hindu and anti-India sentiments. It is believed that these activities are conducted by Jamaat-e-Islami members who clandestinely cross over from Bangladesh.[110]

These developments have created resentment against the illegal migrants among the local population, who feel that they are getting marginalised in their own land. Elsewhere in the country, intermittent protests against Bangladeshis by some political parties have been recorded, especially in the urban centres. In most of the cases, the political parties accuse the illegal migrants of taking away jobs from the local communities.[111] Acknowledging the adverse consequences of illegal migration, the Union Minister of State P.M. Saeed said in Lok Sabha in August 1995, "there has been continuous influx of Bangladeshi nationals into India for a variety of reasons, including religious and economic considerations. The demographic composition of the border areas has been altered with new entrants flooding the areas and the local migrating into the interior."[112]

Ethnic, linguistic and religious commonality between the illegal migrants and the people on the Indian side of the border enables them to find safe shelter. It makes their detection difficult. Newspaper reports focused frequently on the uncanny ability of undocumented immigrants to evade identification and deportation. Bangladeshi Muslim immigrants disappeared *en masse*, adopted Hindu names and practices, took up daily waged labour, and dispersed rapidly to other localities both in and outside Delhi.[113] The few hundred immigrants who were banished in 1992 returned to Delhi shortly after being deported, and they continued to return despite being expelled on several occasions.[114] These acts of defiance were so apparent that a joke circulating among the Delhi police suggested that the deportees were returning to Delhi much before the police team accompanying them to the border did![115]

Sujata Ramachandran informs that several undocumented immigrants revealed to her during interviews that they were allowed to leave the police station when they claimed to have migrated from Bihar or other parts of India. In most cases, this technique worked if the respondent spoke fluent Hindi to convince the local police.[116]

The issues of discontent and despair of the sons-of-the-soil, indigeneity of the autochthons, ethnic homogeneity, cultural integrity of the linguistic groups, religious commonality, resurgence of sub-nationalism, ascendancy of divisive politics, or traditional 'pride' in one's provincial roots, as evidenced throughout the length and breadth of the country—from Maharashtra to Manipur, Jammu & Kashmir to Kanyamumari—are all manifestation of the same disease, the fear of being submerged in "others", of helplessness, of compromising with one's very existence, of losing the territorial integrity, or in broader sense, the "clash of civilization". And this agony and anger of the sons-of-the-soil is a world-wide phenomenon through all ages—from Maharashtra to Malaysia, Kenya to Fiji, though the problems are not exactly the same.

Trump's advocacy of 'America for Americans" is also rooted in this policy.

It is no wonder that many states in India like Andhra Pradesh, Telangana, Tamil Nadu, Karnataka, Maharashtra, Gujarat, Rajasthan, Uttarakhand, U.P., West Bengal, Assam are adopting 'sons of the soil' policies prescribing reservation or preference based on domicile or residence requirement for employment or appointment in government or private concerns or for enrolment in educational institutions. It may be recalled that till the other day the residential qualification for being a member of the Rajya Sabha was strictly adhered to though it has since been dispensed with.

Besides political parties, pressure groups and judiciary, officials also started endorsing the argument that illegal migration does pose a threat to the national security. On 8 November, 1998, Lt. General (Retd.) S.K.Sinha, Governor of Assam, in a lengthy and comprehensive report drew the attention of the President to the problems emanating from large-scale unabated migration from Bangladesh. Xerox copy of this 42-page report to the President on the "illegal Migration into Assam" was later easily available in Guwahati. One was required to spend Rupees 45 for obtaining the same.[117]

Some portions of the report are reproduced below:

> "1. The unabated influx of illegal migrants from Bangladesh into Assam and the consequent perceptible change in the demographic pattern of the State has been a matter of grave concern. It threatens to reduce the Assamese people to a minority in their own State, as happened in Tripura and Sikkim.
>
> 3. There is a tendency to view illegal migration into Assam as a regional matter affecting only the people of Assam. It's more dangerous dimension of greatly undermining our national security is ignored. The long cherished design of Greater East

> Pakistan/Bangladesh, making in-roads into strategic land link of Assam with the rest of the country, can lead to severing the entire land mass of the North-East, with all its rich resources from the rest of the country. They will have disastrous strategic and economic consequences.
>
> 22. The dangerous consequences of large scale illegal migration from Bangladesh, both for the people of Assam and more for the nation as a whole, need to be emphatically stressed. No misconceived and mistaken notions of secularism should be allowed to come in the way of doing so.
>
> 23. As a result of population movement from Bangladesh, the specter looms large of the indigenous people of Assam being reduced to a minority in their home State. Their cultural survival will be in jeopardy, their political control will be weakened and their employment opportunities will be undermined.
>
> 24. The silent and invidious demographic invasion of Assam may result in the loss of the geo-strategically vital districts of lower Assam. The influx of these illegal migrants is turning these districts into a Muslim majority region. It will then only be a matter of time when a demand for their merger with Bangladesh may be made. The rapid growth of international Islamic fundamentalism may provide for driving force for this demand. In this context, it is pertinent that Bangladesh has long discarded secularism and has chosen to become an Islamic State. Loss of lower Assam will severe the entire land mass of the North-East from the rest of India and the rich natural resources of that region will be lost to the nation.[118]

Group of Ministers Report of 2001 states that because of large-scale illegal migration from Bangladesh, "demographic changes have been brought about in the border belts of West Bengal, several districts of Bihar, Assam, Tripura, and Meghalaya".[119] The report goes on to say that "the massive illegal immigration poses a grave danger to our security, social harmony and economic well-being".[120]

Indeed, the number of Muslim majority districts in Assam has increased to 9 in the 2011 Census as against 6 in the 2001Census. Further, the Muslim population in another three districts has crossed the one-third threshold and it is nearing 30 per cent mark in another district. In the 2021

Census, the number of Muslim majority districts in Assam is likely to be in two digits.

Lt. Gen. Sinha had also written an article in *The Assam Tribune* in 2016 to say that in 1998, illegal migrant voters were in a majority or near majority in 40 of the 126 Assembly constituencies in Assam. Their presence has increased in the last 18 years. He further wrote: "The Illegal Migration Detection by Tribunal (IMDT) Act ostensibly to check illegal migration was actually designed to facilitate infiltration into Assam." He even alleged that all the 14 Congress MPs from Assam had written to the President calling for his recall as he was interfering in political matters. He went on to point out: "To this day, hardly anything has been done to implement the recommendations in my report to the President submitted in 1998. Tarun Gogoi as the Chief Minister maintained that illegal migration was a non-issue."[121]

IV

But what is the actual figure of Bangaldeshi infiltrators? Conflicting figures float around as to the number of illegal migrants from Bangladesh. Because of ethnic and language similarities, it is extremely difficult to identify Bangladeshis. As a result, no authentic figure of the number of Bangladeshi infiltrators who have made India their home is available.

One of the frequent refrains of the Government of India on the lack of data on illegal migration is that since illegal migrants enter the country clandestinely and surreptitiously, it is impossible to have data on Bangladeshis illegally staying in various parts of the country.[122] Nonetheless, the Government of India has periodically provided statistics on the estimated number of illegal migrants in India. For example, reports in 1992 indicated that the Indian government, which operates upon the assumption that virtually all cross-border movements from Bangladesh subsequent to the resolution of the India-Pakistan war in 1971 are illegal, estimated that there were somewhere between 7 and 12 million Bangladeshis residing in India.[123]

A study was conducted by the Intelligence Bureau and the Home Ministry in 1992 to find out the extent of demographic changes in the eastern sector, especially in relation to illegal migration from Bangladesh. In view of the sensitive nature of the findings the report was kept a secret. It was ultimately leaked out and the estimated number of illegal migrants from Bangladesh was anywhere between 1.5 crore and 2 crore.[124]

As Union Home Minister, both Indrajit Gupta, India's first communist Home Minister, and his successor L.K.Advani of the BJP must have access to this information. So when Indrajit Gupta told the Lok Sabha on May 6, 1997 that there were one crore illegal Bangladeshi migrants in India[125] or

L.K.Advani said in 2003 that nearly 2 crore Bangladeshis were illegally staying in various parts of India[126], they must have relied on this sensitive report.

On 14 July, 2004, Sriprakash Jaiswal, the then Minister of State for Home Affairs informed the Lok Sabha that 1 crore 20 lakh 53 thousand 950 Bangladeshi infiltrators were staying in India illegally.[127] BJP, which was then the main opposition party, demanded that the 12 million illegal Bangladeshi immigrants be identified and deported. As a political storm brewed in states like Assam, Jaiswal withdrew his reply, dismissing the 12 million figure as one based on "unreliable reports" and "hearsay".[128] The Union Minister of State for Home Kiren Rijiju in the BJP-led NDA-II government again in a written reply to a question posed by Rajya Sabah MP Jharna Das Baidya told the Rajya Sabha on 16 November, 2016 that around 2 crore Bangladeshi immigrants were staying in India illegally.[129] It is rather difficult to believe that there is no accretion of illegal Bangladeshis since 2003, when this figure was first quoted by L.K. Advani.

Table 3.1: Numerical distribution and percentage of Major Religious Communities in Bangladesh, 1901-2001

Year	Total popu-lation	Muslim	Percen-tage	Hindu	Percen-tage
1901	28,927	19,113	66.1	9,545	33.0
1911	31,555	21,202	67.2	9,952	31.5
1921	33,254	22,646	68.1	10,166	30.6
1931	35,604	24,731	69.5	10,453	29.4
1941	41,999	29,509	70.3	11,747	28.0
1951	41,933	32,227	76.9	9,239	22.0
1961	50,840	40,890	80.4	9,380	18.5
1971	71,478	61,039	85.4	9,673	13.5
1981	87,120	74,587	86.7	10,570	12.1
1991	1,06,315	93,881	88.3	11,179	10.5
2001	1,23,851	1,11,079	89.7	11,379	9.2
2011	1,49,772	1,35,394	90.2	12,731	8.5

Source: Population Census 2001, National Report (Provisional) July 2003, Bangladesh Bureau of statistics, Planning Division, Ministry of Planning, Table 8.1, p. 65 and Table 8.2, p. 66. For 2011, Bangladesh—Wikipedia en.wikipedia.org›wiki ›Bangladesh

Since the exact number of illegal Bangladeshi infiltrators is not known, a study of the Census Reports of both India and Bangladesh may give an indication of the magnitude of the problem of infiltration from across the border. The religious composition of the enumerated population in Bangladesh as revealed in the population census of 2001 is shown in Table 3.1.

If it is presumed that large-scale migration of Hindu population from erstwhile East Pakistan, now Bangladesh, in the wake of Partition was over by the end of the Fifties, and that the rate of growth of both the Hindu and the Muslim population were the same, then the proportion of Hindu and Muslim population would have been the same in the 2001 Census as it was in the 1961 Census. That means Hindus would have constituted 18.5 per cent of the total population in 2001 as well. In that case, their number should have been

$$\frac{93{,}80{,}000 \times 11{,}10{,}79{,}000}{4{,}08{,}90{,}000} = 2{,}54{,}81{,}000$$

Given that 1,13,79,000 Hindus were enumerated in the 2001 Census, (2,54,81,000–1,13,79,000) = 1,41,02,000 or 14.1 million Hindus have vanished from Bangladesh during the last four decades (1961-2001). Since under the Indira Gandhi-Mujib Agreement of 1972 all the Bangladeshis coming to India for permanent settlement prior to March 25, 1971 were to be given Indian citizenship, what should have been the population of the Hindus in Bangladesh in 2001 taking 1974 as the base year, in the absence of a Census data of 1971, presuming that the rate of growth of the Hindu as well as of the Muslim population were the same? It would be

$$\frac{96{,}73{,}000 \times 11{,}10{,}79{,}000}{6{,}10{,}39{,}000} = 1{,}76{,}02{,}000$$

That means 1,76,02,000 – 1,13,79,000 = 62,23,000 or 6.2 million Hindus have migrated from Bangladesh after the 1974 Census. And where they have gone? Obviously, they have entered India illegally. This rough estimate, however, does not take into account the migration of Muslim population from Bangladesh to India and other countries. If that figure could have been assessed, then the number of illegal Hindu migrants would register a much higher figure.

Now let us look at the Indian population during 1961-2011, as revealed in the Indian Census reports. As per the Indian Census Report of 2011, the religious composition of the population, mainly Hindu and Muslim, is as given in Table 3.2.

Table 3.2: Population of Hindu and Muslim communities and their Growth Rate in India, 1961-2011

Year	Total population	Hindu population	Percen-tage	Muslim population	Percen-tage
1961	43,92,34,771	36,65,26,866	84.4	4,69,40,799	9.9
1971	54,79,49,809	45,32,92,086	83.5	6,14,17,934	10.4
1981	66,52,87,849	54,97,79,481	83.1	7,55,12,439	10.9
1991	83,85,83,988	68,76,46,721	82.4	10,15,96,057	11.7
2001	1,02,86,10,328	82,75,78,686	81.4	13,81,88,240	12.4
2011	1,21,05,69,573	96,62,57,353	79.8	17,22,45,158	14.2

Source: pp. xxvii-xxviii of the First Report on Religion Data, Census of India, 2001 for the period 1961-2001 and *The Times of India*, August 26, 2015, p. 1 for 2011.

During the period 1961-2001, 14.1 million Hindus, as calculated above, have come over to India from East Pakistan/Bangladesh. If those Hindus had remained in Bangladesh, then the Hindu population of India would have been (966.3–14.1) 952.2 million in 2011.

And if we take into consideration the fall-out of the Indira Gandhi-Mujib Agreement on Hindu migration from Bangladesh, the Hindu population of India would have been (966.3–6.2) 960.1 million in 2011, provided there was no inflow of Hindus from Bangladesh after the Indira Gandhi-Mujib Agreement.

Now let us compare the growth rate of the Muslim population *vis-à-vis* the Hindu population in India during 1961-2011 in the following three situations:

1. total Hindu population as enumerated;
2. total Hindu population sans the Hindu migrants since 1961; and
3. total Hindu population sans the Hindu migrants during the post-1971 period.

The growth rate of the Hindu and the Muslim population in India in each of the three situations is as follows:

(1) Total population as per census report in	1961	2011	growth rate
of Hindus (in million)	366.5	966.3	263.66%
of Muslims (in million)	46.9	172.2	367.16 %

If the growth rate of the Hindus and the Muslims were the same then the Muslims population would have been 123.26 million. That means in India, the Muslim population has increased by (172.2–123.3) 48.9 million more compared to the Hindu population during the same period.

	1961	2011	growth rate
(2) Total population as per census report in of Hindus sans those coming from Bangladesh after 1961(in million)	366.5	952.2	259.81%
of Muslims (in million)	46.9	172.2	367.16%

If the growth rate of the Hindus and the Muslims were the same during this period then the Muslim population would have been 121.85 million. That means in India, the Muslim population has increased by (172.2–121.9) 49.3 million more compared to the Hindu population during this period.

	1971	2011	growth rate
(3) Total population as per census report in of Hindus sans those migrating in the post-1971 period (in million)	453.3	960.1	211.80%
of Muslims (in million)	61.4	172.2	280.46%

If the growth rate of the Hindus and the Muslims in India were the same during this period then the Muslim population would have been 130.05 million. It means in India, the Muslim population has registered an increase of (172.2–130.05) 42.15 million more compared to the Hindu population.

How much of this additional Muslim population of 48.9 million, 49.3 million or 42.15 million, as calculated above, which is roughly between 105 per cent and 90 per cent of its population in 1961, is due to the increased birth rate and how much due to migration from across the border is difficult to say. It cannot, however, altogether be ruled out that migration from across the border did not contribute at all to the comparatively higher incidence of growth of the Muslim population. Like the Hindus, a sizeable number of the Muslims have also migrated to India from East Pakistan/ Bangladesh over the years illegally.[130]

As pointed out by Anirban Kashyap way back in 1988:

> The Muslims of East Pakistan, now Bangladesh, are culturally, linguistically, physiognomically and ethnically akin to the Muslims living in West Bengal, Assam and other Eastern States. Similarly, the Muslims of West Pakistan are akin to their counterparts in the bordering States of India. Only the other day they were members of the same family. Partition of the country has made them nationals of two, now three, independent neighbouring countries. They have relations either in this side or that side of the border. If one comes to this side of India after crossing the border and gets himself mixed up with the population of his ilk, it is difficult to identify him.[131]

V

Smuggling and illegal movement across the border are the major threats to security, territorial integrity and efficient border management of any nation. Illegal immigration or infiltration has become a major problem throughout the world. For instance, the United States is adding about 0.25 per cent to its population every year through legal immigration. And through illegal immigration, the United States is perhaps increasing its population by another 0.50 per cent a year.[132] The "organized smuggling" of illegal migrants by criminal gangs, the problem of overstayal of people entering with valid visas or with false immigration papers are being faced by many countries the world over. They are worried that their democratic structure would crumble if they fail to cope with the influx of foreigners. There is also concern about the rising tide of racism and the popularity of the rightist parties with a xenophobic agenda. The ingress of illegal migrants can not only change the demographic profile of the country but also create a tremendous impact on the socio-economic and political affairs of the country, on the security of the people and may even create an identity problem. That is the reason why almost all the countries the world over have enforced curb on immigration by making visa rules more stringent and have even taken other precautionary and preventive measures like better border management, fencing along the international borders, intensive patrolling so as to make it difficult for the illegal migrants to cross over. In most countries 'economic migrants' are subject to immediate deportation. Effective deterrent and penal actions are taken against those who organise illegal migration or employ undocumented migrants.

All the countries are taking stringent measures against the illegal migrants. For instance, Australia has some of the toughest border protection policies in the world, with mandatory and indefinite immigration detention, offshore processing of asylum claims (including the "regional processing centres" in Christmas Island, Papua New Guinea and Nauru) and a policy of immediately returning people who do not make a claim at first instance that rises persecution or torture concerns in their country of origin. In July 2013, the Australian government announced a "Regional Resettlement Arrangement" in which all persons arriving by boats in Australia would be unable to settle in Australia and would, instead, be sent to Papua New Guinea for resettlement.[133] The Spanish government has reintroduced in 2013 barbed wire to the border fence that divides the enclave of Melilla on the North African coast from Morocco in order to deter immigrants from north and sub-Saharan Africa from crossing over.[134] Hungary has built a six-foot razor wire fence blocking the full length of its 175 km border with Serbia to slow the flow of asylum seekers into northern Europe.[135] Slovenia also erected razor wire fences along parts of its border with Croatia in November, 2015 to control migrant flow.[136] President Trump of the USA, in furtherance of his election promise, started erecting wall on the USA-Mexico border.

Israel has illegally coerced almost 7,000 African migrants into returning to their home countries where some face persecution.[137] The conservative government of the UK, though was a member of the European Union (EU) the other day, even plans to restrict the number of immigrants from the EU which has been rejected by the European Commission being not compatible with EU regulations.[138] Not only the far-right groups of the UK demand stricter border controls against immigrants[139], even sections of the Labour Party are calling for greater immigration controls.[140] As a matter of fact, one of the reasons, if not the main reason, why Britain voted for Brexit in the 23 June referendum was the uncontrolled flow of migrants from the EU countries. Harbouring or in any way helping an illegal immigrant is a crime in Italy.[141]

The first priority should be to prevent any further illegal migration from across the border. The Union Government has increased the number of BSF battalions deployed along the border over the years. In 1991, 40 battalions of BSF were deployed along the Bangladesh border. In the next decade, the strength of the BSF was increased to 60 battalions and presently, 80 battalions of BSF are guarding the India-Bangladesh border.

The 4,096.7 km long Indo-Bangladesh border is marked by a high degree of porosity. In order to prevent illegal migration and illegal activities including anti-national activities from across the border, the Government of India had sanctioned the construction of border roads and fencing with floodlights in two phases. The total length of Indo-Bangladesh border sanctioned for fencing is 3,359.59 km; out of which about 2,823.046 km of fencing has been completed up to 31.03.2014. There have been some problems in the construction of fencing in certain stretches on this border due to riverine/low-lying areas, population residing within 150 yards of the border, pending land acquisition cases and protests by the border population. As a result fencing on 536.55 km —WB (234.85), Assam (4.80), Meghalaya (115.57), Mizoram (115.79) and Tripura (65.54)—were pending as on 31.03.2014. The balance fencing works for the 736.11 km [4.096.7–3,359.59=736.11 km] were not sanctioned due to topographical constraints, i.e., riverine/low-lying/hilly etc. In addition, 3,697.47 km of border patrol roads have also been constructed out of the sanctioned length of about 4,407.11 km. The Government has decided to undertake the work of installation of floodlights in the States of West Bengal, Meghalaya, Assam, Mizoram and Tripura along 2,840 km of the Indo-Bangladesh border at an estimated cost of Rs 1,327 crore. Floodlighting work on 1736.06 km has, however, been complete as on 31 March, 2014.[142] Border fencing and floodlighting works along the entire stretch of Indo-Pakistan border has been more or less completed except for a small part of pending work in Gujarat sector of Indo-Pak border (78.22 km for fencing and 47.00 km for floodlighting) as on 31.03.2014.[143]

Junior home minister Nityanand Rai informed the Lok Sabha on 24 July, 2019 that 2,803 km out of the sanctioned 3,326 km of Bangla border, has already been fenced. He added that work was in progress to fence another 169.64 km and 353.48 km remained to be fenced. "The plan is to complete the fencing of 3,326 km by 2020", Rai said.[144] In the wake of the agitations against the CAA/NRC, the Centre has expedited the process of barbed-wire fencing in South Bengal. An amount of Rs. 88 crore has been sanctioned for purchase of 300 acre of private land in the district of North 24 Parganas for barbed-wire fencing. The district L & LR department will hand over the land to the Centre after purchasing the land from its private owners at market price. This is likely to be completed by mid-2020.[145]

While fencing has been successful to some extent in preventing easy access, it has not altogether stopped people from illegally entering India. This is because the migrants have devised means to surmount the fence or circumvent it. There are numerous reports of migrants either cutting the fences or placing wooden ladders and planks to climb over them.[146] That the fence was never meant to completely stop illegal migration all by itself was not lost on the policymakers. In fact, the Minister of External Affairs, Jaswant Singh, had told the Rajya Sabha in March 2002:

> The nature of the Indo-Bangladesh border is such that it is very difficult to fence the entire border. Out of 4,000 km of the border, there is a proper fencing only in a fraction of it. A large part of this border is riverine, a large part of this border keeps changing as the rivers keep changing their course. On account of these various factors infiltration cannot be stopped simply by putting barbed wire fences on this very difficult terrain, on this very difficult border. There are complex social and economic reasons behind infiltration, the illegal infiltration from Bangladesh. There are economic factors; there are factors of land and unless all these are taken into account it will be impractical and unwise to address it in one particular manner.[147]

Initially, the inter-BOP distance along the Indo-Bangladesh border was approximately 9 km, making it extremely difficult to effectively man the border, but over the years, with increased deployment of the BSF personnel and establishment of 802 BOPs, it was reduced to an average distance of 4–4.5 km. In order to reduce the inter-BOP distance between the existing border outposts (BOPs) on the Indo-Bangladesh border (802) and the India-Pakistan border (609) to 3.5 km for an effective border management, a proposal for the construction of additional 509 BOPs (383 along the Indo-Bangladesh border and 126 along the Indo-Pakistan border) at an estimated cost of 1,832.50 crore was approved by the Government on 16 February, 2009. In addition to the newly sanctioned BOPs as mentioned above, 70 BOPs were sanctioned in the year 2000 under the composite scheme for Gujarat sector of the Indo-Pak border. Construction of these additional BOPs will provide necessary infrastructure for the accommodation, logistic support and the combat functions of the BSF troops deployed on the Indo-Bangladesh and the Indo-Pakistan borders. The target date of completion of these projects by 2013-14, however, could not be adhered to because of delays in land acquisition, clearances from various ministries and protests by local people.[148]

The Government had approved the setting up 13 new Integrated Check Posts (ICP) at major points on land border with Nepal, Myanmar, Pakistan and Bangladesh as a Plan Scheme under the 11th Five Year Plan at an estimated cost of Rs. 635 crore in order to stop illegal migration. As on 31 March, 2014, the ICPs at Attari and Agartala have become functional while those at Petrapole, Raxaul, Jogbani and Moreh are in various stages of construction. Land has been acquired in the case of Rupaidiha (Uttar Pradesh) and it is being acquired for the ICPs at Dwaki and Sunauli (Uttar Pradesh). Further, the selection of land is under process for finalization in case of Hili and Changrabandha in West Bengal, Kwarpuchiah in Mizoram, and Sutarkhandi in Assam.[149]

The BSF plans laser walls to trip infiltrators from Pakistan. The laser beams would form a wall in places such as the riverine parts of Jammu where fencing is not possible. The system will be connected to an alarm which would go off at any breach. So, if anyone infiltrates, the force would be alerted. Other than laser walls in unfenced areas, the force is considering anti-tunnel ground sensors and thermal sensors in the fenced stretches. This would work as an advance alert system where one would have time to reach the area where infiltrators might by trying to cut a fence and enter, or a smuggler may be trying to pass on a contraband packet. Such technologies are already in use in countries such as Israel.[150] The force is acquiring unmanned aerial vehicles and other surveillance equipment to bolster border defence. The move comes even though BSF maintains that there is no infiltration from Pakistan on the borders it guards.[151] In the wake of the Pathankot attack and a similar terror strike in Uri leading to the escalation of tensions between India and Pakistan, Union Home Minister, Rajnath Singh, after a high level meeting attended by the Chief Minister of Rajasthan, Deputy Chief Minister of Punjab, Home Minister of Gujarat and Chief Secretary of Jammu & Kashmir at Jaisalmer, Rajasthan on 7 October, 2016, announced that the entire Indo-Pak border would be "sealed" by December, 2018.[152]

But the same attention is not paid to the eastern border the BSF guards. The highest Court of the land on 17 December, 2014 raised a very simple question. It said: "We are at a loss to understand why 67 years after independence the eastern border is left porous. We have been reliably informed that the entire western border with Pakistan, 3300 km long, is not only properly fenced, but properly manned as well, and is not porous at any point." The same Bench also directed the Union to take the following steps on border fencing, border roads and flood lights:

> The Union will take all effective steps to complete the fencing (double coiled wire fencing) in such parts/portions of the Indo-Bangla border (including the State of Assam) where presently the fencing is yet to be completed. The vigil along the riverine boundary will be effectively maintained by continuous patrolling. Such part of the international border which has been perceived to be inhospitable on account of the difficult terrain will be patrolled and monitored at vulnerable points that could provide means of illegal entry. Motorable roads alongside the international border, wherever incomplete or have not yet been built, will be laid so as to enable effective and intensive patrolling. Flood lights, wherever required, will also be provided while maintaining the present arrangements. The completed part of the border fencing will be maintained and repaired so as to constitute an effective barrier to cross border trafficking.
>
> The progress achieved at the end of 3 months from today as against the position on the ground mentioned in the affidavit of the Union extracted above will be monitored by this Court and, depending on what is revealed upon such monitoring, further directions including a definite time schedule for completion

> of the works relating to border fencing, border roads and flood lights may be made by this Court. (para 46)

This Bench ticked off the Assam government and Central Government on 30 March, 2015 and again on 13 May, 2015 for "dragging their feet" on fencing the Indo-Bangladesh border and even appointed senior advocate Upamanyu Hazarika court commissioner to visit the Indo-Bangladesh border in Assam and report about the progress in fencing.[153] After going through the report filed by the Supreme Court-appointed commissioner, the Bench said on 14 July, 2015 that the report highlighted a lot of deficiencies in the measures taken by governments in handling the situation. The Bench said fencing of the international border had not been completed and sufficient number of police and BSF personnel had not been deployed near the border to check entry of illegal migrants. The Court directed Centre and Assam government to take all corrective steps. They should take steps for improvement of border roads, electrification of flood lights on border areas. This is the least they owed to the nation, the Bench said.[154]

Listing two priorities for the new government in Assam, Sarbanand Sonowal, the CM-designate of Assam, said on 21 May, 2016 that borders with Bangladesh would be completely sealed in two years and the other priority is the early completion of the NRC.[155] Addressing the media on 1 September, 2016 on the completion of his government's 100 days in office, Sonowal said that his government has urged the Centre to seal the Indo-Bangladesh border under the supervision of the Army.[156] Home Minister Rajnath Singh assured on 26 December, 2016 that Indo-Bangladesh border in Assam would be completely sealed within a year and a half.[157] But the Bangladesh-Assam border could not be sealed, as promised. Had it been so, there would have been no illegal infiltration in Assam and the political parties would not have clamoured for such a step.

The provisional census data on population during the decade 2001-2011 shows that the rate of population growth in nine West Bengal districts that share their borders with Bangladesh has come down in the past decade. This trend is attributed mainly to an expansion in barbed-wire fencing in nine West Bengal districts and tighter vigil on illegal immigrants.[158] As a result, West Bengal has registered a growth rate of 13.93 per cent as against the country's overall growth rate of 17.64 per cent. Similarly, the growth rate of population of 16.93 per cent and 14.75 per cent respectively in the States of Assam and Tripura was marginally less than the all-India average of 17.64 per cent.[159] This is a welcome sign. If this decline in the growth rate is due to bringing more areas under the barbed-wire fencing and better vigil on the border, then the question arises what prevented the Central

Government in taking these measures so long. If, however, this decline is due to the migration of the infiltrators to other areas of India after crossing the border because of the hostile attitude of the local population and lack of proper resources in these States, then measures have to be taken to ensure that there is no illegal migration from the other side of the border. The directions of the highest Court of the land on taking effective steps to prevent infiltration should be implemented in letter and spirit.

Indeed, there is no alternative to eternal vigilance along the border in which the assistance, help and cooperation of the inhabitants of the border villages should be enlisted in a meaningful way. It is the primary responsibility of the Centre to man the international borders both on the eastern and the western sectors in such a manner that none can infiltrate from the other side of the border. It cannot shirk its responsibility if there is unabated flow of men and materials through the border. The investigation by the CBI (September-October 2020) on illegal cattle trade on Indo-Bangladesh border has brought to the fore the role of BSF and Customs officials, among others, in the thriving illegal cattle trade. What is true for the cattle smuggling is true for human infiltration as well. The same set of persons is involved in human smuggling, only the merchandise changed. Without the active connivance of the border officials, no infiltration across the border is possible. This stark reality should have been realized by the Centre long ago. Apart from rampant corruption in the ranks of the border officials, inadequate deployment of the BSF and ITBP, lack of coordination between the Central and State forces and their intelligence agencies complicate border control efforts. High power monitoring cell may be constituted to oversee the arrangement in the field.

The Army has significantly improved its electronic surveillance along the Line of Control to check infiltration. It has introduced hybrid model of smart fence which will cost around Rs. 10 lakh per km. The fence will be integrated with the LIDAR (Light Detection and Ranging) sensors, infrared sensors and cameras among others. Troops have also been given drones, both big and small, to monitor the ground. It has resulted in a drop in infiltration in 2020.[160] This hybrid model of 'smart' fence can be tested on the Indo-Bangladesh border as well.

On the eve of the Assam Assembly elections in 2021 April, chief minister Sarbanand Sonowal on 10 March, 2021 claimed that the Indo-Bangladesh border along Assam was no longer porous and had been physically and technologically sealed.[161] It is no doubt a right step in the right direction and it is hoped that there would be no illegal infiltration at least in Assam from the other side of the border from now on. It is the wish of every right-thinking Indian that similar steps would be taken on the other sectors of the Indo-Bangladesh border as well and illegal crossings would be a thing of the past.

VI

But why is India the favoured destination? The truth is that infiltration will continue as long the thought that an "over-populated Bangladesh has a right to an expanded living space" finds fertile ground in the State of West Bengal, and the "distress migration" theory is acceptable to the ruling political class whether out of intellectual conviction or for electoral gains. Another Partition, or another poll victory? That is the question which confronts the political parties.

According to Lin and Paul, there are several fundamental economic and political causes of emigration from Bangladesh to India. First, rural development has failed to provide the social and physical infrastructure necessary to significantly increase food production, stand up against natural calamities, and develop rural industries as alternative sources of income. Second, the population pressure on the land is so great that even under the best of climatic conditions, agriculture simply cannot support the food requirements of the current population. Third, industrial development and trade in the towns have failed to provide alternative avenues of employment to absorb rural labour and challenge the dominance of the landholding classes in the countryside. Fourth, the better relationship between Indira Gandhi and Mujibur Rahaman after the 1971 war of independence encouraged Bangladeshis to cross over to India during 1971-75. Many Bangladeshis believed that the two countries were going to open their mutual borders to free bi-directional travel. Fifth, the shifting political balance after the death of Prime Minister Mujibar Rahaman has made life much more difficult for former Awami League supporters.[162]

Without doubt the most important overall reason given for the decision to emigrate from Bangladesh is economic.[163] Most analysts also agreed that the infiltration is driven in the main by economic reasons. Grinding poverty and severe unemployment is what pushes the Bangladeshis to seek greener pastures. The appalling conditions that prevail across the border are clear when one looks at the existing socio-economic parameters. As the Cato Institute has studied, long ago the US conducted a survey on Puerto Rican immigration. Because of Puerto Rica's special political status the flood of immigrants that came to New York and elsewhere faced no barriers and no controls. But even in the 1980s, nearly half of the immigrants stayed on the main land for only two years. In the 1990s, the traffic ceased on its own accord, as Puerto Rica developed rapidly. So most migrant workers if given a choice usually prefer to go home once jobs open up or once they have achieved their goals—savings for a house or to start a small business.[164]

So another useful step could be to replicate the Puerto Rican experiment for controlling migration. A longer term solution must address the widening economic differentials deriving from unequal development between India as an emerging industrial powerhouse and its neighbours—Bangladesh and Nepal—which remain at the periphery not only of the world capitalist system but also of the South Asian regional market. The developmental gap must be reduced in terms of both the forces of production and the relations of production. An appeal may be made to the international agencies to raise the amount of aid given to the neighbouring countries, especially Bangladesh and Nepal, in the hope that a rise in income and employment would reduce the flow of illegal migrants.

Annada Shankar Roy, the noted Bengali writer and thinker had suggested way back in 1996 that infiltration from Bangladesh would automatically decline if the government of India extend utmost cooperation to the Bangladesh government for the development of their agriculture, industry, trade and even administration and restoration of communal harmony.[165]

An economist has suggested that India should also help Bangladesh upgrade its higher education system, give incentive to our software companies to set up faculties in that country and encourage import of labour-intensive products. These initiatives will help Bangladesh graduate from agriculture to the services sector.[166] It may be recalled that both Barack Obama and Hillary Clinton of the U.S.A. were proponents of more actively promoting economic development in Mexico to decrease the incentive of illegal migration to the U.S.A. Biden administration plans to invest $4 billion in the economies of Central American countries to reduce migration.[167] In an attempt to deter the Syrian refugees in Jordon from moving on to Europe in search of jobs, the EU signed a deal with Jordan in 2016 to provide low-interest loans for labour intensive projects and easier access to European markets in order to create jobs for Syrian refugees.[168] The EU negotiators and Turkey reached a deal on 18 March, 2016 of providing it with more money, early visa-free travel and progress in its EU membership negotiations to halt migration flows to Europe.[169]

In India, apart from the problems of urban and rural unemployment and underemployment, relative wage levels, pressures on land and availability of food as worsening under the impact of continuing migration, the issue of Bangladeshi migration is closely linked with widespread and undeclared trans-border trade between India and Bangladesh. The apparent and irreversible reality of significant cross-border "smuggling" of goods and cattle was investigated by a team of journalists who had toured the border districts. Their report suggested a virtually institutionalized system of border markets based on illegal cross-border trade with the bulk of commodities flowing from India into Bangladesh, and concluded with the observation that "even if the West Bengal Chief Minister vents his feelings about the inability of the BSF and the police to check smuggling, there is precious little that can be done. Ingrained within the society, which used to trade even after Partition, smuggling has come to stay. The only option, according to many people along the border, is to legalize border barter of commodities under official supervision".[170] Paula Banerjee *et al.* also pleaded for legitimate growth in Indo-Bangladesh border trade and better cooperation and coordinated action between these two neighbouring countries.[171]

During the visit of the Prime Minister of Bangladesh to India in January 2010, India and Bangladesh decided to establish border *haats* on a pilot basis at selected places. A Memorandum of Understanding (MoU) on Border *Haats* & Border Trade on India-Bangladesh border was signed on 23 October, 2010 between the two countries. Two border *haats* have already been set up at the following places:

1. Kalaichar (Meghalaya, India) – Baliamari (Kurigram, Bangladesh).
2. Dolora (Sunamganj, Bangladesh) – Balat (Meghalaya, India).

Another 66 border *haats* are in the process of being established along Indo-Bangladesh border as under (West Bengal—35, Assam—4, Meghalaya—22, Tripura—5).[172]

The position has, however, not improved over the years. Illegal movement of people and goods, including timber, cattle, textiles, electronic goods, sugar, drugs, arms, medicine and kerosene is going on unabated. Smuggling of cattle is a daily occurrence. The route is known, the point of dispatch is known, the actors are known, the people in the locality cannot sleep in the night because of this operation, yet the BSF could not be woken from the deep slumber to put a stop to the smuggling of cattle which are transported from several states including Bihar, Odisha, Andhra Pradesh, Haryana, UP and MP. Those involved in the smuggling of cattle are also employed in the smuggling of dreaded drugs like Yaba which come from Myanmar through Bangladesh.[173]

The smuggling across the Indo-Bangladesh border has reached such a proportion that the Governor of West Bengal, Keshri Nath Tripati, in an informal chat with the President of Bangladesh, Mohammad Abdul Hamid, on the occasion of the banquet thrown in his honour on 23 December, 2014 raised the question of cow smuggling to Bangladesh and infiltration as also fake-currency smuggling from Bangladesh.[174]

In the meantime, the problems relating to the Indo-Bangladesh enclaves, also known as Chitmahals, in Bangladesh and the Indian States of West Bengal, Tripura, Assam and Meghalaya have been solved. Prime Minister Modi promised that his government would utilize the land swap pact with Dhaka for a lasting solution of the problem of Bangla influx by sealing all routes across the international border through which "illegal" Bangladeshi immigrants had been entering India.[175] The swapping of the Chitmahals will give India an unprecedented advantage of a secure boundary and will enable it to curb illegal migration, smuggling and other criminal activities.

It is, however, good to find the Bangladeshi economy is picking up and both the World Bank and the Asian Development Bank have projected Bangladesh's GDP growth at 6.3 per cent in 2015-16.[176] Bangladesh brought a big surprise to the world economy when the IMF released the World Economy Outlook in October 2020 to show an extraordinary accomplished performance of the economy over the last five years. The stunning news revealed that Bangladesh is expected to outpace India in securing higher per capita income in 2020 if certain conditions are fulfilled. It could successfully emerge as a global leader in the export of garments to the European Union and the US. Besides export of garments, robust growth has been observed in the export of fish and pharmaceutical products. Efforts of the country in social sector development, particularly the empowerment of women, are commendable over the past several decades. [177]According to the Global Gender Gap Report, 2015 undertaken by World Economic Forum (WEF), out of the 145 countries surveyed, Bangladesh ranked 64th; while India, Pakistan and China ranked 114, 144 and 87, respectively, in terms of Gender Equality Index.[178]

With Bangladesh's growing economic prosperity, trade with India has grown. Indian exports more than doubled over the past five years, from $ 2.7 billion to $6.1 billion in 2013-14. Bangladesh exports in 2014 were at $462 million. India could strengthen Bangladesh's short term liquidity by offering it a currency swap facility similar to the one provided to Sri Lanka. Fresh credit commitments will be needed for road, railways, and waterways connectivity projects. Bangladesh will require help to ensure navigable depth for the Inland water protocol routes, and to develop Ashugunj as a transhipment point, with a railway link from Akhaura to

Agartala. Bangladeshi business and industry will gain from connectivity and infrastructure investments, as also India's north-east. The linking of Nepal, Bhutan, and India's north-east to Bangladeshi ports might help make Bangladesh the natural bridge between South and South-east Asia.[179] India and Bangladesh are seminal to each other's progress and prosperity and there is no reason why these two neighbours cannot work cooperatively for the mutual benefit of each other.

Prime Minister Narendra Modi and Bangladeshi Prime Minister Sheikh Hasina on 17 December, 2020 inaugurated a rail link between Haldibari in Cooch Behar and Chilahati in Bangladesh through a virtual summit. After four operational rail link between India and Bangladesh having been restored—Petrapole (India)-Benapole (Bangladesh), Gede (India)-Darshna (Bangladesh), Singhabad (India)-Rohanpur (Bangladesh) and Radhikapur (India)-Birol (Bangladesh), the Haldibari-Chilahati link being made functional on 17 December is the fifth rail link between India and Bangladesh. Railway officials claimed that the Haldibari-Chilahati route will provide travel connections to Bangladesh from Assam and West Bengal in India. It will strengthen rail network access to the main ports, dry ports as well as land borders to support the growth in regional trade, boosting economic and social development of the region. Common people and businessmen of both the countries will be able to reap the benefit of both goods and passenger traffic.[180] NJP-Dhaka passenger trains started rolling out from 26 March, 2021.[181] Another rail link, between Agartala, India, and Akhaura, Bangladesh, is scheduled to open by the end of 2021. The Mahishashan-Shahbazar line is also planned to reopen.

The 1.9 km "Matri Setu" over the river Feni which flows through Tripura between India and Bangladesh was virtually inaugurated by prime minister Modi and prime minister Hasina on 9 March, 2021. The bridge will link Sabroom in Tripura and Ramgarh in Bangladesh. This road connectivity will not only strengthen the friendship between India and Bangladesh but also as a study by the World Bank reveals, this transport connectivity between two South Asian neighbours would increase national income by as much as17 per cent in Bangladesh and 8 per cent in India.[182] If India's Foreign Secretary Harsh Shringla is to be believed, Prime Minister Modi during his two-day visit to Bangladesh on 26-27 March, 2021 had assured Hasina on Teesta agreement in consultation with relevant stakeholders.[183]

VII

Over the decades, Bangladeshi nationals have sneaked into India. Some of them are feared to be fundamentalists. The 'accidental' blast in Khagragarh of Burdwan town in West Bengal on 2 October, 2014 has brought to the fore the activities of the Bangladeshi *jihadis* like the Jamaat-ul-Mujahideen Bangladesh (JMB) in India. The investigations into the Khagragarh incident revealed that some madrasas and mosques, such as the Simulia mosque in Burdwan, are indeed disseminating religious hatred and intolerance.[184] Incidentally, many of these seminaries have Bangladeshi teachers who have acquired Indian citizenship fraudulently.[185] These teachers highlight the alleged atrocities on Indian Muslims through videos and other provocative materials in order to alienate and radicalise the students. The arrest of a JMB operative from Assam revealed that the top JMB leaders had visited one madrasa in Nalbari to conduct motivational training for the youths to join the outfit with the objective of creating terror modules in Assam and West Bengal, which have fairly large concentrations of Bangladeshi illegal immigrants.[186]

Sleuths of the National Investigation Agency have been visiting certain areas in Assam, Shillong and Garo Hills in Meghalaya since they suspect that some Islamic militants are hiding in the North-East after terrorist activities came to notice in the wake of the Burdwan blast. Apart from blending themselves in Muslim-dominated areas they are also settling in ghettos mostly along the Assam-Nagaland border. Khagen Sarma, the Director-General of Police, Assam told reporters on 21 October, 2014 that several Muslim youths of Assam had undergone training in terrorism in Bangladesh. There is support from the local populace, and the foreign funding has aggravated the situation.[187] In Assam, the 'Jamat-ul-Muzahidin, Bangladesh' (JMB) had set up camps in the areas inhabited by its co-religionists. Gradually, it spread its tentacles to other areas, particularly in Barpeta district. It took full advantage of religious fanaticism of the illiterate section of the immigrant Muslims and succeeded in not only enrolling persons like Idris Ali and Shahanur Alam, but also started trading activities with the help of these recruits. NIA's investigation has revealed that one Zahidulla, a prominent leader of JMB, not only purchased land in village Bhaktardoba of Barpeta district, but also married a local girl, thereby cultivating close relationship with villagers of immigrant stock. Zahidullah indoctrinated a number of local youths for getting actively involved in *jihadi* activities. It is surprising that even without being either an Indian citizen or a permanent resident of the village, Zahidullah could acquire immovable property in violation of laws and rules of the country. But no action has been taken against those officers and employees of the concerned departments who had facilitated the acquisition of immovable property by Zahidullah. Even there are scopes for prosecuting those who had harboured this Bangladeshi *jihadi* leader. It was with Zahidullah's blessings that Sahanur succeeded in spreading the *jihadi* network in areas like Howli, Kayakuchi, Bhabnapur amidst others. Of course, Zahidullah disappeared as soon as Sahanur attracted police action.[188] Sahanur Alam was arrested by the NIA with the help of Assam police from Nalbari on 4 December 2014, while Saidul Islam and Rafiqul Islam were arrested from elsewhere in Assam.[189]

The JMB operatives were active in the districts of Burdwan, Birbhum and Murshidabad in West Bengal. It has been found that the Bangladeshi infiltrators settle down in places along the Indo-Bangladesh border and elsewhere in Murshidabad, a district having at least 100 km long river border with Bangladesh, and easily obtain vital documents like ration cards, voter ID or EPIC card which are required for getting a valid Indian passport. The investigation into the Burdwan blast has revealed that many of such vital documents used by the suspected militants originated from Murhidabad, which is getting prominent on the map of terror networks established and operated by militant outfits like JMB, Laskar-e-Taiba and others. Several Bangladeshi nationals possessing EPIC, PAN and ration cards issued by Indian authorities have been arrested in the Burdwan blast case.[190]

JMB Burdwan module masterminds Abdul Kalim Sheikh and Jamatullah Sheikh, father-in-law of Sheikh Yusuf, were enrolled as voters in the Mongolkote Assembly segment ahead of the 2011 Assembly elections.[191]

The investigation by the NIA, which submitted charge-sheet in the Burdwan blast case on 30 March, 2015, 177 days after the incident, against 21 accused persons revealed that the main motive of the JMB, a proscribed organisation in Bangladesh, was "to overthrow the existing democratic government in Bangladesh through violent terrorist acts and replace it with a hard-line Sharia-based Islamic rule" by setting up bases in India. The NIA also mentioned in the charge-sheet: "The outfit (JMB) established its network in three States here including West Bengal, Assam and Jharkhand." Its attempt was to spread its bases in India for recruitment and training purposes and to carry out terror activities in Bangladesh by engaging the youths who underwent training.[192]

The NIA in its supplementary charge-sheet filed on14 December, 2015 against 28 persons claimed that the JMB had prepared a blueprint to create a "Greater Bangladesh" with Murshidabad, Burdwan and Birbhum. It was with this aim that the JMB had planned to carry out a widespread terror attacks in West Bengal and Bangladesh. The JMB also planned to oust the Sheikh Hasina government in Bangladesh to establish Islamic law in Bangladesh. The NIA has mentioned in the charge-sheet how the terror outfit used to recruit prospective terror activists from the state and trained them in their camps and terror centres in Burdwan, Murshidabad and Birbhum. The JMB had recruited several agents in the state who used to raise funds and collect donations to run its terror camps. The JMB used to screen videos related to Osama Bin Laden and Mullah Omar.[193]

Although the Burdwan blast and the subsequent investigations have revealed that the terrorists and their ideologues were exploiting the vast pool of illegal Bangladeshi migrants in the border areas to target their own country, it does not mean that these terror operatives would not join hands with their Indian counterparts in future to attack India. It is needless to underline that the Indian security and intelligence agencies have to remain alert for any eventuality in the future.[194]

The crackdown on JMB activists following the Khagragarh blast, the unearthing of Al-Qaeda module in the border district of Murshidabad in September 2020, the acquisition of Aadhar Card and Voter Card by Bangladeshi terrorists to establish their credentials as Indians and the use of Madrasas and mosques by the *Jihadis* from Bangladesh for training purposes of the recruits have brought the debate on infiltration from Bangladesh back on the political agenda. Though the Bangladesh government obstinately refuses to accept the fact of illegal Muslim emigration from their territory, the finding from their own latest census report proves otherwise.

It is heartening to note that Bangladesh seems to have finally woken up to the threats posed by illegal cross-border movement. Border Guard Bangladesh is actually taking steps to prevent Bangladeshis from crossing into India. In the past, such movement would be ignored by the agencies on the Bangladesh side. They are also sharing information, leading to apprehensions along the International Border.[195] If this vigil by the Bangladesh Government is maintained, it will have a salutary effect on curbing illegal infiltration from the other side of the border. Bangladesh will also be benefited by cracking down on illegal migration. Its annual remittance inflow has crossed the $15 billion mark in 2014-15[196] and it reached $40.33 billion in 2017.[197] It will further increase if the illegal migration being promoted by agents for huge commissions is effectively stopped. After all, illegal migrants do not send remittances, the legal ones do. Director-General of Border Guard Bangladesh has claimed as late as on 25 December, 2020 that with the economic prosperity of the people, Bangladeshi nationals are no longer crossing the border in search of employment in India.[198] Bangladesh Foreign Minister A.K.Abdul Momen even claimed that Bangladeshi migrants now prefer Italy, England, France or US.[199] Actually, illegal migration of Bangladeshis to Malaysia and Japan came to notice even in the 1990s.[200]

VIII

The migrant issue as a formidable political factor was, however, upgraded into a national issue only when the Sangh Parivar made 'Infiltrators, Quit India' one of their political and ideological slogans in 1992 and the Bharatiya Janata Party (BJP) launched the campaign against migrants from Bangladesh.[201] In April 1992, the BJP national executive passed a resolution claiming that over 15 million Bangladeshis had "illegally" entered India in only a few years, stating that:

> ...this influx has led to a variety of socio-economic tensions in the North-East, in West Bengal, parts of Bihar and even in far-away Delhi and Bombay. All this constitutes a serious strain on the national economy, a severe stress on the national society and, withal, a serious threat to the stability and security of the country. And yet the Congress takes no action to stem this flood or push back illegal immigrants, because it views them as its vote bank.[202]

Infiltration has become the new mantra (chant) for the BJP.[203] The propaganda drive of the BJP and its associated organisations increasingly find expression in mainstream and popular writings. A good example is an article by Shyam Khosla[204] in which he characterizes the process as an 'invisible invasion.' Other articles describe clandestine migration from Bangladesh as a 'silent threat to [national] integrity' [205] or as 'an assault on India'[206] by viewing 'infiltration [as] a growing threat' [207] and 'Bangladesh refugees: a growing menace.'[208] Undocumented immigrants, moreover, are dubbed as 'fortune hunters'[209], 'unwanted' [210] or 'uninvited guests'[211] and as 'Bangladesh's unwanted citizens.'[212] This 'problem from Bangladesh'[213] is perceived as a widespread threat to the social fabric, economy and security of India. Biased perceptions of 'India's Bangla problem'[214] are supplemented by stereotypes of immigrants as individuals engaged in immoral, criminal, anti-national activities.[215]

There has been a continual tension and flux within Bangladesh politics between secularist conceptions of the state and polity and the deployment of "Islamic" themes and political mobilizations by various regimes since its formation. In this way, the Hindu minority in Bangladesh has often been caught between these conflicting political compulsions and, especially at moments of systemic crisis such as in 1971, or in the enactment of "Islamic" political strategies and state policies, has suffered direct persecution and dispossession.[216]

The BJP views Muslim migrants from Bangladesh in totality as "infiltrators" with no right to refugee status in India, regardless of the particular economic or political circumstances that have led to their decision to migrate. In some cases, the BJP has rejected the notion that Muslim migrants have been forced to enter India because of poverty or population pressures. Instead, it has claimed that these migrants form part of an "undeclared" policy of Bangladeshi colonization and invasion of selected districts in order to establish Muslim majorities and facilitate another partition of the country. "Infiltration" has therefore often been projected by Hindu nationalist organisations as a sinister Islamic/ Bangladeshi conspiracy that threatens to drive Hindus from border regions in states such as West Bengal and, indeed, to undermine India's territorial integrity and the demographic basis of a Hindu *Rashtra*. In this vein, the West Bengal unit of the BJP in the RSS weekly stated that there was a deliberate policy to:

> ...convert the border areas into Muslim-dominated areas, so that they can finally raise a plea for their annexation to Bangladesh or to increase the Muslim population in India so that in due course they will be demanding more and more rights for the Muslims in a planned and organised way.[217]

The concern of the BJP to represent Bangladeshi migration as ultimately leading to Muslim majority areas within India is not to be brushed aside as a figment of imagination. With an area of 1,44,000 sq km or only one-fifth the size of France, Bangladesh today is the most densely-populated country in the world. With a largely rural society bound by Islamic mores against artificial birth control and low status of women, some Bangladeshi intellectuals had mooted the applicability of Hitler's "*lebensraum*" (living space) to accommodate the growing numbers of the world's most cramped nation.

Several articles quoting reports in Bangladeshi papers maintain that many Bangladeshi intellectuals are encouraging the migration of Muslims into the north-eastern parts of India.[218] These scholars, it is revealed, invoke a theory of *lebensraum* or living space, to submit that unmitigated population growth along with restrictions of geographical space compels migrant mobility 'in search of land.'[219] In 1992, the Muslim migrants in the

West Bengal districts of Murshidabad, Malda and Coochbehar demanded a separate homeland that they called "Swadeshi Muslim Banga Bhoomi."[220]

The demand of Bangladesh for space in India is a long-standing demand being articulated by many righteous Bangladeshis. Even a pro-India leader like Sheikh Mujibar Rahman in his book *Eastern Pakistan; Its population and Economics* observed:

> Because Eastern Pakistan must have sufficient land for its expansion and because Assam has abundant forests and mineral resources, coal, petroleum etc, Eastern Pakistan must include Assam to be financially and economically strong.[221]

Writing in the 18 October issue of the Weekly *Holiday* of 1991 prominent journalist, Sadiq Khan, argued that "by the first decade of the 21st century, Bangladesh will face a serious crisis of *lebensraum*. No possible performance of population planning, actual or hypothetical, significantly alters that prediction." He further argued that the "colonial devastation of Bengal in the 18th and 19th centuries left the reign of Bangladesh bereft of traditional strength of technology and productivity" and that "a natural overflow of population pressure is therefore very much on the cards and will not be restrainable by barbed wire or border patrol measures."[222]

With a population density of 1,101 persons per square kilometer (in July 2014), the Bangladeshis feel that they have a just cause for conquering their neighbours *lebensraum* or 'living space'. If migration, legal or otherwise, was the answer, so be it. With this aim in view the menace of infiltration from across the border went on unabated, only the intensity, method, manner and mode of infiltration changed. This explains why Bangladesh vehemently opposes fencing of the border and why it is reluctant to accept the repatriated nationals. The motto clearly is that the greater the number of people leaving the country the better it is for its larger interests. From 1971 to 1982, about 38,000 people migrated from Bangladesh to the United Kingdom, between 1977 and 1990 about 80,000 people migrated from the same country to the Middle-East.[223]

As Table 3.3 suggests, the growth of population in Bangladesh has dropped dramatically in the last three decades. In the period 1981 to 2001, the population growth has registered a declining trend—from 2.50 per cent in 1974, to 2.33 per cent in 1981, to 2.15 per cent in 1991, and 1.54 per cent in 2001. A marginal increase is seen in 2011, when it rose to 1.66 per cent. It is naive to argue that this drastic fall in population growth can be attributed to better literacy or effective population control measures. It is emigration and emigration alone which is responsible for such fall in population growth in Bangladesh. Actually, none knows how many Bangladeshis, both Hindus and Muslims, have 'vanished' from Bangladesh since 1971 and landed not only in India, but in far off places like Europe, Japan and elsewhere—either legally or illegally—in search of livelihood, accepting, as Samaddar says, "anything that comes in the way; sweat labour in the brickfields, in three-cropped fields, valley projects, orchards, prostitution, earth cutting, vending, rickshaw pulling, scavenging, semi-serf jobs in farmhouses and farmland, driving, restaurant jobs, headloading—anything, everything."[224] The home country, however, treats their emigration in the spirit of "good riddance."[225]

Table 3.3 : Decadal population growth in Bangladesh of adjusted population—1961-2011

Census year	Population	Growth rates
1961	5,52,22,663	2.23
1974	7,63,98,000	2.50
1981	8,99,12,000	2.33
1991	11,14,55,185	2.15
2001	13,00,29,749	1.54
2011	15,25,18,000	1.66

Source: For the period 1961-2001, Table 4.2 of Population Census 2001, Bangladesh Bureau of Statistics, Planning Division, Ministry of Planning, Government of Bangladesh, July 2003, p. 24.
For 2011—Wikipedia.org/wiki/Demographics of Bangladesh.

Although India faces history's worst immigration crisis, the outside world scarcely knows about its magnitude and the problems it poses for the country. Myron Weiner in his seminal book, *The Global Migration Crisis*, has quoted statistics showing the extent of non-nationals in the population structure of 47 countries, but India does not figure in that list because the government has not publicized the gravity of the immigration crisis.

India is perhaps the lone country in the world which is displaying the proverbial ostrich-like attitude to this burning problem of the day which should have been tackled on a war footing. But political will is simply lacking. And all parties are equally responsible for this state of affairs. Traditionally and irrespective of the party in power at the centre, illegal migration has never been treated as a national issue. After all, international border management is the primary responsibility of the Central Government. The Central Government cannot shirk its responsibility by passing the buck on the State Governments. The influx would not have gone so menacingly out of control if successive governments at the centre had made an honest effort to come to grips with the problem.

There is no doubt that successive Central and State Governments have failed to take appropriate steps to prevent the influx of the 'infiltrators.' The obvious reason why practically no effective step is being taken to deter the influx is that the greater the Muslim influx, the bigger the vote bank. However, a crackdown would undoubtedly result in not only losing the migrant vote, but also of the indigenous Muslim population.

Even the BJP which is so much concerned with illegal infiltration and whose PM aspirant Modi had on the eve of the 2014 Lok Sabha elections even threatened to deport all "illegal migrants from Bangladesh" did precious little to translate the threat into action.

On the other hand, his External Affairs Minister Sushama Swaraj, while describing illegal immigration from Bangladesh as a "sensitive issue", had underlined the need for consultations with all stakeholders to carefully handle the problem along India's border with its eastern neighbour.[226]

Instead of indulging in rhetoric and innuendos it is better to formulate a national policy on infiltration which can be put in operation with least possible delay because far too much time has passed without any result. And a national policy on so explosive an issue cannot be formulated without substantial inter-party coordination. But in India, a sensible policy on immigration is yet to see the light of the day because in this country immigration attracts politics, not policy. However, the successful implementation of any national policy on infiltration, if ever it is drawn up, will depend, as an editorial in *The Statesman* puts it:

> Any possible approach will have to first banish all notions of religion, community, ethnicity from the immigration issue. The only valid mark is citizenship or lack of it. Second, vote bank politics with immigrants, in the garb of secular tolerance, must be stopped. But these sensible policies require sensible governments. Where do we get one?[227]

NOTES

1. *The Times of India,* October 18, 2013, p. 1.
2. *Census of India*, 1931, Vol. III, Part I, p. 49.
3. *Ibid.*
4. *Ibid.*, p. 50.
5. *Ibid.*, pp. 51-52.

6. Guha, Amalendu, *Planter-Raj to Swaraj: Freedom Struggle and Electoral Politics in Assam 1826-1947*, 1977, New Delhi, Indian Council of Historical Research, p. 68.
7. Government of Assam, Home and Political Department, *White Paper on Foreigners' Issue,* October 20, 2012, Para 1.1.3, p. 5.
8. *Government of Assam, Line System Enquiry Report*, Shillong, 1938, p. 3.
9. Guha, Amalendu, *Op. Cit.*, pp. 210-211.
10. Nag, Sajal, *Roots of Ethnic Conflict*, 1990, New Delhi, Manohar, p. 96.
11. *Ibid.*, pp. 96-97.
12. *Ibid.*, p. 147.
13. Moon, Pemdrel. (ed), *Wavell: Viceroy's Journal*, 1977, Delhi, Oxford University Press, p. 41.
14. Nicholas, Mansergh and Moon, Penderel (ed), *The Transfer of Power, 1942-47*, Vol. III, Her Majesty's Stationery Office, p. 254.
15. *Assam Secretariat Records, Confidential B, 1964, File No. C232/46*, quoted by Sandhya Barua, "Assam in National Context and Historical Perspective", in *Social tension in North East India*, J.B. Bhattacharjee (ed), 1982, Shillong, North East Council for Social Science Research, *Op. Cit.,* p. 39.
16. Barua, Sandhya, *Ibid.*, pp. 39-40.
17. *Census of India*, 1951, Vol. XII, Part I-A, pp. 75-76.
18. Government of Assam, Home and Political Department, *White Paper on Foreigners' Issue,* October 20, 2012, Paras 1.5.1.-1.5.4, pp. 8-9.
19. *Ibid.*, Para 1.7.1, p. 11.
20. Chatterjee, Sarajit Kumar, *North-East India: Dispersion and Discontent,* 2010, New Delhi, Abhijeet Publications, p. 662.
21. Government of Assam, Home and Political Department, *White Paper on Foreigners' Issue,* October 20, 2012, Para 1.7.1, pp. 11-12.
22. Guha, Ramachandra, *India After Gandhi*, 2007, Picador India, pp. 556-557.
23. Hazarika, Sanjoy, "Bangladesh and Assam: Land Pressures, Migration and Ethnic Conflict", *Occasional Paper Series* of the project *on Environmental Change and Acute Conflict*, No. 3, March 1993, pp. 56-60.
24. Bhattacharyya, Hiranya Kumar, *Operation Lebensraum Illegal Migration from Bangladesh,* 2018, New Delhi, Bloomsbury, pp. 130-132.
25. Hazarika, Niru, "Asom Gana Parishad", *Indian Journal of Political Science*, Vol. 49, no.1, January-March, 1988, p. 95.
26. Murayama, Mayumi, "Borders, Migration and Sub-Regional Cooperation in Eastern South Asia", *Economic and Political Weekly,* April 8, 2006, p. 1355.
27. Baruah, Sanjib, *India against Itself: Assam and the Politics of Nationality*, 1999, New Delhi, Oxford University Press, p. 162.
28. *CAD*, Vol. IX, dated 12-8-1949, pp. 413-417.
29. Lama, J.B., "Caught up in red tape as alien's' influx continues", *The Statesman*, September 10, 2014, p. 8.

30. Das, Pushpita, *Illegal migration from Bangladesh Deportation,Border fencing and work permit*, IDSA, Monograph Series No. 56, December 2016, pp. 23-24.
31. Rajeswar, T.V., "Serious influx from Bangladesh", *The Statesman*, April 6, 1990, p. 1.
32. *Ibid.*
33. *Ibid.*, April 7, 1990, p. 1.
34. Letters to the Editor, *The Statesman*, April 13, 1990, p. 8.
35. *The Hindustan Times*, February 27, 1989.
36. *Ibid.*, February 28, 1989.
37. *Ibid.*, May 13, 1990.
38. *Ibid.*, December 3, 1991.
39. *Ibid.*
40. *Nai Duniya*, January 25, 1992.
41. *The Hindustan Times*, July 6, 1992, p. 7.
42. Chakravarty, Nikhil, "Neighbouring on Inhospitality", *The Telegraph*, October 19, 1992, p. 6.
43. Karlekar, Hiranmay, "Dispatching Bangladeshis", *The Indian Express*, September 19, 1992, p. 8.
44. *The Times of India*, October 23, 1992, p. 1.
45. *The Statesman*, September 17, 1992, p. 1.
46. Ramachandran, Sujata, "Operation Pushback: Sangh Parivar, State, Slums and Surreptitious Bangladeshis in New Delhi", *Economic and Political Weekly*, 2003, February 15, p. 643.
47. Habib, Haroon, "Angry in Dhaka: Indignation over 'operation push back' ", *Frontline*, November 6, 1992, p. 28.
48. Ahmed, Syed Zubair, "Operation Pushback Grinds to Abrupt Halt", *The Times of India*, November 3, 1992.
49. Lin and Paul, *Op. Cit.*, p. 18.
50. *The Hindustan Times*, September 29, 1992, p. 6.
51. *Ibid.*
52. *The Patriot*, September 29, 1992.
53. *The Hindustan Times*, September 29, 1992, p. 6.
54. *The Statesman*, "CMs for I-Cards to Check Bangla Influx", September 29, 1992, p. 4.
55. Dave, P.K., "Bangladeshis' Deportation stepped up", *The Hindu*, September 11, 1992, p. 8.
56. *Ibid.*
57. Ramachandran, Sujata, "Operation Pushback: Sangh Parivar, State, Slums and Surreptitious Bangladeshis in New Delhi", *Economic and Political Weekly*, 2003, February 15, p. 640.
58. *The Hindustan Times*, "Message from Seemapuri", October 13,, 1992, p. 6.
59. Editorial titled "Stopping the flow", *The Hindu*, May 28, 1994, p. 12.
60. Das, Pushpita, *Op. Cit.*, p. 28.

61. Roy Utpal and Mondal, Soumen, "Shifting residencies from Bangladesh to India and its impacts on regional sustainability: an empirical study on Gaighata Block, North 24 Parganas, W.B." in the Abstract Volume on International Conference on Urbanisation and Regional Sustainability, Regional Science Association, India, Department of Geography, *University of Calcutta*, 2016, p, 130.
62. Guhathakurta, Meghna, "Amidst the Winds of Change: The Hindu Minority in Bangladesh", in Tanweer Fazal (ed.), *Minority Nationalisms in South Asia, South Asian Culture and History*, New York: Routledge, 2013, p. 131, quoted by Das Pushpita, *Op. Cit.*, pp. 29-30.
63. Barkat, Abdul, "Political Economy of Deprivation of Hindu Minority in Bangladesh: Living with the Vested Property Act", in Abhijit Dasgupta, Masahiko Togawa and Abdul Barkat (eds.), *Minorities and the State: Changing Social and Political Landscape of Bengal,* New Delhi: Sage, 2011, p. 93.
64. Samaddar, Ranabir, *The Marginal Nation: Transborder Migration from Bangladesh to West Bengal,* New Delhi: Sage, 1999, p. 93.
65. Barkat, "Political Economy of Deprivation of Hindu Minority in Bangladesh", *Op. Cit.*, p. 104.
66. *The Times of India*, March 20, 2021, p. 11.
67. Mukherji, Shantanu, "Hasina must do more for the Hindus", *The Statesman*, October 13, 2016, p. 7.
68. Chaudhuri, Kalyan, "Influx inbound", *Frontline,* November 6, 1992, pp. 24-25.
69. Lin, Sharat G. and Madan C. Paul, "Bangladeshi migrants in Delhi: Social insecurity, state power, and captive vote banks", *Bulletin of Concerned Asian Scholars,* 27, No. 1, 1995, pp. 12-14.
70. *Ibid.*, pp. 4-6.
71. Ahmed, Imtiaz, "Refugees and Security: The Experience of Bangladesh", In *Refugees and Regional Security in South Asia,* ed. S.D. Mani and Lok Raj Baral, 1996, New Delhi, Konark Publishers, pp. 142-144.
72. Chakrobarty, Debesh, Gautam Gupta and Sabari Bandopadhaya, "Migration from Bangladesh to India, 1971-91: Its magnitude and causes", In *State, development and political culture: Bangladesh and India*, ed. Barun De and Ranabir Samaddar, 1997, New Delhi, Har-Anand Publication, p. 272.
73. Lin and Paul, *Op. Cit.*, pp. 8-9.
74. Bannerjee, Debabrata, *Dainik Statesman*, March 12, 2006, p. 4.
75. Ghosh, Manash, *Dainik Statesman*, January 12, 2006.
76. *Dainik Statesman*, January 8, 2006, p. 3.
77. *The Times of India*, November 25, 2020, p. 9.
78. *Anandabazar Patrika*, March 5, 2006, p. 20.
79. *Dainik Statesman*, February 19, 2006, p. 3.
80. *Anandabazar Patrika*, March 18, 2006, p. 6.
81. *Ibid.*, March 20, 2006, p. 6.
82. *Dainik Statesman*, April 9, 2006, p. 6.

83. *Anandabazar Patrika*, April 8, 2006, p. 5.
84. For further reading on CPI-M's patronage of illegal migrants from Bangladesh, read Chandan Nandy, "Illegal Migration from Bangladesh to India: The Emerging Conflicts", *Mellon–MIT Foundation on NGOs and Forced Migration,* November 2005.
85. Lin and Paul, *Op. Cit.*, p. 10.
86. *The Hindu*, June 7, 1995, p. 2.
87. "Political Pawns", *India Today*, August 10, 1998.
88. *The Statesman*, March 26, 2006, p. 5.
89. *The Times of India*, January 29, 2013, p. 8.
90. Nearly 8500 Bangladeshis Living Illegally in Uttar Pradesh", *DNA*, Lucknow, June 11, 2010.
91. "Bihar: Borderline Cases", *India Today*, July 13, 2012.
92. "Government Identifies 3,987 Bangladeshi Infiltrators in Odisha", *The Economic Times*, Bhubaneswar, March 18, 2013.
93. *The Hindu*, February 7, 2006, p. 6.
94. *Ibid.,* June 21, 2016, p. 7.
95. *Ibid.*, November 23, 2014, p. 7.
96. *The Times of India*, January 30, 2020, p. 9.
97. *The Hindu,* June 4, 2014, p. 1.
98. Chaudhuri, Kalyan, "Influx in bound: problems on the Indo-Bangladesh border", *Frontline*, November 6, 1992, pp. 24-26.
99. *The Times of India*, June 9, 2008, p. 7.
100. Beltran, Gonzalo Aguirre, *Regions of Refuge*, 1979, Washington, The Society for Applied Anthropology Monograph Series, Monograph Number 12, p. 48.
101. Weiner, Myron, "The Political Demography of Assam's Anti-immigrant Movement", *Population and Development Review*, Vol. 9, No. 2, June 1983, p. 285.
102. *The Times of India*, New Delhi, January 22, 2015, p. 2.
103. *White Paper on Foreigners' Issue*, *Op. Cit.*, p. 45.
104. Pramanik, Bimal, "Illegal Migration from Bangladesh: A Case Study of West Bengal", in B.B. Kumar (ed.), *Illegal Migration from Bangladesh*, *Op. Cit.*, p. 140.
105. Lin and Paul, *Op. Cit.,* p. 17.
106. Samaddar, Ranabir, *The Marginal Nation: Transborder Migration from Bangladesh to West Bengal*, New Delhi: Sage, 1999, p. 133.
107. Pramanik, Bimal, "Infiltration from Bangladesh: A Critical Analysis", *Dialogue*, Vol. 10, No. 2, 2008.
108. *Ibid.*
109. Samaddar, Ranabir, *The Marginal Nation, Op. Cit.*, p. 91.
110. Nandy, Chandan, "Illegal Migration from Bangladesh to India: The Emerging Conflicts", Mellon–MIT Foundation on NGOs and Forced Migration, November 2005, pp. 172-173.

111. Das, Pushpita, *Op. Cit.*, p. 47.
112. Bhasin,Avtar Singh, *India-Bangladesh Relations*, *Vol. 1*, New Delhi: Geetika Publishers, 2003, p. xciv.
113. Chaudhuri, Kalyan, "Influx unbound: problems on the Indo-Bangladesh border", *Frontline*, November 6, 1992, pp. 24-26.
114. *Pioneer*, May 21, 1992, "Bangladeshi refugees a growing menace?"
115. Shekhar, Shailesh, "Bangla deportees flocking back to Delhi", *Pioneer*, July 23, 1993, p. 3.
116. Ramachandran, Sujata, "Of Boundaries and Border Crossings", *Interventions,* Vol. 1(2), 1999, p. 250.
117. *The Hindu*, December 20, 1998, p. 8.
118. Quoted in *Sarbananda Sonowal* vs. *Union of India,* AIR 2005 SC 2920 (SC 2931-33).
119. *Reforming National Security System*, Recommendation of the Group of Ministers, February 2001, p. 60.
120. *Ibid.*
121. Sinha, Lt. Gen. S.K., "Tackling illegal migration issue in Assam", *The Assam Tribune*, June 3, 2016.
122. "Infiltration of Bangladeshis in India", Unstarred Question No. 2968, Rajya Sabha, August 6, 2014.
123. Ghosh, Partha S., "Bangladesh at the crossroads: Religion and Politics", *Asian Survey,* 33, No. 7, July, 1993, p. 698.
124. *The Telegraph*, February 13, 2008, p. 1.
125. *The Times of India,* May 7, 1997.
126. Nanda, Prakash, "Immigration Imbroglio", *The Statesman*, February 23, 2003, p. 8.
127. *Bartaman,* September 16, 2014, p. 12.
128. *The Times of India*, November 17, 2016, p. 1.
129. *Ibid.*
130. Chatterjee, Sarajit Kumar, *North-East India: Dispersion and Discontent, Op. Cit.*, pp. 678-681.
131. Kashyap, Anirban, *Communalism and Constitution,* 1988, New Delhi, Lancers Books, p. 89.
132. Burki, Shahid Javed, and Swamy Subramanian, "South Asian Migration to United States; Demand and Supply Factors", *Economic and Political Weekly*, Vol. XXII, No. 12, March 21, 1987, p. 513.
133. Howie, Emily, "Sri Lankan Boat Migration to Australia", *Economic and Political Weekly*, Vol. XLVIII, No. 35, August 31, 2013, p. 100.
134. *The Hindu,* November 3, 2013, p. 7.
135. *The Statesman*, August 27, 2015, p. 10.
136. *The Times of India*, November 12, 2015, p. 10.
137. *The Statesman*, September 10, 2014, p. 9.
138. *The Hindu*, October 21, 2014, p. 10.
139. *The Statesman*, September 29, 2014, p. 10.
140. *The Hindu*, October 21, 2014, p. 10.

141. *Ibid.*, December 26, 2013, p, 8.
142. *Annual Report*, Ministry of Home Affairs, Government of India, 2013-14, paras 3.6 to 3.10, pp. 42-44.
143. *Ibid.*, para 3.14, p. 45.
144. *The Telegraph*, July 25, 2019, p. 7.
145. *Anandabazdr Patrika,* December 5, 2019, p. 3.
146. Das Pushpita, *Op. Cit.*, p. 77.
147. Bhasin, *India-Bangladesh Relations*, Vol. 1, *Op. Cit.*, p. xcvi.
148. *Annual Report*, Ministry of Home Affairs, Government of India, 2013-14, paras 3.17-3.19, p. 46.
149. *Ibid.*, paras 3.75-3.76, pp. 61-62.
150. *The Times of India*, November 27, 2014, p. 1.
151. *Ibid.*
152. *Ei Samay,* October 8, 2016, p. 1.
153. *The Times of India,* April 1, 2015, p. 7 and May 14, 2015, p. 11.
154. *Ibid.*, July 15, 2015, p. 17.
155. *Ibid.*, May 22, 2016, p. 6.
156. *The Hindu*, September 2, 2106, p. 2.
157. *The Statesman*, December 27, 2016, p. 5.
158. *The Telegraph*, April 6, 2011, p. 6.
159. *Census of India, India Series 1, Provisional Population Totals, Paper 1 of 2011, Statement 4*, p. 54.
160. *The Hindu*, October 21, 2020, p. 10.
161. *The Times of India,* March 11, 2021, (flap).
162. Lin and Paul, *Op. Cit.*, pp. 4-5.
163. *Ibid.*, p. 5.
164. Poser, Jonathan, "New thinking on immigration", *The Statesman,* September 21, 2007, p. 7.
165. *The Anandabazar Patrika*, January 18, 1996, p. 4.
166. Jhunjhunwala, Bharat, "Migration and deportation", *The Statesman*, February 14, 2013, p. 6.
167. *The Telegraph*, February 20, 2021, p. 2.
168. *The Statesman*, July 27, 2016, p. 9.
169. *The Hindu*, March 19, 2016, p. 14.
170. *The Statesman*, March 3-5, 1992.
171. Banerjee, Paula, Hazarika, Sanjoy, Hussain, Monirul and Samaddar, Ranabir, "Indo-Bangladesh Cross-Border Migration and Trade", *Economic and Political Weekly,* September 4, 1999, pp. 2550-51.
172. *Annual Report*, Ministry of Home Affairs, Government of India, 2013-14, paras 3.77-3.79, p. 63.
173. *Bartaman,* May 24, 2015, p. 11.
174. *Ei Samay*, December 24, 2014, p. 13.
175. *The Hindu,* December 1, 2014, p. 1.
176. Bhaumik Subir, "Looking towards new prosperity", *The Telegraph*, September 1, 2015, p. 9.

177. Mohanty, Saroj K., "Taka Talks In A Tailored Suit", *Outlook*, December 1, 2020, pp. 42-45.
178. Shibil, Abdullah, "How Bangladesh pipped its bigger neighbours", *The Statesman*, January 18, 2016, p. 7.
179. Prasad, Jayant, "Breakthrough in India-Bangladesh ties", *The Hindu*, May 11, 2015, p. 7.
180. *The Statesman*, December 18, 2020, p. 2.
181. *The Times of India*, February 26, 2021, p. 11.
182. *Ibid.*, March 10, 2021, p. 11.
183. *Ibid.*, March 28, 2021, p. 10.
184. *Ibid.*, October 16, 2014, p. 8.
185. *Ibid.*, November 12, 2014, p. 8.
186. *The Indian Express*, Guwahati, December 7, 2014, p. 2.
187. *Ibid.,* October 22, 2014, p. 11.
188. *The Assam Tribune,* May 2, 2016.
189. *The Statesman*, January 4, 2015, p. 3.
190. *Ibid.*, October 15, 2014, p. 14.
191. *Ibid.*, November 9, 2014, p. 3.
192. *Ibid.*, March 31, 2015, p. 1.
193. *Ibid.*, December 15, 2015, p. 21.
194. Das Pushpita, *Op. Cit.*, p. 48.
195. *The Times of India*, December 2, 2014, p. 12.
196. Bhaumik Subir, "Looking towards new prosperity", *The Telegraph*, September 1, 2015, p. 9.
197. Remittances to India—Wikipedia *en.wikipedia.org* wiki Remittances_to_India for the years 2012-13 to 2017-18.
198. *Anandabazar Patrika*, December 26, 2020, p. 8.
199. In an interview in *The Week*, January 5, 2020, p. 40.
200. Samaddar, Ranabir, *The Marginal Nation, Op. Cit.*, pp. 158-159.
201. Ramachandran, Sujata, "Operation Pushback: Sangh Parivar, State, Slums and Surreptitious Bangladeshis in New Delhi", *Economic and Political Weekly*, 2003, February 15, p. 637.
202. Bharatiya Janata Party, *National Executive Resolution*, April 30, 1992, Gandhi Nagar, Gujarat.
203. Ray, Tapas, "A new mantra: Infiltration, BJP's electoral plank", *Frontline,* November 6, 1992, p. 32.
204. Khosla, Shyam, "Invisible invasion", *The Tribune*, October 9, 1992, p. 9.
205. Kaushish, Poonam, "Silent threat to integrity", *The Tribune*, November 11, 1992.
206. "Bangladeshi infiltration an assault on India", *The Indian Express*, September 15, 1992.
207. Vinayak, M., "Infiltration, a growing threat", *The Hindu*, August 18, 1992.
208. "Bangladeshi refugees a growing menace?" *The Pioneer*, May 21, 1992.
209. Shourie Arun, "How countries kill themselves", *Observer of Business and Politics*, April 30, 1993, p. 11.

210. Shukla, Rajiv, "The unwanted guests: isn't it time that we sorted out the illegal Bangladeshi immigrants issue", *The Sunday*, February 12-18,1995, p. 27.
211. Sharma, Manmohan, "Bharat mein Bangladesh se ek karod bina bulaye mehmanon ki ghuspaith" [The infiltration of one million unwanted guests from Bangladesh into India], *The Punjab Kesari,* February 26, 1990.
212. Kamath, M.V., "A Dump for Bangladesh's unwanted citizens", *Independent*, November 25, 1992.
213. Ghosh, Soumya K., "Problem from Bangladesh", *The Pioneer*, November 25, 1996.
214. Gupta, Kanchan, "India's Bangla problem", *The Pioneer*, June 24, 1992.
215. "Bangla infiltrators a 'serious threat'", *The National Herald*, September 30, 1992.
216. Gillan, Michael, "Refugees or Infiltrators? The Bharatiya Janata Party and 'Illegal' Migration from Bangladesh", *Asian Studies Association of Australia,* 2002, p. 85.
217. *Organiser*, July 21, 1991.
218. Chaudhuri, Kalyan, "Influx unbound: problems on the Indo-Bangladesh border", *Frontline*, November 6, 1992, pp. 24-26.
219. Guruswamy, Mohan, "On search of land?" *The Hindustan Times*, February 16, 1997, p. 5.
220. *The Indian Express*, September 23, 1992.
221. Quoted in *Sarbananda Sonowal* vs. *Union of India,* (2007) 1 SCC 174.
222. Banerjee, Satrujit, "Welcome to a new home", *The Telegraph*, April 9, 2008, p. 10.
223. Samaddar, Ranabir, *The Marginal Nation. Op. Cit.*, p. 89.
224. *Ibid.*, p. 92.
225. *Ibid.*, p. 43.
226. *The Statesman*, June 30, 2014, p. 3.
227. Editorial titled "Passage to India", *The Times of India,* October 18, 2013, p. 16.

4
Detection and Deportation of the Infiltrants—National Register of Citizens

The types of illegal migrants or clandestine migrants or undocumented migrants are as follows:

(a) those who came with valid visa/documents and overstayed;
(b) those who came with forged visa/documents; and
(c) those who entered surreptitiously.

Any national policy on illegal migration in order to be effective has got to be an implementable one providing for measures for the (1) prevention of any infiltration, (2) identification of the infiltrators, and (3) deportation of the infiltrators.

While preventing the infiltration should receive top priority, detection and deportation of the illegal migrants is no less arduous. The statistics released in the Rajya Sabha on 22 October, 2008 show that as many as 62,547 Bangladeshis who entered India with valid visas had just 'disappeared' in 2005-07 (12,338 in 2005, 24,497 in 2006 and 25,712 in 2007) while the corresponding number for the Pakistanis were 22,097 (7,043 in 2005, 7,650 in 2006 and 7,404 in 2007).[1] If the number of 'legal migrants' who did not go back is so high, roughly 85 thousand in 3 years, what should be the number of the 'illegal migrants' can easily be visualised. Since the migrants from Nepal can enter India without any travel documents, how many of them did not go back ultimately is any body's guess.

Considering the seriousness of the matter of persistent influx of illegal migrants, the Government of India went on to formulate the Immigrants (Expulsion from Assam) Act, 1950. This Act which came into effect from 1st March, 1950 mandated expulsion of illegal immigrants from the state of Assam.[2] To identify illegal immigrants, the National Register of Citizens was prepared for the first time in Assam during the conduct of 1951 Census. It was prepared under a directive of the Ministry of Home Affairs containing village-wise information of each and every person enumerated therein. Details such as the number and names of persons, the houses or holdings belonging to them, father's name or husband's name, nationality, age, the means of livelihood were all indicated therein.[3]

However, this measure against illegal migrants suffered a major setback due to the fact that only from October 1952 onwards the regulations of passport and visa became operational between India and Pakistan. Further, "the definition of a foreigner to cover a Pakistan national was only clearly spelt out with the amendment of the Foreigners Act, 1946 in 1957."[4]

Meanwhile, the issue of illegal infiltration was becoming formidable in the state of Assam. The Registrar General of Census in his report on 1961 Census assessed 2,20,691 infiltrators to have entered Assam.[5]

In the year 1965, the Government of India took up with the Government of Assam to expedite completion of the National Register of Citizens and to issue National Identity Cards on the basis of this register to Indian citizens towards identification of illegal immigrants. But in 1966, the Central Government dropped the proposal to issue identity cards in consultation with the Government of Assam, having found the project impracticable.[6]

In a notification issued by the Government of India on 17 February, 1976, the State government was instructed not to deport persons coming from Bangladesh to India prior to March, 1971.[7]

Between 1948 and 1971, there were large scale migrations from East Pakistan to Assam. As is well known, West Pakistan commenced hostilities against East Pakistan on 25th March, 1971 culminating in the war which dismembered the two parts of Pakistan and led to the birth of a new nation, Bangladesh.

The movement for the detection and deportation of illegal migrants in Assam, popularly known as Assam Movement which started in 1979 and continued up to 1985 resulted in the signing of the Assam Accord. However, even after the leaders of the Assam Movement formed the ministry in Assam, the process of detecting and expelling immigrants never really officially took place.

II

As the movement for the 'detection, deletion (from electoral rolls) and deportation of Bangladeshis' was assuming the character of a mass-movement in Assam with the participation of people from all walks of life, the then Congress Government, which had an overwhelming majority in Parliament, enacted the Illegal Migrants (Determination by Tribunals) Act, 1983 which came into force on 25 December, 1983. The Statement of Objects and Reasons of the IMDT Act, 1983 reads as under—

> The influx of foreigners who illegally migrated into India across the borders of the sensitive eastern and north-eastern regions of the country and remained in the country poses a threat to the integrity and security of the said regions. A substantial number of such foreigners who migrated into India after the 25th day of March, 1971 have, by taking advantage of the circumstances of such migration and their ethnic similarities and other connections with the people of India, illegally remained in India without having in their possession lawful authority so to do. The continuance of those persons in India has given rise to serious problems. The clandestine manner in which these persons have been trying to pass off as citizens of India has rendered their detection difficult. After taking into account the need for their speedy detection, the need for protection of genuine citizens of India and the interests of the general public, the President promulgated, on the 15th October, 1983, the Illegal Migrants (Determination by Tribunals) Ordinance, 1983, to provide for the establishment of Tribunals.

Though the IMDT Act was ostensibly enacted for facilitating prompt detection and deportation of illegal immigrants, but, in reality, it was so drafted, thanks to its architect, Abdul Muhib Mazumdar, a senior Congress leader of Assam, and an advocate, and the Rules thereunder were so made that innumerable and insurmountable difficulties were created in the matter of identification and deportation of illegal migrants. Under the IMDT Act, the onus of proving the fact that one is an illegal infiltrator was on the person lodging the complaint and not on the person being charged with the offence. This, in essence, took away the onus of proving nationality from the migrants and transferred it to the citizen who had lodged the complaint before the tribunal and pay a fee to engage its services. The IMDT Act came to the advantage of such illegal migrants as any proceedings initiated against them under the said provision which almost entirely ended in their favour enabled them to have a document having official sanctity to the effect that they were not illegal migrants. Moreover, whereas the rest of India had 19 July, 1948 as the cut-off date for Indian citizenship of migrants, the date for Assam was 25 March, 1971.

The hurdle put forth in effectively detecting and ultimately deporting the illegal migrants by enacting such an Act, encouraged infiltration from across the border. In the Assam Accord there is a clause that states that "the Government will give due consideration to certain difficulties expressed by AASU/AAGSP regarding the implementation of the Illegal Migrant (Determination by Tribunals) Act, 1983" [para 5(9) of the Accord]. But the Congress which was ruling then did precious little to undo it. Then came the Asom Gana Parishad government (1985-90). In spite of tremendous public support and goodwill, the students-turned-politicians were so preoccupied in feathering their nests that they paid little attention to the foreign national issue, on the strength of which they were catapulted to power. In its second term (1996-2001), it merely adopted a resolution demanding the withdrawal of the Act, but refrained from making it an election issue, sensibly for fear of losing the Muslim vote.

The IMDT Act merely preserved the Congress's vote bank (many considered this as an anti-Assam law). The Congress government, however, argued that the legislation safeguarded the interests of genuine Indians because the Foreigners' Act, 1946 allowed the police sweeping powers that could be misused at the prompting of vested interests. Some argued, and with justification, that if the Foreigners' Act, 1946 was good enough for the rest of the country, why should there be a need for a separate law for Assam. So the successive governments could neither put a stop to the unabated infiltration from Bangladesh nor could take any effective and concrete measures to detect and deport the illegal migrants from Assam, mainly due to the IMDT Act. Even the NDA 1 Government at the Centre, of which the AGP was a constituent, could not scrap the Act. As a result, people living on the other side of the border felt that if they were to cross over to India they would somehow be accommodated.

In the meantime, the highest court of the land declared the provisions of the IMDT Act *ultra vires* of the Constitution. In a stinging judgment delivered on 12 July, 2005 by a three-judge Bench headed by the Chief Justice, Mr. Justice R.C. Lahoti, the Court, amongst others, observed:

> 27. To give the exact date of entry into India of a Bangladeshi national, who has illegally and surreptitiously crossed the international border, is not only difficult but virtuously impossible. A citizen doing his duty towards nation of pointing out the presence of a Bangladeshi national to the authorities of the State is put under threat of criminal prosecution, if the contents of the application are found to be false. This is bound to have a cascading effect on citizens who will prefer

to remain a quiet spectator to the continued influx of illegal migrants from Bangladesh rather than to take initiative in their detection or deportation.

28. The analysis of the provisions of IMDT Act and the Rules made thereunder clearly demonstrate that the provisions thereof are very stringent as compared to the provisions of Foreigners Act, 1946 or Foreigners (Tribunals) Order, 1964, in the matter of detection and deportation of illegal migrants. It is far more easier to secure conviction of a person in a criminal trial where he may be awarded a capital punishment or imprisonment for life than to establish that a person is an illegal migrant on account of extremely difficult, cumbersome and time consuming procedure laid down in the IMDT Act and the Rules made thereunder. The Act does not contain any provision for constitution of a screening committee which has been done under the Rules and has been conferred a very wide power of rejecting complaints against which no appeal lies. The figures supplied in the initial affidavit filed by the State of Assam show that more than eighty five per cent enquiries initiated were rejected and no reference was made to the Tribunal. Similarly, the restrictions imposed on an applicant, a citizen of India doing a national duty of pointing out the presence of an illegal migrant in Assam, that he should be resident of same police station or same sub-division where the illegal migrant resides or is found does not carry any sense as these migrants keep moving. The requirement regarding application being accompanied by affidavits of two persons who are residents of same police station or being accompanied by declaration of another person who is resident of same sub-division or that not more than ten such applications can be filed or ten such declarations made do not serve any purpose except to create hurdles in the matter of identification and deportation of illegal migrants. Not every person feels that he owes a duty towards the nation and he should initiate proceedings for deportation of an illegal migrant. The applicant also incurs risk to his own security and safety besides spending time and energy in prosecuting the matter. Similarly, there is hardly any sense in making a provision for mentioning the time and date of visit to a place by an enquiry officer in a diary. A deep analysis of the IMDT Act and the Rules made thereunder

would reveal that they have been purposely so enacted or made so as to give shelter or protection to illegal migrants who came to Assam from Bangladesh on or after 25th March, 1971 rather than to identify and deport them.

32. The foremost duty of the Central Government is to defend the borders of the country, prevent any trespass and make the life of the citizens safe and secure. The Government has also a duty to prevent any internal disturbance and maintain law and order.

38. This being the situation there can be no manner of doubt that the State of Assam is facing "external aggression and internal disturbance" on account of large scale illegal migration of Bangladeshi nationals. It, therefore, becomes the duty of Union of India to take all measures for protection of the State of Assam from such external aggression and internal disturbance as enjoined in Article 355 of the Constitution. Having regard to this constitutional mandate, the question arises whether the Union of India has taken any measures for that purpose.

39. We have considered the provisions of the Foreigners Act, Foreigners (Tribunals) Order, 1964 and also the IMDT Act and the Rules made thereunder in considerable detail in the earlier part of the judgment. They clearly demonstrate that the procedure under the Foreigners Act and also under the Foreigners (Tribunals) Order, 1964 is far more effective in identification and deportation of foreigners as compared to the procedure under the IMDT Act and the Rules made thereunder. There being no corresponding provision like Section 9 of the Foreigners Act which places the burden of proof upon the person concerned who claims to be an Indian citizen, which is absolutely essential in relation to the nature of inquiry being conducted regarding determination of a person's citizenship (where the facts on the basis of which an opinion is to be formed and a decision is taken are entirely within the knowledge of the said person) has made the task of the law enforcement agencies of the State not only difficult but virtually impossible. The IMDT Act has been so enacted and the Rules thereunder have been so made that innumerable and insurmountable difficulties are created in the matter of identification and deportation of

illegal migrants. No elaborate discussion on this aspect is required as the figures disclosed in the affidavits filed by the Union of India and the State of Assam speak for themselves. Though inquiries were initiated in 3,10,759 cases under the IMDT Act but out of this only 10,015 persons were declared as illegal migrants and finally only 1,481 illegal migrants were physically expelled up to 30th April, 2000. This comes to less than half per cent of the cases initiated. In the State of West Bengal, where the Foreigners Act is applicable, 4,89,046 persons were actually deported between 1983 and November 1998, which is a lesser period and even this result was termed as unsatisfactory in the counter affidavit filed by the Union of India. Thus, there cannot be even a slightest doubt that the application of the IMDT Act and the Rules made thereunder in the State of Assam has created the biggest hurdle and is the main impediment or barrier in identification and deportation of illegal migrants. On the contrary, it is coming to the advantage of such illegal migrants as any proceedings initiated against them under the said provision which, as demonstrated above, almost entirely ends in their favour, enables them to have a document having official sanctity to the effect that they are not illegal migrants. As already discussed, the presence of such a large number of illegal migrants from Bangladesh, which runs into millions, is in fact an "aggression" on the State of Assam and has also contributed significantly in causing serious "internal disturbances" in the shape of insurgency of alarming proportion making the life of the people of Assam wholly insecure and the panic generated thereby has created a fear psychosis. This has resulted in seriously hampering the growth of the State of Assam although it has vast natural resources as people from rest of the country have a general perception that it is a disturbed area and this factor has resulted in not generating any employment opportunity which has contributed to a large measure in giving rise to insurgency. The impact is such that it not only affects the State of Assam but it also affects its sister States like Arunachal Pradesh, Meghalaya, Nagaland, etc. as the route to the said places passes through the State of Assam.

57. To sum up our conclusions, the provisions of the Illegal Migrants (Determination by Tribunals) Act, 1983 are *ultra vires* the Constitution of India and are accordingly struck

> down. The Illegal Migrants (Determination by Tribunals) Rules, 1984 are also *ultra vires* and are struck down. As a result, the Tribunals and the Appellate Tribunals constituted under the Illegal Migrants (Determination by Tribunals) Act, 1983 shall cease to function. The Passport (Entry into India) Act, 1920, the Foreigners Act, 1946, the Immigrants (Expulsion from Assam) Act, 1950 and the Passport Act, 1967 shall apply to the State of Assam. All cases pending before the Tribunals under the Illegal Migrants (Determination by Tribunals) Act, 1983 shall stand transferred to the Tribunals constituted under the Foreigners (Tribunals) Order, 1964 and shall be decided in the manner provided in the Foreigners Act, the Rules made thereunder and the procedure prescribed under the Foreigners (Tribunals) Order, 1964. In view of the finding that the competent authority and the Screening Committee had no authority or jurisdiction to reject any proceedings initiated against any alleged illegal migrant, the orders of rejection passed by such authorities are declared to be void and non est in the eye of law. It will be open to the authorities of the Central Government or State Government to initiate fresh proceedings under the Foreigners Act against all such persons whose cases were not referred to the Tribunals constituted under the Illegal Migrants (Determination by Tribunals) Act, 1983 by the competent authority whether on account of the recommendation of the Screening Committee or any other reason whatsoever. The appeals pending before the Appellate Tribunals shall be deemed to have abated.[8]

The Centre and the Assam Governments ignored the tell-tale warning signals from the Supreme Court. Both had even stepped around the above order of the apex court asking them to speed up detection of illegal Bangladeshi migrants. In order to assuage the minority concerns that the Foreigners Act might be used to harass them, the Central Government in exercise of its power under Section 3 of the Foreigners Act, 1946 made an order known as "the Foreigners (Tribunals) Amendment Order, 2006", which amended the Foreigners (Tribunals) Order, 1964 principally making the same inapplicable to the State of Assam, and instead notified the Foreigners (Tribunals for Assam) Order, 2006, which was published in the official Gazette on 10 February, 2006, coincidentally on the eve of the elections to the State Assembly held on 3 and 10 April, 2006. It was nothing but an attempt by way of subordinate legislation to nullify the mandamus issued by the Supreme Court in the IMDT case. Instead of obeying the mandamus issued by the Supreme Court essentially in the interests of national security, preserving the demographic balance of a part of India and implementing the Foreigners (Tribunal) Order 1964 in Assam in letter and spirit, the Central Government succumbed to the political pressure and chose to make the 1964 Order itself inapplicable to Assam.

The Supreme Court, however, on 5 December, 2006 struck down the Foreigners (Tribunals) Amendment Order, 2006 on the same line of reasoning as in the IMDT case. The 2006 Order was found to be unreasonable, arbitrary and in contravention of Article 14 of the Constitution (equality before law) since it applied only to Assam and not to other States bordering Bangladesh. It was held to be violative of the Centre's duty to protect the States under Article 355. The Court even questioned whether the authority that should be interested in the welfare of the nation, its security and integrity, could do so in the light of the facts noticed and relied on in the IMDT case. The Supreme Court directed the Centre to constitute within four months a sufficient number of Tribunals under the 1964 Order to effectively deal with foreigners who have illegally come from Bangladesh or are residing in Assam.[9]

With the scrapping of the IMDT Act and the Foreigners (Tribunals) Amendment Order, 2006, foreigners living in Assam are now being dealt with under the provisions of the Foreigners Act, 1946 and the Foreigners (Tribunal) Order, 1964. The Foreigner's Tribunals are to furnish opinion on the question as to whether a person is or is not a foreigner within the meaning of Foreigner's Act, 1946 whenever such a reference is made to them. The Tribunals have the powers of a civil Court while trying a suit under the Code of Civil Procedure in respect of summoning and enforcing the attendances of any person and examining him on oath, requiring the discovery and production of any document and issuing commissions for the examination of any witness. The number of Foreigner's Tribunals established has varied from time to time, according to the requirements of the situation. A detailed account of the working of the Foreigner's Tribunals and Illegal Migrants (Determination) Tribunals in Assam in respect of detection and deportation of foreigners has been furnished in the White Paper on Foreigners' Issue of the Home and Political Department of the Government of Assam of 20 October, 2012 as follows:

> 2.3.2 In 1983, IM(D)Ts were established under the Illegal Migrants (Determination by Tribunals) Act, 1983. Prior to that an ordinance was passed facilitating the setting up of IM(D)Ts. The State Government had initially decided to set up 20 IM(D)Ts. At the

same time after 1985, the Foreigner's Tribunals co-existed with IM(D)Ts with the signing of the Assam Accord. While IM(D)Ts took up cases of suspected foreigners of the post March 25th, 1971 stream, the existing Foreigners Tribunals were entrusted with the responsibility of disposing of cases pertaining to pre-March 25th, 1971 stream of suspected foreigners. IM(DT) Act was amended by IM(DT) Amendment Act, 1988 on April 25, 1988. With the Hon'ble Supreme Court declaring the IM(DT) Act, 1983 as *ultra vires* in 2005 and striking them down, the Tribunals and Appellate Tribunals have ceased to function. The performance of the IM(DT) during various time periods is summarized below.

2.3.3

IM (DT) Cases

Period	Cases Referred	Cases Disposed	Cases pending (cumulative)	Persons declared as Foreigners	Number of declared foreigners pushed back/ deported
1985-90	22682	6486	16196	6724	521
1991-95	3488	7335	12349	2577	792
1996-2000	17623	4420	25552	902	179
2001-July 2005	68998	5780	88770	2643	55
Total	112791	24021	88770	12846	1547

2.3.3. All cases pending before the Tribunals under the Illegal Migrants (Determination by Tribunals) Act, 1983 shall stand transferred to the Tribunals constituted under the Foreigners (Tribunal) Order, 1964 and shall be decided in the manner provided in the Foreigners Act, the Rules made thereunder and the procedure prescribed under the Foreigners (Tribunals) Order, 1964.

2.3.4. It has been found that due to a variety of reasons – lack of judicial supervision, long vacancies of members, inadequate staff – large number of cases were pending unregistered in some of the tribunals. On specific pursuance from Government of Assam and judicial intervention by Hon'ble Gauhati High Court, the number of unregistered cases has come down but there are still more than 65,000 unregistered cases pending for years together in some of the foreigner's tribunals. Additional staff have been deputed from Border Police so that all cases are registered without further delay.

2.3.5. The 21 IMDTs functioning in Assam were wound up and replaced by 21 new Foreigners Tribunals. The learned judges and staff of IMDT were redeployed in the newly created additional Foreigners Tribunals. As a result, after 2005, 32 (21 new + 11 existing) Foreigners Tribunals started functioning. The number of Foreigners Tribunal has now been raised to 36 with the functioning of 4 new Foreigners Tribunals. The performance of Foreigners Tribunal over different time period is presented in the table below:

Foreigners Tribunal Cases

Period	Cases Referred	Cases Disposed	Cases pending (cumulative)	Persons declared as Foreigners	Number of declared foreigners pushed back/ deported
1985-90	32,991	15,929	17,062	14,801	133
1991-95	482	5,909	11,635	4,005	267
1996-2000	2,986	3,552	11,069	6,026	235
2001-2005	6,094	2,216	14,947	4,593	39
2006-July 2012	65,666	45,456	35,157	12,913	221
Total	1,08,219	73,062	35,157	42,338	895

Consolidated total of deported/pushed back illegal migrants on being declared as foreigners by IMD(T)s and Foreigners Tribunals collectively till July 2012 was – 1547 + 895 = **2442.**

2.3.6. The various Tribunals have since 1985 declared 61,774 persons as foreigners, both from the 1966-1971 stream and the post 25 March, 1971 stream. A table indicating the streams to which these foreigners belong on being so declared by appropriate tribunals at various phases is placed below:

Period	1966-1971 stream	Post-1971	Total stream	'D' Voters declared as voters	Total with 'D' Forei-gners
1985-1990	14,801	6,724	21,525	–	21,525
1991-1995	4,005	2,577	6,582	–	6,582
1996-2000	6,026	902	6,928	6,590 (1998 to 31.7.2012)	–

contd..

Period	1966-1971 stream	Post-1971	Total stream	'D' Voters declared as voters	Total with 'D' Foreigners
2001-2005	4,593	2,643	7,236	–	33,667
2006-2012 July	3,112	9,801	12,913	–	—
Grand total	**32,537**	**22,647**	**55184**	**6,590**	**61,774**

2.3.7. The above table clearly brings out the fact that a majority of the foreigners declared by the tribunals belong to the 1966-1971 stream, who, at any rate, are not to be deported but to be given time for registering themselves as Indian citizens. From the figures collected by Border police from various tribunals, out of 32,537 foreigners belonging to the 1966-1971 stream only 12,914 foreigners have registered themselves with the jurisdictional FRROs. On the other hand, tribunals (IMD(T)s and FTs) have declared 29,237 [22,647 plus 6,590] as foreigners who belong to the post 25 March, 1971 stream. These 29,237 foreigners so declared by the appropriate tribunals over a long period of time were to be deported forthwith. However, records reveal that only 2,442 such persons have been deported/pushed back.

Thus from 1985 to July, 2012, 2,20,910 cases were referred to the Tribunals for a decision. Out of them, as many as 97,083 cases were disposed of and the remaining cases were still pending. Of the 61,774 persons declared foreigners, 29,237 belonged to the post-1971 stream who were to be deported. But so far only 2,442 persons could be deported/pushed back. It may be recalled the affidavits filed by the Union of India and the State of Assam before the Supreme Court in *Sarbananda Sonowal* v. *Union of India* AIR 2005 SC 2920 (para 39) had revealed that up to 30th April, 2000, inquiries were initiated in 3,10,759 cases under the IMDT Act but out of this only 10,015 persons were declared as illegal migrants and finally only 1,481 illegal migrants were physically expelled. This comes to less than half per cent of the cases initiated.

Notwithstanding the major discrepancies with regard to the cases initiated, one thing is, however, clear. During the period up to July 2012, not more than 2,442 persons could be deported/pushed back. Considering the huge cost in maintaining the Tribunals and the euphoria raised in the wake of the Foreigners Movement, it is like a mountain producing a mole.

There has never been any doubt that the unending illegal migration from across the border into Assam is an insoluble problem. Had there been timely action, perhaps the exodus could have been stemmed. But no government in Assam, be it led by the AGP or the Congress, did start the process of detecting, disenfranchising and deporting illegal immigrants or tackle the situation effectively enough because of the lack of political will. During a visit to Darrang and Udalgiri districts in October 2008 following the killing of 50 people in Bodo-Muslim clashes, chief minister Tarun Gogoi said he neither met nor saw anyone who could be termed 'illegal Bangladeshis' and mentioned that those who were living there were mostly indigenous Assamese-Muslims.

The AGP in its manifesto for the 14th Lok Sabha elections promised that the party would strive for updating the National Register of Citizens, time-bound implementation of the Assam Accord and protection of linguistic, cultural and social identities of every ethnic group and would raise in the Parliament the State's burning issues like the detection and expulsion of illegal Bangladeshi migrants.[10] Such tall promises had practically no effect on the people because only one MP could be sent by the AGP to the Lok Sabha.

Even the Ulfa came to the immigrants' defence, saying that political parties who were targeting them in a bid to get Bodo votes were "actually of the indigenous Assamese minority community whose ancestors fought against the Moghuls at Saraighat in preserving the sovereignty of Asom and at the historical Pathughata against the British, and gave their lives to safeguard the Assamese language."[11]

Such being the stand of the parties in Assam, it is no wonder that the State of Assam sought a policy for granting asylum, on humanitarian grounds, to those who were citizens of undivided India and fled to this side of the border during partition due to "religious persecution, atrocities and discrimination." Chief Minister Tarun Gogoi had submitted a memorandum to Prime Minister Dr. Manmohan Singh on 20 April, 2012 to that effect. The State Cabinet decided on 16 July, 2014 to pursue this with the ruling BJP government at the Centre.[12] And what would be their number? The "White Paper on Foreigners' Issue" brought out by the Government of Assam states:

> "Following partition and communal riots in the sub-continent, Assam initially saw an influx of refugees and other migrants from East Pakistan. The number of such migrants other than refugees was initially reported by the State government to be between 1,50,000 and 2,00,000 but later estimated to be around 5,00,000."[13]

Quite predictably, the All Assam Students' Union and the Asom Jatiyatabadi Yuba Chatra Parishad warned of vigorous protests against this decision of the State cabinet. The Assam State Committee of the Communist Party of India (Marxist) also cautioned the State Government against diluting the Assam Accord. The Krishak Mukti Sangram Samiti (KMSS) alleged that the State Government move was aimed at creating a vote bank of illegal Bangladeshi migrants with an eye on the 2016 Assembly elections.[14] The Assam Government, however, passed on the buck to the Centre and told the State Assembly on 6 August, 2014 that only the Centre could take a decision on granting asylum and Indian citizenship to Bangladeshi nationals who entered the State due to alleged persecution.[15] In the meantime, the Modi Government at the Centre had come up with a proposal for allowing visa-free entry to Bangladeshi nationals aged below ten years and above 70 years, which did not find favour with the Assam Government. In 2014, the Centre has undertaken in Assam and West Bengal the task of identification of those Bangladeshis who have not returned back to that country even after expiry of the visa.[16]

III

In 1992, the Election Commission gave a nation-wide directive to 'revise' electoral rolls to disenfranchise undocumented immigrants.[17] Apparently the Commission issued this order after receiving several complaints about the inclusion of many Bangladeshis in the voters' list.[18] Chief Electoral Officers of the States and Union Territories were asked to catalogue areas with large numbers of foreign nationals and take steps to prevent their enrolment as voters.[19] In effect, electoral enumerators would not merely reform voters' lists, but create new sets of names by beginning to from a 'clean slate' and abandoning all previous records.[20] A vital part of this registration exercise would, naturally, involve inquiries into voters' citizenship status, and local police and enumerators would carry out the verifications. Extra special care, it was suggested, would be taken to enlist voters from the already identified areas dominated by Bangladeshi immigrants.

What remained vague, however, was the documentary proof required in order to firmly and, without a doubt, establish Indian nationality. Home ministry officials asserted that while these could be produced as evidence, the simple possession of ration-cards or for that matter registration in old electoral rolls would in itself not constitute as 'automatic Indian citizenship.'[21] Up to this point, ration cards issued through the government's public distribution system had served as the principal means to establish domicile status by Indians, particularly by those who did not have the resources to procure any other documents. Documents like passport, until very recently, were meant largely for those who could afford to travel outside the country.

Similarly, the system of issuing birth certificates has remained rather rudimentary and spotty in India, operating largely in urban areas. Only persons, who hold or have owned land in their native place, can likewise provide documents such as property deeds. Again, this may not always be the case especially for those who existed as landless peasants before shifting to big cities. With the exception of ration cards, *jhuggi* tokens and names in voters' lists, the vast ranks of the urban poor in India have not been issued, and until the verification drive did not desperately need, additional certification. So, in the absence of a standardized system of identifying Indians, this persistent ambiguity surrounding citizenship status, particularly in the case of the extremely large numbers of residents of its numerous slums and resettlement colonies, would before long haunt successive Indian governments. Indeed, even though mostly affecting poverty-stricken Muslim Indians and Bangladeshis easily dispensable in normal circumstances, several Indian governments would through the 1990s periodically face the scathing sting of verbal attacks and open protests against these coerced repatriations.

In fact, the only attempt at detecting foreigners by updating the National Register in Assam was through a Pilot Project which was started in 2 circles (referred to as Tehsil in some states), one in Kamrup district and another in Barpeta district in the year 2010, which ended abruptly within 4 weeks amidst a huge law and order problem involving a mob attack on the Office of the Deputy Commissioner, Barpeta that resulted in police firing killing 4 persons. Considering the volatile nature of the issue, for a long time particularly after the experience of the pilot project, NRC update was considered almost an impossible task.[22]

The preparation of the NRC got momentum when the Supreme Court came into the picture. A public interest petition was filed by Assam Public Works, a non-governmental organization in the Supreme Court for undertaking the exercise for updating the NRC 1951 in Assam. The case (274/2009) took a decisive turn when it was handed over to a Bench of Justices Ranjan Gogoi and Rohinton Nariman on 2 April, 2013. This Bench in September 2013 directed the Union Government and the State Government to complete the update of NRC, to be implemented in adherence to the Citizenship Act, 1955 and the Citizenship Rules, 2003, in all parts of Assam with the objective to rule out immigrants from the state. Pursuant to the directive of the Apex Court, the Registrar General of India via its notification Number S.O. 3591 (E) dated December 6, 2013 notified commencement of NRC. That was the beginning of the gargantuan task of identification of illegal migrants and the Supreme Court thereupon took on the task of monitoring the entire process of NRC update in Assam.

The Bench of Justices Ranjan Gogoi and Rohinton F. Nariman observed that Assam's culture was being eroded and peace and harmony of the area disturbed as it got swamped by persons "who have no right to continue to live in this country, resulting in periodic clashes between citizens and migrants. Not only is there an assault on the life of the citizenry of the state of Assam but there is an assault on their way of life." The Court directed the government to effectively fence the Indo-Bangla border while maintaining strict vigil through effective patrolling to prevent influx of illegal migrants. The Court even said that it would monitor steps taken by the government and sought periodic status report after every three months.[23]

This Bench in its orders dated 27 November, 2014 had directed that preparatory work such as selection of vendor system, appointment of staff and training etc. for the preparation of the NRC had to be completed by the end of January 2015.[24] The Court also fixed a time table for the preparation of the NRC so that the entire updated NRC was published by the end of January 2016.[25]

The NRC is updated as per the provisions of the Citizenship Act, 1955 and the Citizenship (Registration of Citizens and Issue of National Identity Cards) Rules, 2003 (As amended by 1. G.S.R. 803(E), dated 9 November, 2009 (with effect from 9/11/2009), Ministry of Home Affairs (Office of Registrar General, India), Order No. S.O. 596(E), dated 15 March, 2010, published in the Gazette of India, Extra, Part II. No. 504 S.3(ii), dated 16 March, 2010, p. 1. As per the two statutes, the eligibility status would be ascertained based on the NRC, 1951, Electoral Rolls up to 1971 and in their absence the admissible documents up to 24 March (midnight) 1971. As a matter of fact, the documents to be relied upon for deciding the case for inclusion in the NRC were enumerated. Two sets of documents had to be furnished by the applicants for inclusion in the updated NRC. They are—

- List A Documents
- List B Documents.[26]

List A Documents

For inclusion of names of any person in updated NRC, the applicants must produce any one of the following List A documents issued before 24 March (midnight), 1971 where the name of self or ancestor appears (to prove residence in Assam up to 24 March (midnight), 1971):

- 1951 NRC
- Electoral Roll(s) up to 24th March (midnight), 1971
- Land & Tenancy Records
- Citizenship Certificate
- Permanent Residential Certificate
- Refugee Registration Certificate
- Passport
- LIC
- Any Govt. issued License/Certificate
- Govt. Service/Employment Certificate
- Bank/Post Office Accounts
- Birth Certificate
- Board/University Educational Certificate
- Court Records/Processes.

Further, the following two documents are also accepted as supporting documents if accompanied by any one of the documents listed above:

- Circle Officer/GP Secretary Certificate in respect of married women migrating after marriage (can be of any year before or after 24 March (midnight), 1971).
- Ration Card issued up to the midnight of 24 March, 1971 can be adduced as supporting documents.

List B Documents

If any of the documents of List A is not of the applicant himself/herself but that of an ancestor, namely, father or mother or grandfather or grandmother or great grandfather or great grandmother (and so on) the applicant then have to submit List B documents to establish relationship with such ancestor, i.e., father or mother or grandfather or grandmother or great grandfather or great grandmother etc. whose name appears in List A. Such documents shall have to be legally acceptable documents which clearly proves such relationship. The applicants must produce any one of the following List B documents to establish the linkage:

- Birth Certificate
- Land document
- Board/University Certificate
- Bank/LIC/Post Office records
- Circle Officer/GP Secretary Certificate in case of married women
- Electoral Roll
- Ration Card
- Any other legally acceptable document.

To make the process of NRC update smooth, the Supreme Court in its order dated 21 July, 2015 passed the following directions:

1. We make it clear that complaints with regard to any obstruction in the matter of preparation/update of NRC by any person or authority may first be brought to the notice of the Court appointed Committee and the said Committee, upon due enquiry, will submit necessary report to the Registry of this Court where after the same will be brought to notice of the Bench.
2. We expect all authorities to act faithfully and diligently to carry out their assigned tasks to ensure smooth preparation of NRC and publication thereof within the schedule fixed by us.

The Supreme Court directed on 1 December, 2015 that Assam Government must make all efforts to complete upgrading of draft as well as the final National Register of Citizens (NRC) by 1 March, 2016. The apex court also said that the state government shall not assign any other work to the personnel involved in the preparation of the report till the time the "said mammoth task is completed."[27]

The mammoth exercise of updating the National Register of Citizens (NRC) involved enlisting the names of those persons or their descendants whose names appeared in the 1951 database, or any of the electoral rolls up to 1971. Those who have admissible documents, mentioned earlier, that show their presence in the state on or before the midnight of 24 March, 1971 would also be part of the new data base. The process involved scrutinising 3.30 crore applications and 6.6 crore documents submitted by the people of Assam. Around 48,000 persons—officials and contractual workers were deployed for the exercise. 5.77 lakh documents were sent to states/central agencies for verification. 27.61 lakh hearings were held for special verification of married women who had to migrate from their original place of residence.[28] Field verification involved door-to-door checking of applicants by verification teams in each district. Their findings were recorded in a form called the verification team report. In office verification, supporting documents submitted by applicants were sent to issuing authorities for backend verification. Documents issued by other states were sent to the respective chief secretaries for verification. The combined verification report would have the results of both field and office verifications. The next step was the publication of a draft NRC, followed by the publication of the final NRC.[29]

The first draft of the NRC was released at midnight on 31 December, 2017. Altogether 1.9 crore names out of 3.3 crore applicants were included in the first draft. Names of many MPs, MLAs and known personalities did not find place in the list. Registrar General of India Sailesh said the verification process of the remaining 1.4 crore applicants was still on.[30]

Mamata Bannerjee voiced concern about Bengalis in Assam after their non-inclusion in the first phase of the NRC and even warned BJP-ruled Assam not to use the NRC as a ploy to drive away Bengalis from Assam, in an apparent rerun of the "Bongal khoda" campaign in the 1960s and the1970s. Her protests were matched by institution of several cases by the Guwahati police on the basis of FIRs lodged against her.[31] TMC leaders even protested outside the Parliament House and senior party MP Saugata Roy moved an adjournment motion in the Lok Sabha during the zero hour on 4 January, 2018.[32] Assam CM Sadanand Sonowal, however, assured on 31 December that not a single genuine Indian citizen would be excluded from the final NRC. [33]

On 30 July, 2018, the final draft NRC was published. The RGI adjudged that 40,07,707 lakh people in the state were not Indians and hence, ineligible to be included in the NRC. Altogether, 3.29 crore residents of Assam had applied for inclusion in the NRC. Only 2.89 crore have made it to the draft NRC. The RGI gave one more chance to those who couldn't make it to the NRC to prove their citizenship. They would have to file claims between 30 August and 28 September.[34] About 1.5 lakh people, whose names were part of the draft NRC published in December 2017 had been excluded from the final draft. They would be informed of the reason for their exclusion through a letter of information (LOI). These applicants were excluded for one of three reasons—their names had been erroneously included, they were found to have submitted false claims, or panchayat certificates submitted by them were found invalid. The rest of the excluded persons would have to file fresh applications in a prescribed form with the local registrar of citizens' registration between 7 August and 28 September to know the reasons for exclusion.[35]

Though the publication wasn't accompanied by major turbulence, doubts lingered whether the process was indeed foolproof, or even warranted. The omission of 1.5 lakh names from the 19 million that had made it to the first draft in December 2017 was a cause of worry. There was uproar in Parliament over Assam NRC update on 31 July. The Union home minister assured the Lok Sabha that time would be given to file claims. He said: "I want to clarify that even after the final NRC, every person will get an opportunity to approach the Foreigners Tribunal. This means that even those whose names do not figure in the final NRC will get an opportunity to approach the Tribunal. There is no question of any coercive action against anyone."[36]

Ahead of the publication of the draft final updated NRC, Assam chief minister Sarbananda Sonowal again assured that nobody would be treated as a foreigner till the NRC process was over. Even to those people who are illiterate, his government would provide assistance.[37]

The Supreme Court on 19 September gave nod to filing of claims and objections on inclusion and exclusion of names in the final draft NRC in Assam from 25 September, 2018 for 60 days.[38] Ultimately, it was extended to 31 December by the SC. [39] It's like waiting for a seismic event that has been prophesied. As the New Year approached, Assam braced up for a precipitate moment in its political history; the first draft of the updated NRC was published on 31 December. Out of the 2.89 crore names included in the draft NRC published in July 2018, the names of 1,02,462 persons were included in the additional exclusion list published on 26 June, 2019[40], thus taking the total number of ineligible persons to 41,73,169.

On 23 July, 2019, the Supreme Court extended the deadline for the publication of the final NRC for Assam from 31 July to 31 August, 2019. The Bench, however, did not accept the pleas of the Union and Assam governments for a "sample re-verification" of the names included in and excluded from the draft NRC published on 30 July, 2018.[41] But the re-verification of documents continued till the final publication of the NRC. People were asked to attend the NRC hearing giving them just one or two days and summoned to 500-600 km away from their homes. Members of the CPI(M) staged a demonstration outside the office of the State Coordinator for NRC in Guwahati on 6 August to protest the "sudden" notices served on thousands of people belonging to the minority communities who were asked to go to NRC centres 300-500 km away within 24-36 hours for re-verification of their documents.[42]

A group of 131 academics, intellectual, professionals and civil society leaders in Assam even approached the SC on 6 August for direction to the NRC authority to reschedule the hearing either within the district or within the adjoining districts and provide at least a week's time.[43] People continued to receive notices for re-verification of their documents, even 72 hours before the publication of the final citizens' list. The NRC authority said there was nothing unusual about such notice. "Some people may be summoned on Friday (30 August) too. The process will continue until the deadline fixed by the Supreme Court", a spokesperson said.[44]

The Supreme Court on 19 September, 2018 had rejected the Centre's plea to share the draft data and the confidential reports provided by Hajela, the NRC coordinator, to it in sealed cover.[45] The Court on13 August ordered that data collated through the exercise be treated with Aadhar-like secrecy. Only the Centre, state and the NRC coordinator should have complete access to the data, and nothing other than hard copies of the supplementary list and inclusions should be provided to the district offices concerned.[46] But the parliamentary affairs minister Chandra Mohan Patowary informed the House that the percentage of exclusion in the draft final NRC was considerably less in the border districts of South Samara (7.22%), Dhubri (8.26%) and Karimganj (7.67%) as against the state average of 12.15 per cent while it was 14.31 per cent in tribal-majority Karbi Anglong and 13.25 per cent in Tinsukia district in upper Assam.[47] A petition was filed in the Supreme Court contending that this disclosure in the Assembly had interfered with and obstructed the administration of justice and urging the SC to issue notice to Assam government on NRC disclosure. The Congress in Assam also criticized the disclosure calling it politically motivated.[48] The SC, however, on 8 August brushed aside the criticism and statements made in the Assam Assembly and outside relating to the exercise carried out for the NRC and said it wanted he deadline of 31 August he adhered to.

The final NRC was published on 31 August, 2019, as mandated by the Supreme Court. A statement from the NRC State Coordinator's office said that a total of 3,30,27,661 people had applied for inclusion in the NRC. Of them, 3,11,21,004 have been included in the document and 19,06,657 excluded.[49] 4,44,077 persons did not file claims to the NRC authorities.[50] The whereabouts of these 4.44 lakh people, who did not file claims after their names were dropped from last year's draft NRC, have become a matter of mystery to the authorities in Assam. It is presumed that this group would comprise Indians from other states who migrated to Assam for a livelihood and did not think it necessary to get their names enlisted because they intended to return to their roots some day, illegal migrants who might have decided to lie low after their first attempt to get citizenship recognition failed, and persons who have died in between.[51] Swati Bidhan Baruah, Assam's first transgender judge, however, estimates that nearly two thousand Assamese transgender have been left out of the NRC. Many trans persons whose names did not appear in the first NRC draft did not even file claims, to avoid putting themselves through the hearing process.

In response to a RTI application filed by *The Hindu*, the Office of State Coordination of NRC, Assam informed in November 2021that "1,032 number of cases of DV/DF/PFT/DVD/DFD/PFTD categories have been referred to the concerned Deputy Commissioner to take necessary action as per Clause 4(3) & 4(6) of the Schedule 4(A)4 of Rules of the Citizenship (Registration of Citizens and Issue of National Identity Cards) Rules, 2003."[52]

Since the publication of the complete NRC, the fate of 19,06,657 people excluded from the updated list in Assam continues to hang in the balance. The ongoing COVID-19 crisis and the repeated floods have been blamed for the delay in issuing rejection slips to each of the excluded persons, citing the reasons why they were left out. According to the Centre's Standard Operating Procedure, a rejected person would have 120 days from the date of receiving the rejection slip to approach a Foreigners' Tribunal for judging his citizenship status.

More than 19 lakh applicants who were left out of the final NRC have not been able to file appeals till date as they are yet to get rejection slips from the office of State NRC Coordinator. Meanwhile, the Office of the RGI in the Ministry of Home Affairs, New Delhi in a letter to the Assam Government on 23 March, 2021 has made it clear that all activities for the updation of NRC have to be completed within the approved cost of the scheme within 31 March, 2021. There is no further provision of funds for expenditure made under the scheme beyond 31 March, 2021, the letter said. The RGI has written the letter in response to the Assam Government's letter on 4 March, 2021 proposing additional requirement of Rs. 3.22 crore per month beyond 31 March, 2021 to complete pending work for the NRC update exercise. In the letter, the RGI has mentioned that the Cabinet on Economic Affairs has approved the Revised Cost Estimates of Rs. 1602.66 crore up to 31 December, 2019 for the NRC update scheme with a condition that the cost estimates will not be revised further. Taking strong exception to the "inordinate delay" in completion of the entire exercise, the office of the RGI in a letter suggested to the state government to terminate the services of "surplus staff" and hand over the workload to government staff, besides shifting the NRC office to a government building.

"The process of issuing rejection slips to those excluded from NRC is yet to start. The NRC Coordination Committee in its meeting held on 30.01.2020 had directed that the pending work relating to issue of rejection slips should be completed on a mission mode", the letter said. The letter also highlighted that the NRC State Coordinator in a meeting on 2 July last year had informed that rejection slips would be issued to NRC excludees by the end of December 2020.

"The NRC Coordination Committee has been insisting on, since its meeting held on 30th January, 2020 and 2nd July, 2020, to complete the activities within the limit of approved budget of Rs. 1,602.66 crore only", it stressed. The RGI in its letter has asked the Assam Government to shift the NRC Data Centre to the State IT department at the earliest to save on cost. It has also asked to shift the office of State NRC Coordinator to the State Government building. The letter has also requested the State Government to sort out the issue of keeping or discharging staff associated with the NRC at the earliest.[53]

The exclusion of more than 19 lakh people from the NRC in Assam stripped them not only of their citizenship, but also their bare status as human beings. They are left with no forum whatsoever to even assert their 'right to have rights.' Some stakeholders have suggested that the issue of "illegal migrants" could be kept alive for "yet another election." "The government has hushed up NRC that was once their main issue. The BJP's hidden agenda has been exposed after the exclusion of many Bengali Hindus who were flattered to deceive. The list did not go their way and they want the issue to linger for political mileage", State Congress president Rupen Bora said. "We don't think the Centre will do anything before the Assembly election in 2021", AASU general secretary Lurinjyoti Gogoi said. The BJP, however, put the onus on the Supreme Court where a petition for re-verification of at least 10 per cent of the names in districts where demographic changes have been drastic is still pending for a decision.[54]

Assam government has also no specific timeframe for completion of the entire process as yet. On the other hand, the state government is strongly in favour of re-verification of 20 per cent of the updated NRC from districts bordering Bangladesh and 10 per cent from the remaining districts. Assam's senior cabinet minister Chandra Mohan Patowary made this assertion in the Assam Assembly on 31 August, 2020 in response to a query by Congress MLA Sherman Ali Ahmed.[55] And the most important announcement was made by Hemant Biswa Sarma on 6 November, 2020 when he said that Assam would go for a fresh exercise to update the NRC after the 2021 Assembly election if the Supreme Court gave the nod.[56]

It may be noted that the Registrar General of India has not as yet issued a notification on Assam's NRC to make it a legal document. But that has not stopped a Foreigners' Tribunal from recording it as the 'final NRC' because on the official website of NRC Assam the NRC published on 31 August, 2019 has been referred and mentioned as Final NRC.[57]

The non-publication of the final NRC by the RGI has, however, led to Aadhar uncertainty for 27,43,396 people in Assam. The biometrics of these people were collected during the claims and objections phase of the NRC exercise prior to the publication of the complete draft on 31 August, 2019. They include the 19,06,657 people left out of the complete draft. The Aadhar enrolment of these people in Assam has been shrouded in uncertainty because of the delay in completing the process of the NRC. Assam's Minister for General Administration informed the Assam Assembly on 13 July, 2021 that the onus was on the Centre to decide whether or not these 27,43,395 people would be issued Aadhar cards. The biometrics of these people were frozen after the publication of the NRC. The Centre had earlier been asked to unfreeze the biometrics, but without any result.[58]

The Assam government has decided to approach the Supreme Court for directing the Centre to provide Aadhar cards to 19.06 lakh people left out of the updated NRC published in 2019. The lack of Aadhar cards has deprived these people of government schemes such as free rice or housing. The Assam government had earlier sought an amendment to the standard operating procedure (SOP) of the NRC to enable left-out people to get Aadhar cards.[59]Another petition has been filed in the Supreme Court seeking direction to issue Aadhar Cards to nearly 27 lakh people who have been included in the state's supplementary list of NRC and the Supreme Court on 11 April, 2022 sought the response of the Centre, Assam and the UIDAI on this petition.[60]

IV

There was widespread anger and a sense of betrayal among political parties and the people as the final NRC excluded many Indian citizens. Many Hindu Bengalee families who are residing in Assam for generations found their names in the NRC-excluded lists. The family members of freedom fighters and even those serving or served in the Armed Forces or para-military forces like the CRPF have met with the same result. They are now in a quandary as to how to wriggle out of the predicament they find themselves in. It is alleged[61] that vested interests are out to prove that the descendants of the Muslims from erstwhile East Bengal who had settled in Assam in early 20th century today are illegal immigrants. The position was described in a nutshell in an editorial in *The Hindu* thus:

> In the run-up to the final publication, case after case has emerged of persons wrongfully left out of the list. The process has left no group out of its sweep, be it Marwaris or Biharis from elsewhere in the country, people tracing their antecedents to other North-eastern states, people of Nepali origin, and caste Hindu Assamese. The prime targets of this exercise, however, are Hindu Bengalis and Bengali-origin Muslims of Assam.[62]

Kargil war veteran and retired army officer Mohammad Sanaullah who spent a few days in detention in May after being declared a foreigner by a tribunal, was among those excluded from the updated list. AIUDF MLA Ananta Kumar Malo could not make it to the final NRC. His party colleague Ataur Rahaman Mazarbhuyan, a former MLA, and his son and daughter did not figure in the final list.[63] The names of AIUDF leader Abdul Samad Choudhury, his two brothers and a sister, and of Zamal Husain, who recently retired from the Post and Telegraph Department are in the exclusion lists.[64]

Nephew of the former President of India Fakhruddin Ali Ahmed was excluded.[65] The name of the wife of Silchar's BJP MLA, Dilip Kumar Pal did not find place in the final NRC.[66] While names of 6 persons of a joint family of 15 were included in the final NRC, the rest 9 were in the exclusion list.[67] Sanjib Upadhyaya, a resident of Sonitpur district, was declared an Indian citizen by an FT this year. But his name has again been excluded from the final NRC.[68]

Several villagers from Sontoli village in Lower Assam's Kamrup district expressed anger after being left out of the final NRC. Many people in Dibrugarh were dissatisfied with the NRC process because several of them did not make it to the final list.[69]

The exclusion of the names of relatives of Baijayanti Devi, who had died during the Assam Agitation in 1979, and Sahitya Akademi award winner Durga Khatiwada, from the NRC Draft Exclusion list released on 26 June, 2019 has brought the focus back on Gorkhas and the NRC being updated in Assam. Raju Bista, the Darjeeling MP from the BJP, issued a statement on 29 June, 2019, suggesting that the exclusion of the relatives of these two luminaries from Assam had rattled the party leaders in the hills.[70]

According to the president of the Assam state committee of the Bharatiya Gorkha Parisangha, an apolitical association of the Gorkhas, around a lakh Assam Gorkhas have been excluded from the final NRC.[71] Binay Tamang of the Tamang faction of the Gorkha Janmukti Morcha informed on18 September that a 15-member delegation visited six districts of Assam for four days from 13 September and met the affected families. The affected families were told that the GJM would fight for them in the Supreme Court and the Foreigners Tribunals without charging any money. Their main demand would be inclusion of the Gorkhas in the Protected List and making them Original inhabitants.[72]

Bista along with Darjeeling MLA Neeraj Zimba met Assam chief minister on 11 September and discussed the exclusion of Gorkhas from the final NRC and requested him to declare the Gorkhas as Original Inhabitants of Assam.[73] The BGP announced on 22 September, 2019 that "the Gorkhas of Assam will not go to the FTs to prove their citizenship. Trial in an FT is an insult to a Gorkha because we are Indians", BGP national president Sukhman Moktan said.[74] The All Assam Gorkha Students Union's Kamrup district unit protested in front of the Boko circle office in lower Assam's Kamrup district on 1 October against the exclusion of the Gorkhas from the final NRC. Members of the Assam Gorkha Sanmilan, Kamrup Zila Kalyan Samittee, Assam Nepali Sahitya Sabha and the Gorkha Mahila Sanmilan Samittee also participated in the protest.[75]

Most of the political parties were unhappy with the final NRC, though for different reasons. The Congress, Trinamool Congress and the CPIM expressed their concern over exclusion of so many people from the state NRC and said steps should be taken to ensure that no Indian citizen was left out.[76] Former CM Tarun Gogoi accused the ruling BJP of failing to ensure a free and fair NRC even with the entire administrative machinery at its disposal. "The NRC has been published with names of genuine Indian citizens left out and foreigners included", he told the reporters.[77] The AASU, too, was not happy with the NRC. It said the final NRC contained flaws and they would appeal to the Supreme Court to remove all the faults and discrepancies in this NRC.[78] Curiously enough, the AASU only three days earlier, on 28 August, 2019 had said that it had full faith in the updation process of the NRC and claimed that the apprehensions expressed by various political parties was a ploy to confuse people as they wanted to protect their vote-banks.[79] BJP ally Asom Gana Parishad said the number of exclusions appears to be "ridiculously small."[80] Similarly, the Muslim Kalyan Parishad and Asom Garia-Yuba Chhatra Parishad claimed that the final NRC was not acceptable to them as it contained huge anomalies. However, the All India United Democratic Front, Communist Party of India and few others came out with supporting statements for the Assam NRC arguing that it was an outcome of intensive labour and could be considered a first step to solve the burning issue.

The Akhil Bharatiya Vidyarthi Parishad, the student wing of the BJP, on 1 September, 2019 demanded "100 per cent re-verification" of all entries of the NRC; otherwise Assam would soon become an 'Islamic state' if the erroneous list was not rectified.[81] The All Assam Minority Students Union threatened to launch an "intense agitation" if any genuine Indian citizen was excluded and a "single foreigner" included in the NRC.[82]

Publication of the NRC has left the ruling BJP disappointed. It is determined to ensure its political plank retains its credibility. The dissatisfied believe the NRC, billed as the country's most complex and most controversial head count, has legalised the existing nature of Assam's demography, the reason why the state suffered political and ethnic flare-ups.

The state BJP was also critical of the NRC and blamed the state coordinator for carrying out the revision based on his own opinion and those of two or three organisations since the SC asked CM Sarbananda Sonowal not to interfere in the process.[83] They thought more members of the minority community would be detected as illegal immigrants but it did not happen. Actually, the mass migration of Muslims from East Bengal to Assam was more or less over before independence, as discussed in the previous chapter. Constitutionally and legally they are Indian nationals. The Muslims who immigrated after independence, especially after the emergence of Bangladesh as a separate nation did not remain in Assam only but dispersed themselves to other states and cities as well not only within India but beyond it. As a matter of fact, only a minuscule portion of them chose to settle down in Assam. This explains why the number of Bengali-Muslims in the NRC-reject list was much less than the Bengali-Hindus. Another section was critical for exclusion of genuine Indian citizens from the list. Himant Biswa Sarma alleged that names of many persons who came before 1971 had been excluded from the list because the NRC authority refused to accept the Refugee Registration Certificates as valid documents. [84] Actually, many NRC applicants in Assam who had submitted refugee registration certificate to back their residency claims were in a fix after the authorities rejected 60 out of every 100 such documents on ground of unavailability of corresponding records with the government to corroborate their authenticity. Refugee registration certificates were mainly submitted by descents of refugees belonging to Bengali, Koch, Garo, Hajong and Dalu communities that are now spread across the state. According to estimates, 5 lakh Hindu refugees fleeing East Pakistan entered Assam till the 1960s, including those who arrived immediately after Partition in 1947. [85] The NRC authority has found that around two lakh of six crucial documents—refugee registration certificate, citizenship certificate, government employment certificate, land and tenancy record, birth certificate and certified copies of pre-1971 electoral rolls from Tripura—out of one crore were forged. This could be detected because the back-end sources with supporting papers of these six documents were available with authorities who originally issued them.[86]

Himant Biswa Sarma told the channel News Live on 2 September, 2019: "Those who are genuine Indians and whose names are not in the final NRC should not be afraid. And foreigners who got themselves included in the final NRC should not celebrate…because nothing is final till Prime Minister Narendra Modi and Union home minister Amit Shah are there." He even appealed to the AASU and the APW to join hands with the government to appeal to the Supreme Court not to accept the final NRC.[87]

That the NRC was not going the way they thought of was realised by the BJP quite early. That is the reason why on 16 July, 2019, the Centre and the State of Assam made an urgent mention before the Chief Justice of India for an extension of deadline for final publication of the

NRC for the state from 31 July, 2019 to a "future date" to conduct a 20 per cent sample re-verification in districts bordering Bangladesh and a 10 per cent sample re-verification in the remaining districts of Assam of names included in the draft NRC published on 30 July, 2018. The Union Ministry of Home Affairs informed the court that the NRC exercise had created apprehensions in the minds of the citizens and could very well impact social harmony, and law and order in the State. "It is pertinent that the exercise of sample re-verification follow before the publication of the final list", the application said.[88]

The 1951 NRC was based on that year's census. The difference between the 1951 NRC and its updation lies in the layers of verification that went into producing the Updated NRC. The exacting procedures were expected to bring a more lasting and credible set of data than what had been thrown up by the more error-prone methods in use till now. But the reverse had taken place. The petition to the SC was a clear admission by Assam's BJP government that after years of effort, monitored by SC, the whole exercise had been a mess, causing distress to lakhs of people. The list was flawed and original inhabitants were being disenfranchised while as the minister of state for home affairs Nityanand Rai informed the Rajya Sabha twenty-five lakh petitioners had complained to the President regarding inclusion of many undeserving names in the NRC.[89] APW filed a fresh affidavit in the Supreme Court on 18 February, 2020 seeking "100 per cent re-verification" of the final rolls claiming that Assam's updated NRC contained the names of almost 80 lakh foreigners, including arrested "jihadist". While making a case for a comprehensive NRC review, APW has suggested the process be started only after the Constitution Bench hearing two related cases—on cut-off date and regarding sections 3 and 6 of the Citizenship Act, 1955—gives the ruling.[90]

Prateek Hajela, the State Coordinator, was criticized by the state government, the ruling BJP, and other organsiations for doing things on his own, especially after the apex court rejected Assam's demand for re-verification of 20 per cent applicants in the borders and 10 per cent elsewhere.[91] In response to a memorandum by a citizens' group called Sachetan Nagarik Mancha, alleging "wrongful exclusion and inclusions" in the two earlier draft NRCs and doubting if the final NRC would be any different, Hajela responded:

> "Considering the fact that immigration from specified territory (Bangladesh) has been happening for around a century now, it is not known as to how you could assume that post-1971 illegal migrants would be confined only to the border districts.

> "Given your interest in the matter, you may also try to find out from the authorities concerned the figure of illegal migrant declared by the various tribunals for border districts. You have further alleged that names of indigenous people are excluded from the NRC. On this account also, you have not pointed out a single such instance to any of the NRC authorities so far", he said.

Hajela also explained why the system of verifying the citizenship and residency credentials based on legacy data cannot be faulted. "This scale of verification of document through comparison with the backend is definitely a very scientific system of verification. The second system is the family tree-based verification, which involves verification for consistency of all persons claiming to be descendants of the same ancestor. Such a system on this scale has been put in place for the first time in the entire country. This system would certainly qualify to be one of the most scientific methods of verification." Copies of the response were sent to the Centre and the state government.[92]

Complaints were lodged at the police stations against Prateek Hajela, the State Coordinator, for willful negligence in the preparation of the NRC. All Assam Goriya-Moriya Yuva Chatra Parishad (AAGMYCP), an indigenous Muslim students' organization lodged a complaint at Guwahati's Latasil police station on 3 September against the NRC state coordinator for deliberate omission of the names of many indigenous people in the final list.

Chandan Mazumdar, whose name does not figure in the final NRC, lodged a complaint at Dibrugarh police station on 4 September against the NRC state coordinator on charges of criminal conspiracy for deliberate omission of his name in the NRC. Majumdar is a member of the All India Legal Aid Foundation.

Assam Public Works (APW), an NGO and the original petitioner in the SC which led to the updation of the NRC, lodged an FIR at Guwahati's Geetanagar police station on 5 September, 2019 against three Bangladeshi nationals whose names figure in the NRC even though they were declared as foreigners and against the NRC authorities of Morigaon district, allegedly responsible for inclusion of their names in the NRC.[93] Peeved by the institution of cases against him and criticism of the state government and the ruling BJP party for the preparation of the NRC which is widely perceived as faulty, Hajela, an Assam-Meghalaya cadre IAS officer approached the Supreme Court for transfer to Madhya Pradesh, his home state, and the Supreme Court on 18 October, 2019 transferred him accordingly.[94] The ministry of personnel, public grievances and pension on 1 November approved Hajela's deputation to Madhya Pradesh for the "maximum period of three years."[95]

Hajela's association with NRC for all practical purposes thus ended but an editorial in *The Times of India* made it known that Hajela had been given mission impossible in the first place. Instead of scapegoating him, it needed to be understood that NRC was fundamentally flawed. "In essence one had to prove one's citizenship based on documentation. Insisting on rigorous documentation in a county where records are scanty is problematic. Even for people with documents, the NRC exercise was not easy", it adds.[96]

Mander also pointed out that the burden of proof (of citizenship) was shifted to the residents to prove that they were citizens, based on documents such as those linked to birth, schooling and land ownership which impoverished and unlettered rural residents anywhere would find hard to muster. Even when residents succeeded in producing these documents, they were often rejected for small discrepancies, such as in the English-language spelling of Bengali names or in the age even though it is well-known that most rural people do not know the dates of birth. Many of them do not have land records.[97]

BJP spokesman Rupam Goswami, however, demanded of the state government not to release Hajela till he furnished proper account of Rs. 1,600 crore received from the Centre for the NRC project.[98] Assam's finance minister Himant Biswa Sarma disclosed on 28 November, 2019 that the CAG has reported a "huge financial scam" during the NRC update exercise. Assam Public Works (APW), the principal petitioner in the Supreme Court, lodged a complaint with the CBI's anti-corruption branch on 28 November alleging a "huge amount of corruption/misappropriation of government money" in the NRC exercise.[99]

It may be noted that the BJP legislators had raised question of the need of re-verification of the NRC data process in the Assembly on 1 August, 2019.[100] The fact that enough members of the minority community had not been found to be illegal entrants seemed to be annoying the BJP. That might be one of the reasons why the BJP governments at the Centre and the state had been insisting on re-evaluation of 20 per cent of the data in the border districts and 10 per cent in the interior.[101] Since the SC did not accept the thesis of wrongful exclusion/inclusion, the Assam chief minister Sarbananda Sonowal already hinted on 19 August, 2019 that the Centre could consider corrective measures including legislation, to set right wrongful inclusions and exclusions only after the NRC was published as mandated by the Supreme Court.[102] Actually, the low percentage of exclusion in the Bengali-speaking Muslim migrant majority districts, particularly those bordering Bangladesh, has given rise to a belief among those calling the process "flawed" that most illegal migrants have made it into the NRC. Himant Biswa Sarma again said on 22 December, 2019 that the state government would not accept the present NRC under any circumstances. "If the Supreme Court allows 20 per cent re-verification in the border districts and there is no mistake in the re-verification, we will accept it. If there are numerous mistakes again in the re-verification, we may approach the Supreme Court for complete review. We are sure lots of mistakes will be found out in the re-verification process", he said in a press briefing.[103] State NRC coordinator's actions, mentioned earlier, give official backing to this claim of the Assam minister.

At a three-day meeting (7-9 September, 2019) of over 200 delegates of 25 RSS affiliates held at Pushkar concerns were raised on several genuine citizens being left out of the NRC, especially those who settled in Assam from neighbouring states. Leaders also expressed concerns that majority of the 1.9 million people excluded are Hindus. BJP working president J.P. Nadda, general secretary (organisation) B.L.Santosh and general secretary Ram Madhav were also in attendance.[104] RSS joint general secretary Dattatreya Hosabale urged the government to remove those before moving forward. "The final list of the NRC is only a list. It's not law...There are some errors and mistakes in it and so the government should remove those and then move forward", said Hosabale.[105] Speaking at a closed door coordination meeting at Uluberia in Howrah on 22 September, 2019, Sangh Sarsanghachalak Mohan Bhagwat told the representatives of 37 allied organisations that no Hindu would be made to leave the country even if their names do not figure in the NRC.[106] Mohan Bhagwat in a closed door meeting with Assam chief minister at Silchar on 28 September had asked him to ensure that non-Muslims who had fled religious persecution in Bangladesh and Pakistan on or before 31 December, 2014, were exempted from the provisions of the Foreigners' Act in accordance with a home ministry notification issued on 7 September, 2015.[107]

Leaders of the Asom Nagarik Samaj (ANS) made up of retired government officials, social entrepreneurs and journalists also underlined the need to consider the NRC as the primary document for citizenship in Assam.[108]

"I want to make it clear that India will not allow a single *ghuspathiya* (infiltrator) to live here. This is our resolution", Amit Shah told the 68th plenary of the North Eastern Council (NEC) on 8 September, 2019 at Guwahati. Later, a delegation of the BJP Assam unit's president,

Ranjeet Kumar Dass, chief minister Sarbananda Sonowal and North East Democratic Alliance (NEDA) convener Himant Biswa Sarma met Amit Shah for about half an hour and submitted memorandum to him.[109] The state BJP unit's dissatisfaction over exclusion of a large number of serving and retired soldiers, freedom fighters and people from different walks of life and descendants of many refugees, who had settled in Assam from the erstwhile East Pakistan before 1971was apprised through a memorandum to the Home Minister.[110]

The complete NRC list of both included and excluded persons was released on 14 September, 2019. The list which was full of mistakes could be viewed on line. Since it was published in Assamese language, plenty of mistakes cropped up due to phonological dissimilarities between the Bengali and Assamese languages. Moreover, the earlier mistakes were not rectified and new mistakes surfaced. The state BJP demanded re-verification of the list.[111]

The BJP is aware that a "flawed" list that apparently underplays the number of illegals (meaning Bangladeshi Muslim illegal immigrants) and, worse, excludes genuine citizens, will seriously damage its campaign against illegals. After all, the NRC and illegal immigrant issue forms part of the BJP's national security plank and figured in the party's manifesto since 1996. RSS, BJP and various Sangh Parivar affiliates have taken up cudgels on behalf of around 19 lakh people left out of NRC. All Assam Bengali Hindu Association, a Silchar-based organisation had threatened on 26 August, 2019 extreme action if a single Hindu Bengali was left out of the list.[112] Citizens' Rights Protection Co-ordination Committee (CRPCC), a Barak valley-based social organisation, on 27 August said it was afraid that lakhs of people would be excluded from NRC, with linguistic minorities being the worst sufferers.[113] Apprehending a breakdown of law and order situation, All Assam Bengali Youth Students Federation urged the state and the Centre on 27 August not to publish the NRC. [114] But no such breakdown of law and order situation in Assam took place, as apprehended.

The Election Commission has decided that those left out of the NRC but figuring in the electoral rolls can continue to vote until they are declared 'foreigners' after exhausting all remedies available under law.[115] The Election Commission is set to revisit its 1997 order on Assam 'doubtful' voters after taking into account the discussion arising from NRC and past orders of the Guwahati High Court and the Supreme Court on 'D' voters.[116] As per the latest official statistics disclosed in September 2017, there are 1,25,155 D-voters in Assam, a majority of whom are Muslims, and some are Hindu Bengalis and Koch Rajbongshis. Individuals are arbitrarily marked as doubtful without any systematic enquiry. The list is full of mistakes, anomalies and discrepancies [117] like that of the NRC. The Election authorities on 22 December, 2020 said that NRC rejects whose cases were not sub judice in the foreigners' tribunals prior to publication of the final citizenship register on 31 August, 2019 and who are free from the 'D' voters' tag will be able to vote in the 2021 Assembly polls.[118]

Moreover, as an editorial in *The Times of India* put it, "the NRC process has vested enormous power in petty bureaucracy and quasi-judicial bodies called Foreigner Tribunals. Corruption and abuse of power are inevitable."[119] It is no wonder that several NRC officials have been arrested on charges of taking bribes to sneak in foreigners as citizens, while genuine Indians have been left out.[120] There are even allegations of trade in NRC legacy data. The Sachetan Nagarik Manch, Asom (SNM), an Assam-based NGO in a memorandum to the Union home minister has claimed that legacy data pertaining to more than 3,000 persons were traded, thus helping undocumented migrants from Bangladesh to be included in the NRC and demanded a CBI enquiry.[121]

The modalities of NRC updation kept changing from proof about ancestor's belonging to Assam pre-1971 to something called "family tree" to establish full picture and spread of family in terms of an "original forefather" to a post-facto rejection of panchayat documents. Issues like determination of "original inhabitants"—a category that created all the debates and possibility of exclusion from being an equal citizen—is arbitrarily invoked in the NRC modalities in clear violation of the tenet of equal citizenship as enshrined in the Constitution.

Rules framed under section 4A of the Citizenship Registration Rules, 2003 mentioned about "original inhabitants" of Assam (under clause 3.3) which shall be determined by the field-level officers. That has opened up a Pandora's Box, as such a category is only special to Assam and has no reference whatsoever in the provisions of the Citizenship Act,1955 meant for the country as a whole. The state NRC coordinator in a notification had clarified that neither in the draft NRC nor in the final NRC there would be no mention of Original Inhabitant beside any name. But it had been pointed out by noted lawyers and social workers that the proforma in which an officer shall verify the credential of an applicant includes a column for determination of OI. Therefore, even if the NRC does not include any categorization of citizens, there would be datasheets mentioning the status of a person as an OI or non-OI, which can be later invoked for discriminating between citizens. The real issue is the lack of transparency and arbitrary criteria invoked for such a determination by a field-level officer in the absence of any clearly-defined constitutional norms about determining original inhabitants of any state within the Union of India. Determination of OI as the most important criterion (although that is implied) in the preparation of the NRC in Assam alters the very one accepted in the Constitution, which is by birth and naturalisation.[122]

Moreover, in the three Barrack Valley districts of Assam, the NRC authorities did not identify anyone as "original inhabitant" under sub-clause 3(3) of Rule 4A of the Citizenship Rules of 2003. This has resulted in a strange demand for reservation of land rights and representation rights only for "original inhabitants" and not "non-original inhabitants." This directly violates the Constitution as there is no such classificatory definition of who is "original" and who is "non-original" in India. The NRC has put forth this arbitrary distinction due to its discriminatory procedures. Without defining OI, it is stated that OI category people would not have to give any documentation in support of their antecedents, while non-OI people will have to undertake 360 degrees verification. Going by this, only people belonging to some non-descript non-original category are subjected to a procedure of proving citizenship by bloodline. This is happening only in the case of Assam and in complete violation of the Representation of Peoples' Act, 1950 and many other Acts such as the Expulsion of Immigrants Act, 1950.[123]

The NRC authority of Assam has imported terms like "legacy data" and "family tree". The former was published by the NRC authority of Assam allotting code numbers to all the names included in the 1951 Census as well as in electoral rolls up to 1971. The applicants have to refer to such names to establish their antecedents. The matter, however, is more complex than one thinks. Many electoral rolls since 1952 are not available, as undivided Assam, prior to 1971 included the areas now known as Meghalaya, and Mizoram and their electoral rolls were not readily available. Indeed the 1951 Census was so incomplete that many districts and places do not find mention therein. Some places do not exist anymore.

The insertion of legacy in the NRC in Assam has shown how citizenship has become a condition of constitutive belonging. Ranabir Samaddar has seen this constitutive power of citizenship unfold in two ways: as a procedure to arrest the power of the family through the construction of a legal myth called the legacy, and the pruning of the power of the individual to claim citizenship as a *person*. Samaddar calls this a "technical power" that drives a wedge in the "broad continuum of the family reaching up to the state."[124]

Anupama Ray argues that "following this argument, it is possible to see both these practies working through contradictory strands of logic—the substitution of the power of the family to absorb the "awkward" citizen to make her accessible to the State and, on the other hand, reinstalling the order of the State through the power of legacy traced through the family tree verifiable by public evidence. The expulsion of the individual in the new identification regime reinforces the power of the State through its capacity to unsettle the family by exercising its power to summon individual members as nodes that make the family suspect."[125]

As far as the "family tree" is concerned, the NRC authorities have devised such a concept to weed out fake legacy claims in cases where family-wise unrelated people referred to the legacy of the same ancestors. The procedure assumes that the validity of the individual's claim to citizenship lies to generations of his/her belonging to the same line of descent from a common ancestor. But the problem is that families get dispersed, members of the same family get separated and live apart in different corners and hence all of them have to be forced to accept each other as members of the same family. If the Citizenship Act, 1955 has stated such a procedure, it could have been deployed in the whole country and then probably the Assam-specific application of such an invented procedure could have had a reasonable legitimacy.

The Gauhati High Court has come to the aid of a person who was declared a foreign by the FT-III of Western Assam's Barpeta because of his failure to establish linkage with all relatives in the pre-1971 voters' lists. Justice N. Kotiswar Singh, while setting aside the FT's above order, observed that the petitioner's claim would have strengthened had he disclosed the family tree in more detail, "...but failure to disclose the names of all the members of the family cannot weaken his case and render his evidence unreliable, nor reduce the credibility of his evidence, when there are other corroborating evidences", the court's order on 30 March, 2021 said.[126] So reliance on the family tree as the only evidence to prove one's nationality is no longer valid, if there are other corroborative evidences in support of one's Indian nationality.

A day after it emerged that Assam's updated citizenship data had vanished from the website, the NRC coordinator's office on12 February, 2020 filed an FIR against a former official for allegedly not 'surrendering' the central data process password in her custody before quitting the job after her ex-boss Prateek Hajela's transfer. In another FIR filed with the CID, the NGO Assam Public Works accused the former NRC coordinator Prateek Hajela of 'cyber crime' during the six-year NRC exercise conducted under his supervision by tempering with valuable public records.[127]

Hitesh Dev Sarma, the new state coordinator for the NRC exercise in Assam, has raised doubts about the quality of screening done so far on the basis of a list of allegedly "ineligible person" who have made it to the citizenship rolls. In a circular issued on 19 February, 2020, he said he had been informed that people declared as foreigners by tribunals and doubtful voters identified by Election Commission have found their way into the NRC. He has asked deputy commissioners and district registrars of citizen registration to share the details of such persons.[128]

Hitesh Dev Sarma, in a letter to the Deputy Commissioner and District Registrar of Citizen Registration on 13 October, 2020 said some names of ineligible people belonging to the "categories of DF (declared foreigner)/ DV (doubtful voter)/PFT (pending in Foreigners' Tribunal) along with their descendants have found entry to the NRC." He pointed out that the local registrars of citizen registration had prepared and published the supplementary list of names after disposal of claims and objections while the "Registrar General of India is yet to publish the final NRC as per Clause 7 of the Schedule of the Citizenship (Registration of Citizens and Issue of National Identity Cards) Rules, 2003".

Actually, the State NRC Coordinator has asked for in a round about way to start the process of re-verification of the NRC list only for the purpose of deletion of names, so long demanded by the BJP, AGP and the AASU and also the state government, without, however, mentioning the word "re-verification" in his letter, because that would have meant inclusion of names as well. Moreover, the question of "re-verification" of the NRC list is now in the judicial domain. This letter of the Coordinator may put some of the DCs and DRCRs in quandary as the state government is known to have been unkind to officials who have failed to match the expectation of the government in terms of the number of "foreigners" bagged by them when entrusted the job under a different pretext.

Assam NRC Coordinator submitted before the Gauhati High Court that the published list of Indian citizens living in the state contained the names of over 4,000 ineligible people and indicated that the number of such "ineligible" people could be as high as 2.77 lakh.[129]

He also submitted before the High Court in an affidavit that the computer software used in the family tree verification process for updating the list of Indian citizens in the state was designed to help data entry operators with "doubtful integrity" to include names of large number of ineligible persons in the list. He submitted that to evaluate the precise effect of absence of quality checks, a sample check was done in three NRC Seva Kendras and after checking data of 2,346 Legacy Data Code, it was found that names of 943 people were entered into the draft NRC through wrong updating of data. He added that the error will remain unless there is a thorough re-verification of the process.[130] In other words, Hitesh Dev Sarma, the state NRC Coordinator pleaded for re-verification of the entire NRC data process, which was demanded by the state government and the state parties including the BJP so long.

In consonance with his avowed stand on the NRC, the state coordinator Hitesh Dev Sarma moved the Supreme Court on 8 May, 2021 for re-verification of the NRC. "The present draft and supplementary list for inclusion and exclusion of NRC that has been published is not free from errors. Thus, the draft NRC needs to be revisited by ordering a comprehensive and time-bound re-verification of the same", his application stated. Urging the top court that re-verification be done under the supervision of a monitoring committee in respective districts, Sarma suggested that the committee may be represented by the district judge, district magistrate and the district police superintendent.

Sarma's demand not only aligns with the BJP-led state government, but even goes further. Assam government has also no specific timeframe for completion of the entire process as yet. On the other hand, the state government was strongly in favour of re-verification of 20 per cent of the updated NRC from districts bordering Bangladesh and 10 per cent from the remaining districts. Assam's senior cabinet minister Chandra Mohan Patowary made this assertion in the Assam Assembly on 31 August, 2020 in response to a query by Congress MLA Sherman Ali Ahmed.[131] And the most important announcement was made by Hemant Biswa Sarma on 6 November, 2020 when he said that Assam would go for a fresh exercise to update the NRC after the 2021 Assembly election if the Supreme Court gave the nod.[132] Only on 6 May, 2021, the chief minister of Assam Himant Biswa Sarma had said that in border districts "we would want a re-verification of 20 per cent names included, and in other districts, that of 10 per cent names."

The Assam NRC Coordinator who had questioned the accuracy and validity of the NRC data from day one lodged an FIR on 19 May, 2022 with the Assam CID charging former state coordinator of NRC Pratek Hajela with 'antinational act' for facilitating entry of names of ineligible persons as Indian nationals in the document.[133] It may be recalled that the Assam police had in September, 2019 registered two cases against him and other unidentified officials for alleged discrepancies in the complete draft published less than a month before. A businessman in eastern Assam's Dibrugarh and an indigenous Assamese Muslim students' organization (All Assam Goriya-Moriya Yuva Chatra Parishad) in Guwahati had filed those cases against him.[134]

Since the entire exercise was monitored by the Supreme Court, it was assumed that the NRC data was a reasonably correct document and that it had its *bona fides* beyond all doubt. Now that the very correctness of the NRC data has been questioned by the present State NRC Coordinator, the Coordination Committee Against Citizenship Amendment Act, a civil society group opposed to the CAA has written to the CJI of the Supreme N.V. Ramana on 24 May, 2022 asking whether the incumbent NRC Assam coordinator Hitesh Dev Sarma had the Supreme Court's permission to question the accuracy of the register and file a criminal case against his predecessor Pratik Hajela.[135] Four Left parties—CPI, CPI(M), CPI(ML) and the RCPI—have also criticized Sarma for his "desperate bid to sabotage the NRC" and pave the way for reverification of the citizens' list as demanded by the BJP and a few other organisations.[136]

Expressing worries over a police complaint lodged against the former Assam NRC Coordinator Prateek Hajela for deceitfully including names of suspected individuals in the NRC with software tempering, Patriotic People's Front Assam (PPFA), in a statement, urged both the governments in New Delhi and Dispur to support a complete re-verification of NRC with 1951 as the cut-off date.[137] The APW has demanded 1951 as the cut-off year, as applicable in the rest of India. The All Assam Tribal Sangha has questioned the existence of a separate cut-off date for Assam. A forum of citizens in North-east India came out with a statement that Assam cannot have a different year to identify illegal migrants from that of the national one. As Assam has to take the burden of more migrants, the forum insisted that the original inhabitants must be protected under legal provisions.[138]

Hitesh Dev Sarma pleads for a re-verification of the entire NRC, not 20 per cent or 10 per cent of the names. The BJP's manifesto for the state assembly elections in April 2021 had stated they would initiate the "process of the correction and reconciliation of entries under the Supreme Court mandated NRC in a structured manner to protect genuine Indian citizens and exclude all illegal immigrants."[139]

The ball is now in the court of the Supreme Court. Will it accept the plea of the State Coordinator for a total re-verification of the entire process of inclusion and exclusion and order for a comprehensive and time-bound re-verification under the supervision of a monitoring committee? Will it order the publication in Bengalee language of the NRC in the Bengali-dominated areas where it was made in Assamiya language leading to serious discrepancies in the names due to phonological dissimilarities? After all, the purpose should be to make the NRC as much error-free and fool-proof as possible.

However, the validity of Assam NRC hinges on the constitutionality of section 6A of the Citizenship Act which was incorporated to give legal sanction to the Assam Accord (Annexure A). Way back in 2014, the constitutionality of section 6A of the Citizenship Act was examined by the Supreme Court bench of Justice Ranjan Gogoi and Justice Rohington Fali Nariman in Writ Petition (Civil) No. 562 of 2012 Assam Sanmilita Mahasangha & Ors, v. Union of India & Ors. The said bench in their orders gave reasons why the bench passed an order for the implementation of the NRC in Assam in the said judgment delivered on 17 December, 2014.

Whether a state-specific provision can be incorporated in the Citizenship Act was challenged in the Supreme Court. The Supreme Court has not given its verdict on that petition as yet. If the court decides that Section 6A is unconstitutional, the entire exercise for the updation of the NRC in Assam will be null and void. It will mean five years of labour by 50,000 government officials and 7,000 data entry operators and an expenditure of more than Rs. 1,220 crore (or Rs. 1,600 crore?) will go down the river Brahmaputra. It will also mean the end of the Assam Accord. Even if legal impediments could be overcome and the NRC lists are made error-free, a problem will still remain, that is what to do with the NRC-rejects. A sizeable portion of them would get Indian citizenship under the CAA 2019. So the fruits of NRC will not be enjoyed by its protagonists. Is there any way out?

V

From the earliest times, India has received successive waves of foreign peoples with diverse languages, cultures, and racial affiliations. In the Neolithic Age, we find the Neolithic types of East India similar to those of South-East Asia and Southern China—indicating a cultural wave reaching India from that direction. The discovery of several archeological sites in different parts of North-east India has yielded cultural materials of the prehistoric period. The Austric people who were known in ancient Sanskrit as Nisadas entered India from the west and spread all over India. The Mongoloid peoples came from the east and settled mostly in the Himalayan sub-tracts and eastern India. There are strong grounds for believing that the Dravidians came to India from the east Mediterranean region long before the Aryans and particularly Dravidianised the whole of peninsular India. The Vedic Aryans poured into India from the north-west bringing with them an altogether new culture. "By the fourth century before Christ", observes Debala Mitra, "the creation of the 'Indian Man' and the main fabric of Indian civilization is almost accomplished. Behind the creation lies the fusion of four principal language-culture groups (loosely called 'races') in blood, speech, and culture. They are the Austric or Austro-Asiatic (Nisadas), the Mongoloid or Sino-Tibetan (Kiratas), the Dravidian (Dravidas) and the Aryans (Aryas)."[140]

Of them, only the Mongoloid peoples emigrated from the east and the other groups came from the west. It seems likely that from at least the beginning of the first millennium B.C., the Kiratas infiltrating themselves from the east through Assam, occupied the southern slopes of the Himalayas as far west as the Punjab, and gradually spread to the plains of North Bihar and North Bengal and also to East Bengal and Assam.[141]

Ethnic intrusions, however, continued unabated, and the country lay exposed to the successive invasions, and infiltrations, one after the other. From a historical point of view, North-East India which is the sentinel of the Indian continent, seems to have been intended by nature to be the meeting place of various ethnic and linguistic groups, i.e., Austric, Indo-Mongoloid, Tibeto-Burman and Aryan, who entered into the area during different historic and pre-historic periods from all directions. The ethnic history of the region is extremely complicated and the population of the North-East is characterized by an enormous diversity, which this region acquired along with the inflow of varied groups of immigrants over several millenniums, thus creating a melting pot for various cultures and ethnic groups.

The population of North-East India may conveniently be divided into two major categories, namely, tribal and non-tribal. Migration and the practice of inter-tribal marriage have kept the social boundaries of an ethnic group in a state of flux. Even at the dawn of independence "a great proportion of hill people now classed as plains tribals have gone a long way towards assimilation with the people of the plains of Assam" asserts the Bordoloi Committee.[142]

In the tribal population, two major ethnic strains are easily distinguishable. These two are the Australoids (Nishadas) and the Mongoloids (Kiratas). There are reasons to believe that the Australoids appeared to have come to North-East India at a very early time. They probably came to this region before the coming of the Mongoloids.[143] Apart from the Mongoloids, the Caucasoids also came to the North-east from the west. They came in batches and bought with them different ethnic elements like the Mediterranean, Alpine-Armenoid, Irano-Scythian, and Indo-Aryan. It is quite likely that the ancient Australoid elements were wholly or partially absorbed by the later immigrants—Mongoloids and Caucasoids. The recent anthropological researches along the castes of Assam reveal that

Australoid elements are discernible in certain caste groups of Assam.[144] Because of prolonged interaction with the neighbourhood Mongoloid populations through inter-marriage and assimilation, Mongoloid features are not uncommon among the non-tribal plainsmen of Assam.

Then came the Ahoms, a Shan tribe from the ancient kingdom of Mungnau or Pong which was situated on the upper portion of the Irrawaddy in 1228 AD. They ruled Assam for about six centuries (1228-1826 A.D.). From the middle of the eighteenth century, the Ahom monarchy was on the decline. The present name 'Assam' is derived from the name of the Ahom.

The annexation of North-east by the Britishers which started from the twenties of the nineteenth century, was done gradually and obviously, not very peacefully and without resistance. The British occupation of Assam opened a venue of employment both in office and trade to the Bengalees. Need for cultivation of fallow lands saw the migration of the hardy Muslim tillers from East Bengal, who settled mostly in the Brahmaputra valley. Market forces and British colonial policies played their parts in enabling this mass migration, but a demographic anxiety of being overrun by hordes of migrants has existed since before independence. The migrants' progenies and prejudices against them have survived.

Because of the difficult terrain, the multiplicity of languages and tribes and the diversity of economic structure in the hills and the plains, the Britishers assiduously followed a policy of seclusion and isolation of the tribals of North-East India. The effects of the isolation have been disastrous both to the hill people as well as to the plains people. It has prevented the two from working as a single unit. There is very little interrelationship of that praiseworthy unity of purpose and welfare or loyalty to public ends, or mutuality of sympathy which was to make up an ideal society. On the other hand, in the material field the exclusiveness resulting from the isolation has ended in each group having interests of its own, so that the prevailing purpose of each is the protection of that which it possesses, instead of reorganization and progress through wider relationships. In the cultural field it has prevented social osmosis. The militant and ethnic stirs and sub-national uprisings in this region are largely due to the policy of isolation and segregation followed with impunity for more than a century by the Britishers and then even by the rulers of independent India.[145]

The National Register of Citizens exercise in Assam has created a situation in which one claims himself to be "original inhabitant" as opposed to "non-original inhabitant" so that the latter can be presented as encroachers, illegals and termed Bangladeshis, although the Supreme Court judgment stated that the sole purpose of the NRC is to determine whether someone was there in Assam before 25 March, 1971. Identity is constructed on the basis of racist assumptions and turning a blind eye to others' vulnerability of a similar past.[146] The claim of being "original" more-often-than-not ignores the long history of migration to the region. The background of migration and peopling gets obfuscated by narrow notions of who is indigenous and who is not in the context of North-East India. There are exclusivist claims while attributing the privilege of being early than late in migration. The extension of the Inner Line Permit System to newer areas, the introduction of the Sixth Schedule model of administration which was originally conceived of for the hill tribal areas of undivided Assam as a ploy to keep the state united and later extended even to the plains tribal areas, the formation of small states on the basis of ethnicity, the continuation of the Sixth Schedule even in states formed on the basis of ethnicity, all these gave primacy to the so-called indigeneity of the people, contradicting the region's complex history of immigration.

In the middle of the NRC process, an arbitrary category of the 'indigenous' Assamese was introduced. But it is not really possible to identify the first settlers of the North-east, given its long history of population movements. Many tribal and ethnic bodies have demanded the right to make their claim to citizenship on the basis of tribal and ethnic identities and legal provisions and schedules thereto, who are to be treated much more leniently even when they could not produce the required documents.

Some members of the tribal communities in the three districts of Dibrugarh, Tinsukia and Sibsagar in Upper Assam, estimated to be close to 8,000, did not bother to apply for NRC as they are the 'bhumiputras' residing in the area for generations and therefore, didn't need to prove their citizenship.[147] In a memorandum under the aegis of the Ahom Tribal Mahasangha, some 32 tribal communities of Barak Valley as well as Brahmaputra Valley insisted on the inclusion of their names without any document, as tribes are supposed to be original people of the state.[148] Ironically enough, it is widely believed that genuine citizens may not have documents, while illegal immigrants might have all the proof.

The All Koch Rajbongshi Students' Union (AKRSU) observed a 12-hour bandh in the state on 20 September, 2019 over exclusion of members of this Indigenous group and demanded that all such members of its community who have been left out, be included soon. Almost all shops, banks, educational institutes, and offices remained closed in Koch Rajbongshi-dominated areas of Morigaon, Kokrajhar, Chirang, Baksa, Nalbari, Nagaon and Sivsagar districts.[149]

Sadou Asom Goria Moria-Deshi Jatiya Parishad, an organization of indigenous Muslims seeks constitutional safeguard befitting an "ethnic group" so that they are spared the ignominy of being equated with illegal Muslim migrants. The Indigenous Muslim groups comprise three categories of Assamese Muslims—Goriya who converted from various indigenous groups and tribes, Moriya whose ancestors were brought by the Ahom kings to make weapons and utensils and Deshi who converted specifically from the Koch-Rajbongsi community. The Parishad claims around 10,000 Indigenous Muslims, mostly from the Deshi community, were left out of the NRC. In its election manifestos of 2011, 2014 and 2016, the BJP had promised to conduct a census of Indigenous Muslims. It is estimated that Assam has nearly 42 lakh indigenous Muslim people.[150]

The names of indigenous Muslims and Bangladeshi Muslims are the same. As a result, the government faces problems in identifying them during implementation of various welfare schemes for them. Assamese-speaking Muslims could bc officially classified as an "ethnic tribe" instead of the loosely-used nomenclature "indigenous Muslims" to distance them from Bengali-speaking Muslim immigrants who comprise more than 63 per cent of the state's total Muslim population.[151] Assam's BJP-led government started conducting a socio-economic census from March 2020 to identify indigenous Muslims in the State. Segregating indigenous Muslims from migrants from Bangladesh was the objective of the census.[152] Though the proposed census has been welcomed by various organisations, a large chunk of Muslims who migrated before the March 25, 1971 cut-off date are going to be left out of the census. Assam's AASU, however, criticised the Centre for such a step saying that the Centre cannot "bargain with anti-CAA agitators" by granting constitutional safeguards to the indigenous communities of Assam by implementing Clause 6 of the Assam Accord. [153]

The Janagosthiya Samannay Parishad, Assam (JSPA), an organisastion representing the Indigenous Muslims launched on 15 April, 2021, the jspacensus.com portal for conducting the first ever census of Assamese Muslims for distinguishing them from migrant, Bengali-origin or Bengali-speaking counterparts. The nine-month exercise, seen as a small version of the NRC, has a cut-off period corresponding with the British annexation of Assam in 1826. The JSPA considers the pre-British rule Muslims as indigenous, which is why the Jolahas—converts from among tea plantation workers who were brought from central India by British planters—have been kept out of the census. The portal has a list of documents that applicants have to upload for registration. They include voter card, Aadhar card and PAN of each family member (non-mandatory for minors), a certified copy from village head, municipal board, town panel or any other competent authority as well as a certified copy from any of the 17 JSPA empanelled organisations listing all members of an applicant's family.[154]

In July 2021, a panel was formed following a meeting between chief minister Himanta Biswa Sarma and Assamese Muslims from various fields, including writers, doctors, cultural workers, lecturers, historians, and musicians, to discuss the community's socio-economic challenges. During the discussion, CM Sarma highlighted the importance of protecting and preserving the "uniqueness of the indigenous Assamese Muslims." The panel submitted its report in April 2022. Assam CM Himanta Biswa Sarma disclosed on 21 April, 2022 that the BJP-led government had accepted the definition of 'indigenous Muslims' in the context of the state, as recommended by the panel. He, however, did not specify the definition.[155] In July 2022, the Assam cabinet has approved a new nomenclature for five Muslim groups-Goria, Moria, Jolah (only the ones living in tea gardens), Desi and Syed (only the Assamese-speaking). They will henceforth be known as indigenous Assamese Muslims.

VI

As per statutory provisions, once the persons who are not part of the updated NRC are identified, they will be part of the negative list. Anyone who figures on the negative list cannot be allowed to vote. But whether he is a foreigner or not is decided by the foreigner's tribunal. Once it is decided that one is a foreigner, he is not allowed to live like a free man. Normally, the tribunal asks for his deportation to the country of origin and till then, he is detained in a detention centre. The tribunal's decision, however, can be overruled by the High Court/Supreme Court. These are long-drawn process. Till then, he cannot be deported.

The Union ministry of home affairs, in a statement issued on 20 August, 2019 clarified: "Every individual whose name does not figure in the final NRC can represent his/her case in front of the appellate authority, that is foreigner's tribunals. Under the provisions of Foreigners Act, 1946 and Foreigners (Tribunals) Order, 1964, only FTs are empowered to declare a person as a foreigner. Thus, non-inclusion of a person's name in NRC does not by itself amount to him/her being declared a foreigner." In view of this clarification, the Assam government ruled out their detention "in any circumstances till the time FTs decide them foreigners".[156]

Those who have been excluded from the NRC have 120 days, extended from 60 days only on 19 August by the Central Government[157], to appeal against it at Foreigners' Tribunals. If not satisfied with the verdict of the tribunals, they will have the option to move the High Court and the Supreme Court for redress. Till then, they can enjoy all the facilities extended by the state.

The Assam Jamiat Ulema has moved the Supreme Court challenging the Centre's new modalities on disposal of appeals of those excluded in the final NRC. Sub-para 10 of Para 3A, which was incorporated in the order of amendment states:

> "Upon production of the records, if the tribunal finds merit in the appeal, it shall issue a notice to the appellant and the district magistrate for hearing specifying the date of hearing and such date shall be within thirty days from the date of production of the records."

Advocate A.S.Tapadar who is representing the Jamiat said that rejecting an appeal without any hearing is not followed in jurisprudence anywhere.[158]

A long and expensive battle lies ahead for those who fail to make it to the final NRC. Apart from suffering mental agony, reclaiming citizenship can cost each of them up to Rs. 50,000, that too at the first stage.

The costs incurred at a tribunal comprise two components—legal and administrative. The legal cost includes the advocate's fee for filing (one time), the appeal and for appearing (multiple times), which can run up to Rs. 40,000 at the very least. Administrative expenses like application fees for getting copies of the 23 documents listed by the government can touch Rs. 10,000.[159]

The state government had already committed to provide legal aid to the needy people among those excluded from NRC.[160] The free services include fees for processing, drafting, typing, clerkage, and remuneration of lawyers empanelled with legal services authority under the National Legal Services Authority (Free and Competent Legal Services) Registration, 2010. District Legal Service Authorities (DLSA) will bear the expenses. The state government had by a December 2018 order notified that people whose annual income was less than Rs. 3 lakh were eligible for free legal services.[161]

The Congress in Assam has offered legal help to the NRC-excluded persons. Independent MP Naba Sarania would appoint 500 people to aid non-Bodo residents in the Bodoland Territorial Council areas.[162] Some NGOs made similar offers. Silchar-based NGO, Unconditional Citizenship Demand Forum, All India United Democratic Front (AIUDF), a political party, and other organizations are helping the victims of the 'foreigner' conundrum. Purbabangiya Bharatbasi Kalyan Samiti and All India Joint Action Committee of Bengal Refugees are planning to file a Public Interest Litigation petition to the Supreme Court seeking redress.[163] Ashraful Husain, an activist, Rehna Sultana and Sofiqul Islam, Guwahati University research scholars and The Hague-based researcher Mausami Chetia were complained against for raising donations to help poor and illiterate persons belonging to the minority communities and misrepresentation of the NRC. [164]

A grassroots movement in Assam is making the Constitution accessible to those that need it most—the poor and marginalized Muslims of Bengali-origin (Miyas) caught in Assam's citizenship tangle. Since December 2020 community-members, local groups, and lawyers have established Samvidhan Seva Kendras (SSKs) in three districts. The first came up in Barpeta's TND Bazzar in 2020, the next two in Sontali (Kamrup) and Jorhat in January 2021 and the fourth came up in Kalgachia in the minority-dominated district of Barpeta, 120 km from Guwahati on the Republic Day. Working out of unassuming buildings, the SSKs give pride of place to Assamese translations of the Preamble. The SSKs double as legal aid centres and community spaces for people marked "doubtful(D)" Voters, "suspected foreigners" or "declared foreigners" in detention centres. "Our job is to facilitate legal aid for people asked to prove their citizenship. We want to familiarize the community with the Constitution and the rights it guarantees", said Aman Wadud, a human rights lawyer who started this initiative.[165]

The state government has set up 200 more FTs, taking the number of FTs in the state to 300. The 200 additional FTs were set up in six district headquarters of Jorhat, Silchar, Nagaon, Bongaigaon, Tezpur and Guwahati. A panel of 221 new members for Foreigners' Tribunals was selected by the Guwahati High Court less than a fortnight ahead of these FTs becoming operational by 1 September.[166] The MHA has sanctioned around 1000 Tribunals to be set up in Assam in the wake of publication of the final NRC to deal with the cases of NRC exclusions.[167]

A study of the functioning of the Foreigner's Tribunals by Rohini Mohan reveals that their trials are arbitrary, deeply inconsistent, and riddled with errors. 78 per cent of the orders were delivered ex-parte, without the accused ever being heard. Few of the Tribunals followed standard protocol. Justice seemed twisted on its head. The judges presiding over the tribunals are often not judges, but lawyers and going forward, can be bureaucrats. The Centre, however, denies that "working of the FTs is flawed."[168] Unsurprisingly, over the last few months, glaring flaws in the working of the Foreigners Tribunals have come to light. Question in

Parliament showed that as many as 64,000 people have been declared non-citizens in ex-parte proceedings, i.e., without being heard.[169] In the meantime, the Gauhati High Court has observed that proof beyond reasonable doubt is not required in a Foreigner's Tribunal for establishing one's citizenship.[170]

Testimonies reveal these people are often not even served notices telling them that they have been summoned to appear. Alarmingly, an investigative media report featured testimony of a former Tribunal member who stated that his compatriots competed to be what was jokingly referred to as "the highest wicket-taker", i.e, the one who could declare the highest number of individuals as "foreigners."[171] Citing the State's performance appraisal data from the affidavit filed in the High Court, Amnesty International asserted that the Assam Government decides the tenure of a Foreigners' Tribunal member based on how many foreigners he or she declares.[172] And to cap it all, several orders of a Foreigners Tribunal in central Assam declaring some people as non-citizens were found missing from records.[173]

Leah Verghese and Shruthi Naik who are with DAKSH, a non-profit organization based in Bengaluru analysed 818 orders passed by Foreigners Tribunal No. 4 between 16 June, 2017 and 30 December, 2019, obtained through the Right To Information Act, and found that 96 per cent were decided ex parte. Also, the orders were inconsistent, vague and biased.

They found that a majority of the orders followed set templates with only the names of persons, police stations, and dates being changed. In 733 cases, the police claim to have met the suspected foreigners. The police asked these suspected foreigners to produce documentary proof of their citizenship, and 570 of them allegedly produced no documents (the remaining orders did not mention whether any documents were produced). In 218 of these cases, the police went on to declare that the suspected foreigners were from Bangladesh (mostly from Maimansingh). Apart from these alleged meetings with the suspected foreigners, the orders do not allude to any other investigation by the police. Although the police claimed they were able to meet suspected foreigners before submitting their inquiry report, in at least 98 per cent of such cases, they were unable to locate the suspected foreigners subsequently to serve a notice to appear before the tribunal. The police alleged that these persons were not residents of their earlier locality and could not be traced despite their asking local residents and *gaonburahs* (village headmen). A practising advocate revealed that in some of his cases, the *gaonburahs* also appeared as witnesses for the suspected foreigners and confirmed that they were not questioned by the police as to the whereabouts of these suspected foreigners. Foreigners

Tribunals do not allow for the police to be cross-examined, thereby leaving no room to disprove or challenge submissions made by them regarding their alleged meetings with the suspected foreigners and their subsequent inability to find them. All this works out conveniently for the police and the tribunals given the anxiety in Assam about finding and deporting Bangladeshis. Unlike regular criminal trials where an accused is presumed not guilty and the state has to prove that he committed a crime, the burden of proof under the Foreigners Act of 1946 is on the accused. If a person fails to appear before the Foreigners Tribunal, it can pass an order declaring him a foreigner ex parte, without allowing him an opportunity to defend himself. In all the ex parte orders, the police produced no evidence to indicate that the suspected foreigners were not Indian, yet the latter were declared Bangladeshi. Only in 31 cases were the suspected foreigners allowed to refute the allegations made against them. All these 31 orders were passed by the same tribunal member. This tribunal took an average of 10 years to dispose of a case. It is interesting to note that 92 per cent of the cases analysed were disposed of in 2018 and 2019 alone. In 82 per cent of the cases, the police gave the tribunal reports of service of notice in 2018 and 2019, although some cases dated as far back as 1999. The cases appear to have been kept in cold storage for several years and disposed of with undue haste in 2018 and 2019. On average, the tribunal took 39 days from the date of receipt of this report to pass an ex parte order. The tribunal ordered the deportation of the suspected foreigners in 97 per cent of these cases. However, very few, if any, will actually be deported since deportation requires Bangladesh to accept the deportees. Assam's Parliamentary Affairs Minister said only 227 persons were deported between 13 March, 2013 and 31 July, 2020.[174] Sadly enough, neither the High Court nor the Supreme Court took steps to rectify the malfunctioning of the Foreigners' Tribunals. The FT is the most important institution and the ultimate authority for deciding the citizenship of a person. It cannot be allowed to decide the claims of 19 lakh people arbitrarily and callously as they have been in the past.

The Supreme Court in *Abdul Kuddus* has held that the 'opinion' of the FT was to be treated as a 'quasi-judicial order' and was therefore final and binding on all parties including upon the preparation of the NRC. When adjudicating upon a person's citizenship—a determination that can have the drastic and severe result of rendering a human being stateless—only the highest standards of adjudication can ever be morally or ethically justifiable. But in further strengthening the FT, the Supreme Court failed to fulfill its duty as the last protector of human rights under the Constitution. The Court attempted to justify this by observing that "fixing time limits and recording of an order rather than a judgment is to ensure that the cases are disposed of expeditiously and in a time bound manner." This, however, as Gautam Bhatia says, is "the reasoning of a company CEO, not that of the highest Court of the land, adjudicating upon a matter that involves the rights of millions of people. When the stakes are so high, when the consequences entail rendering people stateless, then to allow such departures from the most basic principles of the rule of law is morally grotesque."[175]

There is an urgent need to make the procedure followed by the Foreigners' Tribunal fair and transparent. Or else the Foreigners' Tribunals should be abolished and its task be entrusted to special courts constituted for the purpose, as demanded by the Nagarik Adhikar Raksha Samanvaya Committee, Asom in its memorandum submitted to the Prime Minister, Union Home Minister and Assam's Chief Minister on 19 February, 2022.[176]

In a related case, the Foreigner's Tribunal Bench of the Guwahati High Court has directed in May 2022 that once the Foreigner's Tribunal has decided the Indian citizenship of a person, the validity of that decision cannot again be challenged before the High Court.[177] In the meantime, Hitesh Dev Sarma, State NRC Coordinator had on 18 April, 2022 issued letters to the FT members informing them that "since the Registrar General of Citizens Registration (RGCR) has not declared NRC as final and there are errors, things may change when the final NRC gets published." In view of this position, he reminded members of the FTs across Assam to not consider the draft NRC and its supplementary list as reliable evidence for the disposal of cases. But an FT member questioned this interpretation of the State Coordinator and advised him to "withdraw his letter and stop interfering in the lawful functioning of the FTs which is beyond your jurisdiction and limits of power."[178]

Former chief justice of Delhi High Court Justice A.P. Shah pointed out that citizenship right is one of the most basic, fundamental human rights. Deprivation of citizenship must follow the most rigorous procedure available; the overriding concern must be fairness not quickness or efficiency.[179] In plain words, it should be as flawless as possible and everyone should get a chance to place his points of view. But "the fear of being excluded from the NRC, being declared as foreigner, and finally being sent to a detention centre, has created a situation of permanent paranoia among vulnerable communities, especially Bengal-origin Assamese Muslims and Bengali Hindus living in the state of Assam. This fear has pushed the people to a snapping point and many are committing suicide. Women and their children bear a disproportionately higher burden of the process", said a two-day event on "contested citizenship in Assam;

people's tribunal on constitutional process and human cost."[180] The experience of Assam shows that the NRC is a very exclusionary exercise in the larger context.

But the most damning criticism against the NRC exercise came from Aman Wadud, who takes up cases of suspected foreigners *pro bono*. He says: "The problem lies in the so-called investigation by the Election Commission and the Border Police. Its purpose is only to pander to the prejudices of the Assamese majority and the government, who believe that there are millions of Bangladeshis in Assam. Hence, if they don't find Bangladeshis, they accuse Indian citizens of being Bangladeshis, grossly violating their citizenship rights and making a mockery of the fundamental rights enshrined in the Constitution."[181]

The UN agencies like the UN Human Rights Council (UNHRC), UN High Commissioner for Human Rights (UNHCHR), UN Refugee Agency have taken strong exception to the NRC exercise in Assam, calling it "discriminating between other religious groups and Muslims". Such criticism by the world body is unprecedented, India has not faced it ever, even on the Kashmir issue.

The UN Human Rights Council (UNHRC) employed three rapporteurs to study the NRC issue and their report is critical of the Narendra Modi government. The report also questioned India's Foreigners' Act, which puts the onus on individuals to prove their citizenship status. "In nationality determination processes, the burden of proof should lie with the state and not with the individual", said the report. The experts also highlighted the lack of clarity in the link between the NRC process, electoral roll information and the separate judicial processes of citizenship determination before the Assam Foreigners Tribunals. In a scathing indictment of the Union government, the UN experts said they did not receive any response from concerned authorities despite repeated requests.

Liz Throsell, spokesperson of the UN Refugee Agency, said: "We would urge India not to deport and detain people and deprive them of their basic rights. We know India has sovereign rights and the right to detect foreigners. But it has to understand concerns like human rights violations and statelessness", emphasizing that even foreigners should not be deprived of their basic rights. Adrian Edwards, global spokesperson for the UNHCR, said his organization would seek immediate intervention of the Indian government to restore human rights in Assam. "It is certainly a worrying situation. India is a signatory to the international conventions on statelessness and human rights. It should adhere to those conventions", he said.[182]

There are only six detention camps in Assam. These detention centres are attached to the six central jails of the state. Assam's first detention centre to house foreign convicts and people declared "foreigners" by tribunals is being constructed on 20 bighas of land at Matia in Goalpara district, about 124 km west of Guwahati, at an estimated cost of Rs. 46.51 crore. The entire expense on the facility, with a capacity to house 3,000 detainees, is being borne by the Centre. Incidentally, Goa opened a detention centre at Mapusa for foreigners in May 2019.[183] The Maharashtra Government was planning to construct a detention centre at Nerul, 20 km away from Mumbai on a 1.2 hectare of land. But it did not materialise.[184] Punjab Detention Centre is currently being built in Goindwal Sahib in Taran Taran district and is planned for completion in May 2020.[185] Delhi Detention Centre is spread over three locations in Delhi to hold foreigners waiting for deportation. One of the centres at Lampur is being operated under the Foreigners Regional Registration Office (FRRO). The Special Branch of Delhi Police supervises the ward holding the Pakistanis, while people of other nationalities are under the watch of the FRRO. FRRO and Delhi police both work under the Central Home Ministry.

Karnataka Detention Centre is under construction at Sondekoppa in Nelamangala, located 40 kms from Bangalore. It is planned to be operational from 1 January, 2020. The centre has 10-feet high walls, barbed wires with watchtowers in two corners of the compound.[186]

On 9 January, 2019, the Union government released a "2019 Model Detention Manual", which stated that every city or district, having a major immigration check post, must have a detention centre. The guidelines suggest detention centres with 10 feet high boundary walls covered with barbed wires. It also clarified the difference between a prison and a detention centre.[187] In a written reply MOS home affairs Nityananda Rai informed the Lok Sabha that in keeping with Supreme Court directives, MHA has prepared a model detention centre/holding camp manual in consultation with the stakeholders and it was circulated to all state governments.[188]

Recently, the Supreme Court set the detention period of foreigners at three years. The SC in a judgment on 10 May, 2019 in WP(C) No. 1045/2018 had spelt out tough conditionalities for release of detainees who had served a term of three years in detention camps. As per the judgment, two sureties of one lakh rupees have to be furnished by an Indian citizen for the release of a detainee; the detainee must provide a verifiable address; has to give biometric details and report every week to a police station specified by the Foreigners Tribunal.[189] In its latest judgment on 12

April, 2020, a SC Bench comprising Chief Justice S.A. Bobde, Justices L.N. Rao and M. Shantanagouder ordered the release of detainees who had served for two years in detention camps by recognizing the fact that keeping them during the Covid-19 pandemic posed a grave health risk. The release of many inmates from the detention centres across Assam has brought out tales of a flawed foreigner determination procedure as well as their imprisonment that violates end of justice.

As most of the detainees are poor and illiterate, they were not in a position to bear the high legal costs of defending them as Indian citizens. Instances are galore when genuine citizens with necessary supporting documents were put in the detention camps. On an average their families had to spend over 2 lakh to reestablish their identity as Indian citizens. They sold their cattle, land and crops, even mortgaged their trees for obtaining a bank loan of Rs. 50,000 to get them released. People are turned back from the NRC Seva Kendra when they went to deposit the necessary documents on the pretext that these did not prove their Indian citizenship. Any attempt to show all documents to officials of the foreign tribunals proved futile.[190]

People spent more than one year on an average till the administration declared them citizens of India. They do not receive any compensation from the government for such wrongful detentions.[191] Nikhil Bharat Udbastu Smanway Samiti has taken up the cause of these harassed people which was resented by the AASU.[192] The conditions within such detention centres also have raised concerns from human rights standards that are adopted globally. A columnist says that the detention centres in Assam are the concentration camps of 21st century India where people, stamped as non-citizens, can be kept indefinitely, deprived of all their rights and pending deportation, which will probably never happen, given Bangladesh's friendly relations with India.[193]

Harsh Mander, as a special monitor for the National Human Rights Commission, has submitted a detailed report, which described the enormous and unending human tragedy of the detainees, and the extensive flouting of national and international laws, seeking urgent corrections. His paramount recommendation to the NHRC was to urgently establish a clear legal regime in conformity with Article 21 of the Constitution and international law to govern the condition of detaineees. But he did not receive any communication about action taken on his report.[194]

Twenty-five declared foreigners have already died in the detention camps of Assam. The state's parliamentary affairs minister, Chandra Mohan Patowary, told the Assembly recently that seven detainees each have died in 2019 and 2018, six in 2017, four in 2016 and one in 2011. Till

July 2019, there were a total of 1,145 detainees at six detention centres of whom 335 have remained lodged for more than three years.[195]

And it costs money to keep some body confined in detention camps. Government spends Rs. 13 lakh per month on 885 foreigners—265 Hindus and 618 Muslims—locked up in 6 detention centres.[196] Imagine the number of detention camps required to keep even ten per cent of the 19 lakh NRC-excluded persons and the quantum of money for their upkeep.

Racial hounding has also started in Assam bringing back memories of the Assam Agitation days in the 1980s. Recently, on 11 September, 2019 four persons including a couple in their fifties and an elderly man were subjected to racial profiling on suspicion that they were Bangladeshis and handed over to police by a mob led by suspected AASU workers in Assam's Baksa. The officer-in-charge of Goreswar police station upon verification said they were not Bangladeshis.[197] One Indira, a woman author, who allegedly suggested in a Facebook post that those left out of the NRC be put in detention camps after being sterilized, has been booked by Kerala police on charges of promoting enmity between religion and spreading hatred through social media. Her post has since been deleted.[198] Such instances will multiply in the coming days.

VII

The immediate aim of updating the NRC in Assam is, no doubt, the detection of illegal Bangladeshi and their deportation but it is also equally important to prevent the creation of a new set of 'stateless' people not only in Assam but in the entire country. After this long and painstaking exercise the NRC in Assam has identified the persons who could be put in the exclusion list, though there is considerable doubt about the correctness of the list, discussed earlier. It leads us to the next and ultimate step of their deportation.

In Assam, the influx has reduced considerably over time especially because the north-eastern state has seen regular violent conflicts between natives and 'foreign' settlers. A report titled "Foreigners in Assam; a blast from the past" released by the Rights and Risks Analysis Group on 29 August, 2019 says the State of Assam witnessed a huge influx of immigrants from 1901 to 1971, but the influx reduced drastically thereafter. This study was based on the Census reports. In fact, from 1971 to 2011, Assam had the lowest average (20.9%) decadal population growth rate in the entire north-eastern region. Assam did not witness any noticeable influx of foreigners in the post-1971 period. At least, major influx is not supported by Census statistics.[199] The influx of population during the 70-

year period of 1901-1971 changed the demographic character of Assam. But the AASU had accepted the immigrants of this period as citizens of India under the Assam Accord.

There is no doubt that successive Central and State Governments have failed to take appropriate steps to prevent the influx of the 'infiltrators.' Even after the Assam Accord was put in place and signed, the process of detecting and expelling immigrants never really officially took place in Assam. The obvious reason why practically no effective step was taken to deter the influx is that the greater the Muslim influx, the bigger the vote bank. However, a crackdown would undoubtedly result in not only losing the migrant vote, but also of the indigenous Muslim population. In view of the fact that despite a more than three-decade-long anti-foreigner agitation in Assam, not more than 2,442 persons could be deported/pushed back, the third step of the deportation of the infiltrators is an uphill task. Stopping crossings may be tough, but deportation is no easy task either. The most crucial question, therefore, is how to deport them and where. BJP president Amit Shah promised at the 2019 Lok Sabha poll meetings in Assam to deport all illegal migrants from Assam if Prime Minister Narendra Modi got a second term.[200] PM Narendra Modi kicked off his Assam campaign for 2019 Lok Sabha elections on 30 March, 2019 with promise to grant ST status to six communities in Assam and "free Assam and the country of the illegal migrants and terrorists."[201] Pious wishes, but how!

In an interview published in the 8 October, 2017 issue of *The Week*, Bangladesh's Information Minister Hasanul Huq Inu had clearly stated that Bangladesh would not accept the Indian theory of infiltration of Bangladeshis after 1971.[202] Apparently, Bangladesh, like any other country, vehemently denies the presence of their nationals on Indian soil and seems reluctant to take back any 'infiltrators.' It is also not feasible to forcibly send such a large number of people to Bangladesh.

Actually without the active help and cooperation of Bangladesh, influx of illegal migrants from that country cannot be stopped. India's Foreign Minister Sushma Swaraj expressed the view on 31 March, 2016 that India would take the opportunity of the existing good terms with Bangladesh to ensure a permanent solution to the problem of infiltration from that country.[203] The Supreme Court has also directed the Centre to talk to that country to streamline procedures for deporting illegal migrants.[204]

The NRC which raised concern for many in Bangladesh was published when Bangladesh was going through its own struggle of having to shelter more than a million refugees fleeing from Myanmar. The concern was rather valid as the possibility of deportation of the alleged illegal migrants to Bangladesh was being emphasised time and again in political discourses and media debates in India. Since India had always refrained from bringing up the illegal migration issue in any official meeting with Bangladesh, Bangladesh did not officially expressed any concern over the NRC process.

Home minister Amit Shah raised with Bangladesh India's concerns over the illegal immigration from Bangladesh to the North-east. The issue was flagged before Bangladesh home minister Asaduzzaman Khan at the 7th meeting of India-Bangladesh Home Minister Level Talk (HMLT) held in New Delhi on 7 August, 2019.[205] During his two-day visit to Bangladesh (19-20 August, 2019), India's foreign affairs minister Jaishankar in a joint press conference with his Bangladesh counterpart A.K. Abdul Momen said that the NRC in Assam was India's "internal matter" and Bangladesh has nothing to be worried about. Jaishankar's comments came amid concerns in Bangladesh over the NRC.[206]

Prime Minister of Bangladesh Sheikh Hasina paid a 4-day visit (3-6 October) to New Delhi. Speaking to journalists on the sidelines of a reception by the Bangladesh high commissioner on 3 October, she said she had spoken to Modi on NRC and he assured her it would have no impact on Bangladesh.[207]

Such statements reveal that immediate deportation of illegal Bangladeshi immigrants is not on the cards for New Delhi. So what should be done with the NRC-excluded persons? The BJP has long promised that it will deport all illegally resident Bangladeshis from Assam and the rest of India, a view that it has articulated time and again over the years. But this position does not tally with what the Prime Minister of Bangladesh told the media or Jaishankar told his Bangladeshi counterpart. Apart from promising to confer citizenship on all non-Muslims by amending the law, there is no clarity on what the government plans to do with the lakhs of NRC-excluded persons. The Centre should have a well-laid out plan to deal with the humanitarian crisis in Assam. After all, those excluded must be treated humanely—one can't put away 19 lakh people in detention camps for ever—and given fair legal redress.

But the first priority is the preparation of an error-free NRC—both the inclusion list and the exclusion list should be flawless. Admitting that it is humanly impossible not to make error, it should be the endeavour of the state to prepare the NRC as correctly as possible, at least not to make the silly mistakes enumerated earlier. One can first start with the exclusion list and then move on to the inclusion list.

The Supreme Court while directing the updation of the NRC in Assam has said that it should be implemented in adherence to the Citizenship Act, 1955 and the Citizenship Rules, 2003.

The Citizenship Act 1955, as amended till date, was enacted in pursuance of the directions of Article 11 of the Constitution to deal with all matters relating to citizenship including the acquisition and termination of citizenship. Sections 3 to 7 deal with the matter of acquisition of citizenship by birth (Section 3), descent (Section 4), registration (Section 5), naturalization (Section 6), and incorporation of territory (Section 7). [Annexure B]

Section 3 provides for conferment of Indian citizenship by birth during the three periods, mentioned below, subject to the restrictions imposed in sub-section (2)—

(1) on or after 26 January, 1950 but before the 1st day of July, 1987;
(2) on or after the 1st day of July, 1987, but before the commencement of the Citizenship (Amendment) Act, 2003 (6 of 2004)
(3) on or after the commencement of the Citizenship (Amendment) Act, 2003 (6 of 2004). In the last two cases, certain conditions as to the Indian citizenship of the parents have been stipulated but no such conditions have been provided for those born up to 30 June, 1987.

This fact was not kept in mind while conducting the updation of the NRC in Assam, alleges Prof. Faizan Mustafa, Vice-Chancellor of the NALSAR University of Law. In an interview to the Wire he said: "The NRC is a clear violation of Section 3 of the Citizenship Act. I am clear about it." He said the NRC has 24 March, 1971 as the cut-off date to determine citizenship in India. However, Section 3(1)(a) of the Citizenship Act says that "every person born in India on or after the 26th day of January, 1950 but before the 1st day of July, 1987 shall be a citizen of India by birth", he added.

Prof Mustafa said NRC coordinator Prateek Hajela had told the Supreme Court that "citizenship purely by birth and not by descendance is not eligible for inclusion in NRC." His grounds were that one parent of such persons could be a 'doubtful voter', a 'declared foreigner' or someone 'whose claim for citizenship is pending before a Foreigner's Tribunal.' Prof Mustafa said the refusal to include in the NRC those born in India between the Republic Day 1950 and 30 June, 1987 was "a self-inflicted wound in which the Supreme Court is also a party. I would say that in this matter what was expected from the Court has not been delivered. Our expectation from the Court was that they would ensure that people are not denied citizenship if they have genuine documents. Instead people are becoming stateless because of this strict timeline set by the Court", he further added.[208] It may be recalled that the Tibetan refugees were offered Indian citizenship by the Government of India under Section 3(1) of the Citizenship Act. If it was perfectly legal to accord Indian citizenship to the Tibetans, there is no reason why it would not be legal for the migrants from Bangladesh as well. If this issue is brought before the Apex court of the land, the stand of the NRC coordinator on this will surely be declared illegal. An editorial in the *Economic & Political Weekly* has put it in this way: "Differential requirements of documents from different groups have produced a built-in bias in the process and the requirement of legacy documents makes a departure from the principle of citizenship by birth. Such departures threaten to instituionalise the exclusion of the other and that seems to be the purpose behind the weaponisation of the NRC by the ruling party."[209]

Basu and Das argue that the economy of Assam has not remained in the same place for the last 50 years. The centre of gravity has moved away from agriculture and the rural economy. Muslim peasants who migrated many decades ago have passed on. Their descendants have diversified to other occupations such as trade, transportation, and other skilled professions. They acquired education and are competing in the middle-class job market. There has been a distinct ascent of the community, and this threatens the entrenched groups. In other words, there has been a case of mis-identification. Greater presence and visibility of the migrants' descendants in middle-class urban spaces is being identified as illegal immigration from Bangladesh. Given the history of anxiety over migration, such mis-identification, although unfortunate, is not surprising. The anxieties of losing one's culture are real and serious. It is naïve to believe that cultural anxieties can be resolved through the NRC.[210]

It would have been much better if issues that affect the material lives of the common people are addressed. But obsession with illegal immigrants, manifested in the futile NRC exercise, obscures the vision of an all-round economic development of Assam.

VIII

It may be recalled that following the establishment of British supremacy in the Brahmaputra Valley on the conclusion of the Treaty of Yandabo on 24 February, 1826, the process of gradual incorporation of the hills and dales of the north-eastern region started. Assam was a Division of the Province of Bengal till 1874. When Assam was made a Division under the Bengal Province, the Bengal districts of Goalpara, Sylhet and the plains portion of Cachar were transferred to this new administrative unit. This arrangement continued even when Assam was made a new province in 1874. "The idea was that the surplus revenue of the Surma Valley would balance the deficit of the Brahmaputra Valley." [211] That is the reason why there was heavy concentration of Bengali-speaking population in certain areas like Cachar, Sylhet in the Surma Valley, in Goalpara and certain urban areas in the Assam Valley. The easy availability of cultivable land, the fertility of the soil and the prevalence of low rents induced a section of cultivators in the overcrowded districts of Bengal to find their way to Assam. A certain number of persons from the districts of Mymensing, Dacca, Rangpur and Pabna also settled down in Sylhet and Goalpara but this, according to the 1901 Census Superintendent of Assam, E.A.Gait, could scarcely be called immigration. They moved a few miles from their original homes and the accident of boundary alone brought them within the limits of Assam.[212] "While the Muslim settlements came up only in the rural areas, the Hindus generally settled in the administrative and business centres. No wonder, most of the towns in the region originated with the Bengalis. There are similar reasons behind settlements of the Bengalis in and around Shillong, which was the capital of undivided Assam for a very long time."[213]

In India, migration of people from one region to another is going on for ages. In fact, the resilience of the Hindu culture including its social system depended much on such free movement of people, especially of the Brahmans which "was perhaps meant to correct the imbalance of cultural development."[214] Large scale state sponsored migration from different parts of British India had changed the demographic composition of colonial Assam. As Hutton observed:

> There are many immigrants in the plains of Assam. Some of them are labourers in tea gardens, the bulk of whom are Hindus, as are most of the Assamese proper, while some have been converted to Christianity. They come from all parts of India, but mostly from Chota Nagpur and the neighbouring parts of central India. The majority of the more recent immigrants into Assam, however, were Muslim cultivators from Bengal, sturdy, industrious, but rather turbulent people who tended to oust the Assamese from the south and west of the valley. The Shylet and Kachar districts of southern Assam, which belong geographically to Bengal, had, long before the emergence of Pakistan, already become in effect Bengali colonies, the Kachari, who once ruled there, having become quite unimportant numerically. They are allied in

origin to the Garo, Kochh, and the people of the north bank of the Brahmaputra river, and in the hills still speak their own distinctive language.[215]

The Hindu Bengalis, who had historically been advanced than any other communities, had been the major source of supply of trained and educated manpower. They came in this region as collaborator to British administration and in connection with the growing need for professional services. Educationally forward Bengalis were appointed in important offices in which Indians could expect to be. The revenue and judicial departments became the sole preserve of the newcomers from Bengal. They were placed in an advantageous position in Assam when different administrative changes were effected in 1874, 1905, 1912 and 1921.

This produced the Assamese resentment against the Bengalees and the seeds of tensions were sown in economic, social and political life of Assam which ultimately resulted in the Assamese xenophobia. The deep-rooted machination of the elite of the Assam Valley found its way through the referendum in Sylhet held on 6 and 7 July, 1947 and made a gift of four out of five subdivisions of the Bengalee-majority districts to East Pakistan with all the tea gardens to ensure that the Bengali-dominance in the Assam politics was cut to size. Sylhet referendum was the precursor of what was going to happen to the Bengalis in Assam. "Soon after independence an open clash broke out in 1948 between the Bengalis and the Assamese. In major towns of Assam valley, Bengalees were assaulted on the streets and Bengali signboards were pulled down. The assaulters were drawn from the student community. The social base of the movement was becoming wider and its manifestation more violent. 1948 also ushered in a new phase in the movement. So far the Assamese had viewed expulsion of the Bengalees as a means of reducing the threat to their aspirations. They now found that a thorough Assamesisation of the province would reduce the fear of Bengali acculturation. The pulling down of Bengali signboards and the demands to use Assamese on signboards was one device. The violent outbursts that took place in 1954, 1955 and 1960 were a continuation of the 1948 phase. While in 1954 and 1955, the Assamesisation efforts were more extensive, in 1960 a bolder step was taken. Assamese was sought to be introduced as the official language of Assam. The political leaders of the province also supported the demand and the government took necessary steps to implement it. The Bengaleese mainly in the Cachar Valley and the hill tribes offered massive resistance to the move. Violent disturbances took place in various parts of the State in protest against the forcible imposition of the Assamese language. Loot, arson, assaults, injuries and deaths were followed by the hill peoples' demands for separation from Assam...The 1970 and 1972 outbursts were pre- and post-census (1971) attempts at Assamesisation. In 1970, it was an attempt to terrorise Bengalees to declare Assamese as their mother-tongue in the census. In 1972, it was a reaction to the increase in the Bengalee population. It was suspected that many refugees who entered Assam in the wake of the Banglaldesh War (1971) stayed back illegally and registered themselves as regular Indian citizens in the census which further increased the Bengaleee population."[216]

The Assamese achieved no significant success in these movements. Hence in 1979-1985, the Assam Movement was launched for the expulsion of Bengali-speaking people. The Assam Movement catapulted its protagonists to power not once but twice but only 2442 persons could be deported till date. Bhaskar Jyoti Mahanta, special director-general of police (border) in an interview with *The Week*, however, disclosed that "last year (2018), more than100 people were deported and the Bangladesh Government accepted them. The number in the previous 10 years was just around 70. Last year has seen the largest number of deportation."[217]

The Assam NRC has put names of more than 19 lakh persons in the exclusion list, but the majority of them are Bengali-speaking Hindus. The BJP is committed to give them Indian citizenship. But the Assamese gentry are reticent to accommodate them in Assam. As a matter of fact, the objection of the north-eastern states against the CAA is on that ground—such persons must not be allowed to stay in their states.

Considering the fact that the primary objective of the NGO on whose petition the Supreme Court directed the conduct of the NRC in Assam was "to save the Assamese people from becoming a minority in their own land"[218], this purpose would not be achieved if the Bengali Hindus are allowed to stay in Assam on obtaining Indian citizenship. Other states are not likely to come forward to the rescue of Assam.

The best course is to amend the historical mistake committed way back in 1874 when the merger of Bengali-speaking areas with the new chief commissioner's province of Assam had an unintended effect, even though hiving off Assam was done to assuage Assamese needs of identity. The situation for the Assamese was nothing less than paradoxical. It was a movement for liberation from Bengal, but hardly from the Bengalees. The much needed and desired freedom and right to nurture Assamese identity seemed to have been sabotaged from the very start.

The States Reorganisation Commission (SRC) 1955 which was seized with the question of reorganization of States was requested to transfer Goalpara district of Assam to West Bengal because it was predominantly a Bengali-speaking district. Though the Commission admitted that "the latest Census figures show, as compared to the figures of 1931, very striking variations which cannot be satisfactorily explained", but found "it difficult to admit on that ground alone any claim by West Bengal to Goalpara or any part of it. Such historical connection as there has been between Goalpara and West Bengal has been intermittent and tenuous. The district has now been part of Assam for such a long time that there is no justification for disturbing this position."[219]

The Cachar State Reorganisation Committee submitted a proposal to the SRC for the formation of a Purbachal State with Cachar, Tripura, the Mizo Hills, the Naga Hills, Manipur and the NEFA. In the language of the Commission,

> the genesis of the Purbachal demand is that since the major part of Sylhet was cut off from India at the time of Partition, the Bengalis in Assam, who used to feel that culturally and even geographically they belonged to Bengal, have found themselves somewhat isolated in what they may now be disposed to regard as an uncongenial environment. It has been represented to us that the activities of the Assam Jatiya Mahasabha and the policies of the local government have not only not reconciled the Bengalis in this part of Assam, but have had quite the opposite result. The Bengali-speaking people have cited for instance the fact that the number of government primary schools in Goalpara district with Bengali as the medium of instruction has fallen from 252 in 1947-48 to 1 at the present time.
>
> These complaints in so far as there are some *prima facie* justification for them deserve to be carefully examined. It is difficult for us to believe that the arrangements which have been made at present adequately meet the needs of the Bengali-speaking population in this district, and in particular the problem of primary education in this area should receive early attention.[220]

But the Commission felt that "the creation of a new State, which may well mean only that one set of problems is exchanged for another, is not in our opinion an appropriate remedy for the grievances of the minorities, if any."[221]

The SRC in its recommendations gave highest importance to the preservation and strengthening of the unity and integrity of India rather than on linguistic chauvinism, religious fanaticism, provincialism and ethnic loyalties, although the SRC had found such trends even then, mentioned above. Within 20 years of the submission of the SRC report Assam gave birth to separate states/UTs of Nagaland, Meghalaya, Mizoram, and Arunachal Pradesh—all in the name of identity politics. Ethnicity, regional loyalties, cultural and linguistic fanaticism, particularistic feelings and racial supremacy were in full play in the disintegration of Assam. If so many states could emerge just like that, it is all the more logical that Bengali-speaking people and areas are treated on the same footing and are not discriminated.

Five decades after the submission of the SRC report, the National Commission for Religious and Linguistic Minorities (Justice Ranganath Misra Commission) in its report submitted on 10 May, 2007 placed Assam in 'D' category where "the linguistic tensions have been quite volatile due to their linguistic composition as well as their inner group attitudes."[222] So there is no improvement in the linguistic tensions and resultant conflicts—mainly between the Bengali-speaking and Assamese-speaking people—in Assam in the last fifty years or more and the possibility of any improvement in relations is rather remote. After all, as the Ranganath Misra Commission says, "language is an instrument of culture and identity. It is a powerful master trait for group identity. Therefore, language is essential in the very survival of cultural communities. Languages are also an important part of any curriculum."[223]

According to the language census of 2011, released in 2018, the total population of Assam in 2011 was 3,12,05,576. Of them, 1,50,95,797 (48.80%) were Assamese-speakers, 90,24,324 (28.92%) Bengali-speakers and the rest 70,85,455 (22.28%) were other scheduled language and non-scheduled language speakers like Bodo, Hindi, Manipuri, Nepali, Santhali, Odia etc. So Assamese-speaking population continues to be minority in Assam (that is less than 50%) even according to the 2011 census.[224]

The NRC is not likely to change this position because about 11-12 lakh out of the 19 lakh NRC-rejects are Bengali Hindus who are likely to be granted Indian citizenship, according to the policy of the ruling BJP party. If it happens, Assamese-speaking people will continue to remain minority in Assam as they are now. So the NRC will not solve the core issue which sustains and nurtures the Assamese sub-nationalism whose supporters are agnostic towards Bengalis irrespective of their religious background.

The NRC is also a suspect to the Bengali community. "The NRC is a planned exercise to exclude the name of non-Assamese, particularly the Bengalis of Barak Valley. We fear the creation of a stateless people, who will then be exploited, as India has no treaty with any other country for their deportation", alleges Sadhan Purkayastha of Citizens' Rights Protection Coordination Committee.[225] A programme organised by the All Bengali Youth & Student Organisation (ABYSO) at the Press Club in Kolkata in 26 March, 2019, saw informed discussions by the participants on the harassment, humiliation and torture faced by all sections of Bengali community, especially Bengali Hindus, in Assam in the aftermath of the publication of the NRC. There has been a planned conspiracy to destroy and uproot Bengalis from Assam, it was alleged.[226]

To soothe the heightened concerns in the north-east over the CAB 2016, Raj Nath Singh announced in the Rajya Sabha on 9 January, 2019, the constitution of a high-level committee to recommend measures within six months to protect the cultural, social and linguistic heritage of Assam.[227] The home minister had already assured of reactivating the nine-member committee to deal with Clause 6 of the Assam Accord way back on 26 April, 2017 and a committee was formed on 5 January, 2019 by the Centre even before the introduction of the CAB 2016 in the Lok Sabha because the Centre in principle agreed to give constitutional recognition to Clause 6 of the Assam Accord by widening the ambit of protection given to Assam under Article 371. On 5 January, 2019, the Centre notified the formation of a high level committee under chairmanship of retired IAS officer Madan Prasad Bezbarua to examine the modalities for implementing Clause 6, assess the effectiveness of moves taken since 1985 to implement the clause and recommend the level of reservation of seats for Assamese people in the assembly and local bodies. The panel was to submit its report within six months. The committee comprised former IAS officer Subhash Das, two former presidents of Assam Sahitya Sabha—Nagen Saikia and Rongbong Terang, former editor of *The Sentinel* Dhiren Bezbaruah, educationist Mukunda Rajbongshi, advocate general of Assam Ramesh Borpatragohain and one representative of all Assam Students' Union.[228] But within a week of its formation, as many as five members of the committee including its chairman—M.P. Bezbbruah, Nagen Saikia and Rong bong Terang, both former presidents of the premier literary organization Assam Sahitya Sabha, Mukund Rajbongshi, educationist and the AASU representative declined to be part of the committee.[229]

The MHA on 17 July, 2019 formed a new 13-member committee headed by retired justice of the Gauhati High Court, Biplab Kumar Sharma to suggest ways to implement Clause 6 of Assam Accord which says: "Constitutional, legislative and administrative safeguards, as may be appropriate, shall be provided to protect, preserve and promote the culture, social, linguistic identity and heritage of the Assamese people." The new committee had two members who were a part of the earlier one as well—Ramesh Borpatragohain and Subhash Das. The other new members were Arunachal Pradesh advocate general Niloy Dutta, retired IPS officer Pallav Bhattacharya, retired professor Srishtidhar Dutta, author-columnist Sumanta Chaliha, professor Jaikanta Sharma, journalist Wasbir Hussain, besides Samujjal Bhattacharya, Dipanka Nath and Lurinjyoti Gogoi, the top leadership of AASU. The committee, to be serviced by the north-east division of the MHA through Garg, was to submit its report within six months of its notification.[230]

The Committee was given a month's extension after its six month tenure expired on 17 January, 2020. As the committee completed its recommendations, it could not submit its report to the Union home minister. With no hope of submitting it to the Union home minister, the committee handed over its report to chief minister Sarbananda Sonowal on 25 February, 2020. Since then the government has remained silent.

Frustrated with government inaction, AASU leaders made the entire report public through a press conference on 11 August, 2020. The people of the state came to know about the recommendations made by the Committee to the Centre. The committee recommended that the Assam Accord must be fully implemented in a time-bound manner so as to facilitate detection and deportation of the foreigners in Assam. The Committee noted that the Accord is yet to be fully and effectively implemented even after 35 years of its signing. It sought prompt and adequate measures to completely seal the India-Bangladesh border in the line of India-Pakistan border. Till the deportation of post-1971 stream of declared foreigners is completed, they should be resettled in areas outside Assam as an interim measure, the committee suggested.

After deliberations and consideration of various representations from the stakeholders and further, on the basis of interactions with various organisations and individuals, the committee concluded that the definition of the term "Assamese people" for the specific purpose of implementation of the Clause 6 of the Accord should consist of indigenous tribals as well as other indigenous communities of Assam over and above indigenous Assamese. It recommended that while providing constitutional, legislative and administrative safeguards in terms of Clause 6 of the Accord, the term "Assamese people" shall be construed as regards citizens of India who are part of the Assamese community, any indigenous tribal community of Assam, any other indigenous community of Assam and all other citizens of India residing in Assam on or before 1 January, 1951, and their descendants.

The committee recommended the reservation of seats in Parliament, Assam Legislative Assembly and local bodies. It suggested that 80 to 100 per cent of seats in Parliament, which are allotted to Assam, should be reserved for the "Assamese people". Further, it recommended reservation of seats for the "Assamese people" in the state Assembly and local bodies to the extent of 80 to 100 per cent which will be inclusive of pre-existing reservations. The committee also recommended the making of adequate provisions for an Upper House (Legislative Council of Assam) with reservation of all seats for the "Assamese people."

It suggested that adequate measures be taken for provisions in respect of the Inner Line Permit (ILP) system in Assam, reservation of 80 to 100 per cent of Group C and D level posts in Central Government, semi-Central Government, central PSUs, private sector falling and arising in Assam, 80 to 100 per cent of jobs under state government and its undertakings and 70 to 100 per cent of vacancies arising in private partnerships in the state for the "Assamese people."

As regards land rights, the committee recommended that the provisions of Assam Land Revenue and Regulation, 1886 (as amended) should be strictly followed. In addition, the land rights be confined to the "Assamese people" putting restrictions on transferring the same by any means to other persons other than "Assamese people." It suggested that the policy pertaining to Assam's official language be given appropriate constitutional protection under Article 371B.[231]

This Committee has again put the debate in favour of 1951 as the cut-off year for detecting foreigners, as opposed to the base year of 1971 fixed by the historic Assam Accord. The Assam Sanmilita Mahasangha, which recently knocked the door of the Supreme Court over the matter, has raised the issue. It was later supported by the Indigenous Tribal People's Front, All Assam Ahom Association and Purbotar Hindustani Sanmelan. The Assam Public Works, Prabrajan Virodhi Mancha and Patriotic People's Front Assam came out in favour of 1951. The logic is simple—that the historic students' movement was run with the spirit of 1951 as the base year. All the martyrs of the movement, starting with Khargeswar Talukdar, sacrificed their lives not for a new base year for deportation of illegal migrants. But the accord states that only those who entered Assam before 25 Match, 1971 would be granted Indian citizenships. The state units of Jamiat-Ulema-e-Hind, All India United Democratic Front, Congress supported the 25 March, 1971 cut-off date. While AASU and AGP at one point of time had said that they were determined to honour the Assam Accord,[232] it is not known what their role would be in view of the fact that they were signatories of the Sarma Committee report. Incidentally,

AASU along with the Assam Jatiyabadi Youth Chatra Parishad (AJYCP) formed a new regional party Assam Jatiya Parishad (AJP) on 14 September, 2020, roughly within one month of the press conference releasing the recommendations of the Justice (Retd.) Biplab Kumar Sharma Committee and about 35 years after the formation of the first regional party—Assam Gana Parishad (AGP). The AGP was formed on 14 October, 1985. In the mean time in a new twist to this issue, Assam's most powerful minister Himant Biswa Sarma urged the state government on 10 December, 2020 to declassify the Assam agitation files so that people would know on what grounds did 1951 became 1971 (the cut-off date for detection of illegal migrants in Assam).[233]

It may be recalled that the Speaker of the Assam Legislative Assembly, Pranab Kumar Gogoi, on the last date of the budget session on 31 March, 2015, recommended after consultations with 53 different organizations, that the year 1951 be taken as the cut-off period and the National Register of Citizens 1951 be taken as the basis for the definition of the 'Assamiya People' for the purpose of reservation of seats and constitutional safeguards as required by the Assam Accord. The ruling Congress and the Opposition All-India United Democratic Front (AIUDF) members raised objections to this recommendation of the Speaker. They raised objection on the ground that the Speaker had not consulted the legislators and political parties to firm up the definition of the Assamiya People. The members of the Asam Gana Parishad (AGP), Bharatiya Janata Party (BJP) and the Bodoland People's Front (BPF), however, backed the Speaker's definition and insisted that the Speaker's recommendation be treated as a recommendation of the House.[234]

With the recommendation of this Committee being made public, the question as to who is an Asomiya has again taken over the minds of Assamese people. Since the first decade of the twentieth century, the Assamese middle-class became increasingly conscious of their identity and existence which culminated in the formation of different organisations such as the Assam Association (1903), Assam Sahitya Sabha (1917), Asom Chhatra Association (1919) and the Assam Sangrakshini Sabha (1925). The last named organisation was later transformed into the Asom Jatiya Mahasabha. It needs mention that the Assam Association was based on the sentiment of "Assam nationalism" rather than "Indian nationalism". However, the feeling of Assamese nationalism was submerged by the wave of Indian nationalism when most of its members joined the Congress in 1920. But a section of the Assamese elite did not want the Assamese nationalism to be completely submerged and lost in Indian national movement. Ambikagiri Roychoudhury, a notable writer and poet, clearly distinguished "Asamiya Swaraj" from "Bharatiya Swaraj" and that "Swaraj for India might not bring Swaraj for Assam." This section of the Assamese elite apprehended that the British domination might be replaced by the domination of non-Assamese Indians over the Assamese with Independence. In view of this, the Asom Sangrakshini Sabha demanded the vindication of the right of the children of the soil and pleaded for the "protection of indigenous Assamese people against the aggression of outsiders." In fact, the Sangrakshini Sabha put up a strong case of "Assam for the Assamiya."[235]

In a memorandum presented to Nehru at Rongia on 28 November, 1937, it was stated, amongst others, that "as a means of saving the Assamese race from extinction, a considerable section of the Assamese intelligentsia has even expressed their minds in favour of the secession of Assam from India."[236] In a memorandum submitted to the British Parliamentary Delegation on 29 January, 1946, the Asom Jatiya Mahasabha clealry mentioned that "Assam for the Assamese is the battle cry of all the true sons of Assam."[237] In another memorandum to the members of the All India Congress Committee on 9 June, 1946, the Mahasabha unhesitatingly declared that the Assamese people were even prepared to "plunge the country in desperate struggle" for their "emancipation" and "existence", the consequences of which it thought were never foreseen by the All India leaders.[238]

Thus, it appears that a section of Assamese elite expressed secessionist sentiment in the middle and late forties of the twentieth century. This secessionist urges remained dormant most of the time even in the post-Independence period, but on occasions it came into surface. The separatist sentiments appear to have been articulated in different regional movements such as the Language Movement 1960; Oil Refinery Movement 1967; Medium of Instruction Movement 1972; and finally, the anti-Foreigners' Movement 1979-85 which gave birth to a formal secessionist organisation, i.e., the United Liberation Front of Assam (ULFA) on 7 August, 1979.

The sense of relative deprivation because of being swamped by non-Assamiya, real or imaginary, has resulted in both constitutional and extra-constitutional ethno-political movements. For the protagonists of the "Assam for Assamiya movement" "Assamiya" stands for the settlers in Assam, not those speaking Asamese language, because there are multitude of languages spoken by the tribal groups and even Bodo language has been included in the Eighth Schedule, though the Patriotic People's Front Assam (PPFA) asserted that the illegal migrants who would be allowed to stay in Assam legally should adopt Assamese language as their medium of instruction.[239] So when they speak of the settlers in Assam, what should be the relevant cut-off date of settlement—1 January, 1951, as suggested by the Justice Biplab Sharma Committee, or 25 March, 1971 as mentioned in the Assam Accord or 10 January, 2020, the date of coming into force of the CAA 2019? All these dates raise a big question mark, given the pan-India nature of Indian citizenship which gives the citizens the liberty to move around freely in any part of India and allows every Indian citizen to settle in any place of his choice.

Moreover, Assam, being a multi-lingual, multi-cultural and multi-religious state, formed by slicing off certain territories of eastern Bengal actually comprises a huge area where people of non-Assamese ethnic origin live. Despite occasional differences and struggles for rights, Assam, as it stands today, is a melting pot of cultures, languages, ethnicities and identities. Given its multi-religious, multi-ethnic and multi-lingual populace, no one can say for certain who is an Assamese and who isn't.

However, Assam's powerful minister Himanta Biswa Sarma hit back at AASU for putting a confidential report in public domain, which could possibly complicate matters. He also asserted that no committee could define the term Asomiya apart from the State Legislative Assembly. The minister affirmed that until and unless the Assembly endorses it, the definition of Assamee people cannot be finalized.[240]

Leaving aside the question of constitutional validity of such recommendations, it is a fact that the report of the Justice (Retd.) Biplab Kumar Sharma Committee has added a new dimension to the "Asomiyo question" and the Bengali community, like the previous years, will be the natural target in the coming days. So it is all the more necessary that effective steps should be made to reduce the "linguistic tensions" afflicting this state.

The Assam government on 2 October, 2021 set up an eight-member sub-committee to examine and prepare a framework for the implementation of all clauses of the Assam Accord of 1985. The members of the sub-committee are Ministers Atul Bora, Pijush Hazarika and Ajanta Neog, AASU president Dipanka Kumar Nath, its general secretary Sankar Jyoti Baruah and AASU advisors Samujjal Bhattacharya, Prakash Das and Uddip Jyoti Gogoi. Sujata Suchibrata, Deputy Secretary in the Implementation of Assam Accord Department is its convenor.[241] Though the sub-committee was mandated to submit its report within three months for further course of action, it has not submitted its report till June 2022.

Very few are aware of the grim struggle the Bengaleese of Cachar, Karimganj, Hailakandi and other places waged for their mother tongue in the early Sixties. Eleven Bengalees, including a 16-year old girl student named Kumari Kamala Bhattacharyya—the only woman *shahid* in the language movement anywhere in the world—who were all volunteers of Gana Sangram Parishad—laid down their lives in a police firing while offering a peaceful *satyagraha* at Silchar Railway Station on 19 May, 1961. After the firing, the Assam government relented to some extent and declared Bengali as the second state language for the Bengalee residents.[242] But the animosity between the Assamese—and Bengali-speaking people continued. Moreover, the Barak Valley continues to bristle with the feeling of having been betrayed since the day when Gopinath Bordoloi made a gift of a major portion of Barak Valley to Pakistan in 1947 to ensure that Assamese culture dominate the state. That single act had vivisected families who suddenly found themselves in a new country while their relatives were in another.

BJP Member of Parliament and Minister of state for Railways Rajen Gohain was the most prolific in articulating that Bengalee Hindus committed the historical blunder of organizing a language movement in the 1960s that, according to him, created fear and alienated them from Assamese Hindus. Ever since, the latter could never think of Bengalee Hindus as brethren. Hence, they must now adopt Assamiya as their mother tongue, or alternatively, at least call themselves "Bengali-speaking Assamese." His points of argument were that Bengalee Hindus instead of laying emphasis on their linguistic identity ought to have realized their Hindu identity so as to have been absorbed in the mainstream Assamiya language and culture. Further, had children from Bengalee Hindu homes accepted that they were Hindus first, would by now have been studying in Assamiya medium schools and not found themselves aliens to Assamiya culture and language. Gohain's political colleague, Siladitya Sen, a legislator from the same party who apparently represents Bengalee Hindus of the Brahmaputra Valley went a step further in proclaiming that he felt "proud" to call himself an Assamese and that, too, not a Bengali-speaking one.[243] Gohain's articulation assumes significance when viewed from the dominant-aspirant language's efforts at achieving its objective by swallowing other language groups.

The Gazetteer of Bengal and the North-east compiled by ICS officers led by B.G. Allen and E.A. Gait contains facts, now forgotten, that the undivided Goalpara district of Assam with Dhubri as district headquarters that covers most of Bodoland today was carved out of the large Rangpur district of Bengal and made a district in1822 and transferred to Assam after annexation of the Ahom kingdom on the conclusion of the Treaty of Yandabo on 24 February, 1826. However, till 1867 Goalpara was in the charge of the Commissioner of Cooch Behar and in 1868, it was placed under the Judicial Commissioner of Assam (Bengal Presidency).[244] Assam was a Division of the Province of Bengal till 1874. When Assam was made a Division under the Bengal Province, the Bengal districts of Goalpara, Sylhet and the plains portion of Cachar were transferred to this new administrative unit. This arrangement continued even when Assam was taken out of Bengal Presidency and made a Chief Commissioner's province in 1874. "The idea was that the surplus revenue of the Surma Valley would balance the deficit of the Brahmaputra Valley."[245] That is the reason why there was heavy concentration of Bengali-speaking population in certain areas like Cachar, Sylhet in the Surma Valley, in Goalpara and certain urban areas in the Assam Valley.

It must be noted that most land in Goalpara was under the permanent settlement of Lord Cornwallis, which was peculiar to Bengal, and the *rajas* of large *zamindari* estates of Gauripur, Bijni and Sidli commanded vast tracts and enjoyed status and power in society. The British had already annexed the Eastern Duars in 1865 after a short campaign and added places such as Chirag to Goalpara. The claims of *zamindars* of Bijni and Sidli that they were the proprietors of these lands under the Bhutan King were accepted and the areas were added to their *zamindaris*. The total area of Goalpara was 3,961 sq miles then and had a population of 4,62,052. According to the Census, 69 per cent of the population spoke Bengali while 18 per cent spoke Bodo and Muslims constituted 27 per cent of the population. The district, the *Gazetteer* affirmed, "is not a part of Assam."[246]

The easy availability of cultivable land, the fertility of the soil and the prevalence of low rents induced a section of cultivators in the overcrowded districts of Bengal to find their way to Assam. A certain number of persons from the districts of Mymensing, Dacca, Rangpur and Pabna also settled down in Sylhet and Goalpara but this, according to the 1901 Census Superintendent of Assam, E.A.Gait, could scarcely be called immigration. They moved a few miles from their original homes and the accident of boundary alone brought them within the limits of Assam.[247] "While the Muslim settlements came up only in the rural areas, the Hindus generally settled in the administrative and business centres. No wonder, most of the towns in the region originated with the Bengalis. There are similar reasons behind settlements of the Bengalees in and around Shillong, which was the capital of undivided Assam for a very long time."[248]

Following partition and communal riots in the subcontinent, Assam initially saw an influx of refugees and other migrants from East Pakistan. When fresh communal disturbances occurred in early 1950 in Assam along with East Pakistan, West Bengal and Tripura, some immigrants living in the districts of Goalpara, Kamrup and Darrang fled to East Pakistan leaving their properties behind. In the Nehru-Liaquat Agreement signed on 8th April, 1950, it was agreed by the two Governments—India and Pakistan—that the rights of the immovable property of a migrant shall not be disturbed and the same shall be restored to him, even if it is occupied by another person in his absence, provided he returns to his original home by 31 December, 1950. The agreement facilitated the return of almost all the displaced persons. By 31 December, 1950, there was a net influx of 1,61,360 people into Assam who had entered Assam through recognized routes of travel.[249]

After partition, Muslim politics in Assam was shaped by the immigrants' perceived vulnerability and to deal with it, they as well as the longtime Muslim residents of Goalpara and in all districts of the Brahmaputra Valley put down Assamese as their mother tongue in the 1951 Census and voluntarily opposed the claim of West Bengal for the reversion of Goalpara. The switch over to Assamese was complete right from the primary school stage and to the extent of adoption of a strange yet common stance of not speaking Bengali in public. The movement against foreign nationals was the end of this cozy world for ethnic Bengalee Muslims. They are now back to their Bengali roots they once discarded. This is reflected in the Census figures. But it is debatable whether this move would offset the damage, already inflicted.

The historically Bengali-speaking areas of Goalpara district, now split into four districts of Kokrajhar, Bongaigaon, Dhubri and Goalpara, are no longer Bengali-majority districts, thanks to the policy pursued by the Assamese chauvinism since independence, as admitted way back in 1955 by the States Reorganisaion Commission (SRC) itself. So though these areas are contiguous to Bengal and have a sizeable Bengali population (roughly 35% as against 58% of Assamese population, according to the 2011 census) cannot be returned to Bengal, even though these areas geographically once belonged to Bengal.

We have seen earlier that Cachar represented to the SRC way back in 1955 to be part of a Purbachal State with Tripura, the Mizo Hills, the Naga Hills, Manipur and the NEFA. While all the would-be constituents of the proposed Purbachal state became full-fledged states by this time, Cachar remained as it were. Now the time has come to take a fresh look at the proposal and make Cachar, Karimganj and Hailakandi, the three overwhelmingly Bengali-majority (more than 99%) districts a separate state.

It may be recalled that the Union Territory Demand Committee is spearheading a movement for a separate Union Territory out of the Barak Valley since 1971. Now a demand for a separate state has been made by the All Cachar Karimganj Hailakandi Students Association. "The Brahmaputra Valley has always viewed Barak Valley as a cancer, and the rift between the two has only widened over the NRC and the Citizenship (Amendment) Bill 2016, which, if passed, will grant citizenship to Bengalee Hindus excluded by the NRC. So it is better to cut the cancer away and make Barak a separate State", urges Pradip Dutta Roy, founder president of the All Cachar Karimganj Hailakandi Students Association. In May 2017, he had written to Chief Justice Dipak Misra about a possible conflict of interest involving Justice Ranjan Gogoi, a "resident and voter in Assam" who "is monitoring the NRC process."[250]

Noted intellectuals Hemen Borgohain has asserted that certain parts of Assam, such as the Barak Valley, Dhubri and lower Assam had only been parts of Assam's geography but never a part of its history. Borgohain's argument is that the Bengali-speaking people of the Barak Valley and certain other lower Assam areas have pushed Assamese into being a minority language in the state. So he reasoned that the Barak Valley should be separated from Assam to regain "only the Brahmaputra Valley as the land of Asomiya speakers." [251] A welcome suggestion.

The formation of a separate Cachar state will effectively solve both the problems of saving the Assamese people from becoming a minority in their own land and at the same time allowing the Bengali-speaking people to live a life with dignity and fortitude. With some adjustments here and there, all the NRC-excluded persons will find a safe home without being under constant threat of persecution and deportation. The Assamese people can also preserve and protect their identity and culture and live their own way of life without any let or hindrance.

But the formation of a separate Cachar state may act as an impetus to the protagonist of the Bodoland movement to continue their stir for a separate Bodoland with renewed vigour. Similar demand may find a fertile ground in Karbi Anglong and Dima Hasao, the two tribal majority districts. Moreover, this will not solve the problems of Barpeta, Sonitpur, Karbi Anglong, Dima Hasao and Chirang districts where the Bengali-speaking population far outweigh the Assamese-speaking population. Intolerance to other ethnic and linguistic groups had cost Assam dearly. It made a gift of the populous Sylhet to Pakistan at the dawn of independence to get rid of Bengali-speaking people. The hopes and aspirations of the Assamese that they could absorb the hill districts of Assam within their own cultural stream were doomed from the very outset. The Assamese did not realise that people, however primitive, resent the imposition of alien culture. And so, one by one, the hill districts broke away from the parent state and the people of these states feel safer today than being in Assam. It has been repeatedly balkanized to create the hill states of Nagaland, Meghalaya and Mizoram, has border problems with the newly created states and its people are not welcome in the hill states for fear of demographic changes. It is still intolerant of other communities and suffers from a sense of victimhood. "The state's geographical integrity and territorial oneness", asserts a columnist, "can only be preserved in a condition of mutual and reciprocal respect between ethnic groups and minorities."[252] Assam's rich heritage, marked by immense tolerance, fellow-feeling, mutual participation and appreciation makes it possible to shun differences over matters of culture. But political forces are bent on widening the divide between people in the name of culture. The NRC has placed on Assam the heavy burden of taking a decision between linguistic chauvinism and territorial disintegration.

NOTES

1. *The Times of India*, November 1, 2008, p. 1.
2. Government of Assam, Home and Political Department, *White Paper on Foreigners' Issue*, October 20, 2012, para 12.2, p. 6.
3. *Ibid.*, para 14.1, p. 7.
4. *Ibid.*, para 14.2, p. 7.
5. *Ibid.*, para 15.1, p. 8.
6. *Ibid.*, para 16.2, p. 11.
7. *Ibid.*, para 16.3, p. 11.
8. *Sarbananda Sonowal* v. *Union of India AIR 2005 SC 2920* (paras 27, 28, 32, 38, 39 and 57).
9. *Sarbananda Sonowal (II)* v. *Union of India (2007) SCC 174.*
10. *The Hindu*, March 15, 2014, p. 8.
11. Lama, J.B., "Infiltration row and its implications", *The Statesman*, August 23, 2010, p. 8.
12. *The Hindu*, July 17, 2014, p. 4.
13. *White Paper on Foreigners' Issue, Op. Cit.*, para 1.2.1, p. 6.
14. *The Hindu*, July 18, 2014, p. 4.
15. *Ibid.*, August 7, 2014, p. 2.
16. Dutta, Sambudha, *Bartaman*, November 14, 2014, p. 14.
17. *The National Herald*, September 2, 1992.
18. *Ibid.*
19. *Ibid.*
20. *Ibid.*
21. *Ibid.*
22. *The Times of India*, July 31, 2018, p. 8.
23. *Ibid.*, December 18, 2014, p. 7.
24. Para 48(1) of Judgment in *Writ Petition No. 562 of 2012.*
25. Para 48 of Judgment in *Writ Petition No. 562 of 2012.*
26. https://en.wikipedia.org/wiki/National_Register_of_Citizens_of_India.
27. *The Statesman*, December 2, 2015, p. 1.

28. *Outlook*, August 6, 2018, p. 39.
29. Ahuja, Namrata Biji, "Census and consensus", *The Week*, June 26, 2016, pp. 26-27.
30. *The Times of India,* January 2, 2018, p. 1.
31. *Ibid.*, January 5, 2018, p. 1.
32. *Ibid.*
33. *Ibid.*, January 2, 2018, p. 1 and p. 6.
34. *Ibid.*, July 31, 2018, p. 1.
35. *Ibid.*, July 31, 2018, p. 8.
36. *The Hindu*, July 31, 2018, p. 1.
37. *Ibid.*, July 29, 2018, p. 1.
38. *The Times of India*, September 20, 2018, p. 1.
39. *The Hindu*, January 1, 2019, p. 1.
40. *Ibid.,* July 10, 2019, p. 7.
41. *Ibid.*, July 24, 2019, p. 1.
42. *Ibid.*, August 7, 2019, p. 4.
43. *Ibid.*, August 8, 2019, p. 11.
44. *Ibid.*, August 30, 2019, p. 10.
45. *Ibid.*, August 3, 2019, p. 4.
46. *The Statesman*, August 14, 2019, p. 1.
47. *The Times of India*, August 2, 2019, p. 10.
48. *Ibid.*, August 3, 2019, p. 4.
49. *The Statesman*, September 1, 2019, p. 1.
50. *The Times of India*, September 1, 2019, p. 1.
51. Balakrishnan, Varna and Singh Navsharan, "Gendered Exclusions of the NRC", In *This Land Is Mine, I Am Not of This Land* (ed.) Harsh Mander and Navsharan Singh, 2021, Speaking Tiger Books LLP, New Delhi, p. 266.
52. *The Hindu*, November 17, 2021, p. 1.
53. *The Sentinel*, March 28, 2021, p. 1.
54. *The Hindu*, August 31, 2020, p. 1 and p. 8.
55. *The Telegraph*, September 2, 2020, p. 5.
56. *The Hindu*, November 7, 2020, p. 10.
57. *Ibid.*, September 20, 2021, p. 1. and p. 8.
58. *Ibid.,* July 14, 2021, p. 4.
59. *The Hindu*, March 26, 2022, p. 3.
60. *The Telegraph*, April 12, 2022, p. 3.
61. Hussain, Banaji, "Riots & the bogey of Bangladeshis", *The Hindu*, August 6, 2012, p. 6.
62. Editorial titled "Inclusion over exclusion", *The Hindu*, July 20, 2019, p. 8.
63. *The Statesman*, September 1, 2019, p. 1.
64. *Ei Samay*, September 2, 2019, p. 9.
65. *Anandabazar Patrika,* September 1, 2019, p. 6.
66. *Ibid.*

67. *Ei Samay,* September 1, 2019, p. 1.
68. *The Times of India*, September 2, 2019, p. 7.
69. *Ibid.*, September 1, 2019, p. 4.
70. *The Telegraph*, June 30, 2019, p. 9.
71. *Ibid.*, September 1, 2019, p. 8.
72. *The Statesman*, September 13, 2019, p. 15.
73. *Ibid.*, September 19, 2019, p. 15.
74. *The Times of India*, Septmber 23, 2019, p. 7.
75. *The Telegraph*, October 2, 2019, p. 4.
76. *The Statesman,* September 1, 2019, p. 1.
77. *Ibid.*, September 1, 2019, p. 4.
78. *Ibid.*
79. *Ibid.*, August 29, 2019, p. 3.
80. *The Times of India,* September 1, 2019, p. 11.
81. *Ibid.*, September 2, 2019, p. 7.
82. *The Hindu*, August 25, 2019, p. 1.
83. *The Times of India*, August 27, 2019, p. 6.
84. *Anandabazar Patrika*, September 1, 2019, p. 1.
85. *The Times of India*, August 26, 2019, p. 1 and p. 5.
86. *The Statesman*, August 26, 2019, p. 1.
87. *The Telegraph*, September 3, 2019, p. 1.
88. *The Hindu*, July 17, 2019, p. 1.
89. *The Telegraph*, July 18, 2019, p. 7.
90. *The Times of India,* February10, 2020, p. 10.
91. *The Telegraph*, August 31, 2019, p. 5.
92. *The Times of India*, August 31, 2019, p. 11.
93. *The Statesman*, September 6, 2019, p. 3.
94. *The Telegraph*, October 19, 2019, p. 1 and p. 5.
95. *The Times of India*, November 7, 2019, p. 6.
96. Editorial titled "Mission Impossible", *The Times of India*, October 21, 2019, p. 14.
97. Mander Harsh, "A flawed process". *The Hindu*, September 2, 2019, p. 9.
98. *Anandabazar Patrika,* October 19, 2019, p. 8.
99. *The Times of India*, November 29, 2019, p. 8.
100. *Ibid.,* August 2, 2019, p. 10.
101. *The Telegraph*, August 5, 2019, p. 14.
102. *The Times of India*, August 20, 2019, p. 1.
103. *The Telegraph,* December 24, 2019, p. 7.
104. *The Times of India*, August 20, 2019, p. 1.
105. *The Telegraph*, September 10, 2019, p. 1.
106. *Ibid.*, September 23, 2019, p. 5.
107. *The Times of India*, September 30, 2019, p. 7.
108. *The Hindu*, August 30, 2019, p. 10.
109. *The Telegraph*, September 9, 2019, p. 5.
110. *The Times of India*, September 9, 2019, p. 6.

111. *Anandabazar Patrika*, September 15, 2019, p. 6.
112. *The Times of India*, August 28, 2019, p. 6.
113. *Ibid.*, August 28, 2019, p. 6.
114. *Ibid.*
115. *The Times of India*, September 28, 2019, p. 11.
116. *Ibid.*, September 30, 2019, p. 7.
117. Siddique, Nazimuddin, Discourse of Doubt, *Economic & Political Weekly*, March 9, 2019, Vol. LIV, No. 10, pp. 25-30.
118. *The Times of India*, Decmber 23, 2020, p. 12.
119. Editorial titled "NRC Quagmire", *The Times of India*, July 19, 2019, p. 12.
120. Bhattacharjee, Sudipta and Pal, Sudeshna, "NRC Anarchy", *The Telegraph*, August 25, 2019, p. 15.
121. *The Hindu*, August 18, 2019, p. 10.
122. Biswas, Prasenjit, "Murkier and murkier", *The Statesman*, September 25, 2017, p. 16.
123. Biswas, Prasenjit, "On a slippery slope", *The Statesman,* June 4, 2018, p. 10.
124. Samaddar, Ranabir, "Migrants, NRC, and the paradox of protection and power", *The Wire*, April 12, 2019.
125. Ray, Anupama, "Citizenship Regimes, Law and Belonging", In *This Land Is Mine, I Am Not of This Land* (ed.) Harsh Mander and Navsharan Singh, 2021, Speaking Tiger Books LLP, New Delhi, p. 76.
126. *The Hindu*, April 12, 2021, p. 1.
127. *Ibid.*, February 13, 2020, p. 8.
128. *Ibid.*, February 22, 2020, p. 1.
129. *Ibid.*, December 10, 2020, p. 5.
130. *Ibid.*, December 11, 2020, p. 7.
131. *The Telegraph*, September 2, 2020, p. 5.
132. *The Hindu*, November 7, 2020, p. 10.
133. *Ibid.*, May 21, 2022, p. 11.
134. *Ibid.*, May 23, 2022, p. 10.
135. *The Telegraph*, May 27, 2022, p. 5.
136. *The Hindu*, May 26, 2022, p. 4.
137. *The Statesman,* May 22, 2022, p. 4.
138. Thakuria, Nava, "Exclusion & protection", *The Statesman,* May 30, 2022, p. 11.
139. *Ibid.*, May 14, 2021, p. 1.
140. Mitra, Debala, "*Foreign Elements in Indian Population*" in *The Cultural Heritage of India,* Vol. II, 1982 (Reprint), Calcutta, The Ramakrishna Mission Institute of Culture, p. 610.
141. Chatterjee, Suniti Kumar, "Linguistic Survey of India: Languages and Scripts", In *The Cultural Heritage of India,* Vol. I, 1982 (Reprint), Calcutta, The Ramakrishna Mission Institute of Culture, p. 64.

142. Rao, B. Shiva, (ed.) *The Framing of India's Constitution,* Vol. III, 1967, New Delhi, The Indian Institute of Public Administration, p. 693.
143. Das, B.M. "Some Aspects of Physical Anthropology of the Tribes of North-east India", In *The Tribes of North-east India* (ed.) S. Karotemprel, 1984, Calcutta Firma KLM Private Limited, p. 41.
144. Das, B.M., "North-east India and the People", In *Anthropology for North-east India: A Reader* (eds.) Arabinda Basu, Biman K. Dasgupta, and Jayanata Sarkar, 2004, Calcutta, Indian National Confederation and Academy of Anthropologists, Indian Anthropological Society and National Museum of Mankind, p. 8.
145. Chatterjee, Sarajit Kumar, *North East India: Dispersion and Discontent,* 2010, Delhi, Abhijeet Publications, p. 332.
146. Biswas, Prasenjit, "Questions of Indigeneity", *The Statesman*, October 5, 2020, p. 11.
147. *The Times of India*, September 3, 2019, p. 7.
148. *The Telegraph*, March 31, 2019, p. 8.
149. *The Statesman,* September 21, 2019, p. 2.
150. *Ibid.*, September 9, 2019, p. 9.
151. *The Times of India*, February 12, 2020, p. 9.
152. *Ibid.*, February 9, 2020, p. 6.
153. *Ibid.*
154. *The Hindu*, April 16, 2021, p. 4.
155. *The Times of India*, April 22, 2022, p. 12.
156. *The Statesman*, September 1, 2019, p. 1.
157. *Ibid.*, August 20, 2019, p. 7.
158. *The Times of India*, August 28, 2019, p. 6.
159. *Ibid.,* August 25, 2019, p. 1. and p. 6.
160. *The Telegraph*, August 21, 2019, p. 6.
161. *The Times of India*, August 28, 2019, p. 6.
162. *The Hindu*, August 22, 2019, p. 4.
163. *EI Samay*, September 2, 2019, p. 1 and p. 9.
164. *The Hindu*, August 18, 2019, p. 10.
165. *The Times of India*, January 25, 2021, p. 9.
166. *The Hindu*, August 21, 2019, p. 10.
167. *Ibid.*, June 10, 2019, p. 1 and p. 10.
168. Rohini Mohan, "Prove Your Grandfather Is Indian". *The Times of India*, August 2, 2019, p. 14.
169. *Ibid.*
170. *The Hindu*, March 3, 2020, p. 11.
171. Bhatia, Gautam, "The judicial presumption of non-citizenship", *The Hindu*, July 23, 2019, p. 8.
172. *The Hindu,* March 20, 2020, p. 4.
173. *Ibid.,* September 29, 2019, p. 7.
174. Verghese, Leah and Naik, Shruti, "Flawed Foreigners' Tribunal", *The Hindu*, October 21, 2020, p. 7.

175. Bhatia, Gautam, "The Judicial Presumption of Non-Citizenship", In *This Land Is Mine, I Am Not of This Land* (ed.) Harsh Mander and Navsharan Singh, 2021, Speaking Tiger Books LLP, New Delhi, pp. 191-192.
176. *Ganadabi*, 25 February–3 March, 2022, p. 8.
177. *Ei Samay,* May 7, 2022, p. 5.
178. *The Hindu*, May 16, 2022, p. 8.
179. *Ibid.*, September 9, 2019, p. 11.
180. *Ibid.*
181. Karmakar, Rahul, "Staring at statelessness", *The Hindu*, July 14, 2019, p. 9.
182. Bannerjee, Rabi, "Grouse goes global", *The Week,* August 4, 2019, p. 33.
183. *The Telegraph*, September 8, 2019, p. 9.
184. *Anandabazar Partika*, September 10, 2019, p. 8.
185. *The Hindu*, December 24, 2019, p. 8.
186. en.wikipedia.org-wiki-National_Register_of_Citizens, p. 8.
187. *The Hindu*, December 24, 2019, p. 8.
188. *The Times of India,* February 26, 2020, p. 14.
189. Biswas, Prasenjit, "Statelessness in Assam", *The Statesman*, May 20, 2019, p. 16.
190. Bhattacharjee, Sudipta and Pal, Sudeshna, "NRC Anarchy", *The Telegraph*, August 25, 2019, p. 15.
191. *Ibid.*
192. *Ibid.*
193. Bhattacharje, Govind, "Citizenship tangle", *The Statesman*, May 6, 2018, p. 6.
194. Mander, Harsh, "The Dark Side of Humanity and Legality." In *This Land Is Mine, I Am Not of This Land* (ed.) Harsh Mander and Navsharan Singh, 2021, Speaking Tiger Books LLP, New Delhi, p. 222.
195. Bhattacharjee, Sudipta and Pal, Sudeshna, "NRC Anarchy", *The Telegraph,* August 25, 2019, p. 15.
196. Karmakar, Rahul, "Staring at statelessness", *The Hindu,* July 14, 2019, p. 9.
197. *The Telegraph*, September 17, 2019, p. 6.
198. *The Times of India*, September 5, 2019, p. 7.
199. *The Hindu*, August 30, 2019, p. 10.
200. *The Telegraph* April 6, 2019, p. 7.
201. *The Times of India*, March 31, 2019, p. 7.
202. *The Week*, October 8, 2017, p. 24.
203. *The Statesman*, April 1, 2016, p. 3.
204. *The Hindu*, December 18, 2014, p. 7.
205. *The Statesman*, August 21, 2019, p. 3.
206. *Ibid.*
207. *The Times of India,* October 4, 2019, p. 10.
208. *The Statesman*, September 11, 2019, p. 5.

209. Editorial titled "Quandary of National Register of Citizens", *Economic & Political Weekly,* September 14, 2019, Vol. LIV, No. 37, p. 7.
210. Basu, Deepankar, Das Debaashi, "Assam's politics and the NRC", *Economic and Political Weekly*, Vol. LV, No. 5, February 1, 2020, pp. 61-63.
211. Nag, Sajal, *Roots of Ethnic Conflict*, 1990, New Delhi, Manohar, p. 59.
212. *Census of Imdia*, 1901, Vol. IV, pp. 67-68.
213. Bhttacharjee, Tapodhan, "Tension in North-East", in *Social Tension in North-East India* (ed), J.B. Bhattacharjee, Shillong, North-East India Council for Social Science Research, 1982, p. 127.
214. Sharma, Dr. Brijendra Nath, *Social and Cultural History of Northern India c.1000-1200 A.D.,* New Delhi, Abhinava Publications, 1972, p. 176.
215. Hutton, J.H., *Caste in India*, second edition,1951, Bombay, Oxford University Press, p. 30.
216. Nag, Sajal, *Roots of Ethnic Conflict,* Manohar, New Delhi, 1990, pp. 8-9.
217. *The Week*, August 4, 2019, p. 31.
218. *The Hindu*, July 31, 2019, p. 11.
219. *Report of the States Reorganisation Commission*, para 668, pp. 181-182.
220. *Ibid*., paras 707 and 708, p. 191.
221. *Ibid*., para 708, p. 192.
222. *Ibid*., para 17, p. 38.
223. *Ibid*,, para 5, p. 32.
224. *Census of India 2011*, Paper 1 of 2018 Language, p. 12, pp. 23-24.
225. Karmakar, Rahul, "Staring at statelessness", *The Hindu*, July 14, 2019, p. 9.
226. *The Statesman*, March 26, 2019, p. 15.
227. *The Times of India*, January 10, 2019, p. 8.
228. *Ibid*., January 7, 2019, p. 7.
229. *The Hindu*, January 13, 2019, p. 1.
230. thewire.in "government" home-ministry-reconstitutes-...
231. *The Hindu*, August 12, 2020, p. 6.
232. Thakuria, Nava, "Uncertain future", *The Statesman*, September 11, 2017, p. 16.
233. *The Times of India*, December 11, 2020, p. 7.
234. *The Hindu*, April 1, 2015, p. 2.
235. Phukan, Girin, "*Politics of Secessionism in North-east India*", In *Insurgency in North-east India*" (ed) B. Pakem, 1997, New Delhi, Omsons Publications, p. 261.
236. *AICC File No. 4(1)1937*, Nehru Memorial Museum and Library, New Delhi, quoted In *Ibid*., p. 271.
237. *Ibid*., p. 261.
238. *Ibid.*
239. Thakuria, Nava, "Uncertain future", *The Statesman*, September 11, 2017, p. 16.
240. Thakuria, Nava, Who is an Asomiya? *The Statesman*, August 17, 2020, p. 11.
241. *The Hindu*, October 3, 2021, p. 8.

242. Som, Nirupom, Dying for a language, *The Statesman*, April 1, 2012, p. 6.
243. Biswas, Prasenjit and Gogoi, Suraj, "State & the stateless", *The Statesman*, November 14, 2016, p. 16.
244. Datta, Rangan, "Fight for Civil Rights", *The Statesman*, September 15, 2014, p. 16.
245. Nag, Sajal, *Roots of Ethnic Conflict*, 1990, New Delhi, Manohar, p. 59.
246. Datta, Rangan, "Fight for Civil Rights", *The Statesman*, September 15, 2014, p. 16.
247. *Census of India*, 1901, Vol. IV, pp. 67-68.
248. Bhttacharjee, Tapodhan, "Tension in North-East", in *Social Tension in North-East India* (ed), J.B. Bhattacharjee, Shillong, North-East India Council for Social Science Research, 1982, p. 127.
249. Government of Assam, *White paper on Foreigners' issue*, 2012, para 1.3.1.
250. Karmakar, Rahul, "Staring at statelessness", *The Hindu*, July 14, 2019, p. 9.
251. Biswas, Prasenjit, "Insiders, outsiders & improper legalese", *The Statesman*, January 15, 2018, p. 16.
252. Biswas, Prasenjit, "Bizarre goings-on in Asssam" , *The Statesman*, October 9, 2017, p. 18.

5
Citizenship Amendment Bill, 2016 and Citizenship Amendment Act, 2019

The BJP formed the ministry at the Centre after the 2014 Lok Sabha elections. In consonance with its election manifesto, the BJP Government introduced the Citizenship (Amendment) Bill (CAB 2016) on 15 July, 2016, proposing to grant citizenships to persons belonging to six non-Muslim minority communities—Hindus, Sikhs, Buddhists, Jains, Parsis and Christians—from Bangladesh, Pakistan and Afghanistan. The Bill, described by the opposition as "communally motivated humanitarianism," was referred by the Lok Sabha to the 16-member Joint Parliamentary Committee headed by Rajendra Agarwal of the BJP on 31 July, 2016 for scrutiny.

Apprehending opposition to the Bill from the AASU, the Centre convened a tripartite meeting in Delhi on 26 April, 2017 after a lapse of 12 years. The Home Minister announced that Centre would set up a task force to identify and deport illegal Bangladeshi settlers from Assam. While agreeing to reactivate the nine-member sub-committee to deal with Clause 6 of the Assam Accord, the Home Minister assured the AASU representatives that the spirit of the Assam Accord would not be diluted at any cost.[1] Apparently, the Home Minister was trying to rope in the AASU in favour of the CAB, 2016.

Meanwhile, the Meghalaya High Court on 10 December, 2018 asked the Centre to bring in a law to let people of religious and ethnic minority communities from Afghanistan, Bangladesh and Pakistan to be given citizenship without any cut-off year or any questions asked. Allowing a writ petition filed by Amin Rana, an Army recruit who was denied domicile certificate by the Meghalaya government, Justice S.R. Sen in a 37-page judgment said that the Centre should have a law allowing Hindus, Sikhs, Jains, Bhuddhists, Parsis, Christians, Khasis, Jaintias and Garos from neighbouring countries to live in India "with full dignity without making any cut-off year and be given citizenship without any question or production of any document." He also said that such people "may be allowed to come at any point of time to settle in India and the government may provide rehabilitation properly and declare them citizens of India." He added that Hindus and Sikhs residing elsewhere should be automatically considered for citizenship in India.[2] Though the presiding Judge never mentioned about the pending CAB 2016 in his judgment, it was a clear case for bringing in such a legislation with ethnicity rolled in.

The JPC was given time till the first day of the last week of the Winter Session of Lok Sabha to submit its report. The Committee took six extensions from the Speaker of the Lok Sabha to enable them to complete the study after holding wider consultations. The JPC interviewed many people and conducted some field studies. During the course of its examination and field study visits, the committee met a cross-section of people in Gujarat, Rajasthan, Assam and Meghalaya and heard views of organisations, individuals, experts and others. They conducted public hearings in Guwahati and Silchar in Assam and Shillong in Meghalaya to gather opinion of the people on the proposed Bill. The Committee also heard the views of the chief secretaries and police chiefs of Assam, Bihar, Gujarat, Jharkhand, Maharashtra and West Bengal. The members of the JPC visited Barak Valley, the Bengali-majority area of Assam, and Meghalaya to discuss it with various organisations. They reportedly spoke to about 200 organisations.

The Bill brought to the fore serious fissures in the north-east. Various parts of northeast India, more precisely the Brahrmaputra valley in Assam, witnessed an uproarious situation in the backdrop of the Centre's initiative to amend the citizenship laws.

Various parties and NGOs began campaign in Assam against the Citizenship Amendment Bill. Hurt by the Bill, northeast allies joined hands against the BJP. The AGP president and Minister Atul Bora even said that "it will not hesitate to pull out of the government if the Bill is pushed through."[3] Representatives of 159 organisations and political parties met the JPC on 7 May during its visit to Assam from 7 to 9 May when almost everyone opposed the move and demanded withdrawal of the 'anti-Assam' bill.[4]

The pro-talks faction of the Ulfa and the Banga Bhashi Asomiya Samaj held a meeting in Guwahati on12 November, 2018 and decided to bridge the chasm between the Assamese and the Bengali communities in the northeast state over the CAB 2016. "We are against the bill and it should be withdrawn by the government," the president of the Samaj, Pradip Sen Sarma, said.[5]

Assam Chief Minister Sarbnanda Sonowal while interacting with the editors of print and electronic media on12 May, 2018 told them that he had no reason to continue on his office if he could not protect the interest of the people of the State. He also assured them that he would discuss the matter with senior citizens and intellectuals in the coming days and pleaded for peace in the state.[6]

A delegation of All Arunachal Pradesh Students' Union (AAPSU) met the JPC in Shillong on 10 May and cautioned that the frontier state would burn if New Delhi passed the Citizenship Bill.[7] The Meghalaya cabinet, led by BJP's ally National People's Party conveyed its unanimous opposition to the Citizenship (Amendment) Bill to the JPC when it met on12 May, 2018.[8] The apex bodies of students' unions in Arunachal Pradesh, Mizoram and Nagaland organised sit-ins on 21 May, 2018 morning in their respective State capitals, demanding immediate scrapping of the proposed legislation.[9] A 12-hour Assam bandh against the CAB 2016 on 23 October, 2018 called by 60 organisations evoked total response in the Brahmaputra valley, despite the government's best of efforts to foil it.[10]

The Bill was opposed at the United Nations Human Rights Council in Geneva on 3 July, 2018. Bonnya Barua, 22-year-old daughter of Golap Barua *alias* Anup Chetia, on behalf of the Indigenous Forum, Assam opposed the Bill as it would reduce the indigenous communities of Assam into minorities.[11]

The purpose for bringing in the Amendment Bill was explained to the Assamese people by no less a person than by the Prime Minister himself. Addressing a Vijay Sankalp Samavesh rally at Kalinagar in Silchar on 4 January, 2019, Prime Minister Narendra Modi said India needs the Citizenship (Amendment) Bill to give relief to Hindu, Sikh, Buddhist, Jain, Parsi or Christian who are persecuted in Afghanistan, Bangladesh and Pakistan and as "atonement for the wrongs of Partition." "Mistakes were made in the past when the country was divided and they have to be undone. Some people had stayed back in some place and if they face difficulties there, it is the duty of Mother India to give shelter to them. Those reposing faith in Mother India will be protected," Modi said.[12] All changes moved by the opposition in the Joint Parliamentary Committee of the CAB were defeated on 31 December, 2018.[13] The JPC adopted on 3 January, 2019 amidst protests by Opposition MPs its report on the CAB.[14] The JPC submitted its recommendations on the Citizenship (Amendment) Bill (CAB), 2016 to the Lok Sabha on 7 January, 2019. As there were no consensus in the committee on the final report, members of four opposition parties—Congress, Trinamool Congress, CPM and SP—submitted dissent notes against the final report.[15] The opposition MPs, mainly those belonging to the Trinamool Congress and the Congress was to make the Bill religion and country neutral.[16]

The AGP on 7 January, 2019 severed its ties with the NDA when it failed to dissuade the Union Home Minister from introducing the Bill in the Lok Sabha. And its three ministers in the Assam ministry tendered their resignations from the ministry. NDA allies Shiv Sena and JD(U) also decided to oppose the Bill.[17]

Based on the JPC recommendations a fresh Bill was introduced in the Lok Sabha on 8 January, 2019. Introducing the Bill, the Home Minister Rajnath Singh asserted that the Bill was not against the provisions of the Constitution and would give succour to persecuted minorities in the three neighbouring countries as they "have no place to go to, except India." Seeking to assuage the concerns in the Northeast which saw total shutdown during an 11-hour bandh on 8 January, he said: "The proposed law will not be confined to Assam alone. The burden of persecuted migrants will be shared by the whole country. Assam alone should not have to bear the entire burden. The Government of India is committed to give all help to the State Government and people of Assam."[18] The Lok Sabha passed the Bill the same day amidst walkout by the opposition parties.[19]

II

The passage of the CAB 2016 in the Lok Sabha led to a new phase of turmoil in India's northeast. Violence erupted on 8 January Assam bandh called by AASU which was supported by many indigenous groups in other northeastern states.

Indigenous groups like the Krishak Mukti Sangram Samiti of Assam staged nude protests against the Bill in Delhi, trying to out-radicalise AASU and AGP in the Assamese political space in which illegal migration from Bangladesh has been a recurring theme.[20]

The Ulfa (Independent) purportedly took advantage of widespread resentment in Assam against the bill to recruit disgruntled youth. At least 10 youth from Tinsukia, Udalgiri and Golaghat districts joined the Paresh Barua-led Ulfa(I), but the number could be higher as some cases might have gone unreported to the police.[21] The Assam police on 10 January registered a case of sedition against Sahitya Akademi-award winning writer Hiren Gohain for addressing a rally organized by Forum Against the Citizenship Amendment Bill and Left Democratic Front where some younger elements got up to say they had been pushed to a situation where independence and sovereignty were the only options left.[22] Two days later Hiren Gohain said that he was fighting not only for Assam, but for India. "By raising our voice, we are defending the secular character of citizenship and our Constitution."[23]

While three NDA-ruled states in Northeast—Meghalaya, Mizoram and Nagaland rejected the Bill,[24] Manipur insisted the Centre to insert a clause in the Bill that would exempt Manipur from its purview.[25] Several constituent parties of the North-East Democratic Alliance (Neda), the umbrella organisation of the region's parties floated by the BJP in 2016 asked the Union Home Minister on 18 January not to go ahead with the CAB 2016.[26] The Kuki Inpi Manipur (KIM), the umbrella body of all Kuki civil bodies of Manipur strongly disapproved the CAB 2016.[27] The Mizoram unit of BJP issued an ultimatum on 5 February of dissolving the state unit if the party national leaders insist on the passage of the Bill.[28] Ulfa's pro-talk faction threatened to pull out of the "peace talks" with the Centre if the CAB 2016 was passed in Parliament.[29] Meanwhile, Ram Madhab, the BJP national general secretary rushed to the northeast to deal with the opposition within the NDA and dispel misgivings about the Bill. He said misinformation about the Bill that anyone would be provided citizenship stoked unrest in the Northeast.[30]

Upamanyu Hazarika, convener of anti-immigrant body, the Prabajan Virodhi Manch (PVM) demanded reservation of land, government jobs and other facilities like trade licences for locals, and not mere Assembly seat reservations, for safeguarding the rights of indigenous people of Assam.[31]

Members of NGO Coordination Committee (NCC) gave a call for boycotting the Republic Day celebrations in Mizoram. Mizo protestors stopped the government officers from attending the Republic-Day functions. Mizoram Governor addressed an almost empty Republic-Day venue in Aizwal.[32] Eight militant outfits in the region including Ulfa gave a boycott call in Assam and other northeastern states. At least five organisations of Manipur jointly boycotted the Republic Day celebrations in Manipur.[33]

Normal life came to a grinding halt in Imphal on 11 February due to the 36-hour statewide shutdown called by Peoples' Alliance Manipur, an umbrella body of civil society organisations. Normal life was affected in Nagaland due to 10-hour bandh called by civil society organisations. Students of Dibrugarh University protested against the CAB 2016 on 11 February holding placards written with blood drawn from their hand using syringes and blades.[34] The AGP leaders trooped into Delhi on 10 February to lobby with all non-BJP MPs to foil bid on CAB 2016.[35]

Veteran Manipuri filmmaker Aribam Syam Sharma on 3 February, 2019 announced that he would return the Padma Shri as a mark of protest against the CAB 2016, terming it "anti-Northeast."[36]

Seventy-six of the 855 martyrs' families returned on 30 January, 2019 the honours they had received from the Sarbanand Sonowal government in 2016 in recognition of the sacrifice of the agitators killed during the anti-foreigners' movement in 1979-1985 in protest against the CAB 2016. The remaining families of the martyrs would follow suit in phases.[37]

Chief Ministers of Arunachal Pradesh and Assam, on the other hand, defended the Bill. They said people with vested interests were spreading misinformation.[38] Sonowal explained the proposed amendment would not "open the floodgates to migrants," as had been said, but would, on the contrary, be "a check gate". Reiterating his commitment to "protect the interests of the indigenous communities of the state," he said the Bill aims at checking influx. He explained that three conditions must be met for eligibility. "First, the person seeking citizenship has to be from either of the six religious communities—Hindu, Christian, Jain, Parsi, Buddhist and Sikh—and originate from either Bangladesh, Pakistan or Afghanistan. The cut-off date given in the Bill is 31 December, 2014, which means that any person wanting to apply for citizenship has to prove that he has been living in India for at least seven years till 31 December, 2014. The person also has to prove that he is a victim of religious persecution in his country of origin and if he fulfils all these conditions, only then can one apply." Besides, a person seeking citizenship has to apply to the district magistrate and not to the Centre.[39]

Assam's most powerful minister Himanta Biswa Sarma repeatedly commented that the citizenship amendment initiative was the only way to check demographic change in Assam.[40]

In his address to the joint session of Parliament on 31 January, 2019, President Kovind said: "The Citizenship (Amendment) Bill will help in the securing of Indian citizenship by those victims who were persecuted and were compelled to seek refuge in India. These people cannot be blamed since they were victims of circumstances."[41]

Though the President read out the speech as drafted by the ministry, AASU saw red over this remark and urged the Congress to block the Bill in the Rajya Sabha.[42] That the BJP might not push the Bill in this session of the Rajya Sabha was indicated by Amit Shah, the BJP president when he said on 3 February, 2019 that the BJP would go by consensus on the Bill and the party was talking to all the parties, including those in the northeast.[43]

Amid widespread black-flag protests and nude demonstrations against the CAB 2016, the Prime Minister on 9 February assured once again that his government would ensure the proposed amendment would, at no cost, hurt the language, identity and culture of the people of Assam and the northeast. "I assure you that no damage will be done to Assam and the northeast. Granting citizenship under the provisions of the Bill is a long drawn out process and will depend solely on the discretion of the state governments," he said at a rally in Chengsari, 50 km from Guwahati. He lashed out at Congress and other opposition parties for "spreading misinformation about the Bill."[44] The Tai Ahom Yuba Parishad had called a 12-hour bandh in the state to protest against the Prime Minister's visit and its impact was felt in the upper Assam districts of Tinsukia, Dibrugarh, Sibsagar, Lakhimpur and Jorhat with vehicles remaining off the road and shops and business establishments closed. The bandh was supported by the Krishak Mukti Sangarm Samiti along with 70 other organizations jointly protesting against the Bill.[45]

The Centre failed to table the CAB 2016 in the Rajya Sabha on 13 February, 2019, the last day of the winter session, owing to intense protests from the Congress and other opposition parties.[46] "It was pending for consideration and passing by the Rajya Sabha. Consequent to the dissolution of 16th Lok Sabha, this Bill has lapsed," the Lok Sabha was informed by the Union Minister of Home Affairs Nityanand Rai on 16 July, 2019.[47] It is intriguing that the NDA1 I took nearly two and a half years to table the Bill in the Rajya Sabha, that too, at the fag end of its tenure. Was it a calculated step to please both the vote banks—those opposing the Bill, especially in the Northeast and the expected beneficiaries?

Since the CAB 2016 had lapsed, the agitations against its enactment lost the steam. AGP, AASU, KMSS, AJYCP leaders claimed the Centre's failure to pass the legislation in the RS was a victory of democracy. Celebrations erupted across Assam with opponents of the Bill bursting crackers, distributing sweets and breaking into frenzied dancing on the streets. Civil society groups, student bodies end stir in Mizoram. Manipur Chief Minister N. Biren Singh thanked Prime Minister Narendra Modi, BJP chief Amit Shah and Union Home Minister Rajnath Singh for not tabling the Bill in the Rajya Sabha and opting for consensus. Meghalaya Chief Minister Conard Sangma, a BJP ally who had threatened to pull out of the NDA if the Bill was passed in the Rajya Sabha, called it a great moment for the northeast.[48]

But the BJP was likely to place the Bill in the Parliament again for its enactment. Indeed, the BJP's 2019 Lok Sabha elections manifesto under the heading Nation First, mentions under sub-heading Citizenship Amendment Bill postulated:

> We are committed to the enactment of the Citizenship Amendment Bill for the protection of individuals of religious

> minority communities from neighbouring countries escaping persecution. We will make all efforts to clarify the issues to the sections of population from the Northeastern states who have expressed apprehensions regarding the legislation. We reiterate our commitment to protect the linguistic, cultural and social identity of the people of Northeast. Hindus, Jains, Buddhists and Sikhs escaping persecution from India's neighbouring countries will be given citizenship in India

The Congress in its 2019 Lok Sabha manifesto under heading "38 North Eastern States", serial No. 3, on the other hand said: "We will withdraw immediately the widely resented Citizenship Amendment Bill introduced by the BJP Government against the wishes of the people of the NES." Now that the BJP has returned to power with overwhelming majority, the Congress cannot undo what the BJP plans. But in its election manifesto, the BJP has not mentioned Parsis and Christians among the persecuted religious communities in the neighbouring countries.

The conduct of the NRC in Assam and the conferment of citizenship on the Hindus—Bengali Hindus—detected to be illegal migrants were interlinked. It was earlier thought that an overwhelming number of the undocumented migrants would be Muslims. The result has belied that expectation. So what to do with these huge Bengali-speaking Hindu migrants? They could not go back to Bangladesh nor Bangladesh would like to take them back. After all, they could be driven out of Bangladesh over the years with great efforts and planning. The only alternative was to make them Indian citizens. The same thing applied to Pakistani Hindu refugees.

The CAB 2016, as it stood, excluded the Muslims from its ambit. Whether such a law would survive scrutiny of the Supreme Court is difficult to say. The government surely will argue that the CAB does not discriminate against Muslims *qua* Muslims, that it is merely designed to separate genuine Indian Muslims from illegal Muslim foreigners masquerading as Indian Muslims. Whether such an argument will cut any ice is debatable. M. Mohsin Alam Bhat argues that the CAB violates the Constitution because the classification it adopts is manifestly arbitrary and unjustified. Citizenship law defines a country's political and constitutional identity. Laying down rules that determine membership in our political community only on the basis of one's religious beliefs completely violates this principle.[49]

Though the CAB 2016 caused widespread outrage in the northeastern region, it was not a major determinant of voting preferences in the 2019 Lok Sabha elections and, therefore, did not affect the BJP's prospects in the elections. BJP president and Union Home Minister Amit Shah had indicated in the Kolkata meeting on 1 October, 2019 that the enactment of the CAB would precede the introduction of NRC in the states. But in spite of having an overwhelming majority in the Lok Sabha, the BJP was not ready to table the CAB in the Parliament. Meanwhile, Amit Shah assured the northeastern states at the fourth conference of the North East Democratic Alliance (NEDA) in Guwahati on 9 September, 2019 that the contentious Citizenship Amendment Bill (CAB) would neither affect Article 371, enjoyed by six of the eight northeastern states (except Meghalaya and Tripura), nor the existing laws meant for protection of the indigenous people of the region. Shah gave this assurance following concerns were expressed by the Chief Ministers of Meghalaya, Mizoram and Nagaland about the Bill. Meghalaya Chief Minister Conard Sangma expressed apprehensions that the Bill would allow illegal migrants to enter his state. Nagaland Chief Minister Neiphiu Rio apprehended the Bill would change the demographic pattern of the region, while Mizoram Chief Minister Zoramthanga said it would be "quite meaningful" if the Northeast was kept outside the Bill.[50] Former Chief Minister of Assam Tarun Gogoi of the Congress was quick to point out that if the CAB was passed, the NRC would become a waste paper.[51]

Meanwhile, Home Minister Amit Shah in separate meetings with Mizoram Chief Minister, NGOs and civil society organizations in Aizwal assured that a special clause would be incorporated in the CAB so that their state, along with Nagaland and Arunachal Pradesh, was not affected by settlement of people from Pakistan, Bangladesh and Afghanistan who were granted Indian citizenship.[52]

III

The assurance given to the Northeastern States was honoured by incorporating in the CAB 2019, which was cleared by the Union cabinet on 4 December, 2019[53], clause (4) in Section 6B stipulating that "Nothing in this section shall apply to tribal area of Assam, Meghalaya, Mizoram or Tripura as included in the Sixth Schedule to the Constitution and the area covered under 'the Inner Line' notified under the Bengal Eastern Frontier Regulation, 1873." The States of Arunachal Pradesh, Nagaland and Mizoram are already covered by the Inner Line Permit System. It was promised by Amit Shah in the Lok Sabha on 9 December, 2019 to bring the State of Manipur under the Inner Line Permit System. True to his words, the Government of India notified the extension of the ILP to Manipur in the Gazette of India on 11 December, 2019.[54] With this decision, Manipur achieved two objectives: First, the exemption of Manipur from the purview of the CAA as the Act contains provisions for exemption from its purview the Sixth Schedule areas and ILP states, and second, the fulfilment of the long-standing demand for the implementation of the ILP in the state. Manipur, which otherwise posed as a strong protest centre to the CAA, was thus neutralised, thereby effectively weakening the anti-CAA protest in the region.

Unlike the rest of Nagaland, Dimapur district, Nagaland's commercial capital, was not under the ILP regime so long. Ila Longchar, secretary of the Joint Committee on Prevention of Illegal Immigrants (JCPI), a powerful church-backed organisation, said that Dimapur was completely under the control of outsiders. There were hardly any Nagas left in Dimapur. The Business Association of Nagaland (BAN) estimated that Bengalis, Biharis, Marwaris and Assamese controlled 96 per cent business in Dimapur. "They are doing their business on leased land. Since no ILP is required in Dimapur, many have acquired land there", said Akim Jamir, vice president of BAN.[55] The Nagaland Government extended the Inner Line Permit regime to the Dimapur district, according to a notification issued on 11 December, 2019.[56]

The Bill was placed in the Lok Sabha on 9 December and the Lok Sabha passed the Bill the same day well before midnight by 311-80 votes with no abstention. The parties which voted for the Bill were BJP, Shiv Sena, JD(U), Naveen Patnaik's BJD, Ram Bilas Paswan's LJP, Jagan Reddy's YSRCP, RLD, AIADMK, NDPP(Nagaland), MNF(Mizoram), NPF(Manipur) and NPP(Meghalaya), whereas Congress. Trinamool Congress, TRS, DMK, NCP, BSP, SP, CPM, CPI, AIMIM, IUML, AIUDF, RSP, Sikkim Krantikari Morcha, VCK(Tamil Nadu), Kerala Congress(M) and AAP cast their votes against the Bill.[57]

When the Bill was taken up for discussion in the Rajya Sabha on 11 December, Trinamool Congress MP Sukhendu Shekhar Roy pointed out that "there is no reasonable nexus between the Statement of Objects and Reasons and the Bill. Therefore, the Bill is defective and the debate should be adjourned till such period the bill is rectified."

The statement of objects and reasons, which is usually examined by a court to understand the aim of a law if the matter is challenged legally, attached with the bill points out that "the constitutions of Pakistan, Afghanistan and Bangladesh provide for a specific state religion. As a result, many persons belonging to Hindu, Sikh, Buddhist, Jain, Parsi and Christian communities have faced persecution on grounds of religion in those countries. Some of them also have fears about such persecution in their day-to-day life where right to practise, profess and propagate religion has been obstructed and restricted. Many such persons have fled to India to seek shelter and continued to stay in India even if their travel documents have expired or they have incomplete or no documents." The amendment text did not mention the word "persecution". Rajya Sabha Chairman M.Venkaiah Naidu, however, rejected the objection raised by Roy.[58]

It is not clear why the word "persecution" has been omitted from the main body of the Bill although an impression had been generated that the Bill was aimed at helping those who had been persecuted in the Muslim-majority Bangladesh, Pakistan and Afghanistan.

The vacuum of explanation has been filled by speculation. One view is that it would be difficult for anyone to prove after all these years that he or she had been persecuted. The cut-off date of 31 December, 2014 means at least five years have passed since the migrant reached India. This point was harped on by Congress MP Kapil Sibbal in the Rajya Sabha.[59]

Another theory is whether the omission was intended at accommodating non-Muslims who had been left out of the NRC in Assam. Of the 19 lakh left out, as many as 12 lakh are thought to be Hindus. But it is not clear whether the absence of the word "persecution" alone is enough to cover them under the Citizenship Amendment Act (CAA).

While applying for the NRC entry, all those omitted would naturally have claimed that they were already citizens of India. They might have been omitted because they were unable to back up the claim. This raises the question whether they can change their original claim and describe themselves as refugees or migrants from any of these three countries. If so, that will amount to the state condoning an incongruity.

The Rajya Sabha passed the Bill on 11 December by 125-99 votes with three abstention after a lengthy discussion over its provisions.[60] The amended Act received the assent of the President on 12 December and was published in the Gazette (No.47 of 2019), placed as Annexure C.

The exemptions of several regions in the Northeast from the CAB (CAA) failed to cut ice in Assam. AASU said it was a "divisive ploy" of the Centre to weaken the movement [61], and announced non-stop protests against the Bill from 7 December.[62]

North East, especially the plains of Assam, except the Barrak valley, erupted in protest against the Bill as it sought to give citizenship to all the NRC-excluded Hindus (mostly Bengali Hindus).

Protests against the CAB crippled normal life in parts of Assam. At the instance of the North East Students' Organisation (NSSO), the conglomeration spearheading the movement against the CAB, an 11-hour shutdown was observed in the North East, barring Nagaland, on 10 December.[63]

Universities cancelled examinations. Students of Gauhati University wrote a message in blood against the Bill and invoked the battle of Sarighat in which the Ahom army led by Lalit Barphuwan had fought the invading Mughals.[64] The streets of Guwahati turned into a veritable battle zone littered with burnt tyres, stones and tear gas shells as protests against CAB on10 December turned violent and virulent in parts of northeast.[65]

The Army was called out in Guwahati on 11 December after the administration clamped an indefinite curfew in the city along with a mobile internet ban in 10 districts. The city was under siege all day as thousands of protesters were out on the streets to join a long march. Neither tear gas nor lathi charge and water cannons could deter the protesters, most of whom were students. Paramilitary forces did a flag march in Dibrugarh.[66] Four persons were killed and as many as 26 people had been admitted to the state-run medical college with bullet injuries following the police firing in Guwahati on 12 December as thousands defied curfew.[67] The number of persons killed in CAA-related violence rose to 5 by 15 December.[68]

Private residences of Assam CM and of Dibrugarh MLA Prashant Phukan were pelted with stones. Vandals set ablaze the house of Chabua's BJP MLA Binod Hazarika on 12 December afternoon. In central Assam, BJP minister Ranjit Dutta's residence was attacked, as were houses belonging to fellow party MLAs Padma Hazarika in Sootea and Debananda Hazarika in Binpuria constituency. Protesters also ransacked the AGP headquarters in Guwahai and the party's office in Dergoan. BJP and RSS offices in Dibrugarh and Golaghat districts were ransacked too.

The Kamrup (Metro) district administration ordered the closure of all educational institutions in the city till 22 December. Seventeen columns of the Army and 20 more of Assam Rifles were deployed in five locations, including Guwahati.

Most airlines cancelled flights to and from Dibrugarh and Guwahati. All passenger train services in Assam were suspended while long-distance trains to this region were stopped at Guwahati.[69]

The AASU, in order to put a brake on violence, called for peaceful protests against the CAA.[70] Assam CM Sarbananda Sonowal on 12 December stood up for AASU and various indigenous groups protesting against the CAB, saying the spiral of violence since 10 December was the handiwork of "a negative force that has infiltrated groups of peaceful protesters."[71]

A mammoth gathering of citizens including students at the Latsil Ground on 12 December passed off without any confrontation with the security forces.[72] Though thousands defied curfew for second day in

Guwahati on 13 December and participated in 10-hour hunger strike called by AASU, it was a relatively peaceful day in Assam.[73]

Curfew was lifted in Kamrup (Metro) and Jorhat districts while restrictions were relaxed in Dibrugarh and Tinsukia districts on 17 December. Broadband internet also resumed.[74] The Guwahati High Court in an order on19 December directed the Assam government to restore by 5 pm the mobile internet services which was banned in ten districts from 11 December.[75] Mobile Internet was restored across Assam at 9 am on 20 December.[76] Thousands of women including housewives, elderly women and college girls took to the streets of Guwahati on 21 December demanding unconditional repeal of the CAA.[77]

While PM Modi used his poll rallies in Jharkhand to assure the people of Assam that their right and unique identity would be protected,[78] the Centre on 10 December took to Twitter to bust "myths about the CAB and underlined that it would neither lead to "domination" of Bengali Hindus in Assam nor harm the interests of the indigenous people. However, it said the fact was CAB would not automatically confer citizenship on Bengali Hindus. It is just an enabling legislation.[79]

In Tripura, traders were attacked, shops set on fire in separate attacks by protesters on 10 December in Dhalai and North Tripura districts as the shop owners opened their shops in defiance of a bandh call by tribal parties. At least eight motor bikes were destroyed. Internet services were suspended for 48 hours from 2 pm in Tripura.[80] Assam Rifles units were deployed on 11 December to prevent a re-run of 10 December's violent protests in Dhalai and North Tripura districts. Train services were also suspended[81], which continued on 12 December. Suspension of mobile internet services was extended for another 24 hours after 48-hour blockade ended on 12 December afternoon.[82] The Joint Movement against CAB (JMAC), a platform of regional tribal parties and civil society organisations, however, withdrew their agitation on 12 December after Union Home Minister Amit Shah met JMAC and IPT functionaries and assured them that the government would try to solve their issues in a positive way.[83]

Shillong was put under an indefinite curfew from 10 pm of 12 December and mobile internet and messaging services were blocked after around 25 to 30 youth many of them wielding rods ransacked shops and set ablaze several vehicles at Police Bazar, the commercial hub of Meghalaya's capital.[84] Normalcy returned to Shillong gradually.

These protests continued in the Northeast though the Centre decided to largely exempt the region from the legislation by keeping out Sixth Scheduled areas and Inner Line Permit states from its ambit. The general belief is that those Hindus who have been left out of the NRC would be rehabilitated in this region. Lorho Pfoze of the Naga People's Front, an ally of the BJP in Manipur, and a Lok Sabha member alleged on 6 December, 2019 that the Centre was trying to alter the demographic profile of the Northeast by 'dumping' outsiders in the volatile region under the garb of the Citizenship Bill.[85] Congress leader Rahul Gandhi on 11 December, 2019 alleged that the CAB was an attempt by the 'Modi-Shah government' to ethnically cleanse the Northeast.[86]

After the enactment of the CAA 2019, almost all the non-BJP ruled states like West Bengal, Bihar, Kerala, Delhi, MP, Rajasthan, Chhattisgarh and even the BJP-ruled states of UP, Karnataka and Gujarat saw protests against the CAA by people from all walks of life with students and youth in the forefront.

The national electronic media gave more than expected space for the protest. The regional and local media provided a more realistic picture of the reaction. The social media brought an even fuller reporting. Going by all of these media resources, it was clear that protests had been taking place in more than 300 towns and cities in the country since the day the CAB became an Act.[87]

On occasions the protesters turned violent causing damage to public property and clashing with police. Prohibitory orders under section144 Cr.P.C. were clamped in many cities and towns. Police was quick to take actions against the protesters by resorting to lathi charge to disperse them. When the protesters became violent, police fired tear gas shells and even on occasions opened fire on them resulting in the death of a number of persons in UP and two in Mengaluru in Karnataka.

On 19 December, 1200 protesters, including several opposition leaders, were detained in Delhi.[88] On the following day, as thousands of protesters gathered outside the 17th century Jama Masjid in Delhi after Friday prayers, Bhim Army chief Chandrashekhar Azad appeared on the steps, carrying a picture of B.R. Ambedkar and a copy of the Constitution. He led the peaceful marchers who were stopped at India Gate. Stone throwing followed and a vehicle was torched. Eyewitnesses accused the hoodlums of triggering the violence under the cover of darkness. Police resorted to lathi-charge without any provocation.[89]

Earlier, on 17 December, violence erupted again in Delhi over the CAA when 2,000-odd protesters fought a pitched battle with police in east Delhi's Silampur, attacking cops and residents with stones, bottles and sticks. The situation was, however, brought under control in a few hours.[90] Mobile, Internet, SMS and voice calls were blocked in several areas of these States. 21 Metro stations in Delhi were shut.

At least 600 members of the Hyderabad-based All India Majlis-e-Ittehadul-Muslimeen were charged with sedition and another 200 booked for rioting and disobedience to public servants after they protested against CAA in Old Lucknow on 13 December.[91] Even a former Inspector-General of Police of Uttar Pradesh and a cancer patient Sarwan Ram Darapuri, 77 and a 72-year old advocate Mohammad Shoaib were picked up for questioning and later lodged in Lucknow jail because they were "inciting violence."[92]

Parts of UP including Lucknow witnessed the most violent protests with mobs vandalising public property and clashing with police at several places. Two police outposts, three OB Vans, at least six cars, and a government bus were set ablaze during the violence on 19 December. The police brutally cracked down on the agitators, resulting in deaths and injuries.[93] The agitations against the CAA, however, continued in other parts of the State including Lucknow.

The state government seems to have used an iron fist to retain the grip. Internet and messaging services were shut down at 3 pm on 19 December. In Muslim-dominated areas of Lucknow, the police broke into homes and rounded up 'troublemakers'—including women, children and the elderly. The first death reported was of Mohammed Wakil, 32, a resident of Sajjad Ganj area. The same day, a 15-year-old who was on his way to his aunt's house in Old Lucknow was shot. After the crackdown, Adityanath issued a statement saying that violent protesters had been identified with the help of closed-circuit cameras.

Instead of the usual practice of clamping Section 144 on a limited area when there is an evident threat to peace, it has been liberally imposed on all of Uttar Pradesh interfering with the citizens' constitutional right to peaceful protest. The objective is quite obvious. Stifling dissenting voices, be it with the help of draconian legal provisions or with the storm troopers of the State, comes naturally to dispensations that find the contrarian view untenable, even in a democracy.[94] The strong-arm tactics appear to be the result of the BJP's internal troubles. More than 100 party legislators had staged a sit-in in the assembly on 18 December saying they were being muzzled by the bureaucracy and the police. BJP sources said this unprecedented show of defiance had prompted Shah to give a dressing-down to Chief Minister Yogi Adityanath. "The CM was told in very clear terms that he was losing his grip over the state," said a senior BJP leader.[95] In the fitness of things, an investigating officer tasked with probing the anti-CAA violence in UP's Bijnor has been suspended for allegedly framing some people and naming them in the charge-sheet.[96]

A senior UP police official said on 26 December, 2019 on condition of anonymity that 1,113 persons were arrested, 5,558 kept in preventive detention and 19 persons died in clashes with police—five in Firozabad, four in Meerut, three in Kanpur, two each in Sambal and Bijnor and one each in Muzaffarabad, Rampur and Lucknow. The tally does not include the eight-year-old killed in Varanasi on 20 December. As many as 351 police personnel were also injured in the anti-CAA protests, he said.[97]

UP CM threatened to confiscate rioters' assets and auction them to meet the cost of the damage caused to public property. After two days of UP CM administering such a threat[98], the administration in several districts of the state started proceedings by identifying and sealing properties of the accused.[99] 130 'rioters' across UP were asked to pay up over Rs. 50 lakh for their alleged "violent" role in the anti-CAA protests.[100] Bulandshahr locals paid Rs. 6.27 lakh in demand draft to the DM and Senior Superintendent of Police for the damage to public property during the clashes over the anti-CAA agitations on 20 December.[101]

AIMIM president Asaduddin Owaisi on 5 January, 2020 asked why losses were not recovered from these indulged in damage to public property during the Jat agitation in Haryana in 2015 and during the Patel agitation in Gujarat but were recovered from the Muslims of UP.[102] Since the Allahabad High Court had raised objection to putting up roadside banners with photographs and information of people asked to pay compensation for damage to property during anti-CAA protests,[103] the UP Governor promulgated an ordinance on 15 March, 2020 for recovery of losses due to damage of public and private properties during riots and protests and to provide for setting up tribunals to adjudicate claims for damages and recover them.[104]

The Supreme Court on 11 February, 2022 warned the UP government with consequences if it failed to withdraw 236 notices issued in 2019 to alleged anti-CAA protesters for the recovery of compensation over damage to public properties since the notices had violated its 2009 and 2018 guidelines under which such recovery can be initiated only through judicial tribunals under a high court's supervision. In UP the recovery proceedings were initiated through additional district magistrates who are not judicial officers.[105]

The Supreme Court on 18 February, 2022 asked the UP government to refund recoveries from the anti-CAA protesters and restore to them their properties if attached by the state authorities for the alleged damages.[106]

There have been major clampdowns in BJP-ruled Karnataka too. Dakshina Kannada district was placed under curfew after violent protests resulted in two deaths, allegedly in police firing. "Around 2,000 Muslim youth had gathered for the anti-CAA protests in Mangaluru between 4.15 pm and 5.30 pm on 19 December in violation of the prohibitory orders under Cr.P.C.", said the FIR registered against 29 protesters. "They possessed gravel, sticks, soda bottles and other lethal weapons, and [they] intended to torch the Mangaluru North Police Station."

Congress leader and former Chief Minister Siddaramaiah alleged that the violence was "state-sponsored". "The government has imposed section 144 to clamp down on the protesters. Internet has been shut down. This is the second emergency."

With the opposition riding the anti-CAA wave, the BJP's state unit has come out with a 50-page booklet explaining the provisions of the Act and answering frequently asked questions. The booklet is being circulated state-wide and pro-CAA rallies are being organised to counter the protests.[107]

In West Bengal, the protests against the CAB/CAA were led by the ruling Trinamool Congress and its supremo Mamata Bannerjee. She led at least five protest rallies as on 20 December, 2019 in Kolkata, besides those in Howrah, Purulia, Siliguri, Bangoan, Bankura, Durgapur and spoke in a number of meetings against the CAA.

The state government even gave advertisement in print and electronic media on non-implementation of NRC and CAA in the state. The advertisement, however, was withdrawn on the direction of the High Court.[108] Members of Trinamool Youth Congress' Dabgram-Fulbari unit wrote letters to the President with their blood demanding withdrawal of the CAA.[109]

She asked her party supporters to prepare for a "second freedom movement" against the Centre's bid to grant citizenship to migrants from three neighbouring countries on the "basis of religion,"[110] and even challenged the Prime Minister to face a referendum on the CAA and the NRC under the supervision of the United Nations,[111] later modified it to opinion poll.[112] About a week later, the Assam Congress demanded a referendum on the CAA.[113]

Hundreds of protesters took to the streets on 13 December, 2019 blocking road and traffic across Bengal. The demonstrators turned violent in Howrah's Uluberia and Murshidabad's Beldanga where the protesters blocked national highways, ransacked railway property and attacked cops.[114] Violent agitations over the CAA rocked parts of Bengal on 14 December with four districts—Malda, Murshidabad, North 24 Parganas and Howrah—emerging as flashpoints where protesters torched at least 17 buses, five empty trains, fire engines and police vehicles, vandalized half-a-dozen railway stations, hurled stones at passing vehicles and fought a pitched battle with police in Murshidabad. Across the state, thousands of passengers remained stuck on buses, trains and rail stations as national and state highways remained blocked and at least 28 long distance trains were cancelled.[115]

Isolated pockets of South and North Bengal continued to suffer violent protests against CAA on 15 December, 2019 prompting the state government to suspend internet connectivity in Malda, Murshidabad, North Dinajpur, Bashirhat and Barasat in North 24 Parganas, Baruipur and Canning in South 24 Parganas. NH 34, Kalyani Expressway, Jessore Road, Taki Road, Habra-Naihati Road, Bashirhat-Berachampa Road, Diamond Harbour Road were blocked. Buses were ransacked and set ablaze at Karandighi, North Dinajpur. BJP's Barrakpore MP Arjun Singh was attacked by protesters at Jagatdal. At Bairagipara, Berhampore BJP office was set ablaze. Another group ransacked BJP office at Rejinagar.[116] Acts of violence continued on 16 December, 2019. CAA protest rallies, road-blocks brought Kolkata to a standstill. As CM warned against rampage and blockades at Railway Stations, Highways, State moved decisively and arrested 354 persons.[117]

Barring an incident of attack on a police raiding party led by a Deputy Commissioner of Howrah Commissionerate at Sankrail, the rest of the state remained calm on 17 December.[118] Three districts in West Bengal—Uttar Dinajpur, Malda and Murshidabad—saw clashes between supporters and detractors of the CAA on 18 December in which two men were shot at and one stabbed with a sickle at Uttar Dinajpur's Durgapur.[119] Railway connectivity to North Bengal and Assam which was totally cut off from 15 December was restored on19 December.[120] Since then, violent protests gave way to peaceful rallies, demonstrations, meetings in West Bengal.

Union Home Minister Amit Shah also gave a certificate that Bengal was comparatively peaceful.[121] He might have done it with a view to downplay the effectiveness and intensity of anti-CAA protests in Bengal, but in the face of tirade of BJP functionaries of deteriorating law and order condition in the state, it was nevertheless an admission of Central Government to the contrary.

Apart from Trinamool Congress, parties like Congress, Left Front and other parties and organisations representing the Rajbanshis and the Gorkhas of North Bengal joined the movement against the CAA, while the BJP organised meetings, rallies and processions to mobilise public opinion in favour of the CAA.

Protests against police brutality perpetrated on peaceful protesters in UP, Karnataka and Delhi were registered from all corners of the country.

Some talked to Twitter, others spoke to media. Barring a few, most of them expressed outrage at the crackdown on largely peaceful protests in many cities against the CAA, which they described as discriminatory.

The protests were most damning when one of India's most reputed public intellectuals and acclaimed Mahatma Gandhi biographer, 61-year old Ramchandra Guha, was roughly handled and detained by Bengaluru police on 19 December, 2019 for peacefully protesting[122]—compounding India's international shame. The incident inflamed public anger and triggered criticism from across the political spectrum and intelligentsia alike.

In the fitness of things, octogenarian historian Irfan Habib said that the upsurge of public sentiment against the CAA reflected a struggle for the "idea of India as a modern state" and added that even in the colonial times, the British police had not displayed such an inhuman attitude towards protesters as seen in the past few days in several parts of the country.[123] And Habib was not alone. Mutaba Hussain, a well-known writer in Urdu, has decided to return his Padma Sri award in protest against the "atmosphere of fear and hatred" in the country.[124] Singer Papan on 12 December, 2019 pulled out of a music show in Delhi, saying he would not be able to entertain when his home state Assam was "burning, crying and under curfew" over CAB. He was slated to perform in the capital on 13 December.[125] And there were many such protests.

After the enactment of the CAA 2019, protests against it engulfed the entire length and breadth of the country—from Delhi to Bengaluru, from Lucknow to Kolkata, from Mumbai to Patna, from Chennai to Ahmedabad, from Assam to Kochi. Muslims see this as yet another attempt by the Hindu right wing to subjugate the community, yet another step towards "Hindu Rashtra". For secular liberals, the Act smacks of a religion-based bias, they see it as an extension of similar actions, including the abrogation of Article 370 in Kashmir, a Muslim-majority region. All India Majlis-e-Ittehadul Muslimeen (AIMIM) president and MP Asauddin Owaisi tore a copy of the bill in Parliament and accused the government of "hating" Muslims, conspiring to make them "stateless". And he banked on his stand against CAA/NRC for polls in Bihar held in October 2020.[126] The trustees of the Nakhda mosque, the principal mosque of Kolkata, wrote an open letter to the Chief Justice of India urging the Bench to strike down the "fundamentally discriminatory, divisive and unconstitutional CAA".[127]

There is, however, a wide difference between Assam in the North-East and the rest of India on the ground of agitations against the CAA. Assam's vociferous protests against the CAB/CAA stem from the old Assamese-

Bengali divide, from the primal fear of being overwhelmed by Bengali migrants, who now constitute its second largest linguistic population. As Hiren Gohain, a Sahitya Akademi awardee, candidly puts it: "For in the name of freedom, they (the people of Assam) had not bargained for a loss of their precarious independent identity and culture. The abrupt and massive rise in the number of Bengali speakers, whose identity is secure in West Bengal and Bangladesh, can only mean extinction of our language and culture."[128]

Assam has long been sensitive about migration to their region. Assam is opposing the CAA because it will offer citizenship to the so-called infiltrators to Assam and Assam is not willing to accommodate any non-Assamese in that state lest it compromised with its culture, language and distinct identity. All the North-eastern states are ruled by the BJP and its allies. States with the Inner Line Permit System (ILP)—Nagaland, Arunachal Pradesh and Mizoram are exempt from the operation of the CAA. With the addition of Manipur within its ambit after conceding its long standing demand for extension of the ILP regime to that state, Manipur is also exempt from the operation of the CAA. Sixth Schedule areas of Meghalaya, Assam and Tripura are also covered by the exemption clause. So only the plains of Assam and Tripura are affected by the CAA. But Amit Shah have neutralised the anti-CAA agitators of Tripura and so only the plains of Assam except the Barrack Valley are offering stiff resistance to the CAA. It has been restive to the issue of immigration because of its singular experience with influx and is vehemently protesting against the CAA as it threatens to upend the critical clauses of the Assam Accord. The CAA's cut-off date of 31 December, 2014 for regularising migrants directly contradicts the 1985 Assam Accord which had stipulated 24 March, 1971, as the cut-off date. The Supreme Court also agreed to hear the petitions from Assam and Tripura separately because they are opposing the CAA on a different ground than the rest of the country.[129] Even BJP's Assam ally AGP has demanded certain safeguards like extension of the ILP system to Assam to "protect its indigenous population."[130]

The BJP leadership was trying to win over Assam and the PM while addressing a mammoth gathering at the Bodo Accord function in Assam's Kokrajhar town on 7 February, 2020 said that rumours were being spread that outsiders would be allowed to settle in Assam and other parts of the Northeast but this was not correct.[131] The very next day, AASU's chief adviser Samujjal Bhattacharjee hit back at the PM by saying that people opposing CAA are more patriotic than those supporting the Act. On that very day, AASU and 30 other allied organisations took out torch rallies against CAA across district headquarters of the state.[132]

The agitations in the rest of the country against the CAA are for its discriminatory, divisive, religion-specific and anti-secular stance, much against the equality provisions of the Constitution.

Regardless of which states or regions would be most affected by a sizeable influx of migrants, the CAA changes the character of Indian citizenship and the basis on which it is granted, moving from secular to overtly favouring specific groups—particularly Hindus. It opens the door for the creation of second-class citizenship for non-Hindus and most of all Muslims—not just in the extra-legal practices of discrimination and violence that exist today, but in the law.

Home Minister Amit Shah, who piloted the Bill in both the Houses, did not explain why and how the three countries of Pakistan, Bangladesh and Afghanistan were chosen and why migrants who crossed into India up to 31 December, 2014 were to get citizenship and what will happen to those crossing after this date. He had no answer either why in contravention of Articles 5 to 9 region was made a criterion for being a citizen of India and why migrants of other religious persuasions, i.e. Muslims were excluded.

The CAA creates a path for Hindus and a few other denominations who come from three neighbouring countries, but excluding Muslims, to obtain Indian citizenship. This militates against the basic tenets of secularism as enshrined in the Constitution, particularly Articles 14 and 15 which guarantee equality before the law and forbid discrimination on grounds of religion. BJP's argument is that the permitted religions are minorities who have faced religious persecution in neighbouring countries (though the words 'religious persecution' do not occur in the Act), therefore, India should take them in on humanitarian grounds. But that can be determined only on a case by case basis, not read from a person's religion alone. For example, a Hindu from Bangladesh may well be an economic migrant, while an Ahmediya or Shia Muslim from Pakistan could be persecuted for his religion.

Subhash C. Kashyap, former Secretary-General of the Lok Sabha, had advised the Joint Parliamentary Committee on the Citizenship Amendment Bill as an expert, and held that it should not mention names of the communities to be granted citizenship. "I had taken strong exception to the mention of communities. Mentioning persecuted minorities would have been enough, and the purpose would have been served," he revealed in an interview with Deepak Razdan.[133] While terming the contentious CAA "very good" and "generous", exiled Bangladeshi author Taslima Nasreen on 17 January, 2020 said that the law should make an exception for Muslim "free-thinkers, feminists, and secularists" from the neighbouring countries.[134]

As an editorial in *The Telegraph* says, "the enactment of the CAA is a testimony to the growing distance between India and the idea of India. At the hour of its inception, India, unlike its Western neighbour, had chosen to follow the path of democratic constitutionalism. This implied that citizenship would be viewed as a matter of right, and that such a right would be bestowed on the principle of equality. India's nationhood, a bacon to the world at large, had remained composite in character. The Constitution had, thus far, ensured that the country refused to discriminate citizens on the basis of birth, creed, caste, language, gender and so on. The CAA, which is accorded a pride of place in the electoral manifesto of the ruling Bharatiya Janata Party, has now struck a lethal blow to India's pluralistic ethic by choosing to grant citizenship to Hindus, Sikhs, Buddhists, Jains, Parsis and Christians—but not Muslims—from three neighbouring nation states. What is audacious about the CAA is that it seeks to camouflage the BJP's naked display of exclusion in the garb of humanitarianism. When read in conjunction with the NRC, the CAA resembles an express political and ideological project, one which seeks to transform a secular republic into a majoritarian polity."[135]

On the watch of the Supreme Court and under its unrelenting pressure for the completion of the NRC within a certain time frame, Assam has served as a laboratory for a potentially dangerous experiment. Even though the results belied the expectations, the talk of sending those excluded from the register to detention centres has given credence to the fear that thousands of people are vulnerable to being rendered stateless and rightless.

The implications of these developments have been interpreted by Niraja Gopal Jayal in multiple ways. "From a legal perspective, they imply a foundational shift in the conception of the Indian citizen embodied in the Constitution of India, followed by the Citizenship Act, 1955. This is, first, a move from soil to blood as the basis of citizenship, from a *jus soli* or birth-based principle of citizenship in the direction of a *jus sanguinis* or descent-based principle; and second, a shift from a religion-neutral law to a law that differentiates between religious identity. From the perspective of India's social fabric, they signal an ominous fraying and unravelling of what was a daring and moderately successful experiment in pluralism and diversity. From a political perspective, they point to a possibly tectonic shift from a civic-national to an ethno-national conception of the political community and its terms of membership. From a moral perspective, they prompt us to confront the weakness of our commitment to human rights and to the moral and legal personhood of all human beings. From an international perspective, they remind us of, on the one hand, our longstanding aversion to signing international treaties on refugees and the reduction of statelessness and, on the other, our easy engagement in double speak with a valued neighbour."[136]

There is no denying the fact that the CAA strikes at the root of the rule of law, denying protection from discrimination and arbitrary treatment and secondly, puts the very essence of unity in diversity at a discount because without equality, difference would lead to hierarchy and disunity. The Citizenship Act prohibits illegal immigrants from acquiring Indian citizenship. The CAA 2019 amends this and provides citizenship to Hindus, Sikhs, Buddhists, Jains, Parsis and Christians from Pakistan, Afghanistan and Bangladesh by refusing to treat them as illegal immigrants.

The present government is raising the spectre of persecution of non-Muslim minorities in the three neighbouring Muslim-majority countries while the text of the Act makes no mention of religious persecution. Notwithstanding the absence of the word "persecution" from the amendment Act, the BJP leaders never got tired of telling the people of India that the Act actually aims at ameliorating the conditions of the "persecuted" minorities (read Hindus) of the three neighbouring countries. What is more astonishing is that even our Prime Minister is a party to such disinformation exercise. As late as on 21 April, 2022, in an unprecedented address to the nation from the Red Fort on the 400th Prakash Purab of the ninth Sikh Guru Tegh Bahadur Singh, Prime Minister Modi also defended the CAA, calling it a necessary measure to provide relief and security to the Sikhs and Hindus compelled to flee neighbouring countries because of religious persecution.[137]

Tamil Hindus have been persecuted in Sri Lanka and Rohingya Muslims in Myanmar. These groups are minorities in Buddhist majority countries. But they are being denied this kindness and courtesy.

India granted citizenship to 18,999 people from Afghanistan, Pakistan, Bangladesh, Myanmar and Sri Lanka in six years from 2014 to 2019. Among them, the largest number of 15,036 was from Bangladesh, mainly because of the signing of the Indo-Bangladesh Land Boundary Agreement under which 14,064 Bangladeshi nationals were granted Indian Citizenship as per Section 7 of the Citizenship Act, 1955.

The second largest number of 2935 immigrants was from Pakistan. There were 914 people from Afghanistan, 113 from Sri Lanka and just one from Myanmar. The citizenship was granted under Section 5 by registration and under Section 6 by naturalisation, Minister of State for home affairs Nityanand Rai informed the Rajya Sabha in a written reply on 4 March, 2020.[138] As *The Times of India* points out editorially, "extending this naturalisation facility to illegal migrants fleeing persecution, irrespective of country and religion, would be both humane and helpful in mending CAA-engineered gaping hole in India's secular fabric. Refugee persecution must be assessed on a case by case basis, not on that of religion."[139]

But that can't be. This Act is meant to be a nod to the Hindu nationalist idea of India as a natural homeland of Hindus. The BJP is harping on this fact as well in all its outpourings against the critics of the Act. India's tryst with CAA and NRC will determine if unequal treatment will now assume a formal form and get embedded in citizenship.

The idea of nation emerged out of the realization that humans are primarily territorial and that land determines for humans a lot more than they want it to. Thus, people seen in relation to their land or territory came to be seen as 'nation'. One sense of the term 'nation', was, in its initial form 'conditioned people'.[140] Pakistan, the *bete noire* of Modi, does not have a religious dimension in her citizenship. As Ghazala Jamil points out, Pakistan has had to define its citizenship within a territorial conception of nationhood even as it recognizes that Muslims are the majority. The negation of Pakistan as a natural homeland of Muslims became conclusive after the creation of Bangladesh. Although Muslims in India are frequently told to go to Pakistan, it has not extended any special offers of citizenship to Indian Muslims.[141]

IV

The agitations against the CAA have far reaching implications. G.N. Devy has dealt with them very comprehensively thus: "The response to the CAA from media, jurists, citizen groups, and activists included the grounds mentioned by the opposition during the debate in Parliament and also added more points to it. A bald summary of the issues and arguments raised in the opposition to the CAA would be: the amendment is violative of the principles and basic values of the Constitution since it proposes to club together religion and citizenship. The criterion on which it proposes to offer citizenship is not based on any reasonable classification. No reason has been provided for including Afghanistan in the list of countries covered by the act or for leaving out other neighbouring countries, such as Nepal, Bhutan, Myanmar and Sri Lanka.

> "The Act is not even appropriately comprehensive as it does not talk of 'other minorities', such as the nature worshipping tribal communities who too face discrimination in Bangladesh and several minorities within Islamic subgroups. It makes no reference to other minority ethnic groups such as Meitei, Marma, Tanchangya, Barua, Khasi, Santhal, Chakma, Garo, Biharis, Oraons, Mundas, Tripperas, and Mros, and Hindu

illegal migrants from Sri Lanka. The cut-off date stipulated by the Act has no logical basis; and, if religious persecution is the reason for the grant of citizenship, there is no reason to believe that the perceived persecution has come to an end after the cut-off date. The religion of any person is not ground enough to conclude that the perceived persecution is religious. Besides, in the case of those who migrated to India decades ago, it would be just impossible to provide any proof of such persecution.

"It was also argued that the CAA would lead to a serious deterioration of India's relations with Bangladesh and may result in putting the lives of the non-Muslim communities covered by the Act in the neighbouring countries under threat. The objective of the Act is discriminatory, unlawful and unjust. The classifications created by the Act bear no rational relationship with the stated objective. Besides, it leaves out persecutions of all other kinds arising out of views, culture, thought, expression and political turmoil in the neighbouring countries. Criticism also emerged with reference to the vast range of India's 'undocumented' people, such as the Adivasis, the denotified and nomadic communities, migratory labourers, the homeless and orphans, the zero-literacy sections of the population, single/widowed women, transgender and large migratory population.

"More importantly, the CAA brings into the definition of citizenship the question of religion, specifically excluding Muslims and Jews and, thereby, creates space for legalising an anti-Muslim bias in the proposed NRC and NPR."[142]

Not only does the Act violate the domestic laws, as Manish Tewari, Congress MP and Supreme Court lawyer says, "it is also in contravention of India's international obligations. Customary international law does not permit refoulment of refugees. The law is also blind to considerations of race, religion and nationality, and applies equally to all refugees. Despite not having ratified the refugee convention of 1951 and the 1970 protocol, India is still bound by the clause of non-refoulment due to its commitments under the International Covenant on Civil and Political Rights and customary international law as it is a signatory to the UN Convention Against Torture—Article 3 of the Convention embodies the principle of non-refoulment."[143]

The worst casualty of the agitations, however, is the lack of trust on governmental measures. While the PM says that the CAA is meant to give citizenship, not take it away, many of his detractors believe that CAA, in conjunction with NPR or NRC will declare many persons non-citizens and take away citizenship.[144] The unwillingness of the ruling party to have a dialogue with the proponents of the agitation, both politically and administratively, has deepened the chasm further.

Civil society was at the forefront of the protests against the CAA. Even before the CAB became an Act, over 170 scientists and scholars from several institutions, including some of the most renowned in the country, issued a statement against the CAB saying that the Bill would greatly strain the pluralistic fabric of the country.[145]

As many as 625 people from various walks of life signed a statement on 9 December issued by Indian Cultural Forum—a platform of individuals across the civil society—including prominent intellectuals—condemning the CAB. The signatories include writers Amit Chaudhuri, Nayantara Sehgal, Ashok Vajpayi, Arundhuti Roy, Paul Zakaria, Amitava Ghosh and Shashi Deshpande, artists T.M. Krishna, Anil Dodiya, Vivan Sundarm, Sudhir Patwardhan, Gulam Mohammed Sheikh and Nilima Sheikh, film persons Aparna Sen, Nandita Das and Ananda Patwardhan and scholars Romila Thapar, Prabhat Pattnaik, Ramchandra Guha and Geeta Kapur.[146]

Over 720 jurists, writers, actors, activists and citizens issued a statement on10 December against the CAB and the NRC describing these as "misguided" and worse, "unconstitutional". Among the signatories to the statement are Justice P.B. Sawant, Admiral Ramdas, Javed Akhtar, Naseruddin Shah, Aparna Sen, Mallika Sarabhai, Prabhat Patnaik and Usa Patnaik.[147]

Over 1,000 scientists and academicians have signed a petition demanding that the CAB in its current form be withdrawn as the use of religion as a criterion for citizenship would be inconsistent with the basic structure of the Constitution.[148]

Urdu journalist Shirin Dalvi returned an award from State Urdu Academy in protest against CAB. She said it was her way of civil disobedience against the "unconstitutional" and "divisive" Bill. [149] Yaqoob Yawar, Urdu author-translator has decided to return UP State Urdu Academy Award for translation in protest against the CAA.[150]

Uday Shankar, Assamese choreographer decided to return best choreography award to state government to protest against the CAA.[151] National Award-winning filmmaker Jahnu Barua withdrew his film "Bhoga Khirkee" (Broken Window) from the upcoming Assam film awards in protest against CAB.[152]

Families of the martyrs of the Assam agitation boycotted a state government event at Guwahati on 10 December condemning the BJP-led Union Government for passing the CAB which is against the Assam Accord.[153]

Nine Indian Ramon Magsaysay Award recipients issued a statement on 20 December expressing their concern and anguish at the enactment of the CAA and its linkage with the NRC as both are discriminatory and violative of all the guarantees of right to equality before law.[154]

More than 40 alumni of National University of Judicial Sciences (NUJS), all practising lawyers, signed and published a statement opposing the CAA which was likely to polarise the nation.[155] The Democratic Research Scholars' Organisation (DRSO) organised a protest against CAA-NRC on 9 January, 2020 near Coffee House in College Street, Kolkata. Hundreds of theatre artists took to the Kolkata streets on 17 January to protest against the CAA-NRC.[156]

More than one hundred retired bureaucrats under the aegis of the Constitutional Conduct Group wrote an open letter to the government on 9 January asserting the "constitutional and moral untenability of the CAA and urging it to repeal the controversial legislation. The signatories include three former foreign secretaries Shyam Saran, Shiv Shankar Menon, Sujata Singh, former cabinet secretary K.M. Chadrashekhar, former Delhi LG Najeeb Jung, former Indian ambassador to the UK Shiv Shankar Mukherjee, former telecom regulator Rahul Khullar, former top cops Moran C. Borwankhar and Julio Roberio, among others.[157] Nobel Laureates Avijit Bannerjee and Enther Duflo want reconsideration of the CAA/NRC.[158] Another Nobel Laureates and Bharat Ratna Amartya Sen said CAA was an attempt to divide people.[159]

On the other hand, over 1,000 academicians and intellectuals from various universities and reputed educational institutions across India on 21 December released a statement in support of the CAA. Among those who took the initiative to garner support for the CAA were Delhi University professor Prakash Singh and associate professors Swadeh Singh and Abhinav Prakash.[160]

As many as 154 prominent citizens, including former judges, bureaucrats, armed forces officers and academicians, said a 'false and motivated' campaign was being launched against the CAA, NPR and NCR with a sinister design to harm the nation and sought action against the trouble-makers. In a letter to the President of India the citizens urged the Central Government to look into the ongoing protests and safeguard the democratic institutions of the country. The citizens, including 11 former judges of different High Courts, 24 retired IAS officers, 11 former Indian Foreign Service officers, 16 retired IPS and 18 former Lieutenant Generals, said 'fear' is being spread across the length and breadth of India which appears to be 'motivated and with a sinister design' to harm the nation.[161]

Senior lawyers like Mahesh Jethmalani think that the CAA is constitutionally sound and is unfairly picked apart by its enemies.[162] Another senior lawyer Harish Salve thinks that arguments about the CAA being unconstitutional don't hold water.[163] Articles are also coming up in the newspapers in support of the CAA.[164] An inter-faith delegation comprising prominent spiritual gurus and social reformers from different faiths and sects, including Jain Acharya Dr. Lokeshji, Meditation guru Swami Deepankar Ji, Mufti Shamnoon Qasmi Ji and Sardar Sant Singh Ji met Minister of State for Home Affairs G. Kishan Reddy on 9 January to express solidarity with the government on the issue of the CAA.[165]

Actor-turned-politician Rajnikanth voiced his support for the CAA and stated that he would be the first person to question it and stand by Muslims if any harm was done on them in India due to the CAA.[166]

That the opposition of the CAA came from political parties, a section of the media, organised civil society groups and jurists was not so surprising. What surprised everyone within the establishment and outside was that students on many campuses, Muslim women who had rarely hit protest-podiums and citizens who otherwise stay off political debates started to express their concern over the CAA and the two registers proposed by the government. By early January 2020, according to one source, there were 261 CAA-related protests across 24 states of which 230 were against the citizenship law.[167] Those protests played out for three months without let and, if it were not for the Covid-19 lockdown and the concerted repression mounted by the BJP government and its police, they may well have carried on.

The youth and women at the helm of the protests against the CAA in 2020 brought in a rare phenomenon in India's political space, something that was last seen a century ago, Ganesh Devy, a literary scholar and cultural activist said at a virtual session on 7 March, 2021. "It is equally significant that they are espousing values of the Constitution and humanism and articulating with an unprecedented precision a politics that is non-sectarian, non-divisive and non-abrasive," he said.[168]

"If the BJP did not anticipate the students taking to the streets in such large numbers, the party also does not seem to have expected the citizenship law and the NRC to raise tempers to such a pitch," comments Amulya Ganguli, a former Assistant Editor of *The Statesman*.[169] Protests against the CAA have spread to many university campuses, leading to confrontation with police on some instances. The atrocious police actions on students of Jamia Millia Islamia, an institution founded by the nationalist Muslim leaders and the AMU, a minority institution drew wide and massive indignation. One of the bigger police-protester clashes was seen on 15 December at Delhi's Jamia Millia Islamia when a protest against the CAA led to violent clashes with police that left more than 50 people, including corps, injured. At least four buses were set on fire and a dozen cars and scores of bikes were damaged. Reports emerged of stone-pelting by students on police, while the latter forcibly entered the varsity and lobbed tear gas shells on the campus including the library and even assaulted the students and evicted them. Incidentally, Kerala Chief Minister Pinarayi Vijayan welcomed the students of Jamia Millia Islamia to Kerala house in Delhi when their hostel was shut because of protests.[170]

Jamia Vice Chancellor Njma Akhtar submitted a report to the HRD ministry on17 December. It claimed that police entered the campus without permission or notifying the administration and demanded a high-level enquiry into the 15 December incident.[171] The HRD ministry endorsed the demand for a high level enquiry and forwarded the request to the Home Ministry for the final decision as the matter involved law and order.[172] A seven-member NHRC team, however, inspected Jamia Millia campus on 20 December.[173]

News of police action at Jamia sparked off solidarity protests at more than 30 campuses. Students from Aligarh Muslim University demonstrated, leading to their own clashes with police. Similar scenes were witnessed at Patna University while students of Jadavpur University in Kolkata took out a protest march at midnight. In Hyderabad, hundreds of students of the Maulana Azad National Urdu University took to the streets. Also expressing their solidarity against police action were students of Benaras Hindu University, Pondicherry University and Nawada College in Lucknow. Students from the Tata Institute of Social Sciences of Mumbai, DU, JNU, IIT Madras, IISc, IIM Bangalore and many other educational institutions throughout the country expressed solidarity as well.[174] The ripple effect of protests on campuses across the country reached top educational institutions in the world including Oxford, Harvard, Yale, Columbia, Stanford and Tufts where students and scholars staged demonstrations against the police crackdown on students of Jamia Millia Islamia and Aligarh Muslim University. The protests at various universities abroad were mostly led by Indians studying there.[175]

Nearly 400 students from 19 universities across the United States, including Harvard, Yale, Stanford and Columbia, signed a statement "condemning recent police brutality in Indian universities" and expressing solidarity with protesting students in India. At Oxford in the UK, students carried out anti-CAA demonstrations.[176]

A large section of Bollywood found its voice following Delhi police's crackdown on students at Jamia. While expressing their solidarity with students, they also appealed to them to be non-violent.[177] Uddhav Thackeray, Chief Minister of Maharashtra alleged that a deliberate attempt was being made to create an "atmosphere of unrest and fear" and equated the Jamia crackdown with the Jallianwala Bagh massacre.[178] Minority Affairs Minister Mukhtar Abbas Naqvi condemned the police action, particularly against women students in Jamia Millia Islamia as "unjust and wrong" and said that the role of police and all those involved would be investigated in this case. "I would not call the protesting students anti-national or anarchists. I would say they are misguided and misinformed on the issue of CAA," he said.[179] Amit Shah, however, downplayed the police action in Jamia as it was to contain mob violence. He also said that one should not exaggerate the protests, adding: "One should know that there are over 400 universities in the country and reports of agitation have been reported from around 22."[180] Union Finance Minister Nirmala Sitaraman went one step ahead and cautioned against "jihadist, Maoist and separatist" elements getting into student activism and asserted protests fanned across the country over the CAA would not derail the economic agenda.[181]

Within a short time of the Jamia incident, several hundred students of Aligarh Muslim University gathered to protest against the CAA and the police action in Jamia. Very soon clashes ensued between the police and the students. The police resorted to firing tear gas shells. In all, 60 students were injured in the clashes. Nasir, the research scholar from the Chemistry department, lost his right hand after a tear gas shell exploded on his palm. Students were asked to vacate the hostels. Classes were suspended till 5 January.[182] UP police registered a case against 1200 unidentified people for taking out candle march on AMU campus in violation of the prohibitory orders on 24 December.[183]

A fact finding report by a group of civil society that included ex-civil servant Harsh Mander and DU professor Nandini Sunder alleged that police indulged in "unbridled human rights violation" on the AMU campus on 15 December. Police used tear gas, rubber bullets, sound bombs, lathis and stun grenades on the students protesting against the CAA and NRC.[184]

The alumnus of the AMU hit the street in Kolkata on 19 December to condemn the police actions on students of the AMU and the Jamia.[185] About 5,000 students from various institutions in Kolkata organised a march towards the BJP's state headquarters on Central Avenue on 21 December against the use of brute force on students of Jamia Millia Islamia and AMU as well as against the CAA.[186]

The dean of the Presidency University, Pradip Basu, joined the protest rally led by Presidency University students, teachers and non-teaching staff on 24 December evening and spoke twice—once in the beginning and once again at Shyambazar crossing. At least 30 other professors joined in along with non-teaching staff.[187]

Over 10,000 academics, philosophers and scholars have signed an open letter to "condemn in the strongest possible terms the police brutality" on students of Jamia Millia Islamia and AMU. The lists of signatories, which extended to 125 pages, included American philosopher Noam Chomsky, Sanskrit scholar Sheldon Pollock, Homi K. Bhabha, Rajmohan Gandhi, Partha Chatterjee, Romila Thapar, Akeel Bilgrami and Vena Das.[188]

Evidently the CAA has worked up students at several educational institutions. They along with youth are at the forefront of the demonstrations throughout the country as they feel the need to express themselves on such a vital issue. That, however, does not mean that they can take law and order in their hands. Arson and damaging public property cannot be condoned under any circumstances, but police can't trample upon students' right to protest.

Eminent citizens including former Supreme Court Judge J. Chelameswar, former Army Commander Lt. General Harcharanjit Singh Panang, former Chief Election Commissioner S.Y. Qureshi, filmmaker Adoor Gopalaksrishan, renowned musician T.M. Krishna, former UGC Chairman Sukhdeo Thorat, former Planning Commission member Syeda Hameed and film personality Sharmila Tagore on 17 January issued a statement asking if the Constitution was a "mere administrative manual" which enabled elected Governments to claim legitimacy for abuse of power. The citizens said each generation had a solemn duty to constantly introspect and audit the working of the Constitution. They said: "Peaceful and harmonious reconciliation of conflicting interests, healthy public discourse, and respect for dissenting views are at the heart of democracy. We have to introspect whether Truth and Non-violence—the two values held very dear to the heart of the Father of the Nation—continue to inform our actions in the public sphere... . We appeal to all citizens to utilise the solemn occasion to celebrate our success, reflect on our current concerns, particularly about our plural, secular society and resolve to fulfil the Constitutional goal envisaged by Dr. Ambedkar and our forefathers as summed up in the Preamble."[189] Will this sane advice have any effect on the powers-that-be !

Hundreds of students of the Aligarh Muslim University marched against the CAA on the University campus on 21 January, 2020 raising slogans of "CAA se azadi" and vowing to boycott classes until their demands were met.[190] A large number of girls blocked all traffic within the

AMU campus on 3 February, forming a human chain at the main crossing near the university guesthouse.[191]

Students of Aligarh Muslim University, however, started a relay hunger strike from 21 February evening against the CAA and also to mount pressure on Vice-Chancellor Tariq Mansoor and Registrar Abdul Hamid to step down amid continuing outrage over the varsity's decision to call police to quell a protest that the students started on 15 December last year. The VC had admitted that he had written to the local administration to rein in the protesting students. The UP government too has, in an affidavit in Allahabad High Court in a related case, said the VC had requested local police to enter the campus. Proctor Anfullah Khan resigned on 4 February under pressure from the students.[192]

As a morale booster to the students came the judgment of the Allahabad High Court on 24 February directing the UP DGP to identify and take action against the policemen who were involved in stray cases of damaging motorcycles and unnecessarily caning the apprehended students of AMU during the protest against the CAA in December last. Passing the order on NHRC recommendations, Chief Justice Govind Mathur and Justice Samit Gopal directed the state police chief to adhere to a report of the rights body. The NHRC said a direction should be given to the chief secretary to provide suitable compensation to six AMU students who have been grievously hurt. On 8 January, the High Court had directed the NHRC to probe the allegations levelled in a PIL filed by Mohammed Akram Khan.[193]

V

With protests against the CAA spreading across the country, representatives of at least 12 opposition parties led by Sonia Gandhi knocked on the doors of the President on 17 December, 2019 and sought his intervention on violence in central universities. They also urged him to advise the government to withdraw the "divisive and unconstitutional" law.[194]

Twenty opposition parties on 13 January, 2020 sought to intensify protests against CAA-NRC-NPR. Referring to the CAA, NPR and NRC as inimical to vulnerable sections of society, the opposition demanded withdrawal of CAA and the "immediate stoppage of NRC/NPR". It also asked opposition CMs to dump NPR. The deliberations, however, were not attended by six non-NDA parties like Trinamool Congress, Samajwadi Party, BSP, AAP, UPA member, DMK and the new ally Shiv Sena, making it a UPA-Left affair.[195]

Ravi Shankar Prasad, Law Minister slammed the opposition meeting over the CAA-NRC-NPR and said that the resolution passed in the meeting must have gladdened the heart of Pakistan. The resolution was against national interest and national security.[196]

While as many as eight states—Kerala, Punjab, Bengal, Chhattisgarh, MP, Rajasthan, Telengana and Tamil Nadu have announced that they would not implement the CAA, Central Government sources insisted that granting citizenship was the exclusive domain of the Centre. The role of state was limited to physical verification of the documents to be submitted to the MHA.[197]

Senior BJP leader Rajnath Singh said the threat by some states not to implement the CAA was a challenge to India's federal structure as the legislation has been passed by Parliament and was binding on all states after the presidential assent. "There is no option for the states other than to implement the legislation. There are set rules, which they will have to follow. The federal structure of the country has to be respected by all stakeholders. Any state government can not be driven by its agenda while implementing a legislation through constitutional amendment with presidential assent", he said in an exclusive interview to the *Times of India*. He asserted that due legal process would be followed to enforce implementation of CAA in all states once rules were drafted.[198]

Union finance minister Nirmala Sitaraman was of the view that political parties can make a political statement by passing resolutions against the CAA in the assembly, but states cannot refuse to implement it."[199]

The President of India, Ram Nath Kovind, made an indirect reference to the CAA in his address to the joint sitting of Parliament on 31 January and echoed the stand of the government by saying that the law passed by Parliament should be accepted by citizens and that violence weekened society. The opposition, however, attacked the Modi government for "lowering the dignity" of the President by making him deliver a speech in which the "highly controversial and divisive" CAA was listed as among the government's key accomplishments.[200] Opposition members, mostly from the Congress and DMK, protested in the Lok Sabha on 3 February, 2020 against the CAA. Rajya Sabha was adjourned twice on 3 February as the opposition members continued to disrupt the proceedings of the house demanding discussion over the CAA.[201]

Kerala Legislative Assembly took a unanimous resolution against the Act and Kerala Chief Minister sent a letter to 11 non-BJP Chief Ministers urging them to take similar resolution in their States as well.[202] Following this request, the State Legislative Assemblies of as many as eight States/

UTs of Punjab, West Bengal, Rajasthan, MP, Bihar, Telengana, Tamil Nadu and Puducherry took resolutions against the implementation of the CAA.

Telangana Chief Minister K. Chandrshekhar Rao described the CAA as a "blunder" and announced on 25 January that he would soon hold a conclave of the like-minded Chief Ministers on the issue and the state assembly would pass a resolution against it.[203] While intervening during a discussion on the Governor's address, he said on 7 March, 2020 that the image and reputation of the country had taken a beating globally due to the controversial CAA and the problem with CAA and NRC was not confined to only Muslims but that of every poor, oppressed, homeless and uneducated person in the country.[204]

Maharashtra Home Minister Anil Deshpande of the NCP gave a written assurance to the delegation of "Mumbai Bagh" on 3 February that CAA and NRC would not be implemented in the state and not a single citizen of Maharashtra would have to lose citizenship.[205] His Chief Minister Uddhav Tackeray of Shiv Sena, however, said that CAA did not pose any threat to citizens, but his government would not implement the NRC in Maharashtra.[206] He even said on 21 February, 2020 after meeting the PM that no one needed to fear about the CAA as it was not meant for throwing anyone out of the country.[207] The DMK sent over two crore signatures to the President as a part of an anti-CAA signature campaign by the party-led Secular Progressive Alliance.[208]

Now that so many state governments and state assemblies having taken a decision not to implement the CAA and many more are likely to join them in the foreseeable future, what steps the Central Government will take against them? The Central Government can take the route of Articles 256, 257(1), 365 and ultimately 356. It can also take resort to the mechanism of Inter-State Council—an institution meant specifically for handling such Centre-State situations. There is, however, no indication till now to set in motion this constitutional mechanism for discussion and conflict resolution. For working a successful federal system, the states must work in tandem with the Centre. However, both the Centre and the State must adopt a give and take attitude and eschew confrontation. But the Central Government is still on a denial mode and quite clueless about the extent of the discontent. It has kept harping on its resolve to go ahead with the CAA, while Union Law Minister Ravi Shankar Prasad asserting that state legislatures have no power on citizenship law.[209] But, Chidambaram points out, the Prime Minister is not talking to his critics and they do not have an opportunity to talk to him.[210] So what is the way out? A televised Question and Answer session on CAA, as suggested by him?[211]

With anti-CAA protests spreading to more areas, Prime Minister termed the agitation against the CAA "unfortunate and deeply distressing." In a series of tweets, he said: "This is the time to maintain peace, unity and brotherhood. It is my appeal to everyone to stay away from any sort of rumour-mongering and falsehoods. We cannot allow vested interest groups to divide us and create disturbances."[212] Prime Minister on15 December accused Congress and its allies of stoking violence in the name of protests against the CAA. "When Congress and its friends could not stall the CAB in both Houses, they resorted to such tactics", he said at a rally in Dumka.[213] He even said at the same rally that those indulging in violence over the CAA could be identified by their clothes.[214] It reminded people of his churlish rejection of a Muslim cap on another occasion.

Swapan Dasgupta was more specific when he said: "There is considerable alarm, bordering on fear, at the people who seem to be providing numbers to the anti-CAA stir. In blunt terms, the movement is seen to be a Muslim revolt against a BJP government that has succeeded in pushing the community to the margins of politics."[215]

Attacking Congress and other opposition parties on 17 December, PM challenged them to offer Indian citizenship to all Pakistanis.[216] He also dared them to invalidate the law banning triple talaq and revive Article 370.[217] He mocked CAA stand of Mamata in his by now famous Ramlila Maidan speech[218] and tweeted Sadhguru video to drum up support for CAA.[219] He sought social media support to back the CAA by launching the campaign with the hashtag of "India Supports CAA".[220] He even used the Vivekananda Jayanti at Belur Math on 12 January, 2020 to muster support for the CAA.[221]

He sharpened his attack on anti-CAA protesters for destroying prime property. Addressing a gathering on 25 December that included UP Governor Anandbhen Patel, CM Yogi Adityanath and Defence Minister Rajnath Singh, the PM came out strongly in support of the police. This was the second time since 22 December when he condemned attack on security personnel. His remarks contrasted starkly with the stance of opposition parties as well as certain civil society groups who accused the BJP governments in states of unleashing repression on protestors.[222] In a trenchant criticism of the opposition parties, specially the Congress, for their country-wide agitation against the CAA, the Prime Minister accused them of trying to damage the institution of parliamentary democracy in the country and asked them why they were not raising their voice against Pakistan which had been committing atrocities against its minorities for the past 70 years. He was speaking at a function in connection with the setting up of a memorial museum for Shivakumar Swami at Siddaganga Mutt, 80 km from Bengaluru on 2 January, 2020.[223]

In the backdrop of recent violent protests in various university campuses over the CAA and proposed NRC, he tried to woo the youth by saying that the youth hate anarchy and disorder and dislike casteism, nepotism and favouritism. He also said that the coming decade belongs to them and lauded them for believing in the system and questioning it when it does not respond properly.[224] While addressing the Annual Prime Minister's National Cadet Corps (NCC) Rally on 28 January, 2020, the PM said his government brought in the CAA to correct 'historical' injustices and to fulfil India's 'old promise' to religious minorities in neighbouring countries.[225] He told the Lok Sabha on 6 February that "there will be no impact on any citizen of India, whatever be their faith/religion owing to the implementation of the CAA."[226] RSS chief Mohan Bhagat echoed the Prime Minister when asserted, while addressing a gathering in Guhawati on 21 July, 2021 that "no Muslim will face any harm due to CAA."[227]

For a change, the PM shifted his stand and told a seminar on "Globalising Indian Thought" at IIM Kozhikode on 16 January, among others: "Broadly, there are certain ideals that have remained central to Indian values. They are compassion, harmony, justice, service and openness. For centuries we have welcome the world to our land. In a world seeking to break free from mindless hate, violence, conflict and terrorism, the Indian way of life offers others rays of hope. The Indian way of conflict avoidance is not by brute force but by the power of dialogue."[228]

Amit Shah attempted to reach out to the student community while addressing an election rally in Jharkhand's Pakur and advised them to study the act, which was only meant to accord citizenship to religious minorities in Pakistan, Afghanistan and Bangladesh.[229]

He always supported police action in Jamia. Even on13 February he said: "I stand firmly with police in the Jamia case. No one has the right to burn public property. Police only entered the campus to go after students who indulged in arson."[230]

Amit Shah has said umpteen times that CAA would be implemented at any cost. Asked whether the new citizenship law might be rolled back in view of the protests, he told his interviewer Navika Kumar of the *Times*. Now on 17 December that the government was firm "like a rock" and there was "not even a little, there's not even an iota of possibility" of its rollback.[231] He was so long indirectly accusing the opposition as responsible for dividing the country and on 25 January directly accused Mamata Bannerjee, Aam Admi Party, Congress, Samajwadi Party, Bahujan Samaj Party as being members of the Tukde Tukde gang.[232] It may be recalled that the MHA in response to an RTI application by Netizen Saket Gokhale replied on 20 January that "Ministry of Home Affairs has no information concerning *tukde tukde* gang."[233] The MHA gave this 11-word reply on a gang that had been made out to be the biggest threat to India by its own minister.

Home Minister Amit Shah continued accusing the opposition that the anti-CAA protests were politically motivated[234] and asserted that he would not budge an inch on CAA.[235] He slammed the Opposition for misleading people on the CAA and said that the CAA was not about taking away citizenship but giving it to non-Muslim refugees.[236] Addressing a mammoth rally at the Ram Katha park in the Bangla Bazar area of Lucknow on 21 January, 2020, Shah asserted that there would be no U-turn on CAA, come what may.[237]

Modi also said at Varanasi on 16 February that steps like nullification of Article 370 or promulgation of CAA were taken in the national interest and despite all-round pressure, his government would steadfastly stand by these decisions.[238] BJP's working president J.P. Nadda reiterated on 19 December that both the new citizenship law and the NRC would be implemented across the country. Nadda said BJP's rivals were protesting against the CAA for vote bank politics while ignoring the plight of minorities of three neighbouring countries living in India. He further said: "These people have been living in India for 28-30 years but can not admit their children in schools or buy a house as they do not have citizenship." He quoted Amit Shah's statement in Parliament that opposition parties were speaking the same language as Pakistan on the issue.[239]

BJP spokesperson Sambit Patra accused the opposition of misleading the people and trying to "bifurcate" the country in the name of Hindus and Muslims.[240]

But even the BJP leaders are questioning the exclusion of Muslims from the CAA. Chandra Kumar Bose, a Bengal BJP vice-president tweeted: "If Muslims are not persecuted in their home country, they would not come, so there is no harm in including them. However, this is not entirely true—what about Baluch who live in Pakistan and Afghanistan? What about Ahmediya in Pakistan?" Bose wrote[241], Congress leader and Rajya Sabha MP Partap Singh Bajwa urged President Ram Nath Kovind to have the ambit of new citizenship law expanded to include in it Ahmadiyya community too, facing persecution in Pakistan.[242]

Shiromoni Akali Dal (SAD), an ally of the BJP, has demanded the inclusion of Muslims in the CAA, mentioning that the Sikh gurus had sacrificed their lives for other religions.[243]

Like the Sikhs, Christians also stood up for the Muslims. Christian groups in Bengal submitted a memorandum to the state governor saying, *inter alia*, "some groups are giving open calls to eliminate the religious minorities and convert our democratic, sovereign and secular India into a so-called 'Hindu State'. Minorities feel insecure by such oppressive calls."[244]

Priests from the Kolkata Diocese of the Church of North India (CNI) hit the streets in their white cassocks on 20 January, 2020 to protest against the CAA and the NRC. The Roman Catholic Church under the Archbishop of Calcutta organised a similar walk on 26 December, 2019 after the Christmas celebrations though the clergy had not joined in them. Both the walks followed several heads of churches including "anti-discrimination and anti-CAA" messages in their Christmas sermons.[245] New Year mass in different churches talked of peace, hope and unity.

The metropolitan Archbishop of Bangalore Peter Machdo, who is also the president of the All Karnataka United Christian Forum in a memorandum to the President and the Prime Minister of India through Karnataka governor Vijubhai Vala appealed to the Central Government on 9 January, 2020 not to grant citizenship based on religion but only "on the merit of each individual case."[246] This was the first time that he made such an appeal since protests erupted across the country against the CAA.

Archbishop of Goa on behalf of the Catholic community in Goa released a strongly worded statement on 8 February, 2020 appealing to the Centre to "immediately and unconditionally revoke the CAA and desist from implementing NRC and NPR".[247]

In the meantime, petitions have been filed in the Supreme Court challenging the constitutionality of the Act. The Supreme Court on 18 December entertained the pleas against the CAA, fixed 24 January for hearing and asked the Centre to file the reply on 59 pleas by 22 January. No stay on the operation of the law was, however, issued.[248] The Supreme Court also directed the Centre to give wide publicity about the Act's provisions.[249] Accordingly, the Centre explained the background and the salient features of the Act in all-India English, Hindi and Urdu news papers.

While hearing a PIL to make the CAA mandatory, the Bench of the CJI of the Supreme Court observed on 9 January, 2020 that the country was going through a difficult period due to violent protests against the CAA and requested all concerned to desist from aggravating the situation by further provocation.[250]

Notwithstanding such an observation, taking advantage of the fact that the Supreme Court did not give any stay order on the petitions heard on 18 December, the Centre issued a notice on 10 January announcing the coming into force of the CAA from that day. The one-paragraph notice said: "In exercise of the powers conferred by sub-section (2) of Section 1 of the Citizen (Amendment) Act, 2019 (47 of 2019), the Central Government hereby appoints the 10th day of January as the date on which the provisions of the said Act shall come into force."[251] The Rules for the Act are yet to be framed. The six month period for framing CAA Rules ended on 10 July. The Home Ministry has sought from the Parliamentary Standing Committee three months to frame the CAA Rules.[252] The Home Ministry on 2 February, 2021 informed the Parliament that the Committees on Subordinate Legislation for the Lok Sabha and the Rajya Sabha had granted extension till 9 April and 9 July, respectively, to frame rules under CAA.[253] The third extended deadline of 9 January, 2022 was again extended by another three months.[254] The Parliamentary Committees on subordinate legislation in the Lok Sabha and the Rajya Sabha granted extension for the seventh time to frame Rules for the CAA on 7 January, 2023.[255]

Actually, none knows how many such extensions the party in power would require before it decides to implement the Act. Unless the rules are drafted, clarity will not be available on several issues, such as whether the changes apply only to those who faced religious persecution. And Union Home Minister Amit Shah during his 2021 Assembly election ampaign continued to harp on the BJP-led Central Government's commitment to the framing of the rules of the CAA, the only reason it was being delayed was because of the Covid-19 pandemic.[256]

When the case came up for hearing before the SC on 22 January, the number of petitions filed before the Court swelled to 144. That included the petition filed by the Kerala government challenging the validity of the CAA under Article 131, making it a Centre-State dispute. This is the second time in the last 60 years that a state government has moved the Apex Court resisting the implementation of a Parliament-enacted law. In 1961, the West Bengal government had moved a suit in the Court under Article 131 against Parliament passing the Coal Bearing Areas (Acquisition and Development) Act, 1957, which had empowered the Centre to acquire land vested or owned by the state. The Supreme Court upheld the constitutional edge enjoyed by the Centre to legislate for acquisitioning state-owned property.[257]

Making it clear that it would not stay the CAA without hearing the Centre, the 3-judge bench asked the Centre to file a comprehensive reply within 4 weeks and said that the petitions would be heard by a five-judge bench after five weeks, i.e. not before 22 February. The Court agreed with submissions that petition from Assam and Tripura should be heard separately as they were opposing CAA on a different ground than the rest of the country.[258] Later, the Rajasthan government on 16 March moved the Supreme Court challenging the validity of the CAA.[259] The Centre on 17 March, 2020 filed a 129-page affidavit asserting that the CAA does not seek to recognise or seek to provide answers to all kinds of purported persecution that may be taking place across the world or that may have taken place previously anywhere in the world. CAA is a narrowly tailored legislation seeking to address the problem that awaited India's attention for a solution since several decades. It merely offered "amnesty" without hurting India's secularism. It does not violate any fundamental right. The law does not affect the legal right of Indians.[260] Due to Covid-19 pandemic, the hearing of the case, however, could not be taken up by the Supreme Court. The Supreme Court, however, on 19 March, 2021 *prima facie* found no harm in State Assemblies, such as those in Kerala, Punjab, Rajasthan and West Bengal, passing resolutions against Central laws like the CAA or the controversial farm laws. While hearing a petition filed by a Rajasthan-based NGO, Samta Andolon Samiti that said State Assemblies had no business to pass resolutions against Central laws that come under the Union List of the Seventh Schedule, the Bench headed by CJI Sharad A. Bobde observed: "It is the opinion of the majority in the Kerala Assembly.... They have not told people to disobey the law, they have only told Parliament to abrogate the law. It is only an opinion and does not have the force of law." The Court adjourned the case for four weeks, asking the petitioner to do further research on the issue.[261] Earlier, while refusing to entertain a plea made by advocate Vineet Dhanda to declare the CAA as constitutional, a bench headed by Chief Justice S.A. Bobde and justices B.R. Gavai and Surya Kant had observed on 9 January, 2020 that "the country is going through difficult times and there is so much violence that endeavour should be for peace."[262] The Supreme Court on September 12, 2022 fixed the hearing in 220 petitions challenging the CAA 2019 on October 31, 2022 and referred the case to a three-judge Bench.[263] Senior advocate Indira Jaising has urged the CJI in a letter on 15 September, 2022 to facilitate live-streaming of proceedings relating to important constitutional matters such as the CAA, among others.[264] The CAA hearing in the Supreme Court was put off again on 6 December, 2022 and was adjourned at least till January.[265]

VI

The BJP-led NDA III government on coming to power started implementing the party's promises given in the election manifesto. Or as Swapan Dasgupta says "the second innings of Prime Minister Narendra

Modi...has begun at a searing pace with the Home Minister Amit Shah, leading the charge."[266]

The BJP-led government nixed the special status of Kashmir given in Article 370 and the Supreme Court verdict cleared the obstacle to the construction of Ram temple in Ayodhya. The BJP is embroiled in these two sensitive issues and Kashmir is in turmoil since the scrapping of its special status. Moreover, the people are feeling the pinch of spiralling price rise and mounting unemployment and it could be that the BJP government is deliberately fanning the debate as a cover for its dismal economic performance and negative job creation.

Under such a scenario, one wonders whether it was prudent for the BJP to touch another raw nerve by conferring citizenship on the basis of religion. While scrapping of special status of Kashmir and construction of Ram temple at Ayodhya were in the party's agenda for long, conferring citizenship on the basis of religion was not in the party's agenda earlier. The government was at pain to clarify that the CAA would not affect the Indian citizens. The Ministry of Home Affairs on 17 December, 2019 once again clarified that the CAA does not apply to Indian citizens, who will be completely unaffected by it. The MHA has shared parts of the legislation to allay fears among a section of Indians who have been protesting against the legislation saying that the new law poses a threat to their citizenship. "The CAA does not target any religious community from abroad. It only provides a mechanism for some migrants who may otherwise have been called 'illegal', depriving them of opportunity to apply for Indian citizenship provided they meet certain conditions," the MHA said in a statement.

It further maintained that in the last six years 2830 Pakistani, 912 Afghani and 172 Bangladeshi citizens have been given Indian citizenship. Many of them were from the majority community of these countries.[267]

The CAA mentions three neighbouring countries—Pakistan, Bangladesh and Afghanistan—whose minorities will be granted Indian citizenship. But no country wants to be portrayed as perpetrator of its minorities. So is the case with these countries.

Pakistan's PM never misses an opportunity to criticise India on this issue. Even before the CAB became an Act, Pakistani PM Imran Khan on 10 December tweeted: "We strongly condemn the Indian Lok Sabha citizenship legislation which violates all norms of international human rights law and bilateral agreements with Pakistan."[268]

He even said on 17 December at the Global Refugee Forum in Geneva that India's CAA could not only lead to a refugee crisis in South Asia but trigger a conflict between nuclear armed nations. India was quick to respond with the Foreign Ministry saying the Pakistan PM had again peddled familiar falsehoods at a multilateral platform to advance his narrow political agenda by making "gratuitous and unwarranted" remarks on matters entirely internal to India.[269]

At least two Hindu lawmakers of Pakistan have slammed the NDA government over the CAA, saying it should not "drag' the Hindu minorities across the border into the controversy for its political advantage.[270]

In a diplomatic setback, Bangladeshi Foreign Minister A.K. Abdul Momen cancelled his scheduled visit to New Delhi a day after Parliament passed the CAB and protests broke out in Assam. Bangladeshi Home Minister's three-day trip to Shillong starting from 13 December was also cancelled at the last moment. Only on the previous day of this announcement cancelling the visits, Momen had openly contested Union Home Minister Amit Shah for including Bangladesh in the list of countries where minorities were persecuted.

PTI quoted Momen as saying that "India is historically a tolerant country which believed in secularism (but) their historic position will be weakened if they deviate from that." Momen also claimed that the US ambassador to Bangladesh had shared with him Washington's view that India was weakening its position by passing the CAB.[271]

Momen's Prime Minister was more candid when during a visit to the UAE she broke her long silence on India's new citizenship law and said in an interview to the *Gulf News* on 19 January, 2020: "We don't understand why the Indian government did it. It was not necessary. (Still) it is an internal matter."[272]

Afghanistan's ruling dispensation made no secret of its disapproval for bracketing their country as intolerant of its minorities.

In consonance with the policy of the BJP leadership, UP CM Yogi Adityanath claimed at a rally in Gaya (UP) on 14 January that mass killings, forced exodus and coercive conversion of Hindus in Pakistan spurred CAA.[273] Dharmendra Pradhan, Union Minister for petroleum and natural gas and steel in a signed article did not mention Pakistan but lauded the CAA for securing justice and dignity for those who have suffered religious persecution on the subcontinent.[274]

Though the Indian view of Pakistan is increasingly shaped by a kind of national hysteria, as things stand, Pakistan enjoys a strong relationship with China, has largely repaired its once strained relations with America, and is open to overtures from Russia.[275]

The PM claimed that CAA had exposed to the people of the world Pak's atrocities on its (religious) minorities,[276] and the Home Minister declared the government's resolve not to rest until Pak refugees were made Indian citizens.[277]

But what is their number and who prevented the government from conferring citizenship on them even under the provisions of the existing Citizenship Act remained unanswered. It is naive to say that minorities are fleeing Pakistan in droves being victims of persecution there. The Indo-Pak border is properly fenced and manned making it impossible to cross the border illegally.

They are no doubt coming to India but they are coming with valid visa. Since 2011, when long-term visas (LTVs) were first introduced, nearly 30,000 Pakistanis have been granted LTVs and as on 15 July, 2018, 1,500 such applications were pending.[278] It is a different matter that some of them did not return to Pakistan, and they are not supposed to return to Pakistan either. The LTVs are precursors to citizenship, based on the report given by the state governments. In the meantime, LTVs make them eligible to apply for Aadhar number, PAN Card and buy property in India.[279]

But the Indo-Bangladesh border is still porous at several places making it possible for the enterprising ones to cross the border. The Government of India informed the Lok Sabha on 11 February, 2020 that as many as 21,348 infiltrators were deported and 9,145 arrested by Indian authorities along the border with Bangladesh in the past five years since 2014.[280]

The Hindu population in Bangladesh is decreasing every year but good neighbourly relations with Bangladesh stands in the way of focusing on this stark fact. Not only Hindus but Muslims as well do cross the border in search of greener pastures. So when the state BJP president of Bengal says that 50-70 lakh infiltrators would be identified and sent back[281], he has the Muslim infiltrators in mind, but cannot say it in so many words.

Bangladesh, where 10.7 per cent of the 161 million population is Hindu and 0.6 per cent Buddhist, has, however, denied any migration to India because of religious persecution, *Gulf News* said.[282]

The BSF had apprehended 2,194 Bangladeshis in 2019, but since December a substantial increase in the outflow of illegal Bangladeshi migrants to their home country had been recorded. Those leaving the country were mostly engaged as masons, maids and housekeepers in Bangalore and North India. In January 2020 alone, 268 illegal Bangladeshi migrants were apprehended by the BSF.[283] Bangladeshis who had left by choice in the wake of the NRC/CAA turmoil seem to be returning to their workplaces in cities such as Mumbai and Bengaluru by September 2020.[284] Bangladeshi patients who are a major source of revenue for several private hospitals in Kolkata started trickling back by November 2020 as travel curbs imposed due to Covid-19 pandemic were relaxed.[285]

Punjab Chief Minister Amrinder Singh raised a pertinent question in a letter to Ravi Shankar Prasad, India's Law Minister: "As the Chief Minister of a border state I too have a grave concern. The language of the CAA does not even require that any illegal migrant seeking its benefit need not be of Indian origin in any manner. All they have to be is from Afghanistan, Bangladesh or Pakistan. This could be a citizen or even a resident or even a temporary person in transit through these countries. This could be misused for infiltration into our country, particularly in the border state, converting this misguided legislation into a national security threat." The Union Law Minister, however, did not respond to Amarinder's specific question.[286]

The Supreme Court-monitored NRC in Assam rendered as many as 12 lakh Hindus stateless. This unnerved the BJP and it sought to negate the effect of NRC through the CAA. One wonders if the BJP gave a little more time to settle the controversy raised by the abrogation of Article 370 and construction of Ram temple and undertaken the NPR, as settled in 2010, along with the 2021 Census operations before going for the CAA, the opposition to the CAA would have been that much intensive and all-pervasive. The mixing up of the CAA with the NRC and the NPR has created the problem. But the BJP is in no mood to relent.

Has CAA been formulated because the government having recognised the enormous problems that a nationwide NRC would entail has built an escape route for all denominations, except the Muslims? In that case, CAA fails a basic constitutional test of treating all religions equally. Moreover, will it legalise religious discrimination? If India now accepts the responsibility for all minorities in neighbouring countries, where do we resettle them? Does this responsibility fall on Assam and the northeast—or if not, which other states?[287]

Or was it that the hardliners in the BJP were calling the shots over the heads of the saner elements in the BJP? This was very much evident when a section in the BJP lamented the absence of leaders like Jaitley in this crucial juncture[288] or the PM had to publicly contradict his own Home Minister and in the process laid emphasis on certain facts which are not factually correct. He courted controversy by speaking about the CAA from the precincts of Belur Math on the occasion of the Vivekananda Jayanti and invoked the names of Mahatma Gandhi and even of Pandit Nehru in support of the CAA. Or is it a calculated risk taken by the BJP to encash on its overwhelming majority in the Lok Sabha and near majority in the Rajya Sabha to obtain parliamentary approval on all the sensitive issues as quickly as possible, so that the party get sufficient time to convert the polarising effects of such steps in its favour in the 2024 Lok Sabha elections? The Uniform Civil Code could be the possible target in the near future. There is also speculation, as Saba Sharma says, "about whether the CAA is a means to appease India's Hindu diaspora abroad—an important funding base for the ruling party."[289]

And it could as well simply be a failure on the part of the BJP leadership to foresee the fallout of such a step. It resorted to demonetization process primarily to win the 2018 UP Assembly elections. Similarly, it has taken the CAA/NRC route primarily to win the 2021 Bengal Assembly elections by a thumping majority by polarising Hindu votes. Amit Shah was more specific when he said that the BJP would get two-thirds majority in the 2021 Assembly polls[290] and the BJP general secretary gave out that Bengal would be among the first for CAB rollout.[291] Amit Shah, in his speech in the virtual rally on 9 June, 2020 in the middle of the pandemic and an economic crisis, dusted off the CAA plank with renewed zeal, attacking Mamata Bannerjee for her opposition to the controversial law. Shah's thrust left little doubt that the citizenship matrix would be a key element in the BJP's campaign narrative for the 2021 Assembly polls.[292] Earlier, on 1 March, 2020, Shah had assured in a public rally in Kolkata that "no minority will have to leave" the country owing to the new Citizenship Act.[293]

But what could be the polarising effect on an electorate was best demonstrated in Delhi which was rocked by communal frenzy following a clash between pro- and anti-CAA protestors. If this could happen in our national capital, one fails to comprehend what would be its fallout in the other communal sensitive areas of the country.

Its second objective is to negate the effect of the NRC process on 12 lakh Hindus in Assam by conferring citizenship on them. It expected protests from Assam and Bengal but was confident to turn even the adverse situations in its favour as it did earlier in regard to the demonetization and the GST. It never visualised that the protests against the CAA would assume an all-India character. It is a situation that the party did not bargain for. That the BJP was not prepared for such an eventuality is evident in the BJP ministers talking differently, sometimes at variance with that of the government. Even the Home Minister said one thing in the Parliament and another thing outside it.

Yet, it is still hoping that sooner rather than later the excitement over the CAA would fizzle out under its own weight. But the protest is showing no signs of subsiding; the protesters showing no signs of fatigue.

And what would be the number of beneficiaries of the CAA? RSS estimated that about 1.5 crore would get citizenship under the amended Act. Of them 6 lakh would be in Assam and about 70 lakh in West Bengal, most of whom being SCs/STs.[294] Assam Chief Minister, however, gives a figure of 2 lakh Bengali Hindu migrants who would be eligible for Indian citizenship under the CAA,[295] and later admitted on 23 January that there was no data on the number of people who would be granted citizenship in the state.[296] Union Minister of State for Home Affairs G. Kishan Reddy had, however, informed on 17 July, 2019 in reply to a written question by Congress MP Abdul Khaleque that "up to March 31, 2019, a total of 1,17,164 people have been declared foreigners by tribunals in Assam."[297]

Amit Shah told the Rajya Sabha that the actual number of these persecuted minorities may possibly run into "lakhs or crores."[298] But the government figures tell a different story. As per the JPC report laid in both houses of Parliament on 7 January, 2019, the Intelligence Bureau Director had said 25,447 Hindus, 5017 Sikhs, 55 Christians, two Buddhists and two Parsis (total 31,313) from the three countries would be the immediate beneficiaries.[299]

It is not understood how the RSS or Amit Shah had arrived at such an astronomical figure. It could be a ploy to woo refugees in Bengal[300] using Ritwick films to counter CAA[301], although as many as 24 members of Ritwick's family in a written statement expressed their objection to such efforts of the BJP[302] and to brand Mamata government as anti-SC/ST.[303] BJP all along claimed that Matuas would be the biggest beneficiary of the CAA but its claim was belied when a section of Matua community under the banner of Sara Bharat Matua Mahasangha held several marches across North Bengal against the CAA, the NRC and the NPR.[304]

It is not believable that so many persons had been left out of the voters' lists so long. Amit Shah, however, emphatically said that voter identity card or Aadhar card is no proof of citizenship and only the inclusion of names in the NRC would guarantee citizenship.[305] Article 326 of the Constitution stipulates that voting rights are available only to citizens. Thus, a voter automatically becomes a citizen. Similarly, passports under the Passport Act could only be issued to citizens. Again, agricultural land can only be owned by a citizen. Consequently, by a simple rule of thumb, if a person is on the voters' list, or has a passport, or is having agricultural land, then that person is a citizen. This principle was reflected when a magistrate court in Mumbai ruled that passport and voter ID card are sufficient proof of nationality of a person.[306]

Whatever it is, as it stands, the CAA has come into force from 10 January, according to a notification issued by the Central Government. So there is no question of its rollback or moratorium for certain years. The PM, the Home Minister and other leaders of the BJP have clarified on more than one occasion that the CAA has come to stay. Now everything hinges on the verdict of the Supreme Court.

In the meantime, the CAA takes a back seat in the state BJP programme in West Bengal[307], though the All India Matua Mahasangha, whose support the BJP enjoys, has demanded even on 19 November, 2020 the implementation of the CAA.[308] The Vaishnavite Matua sect was founded by Harichand Thakur, a contemporary of Raja Rammohun Roy, to lead the Namasudras. Ideologically, the movement was claimed to be a movement of social protest and politics of backwardness in pre-industrial society. Pramatha Ranjan Thakur, the then head of the sect and a Member of the Constituent Assembly, acquired a large tract of land in Gaighata police station areas of Bongaon sub-division in North 24-Parganas from the local zaminder, which became known as Thakurnagar. P.R.Thakur shifted the headquarters of the Matua sect from Orakandi of Faridpur district, now in Bangladesh, to Thakurnagar in 1948. 'Refugees' and 'displaced persons' mostly of Namasudra persuasions of the Matua sect have poured in the border areas of Nadia and 24-Parganas districts from across the border, particularly from Khulna, Satkhira, Jessore, Jhikargacha, Barisal, Bhola, Faridpur and other places of the region. These people as also other refugees from Bangladesh under the banner of different Refugee organisations are demanding Indian citizenship, for they know that citizenship is the ultimate passport to a secure identity.

On 28 December, 2012 in a public meeting of the Matua Mahasangha at Kolkata, Gautam Deb of the CPIM forcefully supported the demand of the Matuas. CPIM MP Basudev Acharaia and Prashant Chatterjee raised this demand in the Lok Sabha in April 2012. On 22 May, 2012, CPIM general secretary, Prakash Karat wrote to the Prime Minister Manmohan Singh urging for citizenship of the persecuted minorities in Bangladesh. In the Twentieth Party Congress, the CPIM took a resolution on this issue. The Trinamool Congress all along supported the citizenship demand of the Matuas.[309]

The CAA 2019 allows the Bangladeshi Hindu immigrants including the Matuas, amongst others, to apply for Indian citizenship. But the Act could not be implemented because the rules for the implementation of the Act could not be framed till now. It is also a matter of conjecture when the rules would be framed or whether it will ever be framed.

In the 2019 Lok Sabha elections the Matuas are reported to have supported the BJP on the understanding that the party would ensure that they get citizenship. Local BJP MP Shantanu Thakur was agitating for some time past over the inordinate delay in the implementation of the CAA. In a meeting at Gaighata on 29 November he questioned as to why there was such a long delay in implementing the CAA.[310] He had also written a letter to that effect to the Union Home Minister in the last week of October 2020.[311] Former Trinamool MLA Upen Biswas wrote a letter to the Union Home Minister demanding early implementation of the CAA.[312]

State BJP leadership was aware of the discontent among the Matuas over this issue and was trying to douse it. Union Water Resource Minister Gajendra Singh Sekhawat told the party workers at Bongaon on 6 December, 2020 that the CAA would be implemented within a month and a half.[313] BJP MP Santanu Thakur, however, stayed away from the local programmes of the Union minister.[314]

BJP's Bengal minder and national general secretary Kailash Vijayvargiya met the Matua community in Thakurnagar on 12 December, 2020 and told them that the CAA would be implemented by January or February.[315] Earlier on 6 December, 2020, he had told the journalists that "most probably, from January, the process of providing citizenship would begin."[316] Union Home Minister Amit Shah was scheduled to visit the Matua stronghold of Thakurnagar on 19 December amid a buzz in the saffron camp that Shah would make announcement on implementation of the CAA during his coming tour. Shah's scheduled visit to Thakurnagar was, however, cancelled. BJP sources said the cancellation of the visit suggested that the Centre was not yet ready to implement the CAA, a major demand of the Matuas.[317]

The CM of West Bengal at a rally in Gopalnagar near Bongaon on 9 December, 2020 had said that the Matuas were very much citizens of India and need no new certificate to stay here. Nobody could drive them out of the country.[318] She again said at Ranaghat, a Matua bastion, on 11 January, 2021 that Matuas and Namasudras were already citizens[319] and even said that CAA would put the Matuas in deep trouble as the altered law would force those who had already become Indians to apply for citizenship again.[320]

Meanwhile, the Dalit Adivasi Minority Andolon League (DAMAL) has questioned about the implementability of the CAA.[321] The Joint Forum Against NRC, a public platform associated with the anti-CAA and anti-NRC movement in Bengal, said on 18 December, 2020 that the Centre should come clean on where it stands on the NRC, CAA and NPR before the Bengal elections. It stressed that this was more important for Bengal's people than talks on Trinamool turncoats joining the BJP. "We would like to talk on issues that impact people much more than a few leaders switching parties. The Centre has to spell out clearly if it wants a nationwide National

Register of Citizens (NRC) or not. They have to come clear on this before the Bengal elections. If they do not, we will start a movement that forces them to clear their stand," said Prosenjit Bose, convenor of the Forum.[322] Amit Shah, Union Home Minister, put to rest all speculations over the contentious issue. "Rules for CAA have not been framed as yet. We will plan its implementation after the Covid-19 vaccine reaches people. Let the vaccine come first," he said after a road show in Bolpur on 20 December, 2020.[323] Though Shah's announcement did not assuage the feelings of people like Shantanu Thakur[324], it is an indirect admission of the fact that CAA is no longer an important weapon in the armoury of the BJP for winning elections.

The BJP's election manifesto for the 2021 West Bengal Assembly elections was advertised in all leading newspapers on 23 March, 2021. One of its promises was to "implement Citizenship Amendment Act in first cabinet meeting." Such a promise has raised the question as to when the state cabinet was empowered to take a decision on the implementation of a Central Act, that too when the BJP was so long saying that the CAA was a settled fact and there was no question of its abrogation. Perhaps to dilute the criticism against such a promise, Shamik Bhattacharjee, Bengal BJP's spokesperson said: "CAA is a settled fact and nothing is going to unsettle it. We have announced that in our manifesto that it will be implemented in the first cabinet meeting. The Act is about giving citizenship to people, not snatching anything away from them. We have since 1952 been vocal about the rights of the uprooted people. We are committed to it."[325] It is known to everybody that the Act could not be implemented because of the inability of the Centre to frame Rules for the Act without which no Act can be enforced. Such being the position, why this announcement was made in the manifesto? Apparently, it was to assure the Matuas that their interests would be protected by the BJP. It is no wonder that while the BJP did not broach this subject in a big way in the 2021 Assembly polls in Bengal whereas its opponent the Trinamool Congress cashed on the anti-CAA sentiment of the people of the State and came back to power for the third time in a row with more than two-thirds majority.

Shah reiterated his earlier pronouncement on CAA at the much awaited meeting at the Matua stronghold at Thakurnagar on 11 February, 2021 when he said: "I told you earlier the implementation got delayed during pandemic. We will do that after Covid vaccination (drive) is over."[326] But the Matua BJP leaders of West Bengal continue to harp on the implementation of the CAA at the earliest. The BJP's Ranaghat MP Jagannah Sarkar wrote to the Prime Minister on 17 October, 2021 to implement the CAA in India in order to "protect the Hindus of the whole world." His appeal, apparently, was made with the objective of polarisation ahead of the four by-polls in Bengal on 30 October.[327] The BJP's Haringhata MLA Asim Sarkar even threatened on 20 April, 2022 to resign from the Assembly if the CAA was not implemented in West Bengal at the earliest.[328]

Shah did not change track even after more than one year. While addressing a rally in New Jalpaiguri on 5 May, 2022, he reiterated that CAA would be implemented once Covid-19 situation was "completely over." He claimed that that the CAA implementation was halted only due to pandemic and would be implemented before the 2024 polls.[329] So Covid-19 can some time come to the rescue political parties as well.

The polarising effect of the anti-CAA protests is very much manifest in different parts of the country. For instance, while local residents of ward number eight of Arambag municipality in Hooghly district of West Bengal chased off BJP pro-CAA campaigners[330], in two villages—Navanagar and Ratnaal—of Kuchch district of Gujarat, considered the most Muslim-savvy region of the state, banners calling for boycott of Muslims for their anti-CAA stand had appeared.[331]

Realising that any talk about CAA would harm its poll prospects in Assam, Shah while launching the ruling BJP's re-election bid in the 2021 Assam Assembly polls at Guwahati on 26 December, 2020, steered clear of the contentious CAA that is being widely opposed in the state.[332] While Prime Minister Modi refrained from referring to CAA in his public meeting at Sivsagar on 23 January, 2021[333], his Home Minister Amit Shah emulated him the following day at Kokrajhar.[334] Neither the Prime Minister nor the Home Minister did utter a single word on the implementation of the CAA in their subsequent visits to Assam for electioneering campaign. Congress leader Rahul Gandhi, however, promised not to implement the CAA in Assam if voted to power.[335]And for the Congress, Assam includes the Barrack valley too.[336] Himant Biswa Sarma, Assam's Finance Minister, slammed the opponents of the CAA for separating Assamese nationalism from Hindu or Indian nationalism. He backed the Centre's decision to protect Hindu immigrants by implementing the CAA and said the BJP's agenda for the upcoming Assembly elections would be to strike a fine balance between Assamese interests and Hindu interests.[337] But the BJP's Assam election manifesto was mum on the implementation of the CAA in that State.

Assam BJP chief claimed on 14 March, 2021 that the controversial CAA was not an election issue in the upcoming Assembly elections in the state as people would vote logically, not emotionally.[338] AASU, on the other hand, has asked all political parties in the poll-bound state to clear their latest position on the CAA.[339]

Prime Minister Modi's announcement on 19 November, 2021 to roll back the three contentious farm laws has given a fresh lease of hope to those protesting against the CAA, especially in the Northeast. A few organisations like the AASU, Krishak Mukti Sangram Samiti (KMSS) and Co-ordination Committee Against CAA (CCACAA) have decided to revive the anti-CAA protests. They believe that the CAA is against the 1985 Assam Accord.[340] On 11 December, 2021, "black day" was observed across the region in protest against the "unconstitutional law" at the behest of the influential North East Students' Organisation (NESO).[341]

Agatha Sangma, Meghalaya MP and National People's Party leader demanded at the NDA meeting held on 28 November, 2021 for the repeal of the CAA keeping in mind the same sort of sentiments of the people from the northeast which propelled it to roll back the farm laws.[342] On the other hand, Union Minister Hardeep Singh Puri extolled the virtues of the CAA in the backdrop of the problems faced by the Sikh and Hindu communities in Afghanistan. "Recent developments in our volatile neighbourhood and the way Sikhs and Hindus are going through a harrowing time are precisely why it was necessary to enact the CAA," Puri tweeted on 22 August, 2021.[343]

The diatribe on the CAA now hinges on its implementation. The Ministry of Home Affairs said in reply to an RTI question to *The Hindu* in early December 2020 that rules governing the CAA were still "under preparation."[344] On 2 February, 2021, the ministry informed the Parliament about the extension granted by the Committee on Subordinate Legislation for the Lok Sabha and the Rajya Sabha till 9 April and 9 July, respectively, to frame the rules under CAA.[345] The Parliamentary Committees on Subordinate Legislation for the Rajya Sabha and Lok Sabha on 7 January, 2023 granted extension for the seventh time for a period of 6 months until 30 June, 2023 and 9 July, 2023, respectively, to frame the rules under CAA.[346]

Without the rules being notified, the Act remains ineffective. Now the question arises whether the Centre is really keen to notify the Rules? The Centre passed the controversial farm laws on 20 September, 2020 and notified the rules on 20 and 21 October, 2020. If it can frame rules for the farm laws within a month of their enactment, it could have done so in respect of the CAA as well. The very fact that the Centre did not notify the rules for the Citizenship Amendment Act even after more than 2 years of its enactment means that the Centre is not willing to frame the rules right now. It may be recalled that more than 140 petitions, now escalated to 220, against the CAA are pending before the Supreme Court. The Supreme Court had declined to stay the implementation of the CAA. The petitioners also did not press for any stay order because the Rules were not framed till then. Now, if the Rules are framed and notified, the petitioners may approach the Supreme Court with a prayer for 'stay order' and it is anybody's guess what the Supreme Court will do. Perhaps the BJP finds that it cannot exploit the CAA fully to its advantage right now in view of strong opposition to it in the North East.

The annual report for the year 2020-21 of the Ministry of Home Affairs appears to be trying to correct the negative perceptions about the CAA. It has clarified that the CAA 2019 is a "limited, narrowly tailored, compassionate and ameliorative" legislation that seeks to provide a relaxation to minority communities from three neighbouring countries "with a clear cut-off date"[347], but maintains the suspense on timing of implementation of the Act. The annual report of the Ministry of Home Affairs for the year 2021-22, however, did not mention anything about the implementability of the CAA 2019. Apparently, whether the CAA will at all be implemented is a million dollar question.

NOTES

1. *The Times of India*, April 27, 2017, p. 6.
2. *The Hindu*, December 13, 2018, p. 2.
3. *Ibid.,* May 13, 2018, p. 1.
4. *Ibid.*, May 8, 2018, p. 11.
5. *The Telegraph*, November 13, 2018, p. 7.
6. *The Hindu*, May 14, 2018, p. 3.
7. *Ibid.*, May 12, 2018, p. 11.
8. *The Times of India*, May 11, 2018, p. 12.
9. *The Hindu*, May 22, 2018, p. 3.
10. *The Telegraph*, October 24, 2018, p. 7.
11. *Ibid.*, July 5, 2018, p. 7.
12. *The Hindu*, January 5, 2019, p. 11.
13. *The Statesman*, January 1, 2019, p. 2.
14. *Ibid.,* January 4, 2019, p. 2.
15. *The Times of India*, January 7, 2019, p. 7.
16. *The Hindu*, November 28, 2018, p. 10.
17. *Anandabazar Patrika*, January 8, 2019, p. 7.
18. *The Telegraph*, January 9, 2019, p. 7.
19. *Ibid.*, January 9, 2019, p. 7.
20. Bhaumik, Subir, "It's Playing Risky Games", *The Times of India*, January 14, 2019, p. 12.
21. *The Telegraph*, November 14, 2018, p. 7.
22. *The Times of India*, January 13, 2019, p. 9.
23. *Ibid.*, January 13, 2019, p. 1.

24. *Ibid.*, January 30, 2019, p. 17.
25. *Ibid.*, January 31, 2019, p. 22.
25. *Ibid.,* January19, 2019, p. 8.
27. *Ibid.*, January 18, 2019, p. 7.
28. *Ibid.*, February 6, 2019, p. 7.
29. *Ibid.*, January 13, 2019, p. 9.
30. *Ibid.*, January 18, 2019, p. 7.
31. *Ibid.*
32. *The Hindu*, January 28, 2019, p. 11.
33. *The Times of India*, January 28, 2019, p. 12.
34. *Ibid*, February 12, 2019, p. 9.
35. *Ibid*, February 11, 2019, p. 9.
36. *The Statesman*, February 4, 2019, p. 5.
37. *The Times of India*, January 31, 2019, p. 11.
38. *The Hindu*, January 22, 2019, p. 11.
39. *The Times of India*, January 20, 2019, p. 12.
40. *Ibid.*, January 13, 2019, p. 5.
41. *Ibid.,* February 1, 2019, p. 7.
42. *Ibid.*
43. *Ibid.*, February 4, 2019, p. 1.
44. *Ibid.*, February 10, 2019, p. 7.
45. *The Statesman*, February 10, 2019, p. 1.
46. *The Telegraph*, January 10, 2019, p. 5.
47. *The Statesman*, July 17, 2019, p. 3.
48. *Ibid.*, February 14, 2019, p. 3.
49. Bhat, M. Mohsin Alam, "The Constitutional Case against the Citizenship Amendment Bill", *Economic & Political Weekly,* Vol. LIV, No. 3, January 19, 2019, pp. 12-14.
50. *The Telegraph*, September 10, 2019, p. 8.
51. *Ibid.*
52. *The Times of India,* October 10, 2019, p. 9.
53. *The Telegraph*, December 5, 2019, p. 1.
54. Myrboh, Batskhem, "The politics of Inner Line Permit Extension to Manipur", *Economic & Political Weekly*, Vol. LV, No. 5, Februry 1, 2020, p. 18.
55. Bannerjee, Rabi, "States and the stateless." *The Week*, October 13, 2019, p. 25.
56. *The Times of India,* December 12, 2019, p. 19.
57. *The Telegraph*, December 9, 2019, p. 1.
58. *Ibid.*, December 12, 2019, p. 1 and p. 4.
59. *Ibid.*
60. *The Times of India*, December 12, 2019, p. 1.
61. *The Telegraph*, December 6, 2019, p. 1.
62. *Ibid.*, December 8, 2019, p. 1.
63. *The Times of India*, December 11, 2019, p. 12.

64. *Ibid.*, Dccember 10, 2019, p. 8.
65. *Ibid.*, December 11, 2019, p. 1.
66. *Ibid.*, December 12, 2019, p. 1.
67. *Ibid.*, December 13, 2019, p. 1 and p. 10.
68. *Ei Samay*, December 16, 2019, p. 2.
69. *The Times of India*, December 16, 2019, p. 7.
70. *Anandabazar Patrika*, December 14, 2019, p. 6.
71. *The Times of India*, December 13, p. 10.
72. *Ibid.*, December 13, 2019, p. 10.
73. *Ibid.*, December 14, 2019, p. 1.
74. *Ibid.*, December 18, 2019, p. 12.
75. *Ibid.*, December 20, 2019, p. 6.
75. *The Telegraph*, December 21, 2019, p. 5.
77. *Ibid.*, December 22, 2019, p. 10.
78. *The Times of India*, December 13, 2019, p. 1.
79. *Ibid.*, Deceber 11, 2019, p. 12.
80. *Ibid.*, December 11, 2019, p. 1.
81. *Ibid.*, December 12, p. 1.
82. *Ibid.*, December 13, 2019, p. 1.
83. *Ibid.*, December 13, 2019, p. 10.
84. *Ibid.*, December 13, 2019, p. 1.
86. *The Statesman*, December 7, 2019, p. 2.
86. *Ibid.*, December 12, 2019, p. 3.
87. Devy, G.N., "An Epistemic Change?", *Economic & Political Weekly*, Vol. LV, No. 6, February 8, 2020, p. 11.
88. *The Times of India*, December 20, 2019, p. 1.
89. *The Telegraph*, December 22, 2019, p. 1.
90. *The Times of India*, December 18, 2019, p. 1.
91. *Ibid.*, December 16, 2019, p. 7.
92. Awasthi, Puja, "Unageing Fervour", *The Week*, January 5, 2020, p. 35.
93. *The Times of India*, December 20, 2019, p. 1.
94. Editorial titled "Hear the roar", in *The Telegraph*, December 20, 2019, p. 12.
95. Sharma, Pratul, "The citizenship", *The Week*, January 6, 2020, p. 36.
96. *The Times of India*, October 3, 2020, p. 7.
97. *The Statesman*, December 27, 2019, p. 1.
98. *Ibid.*, December 20, 2019, p. 1.
99. *Ibid.*, December 22, 2019, p. 1.
100. *Ibid.*, December 26, 2019, p. 1.
101. *Ibid.*, December 28, 2019, p. 9.
102. *Ibid.*, January 6, 2020, p. 3.
103. *Ibid.*, March 9, 2020, p. 3.
104. *Ibid.*, March 16, 2020, p. 5.
105. *The Telegraph*, February 12, 2022, p. 1.
106. *The Statesman*, February 19, 2022, p. 1.

107. Sharma, Pratul, "The citizenship", *The Week*, January 6, 2020, pp. 37-39.
108. *The Statesman*, December 24, 2019, p. 13.
109. *Ibid.,* December 18, 2019, p. 6.
110. *Ibid.*, December 7, 2019, p. 1.
111. *The Telegraph*, December 20, 2019, p. 5.
112. *The Times of India*, December 21, 2019, p. 1.
113. *The Telegraph*, December 28, 2019, p. 5.
114. *The Times of India*, December 14, 2019, p. 1.
116. *Ibid.*, December 15, 2019, p. 1.
115. *Ibid.*, December 16, 2019, p. 1.
117. Ibid, December 17, 2019, p. 1, p. 3 and p. 6.
118. *Ibid.*, December 18, 2019, p. 1.
119. *Ibid.*, December 19, 2019, p. 5.
120. *Ibid.*, December 19, 2019, p. 3.
121. *Anandabazar Patrika,* December18, 2019, p. 5.
     Ei Samay, December 25, 2019, p. 1.
122. *The Times of India*, December 20, 2019, p. 1.
123. *The Telegraph*, December 26, 2019, p. 6.
124. *The Times of India*, December 19, 2019, p. 11.
126. *Ibid.*, December 13, 2019, p. 10.
126. *The Hindu*, October 29, 2020, p. 9.
127. *The Statesman*, January 22, 2020, p. 13.
128. *Outlook*, December 23, 2019, p. 27.
129. *The Times of India,* January 23, 2020, p. 1.
130. *Ibid.*, December 6, 2019, p. 8.
131. *The Telegraph,* February 8, 2020, p. 7.
132. *The Times of India*, February 9, 2020, p. 6.
133. Interview with Deepak Razdan, *The Statesman*, May 9, 2020, p. 7.
134. *The Statesman*, January 18, 2020, p. 3.
135. Editorial titled "ignoble tryst", *The Telegraph,* December 13, 2019, p. 12.
136. Jayal, Niraja Gopal, "Faith-Based Citizenship", In *This Land Is Mine, I Am Not of This Land* (ed.) *Harsh Mander and Navsharan Singh*, 2021, Speaking Tiger Books LLP, New Delhi, p. 82.
137. *The Times of India*, April 22, 2022, p. 8.
138. *The Statesman*, March 5, 2020, p. 3.
139. Editorial titled "Strike CAA Down", *The Times of India,* January 24, 2020, p. 14.
140. Devy, G.N., "The pathology of protest", *The Telegraph*, January 2, 2020, p. 12.
141. Ghazala Jamil, "Reconfiguring citizenship", *The Telegraph,* December 10, 2019, p. 12.
142. Devy, G.N., "An Epistemic Change?" *Economic & Political Weekly*, Vol. lV, No. 5, February 8, 2020, pp. 10-11.
143. Tewari, Manish, "The Devil's Arithmetic", *Outlook*, December 23, 2019, p. 34.

144. *The Statesman,* January 14, 2020, p. 3.
145. *The Telegraph*, December 9, 2019, p. 4.
146. *The Times of India,* December 10, 2019, p. 6.
147. *The Telegraph*, December 11, 2019, p. 3.
148. *The Statesman*, December 11, 2019, p. 3.
149. *The Times of India,* December 13, 2019, p. 10.
150. *Ibid.*, December 19, 2019, p. 9.
151. *Ibid.*
152. *Ibid.*, December 20, 2019, p. 12.
153. *Ibid.*, December 11, 2019, p. 1.
154. *Ibid.*, December 21, 2019, p. 11.
156. *Ibid.*, p. 2.
155. *Ibid.*, January 18, 2020, p. 13.
157. *The Times of India*, January 10, 2020, p. 11.
158. *Anandabazar Patrika*, January 3, 2020, p. 6.
159. *The Times of India*, January 9, 2023, p. 1.
160. *Ibid.,* December 22, 2019, p. 7.
161. *The Statesman*, February 18, 2020, p. 3.
162. Jethmalani, Mahesh, "Besieged by Sophistry", *The Times of India*, January 16, 2020, p. 12.
163. Salve, Harish, "CAA is necessary", *The Times of India,* March 5, 2020, p. 16.
164. Kaloch, Dhruv C., "Citizenship (Amendment) Act is a wise legislation: Why none of the objections raised on it are valid", *The Times of India,* February 15, 2020, p. 14.
166. *The Statesman,* January 9, 2020, p. 9.
166. *Ibid.,* February 6, 2020, p. 4.
167. Mala Jay, Contrary to top BJP leaders' claims, anti-CAA-NCR protests are spreading, not losing momentum, *The National Herald*, January 23, 2020.
168. *The Telegraph*, March 13, 2021, p. 8.
169. Ganguli, Amulya, "A troublesome future," *The Statesman*, January 21, 2020, p. 6.
170. *The Week*, January 5, 2020, p. 38.
171. *The Times of India,* December 18, 2019, p. 12.
172. *The Telegraph*, December 25, 2019, p. 4.
173. *The Times of India,* December 21, 2019, p. 12.
174. Editorial titled "Allow Peaceful Stir", in *The Times of India,* December 17, 2019, p. 12.
175. *The Statesman*, December 18, 2019, p. 3.
176. *Ibid.*, December 18, 2019, p. 1.
177. *The Times of India,* December 18, 2019, p. 11.
178. *Ibid.,* December 18, 2019, p. 1.
179. *Ibid.*, December 19, 2019, p. 9.

180. *Ibid.*, February 14, 2020, p. 1.
181. *The Statesman,* December 17, 2019, p. 3.
182. *Anandabazar Patrika*, December 16, 2019, p. 8.
183. *The Times of India,* December 26, 2019, p. 5.
184. *Ibid.,* December 25, 2019, p. 9.
186. *Anandabazar Patrika*, December 20, 2019, p. 11.
186. *The Times of India*, December 22, 2019, p. 2.
187. *Ibid.*, December 26, 2019, p. 1.
188. *Ibid.*, December 20, 2019, p. 10.
189. *The Statesman,* January 13, 2020, p. 1.
190. *Ibid.*, January 22, 2020, p. 3.
191. *Ibid.*, February 4, 2020, p. 5.
192. *The Telegraph*, February 23, 2020, p. 3.
193. *The Times of India*, February 25, 2020, p. 6.
194. *Ibid.,* December 17, 2019, p. 1.
195. *The Telegraph* January 14, 2020, p. 1.
196. *Ibid.*, January 14, 2020, p. 4.
197. *The Times of India*, December14, 2019, p. 1.
198. *Ibid.*, December 17, 2019, p. 8.
199. *Ibid.*, January 20, 2020, p. 9.
200. *Ibid.*, February 1, 2020, p. 12.
201. *The Statesman*, February 4, 2020, p. 1.
202. *The Telegraph,* January 4, 2020, p. 5.
203. *The Statesman*, January 26, 2020, p. 9.
204. *Ibid.,* March 8, 2020, p. 9.
206. *The Times of India*, February 4, 2020, p. 1.
205. *Ibid.*, February 6, 2020, p. 13.
207. *The Statesman*, February 22, 2020, p. 1.
208. *Ibid.,* February 17, 2020, p. 5.
209. *Ibid.*, January 1, 2020, p. 5.
210. *Ibid.,* January 14, 2020, p. 3.
211. *Ibid.*
212. *The Times of India*, December 18, 2019, p. 1.
213. *Ibid.*, December 16, 2019, p. 1.
214. *The Telegraph*, December 16, 2019, p. 1.
215. Dasgupta, Swapan, "Citizens not excluded", *The Telegraph,* December 26, p. 12.
216. *The Times of India*, December 18, 2019, p. 1.
217. *Ibid.*, December 18, 2019, p. 1.
218. *The Telegraph,* December 23, 2019, p. 6.
219. *The Times of India*, December 31, 2019, p. 1.
220. *The Statesman,* December 31, 2029, p. 1.
221. *The Telegraph,* January 13, 2019, p. 1.
222. *Ibid.*, December 26, 2019, p. 1.
223. *The Statesman,* January 3, 2020, p. 1.

224. *Ibid.,* December 30, 2019, p. 1.
225. *Ibid.,* January 29, 2020, p. 3.
226. *Ibid.*, February 7, 2020, p. 1.
227. *Ibid.,* July 22, 2021, p. 4.
228. *Ibid.*, January 17, 2020, p. 1.
229. *The Times of India*, December 17, 2019, p. 1.
230. *Ibid.*, February 14, 2020, p. 1.
231. *The Telegraph*, December 18, 2019, p. 1.
232. *Anandabazar Patrika*, January 26, 2020, p. 1.
233. *The Telegraph,* January 21, 2020, p. 1 and p. 4.
234. *The Times of India*, January 3, 2020, p. 6.
235. *Ibid.*, January 4, 2020, p. 9.
236. *The Statesman*, January 19, 2020, p. 5.
237. *Ibid.*, January 22, 2020, p. 1.
238. *The Times of India,* February 17, 2020, p. 10.
239. *Ibid.*, December 20, 2019, p. 6.
240. *Ibid.*, December 17, 2019, p. 1.
241. *The Telegraph*, December 25, 2019, p. 7.
242. *The Statesman*, December 22, 2019, p. 2.
243. *The Times of India*, December 22, 2019, p. 7.
244. *The Telegraph,* January 21, 2020, p. 1.
245. *The Times of India*, January 5, 2020, p. 1.
246. *The Telegraph*, January 21, 2020, p. 1 and p. 4.
247. *The Times of India*, February 9, 2020, p. 6.
248. *Ibid.,* December 19, 2019, p. 1.
249. *The Telegraph*, December 10, 2019, p. 4.
250. *The Times of India*, January 10, 2020, p. 1.
251. *The Telegraph,* January 11, 2000, p. 1.
252. *The Times of India,* August 3, 2020, p. 8.
253. *Ibid.*, February 3, 2021 (Flap).
254. *Ei Samay,* January 12, 2022, p. 7.
255. *The Hindu*, January 8, 2023, p. 1.
256. *Ibid.,* February 14, 2021, p. 1.
257. *The Times of India,* January 15, 2020, p. 1.
258. *Ibid.,* January 23, 2020, p. 1.
259. *Ibid.*, March 17, 2020, p. 6.
260. *The Times of India*, March 18, 2020, p. 1.
    The Statesman, March 18, 2020, p. 1.
    The Hindu, March 18, 2020, p. 11.
261. *The Hindu*, March 20, 2021, p. 1 and p. 8.
262. *The Statesman,* January 10, 2020, p. 1.
263. *The Hindu*, September 13, 2022, p. 1
264. *The Telegraph*, September 17, 2022, p. 1.
265. *Ibid.*, December 7, 2022, p. 1.

266. Dasgupta, Swapan, "Ideological leaps" *The Telegraph*, December 12, 2019, p. 12.
267. *The Times of India*, December 19, 2019, p. 9.
268. *Ibid.*, December 11, 2019, p. 12.
269. *Ibid.*, December 18, 2019, p. 14.
270. *Ibid.*, December 13, 2019, p. 10.
271. *The Telegraph*, December 13, 2019, p. 4.
272. *The Statesman*, January 20, 2020, p. 3.
273. *The Times of India*, January 15, 2020, p. 13.
274. Pradhan, Dharmendra, "Passing the Morality Test". *The Times of India*, January 8, 2020, p. 16.
275. Dhume, Sadanand, "A Passage to Pakistan", *The Times of India*, February 8, 2020, p. 14.
276. *The Statesman*, January 13, 2020, p. 1.
277. *Ibid.*
278. *The Hindu*, July 17, 2018, p. 11.
279. *Ibid.*
280. *The Times of India*, February 12, 2020, p. 7.
281. *Ibid.*, January 20, 2020, p. 7.
282. *The Statesman,* January 20, 2020, p. 3.
283. *Ibid.*, January 25, 2020, p. 1.
284. *The Times of India*, September 16, 2020, p. 10.
285. *Ibid*, November 28, 2020, p. 2.
286. *The Telegraph*, January 4, 2020, p. 5.
287. Editorial titled "Firefighting Time", *The Times of India*, December 20, 2019, p. 16.
288. *Anandabazar Patrika*, December 29, 2019, p. 8.
289. Sharma, Saba, "A national concern", *The Statesman*, July 23, 2018, p. 16.
290. *Anandabazar Patrika,* January 3, 2020, p. 6.
291. *The Times of India*, December 13, 2019, p. 6.
292. *The Telegraph,* June 10, 2020, p. 1.
293. *The Hindu*, March 2, 2020, p. 1.
294. *The Times of India*, December 11, 2019, p. 6.
295. *Ibid.*, December 10, 2019, p. 8.
296. *The Telegraph,* January 24, 2020, p. 9.
297. *The Times of India,* December 12, 2019, p. 19.
298. *Ibid.*, December 12, 2019, p. 19.
299. *The Statesman*, July 17, 2019, p. 3.
300. *The Times of India,* December 26, 2019, p. 5.
301. *Ibid.*, December 23, 2019, p. 5.
302. *Anndabazar Patrika*, December 25, 2019, p. 5.
303. *The Times of India,* December 24, 2019, p. 6.
304. *The Telegraph*, December 31, 2019, p. 5.
305. *Anandabazar Patrika*, December 18, 2019, p. 1.
306. *The Times of India*, December 15, 2019, p. 1.

307. *The Telegraph*, September 26, 2020, p. 5.
308. *Ibid.,* November 20, 2020, p. 6.
309. Roy, Mohit, "One law, many crisis", *Anandabazar Patrika*, February 10, 2021, p. 4.
310. *Anandabazar Patrika*, November 30, 2020, p. 5.
311. *Ei Samay*, November 2, 2020, p. 2.
312. *Ibid.*, December 8, 2020, p. 5.
313. *Anandabazar Patrika*, December 7, 2020, p. 3.
314. *Ibid.*
315. *The Telegraph*, December 13, 2020, p. 5.
316. *Ibid.*, December 8, 2020, p. 5.
317. *Ibid.*, December 15, 2020, p. 8.
318. *Ibid.*, December 10, 2020, p. 6.
319. *The Times of India*, January 12, 2021, p. 6.
320. *The Telegraph*, January 12, 2021, p. 6.
321. *Anandabazar Patrika*, December 15, 2020, p. 6.
322. *The Telegraph*, December 19, 2020, p. 5.
323. *Ibid.*, December 21, 2020, p. 1.
324. *Anandabazar Patrika*, December 27, 2020, p. 7.
325. *The Times of India,* March 23, 2021, p. 6.
326. *The Statesman*, February 12, 2021, p. 3.
327. *The Telegraph*, October 22, 2021, p. 5.
328. *Ibid.*, April 21, 2022, p. 2.
329. *Ibid.*, May 6, 2022, p. 1.
330. *The Statesman*, February 7, 2020, p. 14.
331. *Ibid.*, February 2, 2020, p. 5.
332. *The Telegraph*, December 27, 2020, p. 5.
333. *The Times of India*, January 24, 2021, p. 7.
334. *Anandabazar Parika*, January 25, 2021, p. 7.
335. *The Telegraph*, February 15, 2021, p. 5.
336. *Anandabazar Patrika*, March 14, 2021, p. 9.
337. *The Hindu*, February 19, 2021, p. 4.
338. *The Statesman*, March 15, 2021, p. 5.
339. *The Hindu*, March 17, 2021, p. 4.
340. *The Telegraph*, November 21, 2021, p. 6.
341. *Ibid.*, December 12, 2021, p. 5.
342. *The Hindu*, November 29, 2021, p. 9.
343. *The Times of India*, August 29, 2021, p. 9.
344. *The Hindu*, December 10, 2020, p. 1.
345. *The Times of India*, February 3, 2021 (Flap).
346. The Hindu, January 8, 2023, p. 1.
347. Annual Report, Ministry of Home Affairs, 2020-2021, para 12.24, p. 208.

6
CAA-NPR-NRC Conundrum

A citizen is defined as someone who is a member of a national or political community and enjoys equal rights and responsibilities with all other citizens.[1] Citizenship has been viewed as a fruit of the modern state in which citizens are expected to be loyal to the cause of the state and willing to make all the sacrifices required, and in the same state, foreigners are suspected to be less trustworthy or even potential security risks.[2] Citizenship is the legally acknowledged membership of a state and is thus not voluntary. It is commonly invoked to convey a state of democratic belonging or inclusion, yet this inclusion is usually premised on a conception of a community that is bounded and exclusive.[3]

Citizenship has been central to the understanding of a nation-state from its very inception. Citizenship or the lack thereof created the boundaries within which social and political life is governed. Everything from who was awarded protection within the state, to how different entities within the State would interact with one another, and whether a particular State was responsible for the well-being of a person would involve question of that person's formal relationship with the State, their citizenship. Historically, citizenship was a mark of rights and commitment to a specific place and the rights and responsibilities of citizenship were performed in this civic context.[4]

However, the process of globalisation, modernization and the ways in which they have played out in specific contexts have led to a conflation of the boundaries between citizenship and nationality, between descent/blood ties and civic and political membership, which had led to great terrors, historically and in our own time.[5] Further developments in the social, political, economic and electoral outcomes of India influenced the boundaries of citizenship.

Citizenship, much like many ideas, is one of the most heavily debated and contested field in the social sciences. Although the field of citizenship studies is vast and varied, the tensions of citizenship are often expressed through normatively loaded binaries, such as 'good' or 'bad' citizenship; active and passive citizenship; thin and thick citizenship; top-down and bottom-up citizenship; universal and group-differentiated citizenship; legal and substantive citizenship, etc.[6], when, in fact, these categories are hardly clear-cut and the complexities of citizenship in India encompass all these categories at the same time.[7]

Citizenship as an idea and as an ideal institution has several regressions, incompleteness, contests, and often represent an axis of subordination, which have been seen as "discontents" by many scholars, and therefore becomes relevant in postcolonial societies like India, which has been marked by hierarchies of caste, class, race, religion, and gender. The principle of equality as an abiding feature of citizenship remains elusive and fettered. It is the civic community, which is often considered as an important goal of citizenship.[8] A human being who is not a member of some political community is without recourse to the universal and inalienable human rights. The loss of a polity is the loss of humanity, for only membership in a political community, i.e., citizenship can give people what Hannah Arendt in her book *The Origins of Totalitarianism* famously called the right to have rights.

In India, at the end of a prolonged debate on citizenship, the Constituent Assembly settled on the principle of *jus soli* or birth-based citizenship as being "enlightened, modern, civilized" as opposed to the "racial citizenship" implied by the rival descent-based principle of *jus sanguinis*. A shift from soil to blood as the basis of citizenship began to occur from 1987 onwards. The CAA and the NRC will only consolidate this shift to a *jus sanguinis* citizenship regime.

Constitutionally, India is a political community whose citizens avow the idea of the nation as a civic entity, transcending ethnic differences. The NRC-CAA combination, argues Niraja Gopal Jayal, signals a transformative shift from a civic-national conception to an ethno-national conception of India, as a political community in which identity—based on creed rather than on birth—determines gradations of citizenship.[9]

The Citizenship (Amendment) Act (CAA) 2019, changes the 2003-04 embargo concerning citizenship rights for illegal migrants. What the 2019 amendment says is that if such illegal migrants have come into India from Bangladesh, Pakistan or Afghanistan, prior to 31 December, 2014 and if such migrants belong to Hindu, Christian, Sikh, Buddhist, Parsi or Jain communities they will be entitled to citizenship by naturalisation if they have stayed in India for five years. Thus, all such persons would be entitled to citizenship by 1 January, 2020. What the CAA does is, for the first time, make religion, and that too only certain groups, a ground for granting or rejecting citizenship. This was not done when the Constitution was framed, nor under the Citizenship Act, nor in its earlier amendments, nor even at the time of the Assam Accord. Despite the backdrop of partition and the communal violence which was unleashed and despite Pakistan having been created along communal lines, the Indian Constitution at no stage did make reference to religion as a criterion for citizenship.

This is in clear violation of the secular nature of the Constitution—which is held by the Supreme Court to be part of the basic structure of the Constitution—and also violates the fundamental rights enshrined in the Constitution. This initiative which could be seen as one of the important Hindutva projects, has serious implications for both the Muslim immigrants as well as Muslims residing in India itself. The Act has created a climate of tension in the country, as it violates the basic principles and secular values of the Constitution since it proposes to club religion and citizenship together.

Mihir Desai, a senior practicing advocate in the Bombay High Court has very cogently argued why the CAA can even be struck down by the Supreme Court because of its discriminatory and arbitrary nature.[10] Rajnath Singh, Union defence minister, speaking at the EI-GBS in Delhi on 7 March, 2020, however, sought to allay fears of Muslims over the CAA by emphasizing that as India believed in the creed of *Vasudhaiva Kutumbakam*, it can never discriminate based on caste, creed or religion.[11]

The Passport (Entry into India) Rules provide that anyone who enters into India without proper travel documents can be prosecuted and expelled from India. Foreigners Order, 1948 (which was passed under the Foreigners Act, 1946) also provides for similar consequences. During the NDA government, in 2015 and 2016, both these rules were amended for granting exemption to persons belonging to minority communities in Afghanistan, Bangladesh and Pakistan, namely Hindus, Sikhs, Buddhists, Jains, Parsis and Christians who were compelled to seek shelter in India due to religious persecution or fear of religious persecution and entered into India on or before 31 December, 2014 without proper travel documents (that is, those who are illegal migrants) from the provisions of these laws.

Thus, such illegal migrants cannot be prosecuted or expelled. What the present amendment does is to provide citizenship to these very persons, provided they satisfy the conditions under the amended Passport Rules and Foreigners Order. The amendment to the rules prescribes persecution or fear of persecution as one of the conditions, and thus, even the CAA would be applicable to only those illegal migrants who satisfy the condition of persecution. These rules are also under challenge in the Supreme Court.[12]

India's vast multi-cultural and multi-ethnic mosaic of communities with a long, shared past would now split up into distinguishable and bounded political identities because of the CAA.[13] One wonders whether it was not possible to extend this benefit by restoring the Citizenship Act to the 1987 position abrogating the 2003 amendment and the other relevant rules. If Indian citizenship could be conferred on Bangladeshi, Pakistani and Afghanistani migrants so long by the pre-CAA Citizenship Act, what was the necessity to modify it lock, stock and barrel. A New Delhi based rights group, National Campaign Against Torture (NCAT) has said on 18 March, 2020 that the CAA has made 6 lakh refugees for ever stateless.[14] The Asom Sangrami Manch, a newly-formed political party in Assam had, in the meantime, on 5 February, 2020 sent formal letters separately to the UNHCR, its Chief of Mission in India and the chairperson of the Indigenous Peoples and Development Branch of the UN's Secretariat of Permanent Forum on Indigenous Issues (SPFII) for evaluating the compliance of the CAA and its validity under the Universal Declaration of Human Rights.[15]

The agitation against the CAA soon spread to the states ruled by parties which supported the CAA in the Parliament. For instance, thousands of protesters under the banner of "We the People of India" took out a massive rally from Exhibition Ground Road to Mahatma Gandhi Marg, a two km-long stretch, in Bhubaneswar on 30 January, 2020 opposing the CAA, the NRC and the NPR. More than 50 organisations and parties, including all political parties except Biju Janata Dal and the BJP had joined hands for the massive protest. They slammed the BJD MPs for supporting the Citizenship Amendment Bill in Parliament.[16] Again on 22 February, 2020 the activists under the banner of "We the People of India" demanded that the State Assembly pass a resolution against the CAA and the NPR, alleging that the CAA was discriminatory on religious grounds and the NPR was a step towards the implementation of the controversial NRC.[17]

Thousands took to the streets across Tamil Nadu on 19 February, 2020, demanding that the State Assembly pass a resolution against the implementation of the CAA.[18] BJP's southern ally, the AIADMK in its 2021 Assembly election manifesto released on 13 March, 2021 asked for repeal of the CAA.[19] It may be noted that the AIADMK had voted in the Lok Sabha on 9 December, 2019 in favour of the CAB 2019. And to cap it all, the BJP-ruled Solu municipal corporation in Parbhani district of Maharashtra unanimously passed a resolution on 20 February, 2020 against the implementation of the CAA.[20]

Even the north-eastern states, most of which have been insulated against the operation of the CAA, are agitating against the CAA. Naga People's Front, the opposition party in Nagaland, protested against the CAA in the Assembly on 8 February, 2020 and insisted that an anti-CAA resolution be passed in the House. Deputy CM Y. Patton, however, rejected the demand because the law would not affect the Nagas, as the states with Inner Line Permit regime have been exempted from its purview.[21] Sikkim joined other north-eastern states in protesting against the CAA as scores of youths and Sikkim Central University students took out a rally on 14 December, 2019. Chief Minister P.S.Golay, however, maintained that the new law would not be applicable in the state as "Sikkim is protected by Article 371F."[22] The Sikkim Krantikari Morcha and its government were, however, working on getting the Inner Line Permit regime extended throughout the state, Sikkim's lone Lok Sabha member Indra Hang Subba said on 23 February, 2020.[23] Once the entire Sikkim is brought under the ILP regime, the CAA cannot be enforced in the state. The Khasi Students' Union has been demanding the extension of the ILP to Meghalaya for the last two decades. The Meghalaya Assembly passed a resolution on 19 December, 2019 for the implementation of the ILP. The Centre has turned down the demand.[24]

As many as 69 people have been killed in various incidents in the 79 days since the CAA was passed by the Parliament on 11 December.[25] While the number of deaths mount, and more than three years have elapsed since Parliament ratified the legislation, the Ministry of Home Affairs is yet to notify the rules that will make the CAA operational. According to the manual on parliamentary work, rules for legislation should be framed within six months of the date of the President's assent or the standing committee on subordinate legislation should be approached for extension of time. The six month period for framing CAA rules ended on 10 July, 2020. Since then it has been extended at least seven of times but the Rules were not framed obviously for political reasons.

Conferring citizenship to all faiths except Islam follows from the questionable idea of Hindu homeland. Nitin Gadkari, transport and highways minister sought to justify the need for CAA by emphasising the fact that India was the only country in the world for Hindus while there were several for Muslims where they can go and get citizenship. CAA is needed as there is no Hindu nation.[26] Echoing Gadkari, Gujarat chief minister Vijay Rupani told a rally in support of the CAA at Ahmedabad on 23 December, 2019 that Muslims can choose any one of the 150 Islamic countries in the world but India is the only country for Hindus.[27] A group of Indian diaspora in the USA has taken strong exception to Gujarat chief minister's such remark. In a letter to the chief minister, Hindus for Human Rights USA (HHR) reminded him about the oath he has taken to uphold the Constitution and told him that "the CAA is clearly a step towards a Hindu Rashtra that seeks to alienate non-Hindus in their own land of birth."[28] Rabi Kishan, BJP MP from Gorakhpur, was candid in admitting that India is a Hindu Rashtra.[29]

This fact was harped upon by people across the political spectrum. Billionaire investor and philanthropist, George Soros in a speech at the World Economic Forum at Davos on 23 January, 2020 said that Prime Minister Narendra Modi was "creating a Hindu nationalist state" in India.[30] Neeti Nair, associate professor of South Asian history at the University of Virginia in the US says that the CAA and the NRC represent steps towards a "Hindu Rastra."[31]

It has been argued that the series of legal actions of the government related to the downgrading of the former Jammu & Kashmir state, the Supreme Court verdict on the long-vexed Babri Masjid–Ram Janmabhoomi dispute and the CAA show a rapid unfolding of the Hindu rashtra agenda of the Rashtriya Swayamsevak Sangh (RSS).[32]

Incidentally, there has been a sharp fall in the freedom index prepared by the Washington-based Freedom House for the year 2019. The sharp fall has been blamed on three actions of the Modi government—the unilateral annulment of the semi-autonomous status of Jammu & Kashmir, the implementation of the NRC in Assam and the passage of the CAA. India has now been placed among "countries in the spotlight" along with Haiti, Nigeria, Sudan, Tunisia, Turkey, Hong Kong and Ukraine. This category lists countries where important developments in 2019 affected the democratic trajectory and deserves special scrutiny in 2020. India's drop could "blur the value-based distinction between Beijing and New Delhi", the India chapter in the *Freedom in the World 2020* report noted.[33] The US State department in its annual International Religious Freedom (IRF) Report for 2019 submitted to the US Congress took note of the change in the status of Jammu & Kashmir, the CAA and the NRC and discussed in detail mob lynchings and anti-conversion laws and related issues.[34] Responding to the criticism, the Ministry of External Affairs said on 11 June, 2020 that it saw no locus standi for a foreign entity to pronounce on the constitutionally protected rights of Indian citizen and that the panel had exhibited its bias and lack of understanding.[35] US Ambassador at large for International Religious Freedom Sam Brownback told reporters on 8 December, 2020 that the US government has and will continue to raise issues like the CAA with the Modi government. "We watch the situation in India very closely. The Secretary travelled there multiple times. These issues have been raised in private discussions at the government-high government level, and they will continue to get raised", he said.[36]

II

The idea of an NPR and NRC comes for the first time with the adoption by Parliament of the 2003 Citizenship Amendment Bill in December 2003, which on obtaining the assent of the President on 7 January, 2004 became an Act (Act 6 of 2004) and the framing of the Citizenship (Registration of Citizens and Issue of National Identity Cards) Rules, 2003. Before this, there was no requirement for every citizen to register on any common list. The need for a separate register was completely otiose. This happened when NDA I was in power at the Centre. A few years earlier, the Kargil Review Committee had recommended compulsory registration of citizens and non-citizens because there was illegal immigration.

Though the Rules are titled the Citizenship (Registration of Citizens and Issue of National Identity Cards) Rules, 2003, they cover the Population Register as well. Population Register is the precursor to the Citizens Register. Unless the Population Register is created, no Register of Indian Citizens can be prepared. The Population Register contains the information of all residents which include non-citizens as well, whereas Register of Indian Citizens is concerned with information pertaining to Indian citizens. Only a part of the information collected for the Population Register is used for the preparation of the Register of Indian Citizens. Population Register is of wider amplitude when considered in relation to the Indian Citizens Register. Under no other law is there a concept of a Population Register. It is carried out only if it is followed up with the Register of Indian Citizens. The objective was to issue national identity cards to citizens and multipurpose residence cards to non-citizens.

There was, however, initial resistance by several states, but a pilot project was soon launched in a dozen states. Bureaucratic hurdles and delays, however, dragged the project into the UPA government's tenure. After Shivraj Patil became the home minister, he had to take a decision on this project. He declared that the Centre was not keen on implementing the project in its original form. He said every person in the country would be provided a national identity card and be given a unique national identity number.

The 26/11 terror attacks in Mumbai in 2008 brought the idea back on the table. Then home minister P. Chidambaram first-tracked a project to priorities identification of people living in border and coastal areas under the NPR by 2020, without waiting for the 2011 census. At one of the meetings with census officials, Chidambaram reportedly said the country could not count its citizens till it knew who its residents were. The stakeholders agreed, and it was decided that the NPR would have to be the bedrock and the NRIC could only be its subset.[37]

In 2010, the NPR was created for the first time with the names of 119 crore residents of India.[38] In 2015-16, the NPR was updated for the entire country, except Assam. Census officials said that it had enlisted around 110 crore people.[39] On 18 June, 2014, the Home Minister Rajnath Singh had given instructions "to take NPR project to its logical conclusion which is creation of National Register of Indian Citizens."[40] Since 2014, the government has stated in the Parliament several times that the National Register of Indian Citizens (NRIC) or NRC is based on the data collected under the NPR, after the verification of the citizenship status of every individual.[41] For the government to now say that the two are not connected is a white lie.

Censusindia.gov.in "2011-Common" IntroductionToNpr, the Census of India website, says that the National Population Register (NPR) is a Register of usual residents of the country. It is being prepared at the local (Village/sub-Town), sub-District, District, State and National level under provisions of the Citizenship Act, 1955 and the Citizenship (Registration of Citizens and issue of National Identity Cards) Rules, 2003. It is mandatory for every usual resident of India to register in the NPR. A usual resident is defined for the purposes of NPR as a person who has resided in a local area for the past 6 months or more or a person who intends to reside in that area for the next 6 months or more. The objective of the NPR is to create a comprehensive identity database of every usual resident in the country. The database would contain demographic as well as biometric particulars.[42]

Rule 2(1) of the Citizenship (Registration of Citizens and Issue of National Identity Cards) Rules, 2003 defines the "Population Register as follows: "Population Register" means the register containing details of persons usually residing in a village or rural area or town or ward or demarcated area (demarcated by the Registrar General of Citizen Registration) within a ward in a town or urban area. Rule 3(4) says that the Central Government may, by an order issued in this regard, decide a date by which the Population Register shall be prepared by collecting information relating to all persons who are usually residing within the jurisdiction of Local Registrar. But what information are to be collected have not been mentioned in the Rules.

However, the following demographic details[43] of every individual are required for every usual resident to be incorporated in the National Population Register:

- Name of person
- Relationship to head of household
- Father's name
- Mother's name
- Spouse's name (if married)
- Sex
- Date of Birth
- Marital status
- Place of birth
- Nationality (as declared)
- Present address of usual residence
- Duration of stay at present address
- Permanent residential address
- Occupation/Activity
- Educational qualification

The Form for the National Population Register 2020, however, contains as many as 12 questions, as in Annexure D.

It shall be the responsibility of the head of every family, during the period specified for preparation of the Population Register, to give the correct details of name and number of members and other particulars, as specified in sub-rule (3) of rule 3, of the family of which he is the head [Rule 7(2)]. Any violation of provisions of this rule shall be punishable with fine which may extend to one thousand rupees [Rule17].

For the purpose of preparation of the National Register of Indian Citizens, the Central Government shall cause to carry throughout the country a house-to-house enumeration for collection of specified particulars relating to each family and individual, residing in a local area including the Citizenship status [(Rule 4(1)] and the Registrar General of Citizen Registration shall notify the period and duration of the enumeration in the Official Gazette [(Rule 4(2)]. The Local Registrar shall, for the purposes of preparation and inclusion in the Local Register of Indian Citizens, verify and scrutinize the particulars collected of every family and individual in the Population Register [Rule 4(3)]. During the verification process, particulars of such individuals, whose Citizenship is doubtful, shall be entered by the Local Registrar with appropriate remark in the Population Register for further enquiry [Rule 4(4)]. The Registrar General of Citizen Registration or any officer authorized by him at any time may call for any records for examination, and issue directions regarding inclusion or exclusion of any individual or family particulars from the Population Register [Rule 16(5)]

The data for National Population Register was collected in 2010 along with the house listing phase of Census of India 2011. The updation of this data was done during 2015-16 by conducting door to door survey. The digitisation of the updated information has been completed. Now it was decided to update the National Population Register along with the House listing phase of Census 2021 during April to September 2020 in all the States/UTs except Assam. A Gazette notification to this effect was published by the Central Government.[44] The NPR database would be updated along with House listing and Housing Census phase of Census of India 2021 during April-September 2020 according to the methodology given in the manual for NPR through mobile app by updating the existing NPR database by verifying the details of all residents by conducting a house to house enumeration by the enumerator (designated Government official) and modifying/correcting the demographic data items, collecting Aadhar number from each resident voluntarily, collecting Mobile number, Election Photo Identity Cards (EPIC) or Voter ID Card number, Indian Passport number and Driving License number, if available with the residents. All new resident(s)/new household(s) found in the local area (HLB) during the field-work will also be included in NPR. The exercise was scheduled to be undertaken between 1 April and 30 September, 2020. The exercise to update NPR was to kick off on 1 April in the New Delhi Municipal Corporation area with President to be the first person to be enrolled. PM and VP were likely to be enumerated the same day.[45]

The Census house-listing and NPR operations, however, could not be undertaken due to Covid-19 pandemic and was postponed indefinitely. Indications are emerging that the onset of Census exercise may have to wait until 2021or even 2022, if the Covid-19 situation continues to be of concern.[46]

In 2010, information on 16 subjects was collected in the NPR. In 2020, seven more subjects were included. These include, apart from Aadhar card and Voter ID card, information on the date of birth and place of birth of the parents. In some states like West Bengal, Bihar, Delhi and Karnataka, biometric details may be collected as this information was not collected in the 2010 exercise. Those having Aadhar card need not furnish this, as the same was furnished at the time of preparation of the Aadhar card.[47]

Since the questions on date and place of birth of parents triggered fears that the exercise might be a precursor to the preparation of NRC, the BJP tried to pass on the blame to the UPA government and asserted that the NPR was started by the UPA regime in 2010 and they are simply following it. But the Congress vehemently objected to that and said that the exercise this time is fundamentally different from that conducted in 2010-11 and is unacceptable. Former union minister Ajay Maken who oversaw the NPR exercise in 2010-11said: "The government's intention is to carry out NRC in the garb of NPR. It is a lie that they are only implementing the law made by the Congress...The biggest problem is the government's intention, the trust deficit with citizens. The government is not telling the truth.

"Whatever is available on social media suggests that the new NPR is fundamentally different. In the 2020 version, new features include: Date and place of birth of parents, last place of residence, Aadhar number, driving license number, Voter ID card and mobile number. These features make the NPR drastically different. They are trying to convert NPR into NRC by subterfuge. This is not expected from an elected government."

The NPR executed by the Congress in accordance with a law brought by the Vajpayee government in 2003, only asked for basic details, Maken said.

"That was an exercise to make a local register of usual residents. That was perfectly in tune with the United Nations definition. Now they are asking for date and place of birth of parents. What does NPR have to do with this information? That's the preparation for NRC", Maken said. He also said: "Nobody objected to NPR because we didn't ask for unnecessary details and then there was no CAA which injected doubts and fear into the minds of people. It is sad that the intention of the government is doubted by the citizens."[48]

Since there is not much difference between the basic data wanted for the NPR and those of the NRC and the NPR preceded the NRC in Assam, people are apprehensive of introduction of NRC in the coming days as well. The Bengal government on 16 December, 2019 stayed the preparations for NPR. An order that no activity regarding NPR can now be undertaken without prior clearance from the state government was issued from the state secretariat for all district magistrates and commissioner of Kolkata and Howrah Municipal Corporations.[49]

Central officials, however, questioned the validity of the Bengal government's decision. Both Census and NPR are mandatory and the states do not have any leeway to interfere with their schedules. According to a notification already issued by the Registrar General of India, the NPR exercise—which is undertaken in accordance with provisions of the Citizenship Act—will be conducted, along with the house listing phase of Census 2021, from April to September 2020 (since deferred) in all states and Union Territories except Assam. The same enumeration will capture data for both Census and NPR", said an official source at the Centre.[50]

It may be recalled that Rule 5 of the 2003 Citizenship Rules stipulates that every official of the Central Government, State Government, local bodies or their undertakings shall assist the Registrar General of Citizen Registration in the preparation of the database relating to each family and every person, and in implementing the provisions of these rules. Any violation of this provision attracts a penalty of Rupees 1000 under Rule 17 of the said Rules.

Kerala government has directed all district collectors to ensure that the NPR is not mentioned while sending communications related to Census. K.R. Jyotilal, principal secretary, general administration department has asked the collectors to personally ensure this as the government has last month stayed all matters relating to NPR which were to be conducted along with the first phase of the 2021 census operations.[51]

Kerala has toughened its stand against updating the NPR and asked its Census officials not to attend training sessions related to the register. The state authorities had taken care to strike down all references related to the NPR in the circular issued by the Director of Census Operations, Kerala regarding the appointment of enumerators, supervisors and field trainer for house-listing and housing census operations and updating of the NPR to be undertaken in the state between 15 April and 29 May, 2020.[52]

On 25 February, 2020, the Bihar Legislative Assembly adopted a resolution not to implement NRC in the state and to implement the NPR only if the conditions set out by the Bihar government are accepted by the Centre.[53] Andhra Pradesh Chief Minister Y.S. Jagan Reddy on 3 March said that the centre should continue with the 2010 questionnaire for the NPR since some of the questions of the new ones caused insecurity among the minority population in the state. He announced that the state assembly would pass a resolution on the issue.[54] The Tamil Nadu government led by BJP ally AIADMK has put on hold the updation of NPR till it gets clarifications from the Centre on the three new questions in the form.[55] The Delhi Assembly on13 March passed a resolution calling upon the Centre not to go ahead with the NPR and the NRC.[56] The Telangana Assembly on 16 March adopted a resolution that urged the state government to "take all necessary steps to safeguard the people of Telangana from exercises such as the NPR and the NRC."[57]

So far only ten states and two Union Territories—West Bengal, Kerala, Punjab, Rajasthan, Bihar, Andhra Pradesh, Madhya Pradesh, Chattisgarh, Tamil Nadu, Telangana, Puducherry and Delhi—have decided either not to implement the NPR at all or to implement the NPR with the 2010 questionnaire. The CPI(M) has taken up a programme of door-to-door campaign beginning from 1 March and ending on 23 March, 2020 to persuade people not to participate in the NPR survey which would lead to implementation of the NRC.[58]

The CM of West Bengal on 20 January, 2020 appealed to the North-eastern States including Sikkim to study the contentious NPR before taking a call on its implementation.[59] She also informed the Assembly on 14 February that she would write to other non-BJP state governments urging them to stop work on the NPR.[60] In view of differences between the allies in Maharashtra on CAA and NPR, Maharashtra CM announced on 23 February, 2020, the setting up of a three-party panel of ministers that would look into problems that could emerge during NPR's implementation in the state.[61]

The Jharkhand Janadhikar Mahasabha (JJM), a forum of progressive organisations, on 24 February urged the Soren government to stop all NPR-related activities and also pass a resolution against the CAA and the NRC in the Assembly.[62]

A few non-BJP-ruled states raised objection at a day-long conference convened by the Union home ministry on 17 January, 2020 over the new methodology to be adopted in the NPR exercise during the house listing phase of the 2021 Census.[63] The Odisha government, however, issued a notification on 5 February, 2020 for carrying out house-listing operations as part of the Census between April and September 2020 while there was no word on conducting the NPR survey during the said period. House-listing and NPR are usually conducted simultaneously. According to the latest information, 31 questions will be asked during the house-listing exercise.[64]

At the NDA meeting on 31 January, 2020 allies like JD(U), LJP and Akali Dal had flagged the apprehension among certain sections of the population about the new NPR form. This led the home minister to say that while dropping columns from the form might not be feasible at this stage, a disclaimer that not replying to questions relating to date and place of birth of parents shall not impact the respondents' citizenship status or put them in the 'doubtful' voters' list could be inserted.[65] This is in consonance with the Cabinet decision that questions pertaining to date and place of birth of parents in the NPR would remain but it would be considered as dropped if someone doesn't remember the date and place of birth of his parents and can't share.[66] But the question is why take the disclaimer route instead of omitting such contentious questions altogether from the form?

In the meantime, the Parliamentary Standing Committee on Home Affairs in its report placed in the Rajya Sabha on 5 March, 2020 recommended that all states and UTs be "fully convinced" on issues pertaining to update of the NPR and a national consensus be evolved to rule out lack of clarity or apprehension among people. This, it was underlined, would facilitate smooth conduct of NPR and Census exercises to be undertaken simultaneously. It was also insisted that Aadhar data should be used for upcoming Census and NPR.[67]

Union minister of home affairs, Nityananda Rai, however, informed the Lok Sabha on 3 March, 2020 while replying to a written question that "the government is in discussion with the states having concern in regard to the preparation of NPR. The demographic and other particulars of each family and individual are to be updated/collected during the exercise of updation of NPR. No document is to be collected during this exercise." Home Ministry source said the Central Government has already started the outreach to alley the apprehensions of states by meeting CMs critical of the exercise. As part of this outreach, Registrar General and Census Commissioner Vivek Joshi met Punjab Chief Minister and apprised him about the preparations for the census and the NPR.[68]

Nobel Laureate Amrtya Sen described the NPR as a crazy and inhuman idea. "I think it is a crazy idea. It is against the form of democracy laid down in the country's Constitution. The Constitution provides there should be no discrimination against any community. It is discriminatory, unconstitutional and inhuman", said Sen referring to NPR.[69] Author, columnist, teacher and activist Harsh Mander even felt that there was a possibility of immense bloodshed in Bengal if NPR was enforced. "If NPR happens, the authorities will get the right to identify people who they feel are doubtful. The CAA will do the rest. The 2003 amendment of the Citizenship Act needs to be withdrawn. There is immense possibility of violence in Bengal as it is the frontline after Assam. Unfortunately, I don't see any clarity or courage among political parties to take on the government. The issue won't be resolved in Parliament or any court. It has to be resolved on the streets and in our hearts." Mander said while delivering the keynote address at a national conference on Statelessness and the Right to Have Right" organized by the Legal Aid Society West Bengal National University of Juridical Science in association with Cornell Law School Human Rights Clinic in Kolkata on 12 February, 2020.[70]

Several academicians and former civil servants like Romila Thapar, Prabhat Patnaik, former ambassador Deb Mukherjee and Mahatma Gandhi's grandson Rajmohan Gandhi have individually petitioned 19 non-BJP chief ministers including BJP allies to join the collective effort towards "civil disobedience" and refuse to implement the NPR and the NCR in their states. They urged the chief ministers to follow the Kerala government and approach the apex court. "If these (CAA, NPR and NRC) are not struck down, the only path for the states to take is to disobey the Union government, even at the risk of dismissal", they said in an open letter.[71] Prime Minister Modi, however, while replying in the Rajya Sabha on 6 February, 2020 to the motion of thanks to the President's address dismissed the additional questions in the NPR as an ordinary administrative process[72], even though critics believe the Indian government will use the list to mark people as doubtful citizens after which they would be asked to prove their citizenship. Actually, the first NPR in 2010-11 was also carried out along with the census. But, since that exercise was before the Assam NRC and the CAA 2019, NPR 2010 did not encounter the kind of resistance it is facing this time round. The reason the NPR is facing such opposition throughout the country is the fear that it will once again form the basis for the pending NRC exercise.

Nearly 200 social scientists and economists that included former Planning Commission member Avijit Sen, Bibhas Saha of the University of Durham (UK), Pulapre Balakrishnan of Ashoka University, Vamsi Vakulabharaman, University of Massachusetts, in a statement said: "There is a real danger that the concerns around the NPR and the fears that are growing among substantial sections that investigators can determine whether a respondent's citizenship is doubtful. This possibility has already led to widespread public distrust and suspicion about NPR" and called for delinking the NPR from the census to "ensure that the exercise of data collection for census 2021 is absolutely safe, comprehensive and uncontaminated by any other factor." [73]

Meanwhile, the Supreme Court on 27 January, 2020 sought government's response to a petition filed by Udgar Khan from Madhubani district in Bihar and two others to quash a Union Home Ministry notification of 31 July, 2019 for the conduct of the NPR exercise from April to September 2020 as the said exercise is a gross invasion of privacy of private citizens.[74]

While participating in the debate on Delhi violence in the Rajya Sabha on 12 March, 2020, Home Minister Amit Shah clarified that no document would have to be submitted for the NPR and no one would be declared 'D' (doubtful).[75]

Rules for Preparation of the National Register of Indian Citizens have been mentioned in details in Rule 4 of the 2003 Citizenship Rules. Sub-Rule (3) of Rule 4 states: "For the purposes of preparation and inclusion in the Local Register of Indian Citizens, the particulars collected of every family and individual in the Population Register shall be verified and scrutinized by the Local Registrar, who may be assisted by one or more persons as specified by the Registrar General of Citizen Registration." And sub-Rule (4) of Rule 4 posits: "During the verification process, particulars of such individuals, whose Citizenship is doubtful, shall be entered by the Local Registrar with appropriate remark in the Population Register for further enquiry and in case of doubtful Citizenship, the individual or the family shall be informed in a specified proforma immediately after the verification process is over."

Sub-sub Rule (a) of sub-Rule (5) of Rule 4 stipulates: "Every person or family specified in sub-rule (4), shall be given an opportunity of being heard by the Sub-district or Taluk Registrar of Citizen Registration, before a final decision is taken to include or to exclude their particulars in the National Register of Indian Citizens."

But when Shah made the statement on 12 March, Rule 4 of the 2003 Citizenship Rules had not undergone any change and they continued to provide for the "doubtful" categorisation.

Unless the relevant rules are suitably changed, assurances given in the Parliament will remain an assurance only and the apprehensions of the general populace over the NPR will continue to haunt them as before. The Politburo of the CPIM demanded on 13 March, 2020 that the government should immediately scrap the relevant rules. [76] Two umbrella groups against the CAA—We the People of India which includes several progressive parties and NGOs such as Swaraj India, Left groups and United Against Hate and Alliance Against CAA-NRC which includes Muslim groups such as Jamaat-e-Islami Hind and Jamiat Ulema-i-Hind jointly demanded on14 March that the Centre amend the rules to preclude people being marked "doubtful" citizens during the NPR update. They also announced they would withdraw their call to boycott the NPR, scheduled to begin from 1 April. However, their movement against the CAA and the NRC would continue.[77]

III

For the ruling BJP establishment in both Assam and at the Centre, expelling 'infiltrators' from Bangladesh has been as integral to their core agenda as abrogating Article 370, building the Ram Temple and introducing a Uniform Civil Code. But in their definition, it is only Bengali-origin Assamese Muslim immigrants who are 'infiltrators'; they constitute a threat to the Indian nation. Bengali Hindus are not infiltrators but refugees for whom India is their 'natural home.' After the repeal of special status of Jammu & Kashmir, the BJP is now banking upon the NRC for its electoral success. The BJP had been raising this issue for decades. Its failure in Assam has dealt a body blow to their campaign of conducting NRC in other states. But despite its failure in Assam, the BJP is not going to abandon it just like that. BJP all-India president Amit Shah had asked all the state units to go to the hilt for the NRC. As a prelude to the introduction of

NRC in other states, the Centre has changed rules regarding constitution of Foreigners Tribunals. So long only the MHA could constitute FTs. The MHA has amended the Foreigners (Tribunals) Order, 1964 by issuing a Gazette notification on 30 May, 2019 in the first week of June 2019 and has empowered the state governments and the district magistrates in all States and UTs to set up tribunals to decide whether a person staying illegally in India is a foreigner or not.[78]

The ruling BJP's election promise to "implement the NRC in a phased manner in other parts of the country in future" contradicts the Centre's stand in the Supreme Court and Parliament. A petition was filed by the Tripura People's Front and some others in the Supreme Court of India to update the NRC in Tripura, as is being done in Assam, in order to detect and deport the "illegal immigrants" from Bangladesh by taking 19 July, 1948 as the cut-off date and the Supreme Court on 8 October, 2018 directed the court registry to tag the petition along with petitions in the Assam NRC case.[79] The SC had subsequently issued a notice to the Centre and State government on the petition. In its response, the Centre had filed an affidavit in the Supreme Court in January that it was not required as adequate laws existed to identify and deport illegal immigrants.

On 19 December, 2018, Union Minister of State for Home Affairs Hansraj Ahir had informed the Lok Sabha that "the exercise to update NRC 1951 is being conducted under the special provisions in respect of State of Assam under the Citizenship Act, 1955 and the Citizenship Rules, 2003. At present, there is no proposal to extend the NRC to States other than Assam."[80]

However, in March 2019, BJP's national president Amit Shah began his election campaign in West Bengal with a pledge to introduce NRC in the State if the Modi government was voted back to power.[81] With the coming back to power at the Centre for the second term, NRC has become a war cry for the BJP and not a day passes without a threat on implementing the NRC and detecting as many as 20 million infiltrators in Bengal. BJP state president Dilip Ghosh claimed around two crore "Bangladeshi Muslim" infiltrators had "illegally" entered India through the border in Bengal and had spread across other parts of the county up to Kashmir. While one crore infiltrators are still staying in Bengal, the others have gone elsewhere in the country.[82]

Not to be left behind, Locket Chatterjee, BJP MP, said on 12 September, 2019 that she would demand NRC in West Bengal and that she was confident that more than 1 crore 'fake voters' would be detected in some areas in Bengal.[83] Smriti Irani, Union minister for women and child development and textiles, like all other BJP leaders assured that no Indian would be left out of NRC.[84] She, however, did not spell out how this should be ensured, through the FT route or special enactment.

West Bengal state unit of the BJP has formed two committees—Mass Awareness Committee and Mass Contact Committee—to steer the movement in support of the demand for introduction of the NRC.[85] The Bharatiya Janata Yuva Morcha (BJYM) would hit the streets with its Jan Jagaran (mass awareness) programme to make the people aware about the NRC.[86] RSS is also trying to spread its organisation in the border areas.[87]

Shah's pledge on NRC in Bengal set off storm in Bengal with the accredited political parties like the TMC, the Left and others accusing the saffron party of polarizing people.[88] A resolution against the implementation of NRC in the state was adopted by the West Bengal Assembly on 6 September, 2019 unanimously with the BJP staging a walkout.[89]

The CPI(M-L) Liberation organised a protest march and later held a meeting at Siliguri on 9 September against the communal and divisive agenda of the RSS-BJP in the name of NRC in Assam.[90] The Darjeeling District Left Front strongly protested against the NRC and highlighted the issue in its public meeting at Siliguri on14 September.[91] Actually, the CPIM proposes to capitalize on the threat to implement NRC in West Bengal to revive its bases in the state.

Binay camp of the GJM is not against the NRC as such but demands that Gorkhas should be included in the Protected List and should be made Original Inhabitants.[92] The Morcha camp put up posters across the Hills and Plains on 7 September to highlight the situation consequent to the publication of the final NRC in Assam and organized protest in the Hills on 12 September.[93] Bista ridiculed Binay for such protests since he thought that Binay had little credibility in the Hills, as evidenced in the recent elections.[94]

Bimal Gurung maintained on 13 September that his faction of the GJM would form several teams to help Gorkha people acquire documents needed for the NRC before the exercise was conducted in West Bengal.[95] Hill Trinamool leader N.B. Khawas warned that the 1950 Indo-Nepal Treaty and the Gazette Notification of 23 August, 1988 would not be entertained if the exercise for the NRC was carried out in West Bengal. He called for a united fight against NRC.[96]

To fish in the troubled water, the Kamtapur Progressive Party (KPP) and the Greater Cooch Behar Peoples' Association (GCPA) formed a joint forum, the Bhumiputra Aikya Mancha (BAM) to spearhead the movement for an NRC for north Bengal. The BAM was floated on 10 June, 2019 to launch a movement for a separate Cooch Behar or Kamtapur state to be carved out of north Bengal districts, except Malda. CCPA general secretary, Bangshi Badan Barman is the chairman of the Mancha while Atul Roy, KPP president, is its vice-chairman. Both the CCPA and the KPP represent the Rajbongshi community, the sons of the soil. The Mancha, among other demands, wants an NRC-like exercise in north Bengal to weed out infiltrators.[97] But these organizations are in a predicament as the majority of the NRC-rejects in Assam belong to the Rajbongshi community, whose interests they profess to protect.

As announced, the TMC organised protest programmes on 7 and 8 September, 2019 and brought out an anti-NRC rally from Sinthir More to the five point crossing at Shyambazar (Kolkata) on 12 September. Bengal chief minister and other leaders of the party participated in the rally. At the gathering at the five point crossing, Bengal CM assured the people so long she was alive NRC would not be implemented in West Bengal. She would scuttle the move at any cost and she would not let the BJP divide the people on the lines of religion and caste, she said.[98] Virtually launching a counter-attack against the CM who led the road show, BJP state president Dilip Ghosh said NRC would be implemented in Bengal and those who would be identified as unwanted Muslims as per the register would have no place in the state.[99]

People in Bengal have become panicky about the NRC and have started collecting any document that could be of help to them in establishing their citizenship. People have started making round of government offices, schools, and banks to arm themselves with documents that can help them prove they are legitimate Indian citizens. Hundreds of panicked citizens in Kolkata have begun flocking to the Kolkata Municipal Corporation health department every day to either obtain birth certificate or incorporate corrections in them.[100] An old woman from a well-to-do family is reported to have paid Rupees thirty thousand to obtain her birth certificate.

Although chief minister Mamata Bannerjee has issued an audio-visual appeal to calm fear about the NRC and the same is broadcast through electronic media every day, the panic is linked to the convergence of three factors: repeated assertions by BJP leaders about an NRC in Bengal, the voter verification programme undertaken by the Election Commission, and the issue of digital ration card by the Bengal government. People are rushing to SBI branches for rectification of Aadhar cards and new Aadhar enrolment, although the NRC has got nothing to do with the Aadhar card.[101] Hundreds of people had been queuing up every day at post offices, which double as Aadhar centres, to get their documents corrected. The government on 19 March, 2020 ordered the closure of Aadhar centres in Bengal for an indefinite period to avoid mass gatherings during the

Covid-19 outbreak. However, people like Mohammad Golam, a villager from Police Station Onda, district Bankura, who wanted to get the spelling of his name corrected, the NRC is a bigger threat than Covid-19.[102]

NRC fears saw a rush in Bengal to seed Aadhar cards with ration cards, as mandated by the Supreme Court. Since the state government launched a drive to link the two in the last week of November, out of 9.16 crore ration cards to be linked with Aadhar cards, around 6.2 crore people have done so by the middle of January 2020. The response was unexpected as people generally have reservations about linking Aadhar cards with other documents.[103]

A rumour spread among the people that the digital ration card is the strongest document in support of one's citizenship. As such, people in large numbers have started flocking to the BDO offices in rural areas and in municipal offices in urban areas where camps were being held by the state government everyday for the ration card. More than 32 lakh people have applied for ration cards within a span of 14 days.[104] About 45 lakh people across Bengal have applied for non-foodgrain ration cards in less than three weeks reflecting the widespread panic about a prospective NRC update in the state and the consequent labelling of sections of residents as non-citizens. The applicants are from well-to-do families. Usually these families have enough documents to claim inclusion in any updated NRC. When these families apply for a non-foodgrain ration card, it's clear that people are panicking.[105] A report, however, indicates that as many as 42 thousand digital ration cards could not be delivered because the applicants could not be traced at the given addresses.[106] The stated government now proposed to introduce e-Ration Card in lieu of digital ration card.[107]

Every day, scores of people are visiting the schools and madrasas where they studied decades ago and trying to obtain school leaving certificates. The certificate, they feel, can help them prove their citizenship and would also be of use in case they need to make any rectification in their identity proofs. As the former students are swarming into the schools and madrasas, the authorities are busy searching for old registers. But it is an uphill task to find old registers and verify particulars of former students who had left schools in the seventies or late sixties.[108]

Some of them became so much panic-stricken that they even committed suicide or died of heart failure. Such cases were reported from various parts of Bengal. Amongst them were Ananda Roy (39) of Moynaguri in Jalpaiguri[109], Mintu Sarkar of Balurghat[110], Soleman Sarkar (55) of Itahar in North Dinajpur[111], Shymal Roy (40) of Dhupguri, Shaber Ali (42) of Jalpaiguri and Ajina Khatum Bibi (27) of Cooch-Behar[112], Alauddin Tarafdar (51) of Baduria[113], Kamal Ghosh (55) of Jamalpur[114],

Nibas Sarkar (55) of Hanskhali, Nadia[115], Umarani Mukherjee (64) of Chittaranjan, Asansole[116]. Sahabuddin Mohmmad (69) of Panidhura village in Jalpaiguri district[117], Shipra Shikdar (36) in East Burdwan's Jougram[118], Abdul Sattar (63) of Katwa's Natungram Purbapara and Kasem Ali (62) Katwa's Natungram Paschimpara[119], Giyasuddin Mian (74) of Shibdaha village near Guskara Municipal town, Sarfuddin Mirza (72) of Deudi Jamboni village, Karsa gram panchayat under Garbeta-3 Block of West Midnapore district[120], Nizamuddin Sheikh (69) of Mukshimpara gram panchayat and Liyakat Karigar of Nimdaha gram pahchayat, both under Purbasthali Police station[121], and Mithu Saha (46) of Binpara village under the Ratua police station in Malda district.[122]

All government surveys in Birbhum district as well as in Murshidabad district of Bengal had to be suspended as people are panicking over any kind of surveys or data collection. They suspect that any collection of information is connected with an NRC-like exercise.[123] The fear against the NRC exercise was so great that four women and a girl of Kacharewadi village of Maharashtra's Solapur who had travelled to Illambazar area in Birbhum for financial aid in the wake of purported crop failure due to heavy and untimely rain in December last, were detained on 9 February, 2020 by the villagers of Choto Chak village of Illambazar on suspicion that they were collecting data for NRC.[124] A four-member team from the Survey of India were detained for an hour and physically prevented from conducting field work in East Burdwan's Galsi on 12 March as villagers got apprehensive that they were there to do the groundwork for an NRC exercise.[125]

BJP state president Dilip Ghosh blamed the Chief Minister for the panic deaths.[126] Bengal CM also brought to the notice of the Union home minister during her meeting with him on 19 September, 2019 that Assam's NRC exercise has spread fear in West Bengal.[127] The all-pervading fear of the general populace of NRC had had its toll on the overall economic situation of the country, asserts Sugata Marjit, the noted economist.[128] A columnist apprehends that the initiatives taken under the Act East Policy of Modi 1.0 for the development of the North-East might well get derailed by the NRC-CAA of Modi 2.0 government.[129]

Meanwhile, apolitical organizations like the Bangla Sanskriti Manch have launched drives in several districts against the possible implementation of the NRC.[130] In the meantime, the West Bengal government decided to regularise the colonies sprung up in the suburbs of Kolkata in the post-partition period. On 28 January, 2019, it gave freehold land rights to residents of 94 refugee colonies set up on state government plots, a move expected to benefit 30,00 families.[131] In October 2020, the Land and Land Reforms Department had issued an order to grant freehold land rights to the possessors occupying land in 119 colonies. Of them, 40-odd colonies were set up on Central Government land and the remaining colonies were set up on state government and private land.[132] The idea is that "anybody who lives in a refugee colony will get a *patta*, in phases, so that no one can take away the land from them", the CM said on 4 November, 2020 after a meeting at the Nabanna with representatives of numerous backward classes and communities.[133] The State government decided to hand over deed to about 25 thousand by 15 December and to hand over assurance paper to another one lakh refugee families. It may take two years to sort out the legal problem to hand over deed to them.[134] The state government was determined to give free-hold land rights to the residents of 300-odd refugee colonies. Residents of 96 refugee colonies already got the land rights and the process had begun to provide free-hold deeds to 213 more colonies, the chief minister said on 11 January, 2021.[135] The state government claimed in February 2021 that 30 thousand land rights and *pattas* had already been given and land of 244 refugee colonies had been brought under private ownership.[136] This step fulfils a long-standing demand of the erstwhile refugees from East Pakistan, now Bangladesh. The refugee colonies in other states are being similarly regularized. The Maharashtra government has set up a sub-committee to regularize residential and commercial transfers without sanction in refugee colonies in Mumbai and its suburbs. These colonies house Sindhi and Punjabi communities who travelled to Mumbai after Partition.[137] The Union Cabinet on 23 October, 2019 approved a proposal to grant ownership and transfer rights for properties in 1,797 colonies that had been identified in 2014. About 40 lakh people would benefit from this decision.[138] The issue of granting rights to the affluent unauthorised colonies would be taken up separately.[139] PM Modi gave papers for land rights to more than 1 lakh families belonging to 70-odd indigenous communities of Sivsagar—the heart of protests against the CAA in December 2019 in Assam—on 23 January, 2021.[140]

Union home minister Amit Shah told a seminar organised by the BJP at the Netaji Indoor Stadium on 1 October, 2019 that NRC would be implemented in the entire country but it would be done after the passage of the CAB that grants nationality to all non-Muslim refugees. He also said that not a single infiltrator would be allowed to stay in the country[141], but where they would go none knows! NRC has become a favourite election issue of the BJP throughout India. BJP president Amit Shah never forgot to reiterate during electioneering campaigns in other states that the NRC would identify illegal immigrants who would be sent home before the next parliamentary elections in 2024.[142] But the union minister for home Nitynanda Rai informed the Lok Sabha on 4 February, 2020 that no decision for pan-India NRC had been taken by the government.[143]

At one point of time it was thought that in the 2021 West Bengal Assembly elections, infiltration was going to be a big issue.[144] The BJP was clearly viewing NRC in Bengal as its ace in the hole that would help it topple the Trinamool government in the 2021 assembly polls. But the dubbing at the hustings in the November by-elections in West Bengal should be an eye opener for the BJP. The NRC fear caught the electorate so much that the BJP lost all the three Assembly seats including the Khargapur seat so long held by the state party president Dilip Ghosh. An inner party probe into the bye-poll debacle revealed that apart from the NRC fear factor, shifting of Congress vote bank, weaker campaign machinery and complacence among party workers played a crucial role in pulling down votes in the bye-polls.[145] An internal report of the BJP, however, claimed later that self-satisfaction, lackadaisical campaign and groupism over selection of candidates, rather than the NRC, were the reasons for the BJP's debacle in the by-elections.[146] Chandra Bose, a state vice-president tweeted after the drubbing in the by-poll that "it's essential for@BJP4Bengal to cleanse the party system & devise a strategy specific to Bengal. Pan India strategy would not apply to the land of Swami Vivekananda and Netaji Subhas Chandra Bose", and called for introspection.[147] In the 2021 Assembly elections in West Bengal, the BJP made a passing reference to the infiltration issue in its manifesto promising to "completely stop border infiltration and trafficking" on coming to power, as if "infiltration" and "border management" come under the state domain but did not utter a single word on the implementation of the NRC in the State. The Trinamool supremo Mamata Banerjee, on the other hand, resurrected the Narendra Mod government's contentious citizenship matrix as a prominent poll plank for the Bengal campaign on 18 March, 2021 and asked the people to be cautious about the NPR and the NRC.[148]

A study conducted by the Calcutta Research Group revealed that the Bengal Assembly elections in April-May 2021 triggered the return of the migrant workers who voted in huge numbers, apprehending that if they did not vote, their names would be struck from the voter list. NRC and the contentious issue of citizenship was a major part of the political milieu in which the Assembly election was held in 2021.[149]

The Central Government's latest stand on the implementation of the NRC throughout the country was explained by the Union Minister of State for Home Nityananda Rai in the Rajya Sabha on 17 March, 2021. In a written reply to Indian Union Muslim League member Abdul Wahab he informed that "till now" the Union Government had not taken any decision to prepare the NRC at the national level.[150] He again informed the Lok Sabha on 30 November, 2021 in reply to a question by Mala Roy that the Centre had not taken any decision on the implementation of the NRC at the all-India level.[151]

IV

There were genuine apprehensions that those who don't make it to the NRC in Assam would spill-over to Meghalaya, Nagaland, Manipur and Arunachal Pradesh. The Manipur government took adequate measures to stem that spill-over by posting special police team in Jiribam, Babupara Bazar and along the Barak River bordering Mizoram. Special police teams were deployed at Mao Gate, in Manipur's Senapati district bordering Nagaland and the Tamei-Haflong road in Tamenglong district bordering Assam, to check the entry points.[152] Manipur chief minister informed on 2 August, 2018 that the state government had constituted two separate committees—one at the state level and another at the district level—to prevent entry of "illegal immigrants" into the state post publication of the final draft NRC in Assam on 30 July.[153] The Arunachal Pradesh government too was alert to this imminent danger of spill-over into that state.[154]

The Mizoram government has ordered strengthening of all entry points and border check gates manned by the police to prevent any possible influx from Assam. Round-the-clock vigil was maintained at Vairengte, Bairabi, Saiphai and Phaisen police outposts while additional patrolling gate was erected at a place between Vairengte and Phainuam village. Second-line checking was also maintained at Kawnpui and Serkhan to double-check that no one enters the gate without valid Inner Line Permit (ILP). [155] Mizoram police arrested 1098 non-tribals—865 people in Aizawl district, 111 in Kolasib district, 52 in Momit district, 43 in Serchip district and 27 in Champhai—for not having a valid Inner Line Permit and have pushed back 92 of them to Assam, the Deputy Inspector-General of Police of Northern Range informed on 2 August, 2019.[156]

Cooch Behar, Alipurduar and Jalpaiguri districts in North Bengal apprehended influx of Bengali-speaking people from Assam whose names were excluded from the Assam NRC and the district administrations were geared up to provide them food and shelter.[157] But there was no such influx following the publication of the final draft NRC on 30 July, 2018.

Senior Congress leader and former chief minister of Meghalaya Mukul Sangma, during discussions in the Assembly on 10 September, 2019 claimed that the final NRC of Assam has left out all the Indian women who had come to Assam as brides from other states like West Bengal, Nagaland, Bihar and Meghalaya, adding that he received frantic calls from such victims in Assam.[158]

A claim by a Bengali outfit Bengali Janamukhi Bahini (BJB) that between 11 to 12 lakh Bengali Hindus and a lakh Gorkha residents of Assam were excluded from the final NRC has spread panic among the Bengali-speaking population in neighbouring Cooch Behar, Alipurduar and Jalpaiguri districts in West Bengal.[159] The NRC-hit families have started contacting Trinamool leaders for assistance. The response is seen as a boost for the ruling Trinamool after it suffered setbacks in the area in the Lok Sabha elections.[160]

The publication of the NRC in Assam has led to renewed demand for a similar exercise in almost all the north-eastern states and Mizoram and Nagaland have taken steps to identify the real inhabitants.

Manipur is the first state after Assam to formally resolve to adopt the NRC. The state cabinet has already greenlighted the controversial project. In an interview Manipur's chief minister N.Biren Singh told *The Week* that his state was facing threat from the continued influx of migrants, especially from Myanmar. He said that Manipur has a free movement regime (FMR) up to 16 km on both sides of the border with Myanmar. While Manipur ensures that the people who cross over to Myanmar come back, it does not happen the other way round. People take advantage of it and settle in Manipur state. It is very difficult to identify and check Myanmarese citizens because of their ethnic similarities with the people of Manipur. The Rohingyas also make use of the FMR and sneak through Manipur border. Many Gorkhas of Nepali origin also stay in Manipur. They do not have land rights. They take land on lease in the hills and stay. All foreigners will have to go, he said.[161] With the introduction of the Inner Line Permit System from 31 December, 2019, people from other states will not be able to live and work there permanently any more. The Manipuris feel that the ILPS will ensure that they are not swamped by outsiders. But the pro- NRC tribal organizations said the ILP was not enough as Manipur could not come up with the definition of "indigenous inhabitants" and demanded the NRC. At least 19 apex tribal organizations and their affiliates had on 12 July, 2022 written to the Prime Minister demanding NRC and other mechanism to insulate the indigenous people from the "ever-increasing number of non-local residents." Bowing to demands from tribal groups, the Manipur Assembly on 5 August, 2022 resolved to implement NRC and establish a State Population Commission (SPC).

Mizo Zirlai Pawl (MZP), the apex students' body of Mizoram, sought to have foreigners' tribunals and an NRC, but the cut-off year should be as enshrined in the Constitution. Mizoram's NGO Coordination Committee, a conglomerate of major civil societies and student associations, too echoed the demand.[162] The Mizoram Assembly on 18 March, 2019 unanimously passed the Mizoram Maintenance of Household Registers Bill, 2019 to provide credible individual identification system and to prevent "usurpation" of benefits of developmental schemes by those who are not entitled. The Bill will enable the state to detect illegal foreigners and develop database of residents.[163] Mizoram government has formed "special task force committees", both at the district level and the subdivision level, in three districts of the state—Longlei, Mumit and Lawngthai—to detect and deport illegal Bangladeshi immigrants (mainly Chakmas), the state Assembly was informed by the state Home Minister Lalchamillana on 21 February, 2020.[164] Mizoram chief minister Zoramthanga told *The Week* in an interview that he wants "the NRC because Bangladeshi infiltrators in the form of Chakmas. I am not against Bengalis from West Bengal or elsewhere who are here with the inner line permit."[165]

Meghalaya government was contemplating to add more teeth to the Meghalaya Resident Safety and Security (MRSS) Act, 2016 to check illegal immigration into the State[166], and on 1 November issued an ordinance under this Act making registration on entry mandatory for visitors who intend to spend more than 24 hours in the state. Central and state government employees are exempt from the new entry rule.[167] An influential students' body, the Khasi Students Union (KSU) put up banners and posters reading "All Meghalaya Bengalese are Bangladeshis" in different places in Shillong town on 21 October, 2020. The police, however, removed the posters and banners and warned of action against those trying to "incite communal disharmony".[168]

On 29 June, 2019, Nagaland Home Commissioner issued a notification for the setting up of the Register of Indigenous Inhabitants of Nagaland (RIN), a Nagaland variant of Assam NRC. It will be prepared under the supervision of each district administration. To be monitored by the Home Commissioner, Nagaland's exercise for collecting information on locals and non-locals has a 60-day deadline effective from 10 July. Detailed instructions on the preparation of the RIN were issued to all Deputy Commissioners asking them to ensure that the teams were constituted by name within a week of the publication of the notification, make the information about the team public, and communicate to the village council chairmen, Village Development Board secretaries, ward authorities, tribal hohos, church authorities, and NGOs. Hoho is the apex body of each Naga group.

The survey teams have been instructed to visit each house and make a list of indigenous inhabitants living there. Each family member will be listed in the village of their original residence and mention will be made of any member living elsewhere. The format for making the list will mention "permanent residence and present residence" separately. Aadhar number, wherever available, will also be recorded.

The list will be published in the respective village and wards which will then be authenticated by village and ward authorities under the supervision of the district administration. Each list will then be signed by the team concerned as also the village and ward authorities. The provisional lists will then be published in the villages and wards and also on the websites of the district and the state government on 11 September. Time will be given till 10 October for any claims and objections after the publication of the provisional lists. The RIN process will be completed on or before 10 December and copies of the final list will be provided to every village and ward besides being placed at the district and state levels.[169]

The Nagaland government on 27 July constituted a commission to frame the modalities of creating the RIN. The commission would recommend the eligibility criteria to be an indigenous inhabitant, the documents to be acceptable proof for being an indigenous inhabitant, the manner in which the exercise to be carried out and any other issue relating to implementation of the RIN. The commission would submit its report within three months.[170] Apparently, the actual enumeration would begin much later than what was originally thought of. In the meantime, divergence of opinion has surfaced over the cut-off date—1 December, 1963 or 28 April, 1977.[171]

Although the Joint Committee on Prevention of Illegal Immigrants (JCPI) supports the NRC in Nagaland, the Naga Hoho, the apex tribal organization of the state, and major insurgent groups like the National Socialist Council of Nagaland (IM) are opposed to the process. They believe that the NRC will hurt the prospects of greater Nagaland, an entity they hope to set up one day by merging the Naga-dominated territories of Manipur, Arunachal Pradesh, Assam and Myanmar with Nagaland. Moreover, they disapprove the move to target the Nagas from Myanmar. Curiously enough, the Nagaland Assembly on 28 March, 2017 had adopted a resolution appealing the Centre to urge the Myanmar government to permanently drop the Indo-Myanmar border fencing project in Nagaland for continuing with the cordial and fraternal relations among the Nagas living on both sides of the border.[172] The exercise was, however, suspended following protests from community-based and extremist organizations. The Nagaland government has reportedly been trying to revive the RIN exercise. The Naga Hoho, the apex body that had objected to the RIN in 2019, has reacted to the State Government's alleged bid to implement it. It was apprehensive of "dreadful consequences" if the "advocates of RIN" implement the identification process with 1 December, 1963—the day Nagaland attained Statehood—as the cut-off date for determining the "permanent residents" of the State as the date was likely to exclude Nagas who had come from beyond the boundaries of Nagaland.[173]

After Assam, the demand for a NRC gained momentum in Tripura. All the tribal parties, who otherwise are political adversaries to each other are on the same page regarding the NRC. The Indigenous Nationalist Party of Tripura (INPT), the oldest existing tribal party in the state, is trying to make it an important issue and even held a demonstration in Agartala on 25 August, 2018. The main rival of INPT, the Indigenous People's Front of Tripura (IPFT), the junior partner in the BJP-led government, is too in favour of the NRC. Other smaller tribal parties like IPFT(Tipraha), a splinter group of the IPFT(NC) and the National Conference of Tripura have also joined the chorus.[174] The Tipraha Indigenous Progressive Regional Alliance (TIPRA), which was formed in February 2021 by Pradyot Manikya after quitting as president of Tripura Pradesh Congress Committee over difference with the party's stand on the CAA and NRC, won 18 of the 28 seats in the Tripura Tribal Autonomous Council election held in April 2021. While the Congress was opposed to the NRC, Manikya who was then state president of the Congress went to the Supreme Court seeking an NRC in the State. He also shared the anti-CAA sentiment because "it is a matter of survival of the indigenous people, protecting their interests, language, culture and identity."[175]

It is a fact that Tripura was a tribal majority state but the continued influx of Hindu Bengalis from the then East Pakistan has altered the state's demography. Even Buddhist Chakmas also left behind their homes in East Pakistan. The demand for NRC updation in Tripura is not wrong but the motives behind it are guided by a communal agenda. All the tribal parties are unanimous that the cut-off year should be 1951, which seems to be an absurd demand. It would entail that most Hindu Bengalis—currently the largest linguistic group in the state—and the Buddhist Chakmas who came after 1951 would lose citizenship. That would cause absolute chaos. Tripura witnessed horrific riots between Bengalis and tribals in 1960 and memories of that period are still fresh among non-tribal communities living in the state. The NRC is for identification of illegal immigrants, not to make people stateless.

After Assam released its final NRC list, Uttar Pradesh, Uttarakhand, Jharkhand and Haryana have also pitched for NRC.[176] Congress leader and former chief minister Bhupinder Singh Hooda of Haryana was quick to support the NRC plan for the state[177], but Congress veteran Harish Rawat warned that NRC, an Assam-specific exercise, would boomerang if it was extended beyond Assam.[178] Manoj Tiwari, president of the Delhi unit of the BJP, demanded NRC in the national capital to identify those who had crossed the border illegally to stay there permanently.[179] The Director-General of Police of Uttar Pradesh, O.P. Singh has issued a circular asking all the district Superintendents of Police to identify the Bangladeshi nationals. The construction companies have been especially directed not to employ any Bangladeshi nationals not in possession of valid identity papers.[180]

The B.S.Yediyurappa government is also keen on implementing NRC in Karnataka and the state has already held two meetings on the possibilities of rolling out NRC.[181] The remaining BJP-ruled states would fall in line in no time, because as Haryana chief minister Manohar Lal Khattar said on 21 September, 2019, the NRC was not a political issue for the BJP but a step towards saving the nation's interest.[182]

But what is happening in Bengaluru is an eye opener. The inability to distinguish between people from Bengal and Bangladesh is leading to prejudice against all Bengalis. The anti-Bangladeshi sentiment has morphed into anti-Bengali prejudice and the apartment complexes in Bengaluru's tech corridor have been directing recruitment agencies not to send them Bengali speaking workers. This comes at a time when the police have launched a crackdown on illegal Bangladeshi migrants in Bengaluru.[183] An editorial in *The Times of India* has put the matter in the correct perspective thus: "If the anti-Bengali drive in Bengaluru balloons out of control, it is bound to hurt Bengaluru's cosmopolitan image and its lucrative tech industry that employs a considerable number of Bengalis. Prejudice and development cannot go hand in hand. Moreover, if states start expelling or otherwise harshly discriminating against people from other states, this will loosen bond that hold the country together.[184] About 8 years earlier, on 29 August, 2012, to be precise, members of the Akhil Bhartiya Vidyarthi Parishad (ABVP) had assaulted 98 migrant workers after dragging them out of a train in Mandya in Karnataka branding them as "illegal Bangladeshis". The workers hailing from West Bengal, Odisha, Rajasthan, Bihar and other states were going to Mangalore on the Yashantipur-Kannur Express.[185]

The protests against the CAA/NPR/NRC were mounting both at the political level as well as apolitical level throughput the length and breadth of the country and as many as nine CMs, those of Kerala, Andhra Pradesh, Chattisgarh, Punjab, Bihar, West Bengal, Odisha, Rajasthan and Madhya Pradesh, had registered their intention by 20 December, 2019 not to implement the NRC in their states.[186] BJP's ally in Bihar JD(U) opposed the BJP's demand to implement NRC in Bihar. States and UTs like Telangana, Puducherry and Delhi also joined them later. In the backdrop of resentment of such a magnitude, PM Modi had made an announcement of far-reaching consequences. While addressing a mammoth rally at Ramlila Maidan on 22 December, 2019, Modi had said: "I wish to tell 130 crore Indians that after my government came to power in 2014 and until today, not a word has been uttered on NRC within the government. No rules have been framed. We had to carry out the NRC only in Assam on instructions of the Supreme Court. Congress and some urban naxals are spreading canards that all Muslims will be sent to detention camps. This is false and politically motivated campaign."[187]

It is not known whether Modi was jumping the NRC ship or buying time, but the groundwork for such a statement was prepared by the Union ministers who sought to deemphasise the government's declared intent to prepare an NRC even as they stood by the proposed exercise to identify and document citizens. Finance minister Nirmala Sitaraman said on 20 December, 2019, the NRC process would not start without taking into account the concerns of all concerned. She also asserted that details of the exercise were yet to be worked out. Shah's junior in the home ministry, G. Kishan Reddy said: "I clarify that NRC exercise is yet to be formally announced and as and when it is done, rules and regulations will be so framed to rule out any harassment to Indian Citizens." I&B minister Prakash Javdekar asserted that the NRC exercise would not hurt Indian citizens, while law minister Ravi Shankar Prasad made a strong pitch against the opposition bid to dub the CAA as anti-Muslim. [188] BJP working president J.P. Nadda had reiterated on 19 December, 2019 that both the CAA and the NRC would be implemented across the country.[189] NRC panic saw as many as 80 lakh people applying for revision in the voter's lists in Bengal alone.[190]

Modi's clarification may have been meant to underline that the NRC is not on immediate priority even though the intent to have NRC done across the country has been declared in BJP's 2019 manifesto as well as in multiple statements by senior members including Amit Shah. Or is it a mere division of political labour for the longer term project of ushering in a Hindu-majoritiarain State? Or it might be the Prime Minister and the Home Minister were saying different things at different times. That is their way of trying to confuse the people. As Pamela Philipose says, the Modi-Shah partnership has decisively transformed Indian politics, first at the Gujarat state level and later on the national stage. Together it spelt a rare unity of purpose and a cogent ideological vision developed through the long personal associations both men have had with the RSS. Both men are extremely aware that their ultimate goal is to promote the twin Savarkarite tests of full citizenship—*pitribhumi* (India as the citizen's ancestral land) and *punyabhumi* (India as the land of the citizen's religion). They also understand how central the CAA-NPR-NRC architecture is to the political consolidation of the Hindu community along the axis of citizenship.[191]

The President of India, Ram Nath Kovind in his Address to the joint session of Parliament on 20 June, 2019, however, had said: "My government has decided to implement the process of National Register of Citizens on priority basis in areas affected by infiltration."[192] Incidentally, President's speech is prepared by the ministry and is approved by the Cabinet which is normally presided over by the Prime Minister.

On 1 May, 2019, addressing a rally in West Bengal Shah had said: "First, we will pass the CAB and ensure that all refugees from the neighbouring nations get Indian citizenship. After that, NRC will be made and we will detect and deport every infiltrator from our motherland."[193] Again, while addressing a seminar on NRC at Netaji Indoor Stadium on 1 October, 2019, Amit Shah categorically said the NRC would be carried out in Bengal and no one can stop it.[194]

Launching his party's campaign for the forthcoming Haryana Assembly polls at a public meeting at Kaithal, Amit Shah said on 9 October, 2019 that by 2024 when the next general elections take place in the country, there would be no illegal immigrant in the country because of the NRC.[195]

Amit Shah had told the Rajya Sabha on 20 November, 2019 that NRC would be conducted across India and it would be repeated in Assam as well. He also assured that "no one, irrespective of their religion, should be worried. It is just a process to get everyone under NRC."[196] Official sources, however, said that nation-wide NRC could only happen after the NPR was updated, which would be done alongside the Census 2021. After NPR's verification process was over, the process of NRC could begin. As of now, the NPR exercise was not being taken up in Assam and the final NRC published recently would be updated along with the NRC.[197]

To dispel any doubt of the leaders of the north-eastern states about the CAB, Amit Shah had argued that "economic" influx of Bangladeshis would be countered through the NRC, which would work in tandem with the CAB. The NRC would work to provide verified citizenship lists while the CAB offered relief only to minorities whose cases were viewed sympathetically by India on grounds of religious persecution.[198] Addressing poll rallies at Chakradharpur and Biharagora on 2 December, 2019, Amit Shah had set a deadline for completing the NRC across the country by 2024 and declared that "each and every infiltrator will be expelled before the next general elections."[199]

The most credible declaration of the government's intent to have an all-India NRC came during Shah's reply to the debate on CAB in Lok Sabha on 9 December. Shah had categorically said NRC would be brought across the country. "There is no need to connect CAB with NRC. I will explain it (NRC) the same way in Parliament as CAB. Rest assured, NRC will be brought soon", Shah had said.[200] The intent was reiterated in the Rajya Sabha a couple of days later.[201] All these pronouncements by the Union Home Minister were made before the by-now-famous Ramlila Maidan speech of the Prime Minister on 22 December, 2019.

Even after the anti-CAA protests began, there were some statements from Shah on NRC. Subsequently, the government's publicity wing, Press Information Bureau, put out a document answering FAQs on NRC, an indication that the concept had been discussed at some level even if details remain to be worked out and the issue had not formally figured in the meeting of the Cabinet. Soon afterwards, the home ministry said that rules regarding NRC had not been worked out. [202]

Again, on 4 February, 2020, Union Minister of State for Home Nityananda Rai informed the Lok Sabha that no decision had yet been taken to prepare the NRC. "Till now, the government has not taken any decision to prepare the National Register of Indian Citizens at the national level."[203]

Two days after Modi's Ramlila Maidan speech, Shah appeared on television to be interviewed by the news agency ANI on 25 December to firmly deny any link between the NPR exercise and the proposed contentious NRC exercise. "NPR process cannot be used for NRC. They are different laws." But he did not rule out the rollout of a nationwide NRC, promised by him on several occasions.[204]

While the statement by the home minister is welcome, this needs to be backed by an administrative order delinking NPR from the process of preparing the NRC. The important question would then pertain to the use of the NPR data, collected with enormous physical and financial cost, when Aadhar-based bio-metric identification numbers having a higher coverage linked to almost all welfare programmes are available.

The present government has made an electoral promise to implement the NRC, and the Parliament has been informed, time and again, that it will be implemented throughout the country. The process begins with the Central Government preparing the National Population Register (NPR), a list of all people residing in India, including the non-citizens. This was done as part of the house-listing operation of 2011 Census and updated in 2015. Given the present level of decadal migration, roughly 12 per cent of the people would not be found in the place where they were enumerated in 2011. It would, therefore, be erroneous to consider 2021 NPR as a mere updating exercise. The NPR is a location-based register unlike the Aadhar database. Updating the NPR is possible only if the current and past records can be unambiguously matched, which will be a serious concern for people who have migrated since the last census. Mismatch of any information can create serious problems for an individual, including their claim of citizenship. Given the present social tension and uncertainties, this could result in massive corruption and violence at the ground level. Furthermore, a lot of data in the NPR, like educational status, marital status, occupation, etc., are not constant for a person, and given the time lag between the enumeration and finalisation of the citizenship register, these would have limited validity.[205]

The population census with which the NPR is tagged, suffers from a serious coverage error by missing out 2.3 per cent of the population, as determined through the Post Enumeration Check in 2001 and 2011. The degree of undercount did not go down with computerisation and the use of digital technology since the undercount in 1991 and 1981 was less—only 1.8 per cent. The undercount in 2011 was even larger in urban areas, that is, 4 per cent, where a larger percentage of Muslims reside. In any case, not counting 2 per cent of the population implies exclusion of 30 million people in India. Increased mobility is likely to increase this figure. The NPR prepared the electronic database for 1,180 million persons only, against the census figure of 1,210 million. Considering the undercount of another 30 million in the census itself, it is evident that 60 million people were missed in this NPR exercise. One does not know the extent of exclusion when the register was updated in 2015 by linking with biometric information from the Aadhar database, since this is not in public domain.[206]

Large-scale exclusion inevitable in the NPR exercise will therefore be a nightmare for all usual residents of the country. That the government has not revealed the existing NPR for any kind of public scrutiny makes any statement on its accuracy a matter of conjecture. The call given by several political leaders and activists in the country to boycott NPR gives rise to serious administrative difficulties. For the census staff, it will be a nightmare to organise its operation amidst the threats and frets of disenfranchisement, without losing credibility of the information collected.

The apprehension that the NPR would be the base document for NRC would compromise the reliability of the 2021 Census data. It may be reiterated that the NPR is prepared as per the Citizenship Rules, 2003 and not under the Census Act. Consequently, while registration in the NPR is compulsory for all "usual residents of India", the confidentiality umbrella provided by the Census Act is no longer available for the data collected for the NPR.

In response to a question filed by *The Hindu* under the RTI seeking information on the expected date of the first phase of the Census—House listing and Housing census—and an update of the NPR that was earlier scheduled to begin from 1 April, the office of the Registrar General of India (RGI) has said on 17 November, 2020 that the schedule of the questionnaire of the NPR is "being finalised" and the information about the expected date of the first phase of the Census 2021 is "not available."[207] The parliamentary committee on Home headed by the Congress's Ananda Sharma, while discussing the demands for grants report on 18 February, 2020 had observed that there was a lot of dissatisfaction and fear among people regarding the coming NPR and Census. The Union Home Ministry in its 226th action taken report on the recommendations/observations contained in the 224th on demand for grants (2020-21) has informed that "a 360 degree approach for communicating the right and clear message on the NPR has been planned to be followed. All kinds of media, i.e., social media, AV[Audio visual], digital, outdoor, print and word of mouth publicity tools are part of the planned media strategy. Right kind of messaging will be done to tackle the miscommunication and rumours around NPR and Census 2021." The report was presented to the Rajya Sabha Chairman M.Venkaiah Naidu in December 2020 and was laid on the table of the House on 2 February, 2021.[208]

A senior government official told *The Hindu* that the Registrar General of India was preparing to conduct pre-tests or field trials of the first phase of the Census and the NPR using a mobile application in all States and Union Territories. On 9 February, 2021, Vivek Joshi, RGI and Census Commissioner of India, chaired a virtual meeting of the Directors of Census Operations of all States to review the preparations for the coming census where field trials using the app were discussed. On 10 February, Union Minister of State for Home Nityanand Rai informed the Rajya Sabha that "an app for the collection of data and a census portal for the management and monitoring of various Census related activities has been developed." "Instruction manuals for enumerators and other Census functionaries have been prepared. A pre-test of the Census was undertaken from August 12, 2019 to September 20, 2019 in selected areas of all the States and Union Territories to test the Census questionnaire and methodology", he added.[209]

The pre-test conducted in selected areas of the States and UTs except Assam involving 30 lakh population included questions such as date and place of birth of father and mother, last place of residence, mother tongue, Aadhar (optional), voter ID card, apart from mobile phone, ration card and driving license numbers.[210]

According to the annual report of the Ministry of Home Affairs for the year 2019-20, there will be a three-pronged approach for updating the NPR database—self updating, updating of the NPR data in paper format and the mobile mode. The Centre will allow residents to fill the National Population Register (NPR) form on their own, through the online mode, a month before the door-to-door enumeration by Census officials starts. After filling the form online, residents will get a reference code that they can mention to the field enumerator at the time of his or her visit. The details of the resident would be displayed on a mobile application developed for conducting the Census exercise but no biometrics or documents would be collected. These details would then be stored in the system for future use.[211]

The first phase of census and the collection of details to update the NPR have been postponed at least till September 2022.[212] The RGI pulled down after 26 October, 2021, the document with the latest form of the NPR which had retained contentious questions such as the "mother tongue, place of birth of father and mother, and last place of residence", from its website censusindia.gov.in. A Home ministry official, however, explained on 29 October, 2021 that "the NPR proforma was yet to be finalised."[213] Junior Home Minister Nityanand Rai, in reply to a question, reassured the Rajya Sabha on 20 July, 2022 that individual data to be collected as part of the Census would not be used for preparation of any other database including the NRC.

V

The CAA provides that "any person belonging to Hindu, Sikh, Buddhist, Jain, Parsi or Christian community from Afghanistan, Bangladesh or Pakistan, who entered into India on or before the 31st day of December, 2014 and who has been exempted by the Central Government by or under clause (c) of sub-section (2) of section 3 of the Passport (Entry into India) Act, 1920 or from the application of the provisions of the Foreigners Act, 1946 or any rule or order made thereunder, shall not be treated as illegal migrant for the purposes of" the Citizenship Act. In other words, they will be treated as "legal migrant" who needed shelter in India because of their religious background. This Amendment is criticised for singling out the "migrants" (not refugees) on the basis of religion.

It is well known that the Partition of India in 1947 along ostensibly religious lines into India, Pakistan, and what eventually became Bangladesh was heralded by the largest bilateral flow of refugees in South Asia and perhaps the largest and the most rapid human migrations in human history. Some 10 million people were displaced and between 1.5 and 2.0 million people perished in an orgy of violence and bloodshed. Indeed two millions of Indians and Pakistanis who actually lived through that horrendous event and to their children and grand children, the word Partition triggers traumatic memories of indescribable bloodshed, murder, rape, torture, arson and looting of a scale unknown in human history.

Partition had left the country with an obligation to rehabilitate the Hindu, Sikh, and other non-Muslim immigrants from Pakistan. Our national leaders gave such assurances to the minorities of Pakistan day in and day out as soon as the proposal of partition took a concrete shape. Md. Zinnah's proposal for exchange of 'Hindu', 'Sikh' and 'Muslim' population was turned down by the Congress leadership as that would have given a seal of approval to the Muslim League's two-nation theory. While the problem of West Pakistan was solved by a spontaneous exchange of population and permanent rehabilitation of the West Pakistani refugees, the same thing did not happen in the eastern sector. There was no exchange of population in an organized manner. Only a minuscule of Muslim population migrated to Pakistan. On the other hand, Bengali Hindus and other non-Muslims from East Pakistan were compelled to take shelter in different States of India particularly Assam, Tripura and West Bengal. There was no effort to permanently rehabilitate them as was done in respect of the refugees in the western sector. They were compelled to live on weekly doles. And to cap it all, the porous Indo-Bangladesh border remained unfenced till now at many places allowing infiltration from across the border, due to the cooperation of the BSF, the local police and the local political parties. It is the primary duty and responsibility of the Central Government to guard the border. If it could discharge such obligations so effectively in the western sector, it is not understood why it failed to discharge its obligations in the eastern sector allowing infiltration not only from Bangladesh but from Myanmar and Nepal as well.

As a matter of fact, starting with Noakhali riots in October 1946, the influx of refugees from East Pakistan continued in spurts and by the end of 1951, 28 lakhs of Hindus crossed the border and entered Assam, Tripura and West Bengal. By the end of 1956, the total figure, as noted in the government registers reached up to 39.84 lakhs. By 1960, more than

30 lakhs of migrants came only to West Bengal. It seemed as if this stream of refugees would never stop. The mass migration of the people, on a scale unprecedented in modern history, posed terrible and pressing problems for India.[214] It has been estimated that up to the census of 1971, altogether 91 lakh immigrants had come to India from different neighbouring countries. Of the 81.8 lakh who came from Pakistan, 52.31 lakh belonged to the eastern wing. Of them, 9.90 lakh came to Assam, 32 lakh to West Bengal, 5.3 lakh to Tripura and the rest 5.11 lakh were distributed among other States.[215]

The routine, long-term, low-level violence perpetrated on the minorities, particularly the Hindus in Bangladesh, did not, however, end with the liberation of Bangladesh. The emergence of Bangladesh in 1971 as an independent country with secularism as one of the pillars of the constitution did not change the fate of the Hindus in that country. In fact, with each succeeding year, the Bangladeshi political regime was growing more hostile to the minority communities. Whenever a communal riot takes place anywhere in India, retaliatory attacks on the Hindus in Bangladesh are often reported. They lived under a shadow of violence: they witnessed violence on others and themselves faced other kinds of violence such as loss of religion, property and threats to their lives. The common forms of persecution are rape, torture, killings and arson. As a result, migration of the Hindus from Bangladesh still continues.

The migration of Hindus from the eastern border may conveniently be divided into two phases—those coming before 25 March, 1971 and those coming after 25 March, 1971. Those who came before 25 March, 1971 came from the territory known as East Pakistan but those who came after 25 March, 1971 were citizens of an independent country called Bangladesh.

The Assam Accord fixed 25 March, 1971 as the cut-off date for being considered as an Indian citizen. The Accord was signed on 15 August 1985 but much before the signing of the Accord, the Central Government had started operating on the assumption that subsequent to the resolution of the India-Pakistan war in 1971 leading to the emergence of a free Bangladesh migration of Hindu and other minorities from Bangladesh had virtually stopped and that they were not to be treated as refugees. In fact, the Central Government in a letter dated 29 November, 1971 addressed to the Chief Secretaries of the States/UTs informed them that after 25 March, 1971, the application for citizenship under section 5 of the Citizenship Act should not be entertained. After the emergence of independent Bangladesh, another circular was issued by the Central Government on 5 July, 1975, intimating that consequent to the adoption of a resolution in Parliament on 9 May,

1975 no migration from Bangladesh would be tolerated by the Central Government and all such infiltrants should be deported forthwith.[216]

The political repression against Awami League supporters subsequent to the assassination of Sk. Mujibur Rahman in a military coup in August 1975, among others, triggered the first wave of emigration of the Hindus after the liberation of Bangladesh. In the ensuing political crisis, Mujibar Rahman's successor, Khandakar Mushtaq Ahmed, was himself toppled in a countercoup that placed Bangladesh under the rule of a martial law administration ultimately headed by General Ziaur Rahman. In 1982, a third military coup brought Lt. General Mohammad Ershad to power. Though perhaps less dramatic and spread over a longer interval of time, a second wave of emigration occurred throughout the 1980s.

After the demolition of the Babri Masjid in Ayodha, Uttar Pradesh on 6 December, 1992, communal violence in Bangladesh against Hindus reached unprecedented proportions, spawning a third wave of emigration, although smaller in magnitude and duration than its predecessors.

The election slogan of the BNP/Jamaat in the October 2001 election was: *Hare Krishna hare Ram, Hasinar baper nam; Hindu joḍi bachte chao, Bangla chere Bharat jao* (Hasina's father is Hare Krishna, Hare Ram; if you want to survive, Hindus leave Bangladesh and go to India). It is, therefore, no wonder that ever since Khaleda Zia of the BNP came to power in October 2001, the minority communities, particularly Hindus, have had to face the wrath of the Bangladesh Nationalist Party and Jamaati activists who had gone on a rampage against them. Fearing for their lives, Hindus fled Bangladesh in the thousands culminating in the fourth wave of emigration.[217]

The violence before and after the elections in Bangladesh in January 2014 showed how, even under the Awami League dispensation, the Hindus had become easy targets of anti-election activists who ransacked their houses and other properties, on the assumption that they voted for the ruling Awami League flouting the directive to refrain from voting, forcing them to leave the country.[218]

But what is the actual figure of Bangladeshi Hindu infiltrators? Conflicting figures float around as to the number of illegal migrants from Bangladesh. Because of ethnic and language similarities it is extremely difficult to identify Bangladeshis. As a result, no authentic figure of the number of Bangladeshi Hindu infiltrators who have made India their home is available. The 1981 Census revealed that in the eight border districts of West Bengal, the population had grown by over 30 per cent between 1971 and 1981 whereas in the remaining districts reported growth rates were below 20 per cent. In one town, population had jumped from 10,000 to

1,50,000. One scholar cited a report which showed a 100 per cent increase in the population of 37 villages in those eight border districts. [219] The border authorities reported the interception of over 55,000 Bangladeshis attempting to cross the border in 1990 and over 73,000 in 1991. These figures, if accurate, may provide some indication of how many migrants succeeded in entering the state in the early 1990s.[220]

Crossing the border illegally and entering India surreptitiously is not the only way in which undocumented Bangladeshi nationals settle down in the country; a large number of Bangladeshis arrive with valid documents but do not return and continue to reside in India illegally. According to the government data, between 1972 and 1997, a total of 9,91,031 Bangladeshis entered India with valid documents but did not return.[221] The latest data on such visa violators, as on 31 December, 2012, reveal that 16,350 Bangladeshis who came on valid travel documents were overstaying in India.[222] If the number of persons coming with valid travel documents but overstaying is of that magnitude, it is anybody's guess what the number of illegal migrants from Bangladesh would be. It is however, the difficult nature of obtaining an accurate estimation of this process that has allowed a great deal of alarmism and political opportunism in regard to this issue.

A study was conducted by the Intelligence Bureau and the Home Ministry in 1992 to find out the extent of demographic changes in the eastern sector, especially in relation to illegal migration from Bangladesh. In view of the sensitive nature of the findings, the report was kept a secret. It was ultimately leaked out and the estimated number of illegal migrants from Bangladesh was anywhere between 1.5 crore and 2 crore.[223]

Quoting Home Ministry/Intelligence Bureau sources the August 10, 1998 issue of *India Today* has given the breakdown of these illegal migrants by States:

- West Bengal 5.4 million
- Assam 4.0 million
- Tripura 0.8 million
- Bihar 0.5 million
- Maharashtra 0.05 million
- Rajasthan 0.05 million
- Delhi 0.03 million
- making a total of 10.83 million.

During the period 2001-2011, there is an alarming decrease of Hindu population in Bangladesh. According to statistics available with the government sources, the proportionate decrease in Hindu population is around nine hundred thousand. The statistics show almost elimination of Hindu population in fifteen districts in that country. Most of the Hindu families in those districts were forced to leave the country. Currently 8.5 per cent of the total population of Bangladesh are Hindus, while in 2001 it was 9.2 per cent. The proportion of Christian, Buddhist and other religious minority population did not see any decline in the past. The district-wise statistics of population show "huge decline" or "almost elimination" of Hindu population in fifteen districts, though the statistics terms the decline of Hindu population as "missing population".[224]

During the World Alliance of Religions Peace Summit in Seoul (17-18 September, 2014), a delegate of Bangladesh Hindu, Buddhist and Christian Unity Council drew attention to the gruesome fact that 49 million people (non-Muslims) are missing from Bangladesh since 1947 (then East Pakistan) and that the non-Muslim population in that country has dwindled to 8.9 per cent from 19.6 per cent in a span of 40 years. This is nothing short of a demographic disaster. The report stated that in Bangladesh abduction of young girls from religious minority communities, indiscriminate rape, and conversion to Islam under threats are rampant; they are used as tools for the persecution of minorities, indeed to eject them from the country.[225]

Dr. Abdul Barkat, a Dhaka university professor said in his book *Political economy of reforming agriculture-land-water bodies in Bangladesh* which was published on 19 November, 2016 that there would be no Hindus left in Bangladesh three decades from then if the current rate of "exodus" continued. "From 1964 to 2013, around 11.3 million Hindus left due to religious persecution and discrimination which means on an average 632 Hindus left the country each day and 2,30,612 annually", he said at the book launch ceremony at the Dhaka University. From his 30-year long research, Barkat found that the exodus mostly took place during military governments after independence in 1971. Before the Liberation War, the daily rate of migration was 705 while it was 512 during 1971-1981 and 438 during 1981-1991. The number increased to 767 persons each year during 1991-2001 while around 774 persons left the country during 2001-2012, the book says.[226]

A recent survey by the *Nikhil Bharat Udbastu Samanay Samiiti* (All India Bengali Refugee Coordination Committee) reveals that even after 70 years of partition of India more than 1.50 crore Bengali refugees are living in various places in India—Assam (75 lakh), UP and Uttarakhand (25 lakh), Odisha (30 lakh), MP (11 lakh), Chhattisgarh (5 lakh) and Jharkhand (5 lakh), Rajasthan (1.20 lakh), and Karnataka (35 thousand). They are in search of their roots. They have more or less forgotten their mother tongue and are afraid of disclosing their Bengali identity, especially after the controversy over the National Register of Citizen (NRC).[227] And if the Bangladeshi migrants living in West Bengal are added with it, the number will be more than 2.5 crore. This figure is in consonance with the census figures of Bangladesh. The percentage of Hindu population to the total population in Bangladesh was 22 per cent in 1951 and it has dwindled to 9.2 per cent in 2001 and to 8.5 per cent in 2011. Where did the Hindus migrate? Obviously to India. But what is their number? Since there is no authentic number of Bangladeshi illegal immigrants in India, it is preposterous to expect an authentic figure of their religious composition. But a rudimentary idea can be had from the following figures of overstayals. Between 1972 and 1993, of the total arrival figure of 41,25,516, Hindus constituted 23,70,559 (57.5%), and Muslims constituted 1,72,652 (41.8%); of the total overstay figure of 8,36,524, 5,38,501 (64%) were Hindus and 2,94,104 (35%) Muslims.[228]

So roughly, one-third of Bangladeshi illegal immigrants can be said to be Muslims. But if we look at the number of persons detected at the border it will give a different picture. For instance, out of 55,553 illegal immigrants apprehended by the BSF in 1991, 13,457 were Hindus and 42,090 were Muslims. The number of Muslims is usually twice or more than that of the Hindus.[229]

The NDA I brought a major amendment to the Citizenship Act in 2003. For the first time, "illegal immigrants" were defined as a person who entered India without proper travel documents or entered India with proper travel documents but overstayed without permission. Ordinarily, such an illegal migrant could have applied for citizenship by registration or naturalisation by staying for certain number of years in India. But, the 2003 amendment also provided that such an illegal migrant cannot apply at all for Indian citizenship either by registration or naturalisation. Thus, if a Bangladeshi Hindu crossed the border and came into India, they will not be entitled to Indian citizenship ever even if they get married here to an Indian citizen, stay for 60 years and have children in India. Even such children would not ever be entitled to Indian citizenship. That such a law would be to the detriment of the interests of the Hindus fleeing Bangladesh due to persecution in that country was known to our leaders.

As a matter of fact, when the CAB 2003 was introduced in the Rajya Sabha on 18 December, 2003, Dr. Manmohan Singh, leader of the opposition said that "after the partition of our country, the minorities in countries like Bangladesh, have faced persecution, and it is our moral obligation that if circumstances force people, these unfortunate people, to seek refuge in our country, our approach to granting citizenship to these unfortunate persons should be more liberal. I sincerely hope that the hon. Deputy Prime Minister will bear this in mind in charting out the future course of action with regard to the Citizenship Act.[230] General (Retd.) Shankar Roy Choudhury also pointed out that "from Bangladesh, we are getting a wide variety of people who are entering into our country illegally, all of them. Some are economic migrants whom you see all over the country, be it Mumbai, Delhi or Calcutta. Some are infiltrators, terrorists. But a large number of them are religious minorities facing persecution, Chakmas, Hindus, Buddhists, many of them. I urge the Government again, through you, Madam—I earnestly urge the Government—minorities fleeing Bangladesh for the fear of persecution should be given citizenship and should be treated in a supportive and kind manner."[231] L.K. Advani while endorsing his full agreement with the views expressed by Dr. Singh and General (Retd.) Choudhury, added: "Very often, in the past, we have faced this kind of situation when we have adopted an approach of that kind. There were various kinds of allegations made that 'you are making discrimination between this and that' which we do not propose to do. We always say that a person who has to flee because of religious persecution is a refugee, *bona fide* refugee, and he cannot be regarded on par with the illegal immigrant who may have come for any reason, even for economic reasons. If he is an illegal immigrant, he is an illegal immigrant. So, I take note of what has been said and endorse it."[232]

Though Advani was in full agreement for granting citizenship liberally to those Bangladeshis who were fleeing the country due to religious persecution, he did precious little to translate his promise into action for reasons best known to him. That, however, did not prevent him or rather the ruling NDA I to make special provisions for the West Pakistani Hindus and Sikhs.

Within two months of the enactment of the 2003 CAA, the Citizenship Rules, 1956 was amended on 28 February, 2004 to address the claims to citizenship of about 17,000 Hindu and Sikh migrants from Pakistan who had travelled on Indian visas into the states of Gujarat and Rajasthan but overstayed. But no such measures were initiated in the eastern sector where the problem was of gigantic proportions and needed a far more careful handling because of presence of a large number of people who crossed over without any valid travel documents but also of those travelling with valid travel documents but overstayed over a considerably long period of time. A more humane and compassionate step was expected from the two tallest leaders of the ruling dispensation—L.K. Advani, himself a refugee from West Pakistan, and Vajpayee, a known sympathizer of the Bengali refugees. Why this step-motherly attitude towards the Bangladeshi Hindu immigrants is a question which defies any answer.

Moreover, in spite of the assertion of Advani that those fleeing Bangladesh due to fear of religious persecution were *bona fide* refugees, no official endorsements were made to treat them as such. As a result, the Bangladeshi Hindu immigrants are in a state of perpetual threat of being deported to a country where they are not wanted. These people crossed over to a country for refuge and shelter under compelling circumstances but that country refused to treat them as such.

As a matter of fact, the enactment of the 2003 Citizenship Amendment Act has opened a Pandora's box so far as acquisition of citizenship is concerned. It not only created a new category known as "illegal migrants" and prohibited citizenship to them and to their progeny but also introduced the concept of NRC/NPR, which no government has been able to implement till now. Moreover, even the Citizenship Identity Card for all Indian citizens could not be prepared. One wonders whether the enactment of the 2019 CAA would at all have been necessary if the Government of India had changed its policy with regard to Bangladeshi Hindu "infiltrators", and reverted to pre-2003 position.

Boris Johnson on becoming prime minister of UK announced amnesty for all illegal immigrants into Britain who have lived there for 10 years or more.[233] Switzerland eased passport rules for third generation of immigrants.[234] Canada invited a record 27,332 candidates to apply for permanent residency following a draw for the Canadian Experience Class' category on 13 February, 2021.[235] Tens of thousands of stateless people in oil-rich Kuwait will be offered citizenship of the impoverished African nation of Comoros to end their decade-old problem.[236] The US Citizenship Act of 2021 promises to provide a path to citizenship for 11 million undocumented immigrants.[237] Prabhat Patnaik, Professor Emeritus, Centre for Economic Studies, JNU, has pleaded for amnesty for the NRC-rejects in Assam.[238] The Citizenship Amendment Act will effectively amnesty all illegal immigrants except Muslims.

It may be recalled that India had, in fact, granted permanent amnesty in 1971 to lakhs of East Bengalis/East Pakistanis who had crossed over to India during the 1950s and 1960s. The move was not initiated to curb illegal migration, but was more a friendly gesture to a new country. As part of extending all possible political and economic assistance to Bangladesh, India had agreed to Bangladesh's request that only those who entered India as refugees after its declaration of independence shall be repatriated to Bangladesh.[239] In other words, Bangladesh refused to accept those persons who entered India illegally prior to or on March 24, 1971 as its citizens. The

Bangladeshi refusal to accept illegal entrants as its own citizens left India with no option but to agree to take the responsibility of the illegal migrants and grant them Indian citizenship. This regularisation of Bangladeshis illegally staying in India by the Central Government was later formalised in the Assam Accord of 1985.

As the history of Assam agitation shows, regularising lakhs of East Bengalis/Pakistanis did not result in addressing the issue of illegal migration. On the contrary, it acted as a catalyst for further unauthorised crossings into India. In fact, the Government of India realised as early as 1974 that illegal migration from Bangladesh had restarted. In 1974, controversy broke out over the validity of the so-called exit permits issued by Bangladesh to those willing to go back to India on the ground that they were Indians and had come to Bangladesh after the liberation. And by 1975 numerous reports started appearing in Indian newspapers about illegal Bangladeshi emigrations to Assam, Meghalaya, West Bengal, Tripura and other border states of India. The external affairs minister reported to the Parliament that the number of illegal migrants in India from Bangladesh between April to December 1974 was 15,278, in 1975 it was 38,445 and in 1976 it stood at 7,014. *The Statesman* contradicted the 'low figures' and claimed quoting home ministry (BSF) figures that as 'high' a figure as 78,808 persons had been detected and sent back.[240]

European countries, such as Spain, Italy and Portugal, have been regularising illegal migrants since the 1970s. Between 1996 and 2007, these countries have regularised 5 million illegal migrants through various programmes. One of the reasons for such amnesty processes in these countries is the argument that Italy, Spain and Portugal do not possess the administrative capacities to admit large-scale legal migrants, nor do they have the wherewithal to effectively secure their borders against the illegal migrants entering their territories mostly from Africa.[241] In fact, experiences of various countries who have taken recourse to amnesty schemes showed that they have not been successful in preventing illegal migration into their territories. Various studies and statistics have proven that instead of preventing illegal migration, these programmes have, in reality, proved to be an incentive for migrants to cross the border illegally, find work and settle down in these economically developed countries.[242] Actually, the regularization programme is not designed to prevent illegal immigration. This is more a humanitarian programme and should be considered as such. So far the Bangladeshi Hindus are concerned, India has a moral obligation to grant citizenship to them, if they happen to be the victims of persecution.

When it became quite clear to the Central Government that Bangladeshi Hindus were fleeing Bangladesh in droves due to fear of persecution even after its emergence as an independent state, it should have amended its circulars of 29 November, 1971 and 5 July, 1975 on Bangladeshi immigrants and statutorily defined in clear terms which migrants from Bangladesh (and Pakistan) would be treated as "refugees" and formulated a concrete policy with a legal framework to deal with such "refugees." Once officially recognised under an appropriate legal framework as "refugees", the issue of (illegal) Hindu migrants from Bangladesh (and Pakistan) could have been tackled in a meaningful way and the issue would not have become such an intractable problem as at present.

The BJP manifesto for the 2021 West Bengal Assembly elections advertised in all major Newspapers on 23 March, 2021 promised to "provide Rupees 10,000 per annum to each refugee family for 5 years." This announcement presupposes the existence of refugee families in West Bengal but none knows who are they, when they were so categorized and what is their number. It is also presumed that the West Bengal state government has, or at least the state government of West Bengal under the stewardship of the BJP will have, the unfettered power to enlist anyone as refugees, irrespective of country of origin and religious background. But our law does not distinguish between "foreigners" and "refugees". In the absence of explicit recognition by Indian law of the category of refugees, or of their legally binding rights, even the guarantees of Fundamental Rights to life, equality and non-discrimination and humanitarian obligations did not prevent India from violating the crore principle of non-refoulement, of not sending back people to situations of persecution.

It is also presumed that enlistment as refugees will pave the way for granting of Indian citizenship by the Central Government in the near future. But if the "refugees" are already enlisted as voters in the electoral rolls, will they again be treated as "illegal infiltrators" and their names deleted from the voters' lists? Will such "illegal infiltrators" then be treated as "refugees" so as to make them eligible to be Indian citizens? Will the state government play any role in conferring such "citizenship" which is in the exclusive domain of the Union government? It will also open the larger question whether only a citizen can be enlisted as a voter or a non-citizen can also be a voter and thus decide the destiny of the nation.

NOTES

1. Macfoy, M.K., "Introduction: Who is a Citizen? Feminism, Multiculturalism and Immigration", In *Citizenship*, R. Bellamy and M.K. Macfoy (eds), Vol. II, 2014, New York: Routledge.
2. Hammar, T., "Citizenship: Membership of a Nation and of a State", *International Migration*, Vol. 24, 1986, pp. 735-48.
3. Bosniak, L., *The Citizen and the Alien: Dilemmas of Contemporary Membership*, 2006, New Jersey: Princeton University Press.
4. Desforges, L., Jones, R. and Woods, M., "New geographies of citizenship", *Citizenship Studies*, Vol. 9, No, 5 (2005), pp. 439-51, quoted by, Chanchani, Mihika and Balakrishnan, Varna, "Citizenship in India and Assam", In *This Land Is Mine, I Am Not of This Land* (ed.) Harsh Mander and Navsharan Singh, 2021, Speaking Tiger Books, LLP, New Delhi, p. 118.
5. Roy, Anupama, *Mapping Citizenship in India*, New Delhi, Oxford University Press, 2010, quoted by, Chanchani, Mihika and Balakrishnan, Varna, "Citizenship in India and Assam", In *This Land Is Mine, I Am Not of This Land* (ed.) Harsh Mander and Navsharan Singh, 2021, Speaking Tiger Books, LLP, New Delhi, p. 118.
6. Jayal, Niraja Gopal, *Citizenship and Its Discontents: An Indian History*, Cambridge, MA, Harvard University Press, 2013, quoted by Chanchani, Mihika and Balakrishnan, Varna, "Citizenship in India and Assam", In *This Land Is Mine, I Am Not of This Land* (ed.) Harsh Mander and Navsharan Singh, 2021, Speaking Tiger Books, LLP, New Delhi, p. 119.
7. Chanchani, Mihika and Balakrishnan, Varna, "Citizenship in India and Assam", In *This Land Is Mine, I Am Not of This Land* (ed.) Harsh Mander and Navsharan Singh, 2021, Speaking Tiger Books, LLP, New Delhi, p. 119.
8. Jayal, N.G., *Citizenship and Its Discontents: An Indian History*, 2013, US: Harvard University Press.
9. Jayal, Niraja Gopal, "The misadventure of a new citizenship regime", *The Hindu,* November 27, 2019, p. 6.
10. Desai, Mihir, "CAA-NRC-NPR and its Discontents", *Economic & Political Weekly*, Vol. LV, No. 7, February 15, 2020, pp. 28-29.
11. *The Times of India*, March 8, 2020, p. 12.
12. Desai, Mihir, *Op. Cit.*, p. 29.
13. Biswas, Prasenjit, "Designating the 'other'", *The Statesman*, December 16, 2019, p. 16.
14. *The Hindu*, March 19, 2020, p. 4.
15. *Ibid.*, February 6, 2020, p. 11.
16. *Ibid.*, January 31, 2020, p. 4.
17. *Ibid.*, February 23, 2020, p. 5.
18. *Ibid.*, February 20, 2020, p. 7.
19. *Anandabazar Patrika*, March 14, 2021, p. 8.
20. *The Telegraph*, March 3, 2020, p. 5.

21. *Ibid.*, February 9, 2020, p. 5.
22. *The Times of India,* December 15, 2019, p. 10.
23. *The Telegraph*, February 24, 2020, p. 6.
24. Haokip, Thongkholal, "Enduring fault lines", *The Statesman*, March 16, 2020, p. 16.
25. *The Hindu*, February 29, 2020, p. 19.
26. *The Telegraph*, December 19, 2019, p. 4.
27. *The Statesman*, December 24, 2019, p. 3.
28. *Ibid.*, January 3, 2020, p. 3.
29. *Anandabazar Patrika*, December 5, 2019, p. 6.
30. *The Times of India*, January 25, 2020, p. 1.
31. *The Telegraph*, December18, 2019, p. 5.
32. Davy, G.N., "An Epistemic Change?", *Economic & Political Weekly,* Vol. IV, No. 6, February 8, 2020, pp. 10-11.
33. *Ibid.*, March 5, 2020, p. 1.
34. *The Hindu*, June 11, 2020, p. 10.
35. *The Times of India*, June 12, 2020, p. 7.
36. *The Hindu*, December 10, 2020, p. 11.
37. Ahuja, Namrata Biji, "Clash register", *The Week*, January 5, 2020, p. 42.
38. *The Hindu*, December 24, 2019, p. 11.
39. Ahuja, Namrata Biji, "Clash register", *The Week*, January 5, 2020, p. 42.
40. *The Hindu*, December 25, 2019, p. 11.
41. *Ibid.*
42. censusindia.gov.in "2011-Common" IntroductionToNpr
43. *Ibid.*
44. *Ibid.*
45. *The Times of India*, February 17, 2020, p. 10.
46. *Ibid.*, September 29, 2020, p. 10.
47. *Anandabazar Patrika,* January 2, 2020, p. 1.
48. *The Telegraph*, December 26, 2019, p. 6.
49. *The Times of India*, December 17, 2019, p. 5.
50. *The Telegraph*, January 18, 2020, p. 5.
51. *The Times of India,* December 17, 2019, p. 1.
52. *The Hindu*, February 28, 2020, p. 6.
53. *Anandabazar Patrika,* February 26, 2020, p. 8.
54. *The Statesman*, March 4, 2020, p. 4.
55. *The Times of India*, March 13, 2020, p. 1.
56. *The Telegraph*, March 14, 2020, p. 5.
57. *Ibid.*, March 16, 2020, p. 1 and p. 4.
58. *The Hindu,* February14, 2020, p. 11.
59. *The Statesman*, January 21, 2020, p. 15.
60. *The Telegraph*, February 15, 2020, p. 5.
61. *The Times of India*, February 24, 2020, p. 6.
62. *Ibid.*, February 13, 2020, p. 4.
63. The Statesman, January 18, 2020, p. 1.

64. *The Hindu*, February 6, 2020, p. 1.
65. *The Times of India*, February 1, 2020, p. 1.
66. *Ibid.*, January 23, 2020, p. 9.
67. *The Statesman*, March 6, 2020, p. 4.
68. *The Telegraph*, March 5, 2020, p. 6.
69. *The Times of India*, February 20, 2020, p. 4,
70. *The Telegraph*, February 15, 2020, p. 5.
71. *Ibid.*, January 13, 2020, p. 5.
72. *Ibid.*, February 7, 2020, p. 1.
73. *Ibid.*, March 6, 2020, p. 5.
74. *The Hindu*, January 28, 2020, p. 11.
75. *The Statesman*, March 13, 2020, p. 1.
76. *The Telegraph*, March 14, 2020, p. 4.
77. *Ibid.*, March 15, 2020, p. 4.
78. *The Times of India,* June 10, 2019, p. 1 and p. 10.
79. *Ibid.,* October 9, 2018, p. 1.
80. *Ibid.*, May 18, 2019, p. 7.
81. *Ibid.*, March 30, 2019 , p. 2.
82. *The Telegraph*, September 11, 2019, p. 5.
83. *Ibid.*, September 13, 2019, p. 15.
84. *Ibid.*, September 11, 2019, p. 5.
85. *The Statesman*, September 3, 2019, p. 5.
86. *Ibid.*, September 16, 2019, p. 14.
87. *Anandabazar Patrika*, September 2, 2019, p. 3.
88. *The Telegraph*, March 31, 2019, p. 8.
89. *The Statesman*, September 7, 2019, p. 5.
90. *Ibid.*, September 10, 2019, p. 15.
91. *Ibid.*, September 9, 2019, p. 13.
92. *Ibid.*, September 5, 2019, p. 15.
93. *Ibid.*, September 6, 2019, p. 15.
94. *Ibid.*
95. *Ibid.*, September 14, 2019, p. 15.
96. *Ibid.*, September 20, 2019, p. 15.
97. *Ibid.*, September 5, 2019, p. 15.
98. *Ibid.*
99. *Ibid.*
100. *Ibid.,* September 25, 2019, p. 14.
101. *Ibid.*
102. *The Telegraph*, March 20, 2020, p. 6.
103. *Ibid.*, January15, 2020, p. 7.
104. *Anandabazar Patrika*, September 25, 2019, p. 5.
105. *The Telegraph*, December 1, 2019, p. 1.
106. *Ei Samay*, November 19, 2020, p. 5.
107. *Ibid.*, January 15, 2021, p. 7.
108. *The Telegraph*, January 5, 2020, p. 6.
109. *The Statesman*, September 21, 2019, p. 14.
110. *The Telegraph,* September 11, 2019, p. 5.

111. *The Times of India*, September 21, 2019, p. 9.
112. *The Telegraph,* September 25, 2019, p. 7.
113. *Ei Samay*, October 2, 2019, p. 6.
114. *Ibid.*, September 28, 2019, p. 7.
115. *Anandabazar Patrika*, October 5, 2019, p. 5.
116. *Ei Samay,* October 14, 2019, p. 2.
117. *The Telegraph,* December 6, 2019, p. 7.
118. *Ibid.*, December 15, 2019, p. 9.
119. *The Times of India,* December 21, 2019, p. 10.
120. *Ei Samay*, December 22, 2019, p. 10.
121. *Ibid.*, December 26, 2019, p. 5.
122. *The Statesman*, January 28, 2020, p. 15.
123. *The Telegraph,* January 15, 2020, p. 7.
124. *The Times of India,* December 8, 2019, p. 6.
125. *The Telegraph,* March 13, 2020, p. 9.
126. *The Statesman*, September 25, 2019, p. 5.
127. *The Times of India,* September 20, 2019, p. 8.
128. Marjit, Sugata, "Aam Admi are terror-stricken, its bad effect on economy", *Ei Samay*, January 21, 2020, p. 8.
129. Bhattacharya, Rakhee, "NRC-CAA may derail NE growth", *The Statesman*, December 30, 2019, p. 16.
130. *The Telegraph*, October 27, 2019, p. 8.
131. *Ibid.,* January 29, 2019, p. 1.
132. *Ibid.,* October 7, 2002, p. 6.
133. *The Times of India*, November 5, 2020, p. 7.
134. *Ei Samay*, November 17, 2020, p. 4.
135. *The Telegraph*, January 12, 2021, p. 6.
136. *Anandabazar Patrika*, February 6, 2021, p. 11.
137. *The Hindu*, September 10, 2019, p. 5.
138. *Ibid.*, October 24, 2019, p. 1.
139. *Ibid.*, October 15, 2019, p. 2.
140. *The Times of India,* January 24, 2021, p. 7.
141. *Ibid.,* October 2, 2019, p. 1.
142. *The Statesman,* October 10, 2019, p. 3.
143. *Ibid.*, February 5, 2020, p. 1.
144. *Ei Samay*, August 28, 2019, p. 7.
145. *The Telegraph*, February 10, 2020, p. 5.
146. *Anandabazar Patrika*, December 13, 2019, p. 5.
147. *The Telegraph*, November 30, 2019, p. 6.
148. *Ibid.*, March 19, 2021, p. 6.
149. *Ibid.*, May 25, 2022, p. 8.
150. *The Hindu*, March 18, 2021, p. 1.
151. *Ei Samay*, December 1, 2021, p. 2
152. Patricia, Mukhim, "Far-reaching Implications", *The Statesman*, January 8, 2018, p. 16.
153. *The Hindu*, August 4, 2018, p. 11.
154. Patricia, Mukhim, "Far-reaching implications", *The Statesman*, January 8, 2018, p. 16.

155. *The Statesman*, September 6, 2019, p. 3.
156. *The Hindu*, August 3, 2019, p. 4.
157. *The Times of India*, June 13, 2018, p. 12.
158. *The Statesman*, September 11, 2019, p. 5.
159. *The Times of India*, September 3, 2019, p. 5.
160. *The Telegraph*, September 10, 2019, p. 8.
161. Bannerjee, Rabi, "Interview of N. Biren Singh, Chief Minister of Manipur", *The Week*, October 13, 2019, p. 27.
162. *The Times of India,* September 1, 2019, p. 11.
163. *The Hindu*, March 19, 2019, p. 3.
164. *Ibid.*, February 22, 2020, p. 4.
165. Bannerjee, Rabi, "Interview of Zoramthanga, Chief Minister of Mizoram", *The Week*, October 13, 2019, p. 28.
166. *The Hindu*, September 23, 2019, p. 10.
167. *The Times of India*, November 2, 2019, p. 1.
168. *Ibid.*, October 23, 2020, p. 8.
169. *The Statesman,* July 1, 2019, p. 1 and p. 10.
170. *The Hindu*, July 28, 2019, p. 7.
171. *Ibid.*, August 15, 2019, p. 10.
172. *Ibid.,* March 28, 2017, p. 3.
173. *Ibid.*, April 14, 20021, p. 1.
174. Sinha, Sagarneel, "Ripple effect", *The Statesman*, September 10, 2018, p. 16.
175. *The Hindu*, April 12, 2021, p. 9.
176. *The Times of India*, October 4, 2019, p. 10.
177. *Ibid.,* September 16, 2019, p. 7.
178. *Ibid.*, September 27, 2019, p. 7.
179. *The Statesman*, September 14, 2019, p. 7.
180. *Ei Samay*, October 2, 2019, p. 19.
181. *The Statesman*, October 4, 2019, p. 4.
182. *The Hindu,* September 22, 2019, p. 10.
183. *The Times of India*, November 5, 2019, p. 8.
184. Editorial titled "NRC Fallout", *The Times of India,* November 7, 2019, p. 14.
185. *The Hindu*, August 31, 2012, p. 1.
186. *The Times of India*, December 21, 2019, p. 1.
187. *Ibid.*, December 23, 2019, p. 1.
188. *Ibid.*, December 21, 2019, p. 11.
189. *Ibid.*, December 20, 2019, p. 6.
190. *Ei Samay*, February 10, 2020, p. 6.
191. Philipose, Pamela, "A Tool Kit for Hindu Rashtra?", In *This Land Is Mine, I Am Not of This Land* (ed.) Harsh Mander and Navsharan Singh, 2021, Speaking Tiger Books, LLP, New Delhi, p. 100.
192. *The Statesman*, June 21, 2019, p. 1.
193. *The Telegraph*, May 3, 2019, p. 1.
194. *The Statesman*, October 2, 2019, p. 1.
195. *Ibid.*, October 10, 2019, p. 3.
196. *The Times of India*, November 21, 2019, p. 1.
197. *Ibid.*, November 21, 2019, p. 1.

198. *Ibid.*, December 5, 2019, p. 6.
199. *Ibid.*, December 3, 2019, p. 1.
200. *Ibid.*, December 10, 2019, p. 1.
201. *Ibid.*, December 12, 2019, p. 1.
202. *Ibid.*, December 24, 2019, p. 7.
203. *The Statesman*, February 5, 2020, p. 1.
204. *The Telegraph*, December 25, 2019, p. 6.
205. *The Times of India*, December 25, 2019, p. 13.
206. Kundu, Amitava, Mohanan P.C., "Citizenship (Amendment) Act How Do We Move Forward?" *Economic & Political Weekly,* Vol. IV, No. 12, March 21, 2020, pp. 15-16.
207. *The Hindu*, November 19, 2020, p. 1.
208. *Ibid.*, February 3, 2021, p. 9.
209. *Ibid.*, March 4, 2021, p. 9.
210. *Ibid.*, March 15, 2021, p. 10.
211. *Ibid.*, p. 1.
212. *The Hindu*, January 3, 2022, p. 1.
213. *The Hindu*, October 30, 2021, p. 9.
214. Gupta, Saibal, *Dandakaranaya: A Survey of Rehabilitation*, 1999, Calcutta, Bibhasa, p. 3.
215. *The Assam Tribune*, September 17, 1980.
216. Roy, Mohit, "One law, many crisis", *Anandabazar Patrika*, February 10, 2021, p. 4.
217. Biswas, Ashis K., "The Demand and the Forgotten", *Outlook*, November 19, 2001, p. 42.
218. Chowdhury, Prasenjit, "Targeting minorities", *The Statesman*, October 18, 2014, p. 6.
219. Samaddar, Ranabir, *The Marginal Nation*, *Op. Cit.*, p. 200.
220. Ahmed, Imtiaz, *Op. Cit.*, p. 144.
221. "Writ Petition (Civil) No. 125 of 1998, All Indian Lawyers Forum for Civil Liberties AILFCL) & Another Vs. Union of India and Others, Counter Affidavit on behalf of the Respondent No. 3", quoted by Bimal Pramanik in B.B. Kumar (ed.), *Illegal Migration from Bangladesh*, p. 140.
222. "Infiltration of Bangladeshis in India", Unstarred Question No. 2968, Rajya Sabha, August 6, 2014.
223. *The Telegraph*, February 13, 2008, p. 1.
224. https://www.facebook.com/...hindu...bangladesh...hindu.../24959253516...
225. *Ibid.*
226. *The Statesman*, November 23, 2016, p. 9.
227. *Ei Samay*, January 2, 2019, p. 5.
228. Samaddar, Ranabir, *The Marginal Nation*, *Op. Cit.*, p. 202.
229. *Ibid.*, p. 206.
230. Rajya Sabha Debates, 2003, dated December 18, 2003, p. 383.
231. *Ibid.*
232. *Ibid.*, dated February 18, 2003, pp. 383-394.
233. Patnaik, Prabhat, "Matter of principle", *The Telegraph*, August 9, 2019, p. 12.
234. *The Statesman*, February 13, 2020, p. 10.
235. *The Times of India*, February 17, 2021, p. 6.

236. *The Statesman*, November 10, 2019, p. 9.
237. *The Telegraph*, February 20, 2021, p. 2.
238. Patnaik, Prabhat, "Matter of principle", *The Telegraph*, August 9, 2019, p. 12.
239. "Joint Communique Issued at the End of the Visit of the Prime Minister of Bangladesh Sheikh Mujibur Rahman to India, Calcutta, February 8, 1972", in Avtar Singh Bhasin, *India-Bangladesh Relations: Documents 1971-2002,* Vol. I, New Delhi: Geetika Publishers, 2003, p. 2651.
240. Samaddar, Ranabir, *The Marginal Nation, Transformer migration from Bangladesh to West Bengal,* 1999, Sage, pp. 199-200.
241. Das, Pushpita, *Op. Cit.*, p. 106.
242. *Ibid.*, p. 113.

7
The Reality

Infiltration is an emotive issue and it will remain so for ever. The complicated legal process of detecting illegal immigrants has made it even more intractable. To segregate the citizens from the non-citizens by itself is a gigantic task. Vote-bank politics has ensured that a great majority of them had been issued ration cards for obtaining subsidized food rations under the government's public distribution scheme, given identification tokens, their names recorded in the electoral rolls and provided with photo-identity cards by the Election Commission, the final documentary proof of Indian citizenship.

BJP leaders have tried to paint "infiltrators" as enemies of the nation who need to be crushed and "weeded out" like a vermin. They are insisting on setting up NRCs across India in order to identify and then deport "illegal migrants" knowing full well that no such deportation is possible and that India has never broached the issue with Bangladesh, the country of origin of most of such infiltrators. She has not yet been able to sign a new Indo-Nepal Treaty to forestall the easy migration of Nepali-speaking people to this country. The Indo-Myanmar border is still open at many places allowing people easy access to come over to this side of the border and settle down. The bare truth is that most of the migrants—whether they come from across an international border or an inter-state border—are desperately poor people who work for a pittance and contribute much more to the economy than they take away. This is a global phenomenon and India is no exception.

The flow from the other side of the border continues unabated. Deputy Prime Minister L.K. Advani revealed on 7 January, 2003 that 11,500 or so Pakistanis and half a crore or so Bangladeshis had remained in India after the expiry of their visas. They posed a security threat to the country's internal security and needed to be identified and deported.[1] They all came with legal documents and overstayed. If their number is so high, what the total number of illegal infiltrants from Bangladesh would be is anybody's guess.

In West Bengal, the inflow has remained unending as ethnic, linguistic and religious homogeneity has ensured that immigrants, both Muslims and Hindus, have been able to 'lose' themselves in the teeming multitude. The recent decision of the Modi government to confer citizenship on the religious minorities like Hindus, Christians, Buddhists, Jains, Sikhs and Parsis who have come from Afghanistan, Pakistan and Bangladesh on or before 31 December, 2014 has more or less insulated the persons belonging to these communities from the spectre of "deportation." Now the size of infiltrators has been considerably reduced; the targeted infiltrators are only the Muslims.

Bangladeshi migrants who crossed over to other states to avoid deportation have ended up creating a category of stateless persons working and residing in India sans citizenship. After all, the problem of Bangladeshi migrants is not limited to Assam alone any more. It has assumed an all-India character.

The public narrative of clandestine migration clearly endorses the forcible deportation of 'illegal' migrants. To this end, an editorial in *The Hindustan Times* titled 'Send them back' provides the following suggestions: "New Delhi…has to do two things—one, stop the influx and two, send those back who have already come from Bangladesh."[2]

But, there is no guarantee that Bangladesh would take back all these "stateless" persons. Will they be permanent residents in Jails or detention centres the Narendra Modi government at the Centre has decided to build in every State in consultation with the States to house illegal immigrants arrested and jailed under the Foreigners Act for illegally entering India?[3] And what about their number? In a written answer to a Lok Sabha question Minister of State for Home Affairs, Kiran Rijiju informed the House on 21 April, 2015 that it was not possible to state the exact figures of Bangladeshi infiltrators.[4] If the Central Government cannot give even the rudimentary figure of Bangladeshi infiltrators, it casts an aspersion on the intention of the Central Government to tackle this burning issue. And it is better to remember that it devolves on the Central Government to guard India's border by fencing it and manning it in such a manner that none can cross the border without documents. Apparently, the Central Government ignored this primary duty.

It is one thing to detect and deport illegal immigrants instantly when they cross the border. But when people have been allowed or they have managed to be in India for so long, when they have built their lives and became part of local economics and communities, can they be rendered stateless on the basis of a list. This pertinent question has been raised in an editorial in *The Hindu*.[5]

The CAA/NRC process has attracted international attention. As a matter of fact, the BJP government has a trying time fighting CAA/NRC battle abroad. Imran Khan, Prime Minister of Pakistan on 19 August, 2019 sought to draw the attention of the international community towards the mega exercise in Assam, alleging that 40 lakh Muslims could lose their citizenship.[6] He, however, kept mum when in the final list of NRC-rejects, the number of Muslims was a mere 1 lakh or so. The Assistant Secretary of State of the USA in charge of South and Middle Asia, Alice G. Wells has referred to the19 lakh NRC-rejects who are counting days for becoming stateless as questions have been raised about their citizenship.[7]

The UN High Commissioner for Refugees has already issued a statement urging India to ensure that no one ends up stateless. "Any process that could leave large numbers of people without a nationality would be an enormous blow to global efforts to eradicate statelessness", he said on 1 September, 2019 in Geneva.[8]

The external ministry clarified that those left out would not be treated as 'stateless' and would continue to enjoy all the rights as before till they exhausted all the remedies available under the law. He, however, did not say what would happen after that phase was over. Would the state permanently consign a sizeable section of the population to a life of statelessness?

The Indo-Japan annual summit between the Prime Ministers of India and Japan, scheduled for 15-17 December, 2019 at Guwahati, was postponed due to violent protests in Assam.[9] This is a big blow to India's 'Act East' policy. Simultaneously, UN Human Rights Office in a statement issued on13 December, 2019 expressed its concern at "fundamentally discriminatory" Citizenship Act and said that "amended law would appear to undermine the commitment to equality before the law enshrined in India's Constitution...hope it (SC) will consider carefully the compatibility of the law with India's international human rights obligations."[10]

UN Secretary General Antonio Guterres has called for respect for the rights of freedom of opinion and expression as he voiced concern over the violence and alleged use of excessive force by security personnel in India during protest against the CAA.[11]

During his four-day visit to Pakistan in February 2020, the UN chief in an interview to the *Dawn* newspaper said that India's new citizenship law might render a large number of Muslims stateless and that he was personally concerned about the future of minorities in India.[12]

The United States Commission on International Religious Freedom (USCIRF) has urged Washington on 9 December, 2019 to consider sanctions against the Union home minister and "other principal leadership" over the religion specific Bill (CAB). "The CAB is a dangerous turn in the wrong direction; it runs counter to India's rich history of secular pluralism and the Indian Constitution, which guarantees equality before the law regardless of faith", the Commission said.

> "In conjunction with the ongoing National Register of Citizen process in Assam and the nationwide NRC that home minister seeks to propose, the USCIRF fears that the Indian government is creating a religious test for Indian citizenship that would strip citizenship from millions of Muslims", the statement added.

Though New Delhi protested that the statement was inaccurate and unwarranted, the statement opens up another front, apart from Kashmir. It may be recalled that because of this commission the then chief minister Modi was denied a US visa in 2005 following the Gujarat carnage.

In a related statement, the House of Representatives foreign affairs committee tweeted: "Religious pluralism is central to the foundations of both India and the United States and is one of our core shared values. Any religious test for citizenship undermines the most basic democratic tenet."[13]

The Central Government pushed back against US criticism of CAB the next day. "Every nation, including the United States, has the right to enumerate and validate its citizenry and to exercise this prerogative through various policies", the external affairs ministry said in a strongly worded statement, clarifying that the Bill provided "expedited consideration for Indian citizenship to persecuted religious minorities already in India from certain contiguous countries."[14]

The Trump administration on 17 December, 2019 urged Indian authorities to "protect and respect the right of peaceful assembly" while asking protesters to refrain from violence.[15] The next day, US Secretary of State Mike Pompeo said that US cares deeply and always will about protecting minorities and religious rights but "we honour Indian democracy as they have a robust debate inside of India on the issue."[16]

The US Congress' thinktank, Congressional Research Service (CRS), in a report said: "In tandem with a National Register of Citizens (NRC) planned by the federal government, the CAA may affect the status of India's large Muslim minority of roughly 200 million." The report echoes many who have suggested BJP government is trying to consolidate Hindu support through the CAA.[17]

The United States Commission on Inernational Religious Freedom (USCIRF) in a new report released just a few days prior to the visit of President Trump to India (24-25 February, 2020) raised serious concerns about comments from various BJP leaders about the party's intention to create a new, exclusively Hindu country in India. "With the CAA in place, Muslims would primarily bear the punitive consequences of exclusion from the NRC which could include statelessness, deportation, or prolonged detention", said a new fact sheet on the CAA produced by the USCIRF. Official sources responded on 20 February by saying that the PM had made it clear that country would not budge an inch on the CAA.[18] As a matter of fact, Modi had indicated on 16 February, 2020 itself that this government was firm on implementing the CAA and there was no rethink on the Citizenship Act.[19]

Trump, however, refused to be drawn into a discussion on CAA as he wrapped up a high-octane two-day visit (24-25 February) and merely said: "CAA is up to India. I hope it will take the right decision for its people." He also said that he had discussed the issue of religious freedom with Prime Minister Modi during the official talks at Hyderabad House.[20]

The USCIRF has downgraded India in the lowest ranking "countries of particular concern" in its 2020 report. India was categorised as a "Tier 2 country" in last year's listing. This is the first time since 2004 that India has been placed in this category. The Centre reacted sharply to the USCIRF report on 28 April, 2020, terming it "biased and tendentious" and rejected its observations.[21]

Not only the Trump administration but also the Baiden administration is also similarly concerned with the CAA. The Chairman of the Senate Foreign Relations Committee, Senator Bob Menendez had written to the US Secretary of Defence Lloyd Austin on 17 March, 2021 asking him to raise concern about the CAA, amongst others, during his visit to New Delhi on 19-21 March.[22]

The European Parliament also discussed the situation arising out of the CAA and the NRC. Though India succeeded in postponing the 30 January vote on the joint resolution on the CAA to one-month-and-a-half later, a couple of the members like the envoy of the UK were insisting that India should be held to account for bringing in such a discriminatory law.[23]

India came under fire in the House of Commons on 3 March, 2020 with Labour, SNP, Liberal Democrats and Conservative MPs, including India-origin MPs queuing up to criticise the government for the recent violence in Delhi and the CAA and urging the UK government to take stronger action.[24]

Meanwhile, in an unprecedented move, the UN High Commissioner for Human Rights (UNHCHR) has filed an intervention application in the Supreme Court on 2 March in connection with the CAA prompting India to assert that no foreign party has locus standi on issues related to the country's sovereignty. UNHCHR Michelle Bachelet had earlier expressed serious concern at the CAA and riots in North-east Delhi and called on Indian leadership to prevent further violence. In its petition to the Supreme Court, the UN human rights chief said the CAA in its present form has raised important issues with respect to international human rights law and its application to migrants, including refugees.[25]

The United States Commission on International Religious Freedom for the third straight year has recommended to the state department that it designate India as a "country of particular concern", where the government "engages in or tolerates 'particularly severe' violations of religious freedom." The India chapter of the report says: "In 2021, religious freedom conditions in India significantly worsened. During the year, the Indian government escalated its promotion and enforcement of policies—including those promoting a Hindu-nationalist agenda—that negatively affect Muslims, Christians, Sikhs, *Dalits* and other religious minorities. The Indian government repressed critical voices—especially religious minorities and those reporting on and advocating for them—through harassment, investigation, detention, and prosecution under laws such as the Unlawful Acivities Prevention Act (UAPA) and the sedition law." It cites the examples of octogenarian Jesuit priest Stan Swamy who died in custody, the arrest of Kashmiri human rights activist Khurram Parvez, and the difficulties created for NGOs.[26]

Former National Security Adviser Shiv Shankar Menon lamented that the perception of India has changed since the CAA was passed. There has been no international support, except diasporic and extreme right voices in favour of the CAA. Even friends have been taken aback. India has isolated itself through the move and the list of critical votes in the international community was also pretty long now. [27] One of the things for which the Modi government rightly deserves credit is strengthening India's foreign policy heft and outreach. It will be a real tragedy if CAA jeopardises India's foreign policy objectives.

II

The prime minister, who had earlier been inspirational with his clarion call to make development inclusive, has now attempted to give a blatantly divisive spin to the unrest over CAA/NPR/NRC by saying that one could make out the identity of the agitators from their clothes.

The BJP leadership including the PM launched attack on continuing anti-CAA agitation at Jamia Millia, Shaheen Bagh and other places saying they marked an effort to disrupt harmony by protesters who were using the tricolour and Constitution to musk their real intent.[28] The party has adopted a confrontationist stand under the assumption that the politically divisive climate and long-drawn protests would eventually corner the Opposition.

But BJP cut a sorry figure in both the Assembly elections held in December 2019 in Jharkhand and on 8 February, 2020 in Delhi after the CAA was enacted. Its policy of polarising the Delhi electorate backfired while Kejriwal won the elections hands down on the plank of development. The AAP has been particularly careful not to associate with anti-CAA protests for fear of giving the BJP an opportunity to characterize it as a Muslim-appeasing party. The Muslims did not hold a grudge against AAP for its muted stand on the CAA-NRC or Shaheen Bagh protests. They understood the compulsions sympathetically as a tactical necessity in the context of contemporary politics and clearly chose AAP in preference to the Congress. Even Amit Shah admitted that BJP might have suffered because of provocative statements (*goli maaro*, and 'Indo-Pak match') but he was quick to add that there was no way to really know "why people pushed which bottom" inside polling booth.[29] Residents of Shaheen Bagh, the epicentre of the anti-CAA protest, on 11 February, 2020 celebrated the stupendous success of the AAP in the Delhi Assembly elections.[30]

The opposition parties in unison said the BJP's defeat in the elections showed that politics of polarisation and division didn't pay dividends.[31] BJP, however, believed CAA boosted its vote share (from 32.3% in 2015 to 40.1% in 2020) and, therefore, unlikely to back down from its plan of polarising the voters on the plank of the new legislation.[32] The BJP-led NDA's narrow win in the Bihar elections held in October 2020 has somehow saved its stature as an all-India party.

There is already a sign of restlessness and desperation among the BJP leaders and workers in the states against the policy of the party. For instance, as many as twelve Assam BJP legislators met Assam CM on 19 December, 2020 and asked him to allay fears of the people and tell them how the state government planned to protect their language and culture. Sootea MLA Padma Hazarika, who led the group, said that houses of many party leaders, workers and MLAs including his, had been attacked. They had been abused and many workers could not come out of their houses. There was "mistrust in BJP and its members" he said, adding that anger against BJP MLAs had aggravated due to certain statements made by some members. "People in our respective constituencies are demanding our resignations and I want to assure them that if our resignations can resolve the problem then we are prepared to resign", Hazarika said.[33]

In West Bengal, Lipika Roy, South Dinajpur Zilla Parishad president joined the TMC on 22 December, 2019 in protest against the CAA. On that very day Sant Bahadur Gurung of Kalimpong also left the BJP to join the TMC.[34] Three BJP Gram Panchayat Pradhans of South Dinajpur district joined the TMC on 13 January but one of them returned to the BJP fold later.[35] In Madhya Pradesh, as many as 80 Muslim leaders of the BJP resigned on 24 January from the primary membership of the party in protest over the CAA calling it a 'divisive' measure.[36]

Darjeeling BJP MLA Neeraj Zimba, who was earlier in the GNLF but joined the BJP during last year's assembly bye-poll, has mocked the party's Bengal chief Dilip Ghosh with a cartoon that shows him with big red lips and an accompanying comments "The Lip is Dilip." The cartoon and the comments sums up Gorkha anger against Ghosh over his recent remarks on the community.[37] Dilip Ghosh had stated in Siliguri on 24 January, 2020 that people who have come from Nepal and settled in India are Indians, and that Gorkhas need not fear the CAA, NPR and the NRC.[38]

Not only BJP leaders and workers are venting their opposition to party policy, its allies are also demanding re-appraisal of NDA policies. Two BJP allies, the Shiromoni Akali Dal (SAD) and Ram Vilas Paswan's Lok Janashakti Party (LJP) on 20 January, 2020 strongly opposed the government's move to ride roughshod over objections and push the contentious CAA-NRC combination.

The Akali Dal declared that it had decided not to contest the upcoming Delhi Assembly elections in alliance with the BJP to protest against government's firmness about not including Muslims in the CAA. It also declared that it was firmly against forcing citizens to stand in queues to prove their citizenship under the proposed NRC. "During our meeting with the BJP, we were asked to reconsider our stand on the CAA, but we declined to do so. The Shiromoni Akali Dal is of the firm stand that Muslims cannot be left out of the CAA", Akali Dal MLA Maninder Singh Sirsa told reporters in Delhi.[39] Giani Harpreet Singh, chief priest of the highest Sikh temporal seat Akal Takht had extended support to Muslim groups which have been protesting against the CAA and the NRC saying Sikhs had always stood by the oppressed and would continue to do so.[40]

Union minister Paswan expressed displeasure at the way the CAA, the abrogation of key provisions of Article 370 and the Ram temple verdict had come in quick succession. On the NRC, Paswan said it was not going to be implemented. He added that it was beyond the power of any political party to take away the citizenship of people belonging to any religion.[41]

It may be recalled that Sikhs as well as *Dalits*, the core support bases of the SAD and the LJP, have joined the protests against the CAA-NRC in large numbers.

Paswan had said earlier on 3 January that "be it *Dalits*, tribals, backwards, minorities of upper castes, they are all original citizens of the country. Citizenship is their birthright. No government can snatch it away. No Indian citizen will be bothered unnecessarily."[42]

BJP's hill ally, the Gorkha National Liberation Front, expressed its disapproval of the NRC and the CAA. The party said that in their present forms, both would affect the Gorkha community.[43]

Assam Chief Minister Sarbananda Sonowal gave a fresh twist to the debate over the contentious CAA. He tweeted saying: "As a son of Assam, I will never settle foreigners in my state. This Sarbananda Sonowal will never allow this..."[44]

The Congress told home minister Amit Shah on 3 January, 2020 that NDA constituents and chief ministers of the ruling BJP were not accepting the CAA but Prime Minister and he continued to abuse the Opposition. Congress's chief spokesperson Randeep Surjewala even dared the PM to dismiss his own chief minister for openly opposing the CAA and declare him an "anti-national" for doing so.[45] Surjewala's "anti-national" jibe is a gruesome reminder to the BJP's endeavour to paint the critiques of the CAA/NRC/NRP combo with the "anti-national" brush, thus negating the constitutional prerogative of organising peaceful protests.

But peaceful protests are not to be construed as an "anti-national" act. The Aurangabad Bench of the Bombay High Court has made it clear that people wanting to agitate in a peaceful way "cannot be called as traitors, anti-nationals only because they want to oppose one law." "It can be said that it is unfortunate but the people are required to agitate against their own government now but only on that ground the agitation cannot be suppressed", a Bench consisting of Justices T.V. Nalawade and M.G. Sewlikar said.[46]

Justice Deepk Gupta of the Supreme Court while delivering a lecture on "Democracy and Dissent" organised by the Supreme Court Bar Association, said that majoratianism is anti-thesis to democracy and criticism of the executive, judiciary, bureaucracy or the armed forces cannot be termed "anti-national" or is against the country. "In case we stifle criticism of the institutions whether it be the legislature, the executive or judiciary or other bodies of the state, we shall become a police state instead of a democracy. Dissent is essential to a democracy. If a country has to grow in a holistic manner where not only the economic rights but also the civil rights of the citizen are to be protected; dissent and disagreement have to be permitted, and in fact should be encouraged. It is only if there is discussion, disagreement and dialogue that we can arrive at better ways to run the country", he said. "The right to dissent, disagree and have another point of view is not only a constitutional right but also a part of human rights and no one should be deprived of that right in a democracy", he added.[47]

The agitators against the CAA/NRC/NPR all over India largely remained peaceful unless provoked by the police. For instance, tens of thousands of people hit the streets in Kolkata on 18 December, 2019 to protest the CAA and the NRC. The processions came like waves through lanes and thoroughfares and meetings were held in the heart of the city. Many of the participants never walked in a protest march before. And all without much of a preparation and without any party flag.[48]

Nearly one lakh people marched through the streets of Bhiwandi, hub of the power loom industry in Thane and is considered communally sensitive, on 20 December, 2019 and took part in a protest march against the CAA and the proposed NRC. The protest march passed off peacefully, ending after a memorandum was submitted to the local authorities. Residents of Bhiwandi on 25 December felicitated the deputy commissioner of police Rajkumr Shinde in the traditional Maharashtrian way for the force's deft handling of the huge protest march.[49]

Around 1 lakh people from different faiths crammed into the Khuddus Saheb Idgah grounds in Bengaluru on 23 December, 2019 while another two lakh thronged the streets and lanes outside, all pledging not to furnish any documents if the NRC was updated nationwide and the CAA enforced.[50]

On 1 January, 2020 in Kochi, the commercial capital of Kerala, at the call of Muslim organisations, supported by people of other faiths and members of the civil society, around 5 lakh people participated in one of the biggest rallies in the country since the citizenship-related protests began. The marchers carrying placards with pictures of Mahatma Gandhi, B.R. Ambedkar and Maulana Abdul Kalam Azad assembled in a stadium from 1 pm before they began their long march to Marine Drive about 5 km away. The sweep and breadth of the crowd and the peaceful conduct prompted a senior lawyer of the Supreme Court to suggest that such non-violent political processes were the best alternative under the circumstances instead of every politician rushing to the court to challenge the changes to the citizenship law.[51]

One lakh protesters, many carrying the Tricolour, marched peacefully in Hyderabad on 4 January, 2020 chanting slogans against the CAA. The protest, dubbed as the "million march", was organised by an umbrella group of Muslim and civil society organisations.[52] Samajwadi Vichar Yatra started from New Delhi on 30 January and culminated in Hyderabad on 23 March after travelling through more than 13 States. The members of the Yatra created awareness against CAA, NPR and NRC. Apart from 'Smajwadi Samagam', several other organisations such as Rashtra Seva Dal, National Coordination of Public Movement (NAPM), Hind Mazdoor Sabha, Ham Bharat Ke Log, Yusuf Meher Ali Centre, Peoples' Association in Grassroots Action and Movement Federation were supporters of the Yatra.[53]

And not to forget the peaceful sit-in demonstration by Muslim women with baby in their arms blocking Road 13A that connects Delhi to Noida at Shaheen Bagh in Delhi against the CAA-NRC-NPR combo which crossed the 60-day mark on 12 February, 2020. Due to the efforts of the Supreme Court-appointed mediators—Sanjay Hegde and Sadhana Ramachandran—the protestors opened Kalindi Kunj Road which leads to Noida Sector 37 at around 5 pm on 22 February, 2020.[54]

The humble demonstration which started against the Delhi Police beating Jamia Millia Islamia university students on 13 December, 2019 at Shaheen Bagh, turned it, following the brutal police crackdown in Jamia on the evening of 15 December, as the epicentre of nationwide opposition to the CAA-NPR-NRC combo.

The 40-foot iron and mesh map of India inscribed with the words *Hum Bharat ke log CAA-NPR-NCR nahin maante* (We, the people of India, reject the CAA-NPR-NCR), overlooked the site. It gave the strength and the desire to the participants to stand firmly and unitedly for a cause. As an observer put it, it was a reminder to people's humble-yet stunning response to state's excessive urge to define and dominate.[55]

Most of the women of Shaheen Bagh who were part of the sit-in were protesting for the first time in their lives. However, as of now, it was a mix of various people—3women of all ages, all faiths, all professions—who had decided to come together to register their protest against a discriminatory law, thus making it a truly people's protest movement.

Shaheen Baghs were replicated at Park Circus in Kolkata, Rakhial in Ahmedabad, Sabjibagh in Patna, YMCA Maidan Park in Mumbai, Nazrulbagh in Asansole[56], and in Gaya, Kanpur, Allahabad, Aligarh, Bengaluru, and Deoband. In Delhi itself, peaceful sit-ins at Khureji, Seelampur, Turkman Gate, Kardam Puri, Mustafabad, and Inderlok had registered their presence.[57]

When a group of women braved the Delhi winter to protest against CAA-NPR-NRC, they'd have hardly thought it'd prompt so many others across the country to follow their lead. But it did happen without any organisational help or political backing. As a columnist says: "By appropriating the flag, the map and the Constitution, the protesters at Shaheen Bagh have made the case for secular republic peopled by equal citizens in the broadest way possible. They have returned to the liberals and progressives the totems of the republic sharpened by tools with which to build a broader coalition...Shaheen Bagh has demonstrated that it is still possible to galvanise the people on a pan Indian scale around a republican principle."[58]

For the first time, we saw the movement being led and represented by Muslim women. Muslim women as anti-CAA activists also raised a more universal concern that the protcsts were not just about citizenship for Muslims, but about saving democracy and the Constitution. Protests by Muslim women, and more importantly elderly women, made a perceptible difference in the way the movement was received. It carried a different moral weight.

Elsewhere, the agitators devised novel methods to register their protests. For instance, in Kolkata, they painted streets with anti-CAA messages.[59] Artists from Bengal organised an art exhibition near Esplanade metro station as a silent protest against CAA and NRC.[60] In Gujarat, people voiced their protests against the CAA and the NRC by flying kites with messages like "India against CAA", "No NPR, No NRC", on the occasion of Uttarayan Festival on 14 January.[61] Activists of the Chutia Students' Union gave the community feast 'Uruka', held on the eve of the 'Bhogali Bihu' festival in Assam, a miss to stage a 10-hour hunger strike at Titabor in Jorhat district from 5 am on14 January, 2020 against the CAA.[62] The youth wing of the Congress has started a National Register of Unemployed ((NRU) to counter BJP's NRC, NPR.[63] In an interesting way of protest against the CAA, the Imam of Shahi Maszid at Public Gardens of Hyderabad distributed the Tricolour among those attending Friday prayers and urged them to hoist the National Flag at the rooftops of their residences and places of business to send out the message that they, too, were patriotic citizens of the country.[64]

III

Events that unfolded during the post-CAA/NPR/NRC days and the symbols that stood out articulated not just a deep-rooted insecurity and sense of letdown but also the thin line on which the minority community is being compelled to work in contemporary India. The voiding of Article 370, the ban on triple talaq and the Ayodhya verdict were seen as decisions that pushed Muslims to the fringes. The coupling of the CAA with the NRC stoked fears among them. Saba Naqvi, the renowned journalist, thinks that the "CAB (CAA) in conjunction with the NRC actually weaponises the state and law enforcement agencies against Muslims. It continues the process of viciously encircling Muslims, be it in Kashmir, or through cow politics and consequent lynchings or through diminished representation in Parliament and assemblies, or through multiple hysterical public debates drawn from stoking the historical Hindu-Muslim fault line. It does appear to India's 200 million Muslims that isolating, hating and disenfranchising the community is not a mere consequence of a new kind of nationalism, but its principal purpose."[65]

Though the Muslims are the natural target of the BJP for the implementation of the NRC, the members of the Muslim community are not willing to start a separate movement over the NRC issue. The community is aware that any overt show of protest would set the stage for polarisation which would eventually help parties like the BJP in the elections. They see it as a ploy to polarize the people on religious line. Rather they would like to be a part of the movement being organised by the political parties.

From Kolkata to Kozhikode, community leaders repeatedly appealed for peace and underscored the need to keep protests against the religion-specific legislation non-violent, inclusive and secular. The community elders appealed to people from all walks of life and faiths to spearhead the movement. Several speakers reiterated their faith in the Constitution and requested other communities to join the protests. The point they were trying to hammer home, the Muslims are not fighting for themselves but to preserve the idea of India. Najeeb Kanthapuram, Vice-president of the IUML Youth League in Kerala said: "We want all sections of people who are concerned about the legislation to join us to send a combined message of unity and harmony."[66]

Chants of '*Hindustan Zindabad*' were heard at almost all the venues in Kolkata, Delhi and elsewhere. Some instances of violence and vandalism—in Murshidabad, Hooghly and Uluberia in Howrah of West Bengal did take place which had the potential to take a communal colour. But the timely action of the administration and the cooperation of the community leaders did stave off such a catastrophe. The BJP was, however, quick to blame the 'infiltrators', the segment party wants to uproot through the process of NRC backed by legislation like the CAA, for the instances of violence.

The Muslims of Prime Minister Narendra Modi and Home Minister Amit Shah's home state of Gujarat are not concerned about the CAA, NPR or the NRC, not because they have all the necessary documents but because they have already been made second-class citizens. The much-touted "Gujarat development model" has bypassed them. Today they live segregated, ghettoised lives, marginalised by the state, all political parties and even other Gujaratis. The two and a half decades of BJP rule has been marked by 'demonising' and 'othering', topped off by a state-sponsored programme that deprived Muslims of family members, homes, jobs, businesses, a sense of security and even the hope of a brighter future, says Sajeda Momin in an article in *The Telegraph.*[67]

At every twist and turn, the Muslim community in India is now running into a paradox. Wearing skullcaps never drew attention in the country earlier, but a sighting of rows of such headgear at a protest rally nowadays inspires devious interpretations. "Our community feels dejected with the passage of the Bill at a time they are already worried about the possible repercussions of a rollout of an NRC exercise in Bengal. But it is also true that the protest will have legitimacy if they keep it non-violent and secular", said Imtiaz Mollah, the convenor of the Joint Forum Against NRC, a rights group in Bengal.

IUML Kerala secretary M.C.Mayin Haji told *The Telegraph:* "The state has always been an example of a syncretic culture with the only difference between Hindus and Muslims being that one community goes to temples and the other goes to mosques. If the CAB and the NRC are implemented, such brotherhood will disappear forever, and we won't allow that."[68]

However, realising that NRC might be enforced in West Bengal at the first opportunity, the All India Imam-Muzziman and Social Welfare Organisation has started educating the people to keep ready the required documents needed to prove one's citizenship. They are distributing leaflets and propagating through mike, etc.[69]

At the instance of All Bengal Imam-Muzziman Council, the Nagarik Sangram Suraksha Manch was formed at a convention held on 3 October, 2019 under the chairmanship of Mamatabala Thakur. A faction of the Matuas, Minority Yuba Federation, All India Sunnatul Samity, Forum for Bengali Refuges, some Dalit and Adibasi organisations have joined this Manch. The Manch will work to ensure that people are not deprived of their citizenship in the name of the NRC. [70]

Apart from the Muslims, social activists and lawyers fear that women, particularly from the Muslim and tribal communities, will be worst hit if the NRC is carried out since many of them dropped out of school or married young and don't have proper documents. Moreover, Muslims have a second name on the basis of gender, like Khatun or Begum. After marriage, the second name is often changed to show the marital status. Hence, names on documents end up not matching. Concern about trouble that women may face has prompted many activists and lawyers to volunteer help and allay fears and insecurity that may have gripped them from time to time.[71]

In Assam, women outnumbered men in the category of 'doubtful voters'. These included the cases that were referred to the Foreigners' Tribunals and those who have been declared illegal migrants already because they failed to produce the relevant legacy documents and establish their patrilineal links. Legal experts and rights' groups feel women across the country will find themselves facing the same disadvantages if they have to prove they are the citizens of the country. Legal experts also pointed out that it may not be restricted only to the Muslim community.

The process followed by the NRC is exclusionary and discriminatory towards women, particularly from the marginalised sections. "Majority women in rural areas get married before the age of 18. Their names are linked with those of their husbands' on the electoral rolls when they became eligible to vote. Many women are not educated beyond primary school. So they don't have their school leaving certificates. Moreover, women hardly have a share in family property making it impossible for them to establish their patrilineal links", said Oliullah Laskar, a Gauhati High Court advocate.

In an order, the Gauhati High Court rejected the petition of Jabeda Begum—who was declared a foreigner by a tribunal though she had submitted land revenue payment receipts, PAN and bank accounts—because she "failed to prove her links with her projected parents and projected brother." "The already disadvantaged women are being rendered stateless through a completely arbitrary process", said Mustafa Khaddam Hussain, another advocate from Gauhati High Court. If the Assam exercise is any indication, there will be huge social crisis, if women become stateless—even if they are to go through the arbitrary process.[72] Jabeda Begum, rejected despite submitting 15 documents, is a symbol of widespread despair in Assam. Fear of statelessness haunts thousands rejected by NRC.[73]

However, the anti-CAA-NPR-NRC protests by women, especially Muslim women, across the country have revealed how they are not only fighting to save the Constitution, they are also grappling with a social battle within the community. It is the beginning of a new era. Many men are discovering the latent talent of their women during these protests as many of the protesters themselves never thought they could hold the stage so convincingly. Such was the impact of the polite rejection of the advice of the Vice-Chancellor of Darul Uloom Deoband of calling off the protests that the seminary had to issue a clarification within 24 hours that it was not against the protest.

Similarly, in Aligarh's Shahjamal area hundreds of *burqa*-clad women, mostly from poor and lower-middle class families are sitting on protest since the last week of January 2020. Their concern is that they might not have papers to pass the NRC test. The Mufti was under so much pressure of the administration that he did not stand with them after a couple of days. The district authorities in these cities are also feeling the heat because they don't know how to engage with the women in *burqa*. Involving the clergy in negotiating with women was not as effective as it was normally with men.[74]

Jamiat Ulema-e-Hind secretary Maulana Mahmood Madani extended full support to the protesting women and praised them for their "great courage" to stand up against the "black Act." [75]

Prof. Ayesha Munita, professor of English in Aligarh Muslim University, who specialises in gender studies, feels the protests are "life-changing" and "empowering" for many Muslim women, particularly from weaker sections. "They have come out on their own. Once the protest ends, women will be easily relegated to four walls. They know their voices are being heard by the country and they are leading a movement", she said.[76]

The Shaheen Bagh protest has shown that women, especially Muslim women, can also be the nucleus of a movement. It has become the inspiration for a large number of similar peaceful and determined protests by groups of women—both Muslims and non-Muslims—across India, from metropolis to obscure cities and towns.

A columnist has pointed out that there are three distinct takeaways from the Shaheen Bagh phenomenon. First, the Muslims as a community have emerged from a state of withdrawal and firmly demanded their rights as citizens of India, without seeking any crunches of political support. Second, Muslim women have liberated themselves from the taboos that kept them confined to their homes in large parts of India. Veiled women have been seen able to look their interlocutor in the eye and firmly claim that neither "*mard*" nor "*maulvi*" would stand in the way of their demanding a just future. Whatever the eventual political outcome of their demands, the liberation of the spirit of the community, and its women in particular, will be here to stay. Third, the women of Shaheen Bagh have reclaimed for the nation what others had ceded to an aggressive nationalism of violence, hatred and divisiveness—our flag and our national anthem. Besides, the nation has been reminded that the ultimate guarantor of our freedom is the Constitution of India.[77]

In India, points out Aditi Singh and Nergish Sunawala, mothers have consistently and tirelessly been a driving force in shaping India's image as a bastion of non-violent, peaceful protests. From the Chipko Andolan, India's most popular forest conservation movement, to the struggle for striking down Article 377, mothers have been at the forefront. During Chipko, women were steadfast in their desire to protect their families from the perils of deforestation, while men wavered in the face of external pressure. In Mahul, a neighbourhood dubbed Mumbai's 'gas chamber', mothers were vociferous, posting petitions, meeting with political leaders, and holding 'dharnas'. Shaheen Bagh—the longest sit-in protest against the CAA and NRC—and the hundreds of similar movements it has inspired hold a candle to the power that mother-driven movements have always had.[78] In other countries also women led political and social movements. For instance, in a country whose strongman President Alexander Lukashenko has openly scoffed at women as too weak for politics and told them that their place was in the kitchen, Belarusian women became the face and driving force of a movement aimed at toppling a leader known as "Europe's last dictator."[79]

Harsh Mander lists the following success of the battle against the CAA-NRC-NPR. Its paramount success was that it was the first national movement for Hindu-Muslim unity after Mahama Gandhi was taken away from us by an assassin's bullet in 1948. Indeed it was a movement for the unity of people of various religious and caste identities. A second success of the movement has been the repoliticization of students in universities across India. In this movement, students were teaching their elders not to hate, showing the way to a more caring and equal country. A third accomplishment was the reassurance to India's Muslim people. In the protests led by Muslim women, the mood was electrically festive. Less protests, these were more celebrations of the reassurance that India was still equally their country, that we all stand together. A fourth achievement was the reclaiming of the idea of nationalism by those Indians who unite rather than divide. Those who truly love their country would not want it to be divided by hate, fear and violence. A fifth victory was in making the Constitution the soul of the people's movement. What could be more apt than "We, the people of India" coming together to defend the Constitution at a time when it was most threatened. The final triumph of the movement was that it compelled the reluctant, morally ambiguous non-BJP parties to take a public stand at last to defend the Consitution, which they were willing to betray for petty electoral considerations. It also clearly rattled the Union government, leading to the lie that the NRIC had not been its agenda.[80]

IV

The worst thing that could have happened befell on North-east Delhi when a clash between the pro-and anti-CAA protesters turned into communal riots taking a toll of 53 lives (up to 5 March, 2020). A 500-strong group dominated by women staged a sit-in on 22 February night on the stretch below Jafrabad Metro Station in north-east Delhi demanding a rollback of the contentious CAA. On 23 February, a group of pro-CAA protesters reached the Maujpur-Babarpur Metro Station, less than a kilometre away. They were demanding that police remove the barricades. They were led by former BJP MLA Kapil Mishra who had given a call in a Tweetter for people to gather near the Maujpur traffic signal in support of the CAA. A video clip doing the rounds showed the BJP leader Kapil Mishra with a DCP by his side issuing an ultimatum to Delhi police on 23 February to get Jafrabad anti-CAA sit-in cleared in three days. Later in the afternoon around 3.30 pm, clashes broke out between the pro- and anti-CAA groups near Jafrabad.

On 24 February, 2020 violent clashes broke out between the pro- and anti-CAA groups of people in various areas such as Jafrabad, Maujpur, Chandbagh, Khureji Khas and Bhajanpura. The violent mobs torched houses, shops and vehicles and indulged in heavy stone-pelting at each other.[81] The riot-affected areas fell on the other side of the Yamuna, with lower middle class Muslims and migrants forming the majority of the population.[82]

Both Hindus and Muslims blamed police inaction for the escalation on 24 February. Some openly accused the police of siding with the pro-CAA groups. Residents said on 24 February night that a crowd, in the presence of the police, was raiding the area and torching shops. Zaharul Islam Khan, chairman of the Delhi Minorities Commission, tweeted at 11.56 pm on 24 February: "Several parts of Delhi especially north-east Delhi, are burning. Armed goons are attacking Muslim localities, markets, shops, mosques..." (Delhi Police Special Cell on 2 May registered an FIR against him on charges of sedition for his tweet for which he later apologised.[83]) For several hours, Reuters news agency witnesses saw the outnumbered policemen mostly stand beside those backing the citizenship law and do little to quell the violence. The police also stood by as a mob vandalised a store with Muslim name, pulling out vehicles and setting them alight. Saffron flags were seen hoisted on the houses and shops belonging to the majority community in Seelampur, Maujpur and Jafrabad areas. This attempt was being seen as an effort to mark the houses and shield them from pro-CAA groups during rioting. Civil rights groups said that a large number of Bajrang Dal activists had entered Delhi from Loni in Haryana and were involved in the violence. In the adjoining Noor-e-Ilahi locality, several Muslim families fled their homes in panic amid reports of police entering Muslim homes with rioters. Delhi police later in the day appealed to the people to maintain peace and not to believe in rumours in the wake of violence.[84] The violence continued on 25 February as well. Smoke was seen going up in some places, including in the epicentre of the trouble Maujpur, which were littered with stones, bricks and burnt tyres, testimony to the spiralling violence and bloodshed. The death toll in the violence climbed to 13—12 civilians and Delhi police head constable Ratan Lal. Four of them including the police personnel had died the previous day.

It was evident early on 25 February that the riot had taken on a communal taint and the violence was only getting worse with reports of night-long incidents of vandalism, arson and stone-pelting. The area remained in the grip of violence all through 25 February with even media persons being attacked for doing their job. One journalist was shot in Maujpur and many others were assaulted. A statement by the Press Club of India and Indian Women's Press Corps said the attackers actively sought to prevent videography or photography that might have led to them being identified. Police were either absent or did not come to help. Shockingly, the mobs were checking the religious credentials of journalists. Incidents of stone-pelting and arson were reported from Jafrabad, Babarpur, Maujpur, Bhjanpura, Kabir Nagar, Chand Bagh, Gokulpuri, Karawal Nagar, Khajuri Khas and Kurdampuri. Rioting spread to new areas like Gorakh Park, Brahmpuri and Chajjupur. Many places witnessed throwing of an acid-like substance and hot water on people and security forces. Five people including four security personnel with acid burns were admitted in Lok Nayak Hospital.

Gopal Rai, AAP Minister told *The Week* that "we were in touch with the lieutenant governor and the police. It is another matter that the police commissioner did not attend my calls even once since the violence started. We went to the lieutenant governor's house on Monday night (24 February), and we were assured that additional police force would be brought in. But that did not happen. Yesterday (Tuesday, 25 February), some additional force was deployed, and curfew was imposed in some areas. However, the violence had not stopped. The rioters have only shifted their place of action. The whole of last night (25 February), arson and firing have taken place."[85]

Heavy deployment of Delhi police personnel including Rapid Action Force and para-military forces like CRPF was visible in the riot-hit areas amidst announcements that shoot-at-sight orders had been issued (and curfew imposed though there was no official confirmation of the same. (G.Kishan Reddy, minister of state for home affairs, however, said that no shoot-at-sight orders were issued.[86]) Some 35 companies of CRPF were deployed. In the Maujpur-Jafrabad area, there was random shooting from rooftops for the first time, making it quite risky to move through the streets. At least 20 people with gunshot wounds were admitted in hospitals. In all, over 200 people, including rioters and bystanders, have been injured and over 100 vehicles damaged. The injured included 48 police personnel including the deputy commissioner of police Shahdara, Amit Sharma, and three firemen. Police fired tear gas shells and also resorted to lathi charge to disperse the violent crowd of protesters. Security personnel conducted flag marches to disperse the mobs and restore law and order.

Five stations on Delhi Metro's Pink Line were closed for the second consecutive day on 25 February. Schools were shut with examinations being postponed, and fearful residents stayed indoors as the area smouldered with tension. Prohibitory orders, banning the assembly of more than four persons, were imposed on 25 February and would continue to be in force till 24 March.[87]

Normalcy gradually restored in the beleaguered city from 26 February. The death toll, however, increased to 27 on 26 February, 38 on 27 February, 42 on 28 February, 46 on 1 March and 53 on 5 March. The dead body of IB constable Ankit Sharma, a resident of Chandbagh, was found in a drain in Chandbagh, a riot ravaged area in north-east Delhi, on 26 February. Delhi police said on 1 March that it had registered 254 FIRs including 41 cases under the Arms Act and arrested or detained 903 persons in connection with the violence so far.[88] According to a police investigation report, Ankit Sharma was killed when he was trying to pacify the crowd on both sides near the suspended AAP Councillor Tahir Husain's house.[89]

Union home minister Amit Shah held a meeting on 25 February with Delhi Lieutenant Governor Anil Baijal, Chief Minister Arvind Kejriwal, Commissioner of Police Amulya Patnaik, Congress leader Subash Chopra, BJP's Manoj Tewari and Ranvir Bidhuri to discuss the present situation in the national capital. Union Home Secretary Ajay Bhalla, and Director of Intelligence Bureau Arvind Kumar were also present. The move came after the home minister had reviewed the law and order situation in the national capital the previous night as violence rocked north-east Delhi. Shah suggested the local peace committees comprising eminent citizens and elected representatives be reactivated and their meetings held to diffuse the tension, quell rumours and ensure coordination with the Delhi police. Shah advised the leaders of political parties in Delhi to exercise restraint and refrain from making any provocative speeches. He suggested that all should rise above politics to jointly work towards restoring peace and order. He said professional assessment was that the violent protests were spontaneous. Minister of State for Home G. Kishan Reddy, however, held the view that the violence in parts of Delhi on 24 February when US President Donald Trump was visiting India "is a conspiracy to defame India."[90]

Throughout the campaign for the assembly elections in Delhi, Arvind Kejriwal and AAP had steered clear of the debate on the CAA. Asked about the protests against the controversial legislation, the trite response was that the police was under Union Home Minister Amit Shah's command. Liberal-minded people had criticised Kejriwal for not taking a clear stand on the CAA issue. Ironically, barely a week after Kejriwal was re-elected as Delhi chief minister, his government found itself in a sticky situation as simmering tensions boiled over and fuelled violent clashes between the pro- and anti-CAA camps. AAP leaders were at pains to explain their proactive steps, even as they attacked Shah and the Union government for failing to take adequate measures to quell the riots. AAP's national spokesman, Raghav Chadha gave out that the Delhi riots were engineered by outsiders who had crossed into the city from the border areas.[91]

Kejriwal himself undertook a series of measures—meeting MLAs of all parties and officials from affected areas, instructing district magistrates to take out peace marches, touring riot-affected areas, asking people to refrain from violence and telling them that all issues could be dealt with through dialogue and meeting Shah and asking him to increase police presence in violence-hit areas. He made a statement appealing for peace.[92] He finally asked Union home minister on 26 February morning to call in the Army to control the situation in the city.[93] He discussed Delhi violence with Prime Minister Modi for the first time only on 3 March, 2020.[94]

Conceding the fact that the Delhi violence cannot be tackled by administrative means alone, which in any case were out of bounds of the Delhi government, the role of the Delhi government and its political leadership during the ongoing crisis left much to be desired. As an editorial in the *Economic & Political Weekly* points out "it necessitates a political response that entails reaching out to the affected areas and using one's popular legitimacy to build pressure on the Central Government to act swiftly. The Aam Aadmi Party's (AAP) passivity points towards the limits of pragmatism in countering the ideological challenge posed by the ruling party."[95]

Prafulla Sharma of *The Week* attributed the violence in the capital "to several slippages, including slow response from political parties, no curb on provocative speeches and a largely ineffective Delhi police."[96]

The CM of West Bengal said on 25 February she was deeply disturbed over the continuing violence in Delhi and appealed to all to restore peace.[97] Later she alleged the communal violence in Delhi was "state-sponsored genocide" and the BJP was trying to replicate the "Gujarat model of riots" across the country.[98] Trinamool Congress hit the streets on 4 March to protest against the Delhi carnage. It also set up a fund to aid victims of "genocide" across the country.[99] Bengali film actors took to Twitter on 26 and 27 February, 2020 to condemn the communal clashes in Delhi and called for peace and amity at this critical hour.[100]

Jamiat Ulama-i-Hind president Maulana Arshad Madani alleged that the Delhi violence was a well-planned conspiracy to derail the peaceful movement against the CAA, while AIMIM chief Asaduddin Owaisi said that clashes in the national capital Delhi brought back memories of the 2002 Gujarat riots. Shiv Sena said that the Delhi violence which was akin to a "horror film depicting the grim reality of the 1984 anti-Sikh riots" brought disrepute to the national capital like never before while US president Donald Trump was in India.[101]

The Jafrabad protesters called off the sit-in around 7.30 p.m. of 25 February as the surrounding areas went up in flames. One of the protesters said they decided to vacate the site after appeals from local leaders, police, clerics and activists and moved to a site in Seelampur, 1 km away.[102]

National Security Adviser, Ajiit Doval, who was later given charge to quell disturbances and restore peace in the riot-hit north-east Delhi, visited the affected areas late on the night of 25 February and again on 26 February afternoon when he met a cross section of people and assured them of full protection and restoration of peace in the areas before long.[103]

The BJP's two top leaders, Narendra Modi and Amit Shah, maintained public silence over the spiralling Delhi violence. Prime Minister Modi, however, broke his silence after three days of uncontrolled violence and appealed for "peace and brotherhood." In a tweet at 1.52 pm on 26 February he said: "Had an extensive review on the situation prevailing in various parts of Delhi. Police and other agencies are working on the ground to ensure peace and normalcy. Peace and harmony are central to our ethos. I appeal to my brothers and sisters of Delhi to maintain peace and brotherhood at all times."

About half an hour earlier of this appeal, around 1 pm, Sonia Gandhi after holding an emergency meeting of the Congress Working Committee, had addressed one of those rare press conferences to assert that what had happened in Delhi was a "colossal failure of duty" for which the "entire responsibility" rested with the Centre and particularly the home minister and called for his immediate resignation.[104]

The BJP leadership fielded Information and Broadcasting minister Prakash Javadekar and law minister Ravi Shankar Prasad to launch a political attack on the Congress chief, but the custodian of Delhi's security continued to maintain public silence.[105] One wonders whether such silence itself was a continuing presence by other means.

A delegation led by Congress chief Sonia Gandhi called on the President on 27 February submitted a memorandum to him urging him to sack Amit Shah. The delegation also asked the President to remind the Modi government of its "rajdharma."[106] Leaders of Left and other Opposition parties, who could not meet the President because of his engagements,, urged him on 28 February to direct the Lt. Governor of Delhi to ensure speedy recovery of normality in the riot-affected parts of the city.[107]

In the meantime, ally LJP slammed BJP netas and asked the top BJP leadership to take immediate action against the leaders like Kapil Mishra, Anurag Thakur, Parvesh Verma and Giriraj Singh for their hate speeches and statements.[108] The BJP, however, said on 28 February that it disapproved of the allegedly inflammatory statements by Kapil Mishra and other party functionaries.[109] The Election Commission on 29 January, 2020 ordered the removal of BJP leaders Anurag Thakur and Parvesh Verma from the BJP's list of star campaigners for Delhi polls over their controversial remarks.[110] Jamia Millia Islamia alumni association president Shifa-Ur-Rehman, arrested under the UAPA, raised the awkward question before the Additional Sessions Judge Abhishek Rawat on 24 August, 2021 why no FIR was lodged against Union Minister Anurag Thakur, BJP leader Kapil Mishra and others for allegedly instigating the riots.[111]

It is perhaps no coincidence that the violence in Delhi has largely been concentrated in areas that the BJP managed to win in the recent Assembly elections on the back of a vicious and polarising campaign by Union home minister Amit Shah. Five of the eight seats the BJP won in the 70-member Assembly, fall in the north-east Delhi where rioting took place. "The communal polarisation in these areas had worsened in the run-up to the election as several BJP leaders had delivered hate speeches. The seeds of hatred were sown then and it was waiting to erupt. The provocative statements by BJP leader Kapil Mishra on Sunday (23 February) only stirred the communal pot already simmering for nearly a month", a retired Delhi Police Commissioner told *The Telegraph*.[112]

There were allegations of inaction, non-action and even of partisan action against the Delhi police. Several disturbing videos have come up showing policemen purportedly aiding and abetting the violence. In many cases, they were seen watching murderous mobs running amok, while in some cases they were even participating in the violence.[113] Reports of violent mobs raising sectarian slogans being shielded by the police, or the police themselves indulging in heinous acts of beating up the injured from a particular community and asking them to sing the national anthem, or preventing the ambulances from reaching the grievously injured are indicators of the abdication of their duty to uphold the rule of law. Moreover, there are reports of the Delhi police not acting on intelligence reports indicating the possibility of violence. As if to lend credence to such complaints against the police, Naresh Gujral, MP of key constituent Shiromani Akali Dal, in a letter addressed to the Delhi Police Commissioner alleged that police didn't take action on his complaint seeking help for 16 people trapped in riot-hit areas.[114] Home minister Amit Shah, however, ducked pointed questions on police brutality both in the Lok Sabha on 11 March and in the Rajya Sabha on 12 March.[115]

As a columnist points out, we know from studies of riots the world over that what is vital for their prevention is the effective deployment of force by the state in the 12-24-hour lull between the first incident and the major outbreak of violence. Where the required will is weak or absent, the horrors of mass violence soon overcome any effort at their containment, the fire can no longer be controlled even by those who were involved in lighting it in the first place.[116] M.K.Narayanan, a former Director of IB and a former Governor, points out that the riots were stoked by a series of factors, but it is the stark police ineptitude that must cause much introspection.[117] Former Supreme Court Judges, Justice A.K.Patnaik and Justice Kurian Joseph said the State has failed to do its job.[118] Kapil Sibal lamented that the police, the government and the courts have been found wanting amidst another outbreak of communal violence.[119]

More than mere communal violence, the recent events mark a disturbing turning point in contemporary Indian politics.[120] The violence that had engulfed parts of Delhi is a severe human tragedy and signifies the acute moral and political crises that our republic is facing. It is a symptom of a vastly altered India[121], where intolerance to others' views tends to pass off as nationalism. Amartya Sen was 'deeply concerned' and 'disturbed' with violence in Delhi and was worried lest the secular name of the country was tarnished.[122]

As an editorial in *The Times of India* says: "The Delhi riot is a manifestation of Delhi Police's monumental incompetence."[123] At the first sign of trouble, a more professional police force would have intensified patrolling, posted police camps at strategic places in strength, registered cases against the perpetrators, even if unknown, made preventive arrests, combed the area for illegal arms and outsiders, convened peace committees, ramped up intelligence and called up Army as a last resort. Sadly, the Delhi police did nothing to quell the disturbances inviting adverse criticism from both the Delhi High Court and the Supreme Court.

The Supreme Court Bench consisting of Justices S.K. Kaul and K.M. Jospeh while hearing the Shaheen Bagh case, pulled up the Centre for the way it has responded to the violence in Delhi. Justice Joseph spoke of inaction of police. "The problem is that there is lack of independence and professionalism in the police force. If this (subsequent action by police and paramilitary force) had been taken before, this situation would not have arisen", he commented.[124]

The Bench of Justice S.Muralidhar and Justice Talwant Singh of Delhi High Court expressed "anguish" at the delay in filing of FIRs against the hate speeches by BJP leaders Anurag Thakur, Parvesh Verma, Abhay Verma and Kapil Mishra and asked the government to take a decision by 27 February. The Bench said it could not remain "blind" to what was happening and that it could not allow a repeat of the 1984 riots. The court also passed the following directions:

- Safe passage for the dead and assurance that their burial takes place with utmost dignity in consultation with the relatives.
- Setting up of helplines and helpdesks. Officials at the district legal services authorities to ensure the helplines work 24×7 at least for two weeks.
- Police to ensure safe passage for ambulances and requisition sufficient private ambulances.
- The government should ensure there are adequate shelters with basic amenities, including blanket, medicines, sanitation and clean drinking water.[125]

Justice S. Muralidhar who passed the order for immediate action for the hate speech was transferred to the Punjab High Court and a new Bench consisting of Chief Justice D.N.Patel and Justice C. Hari Shankar on 27 February allowed the plea of the Solicitor General Tushar Mehta that the police had decided to defer registering FIRs now "looking at the complexity of the situation" and agreed to grant four weeks for a reply to be filed.[126] In the meantime, a PIL seeking action against Sonia Gandhi, Rahul Gandhi, Priyanka Gandhi and others for hate speech was filed before the same Bench. The Bench issued notices to the Centre, Delhi government and Delhi police on 27 February and fixed 13 April for hearing.[127] The Supreme Court on 4 March asked the High Court to advance to 6 March the hearing of the hate speech cases.[128]

Union home minister Amit Shah while participating in the debate on Delhi riots in the Lok Sabha on 11 March, however, appreciated the role of the Delhi police for not allowing the riots to spread and in controlling the riots within 36 hour. He also informed the Lok Sabha that police had fired 400 rounds, lobbed five thousand tear gas shells, arrested or detained 2647 persons and registered 712 complaints on the violence in which 52 persons had lost their lives and 526 persons sustained injuries. Around 300 persons from UP had infiltrated into the area. Two Special Investigation Teams had been formed. In addition, around forty police teams were active.[129] Delhi police with the help of facial recognition software had identified 1922 persons.[130] The Delhi High Court had designated two sessions and two magisterial courts for trial of the Delhi riot cases.[131]

Alarmed by the Delhi riots multiple international agencies and opinion makers have expressed concern and criticism. Both the USCIRF and the OIC have condemned the violence against Muslims, while UN human rights chief expressed "great concern" over the discriminatory CAA and police action in the riots. The Democrat and Republican co-chairs of the Senate's India Caucus have issued a joint statement of concern over the riots.[132] Though India hit out at OIC, USCIRF's 'selective criticism' of India[133], their concern over the riots needed to be addressed.

Iran's spiritual leader Ayatollah All Khomenei on 5 March joined the growing chorus of concern across the world at the Delhi riots. "The hearts of Muslims all over the world are grieving over the massacre of Muslims in India. The Government of India should confront extremist Hindus and their parties and stop the massacre of Muslims in order to prevent India's isolation from the world of Islam", Khomenei said in a tweet. The tweet carried the heading "Indian Muslim in Danger." Khomenei spoke out two days after India had summoned the Iranian ambassador to register strong protest over foreign minister Javad Zarif's scathing tweet on the Delhi riots.[134]

Police after investigation submitted charge-sheet in a number of cases. The second charge-sheet filed by police on 2 June alleged that Tahir Hussain, the suspended AAP Councillor played a pivotal role in the Delhi riots. It claimed that Hussain transferred Rs. 11 crore to shell companies in the second week of January and later got that amount in cash.[135] In the charge-sheet filed in the murder of Dilber Negi, a sweet shop employee, the Delhi Police have mentioned that all the 12 accused in the case were under the apprehension that if they failed to produce "documents" they would lose their citizenship.[136] The charge-sheet in the Delhi riot conspiracy case has concluded that a "secret meeting" held on the midnight of

16-17 February at Chand Bagh was the "genesis" of several brutal murders, including that of head constable Ratan Lal and IB staffer Ankit Sharma.[137]

Delhi Police arrested Jamia Millia Islamia Alumni Association president Shafi-Ur-Rehman under the UAPA on 27 April, 2020 for allegedly hatching a conspiracy to provoke communal riots.[138] Earlier suspended AAP leader Tahir Hussain was booked under the UAPA on 22 April.[139] Umar Khalid, a former JNU student, was arrested under UAPA on 13 September, 2020 after more than 10 hours of questioning. His arrest triggered a wave of condemnation while eminent citizens and retired IPS officers issued statements censuring the way Delhi police were probing the riot cases.[140] Before he was arrested, Umar Khalid had made a video alleging that Delhi Police was trying to frame on false charges those who were protesting against the government. This particular clip was played out at a press conference called by activists on16 September in which senior advocate Prashant Bhushan claimed that the investigation into Delhi riots was a criminal conspiracy and police had been trying to frame innocent people protesting peacefully against CAA and NRC.[141] A statement signed by 36 persons including Delhi University professor Apoorvananda and JNU professor Jayati Ghosh said the arrest by the Delhi police was part of a brazen attempt to try to suppress Mr. Khalid's voice of dissent.[142]

Amidst protests by the civil rights groups that Umar Khalid had been framed in the riot cases because he had protested against the CAA regime, the Centre and Delhi's AAP government on 6 November, 2020 sanctioned the prosecution of Umar Khalid under the UAPA.[143] Though discharged from a stone-pelting case on 3 December, 2022, Umer Khalid is still languishing in jail and not getting bail because he was charged under the UAPA, the very constitutionality of which the Supreme Court has promised to look into.

On 19 May, 2020, Delhi police arrested Jamia Millia Islamia student Asif Iqbal Tanha under the UAPA in connection with the north-east Delhi riots. On 23 May, 2020, police arrested JNU students Ms.Natasha Narwal and Ms. Devangana Kalita in a riot case. On 24 May, 2020, they were granted bail but were arrested in another case moments later. On 29 May, 2020 both of them were arrested in UAPA case.[144] After more than a year's incarnation in Tihar jail, on 15 June, 2021 they were granted bail by a bench of Justices Siddharth Mridul and Anup J. Bhambhani of the Delhi High Court holding that "the right to protest is a fundamental right that flows from the constitutionally guaranteed right to assemble peaceably and without arms enshrined in Article 19(1)(b) of our Constitution" and pointing out that "surely the right to protest is not outlawed and cannot be termed as a 'terrorist act' within the meaning of the UAPA, unless of course the ingredients of the offences under Sections 15, 17 and/or 18 of the UAPA are clearly discernible from the factual allegations contained in the charge-sheet and the materials filed."[145] Within twenty-four hours of this order Delhi Police moved the Supreme Court against the bail order to these 3 students.[146] The Supreme Court on 18 June did not intervene in the Delhi High Court decision granting bail to these 3 students but said the High Court's order of 15 June would neither be treated as a precedent in any proceedings nor be relied on by the parties.[147] The Supreme Court on 31 January, 2023 expressed displeasure at Delhi police seeking adjournment of hearing on pleas against the bail granted to these three student activists on the ground that a senior law officer representing them was busy in another court.[148] The Additional Sessions Judge Amitabh Rawat granted bail to former Congress councillor Ishrat Jahan on 14 March, 2022, though arrested under the stringent UAPA. Jahan was the first to get bail from a sessions court in a case instituted under the UAPA.[149] Earlier, the Delhi High Court had granted bail to persons arrested under the UAPA.

Both print and electronic media reported on 12 September that the names of CPIM general secretary Sitaram Yechury, Swaraj Abhiyan leader Yogendra Yadav, economist Jayati Ghosh, Delhi University professor Apoorvananda, filmmaker Rahul Roy figured in a supplementary charge sheet filed by Delhi police on the riot cases, allegedly for "provoking and mobilising" anti-CAA protesters.[150] Delhi police, however, on the same day denied media reports that it had named CPIM general secretary Sitaram Yechury, Swaraj Abhiyan leader Yogendra Yadav, economist Jayati Ghosh, Delhi University professor Apoorvananda, filmmaker Rahul Roy, as co-conspirators in a supplementary charge sheet filed in the north-east Delhi riot case.[151] But *The Hindu* reported on 13 September that a supplementary chargesheet in the communal riots issue filed by the Delhi police Crime Branch had named CPIM General Secretary Sitaram Yechury along with Swaraj India president Yogendra Yadav and some other prominent individuals.[152] On 24 September, it came to light that the Delhi Police had named veteran Congress leader Salman Khurshid, CPIM Politburo member Brinda Karat and senior lawyer Prashant Bhusan, as co-conspirators in the Delhi riots cases.[153]

On 17 September, 2020, a delegation of opposition leaders consisting of Congress MP Ahmed Patel, CPI general secretary D. Raja, CPI-M general secretary Sitaram Yechury, DMK MP Kanimozhi and RJD MP Manoj Jha met President Kovind at Rashtrapati Bhavan and submitted a memorandum to him expressing concern over the probe into the Delhi riots being conducted by the Delhi Police and sought his intervention in ensuring a "credible and unbiased" probe into the Delhi riots by a sitting or retired judge under the Commission of Inquiry Act.[154] The intervention, however, remained elusive.

The Delhi Minorities Commission in an assessment report of the Delhi riots has concluded that the violence was 'one-sided, well-planned' with support from local people and most damage was done to shops and houses belonging to the minority community.[155] A Delhi court has remarked that police investigation has targeted only towards one end in riots case and asked the Delhi police to ensure fair investigation.[156] The Delhi Assembly's Minority Welfare Committee has directed Principal Secretary (Home) B.S.Bhalla to take prompt action against BJP MP Parvesh Verma and party leader Kapil Mishra for their provocative hate speeches before the Delhi riots as also against the Delhi police for its alleged refusal to share copies of FIRs registered in riots cases.[157]

The role of the Delhi police in investigating the riot cases was questioned. Radhika Chitkara and Vilas Kumar, secretaries of Peoples Union for Democratic Rights (PUDR), a Delhi-based civil rights group, in a signed article published in *The Hindu* alleged that while 38 out of the 53 persons recorded killed in the riots were Muslims, as were majority of those otherwise affected, most of the anti-CAA protest organisers being targeted by the police under the supposed "conspiracy" angle are Muslims. About 40 FIRs related to the Delhi riots cases accessed by the PUDR and in its possession, reveal crucial discrepancies. One, several Muslim victims have faced problems while trying to lodge FIRs. Two, in few where they have managed to, charges have been diluted and non-bailable sections against Hindu names have been visibly dropped. Three, there is evidence of a single FIR combining multiple incidents. Four, the police have chosen to be the complainant even in those instances where there were independent witnesses. But the most serious charge is that no FIR still exists against BJP leader Kapil Mishra or other leaders and there are many instances of communal bias of the police, including illegal detentions of Muslims and refusal to lodge 'missing person' complaints by Muslims.[158]

The trial of the charge-sheeted cases would have put to rest all doubts as to whether the police did conduct a fair and unbiased probe into the cases maintaining the standard of neutrality expected of them. But this did not happen. On the contrary, the observations of the trial judges proved that the charge that the cases were instituted and investigated with the sole aim of teaching a lesson to the members of one particular community. For instance, Karkardooma court judge Vinod Yadav slapped a fine of Rs. 25,000 on the station house officer (SHO) of Bhajanpura police station and his supervising officers for not registering an FIR on the complaint of Mohammed Nasir who lost his left eye after suffering a gun-shot injury during the riots.[159] In another case, the same judge while framing charges against Rohit in a north-east Delhi riots case, observed that the investigation appeared to be "callous", "inefficient" and "unproductive", because charge-sheet could be submitted only against one man while 400-500 people were involved in that case related to the alleged vandalism, loosing and putting ablaze the houses of Anwar Ali, Ashiq Ali and Irshad during the riots in Gokalpuri.[160] While discharging Shah Alam, Rashid Saifi and Shadab of all charges related to alleged vandalism, looting and setting on fire the shop of one Harpreet Singh by a mob, the same judge observed on 2 September, 2021 that police's failure to conduct a proper investigation was a "colossal" and "criminal" waste of taxpayers' time and money.[161] Additional Session Judge Vinod Yadav on 11 September revoked arson charge against 8 persons because the complainants did not allege commission of arson in their shops.[162] Chief Metropolitan Magistrate Arun Kumar Garg on 17 September came down heavily on the city police for its "lackadaisical approach" and said no steps for the proper prosecution of the 2020 riots cases have been taken by the Police Commissioner and other top officials.[163] Additional Sessions Judge Amitabh Rawat discharged Amir, Saddam, Mohd. Rahis, Amir, Akram and Wasim from a case registered at the Jyoti Nagar police station pertaining to rioting and arson as the only 'incriminating' material against them were their own disclosure statements made after their arrests which "has no value in the eyes of law."[164]

Not only the PUDR, but also a senior retired police officer raised the same question. Julio Ribeiro, the former Commissioner of Mumbai Police, in a letter addressed to the Delhi Police Commissioner on 12 September, 2020 raised question over actions taken by Delhi police against peaceful protesters who "rightly apprehend injustices born from bias and hate against a minority community", and sought "a fair probe into the 753 FIRs registered against peaceful protesters." He even questioned "why Kapil Mishra, Anurag Thakur and Parvesh Sharma have not been arraigned before the courts of law" and urged him to "revisit the actions of the police under your command in Delhi to determine if they have been true to their oaths taken at the time of their induction into the service".[165] Neeraj Kumar, a former Delhi Police Commissioner said that Delhi riots were the culmination of mishandling of many incidents, failure of intelligence, and lack of proper planning. It was a reflection of poor police leadership.[166]

And in a new twist to the investigation of the Delhi riot cases, the Delhi police raided the office of advocate Mehmood Pracha's firm Legal Axis which is handling around 150 riot cases, that is, about a sixth of the total riot cases. The police are investigating Pracha for allegedly coercing a witness to make a statement, a claim the witness has denied. The police searched Pracha's office on 24 December, 2020 to examine his email outbox, and later charged him with obstructing their search. Retired Justice B.G. Kolse-Patil of the Bombay High Court, Supreme Court lawyers Prashant Bhushan and Chander Uday Singh in a statement on 13 January, 2021 condemned the raid. Several Bar associations have also spoken out against the raid.[167]

Justice A.P. Shah, retired chief justice of Delhi and Madras High Courts and former Chairman of the Law Commission, while delivering a lecture on 19 September, 2020 on the topic "The Supreme Court in Decline: Forgotten Freedoms and Eroded Rights", said the Supreme Court was a mute spectator while the police charged protesters, students, academics and poets with sedition and booked them under the provisions of the Unlawful Activities (Prevention) Act in Delhi riots cases this year. He said protesters were labelled anti-nationals and accused of "destabilising the government", but the apex court found reasons not to address the case.[168]

In the light of "extensive critical commentary" of the investigations by Delhi police, a "Citizens' Committee on the Delhi Riots of February 2020: Context, Events and Aftermath" headed by former Supreme Court judge Justice M.B.Lokur was formed in October 2020 to probe into Delhi riots independently. Besides Justice Lokur, others in the committee include, Justice A.P. Shah, former Chief Justice of Delhi High Court and former chairman of the Law Commission, Justice R.S.Sodhi, former judge of Delhi High Court, Justice Anjana Prakash, former judge of Delhi High Court, former Union home secretary, G.K.Pillai and Meeran Chadha Borwankar, former D.G., Bureau of Police Research and Development. All of them are part of the Constitutional Conduct Group (CCG), a collective that has spoken out against the harassment of anti-CAA activists on the pretext of investigation into the Delhi riots. The collective said in a statement: "Considering the horrific nature of the riots in North-East Delhi in February 2020, the scale of violence, the loss of lives and the resulting communal divide between the communities, we felt that an expert body should carry out a thorough examination of what transpired before, during and after the riots. This has become even more necessary as the investigation carried out into the riots by the Delhi police has evoked extensive critical commentary in recent times. We therefore conclude that a Committee with credible reputations in the judiciary, the civil service and the police would be best suited to contribute to an objective and fair understanding of the riots and their aftermath."[169]

A fact-finding report titled Communal Violence in North East Delhi, February 2020 steered by CPM Politburo member Brinda Karat and Delhi state secretary K.M.Tewari released by the CPIM on 9 December, 2020 has held Union home minister Amit Shah responsible for the escalation of the violence and prejudicing the probe. The report breaks new ground by listing several specific instances of violence that go against the general narrative pushed by the police and highlights several identical FIRs and confessions cited by the police as well as complaints of torture. The report adds: "Before any investigation was done, the home minister laid down its findings (in the Lok Sabha on 11 March, 2020). The subsequent investigation was only to substantiate and validate this narrative."[170]

Another committee, People's Tibunal, was organised by the CPI-backed National Federation of Indian Women, CPM-backed All India Democratic Women's Association, ex-civil servants' forum Constitutional Conduct Group, human rights groups such as the People's Union of Civil Liberties, United Against Hate and the Karwan-e-Mohabbat led by former bureaucrat Harsh Mander. The findings by the People's Tribunal which included a group of citizens like former Union home secretary G.K. Pillai, former ambassador Deb Mukherjee, historian Mridula Mukherjee, journalist Pamela Philipose and former Planning Commission member Syeda Hameed were released on 26 February, 2022. The tribunal has accused Delhi Police of misconduct and bias during and after the Delhi communal violence and criticised the state government especially for its failure in providing adequate relief. The report echoes past reports by the Delhi Minorities Commission and the CPM. It reiterates a recommendation made by several civil society groups that have worked on the riots and its victims—that for a judicial probe by a retired Supreme Court judge.[171] Even after two years of riots, many of the affected are still running around incessantly, submitting documents to the sub-divisional magistrate, hoping for compensation that they feel is their due. Unfortunately, most of them happen to be Muslims.[172]

But a review of the home ministry's major decisions and initiatives during the year 2020, put out on 7 January, 2021 by the Press Information Bureau underscores home minister Amit Shah's intervention to bring the law and order situation in Delhi under control in the wake of riots that broke out in parts of the national capital in February 2020. The year-end review records how the home minister had chaired a meeting with political parties and senior officers on 25 February and directed deployment of additional forces in the affected areas.[173]

Delhi police on 22 February, 2021 said in a statement that 365 out of 755 cases registered in connection with the Delhi riots were yet to be solved and the investigations were on in "full swing." The police claimed that "efforts resulted in genuine arrests, presentation of best-in-class evidence before the honourable court" and "even as on date, a total of 1204 arrested accused have been consistently denied any kind of relief from the courts." The Delhi High Court on 19 February, 2021 had rebuked Delhi police for arresting three men from the minority community and objecting to their bail with "no evidence whatsoever either direct or circumstantial or forensic."

Calling the riots a "well-calculated conspiracy", Delhi police said: "The timings of the north-east district riots were almost meticulously executed by key conspirators. They were aware of the fact that any communal violence in Delhi during US President Donald Trunp's visit would immediately be picked up by international media and would cause huge embarrassment to the Indian government. They decided to resort to '*chakka jam*' at communally sensitive spots and attacked police personnel to escalate violence which coincided with the visit of the US President."[174]

Delhi police said after the riots they had conducted 471 peace committee meetings to maintain peace and harmony in the area. The police claimed that they were also facilitating the victims with submission of forms to the Riot Commission. "As on date, as many as 2,599 forms were submitted to the Commission."[175] The Delhi government had disbursed compensation amounting to Rupees 26,09,78,415 to a total of 2,221 claimants so far.[176] The first report of the Committee on Welfare of Minorities, instituted to review the compensation paid to the riot victims was presented to the Delhi Assembly on 11 March, 2021 by its chairman, AAP Okhla MLA Amanullah Khan. While presenting the report, Khan alleged that the riots in February 2020 were orchestrated by the 'opposition' BJP and its members, including Ragini Tewari, Kapil Mishra, Anurag Thakur and Pravesh Verma. The reference to the BJP, which triggered pandemonium in the House was, however, later expunged at the instance of the Leader of the Opposition, Ramuir Singh Bidhuri.[177]

The latest factual position of the cases instituted over the Delhi riots was disclosed by Delhi Police Commissioner S.N.Srivastava in an interview published in *The Week* on 25 April, 2021. He said: "53 people had died and more than 500 were injured in the Delhi riots. A total of 755 cases were registered over a few days. Important cases were handed over to the special investigation teams created in the crime branch. One case was registered with the special cell to unearth conspiracy behind the riots and the remaining cases were assigned to police stations. More than 400 of the 755 cases registered have been worked out and charge-sheets filed, in most cases. Over 1,800 people were arrested."[178]

Just after two years of the Delhi riots, the Human Righst Watch in a statement on 21 February, 2022 said that police investigations into the riot cases have been marked by bias, delays, inaccuracy, lack of proper evidence and failure to follow poper procedures." Indian authorities have been targeting activists instead of impartially investigating BJP leaders who allegedly incited violence. The Delhi police were also allegedly complicit in attacks", said Meenakshi Ganguly, South Asia director at Human Rights Watch.[179]

Delhi police, who report to the Union Home ministry, have been accused of bias in their investigation of the Delhi riot cases that killed 53 people, not only by the different non-governmental organizations probing the incidents and members of the civil society but also by the trial courts as well, discussed ealier. But what appears to be mysterious as to why the investigation of these cases was not assigned to a central body like the CBI. If a not-so complicated case of rape and murder of a minor girl can be handed over to the CBI by the Calcutta High Court in order to have a 'fair investigation' and instil confidence in the family members of the victim and also residents of the locality and the state,[180] one fails to understand why under the same logic the investigation of the Delhi riot cases was not handed over to the CBI, or to a SIT under the direct supervision of the High Court/Superme Court especially when the role of the Delhi police in this riot case was not above board from the very beginning. If the Delhi High Court or the Supreme Court had taken such a step, the real culprits in these cases would have been punished, the 'conspiracy angle' would have been probed properly and the role of the Delhi Police would have been laid bare. But this did not happen. As a result, again there was a violent communl incident on 16 April, 2022 in Jahangirpuri neighbourhood, a highly communally sensitive area, when "outsiders" from within a Hanuman Jayanti procession, which had not the nod from the police to take out the procession, stopped before a mosque at 6 pm, when the *namaz* was being held before the break of the *Roza*, shouted abusive slogans, threw brickbats and entered it to try and plant a saffron flag.[181] Photo of saffron flags and brickbats at the entrance and on the premises of a mosque at Jahangirpuri was published in the front page of a leading newspaper.[182] Additional session judge Gagandeep Singh of the Rohini Court on 7 May, 2022 has castigated Delhi police for failing to stop the unauthorized Hanuman Jayanti procession. "It prima facie reflects the utter failure on the part of local police in stopping the said procession having no permission. The issue seems to have been simply brushed aside by the senior officers. The liability on the part of the concerned officials needs to be fixed so that in future no such incident takes place and the police is not complacent in preventing illegal activities. Their complicity, if any, also needs to be investigated", the judge said in his orders.[183] Earlier,

Muslim residents of Jahangirpuri have accused Delhi police of a one-sided investigation into the 16 April communal clash, alleging that the force was portraying the minorities as "aggressors" and treating the armed provocateurs from the Hanuman Jayanti procession with "kid gloves."[184] Several retired intelligence and police officers had told *The Telegraph* that the police seemed to have played a "dubious" role in Jahangirpuri.[185] Apparently, the role of the Delhi police is not above board either in preventing the communal incidents or in investigating cases instituted over the communal clashes in Delhi.

Political stake in the Delhi riots was quite high for the BJP and it exploited it to the hilt. Amit Shah attacked the opposition parties for instigating riots over the CAA in his first public speech at Bhubaneswar on 28 February, 2020 since the communal carnage in Delhi[186] and followed it up in the Kolkata meeting on 1 March, 2020 by accusing TMC chief of "triggering riots."[187] The Prime Minister, on the other hand, indirectly talked of "rajdharma" when he admitted that a government was obliged to ensure justice and equal benefits for all sections of society.[188]

And all these while the BJP cadres in Delhi and Kolkata chanted "Goli Maaro" slogan.[189] AAP, the ruling party in Delhi, also failed to rise to the occasion and discharge its constitutional obligations to the electorate. It has been criticised for not taking any pro-active role in quelling the riots. The other political parties in the fringe could make their presence felt by creating appropriate noises in the corridor of power and leading delegation to the President or making statements in the media. What was the role of the President during those crucial 'three days' is, however, not known.

V

Chief Justice of India Ranjan Gogoi in a book-launching function held on 3 November, 2019 defended the NRC in Assam, an exercise he had supervised and driven, as a reference to determine the future claims. "Nineteen lakh or 40 lakh is not the point. But it is a base document for the future. A document on which we can refer to determine future claims. The intrinsic value of the NRC, in my view, is mutual peaceful co-existence. Progressive societies are meant to be inclusive," he said.[190] He also warned people raising objections against the NRC process, saying they "are playing with fire."[191] He described the critics of this process variously as "armchair commentators", "iresponsible", "careless", contributing to "worsening the situation", who "thrive through their double speak", are "far removed from the citizenry", and have "vile intentions". Many of these critics were litigants in his Court.

It is extremely unusual for an incumbent Chief Justice of India's Supreme Court to publicly declare his views about issues which are highly politically fraught, and which are still being considered in his Court. It is even more unusual for him to publicly disparage, using harshest language, those who contest his views.[192] His dealing with the Assam-specific question of NRC raised eyebrows, he himself being a resident of Assam, and some even sought the refusal of Chief Justice Gogoi from hearing the related cases but in vain. He also set a precedent by being part of the bench that heard the matter related to sexual harassment allegations against him.

After his retirement as the CJI of India, Jusitce Gogoi was nominated to the Rajya Sabha on 16 March, 2020[193] by the Modi government. His critiques, however, say the nomination was a reward for the judgment deliverd on November 9, 2019[194] in the Ayodhaya land dispute case by the Supreme Court bench headed by him. This judgment paved the way for the construction of the Ram Mandir at Ayodhaya by the BJP, the *Bhumi Pujan* for which was performed by no less a person than by the Prime Minister himself when on 5 August, 2020 he laid a 40 kg silver brick to symbolize the start of the construction of the temple.[195]

After his retirement, Justice Gogoi has penned his autobiograhy tited *Jusitce for the Judge: An Autobiography.* In this book he proffered reasons for some of the judgments delivered by him. However, as Akshat Agarwal says, "Justice Gogoi's justification of some of his judicial decisions show the complete substitution of traditional legal reasoning with considerations for political factors. This unequivocal acknowledgment of political circumstances as a justification for judicial decision-making, which many legal scholars would consider extraneous to legal reasoning, is significant. While the Indian judiciary has always had a reputation of being activist, at least judges have sought to emphasise legal reasoning in justifying their decisions, Justice Gogoi enbraces the political circumstances behind his judicial decisions."[196]

Another question which merits consideration is whether the Supreme Court should be involved in deporting illegal immigrants. More often than not PILs are filed in the Supreme Court seeking court's intervention for deportation of illegal immigrants. Very recently, in May 2022, the Jhakhand government has told the Supreme Court that the Centre and the States are taking necesasay steps for identifying and deporting of illegal migranst and the Supreme Court needn't step in.[197] The Supreme Court monitored NRC exercise in Assam has brought to the fore what could be the result if such an exercise is undertaken. Even after three years of publication of the draft final report, the final report could not be published till now. Such being the position, one should think thrice before asking for such an exercise.

It is, however, difficult to oppose the rationale behind drawing up a citizenship register. Almost all the countries in the world do have it. But implementing the NRC has numerous challenges. The task is not just detecting illegal Bangladeshi migrants and deporting them, but also preventing the creation of a new set of 'stateless' people in the entire country. So the first step should be to ensure that no illegal immigration takes place. No doubt this is a world-wide problem but all the countries are tackling the problem in their own light. Trump fought with the House of Representatives to get fund for building wall on the Mexico border and had succeeded at least in starting it. Along the Sahel, from Mauritania to Chad in North Africa, the Europeans and the US have begun to build what amounts to a highly militarised border. Europe has moved its border from the northern edge of the Mediterranean Sea to the southern edge of the Sahara desert to prevent migrants from reaching the Mediterranean.[198] The U.K. left the European Union because of unabated inflow of people from the less developed nations of Europe. There have been rallies for an all-white Europe on Independence Day in Poland and Hungary is threatening to opt out of the Eurozone to clamp down on Syrian refugees.

But the Central Government does not think it necessary to give that much importance to the eastern border of the country. Keeping the door ajar for the ingress of people from the other side of the border and then conduct the NRC to find them out is the worst kind of hypocrisy. While the NRC's predecessor were counting 'residents' rather than 'citizens', the objective of the NRC is to count citizens—specifically to sift and sort citizens from non-citizens, to include and exclude, and having done so to weed out "infiltrators" destined for detention camps and potential deportation. "With what justification can a state that does not have the ability to "detect' aliens, or even to secure its borders against illegal migrants, set out to find aliens by elimination? This is tantamount not only to using an elephant to crush an ant, but of torturing the elephant to do it", observes a columnist.[199]

So, the first step to be taken before the conduct of the NRC is to seal the border. But only half of the 4,096-km border with Bangladesh could be fenced by February end of 2017.[200] Complete sealing of the Indo-Bangladesh border is no doubt a challenging task and it is anybody's guess whether the Central Government is really serious to finish the work within a definite time-frame, say by the end of 2019 or even 2021.

As an observer put it, the NRC mess in Assam should serve as a cautionary tale. The exercise exposed the people of that state to untold harassment, stress and misery. The poor lost their meagre savings and sacrificed their daily earnings to pursue their claim, sometimes only to be cheated by middlemen. Errors in implementation occurred on a horrific scale: overlooking soldiers and freedom fighters, registering the child but not the parent, one sibling but not another; in one reported case, only one of a pair of twins. People were placed in detention centres not only on grounds later overruled but owing to clerical blunders and mistaken identity. The exercise cost the nation Rs. 1,600 crores, leaving out of account the situation of the 19 lakh individuals excluded from the register. An untold number who finally made it lost their worldly security and peace of mind along the way: their lives will never be the same. The NRC was touted as stopping foreign infiltrators from depriving genuine citizens of their income and benefits. Yet the NRC itself has done just that for very many Assamese, alleges an observer.[201]

It is all the more astonishing that even after BJP itself had rejected the NRC exercise in Assam which excluded 19 lakh people from the polls including around 12 lakh Hindus, BJP has pitched for a pan-India NRC to weed out illegal immigrants. It's worth keeping in mind that NRC verification isn't as simple as producing voter ID card or a passport. In the Assam NRC, one first had to produce documentary proof issued before 24 March, 1971—like the 1951 NRC or electoral rolls up to 24 March, 1971—to prove that one's ancestor were residing in India before that date. The next step was producing documents for oneself to establish relationship with those ancestors. In a country with a poor documentation culture and crores of people with meagre financial resources, such onerous requirements are often beyond one's means.

One needs to take a step back and think through what the move entails conceptually. It is, as an editorial in *The Times of India* says, akin to asking 135 crore Indians reapply citizenship.[202] It "would place each of India's 1.35 billion people under suspicion of falsely claiming citizenship, and task them with exonerating themselves. In other words, they would be assumed guilty until they proved themselves innocent. Is there any instance in history of any nation, let alone one so large and, all told, so stable and politically organized as India, consigning its entire population to such an inquisition?", asks Sukanta Chaudhuri, Professor Emeritus, Jadavpur University.[203]

If the NRC is implemented, the nation could witness the largest 'statelessness' crisis the world has ever witnessed. Though the Chief Justice of India Ranjan Gogoi, the head of the Bench under whose orders the NRC was implemented in Assam, had said on 3 November, 2019 that the Assam NRC process to identify illegal migrants residing in the border state, was "neither a new or novel idea" but only an attempt to update the 1951 NRC data,[204] its fallout is there for all to see.

Since Amit Shah proposes to conduct the NRC throughout the country, what would ultimately be the number of the NRC-rejects is anybody's guess—it could be one crore, two crore or anything, as the BJP leaders often blurt out. And what resources would be needed to conduct such an NRC? The Assam NRC is reported to have cost 1,600 crore with 48,000 persons (both officials and contractual workers) deployed to scrutinize almost 3.3 crore applicants. On this basis, a perceptive analyst has calculated that for an Indian electorate of 87.9 crore, a nationwide NRC would require an outlay of Rs. 4.26 lakh crore, which is more than double the presumptive loss in the 2G scam, and four times the budgetary outlay for education this year and deployment of 1.33 crore officials, whereas in 2011-12 (the most recent official data available), the total number of government employees in India was 2.9 crore.[205] Is the country prepared to mobilize the resources of such a scale for an exercise which is flawed on several accounts, if the Assam experience is any indication.

The Central Government has said time and again that none will be treated as a foreigner unless the legal remedies available to him are exhausted. That means the trial in the FTs, the appeal in the High Court/ Supreme Court and their verdict. Till then they are to be treated as citizens of the country with all rights and privileges. The action against them will start after the infiltrators are branded as foreigners by the judicial process.

The next question which is required to be resolved is what to do with these foreigners. Union home minister Amit Shah, as late as on 17 July, 2019 informed the Rajya Sabha that all the illegal immigrants would be "deported in accordance to prevailing international laws."[206] A politically-correct answer! But where will this huge number of illegal immigrants, if the estimates of the BJP leaders turn out to be correct, be deported? Deportation to Bangladesh is out of the question. Harsh Shringla, Foreign Secretary, the senior most Indian official to visit Bangladesh after the CAA-NRC controversy broke out here, told a high-powered audience in Dhaka on 2 March, 2020 that "the NRC exercise is a process that is entirely internal to India. Therefore, there will be no implications for the government and the people of Bangladesh. You have our assurance on that count."[207]

If they cannot be deported, they will have to be kept in detention camps or be allowed to live on with some restrictions and without most of the rights guaranteed by the Constitution. What would be the infrastructural costs involved in holding these prisoners with basic dignity in place? How long would these detentions last? Who will provide the fund for their maintenance and how long? Is the country that much strong to bear the economic burden and face international criticism? And who will ensure that the Foreigners Tribunals while adjudicating upon a person's citizenship will maintain the highest standards of adjudication required of such a body whose verdict would render a human being stateless? What is our experience in Assam about the FTs?

Aakar Patel, India head of the global rights body, Amnesty International said on 27 November, 2019 that the Supreme Court and the Gauhati High Court have enabled the Foreigners' Tribunals to create a statelessness crisis in Assam. FTs that determine the paramount right to citizenship in Assam are often dismissive, use derogatory language, control their own procedures and apply them in arbitrary ways. The judiciary has in the case of Assam aided the government institutions and the FTs to commit abuses with impunity. Amnesty International cited the case of a Muslim woman who was declared a foreigner because she could not remember the constituency where her grandfather cast his vote in 1966, and that of a Muslim man whose grandfather's name was spelt differently in two documents. Alleging that the FTs have created havoc in Assam, it said they have not been held accountable by the courts, the Centre and the state government.[208]

On being declared 'foreigners' by the judicial body, the infiltrators' voting rights would be taken away. Apart from losing their voting rights, would they also be shorn of their rights to land and property? How would the state deal with those declared stateless but who already own property including cultivable land? Would the stateless people not be allowed to acquire land and property? What about their children? Will they ever be considered citizens of India? What would the status of these people be after they are released on completion of the specified period?

What would be the nationality of the person dying in captivity? Would he regain his citizenship after his death? This question haunted the district administration of Sonitpur district when the sons of Dulal Chandra Paul (65) refused to accept the body unless their father was declared an Indian national. Paul was in detention since 2017 on being declared foreigner by an FT and died on 13 October, 2019 at Gauhati Medical College and Hospital where he was admitted on 25 September. His relatives complained that he was not administered proper treatment.[209] After a lot of persuasion, the sons accepted the dead boy after 10 days. Chief minister Sarbananda Sonowal promised to remain personally present on the occasion of his last rites performance. Another such incident happened when Falu Das (72), a resident of Chate Mari village under Mukalmua police station of Nalbari, who had been in a detention camp in Goalpara since July 2017, died on

24 October, 2019. His sons refused to accept the dead body unless all the members of the family were included in the NRC.[210] At the intervention of the local BJP MLA Narayan Deka, the relatives accepted the dead body without any conditions and the cremation was performed on 28 October.[211]

More such deaths would be reported as more and more persons are incarcerated in the coming days. The Supreme Court has to decide the maximum period of detention and what would be their nationality after release from detention or if dying while in captivity. It would be most inhumane to deprive a person of his last rites as per his religion and customs. The state can take away the voting rights but not the right to be cremated with full dignity, solemnity and honours. The Supreme Court is the last protector of human rights under the Constitution and therefore has a duty to look into this.

Is there any other alternative to creating a generation of stateless people? Senior leaders in the BJP-led government at the Centre during the period 1999-2004 such as L.K.Advani, the Home Minister, and A.B.Vajpayee, the Prime Minister, had gone so far as to indicate that a more practical solution to the infiltration issue could involve some form of "work permit" system for immigrants already in India.[212] In 1999, Paula Banerjee et al. gave a detailed outline of such a "work permit" system.[213] Although such suggestions were not acted upon, nevertheless they represent an alternative to forcible deportation. Once the infiltrators are identified, apart from disenfranchisement, they could be given Temporary Work Permit (TWP). If one stays back even after the expiry of the period mentioned in the permit he will not get job anywhere in the country and without any means of livelihood, will be forced to leave the country.

So apart from the question of deportation, detention in camps, disenfranchisment, there is the option of declaring an amnesty as was done in many other countries. But, as we have seen, such an amnesty could not prevent infiltration into the countries which offered such an amnesty. Actually, there is no fool-proof system of dealing with the infiltrators, except preventing them from crossing, be it from Bangladesh, Myanmar or Nepal.

Many such questions bring to the fore the humanitarian dimensions of the problem. These have far-reaching consequences in a country like ours with multi-cultural, multi-lingual, multi-religious, multi-racial and multi-ethnic polity and need to be resolved before the NRC in other states of India is actually undertaken. At the same time, it should be remembered that no country can sustain pressure of unending flow of infiltrators for long and that displacement of millions of people for the submergence of low lying coastal areas including islands due to the rise of water level of the seas as a result of global warming will take place not only in India but in many other countries of the world within the coming decades. As climate and economic changes are rendering more people footloose migrants, the 'indigenous' have directed their ire against migrants.Tuvalu, an island state in the western Pacific is expected to become uninhabitable by 2050. The Tuvaluians have requested New Zealand to accept its entire population, although no decision has been reached yet. Many such cases will be reported from different corners of the world. Environmental refugees due to climate change will be a big problem in the coming days. It has to be tackled with ingenuity, compassion and a humane face. One finds an echo of such anxieties in many countries around the world.

VI

Infiltration of Bangladeshis, both Hindus and Muslims, continued unabated even after the emergence of Bangladesh as an independent country. Various measures like strict vigil on the border, strengthening the border posts, fencing of the unfenced portion of the border, technology-driven border management, strengthening border patrolling and gearing up the intelligence machinery were undertaken to stop this "demographic invasion". One of such measures was to issue identity cards to the residents of the border districts. In 1965, the Union government considered introducing a scheme of providing identity cards to the people residing along the India—Bangladesh border belt. The purpose was to identify and differentiate Indian citizens from foreigners. Persons who were issued identity cards were required to carry the cards voluntarily so that they could be easily identified as genuine citizens and not harassed by the police checking people against illegal migration. Incidentally, the proposal of issuing identity cards to border people was cancelled a year later after it was found that the proposal was not feasible.[214]

In 1986, the exercise was introduced in three border districts of Rajasthan in 1986 on an experimental basis and the results were encouraging.[215] The project of identity cards was again revived in 1991 when the Government of India approved a "scheme for issue of identity cards in the specified areas in the states of Assam, Mizoram, Tripura, and West Bengal to check illegal migration."[216] A resolution was adopted at a meeting the Union Home Minister S.B.Chavan had with the Chief Ministers of different states in Delhi on 28 September, 1992 of issuing identity cards to inhabitants of the border districts adjacent to Bangladesh. The West Bengal State Committee of All India Majlis-e-Ittehadul Muslimeen opposed the adoption of such a scheme. The organisation in a statement issued in Calcutta on 5 October, 1992 said the resolution was "unacceptable" as it intended to send innocent people residing in the border areas to Bangladesh "forcibly".[217] The project was, however, not taken up in earnest for a long time as the administration concluded that "creating database of 1 billion people is a gigantic exercise".[218]

The Union Home Ministry decided in 1993 to issue photo-identity cards to all those living in the notified international border areas of six states—Punjab, Rajasthan, Jammu & Kashmir, Assam, Mizoram and Tripura. The identity cards would be given to the entire population of Mizoram and Tripura while in the other states it would be issued only to the residents of bordering areas. The Bhabha Atomic Research Centre (BARC), Bombay, had developed a scientific computerised laser image printing (CLIP) system that produces cards which could not be duplicated. The Electronic Corporation of India Limited (ECIL) had the facilities to manufacture the CLIP and was approved by the BARC. Each card was given a distinct computer identity, based on a numbering system. It was not possible to remove photograph and the number from the card.[219] The Tripura government took a decision on 18 November, 1993 to issue photo-affixed identity cards to all its citizens.[220]

More or less during the time when the central and some state governments were embroiled with the issue of photo identity cards to the inhabitants of the border districts, the Election Commission of India took up the project to issue EPIC (Electoral Photo Identity Card) to each and every voter of India. After initial hiccups and resistance from some political parties and even state governments, the project ultimately got through, thanks to the insistence of the then Chief Election Commissioner, T.N.Sheshan who even threatened that there would be no election unless the process of issuing identity cards to each and every voter was completed by 31 December, 1994.

With too many shady characters entering the fray, the rate of malpractices—rigging, impersonation, bogus voting etc.—reached an all-time high in India. Some of these elements successfully nullified even photo-identity cards issued for local elections by replacing the originally affixed photos with their own, giving a tough time to election authorities. Public opinion was also building up in favour of the efforts made by Seshan to clean up the electoral system.

It may be recalled that in 1972, the Joint Parliamentary Committee on electoral reforms had proposed the introduction of identity cards. Later, every official and non-official committee, constituted to look into poll reforms, had made similar recommendations.[221]

The Electronic Corporation of India came out with a solution to the identity problem under which the photograph of the voter along with other details—name, name of father/mother/husband, sex, age, village, permanent address and Assembly constituency, date of issue were printed on a specially made watermark stationery supplied by the government mint in Nasik, which is normally used for currency notes. Also printed on the card was an alphabetical code, allotted to each voter based on six phonetic characters of each Indian language and the electoral officer then affixed his hologram. The comfortably sized card (10 cm by 8 cm), which can easily be kept in a pocket, was then laminated and issued to the voter. The size of the card has, however, been reduced since then.

The system was first developed by the Bhabha Atomic Research Centre, Mumbai in 1985 but in a different form to issue identity cards to all citizens in the border states which faced security risks following infiltration of foreign nationals—Mizoram, Assam, Tripura, West Bengal, Punjab, Rajasthan, Gujarat, etc. as sought by the Home Ministry. The ECIL developed it into what it is today in collaboration with the Centre for Development of Advanced Computing, Pune.[222]

Photo identity cards to people of border States and EPIC to all voters were not enough to the BJP. It was in favour of a multi-purpose identity card for the people of India. L.K.Advani, BJP's all-India president said even on 11 November, 1994 that the voter identity card as envisaged by the Election Commission ought to serve as a "multipurpose card" for the people as well.[223]

Again on 2 April, 1998, while on a day's visit to Gandhinagar, L.K.Advani revealed that the BJP has mooted the idea of citizen's identity card which would be multi-purpose and would also serve as a voter's identity card.[224] Advani was criticised by the CPIM for announcing the above scheme. In a statement issued on 4 April, 1998, the politburo of the CPIM said: "One fails to understand why such a decision has been taken when after a thorough discussions, the Election Commission of India has already undertaken a scheme of issuing identity cards to all voters." The politburo said that after discussion with all political parties it was understood that these cards would serve as multi-purpose identity cards for citizens.[225] It may be noted that the Chief Electoral Officers of States at a meeting in New Delhi in January 1997 had suggested to the Election Commission and the Union Government to consider a Permanent Citizenship number to all Indians with a provision for change of addresses temporarily as well so that it could serve as a multi-purpose identity card. The suggestion was being examined by the Election Commission.[226]

On coming to power at the Centre, the Vajpayee administration wanted to use the I-card in a number of ways like using the card to ensure opening of individual bank accounts, widening the income-tax net, plugging loopholes in the education and health care systems and setting up an easily accessible citizenship documentation network.[227]

In 1998 itself, the Ministry of Home Affairs under the stewardship of Advani thought of introducing national identity cards by issuing Green Cards to resident Indians and Red Cards to illegal immigrants. The ministry found that manually prepared and maintained electoral rolls had an error margin of 5 per cent. In order to avoid error, the ministry would rely on documents applying information on citizens. These include electoral rolls, birth certificates, land holding records, rent receipts issued by revenue officials, refugee registration certificates and passports. The ministry proposed to have 10 teams in every district, mobile vans, a district registry to maintain records, prepare and distribute identity cards and a complaint redressal system to look into appeals against the designated officials for issue of green/red cards.[228]

In 1999, the Union Government commissioned a detailed feasibility study for implementing National Identity Card Scheme (NICS), which submitted its report in March 2000. Finally, in "a few selected sub-districts of 13 States and Union territories, namely, Jammu & Kashmir, Gujarat, Uttaranchal, Rajasthan, Uttar Pradesh, Assam, Andhra Pradesh, West Bengal, Tripura, Goa, Tamil Nadu, Pondicherry and Delhi in April 2003, the Union Government launched a pilot project of granting multipurpose identity cards covering a total population of 30.5 lakh."[229] The project work was to complete by August 2004, but the early elections disturbed the schedule.[230] Apart from being a proof of citizenship, this Card would be used as Voter Card, Ration Card, admission to school and colleges etc. But even after four years of this project, the Home Ministry officials were not sure whether this NIC would at all be able to stop infiltration because of the inherent loopholes in this project, that is, the certificate of the local functionaries and the affidavits before the magistrates.[231] The project was completed in March 2009.[232] Unfortunately, the project could not be implemented in Assam because the verification of citizens in the state had not been completed.[233]

On a public interest litigation petition filed by O.P.Saxena, president, All India Lawyers Forum for Civil Liberties seeking a direction to the authorities to deport about 2 core Bangladeshi migrants staying illegally in India, a bench consisting of Chief Justice K.G. Balakrishnan, Justice P. Sathasivam and Justice J.M. Panchal of the Supreme Court on 15 January,

2009 directed the Union Government to take immediate steps for issue of Multi-Purpose National Identity Cards (MPNIC) to all Indian citizens, starting with Assam and other north-eastern States. This Card should be the basis for the citizens to avail themselves of benefits such as ration card, school admission and inclusion of name in electoral rolls. The Court also asked the Union Government to prepare a National Identity Register (NIR) to check the infiltration of Bangladeshis. In fact, the Union Government in its affidavit filed in 2009 had proposed to issue the MPNIC to citizens in the border States and create an NIR to provide a credible identification system through e-governance. The Court even commented that the Bangladeshi migrants get better facilities than normal Indian citizens. No country will allow that. If the infiltrators enjoy all facilities it will be difficult to separate them.[234] The court also referred to the government's statement on fencing India-Bangladesh border in two phases and wanted land acquisition for fencing to be completed at the earliest.

On the petitioner's argument that sufficient number of tribunals have not been set up for identification of Bangladeshis, the bench asked the government to set up adequate number of tribunals for quick disposal of all pending cases. It asked the government to file a report in eight weeks on the steps taken to identify illegal Bangladeshis, number of tribunals set up and cases disposed of.

The petitioner's counsel said that infiltration from Bangladesh was on the rise and the illegal migrants were securing ration cards, getting their names enlisted in the voters roll and exercising their franchises. Referring to senior lawyer K.K. Venugopal appearing for West Bengal government, the bench said that a number of Bangladeshis had been living in camps as Bangladesh refused to take them back. The Indian government was asked to hold talks with Bangladesh authorities on the issue, it added.

The Supreme Court has observed that "there is a lack of will (on the part of the Centre) in the matter of ensuring that illegal migrants are sent out of the country."[235] Even such stinging rebukes from the highest court of the land have failed to wake up the executive from the deep slumber. The Supreme Court had warned on 14 June, 2008 that foreigners found without valid travel documents would not be shown any leniency by the judicial forums in imposing stricter sentence under the Foreigners Act.[236] The Supreme Court has again asked the Central Government on 15 April, 2009 to take all possible measures to ensure that no illegal immigration and infiltration of Bangladeshis into India takes place.[237]

In 2012, a special identity card, Resident Card, was designed for issue to the inhabitants of the Chicken Neck Corridor of Siliguri, because of strategic importance of the area, being surrounded by Nepal, Bangladesh on two sides while China was only128 km north of the area.[238]

Amit Shah, in consonance with the BJP's avowed stand on ID Cards, mooted the idea of a multi-purpose identity card for citizens with all utilities like Aadhar, passport, bank account, driving license, voter card, while laying the foundation stone of a new building of the Registrar General of India and Census Commissioner in New Delhi on 23 September, 2019. He spoke of a system that all data should be put together in a single card.[239] This is, no doubt, a worthwhile proposal and should be examined in greater details.

Many statutory authorities and government departments like the Election Commission of India, Unique Identification Authority of India, Ministry of External Affairs, Income Tax Department of the Ministry of Finance, Transport Department and Food & Supplies Department of state governments issue identity cards for various purposes. For instance, the Election Commission of India issue Identity Card to the voter; the Unique Identification Authority of India issue Aadhar, MEA issue passport, Income Tax Department issue PAN Card, Transport Department of state governments issue Driving Licence and Food & Supplies Department of state governments issue Ration Card. These cards are issued to meet the specific needs of the authorities concerned. Besides, local DM/SDO issue SC/ST/OBC certificates to the concerned persons. Birth certificates are issued by local-self government like Municipalities, Panchayats. Revenue receipts are issued by the L & LR Department of the state Government. Trade Licence is issued by the Municipality/Panchayats. Fire Licence is issued by the Fire Services Department of state governments. Electricity Bills are issued by the respective State Electricity Boards/Electricity Companies. Telephone Bills are issued by the BSNL/ telephone companies. Bank Passbooks are issued to the holders of Bank Accounts. Many of these documents are relied upon as address proof documents. Banks insist on production of KYC like Aadhar, PAN Card, Voter Card, etc. for the opening of an account.

The National Identity Card Scheme (NICS) envisages granting identity cards to all citizens above 18 years of age and continuous updating of the NICS by linking it up with the Births and Deaths system. To provide legal sanction for the project, the Citizenship Act, 1955 has been amended and a specific section (14A) on registration of citizens and issuing cards has been inserted by the Citizenship (Amendment) Act, 2003 (Act 6 of 2004). The section provides that the "Central Government may compulsorily register every citizen of India and issue National Identity Card to him."[240]

The National Identity Card is issued by the National Registration Authority. The Registrar General of India acts as the National Registration Authority and functions as the Registrar General of Citizen Registration. For implementing this scheme, the Citizenship (Registration of Citizens and Issue of National Identity Cards) Rules, 2003 was notified on December 10, 2003. The 2003 Citizenship Rules provide for preparation of NPR for all residents, irrespective of citizenship and NRC for Indian citizens.NPR/ NRC is prepared on the basis of Rules framed under the Citizenship Act. If the Rules are abrogated, NPR/NRC loses its statutory backing. Now NPR/ NRC has assumed the pride of place because of their punitive prerogative of making a person non-citizen.

The NRC was envisaged as an instrument to end a decade of violence in Assam and to address the legitimate anxieties of vulnerable communities about culture, land and migration. But the objection was against the way it was implemented—mostly under the watchful eye of the Supreme Court—because it violated constitutional guarantees and due process and caused severe and avoidable suffering to recently immigrant communities. In view of the apprehensions raised throughout the length and breadth of the country against the NPR/NRC, it is perhaps meet and proper to delve into the possibilities of preparing a citizenship register without going through the decennial process of NPR/NRC along with the Census operations. Actually, the preparation of a citizenship register is a continuous process and is to be updated daily in order to make it useful. This daily updation of the citizenship register is possible if the citizenship identity card is updated daily. After all, a citizenship register is nothing but a summation of the citizenship identity cards.

Of all the cards, enumerated above, a voter card (EPIC) can only be issued to a person when he/she attains the age of voting, i.e., 18 years. Persons of the age group 0-18 years are left out from its purview. Central Government has given the Election Commission legal power to link Aadhar and voter ID. Linking Aadhar number with electoral rolls will help rid voters' list of bogus and duplicate entries. It will also help realise EC's plan to work towards a secure, possibly electronic, voting to help migrant voters exercise franchise even if they are not in the constituency.[241] Questions have, however, been raised whether it would at all be feasible to eliminate bogus and duplicate voters from the voters' list, given that there were loopholes in the preparation of Aadhar itself.[242] On 25 January, 2021, the National Voters' Day, the Election Commission rolled out the 'e-EPIC', a non-editable and secure PDF version of the EPIC that can be downloaded on the mobile phone or in a self-printable form on the computer. The e-EPIC facility will eliminate the wait for delivery of the physical EPIC card after it is approved.[243] The law ministry, after consultation with the Election Commission, has amended the the Registration of Electors Rules, 1960 and Conduct of Elections Rules,1961, to give effect to the electoral reforms enacted in 2021 including the linking of voter ID with Aadhar. The gazette documents issued on17 June, 2022 specify 1 April, 2023 as the date on or before which every person whose name exists in the electoral rolls "may" intimate his Aadhar number. Furnishing Aadhar for voter authentication will, however, be entirely voluntary.[244]

Passports can be issued to persons of all age group but only a miniscule portion of the populace do possess passports which is required only when one travels abroad. PAN card can be issued to any person of any age group. So far 48 crore PAN Cards have been issued and the process of linking a PAN Card with Aadhar was to be completed by 31 March, 2023.[245] Unless this seeding is done, a PAN Card will become invalid. So far, 17.58 crore PAN Cards have not been seeded with Aadhar and the Income Tax Department is going to declare them invalid. Since there is no system of cancellation of PAN Card of dead persons, this figure may include the PAN Cards of dead persons as well.[246] PAN-Aadhaar link became mandatory from 1 July, 2017 for filing ITR and obtaining a new Permanent Account Number. This has been done in order to weed out fake PAN cards which was being used in drug financing and terror financing. The idea behind bringing Aadhaar was to have a secure and robust system to ensure that the identity of a person cannot be faked. Only 5.95 crore of people have filed Income Tax returns up to 10 January, 2021 for the F.Y. 2019-2020[247], i.e., 12-13 per cent of the PAN Card holders are Income Tax payees. Since such a small number file Income Tax Returns, the outreach of the PAN card is very limited. Now instant PAN allotment is available for anyone who has a valid Aadhar number and a mobile number registered with the Aadhar. This scheme was formally launched by the Union finance minister Nirmala Sitaraman on 28 May, 2020.[248]

The Driving licence is issued to a person above the age of 18. Its possession entitles its holder to drive a vehicle as stipulated in the licence. Ration Cards are issued to persons of all age groups. Since income is a precondition for drawal of rations at subsidised rates, now non-food grain ration cards are being issued to those above the stipulated income category, more as an identity document than for drawing rations. The Central Government has started 'One Nation, One Ration Card' scheme from 1 June, 2019. As on 1 August, 2020, as many as 24 States/UTs— Andhra Pradesh, Bihar, Dadra & Nagar Haveli and Daman & Diu, Goa, Gujarat, Haryana, Himachal Pradesh, Jammu & Kashmir, Jharkhand, Karnataka, Kerala, Madhya Pradesh, Maharashtra, Manipur, Mizoram,

Nagaland, Odisha, Punjab, Rajasthan, Sikkim, Telangana, Tripura, Uttar Pradesh and Uttarakhand—have implemented the scheme.[249] By the second week of November, 2020, as many as 28 States/UTs have joined the scheme enabling 68.8 crore beneficiaries to get subsidized foodgrains from their place of work or residence under the National Food Security Act (NFSA).[250] Under the scheme, beneficiaries can buy subsidised food grain from ration shops in any part of the country.[251] States across the country are taking steps towards providing digital identities to beneficiaries of the public distribution system to reduce leakage of grains into the open market and ensure better availability of grains to genuine beneficiaries. In doing so, the use of Aadhar-based biometric seems to be the preferred choice. It has been found that despite other alternatives being available, the biometric mode of authentication seems to be more effective in the registration process. Consequently, the exercise of seeding Aadhar numbers with ration cards is a promising step towards strengthening the states' Ration Card Management System (RCMS).[252]

Now, Ration Cards and Phone Numbers are linked to the Aadhar. The West Bengal government scrapped 30.93 lakh ration cards between November 2021 and January 2022 after inspections revealed that a huge number of beneficiaries were dead or traceless but their cards stayed acitve. Seeding Aadhar cards with ration cards helped identify bogus ones.[253]

Unique Identification Authority of India (UIDAI) issue Aadhar to persons of all age group above the age of five years, because the biometric details of a person are not developed before that age. It may be recalled that in 2010 when the NPR exercise was undertaken, a simultaneous project—Aadhar—was formed under the Unique Identification Authority of India. The UIDAI was under the Planning Commission and Aadhar was to be used to roll out benefits of government schemes. Bureaucratic wrangling, a race for funds, duplication of efforts and questions of authenticity led to an intervention by the home ministry. Finally, both were allowed to continue and both captured the biometric data of residents, and provisions were made to eliminate any overlap. While the NPR was based on census figures and the enumeration was house to house, which took each unit (family) into account, Aadhar was issued to each resident and with its minimum qualification of three months to be a resident, it got distributed loosely and even illegal migrants got it. There was also no way to determine whether a set of residents belonged to the same unit.[254]

Both the Central Government as well as the State governments spend a substantial amount of money for the issue and updation of these cards. For instance, the state government of West Bengal is reported to have spent around Rupees 200 crore only for issuing digital ration cards.[255]

It is worthwhile to examine if any of these cards can be suitably converted as citizenship identity card in lieu of the national identity card stipulated in section 14A of the Citizenship Act. It may be recalled that section 14A, which was inserted in the Citizenship Act by virtue of the Citizenship (Amendment) Act, 2003 (Act 6 of 2004), stipulated that the Central Government would issue national identity card to every citizen of India and the Registrar General of India, shall act as the National Registration Authority and he shall function as the Registrar General of Citizen Registration. This pious wish, however, remained in the contemplation stage and never materialized.

Instead of first preparing the NPR, then the NRC and lastly the National Identity Card, the process can be reversed, keeping in mind peoples' aversion to the NPR/NRC exercise in the wake of the Assam fiasco. Moreover, if the National Identity Card or the Citizen Identity Card, whatever it is called, is prepared first, it would enable the authority to prepare the NRC easily because the NRC is nothing but a summation of the CICs.

Of the cards mentioned above, only Aadhar is linked with voter card, PAN card, Driving licence, Ration Card, bank accounts and Sim cards. No Sim card is issued without the Aadhar. No Bank Account can be opened unless vetted by an Aadhar. Services that most commonly use Aadhar authentication include issue of mobile SIM (new or replacement), banks, public distribution system and office attendance at government offices.[256] Aadhar cards are now valid travel documents for Indians under 15 and over 65 travelling to Nepal and Bhutan. Indians other than in these two age groups can travel if they have a valid passport, a photo identity card issued by the government of India or an EPIC issued by the Election Commission.[257] The Centre has asked all state governments' revenue departments to register all land records online and link Aadhar numbers to each of these transactions, including existing records. An inter-ministerial committee has recommended to the Ministry of External Affairs to make Aadhar mandatory for the registration of NRI marriages in India to tackle desertion and other marital issues. And to cap it all, the Food and Drug Administration of Maharashtra has issued a circular making it mandatory for the relatives of Covid patients to produce Aadhar card details, along with other documents for the purchase of two Covid drugs in Maharashtra.[258] Aadhar cards, however, cannot be made mandatory by the government for extending benefits of social welfare schemes. But the government policy is such that linking of Aadhar has become mandatory for all such schemes though in a roundabout way.

If a COVID-19 vaccine seeker provides his/her Aadhar as identity proof to be inoculated, the government of Karnataka will immediately generate a unique health identity (UHID) for the individual. Eyeing this as an opportunity, authorities now are planning to use the vaccination programme to get digital health IDs for citizens. Once a UHID is generated, a person's health records are digitally maintained in hospitals and become a part of government records, though the Karnataka government has expressly stated that using Aadhar as ID proof could have "legal implications."[259] Aadhar number is mandatory while going for COVID-19 test. It enables the civic authority and the government to track down the Covid-19 positive cases and follow upon patients who are in home isolation.[260] It is also mandatory to produce Aadhar for Covid-19 vaccination. Now some physicians insist on Aadhar of a patient before treating him/her. Over the last few years, Aadhar has become the most trusted identity proof with hospitals, hotels and employers insisting on Aadhar photocopies, although it is "voluntary." Many people in a document-poor country didn't have any means to prove identity when, say, applying for a SIM card. The Government of India specifically allowed telecom companies to use Aadhar e-KYC. This calls for according it *de jure* recognition by an enabling Act.

Unique Identification Authority of India (UIDAI) has introduced a more secured Aadhar card called Aadhar polyvinyl chloride (PVC) Card. It is completely weather-proof, more durable and convenient to carry even in wallets. Its security features include a hologram, Guilloche Pattern, ghost image & Microtext, issue date and print date. It contains the embossed Aadhar Logo. Instant offline verification is possible by QR code. Once the request is raised, the UIDAI will hand over the card to the post office within five working days (excluding the date of request) and the PVC card will be delivered using Speed Post services. While ordering the PVC Aadhar card, an individual will have to pay Rs. 50 (inclusive of GST and speed post charges).[261] With the introduction of the PVC Aadhar Card, it is one step closer to being converted into a Citizen Identity Card. It may be recalled that the Supreme Court in the matter of *Assam Public Works* V. *Union of India WP (C) 274* of 2009 in several orders including order dated 13.8.2019 [2019 (9) SCC 70)] specifically directed Union of India to update NRC on the pattern of Aadhar.

It has been said time and again that Aadhar is not a citizenship document because, as Nilekani *et al*. say, Aadhar collects only four pieces of personal information – name, age, gender and address – along with biometric data.[262] But with the linking of Voter Card, PAN Card, Ration

Card, Bank accounts, Sim Card etc., all these information can be accessed by the UIDAI. Over the years, Aadhar has become the storehouse of multiple information about each individual. The Haryana government has decided to prepare Aadhar-based state resident database (SRDB) to provide benefits of various schemes to every people of the state. The Health department would prepare the Aadhar cards of new-born babies and the education department would update the Aadhar of the child by taking finger prints when he or she turns three year old. This Haryana model can be further modified to accord Aadhar the *de jure* recognition of a Citizen Identity Card by an enabling Act. If there is any dearth of information as collected or linked with Aadhar for declaring a person a citizen of India, that has to be taken care of by amending the enabling Act. As a matter of fact, the Citizen Identity Card will be so designed as to supersede all existing identity cards issued by the different authorities.

For instance, the birth certificate. It should henceforth include the Aadhar number of the parents as well. But all births are not registered even now under the Compulsory Registration of Births and Deaths Act, 1969. National birth registration coverage was 41.2 per cent in 2005 and it improved to 79.6 per cent in 2015.[263] The non-registration would be more frequent amongst tribals, *dalits* and poor communities. In addition, millions of people are migrant workers within India who have hardly any birth certificate or for that matter any documentation. If the example of Assam is anything to go by, a large number of persons have been excluded because in their documents, there was a slight discrepancy in the spelling. Women are the biggest victims there because in the villages in which they are born, there is no documentation, and in the villages, where they are married into, the documentation, at the best, will be from the date of marriage, and not birth. Besides, names are changed after marriage, and there is often nothing to connect the previous name to the new spouse. Problems will also arise for those belonging to the transgender community.[264] Unless all births are registered, both the individual and the state will forever lose this vital document of proof of citizenship. Once it is made known and general public realises that birth certificate is required as a proof of citizenship, people will procure and preserve it for obvious reason.

Now Aadhar is issued to persons of all age group above the age of five years, because the biometric details of a person are not developed before that age. But India Post Payments Bank (IPPB) has for the last one year started to enrol the new born babies in the hospitals for the issuance of Aadhar card.[265] While hearing a PIL on Aadhar, the Apex Court made it clear way back in 2013 that no illegal immigrant should be issued Aadhar no.[266] Since an Aadhar can technically be issued to a non-citizen as well,

Aadhar issued to a citizen must be of a different colour to differentiate it from the one issued to a non-citizen. It may be remembered that the MHA in 1998 thought of introducing national identity cards by issuing Green Cards to resident Indians and Red Cards to illegal immigrants. A person in possession of a non-citizen Aadhar will know that he is not a citizen of the country. If he is a citizen of the country, he will find out why his name has been included in the non-citizen category and will rectify the mistakes by producing the relevant documents. He gets enough time to get his name included in the citizen category. Once in the citizen category, one continues in that category till death or till he acquires citizenship of another country.

India being a secular state, there should not, however, be any provision to indicate the religious identity of the person concerned. Even in an Islamic country like Pakistan, the minorities oppose the government decision to note the religion of all Pakistanis in the Identity cards and the Bishop of Faisalabad even threatened to court arrest before Christmas and remained in jail on 25 December in protest against the Government decision.[267]

Initially, UIDAI collected only four pieces of personal information—name, age, gender and address of the applicant for Aadhar Card along with biometric data. But with the linking of Voter Card, PAN Card, Ration Card, Bank Accounts, Sim Card etc., it is now a repository of multiple information. So it devolves on the UIDAI to protect the data so collected in order to ensure that the privacy of the holders of Aadhar is not breached. However, a petition has been filed in the Madras High Court alleging that local BJP candidates of Puducherry unit had obtained the mobile phone numbers of voters that are linked with Aadhar and were using them to create WhatsApp groups in their respective constituencies for campaigning in the 2021 Assembly elections. 952 WhatsApp groups had thus been created with voter details obtained from Aadhar data. The Division Bench of the Madras High Court consisting of Chief Justice Sanjib Bannerjee and Justice Senthilkumar Ramamurthy on 24 March, 2021 lambasted the Election Commission of India over its failure to probe complaints about the Puducherry unit of BJP illegally accessing Aadhar data and using it to reach voters in the Union Territory and asked it to file a report by 26 March.[268] The same Bench on 1 April, 2021 rejected the BJP's claim that mobile numbers of voters linked to Aadhar were collected by their party workers going door-to-door in Puducherry and asked the UIDAI to answer how information furnished to it by citizens in the hope that confidentiality would be preserved had been breached. The HC also made it clear that the Election Commission of India should deal with the perceived breach of code of conduct without putting a lid on the issue and a separate criminal investigation against the party should go on.[269] This incident has put a question mark on the security of the data stored by the UIDAI and called for an in-depth study of the entire matter relating to the security of the data collected by it.

The Kolkata police issued a fraud warning—for the second time in two months—asking the citizens to be careful when submitting Aadhar details, both online and offline.[270] Telangana police have issued an alert on Aadhar-enabled payment system (AePS) fraud. It comes after a series of instances of AePS fraud in Haryana, Jharkhand and other areas.[271] The modus operandi followed by scammers is varied. Some infect the victim's phone with malware or mirror the screen and steal OTPs. Others trick victims into sharing OTPs under false pretexts. Biometrics are also susceptible to theft. A victim's fingerprints are also lifted from objects she has touched. Or her iris scans can be captured using advanced cameras from a distance. Once a scammer has access to OTP or biometrics, it becomes easier to commit financial frauds. Data security expert Kodali Srinivas said: "Criminals had stolen biometric data, including thumbprints, from Haryana's land records website. They created duplicate prints on silicon and withdrew funds from Aadhar-linked bank accounts of victims." The Supreme Court, in its judgment, had cleary ordered banks to not link Aadhar to bank accounts", Srinivas said. [272]

Not only UIDAI data could be accessed, the personal health data of Aarogya Setu are being shared. This happened in Jammu & Kashmir when it was revealed in an RTI reply that the J&K administration in a breach of protocol had shared sensitive medical information with the police department.[273] It may be noted that over 172 million Indians had offered personal information while signing up with the Aarogya Setu App. The data was given following repeated assurances by the government that it would be used for health-specific purposes only and the users' privacy would be respected. The RTI reply shows that isn't the case in J&K. What is more worrying is that one cannot rule out the possibility that other states might have shared the information with law enforcement agencies or other government entities. The UIDAI has, however, told the Delhi High Court that it cannot share Aadhar details such as core biometrics information with investigating agencies to match chance prints and photographs from crime scenes because the objective of the Aadhar Act 2016 is to empower the people with a unique identity and digital platform only for the purpose of "identity proof."[274] To protect the public against misuse of Aadhar data, a data protection law is critical. Without it, we are at the mercy of every hotel, movie theatre, school or employer who wants to check if we are who we claim we are. Confidence and trust is fundamental to the relationship between the state and its citizens. The price to be paid if that is eroded is enormous.

It may be recalled that the UPA government could not get the Aadhar Bill, 2010 passed due to intense opposition from the BJP and other opposition parties. During the 2014 Lok Sabha elections, the BJP had opposed Aadhar. However, after coming to power the party thought it was a good proposition, as with the help of the Unique Identity (UID) residents' financial subsidies and other public services could be targeted more efficiently. The Aadhar (Targeted Delivery of Financial and Other Subsidies, Benefits and Services) Bill, 2016 was passed by Parliament as a Money Bill to facilitate its safe passage. The ruling NDA lacked a majority in the Rajya Sabha and thus wanted to avoid the embarrassment. The 2016 Act also takes care of the apprehensions expressed about the assault on privacy by making statutory provisions. According to the current legislation, information related to a holder's finger print and iris scan shall not be published or displayed publicly except for purposes specified by regulations. When authenticating an individual's identity, the UIDAI authority cannot reveal information related to finger print and iris scan to the entity requiring for authentication. The Supreme Court has barred private entities from using Aadhar for know-your-customer (KYC) authentication. So, a bank or a mobile company cannot insist on Aadhar. It is not mandatory even for school admissions. But it is needed for direct transfer of benefits and government subsidies to the beneficiaries account. Nonetheless, ration and pension cannot be denied for want of Aadhar. It is mandatory for getting a Permanent Account Number or filing income tax returns. Those who have a PAN need to link it with their Aadhar as a precaution against misuse. "Aadhar card should be freely used for providing identity and doing transactions, but should not be put on public platforms like Twitter, Facebook, etc. While using Aadhar, you should do the same level of due diligence as you do in case of other ID cards—not more, not less", a post on the UIDAI website said.[275] "Aadhar identiy authentication ecosystem has provided adequate features for protecting and safeguarding the identity and privacy of the Aadhar holder", the Ministry of Electronics and Information Technology (MEIT), the parent body of the UIDAI, said in a statement issued on 29 May, 2022.[276] Therefore, one can say that an attempt has been made to address concerns about privacy.

It has been reported that out of 23.58 crore Ration Cards issued in India, 89 per cent are Aadhar-seeded, while remaining 11 per cent that is about 2.59 crore are not Aadhar-seeded resulting in their cancellation.[277]

"The insistence on Aadhar and biometric authentication had resulted to the cancellation of nearly four crore ration cards in the country, according to the Union of India. The Union of India gives an explanation that these cancelled cards are bogus. The real reason is that the technological system based on iris identification, thumb prints, non-possession of Aadhar, non-functioning of the internet in rural and remote areas etc., led to large scale cancellation of ration cards, without notice to the family concerned", said a report submitted by the petitioner Kolli Devi to the Supreme Court. The Supreme Court on 17 March, 2021 said it was a "very serious" matter if the Centre had cancelled around three crore ration cards and asked the Centre to respond to the allegation made by the petitioner Kolli Devi who was represented by senior advocate Colin Gonsalves.[278]

The allegation of cancellation of about three crore ration cards for not being linked with the Aadhar database has severely challenged the case of Aadhahr Card being converted into the Citizen Identity Card. An editorial in *The Hindu* written immediately after the Ration Card cancellation fiasco has put the issue in proper perspective thus: "Biometric authentication failures are but expected of a large-scale and technology-intensive project such as the UID. Despite being designed to store finger and iris scans of most users, doubts about the success rates of authentication and the generation of "false negatives" have always persisted, more so for labourers and tribal people. Those engaged in manual and hard labour, for example, are susceptible to fingerprint changes over time. In practice, beneficiaries have tended to use Aadhar cards as identity markers."[279] It is a fact that Aadhar link to ration card doesn't always work primarily due to migration and fingerprint problems, among others. If Aadhar aspires to double up as a Citizen Identity Card as well the obstacles pointed out in the petition to the Supreme Court have got to be addressed. After all, there cannot be any hurdle which cannot be surmounted provided there is a will to scale it.

Aadhar is ubiquitous. As of 31 December, 2019, 125 crore residents of India have Aadhar.[280] By now, around 1.3 billion residents, including 99.9 per cent adults, have been assigned this pan-India biometric identifier. Consequently, it is the single most important database in India and one which is the *de facto* yardstick for all other databases. It's an unprecedented phenomenon as the first Aadhar was issued only in September 2010. It took a mere four years from its tentative conceptualisation to issuing the first 12-digit number, and then just another six years to cover a billion people.

CAG presented its performance audit of Aadhar's regulator, Unique Identification Authority of India (UIDAI) in April 2022. The audit covered its mature phase, from 2014-15 to 2018-19. By this time it had already generated about 800 million Aadhar numbers. Given this backdrop, CAG's audit report portrays an unsatisfactory picture of the systems and processes in UIDAI.

The Comptroller and Auditor General of India has pointed out that all Aadhar numbers were not paired with the documents relating to personal infomation of their holders, and even after nearly 10 years, the UIDAI could not identify the exact extent of mismatch, as a result the UIDAI had to cancel more than 4.7 lakh Aadhars "for being duplicate." "There were instances of issue of Aadhars with the same biometric data to different residents indicating flaws in the de-duplication process and issue of Aadhars on faulty biometrics and documents", the CAG said in a report tabled in Parliament on 6 April, 2022.[281] The main takeaway is the laxity in the organization, which not only generates data for India's most important identity, but also is entrusted with safely storing it. This level of laxity is worrying becsue of the risk it entails.

UIDAI operates Aadhar through a layer of subcontractors. It appoints registrars for enrolment who, in turn subcontract. So, when an applicant's biometrics are uploaded to the Central Identities Data Repository, it may be executed by the third layer of sub-conracts. A similar system is in place when a financial intermediary seeks to authenticate the identity of a potential customer by using the Aadhar database. CAG's report shows looseness in the pocess all through. Often UIDAI neither has granular data nor is it able to pinpoint the cause for failures. A consequence is that it forces people to pay to update their biometrics. In 2018-19, there were about 30 million biometric updates, of which 73 per cent were voluntary updates. CAG observed they were mostly on account of authenticaion failures.

The audit also showed that even at the first stage of enrolment there were problems of duplicate Aadhars. Most wearisome perhaps is the lack of oversight of subcontractors. Many failed to comply with UIDAI's requirements on getting their operations audited annually by information systems auditors. This has a bearing on data security. [282]

It is a matter of concern whether such vast data of all the Indians can be allowed to be handled by the UIDAI which mainly outsources its operations. This calls for vesting its operations to only a governmental organization. It should be the responsibility of the Government to issue the CIC and of nobody else. It is better if a full-fledged ministry of the Union Government under the charge of a cabinet minister is created at the union level to handle the citizenship issue with units up at all states and UTs up to the panchayat level. In any case, if the Aadhar Card is converted into a

Citizen Identity Card, a comprehensive Act has got to be enacted to ensure that the processes and systems of issuing Aadhar Card and the storing of the datas are as foolproof as possible. It should be clearly stated in the Act that it would be a crime to obtain the Aadhar details by organisations that have not obtained User License from the authority. It would be much better if along with the CIC a masked CIC which displays only the last 4 digits of the CIC number is also issued to be used as an "identity proof", so that the data stored in the system are not accessed by unscrupulous people. Aadhar should be updated every fifth year to include all the changes taking place in between like the educational qualification, marital status, biometric details of those not included earlier, and the like. (The Government has mandated that Aadhar should be updated 'at least ones' in 10 years.) Whatever steps are taken that should be preceded by ample public discussions and debates to work out a smooth, non-invasive and equitable process. After all, the Aadhar Act, 2016 is primarily meant to make it easier to transfer LPG subsidy, food subsidy, MGNREGA wages and many other benefits directly to the targeted beneficiaries without any leakage. It was not designed to serve as the Citizen Identity Card.

If Aadhar Card is converted into a Citizen Identity Card, the apprehensions of the people of being declared as "doubtful citizen" at every 10th year would be considerably minimised because the citizen knows that the legacy documents are already with the accredited body. In case of any doubt about the bona fide of any document that could be sorted out within the parameter of the existing laws and would not be left to the whims and caprices of the 'village level or ward level' officers as in the 2003 Citizenship Rules, a nightmarish prospect for poor and unlettered citizens.

It will call for the scrapping of section 14A of the Citizenship Act and the 2003 Citizenship Rules, thus divesting the Registrar General of India of the responsibility of issuing the National Identity Card and preparation of the NRC, which many think carves out paths to statelessness for groups that are disfavoured.[283] With the scrapping of Section 14A of the Citizenship Act, the Citizenship Act will be restored to its pre-2003 position when the NRC and NPR were not part of the citizenship exercise.

In September 2013, Justice K.U.Chandiwal of Bombay High Court gave a judgment that a birth certificate, passport or even an Aadhar card alone may not be enough to prove Indian citizenship if one is born after 1 July, 1987. Citizenship laws say a person born in India after 1 July, 1987 cannot claim automatic citizenship unless at least one of the parents is an Indian citizen.[284] The division bench of Gauhati High Court comprising Justices Manojit Bhuyan and Parthivjyoti Saikia dismissed on 12 February, 2020, the citizenship claim by Jabeda Begum of Assam's Baksa district, who produced as many as 15 documents including land revenue paying receipt, bank passbook, voter list and Permanent Account Number (PAN), because she was not able to link her relationship with her parents by submitting documents. (*Jabeda Begum @ Jabeda Khatun* vs. *the Union of India and 5 others* in case no. WP(C) 7451/2019). The same Bench has held in *Md. Babul Islam* vs. *Union of India* (WP(C)/3547/2016) that PAN Card and bank documents are not proof of citizenship.[285]

In view of these judicial pronouncements, there should be clear indication in the Act itself as to what document/documents are to be relied on for declaring a person an Indian citizen. If a Muslim woman law student is asked by the public information officer to prove citizenship before her application under the RTI could be considered, as happened in Gujarat[286], what documents would she produce to conclusively prove her Indian citizenship? Where it is codified that such and such documents the administration and the judiciary should rely on as proof of one's citizenship? In the backdrop of the raging controversies, apprehensions, threats and litigations over citizenship, it is better to address this great lacuna in our citizenship law once for all, the earlier the better. After all, it is the continuing obfuscation on the issue of citizenship that has caused the Anti-CAA/NPR/NRC protests across India[287], billed as the third Pan-Indian stir after the JP movement in 1975-77 and the Jan Lokpal movement against rampant corruption by Anna Hazare in 2011.[288] In any case, it should be the endeavour of an elected government in a functioning democracy to enlist the trust and goodwill of all sections of the population, even of those who are not the followers of the party in power and no government can afford to antagonise a sizeable section of the population for long or keep them hostage to a perpetual threat of disenfranchisement and deportation.

NOTES

1. *The Hindu*, January 8, 2003, p. 1.
2. Editorial entitled "send them back", *The Hindustan Times*, September 30, 1992.
3. *The Telegraph*, August 1, 2014, p. 7.
4. *Bartaman*, April 22, 2015, p. 4.
5. Editorial titled "Numbing numbers" in *The Hindu,* August 1, 2019, p. 8.
6. *The Times of India,* August 20, 2019, p. 7.

7. *Anandabazar Patrika*, October 23, 2019, p. 6.
8. *The Telegraph*, September 2, 2019, p. 1.
9. *The Times of India*, December 14, 2019, p. 1.
10. *Ibid.*
11. *Ibid.*, December 19, 2019, p. 9.
12. *The Hindu*, February 20, 2020, p. 11.
13. *The Telegraph*, December 11, 2019, p. 1.
14. *The Times of India*, December 11, 2019, p. 1.
15. *Ibid.*, December 18, 2019, p. 1.
16. *Ibid.*, December 20, 2019, p. 1.
17. *Ibid.*, December 28, 2019, p. 1.
18. *The Hindu*, February 21, 2020, p. 1.
19. *The Statesman*, February 17, 2020, p. 1
20. *The Times of India*, February 26, 2020, p. 1.
21. *The Hindu*, April 29, 2020, p. 8.
22. *Ibid.*, March 19, 2021, p. 10.
23. *The Telegraph*, January 31, 2020, p. 3.
24. *The Times of India*, March 4, 2020, p. 6.
25. *The Hindu*, February 15, 2020, p. 11. *The Statesman*, March 4, 2020, p. 1.
26. *The Telegraph,* April 26, 2022, p. 1. & p. 4.
27. *The Statesman,* January 4, 2020, p. 3.
28. *The Telegraph,* February 4, 2020, p. 1.
29. *Ibid.*, February 14, 2020, p. 1.
30. *The Statesman*, February12, 2020, p. 5.
31. *The Hindu*, February 12, 2020, p. 11.
32. *The Telegraph*, February 12, 2020, p. 1.
33. *The Times of India,* December 20, 2019, p. 10.
34. *Ei Samay,* December 23, 2019, p. 5.
35. *The Statesman*, January 14, 2020, p. 15.
36. *The Telegraph*, January 25, 2020, p. 5.
37. *Ibid.*, January 28, 2020, p. 5.
38. *The Statesman*, January 28, 2020, p. 15.
39. *The Telegraph,* January 10, 2020, p. 5.
40. *The Hindu*, February 16, 2020, p. 9.
41. *The Telegraph*, January 21, 2020, p. 4.
42. *The Statesman,* January 4, 2020, p. 3.
43. *The Times of India*, January 22, 2020, p. 9.
44. *Ibid.*
45. *Ibid.*
46. *Ibid.*, February 15, 2020, p. 1.
47. *Ibid.*, February 25, 2020, p. 7.
48. *The Telegraph*, December 20, 2019, p. 7.
49. *Ibid.*, December 26, 2019, p. 6.
50. *The Times of India*, December 24, 2019, p. 1.

51. *Ibid.*, January 2, 2020, p. 1.
52. *Ibid.*, January 5, 2020, p. 5.
53. *The Hindu*, March 15, 2020, p. 5.
54. *The Statesman,* February 23, 2020, p. 4.
55. Farooqi Irfanullah, "Citizenship as Participation; Muslim Women Protestors of Shaheen Bagh", *Economic and Political Weekly*, Vol. LV, No. 4, January 25, 2020, pp. 14-15.
56. *Ei Samay*, January 19, 2020, p. 5.
57. Farooqi Irfanullah, *Op. Cit.*, p. 13.
58. Kesavan, Mukul, "Blocking the way", *The Telegraph*, February 9, 2020, p. 16.
59. *The Telegraph*, January 5, 2020, p. 5.
60. *The Statesman,* February 13, 2020, p. 15.
61. *Ibid.,* January 15, 2020, p. 3.
62. *Ibid.*
63. *Ibid.,* January 25, 2020, p. 5.
64. *Ibid.,* January 4, 2020, p. 3.
65. Naqvi, Saba, "Noose Around Our Necks", *Outlook*, December 23, 2019, p. 36.
66. *The Telegraph*, December 14, 2019, p. 1.
67. Momin Sajeda, "Why NRC doesn't worry Gujarat", *The Telegraph,* March 9, 2020, p. 5.
68. *Ibid.*, December 14, 2029, p. 1.
69. *Aṇandabazar Patrika*, September 3, 2019, p. 3.
70. *Ei Samay,* October 22, 2019, p. 7.
71. *The Times of India,* December 29, 2019, p. 3.
72. *Ibid.*
73. *The Hindu*, March 16, 2020, p. 1.
74. *Ibid.*, February 10, 2020, p. 2.
75. *Ibid.*, February 12, 2020, p. 5.
76. *Ibid.*, February 10, 2020, p. 2.
77. Mukherjee, Deb, "Shaheen soars as women raise flag", *The Telegraph*, March 5, 2020, p. 5.
78. Singh Aditi and Sunawala, Nergish, "Chipko to Shaheen Bagh: why mom-driven movements work", *The Times of India*, March 8, 2020, p. 16.
79. *The Hindu*, October 12, 2020, p. 11.
80. Mander, Harsh, Introduction, *This Land is Mine, I Am Not of This Land* (edited by Harsh Mander and Navsharan Singh), New Delhi, Speaking Tiger Books, 2021, pp. 30-32.
81. *The Hindu,* February 25, 2020, p. 1.
82. Sharma, Prafulla, "Riots and Wrongs" *The Week*, March 8, 2020, p. 44.
83. *The Hindu*, May 3, 2020, p. 2.
84. *The Telegraph*, February 25, 2020, p. 1 and p. 5.
85. Interview of Gopal Rai in *The Week*, March 8, 2020, p. 33.
86. Interview of G. Kishan Reddy in *The Week,* March 8, 2020, p. 51.

87. *The Statesman,* February 26, 2020, p. 1.
    The Times of India, February 26, 2020, p. 1, pp. 7-8 and pp. 12-14.
88. *The Statesman*, March 2, 2020, p. 1.
89. *The Hindu*, June 4, 2020, p. 1.
90. *The Statesman,* February 25, 2020, p. 6.
91. Interview with Shabani Banerjee, *The Statesman*, March 14, 2020, p. 7.
92. Mishra, Soni, "Broom for manoeuvre", *The Week*, March 8, 2020, p. 54.
93. *The Telegraph*, 27 February, 2020, p. 5.
94. *The Statesman*, March 4, 2020, p. 2.
95. Editorial titled "Politics of Communal Violence in Delhi", in *The Economic & Political Weekly,* Vol. LV, No. 9, February 29, 2020, p. 7.
96. Sharma, Prafulla, "Riots and Wrongs", *The Week*, March 8, 2020, p. 41.
97. *The Times of India*, February 26, 2020, p. 14.
98. *The Statesman*, March 3, 2020, p. 1.
99. *Ibid.*, March 4, 2020, p. 13.
100. *Ibid.*, February 28, 2020, p. 13.
101. *The Times of India*, February 27, 2020, p. 6.
102. *Ibid.*, February 26, 2020, p. 6.
103. *Ibid.*, February 27, 2020, p. 10.
104. *The Statesman*, February 27, 2020, p. 1.
105. *The Telegraph*, February 27, 2020, p. 5.
106. *The Statesman*, February 28, 2020, p. 1.
107. *Ibid.*, February 29, 2020, p. 1.
108. *The Telegraph,* February 28, 2020, p. 13.
109. *Ibid.*, February 29, 2020, p. 10.
110. *The Statesman*, January 30, 2020, p. 1.
111. *The Hindu*, August 25, 2021, p. 3
112. *The Telegraph*, February 27, 2020, p. 1.
113. *Ibid.*, February 27, 2020, p. 3.
114. *The Times of India*, February 28, 2020, p. 13.
115. *The Hindu*, March 14, 2020, p. 11.
116. Kakar, Sudhir, "The Psychology of Riots", *The Times of India*, March 4, 2020, p. 16.
117. Narayanan, M.K., "Delhi's shame is India's shame", *The Hindu*, March 13, 2020, p. 8.
118. *The Hindu*, March 2, 2020, p. 11.
119. Sibal, Kapil, "A tragic pattern of inaction", *The Hindu*, March 3, 2020, p. 9.
120. Deshpande, Satish, "The message from Delhi", *The Hindu*, March 3, 2020, p. 8.
121. Thakur, Sankarshan, "World of tomorrow", *The Telegraph*, March 4, 2020, p. 6.
122. *The Times of India*, March 1, 2020, p. 6.
123. Editorial titled "Delhi Riots, Again", *The Times of India,* February 26, 2020, p. 20.

124. *The Telegraph*, February 27, 2020, p. 3.
125. *Ibid.*, February 27, 2020, p. 1 and p. 4.
126. *The Times of India*, February 28, 2020, p. 1.
127. *The Telegraph*, February 29, 2020, p. 4.
128. *Ibid.*, March 5, 2020, p. 1.
129. *Anandabazar Patrika*, March 12, 2020, p. 12.
130. *The Times of India*, March 13, 2020, p. 1.
131. *The Hindu*, June 17, 2020, p. 2.
132. Editorial titled "Correct Course" in *The Times of India,* February 29, 2020, p. 14.
133. *The Times of India*, February 28, 2020, p. 8.
134. *The Telegraph*, March 6, 2020, p. 1.
135. *The Times of India*, June 3, 2020, p. 11.
136. *The Hindu,* July 6, 2020, p. 3.
137. *The Times of India*, September 23, 2020, p. 1.
138. *The Hindu*, April 29, 2020, p. 2.
139. *Ibid.*, April 23, 2020, p. 2.
140. *The Telegraph*, September 15, 2020, p. 1.
141. *The Times of India*, September 17, 2020, p. 8.
142. *The Hindu*, September 15, 2020, p. 10.
143. *The Telegraph*, December 4, 2022, p. 1.
144. *The Hindu*, June 16, 2021, p. 1.
145. *The Times of India,* June 16,2021, p. 7.
146. *The Hindu*, June 17, 2021, p. 1.
147. *Ibid.*, June 19, 2021, p. 1.
148. *The Telegraph*, February 1, 2023, p. 4.
149. *The Times of India*, March 15, 2022, p. 10.
150. *The Telegraph*, September 13, 2020, p. 1.
151. *The Times of India*, September 13, 2020, p. 1.
152. *The Hindu*, September 13, 2020, p. 1.
153. *Ei Samay*, September 25, 2020, p. 1.
154. *The Times of India*, September 18, 2020, p. 7.
155. *The Hindu*, March 5, 2020, p. 11.
156. *Ibid.*, May 29, 2020, p. 3.
157. *Ibid.*, October 30, 2020, p. 3.
158. Chitkara, Radhika and Vilas Kumar, "Rescripting North-east Delhi riots—and the question of justice", *The Hindu*, May 16, 2020, p. 2.
159. *The Telegraph*, July 15, 2021, p. 1.
160. *The Times of India,* August 29, 2021, p. 12.
161. *Ibid.*, September 3, 2021, p. 9.
162. *Ibid.*, September 12, 2021, p. 7.
163. *The Hindu*, September 18, 2021, p. 3.
164. *Ibid.*, January 12. 2022, p. 3.
165. *Ibid.*, September 14, 2020, p. 3.

166. Interview with Vijay Thakur, *The Statesman*, September 12, 2020, p. 7.
167. *The Telegraph*, January 14, 2021, p. 5.
168. *The Hindu*, September 20, 2020, p. 5.
169. *The Telegraph*, October 13, 2020, p. 4.
170. *Ibid.*, December 10, 2020, p. 1 and p. 4.
171. *The Telegraph*, March 1, 2022, p. 1. and p. 4.
172. *TheTimes of India*, March 2, 2022, p. 14.
173. *Ibid.*, January 8, 2021, p. 10.
174. *The Hindu*, February 23, 2021, p. 3.
175. *Ibid.*
176. *Ibid.*
177. *Ibid.*, March 12, 2021, p. 3.
178. Ahuja, Namrata Biji, "Due procedure followed in cases against activists", *The Week*, April 25, 2021, p. 26.
179. *The Hindu*, February 22, 2022, p. 3.
180. *The Times of India*, 13 April, 2022, p. 1.
181. *The Telegraph,* April 19, 2022, p. 1.
182. *Ibid.*, April 18, 2022, p. 1.
183. *Ibid.*, May 9, 2022, p. 1.
184. *Ibid.*, April 25, 2022, p. 1.
185. *Ibid.*, May 9, 2022, p. 1.
186. *The Hindu,* February 29, 2020, p. 11.
187. *The Statesman*, March 2, 2020, p. 1.
188. *The Times of India*, March 1, 2020, p. 1.
189. *The Statesman,* February 29, 2020, p. 1.
190. *Ibid.*, November 4, 2019, p. 1.
191. *The Times of India*, November 4, 2019, p. 1.
192. Mander, Harsh, "The Dark Side of Humanity and Legality", In *This Land is Mine, I Am Not of This Land* (edited by Harsh Mander and Navsharan Singh), New Delhi, Speaking Tiger Books, 2021, pp. 230-31.
193. *The Hindu*, March 17, 2020, p. 1.
194. *Ibid.*, November 20, 2019, p. 1.
195. *Ibid.*, August 6, 2020, p. 1.
196. Agarwal, Akshat, "An injured voice", *The Telegraph*, June 3, 2022, XXCE.
197. *The Times of India*, May 23, 2022, p. 8.
198. Prashad, Vijay, "A World of Migrants", *Economic & Political Weekly*, June 1, 2019, Vol. LIV, No. 22, pp. 20-22.
199. Jayal, Niraja Gopal, "The misadventure of a new citizenship regime", *The Hindu*, November 27, 2019, p. 8.
200. *The Hindu*, March 3, 2017, p. 10.
201. Chaudhuri, Sukanta, "Groping in the dark", *The Telegraph*, December 11, 2019, p. 10.
202. Editorial titled "Tread Carefully", *The Times of India*, November 21, 2019, p. 14.

203. Chaudhuri, Sukanta, "Groping in the dark", *The Telegraph*, December 11, 2019, p. 10..
204. *The Hindu*, November 4, 2019, p. 1.
205. Jayal, Niraja Gopal, The misadventure of a new citizenship regime", *The Hindu*, November 27, 2019, p. 8.
206. *The Hindu*, July 18, 2019, p. 1.
207. *The Times of India*, February 28, 2020, p. 13.
208. *The Hindu*, November 28, 2019, p. 4.
209. *The Telegraph*, October 17, 2019, p. 6.
210. *Ibid.*, October 26, 2019, p. 5.
211. *Anandabazar Patrika,* October 29, 2019, p. 6.
212. *The Hindu*, September 10, 1998. *The Statesman,* May 8, 2001.
213. Banerjee Paula, Hazarika Sanjoy, Hussain Monirul and Samaddar Ranabir, "Indo-Bangladesh Cross-Border Migration and Trade", *Economic and Political Weekly,* September 4, 1999, p. 2550.
214. *White Paper on Foreigners' Issue*, *Op. Cit.*, pp. 10-11.
215. Editorial titled "Aliens and Identity", *The Statesman*, November 28,1993, p. 6.
216. Government of India, *Annual Report 1991-1992*, New Delhi: Ministry of Home Affairs, 1992, p. 13.
217. *The Statesman*, October 7, 1992, p. 7.
218. Government of India, *Annual Report 1999-2000*, New Delhi: Ministry of Home Affairs 2000, p. 12.
219. *The Statesman,* June 28, 1993, p. 7.
220. *Ibid.*, November 20, 1993, p. 1.
221. *Ibid.*, August 29, 1994, p. 1.
222. Rao, M. Maheswara, "Technique for foolproof ID cards", *The Hindu*, November 9, 1994, p. 11.
223. *The Statesman*, November 12, 1994, p. 4.
224. *Ibid.*, April 3, 1998, p. 1.
225. *The Times of India*, April 5, 1998, p. 8.
226. *The Hindu*, February 2, 1997, p. 4.
227. Majumdar, Diptosh, "I-card tabs on personal details", *The Telegraph*, May 8, 1998, p. 1.
228. *The Statesman*, July 27, 1998, p. 5.
229. Government of India, *Annual Report 2003-2004*, New Delhi: Ministry of Home Affairs, 2004, p. 5.
230. *The Telegraph*, July 11, 2004, p. 8.
231. Bannerjee, Diganta, *Anandabazar Patrika*, April 16, 2007, p. 7.
232. Government of India, *Annual Report 2009-2010*, New Delhi: Ministry of Home Affairs, 2010, p. 177.
233. Government of India, *Annual Report 2006-2007*, New Delhi: Ministry of Home Affairs, 2007, p. 42.
234. *The Telegraph*, January 16, 2009, p. 4.
235. *Sarbananda Sonowal* vs. *Union of India* (2007) 1 SCC 174 (para 64).

236. *The Times of India*, June 15, 2008, p. 6.
237. *The Statesman*, April 16, 2009, p. 3.
238. *Anandabazar Parika*, August 17, 2012, p. 1.
239. *The Statesman,* September 24, 2019, p. 1.
240. Government of India, *Annual Report 2014-15*, New Delhi: Ministry of Home Affairs, 2015, p. 245.
241. *The Times of India*, February19, 2020, p. 1.
242. Sengupta Suman, *Ei Samay,* March 7, 2020, p. 8.
243. *The Times of India*, January 25, 2021, p. 8.
244. *Ibid.*, June 19, 2022, p. 7.
245. *The Telegraph*, December 25, 2022, p. 7.
246. *Ei Samay,* February 10, 2020, p. 12.
247. *Ibid.*, January 13, 2020, p. 10.
248. *The Hindu*, May 29, 2020, p. 11.
249. *The Economic Times*, August 2, 2020, p. 1.
250. *The Times of India*, November 13, 2020, (*Times Business*).
251. *Ibid.*, February 25, 2020, p. 8.
252. Allu, Rakesh, Deo, Sarang, Devalkar, Sripad, "Alternative to Aadhar-based Biometrics in the Public Distribution System", *Economic & Political Weekly*, Vol. LIV, No. 12, dated March 23, 2029, pp. 30-37.
253. *The Telegraph*, February 9, 2022, p. 9.
254. Ahuja, Namrata Biji, "Clash register", *The Week*, January 5, 2020, pp. 42-43.
255. *The Times of India*, February 25, 2020, p. 8.
256. *Ibid.*, March 28, 2017, p. 1.
257. *Ibid.*, January 21, 2019, p. 10.
258. *Ibid.*, July 11, 2020, p. 14.
259. *Ibid.*, January 11, 2021, p. 7.
260. *Ibid.*, November 18, 2020, p. 4.
261. *Anandabazar Patrika,* November 17, 2020, p. 9.
262. Nilekani, Nandan and Kudva, Roopa, "Aadhar at 10: taking stock—The unfinished work lies with the most vulnerable sectiosn of society", *The Times of India*, January 7, 2020, p. 12.
263. https://www.sciencedirect.com/science/article/pii/S2352827321000033, para 3.2.
264. Desai, Mihir, *Op. Cit.*
265. *Ei Samay*, June 8, 2022, p. 4.
266. *The New Indian Express*, New Delhi, September 23, 2013.
267. *The Statesman*, December 24, 1992, p. 5.
268. *The Times of India*, March 25, 2021, p. 18.
269. *Ibid.*, April 2, 2021, p. 1.
270. *Ibid.*, February 13, 2021, p. 4.
271. *Ibid.*, May 30, 2022, p. 6.
272. *Ibid.*, May 30, 2022, p. 6.
273. *Ibid.*, March 31, 2021, p. 7.

274. *The Hindu*, May 6, 2022, p. 4.
275. *The Times of India*, June 2, 2022, p. 9.
276. *The Hindu*, May 30, 2022, p. 1
277. *Ibid.*, March 18, 2021, p. 1.
278. *Ibid.*
279. Editorial titled "Aadhar as a hurdle", *The Hindu*, March 19, 2021, p. 6.
280. Unique Identification Authority of India website.
281. *The Times of India*, April 7, 2022, p. 10.
282. Editorial titled "Safeguard Aadhar", *The Times of India*, April 8, 2022, p. 12.
283. Jayal, Niraja Gopal, *Op. Cit.* p. 8.
284. *The Times of India*, September 3, 2013.
285. *National Herald*, February 19, 2020. www.nationalheraldindia.com "NEWS" India.
286. *The Statesman*, December 9, 2020, p. 5.
287. *The Times of India*, February19, 2020, p. 1.
288. Rajappa, Sam, "Third Pan-Indian Stir", *The Statesman,* March 8, 2020, p. 6.

Annexures

Annexure A
Assam Accord
15th August, 1985
(Accord between AASU, AAGSP, Central and State Government on the Foreigner Problem Issue)

MEMORANDUM OF SETTLEMENT

1. Government have all along been most anxious to find a satisfactory solution to the problem of Foreigners in Assam. The All Assam Students' Union (AASU) and the All Assam Gana Sangram Parishad (AAGSP) have also expressed their keenness to find such a solution.
2. The AASU through their Memorandum dated 2nd February, 1980 presented to the Late Prime Minister Smt. Indira Gandhi, conveyed their profound sense of apprehensions regarding the continuing influx of foreign nationals into Assam and the fear about adverse affects upon the political, social, cultural and economic life of the State.
3. Being fully alive to the genuine apprehensions of the people of Assam, the then Prime Minister initiated the dialogue with the AASU/AAGSP. Subsequently, talks were held at the Prime Minister's and Home Ministers levels during the period 1980-83. Several rounds of informal talks were held during 1984. Formal discussions were resumed in March, 1985.
4. Keeping all aspects of the problem including constitutional and legal provisions, international agreements, national commitments and humanitarian considerations, it has been decided to proceed as follows:—

Foreigners Issue:

5.(1) For purpose of detection and deletion of foreigners, 1-1-1966 shall be the base date and year.

(2) All persons who came to Assam prior to 1-1-1966, including those amongst them whose names appeared on the electoral rolls used in 1967 elections, shall be regularized.

(3) Foreigners who came to Assam after 1-1-1966 (inclusive) and up to 24th March, 1971 shall be detected in accordance with the provisions of the Foreigners Act, 1946 and the Foreigners (Tribunals) Order, 1939.

(4) Names of foreigners so detected will be deleted from the electoral rolls in force. Such persons will be required to register themselves before the Registration Officers of the respective districts in accordance with the provisions of the Registration of Foreigners Act, 1939 and the Registration of Foreigners Rules, 1939.

(5) For this purpose, Government of India will undertake suitable strengthening of the governmental machinery.

(6) On the expiry of the period of ten year following the date of detection, the names of all such persons which have been deleted from the electoral rolls shall be restored.

(7) All persons who were expelled earlier, but have since re-entered illegally into Assam, shall be expelled.

(8) Foreigners who came to Assam on or after March 25, 1971 shall continue to be detected, deleted and expelled in accordance with law. Immediate and practical steps shall be taken to expel such foreigners.

(9) The Government will give due consideration to certain difficulties expressed by the AASU/AAGSP regarding the implementation of the illegal Migrants (Determination by Tribunals) Act, 1983.

Safeguards and Economic Development:

6. Constitutional, legislative and administrative safeguards, as many be appropriate, shall be provided to protect, preserve and promote the cultural, social, linguistic identity and heritage of the Assamese people.
7. The Government takes this opportunity to renew their commitment for the speedy all round economic development of Assam, so as to improve the standard of living of the people. Special emphasis will be placed on the education and Science & Technology through establishment of national institutions.

Other Issues :

8(1). The Government will arrange for the issue of citizenship certificate in future only by the authorities of the Central Government.

(2) Specific complaints that may be made by the AASU/AAGSP about irregular issuance of Indian Citizenship Certificates (ICC) will be looked into.

9 (1). The international border shall be made secure against future infiltration by erection of physical barriers like walls barbed wire fencing and other obstacles at appropriate places. Patrolling by security forces on land and riverine routes all along the international border shall be adequately intensified. In order to further strengthen the security arrangements, to prevent effectively future infiltration, an adequate number of check-posts shall be set up.

(2) Besides the arrangements mentioned above and keeping in view security considerations, a road all along the international border shall be constructed so as to facilitate patrolling by security forces. Land between border and the road would be kept free of human habitation, wherever possible. Riverine patrolling along the international border would be intensified. All effective measures would be adopted to prevent infiltrators crossing or attempting to cross the international border.

10. It will be ensured that relevant laws for prevention of encroachment of government lands and lands in tribal belts and blocks are strictly enforced and unauthorized encroachers evicted as laid down under such laws.

11. It will be ensured that the law restricting acquisition of immovable property by foreigners in Assam is strictly enforced.

12. It will be ensured that Birth and Death Registers are duly maintained.

Restoration of Normalcy:

13. The All Assam Students Union (AASU) and the All Assam Gana Sangram Parishad (AAGSP) call off the agitation, assure full co-operation and dedicate themselves towards the development of the Country.

14. The Central and the State Government have agreed to :

a. Review with sympathy and withdraw cases of disciplinary action taken against employees in the context of the agitation and to ensure that there is no victimization;

b. Frame a scheme for ex-gratia payment to next of kin of those who were killed in the course in the agitation.
c. Give sympathetic consideration to proposal for relaxation of upper age limit for employment in public service in Assam, having regard to exceptional situation that prevailed in holding academic and competitive examinations etc. in the context of agitation in Assam.
d. Undertake review of detention cases, if any, as well as cases against persons charged with criminal offences in connection with the agitation, except those charged with commission of heinous offences.
e. Consider withdrawal of the prohibitory orders/notifications in force, if any.

15. The Ministry of Home Affairs will be the nodal Ministry for the implementation of the above.

Sd/-	Sd/-
(P.K. Mahanta)	(R.D. Pradhan)
President	Home Secretary
All Assam Students'	Union Government of India

Annexure B
Extracts from the Citizenship Act, 1955

3. Citizenship by birth.—
   (1) Except as provided in sub-section (2) every person born in India—
      (a) on or after the 26th day of January, 1950, but before the 1st day of July, 1987;
      (b) on or after the 1st day of July, 1987, but before the commencement of the Citizenship (Amendment) Act, 2003 (6 of 2004) and either of whose parents is a citizen of India at the time of his birth;
      (c) on or after the commencement of the Citizenship (Amendment) Act, 2003 (6 of 2004), where— (i) both of his parents are citizens of India; or (ii) one of whose parents is a citizen of India and the other is not an illegal migrant at the time of his birth, shall be a citizen of India by birth.
   (2) A person shall not be a citizen of India by virtue of this section if at the time of his birth—
      (a) either his father or mother possesses such immunity from suits and legal process as is accorded to an envoy of a foreign sovereign power accredited to the President of India and he or she, as the case may be, is not a citizen of India; or
      (b) his father or mother is an enemy alien and the birth occurs in a place then under occupation by the enemy.
4. Citizenship by descent.—(1) A person born outside India shall be a citizen of India by descent,—
   (a) on or after the 26th day of January, 1950, but before the 10th day of December, 1992, if his father is a citizen of India at the time of his birth; or

(b) on or after the 10th day of December, 1992, if either of his parents is a citizen of India at the time of his birth:

Provided that if the father of a person referred to in clause (a) was a citizen of India by descent only, that person shall not be a citizen of India by virtue of this section unless—

(a) his birth is registered at an Indian consulate within one year of its occurrence or the commencement of this Act, whichever is later, or, with the permission of the Central Government, after the expiry of the said period; or

(b) his father is, at the time of his birth, in service under a Government in India:

Provided further that if either of the parents of a person referred to in clause (b) was a citizen of India by descent only, that person shall not be a citizen of India by virtue of this section, unless—

(a) his birth is registered at an Indian consulate within one year of its occurrence or on or after the 10th day of December, 1992, whichever is later, or,

(b) with the permission of the Central Government, after the expiry of the said period; or

(c) either of his parents is, at the time of his birth, in service under a Government in India:

Provided also that on or after the commencement of the Citizenship (Amendment) Act, 2003 (6 of 2004), a person shall not be a citizen of India by virtue of this section, unless his birth is registered at an Indian consulate in such form and in such manner, as may be prescribed,—

(i) within one year of its occurrence or the commencement of the Citizenship (Amendment) Act, 2003 (6 of 2004), whichever is later; or

(ii) with the permission of the Central Government, after the expiry of the said period:

Provided also that no such birth shall be registered unless the parents of such person declare, in such form and in such manner as may be prescribed, that the minor does not hold the passport of another country.

(1A) A minor who is a citizen of India by virtue of this section and is also a citizen of any other country shall cease to be a citizen of India if he does not renounce the citizenship or nationality of another country within six months of attaining full age.

(2) If the Central Government so directs, a birth shall be deemed for the purposes of this section to have been registered with its permission, notwithstanding that its permission was not obtained before the registration.

(3) For the purposes of the proviso to sub-section (1), [any person] born outside undivided India who was, or was deemed to be, a citizen of India at the commencement of the Constitution shall be deemed to be a citizen of India by descent only.

5. Citizenship by registration.—(1) Subject to the provisions of this section and such other conditions and restrictions as may be prescribed, the Central Government may, on an application made in this behalf, register as a citizen of India any person not being an illegal migrant who is not already such citizen by virtue of the Constitution or of any other provision of this Act if he belongs to any of the following categories, namely:—

(a) a person of Indian origin who is ordinarily resident in India for seven years before making an application for registration;

(b) a person of Indian origin who is ordinarily resident in any country or place outside undivided India;

(c) a person who is married to a citizen of India and is ordinarily resident in India for seven years before making an application for registration;

(d) minor children of persons who are citizens of India;

(e) a person of full age and capacity whose parents are registered as citizens of India under clause (a) of this sub-section or sub-section (1) of section 6;

(f) a person of full age and capacity who, or either of his parents, was earlier citizen of independent India, and [is ordinarily resident in India for twelve months] immediately before making an application for registration;

(g) a person of full age and capacity who has been registered as an [Overseas Citizen of India Cardholder] for five years, and who [is ordinarily resident in India for twelve months] before making an application for registration.

Explanation 1.—For the purposes of clauses (a) and (c), an applicant shall be deemed to be ordinarily resident in India if— (i) he has resided in India throughout the period of twelve months immediately before making an application for registration; and (ii) he has resided in India during the eight years immediately preceding the said period of twelve months for a period of not less than six years.

Explanation 2.—For the purposes of this sub-section, a person shall be deemed to be of Indian origin if he, or either of his parents, was born in undivided India or in such other territory which became part of India after the 15th day of August, 1947.

(1A) The Central Government, if it is satisfied that special circumstances exist, may after recording the circumstances in writing, relax the period of twelve months, specified in clauses (f) and (g) and clause (i) of Explanation 1 of sub-section (1), up to a maximum of thirty days which may be in different breaks.

(2) No person being of full age shall be registered as a citizen of India under sub-section (1) until he has taken the oath of allegiance in the form specified in the Second Schedule.

(3) No person who has renounced, or has been deprived of, his Indian citizenship or whose Indian citizenship has terminated, under this Act shall be registered as a citizen of India under sub-section (1) except by order of the Central Government.

(4) The Central Government may, if satisfied that there are special circumstances justifying such registration, cause any minor to be registered as a citizen of India.

(5) A person registered under this section shall be a citizen of India by registration as from the date on which he is so registered; and a person registered under the provisions of clause (b)(ii) of article 6 or article 8 of the Constitution shall be deemed to be a citizen of India by registration as from the commencement of the Constitution or the date on which he was so registered, whichever may be later.

(6) If the Central Government is satisfied that circumstances exist which render it necessary to grant exemption from the residential requirement under clause (c) of sub-section(1) to any person or a class of persons, it may, for reasons to be recorded in writing, grant such exemption.

6. Citizenship by naturalisation.—(1) Where an application is made in the prescribed manner by any person of full age and capacity [not being an illegal migrant] for the grant of a certificate of naturalisation to him, the Central Government may, if satisfied that the applicant is qualified for naturalisation under the provisions of the Third Schedule, grant to him a certificate of naturalisation:

Provided that, if in the opinion of the Central Government, the applicant is a person who has rendered distinguished service to the cause of science, philosophy, art, literature, world peace or human progress generally, it may waive all or any of the conditions specified in the Third Schedule.

(2) The person to whom a certificate of naturalisation is granted under sub-section (1) shall, on taking the oath of allegiance in the form specified in the Second Schedule, be a citizen of India by naturalisation as from the date on which that certificate is granted.

6A. Special provisions as to citizenship of persons covered by the Assam Accord.—

(1) For the purposes of this section—

(a) "Assam" means the territories included in the State of Assam immediately before the commencement of the Citizenship (Amendment) Act, 1985 (65 of 1985);

(b) "detected to be a foreigner" means detected to be a foreigner in accordance with the provisions of the Foreigners Act, 1946 (31 of 1946) and the Foreigners (Tribunals) Order, 1964 by a Tribunal constituted under the said Order;

(c) "specified territory" means the territories included in Bangladesh immediately before the commencement of the Citizenship (Amendment) Act, 1985 (65 of 1985);

(d) a person shall be deemed to be Indian origin, if he, or either of his parents or any of his grand-parents was born in undivided India; (e) a person shall be deemed to have been detected to be a foreigner on the date on which a Tribunal constituted under the Foreigners (Tribunals) Order, 1964 submits its opinion to the effect that he is a foreigner to the officer or authority concerned.

(2) Subject to the provisions of sub-sections (6) and (7), all persons of Indian origin who came before the lst day of January, 1966 to Assam from the specified territory (including such of those whose names were included in the electoral rolls used for the purposes of the General Election to the House of the People held in 1967) and who have been ordinarily resident in Assam since the dates of their entry into Assam shall be deemed to be citizens of India as from the lst day of January, 1966.

(3) Subject to the provisions of sub-sections (6) and (7), every person of Indian origin who—

(a) came to Assam on or after the lst day of January, 1966 but before the 25th day of March, 1971 from the specified territory; and

(b) has, since the date of his entry into Assam, been ordinarily resident in Assam; and

(c) has been detected to be a foreigner;

shall register himself in accordance with the rules made by the Central Government in this behalf under section 18 with such authority (hereafter in this sub-section referred to as the registering authority) as may be specified in such rules and if his name is included in any electoral roll for any Assembly or Parliamentary constituency in force on the date of such detection, his name shall be deleted therefrom.

Explanation.—In the case of every person seeking registration under this sub-section, the opinion of the Tribunal constituted under the Foreigners (Tribunals) Order, 1964 holding such person to be a foreigner, shall be deemed to be sufficient proof of the requirement under clause (c) of this sub-section and if any question arises as to whether such person complies with any other requirement under this sub-section, the registering authority shall,—

- if such opinion contains a finding with respect to such other requirement, decide the question in conformity with such finding;
- if such opinion does not contain a finding with respect to such other requirement, refer the question to a Tribunal constituted under the said Order hang jurisdiction in accordance with such rules as the Central Government may make in this behalf under section 18 and decide the question in conformity with the opinion received on such reference.

(4) A person registered under sub-section (3) shall have, as from the date on which he has been detected to be a foreigner and till the expiry of a period of ten years from that date, the same rights and obligations as a citizen of India (including the right to obtain a passport under the Passports Act, 1967 (15 of 1967) and the obligations connected therewith), but shall not entitled to have his name included in any electoral roll for any Assembly or Parliamentary constituency at any time before the expiry of the said period of ten years.

(5) A person registered under sub-section (3) shall be deemed to be a citizen of India for all purposes as from the date of expiry of a period of ten years from the date on which he has been detected to be a foreigner.

(6) Without prejudice to the provisions of section 8—

(a) if any person referred to in sub-section (2) submits in the prescribed manner and form and to the prescribed authority within sixty days from the date of commencement of the Citizenship (Amendment) Act, 1985 (65 of 1985), a declaration that he does not wish to be a citizen of India, such person shall not be deemed to have become a citizen of India under that sub-section;

(b) if any person referred to in sub-section (3) submits in the prescribed manner and form and to the prescribed authority within sixty days from the date of commencement of the Citizenship (Amendment) Act, 1985 (65 of 1985), or from the date on which he has been detected to be a foreigner, whichever is later, a declaration that he does not wish to be governed by the provisions of that sub-section and sub-sections (4) and (5), it shall not be necessary for such person to register himself under sub-section (3).

Explanation.—Where a person required to file a declaration under this sub-section does not have the capacity to enter into a contract, such declaration may be filed on his behalf by any person competent under the law for the time being in force to act on his behalf.

(7) Nothing in sub-sections (2) to (6) shall apply in relation to any person—

(a) who, immediately before the commencement of the Citizenship (Amendment) Act, 1985 (65 of 1985), is a citizen of India;

(b) who was expelled from India before the commencement of the Citizenship (Amendment) Act, 1985, under the Foreigners Act, 1946 (31 of 1946).

(8) Save as otherwise expressly provided in this section, the provisions of this section shall have effect notwithstanding anything contained in any other law for the time being in force.

7. Citizenship by incorporation of territory.—If any territory becomes a part of India, the Central Government may, by order notified in the Official Gazette, specify the persons who shall be citizens of

India by reason of their connection with that territory; and those persons shall be citizens of India as from the date to be specified in the order.

OVERSEAS CITIZENSHIP

7A. Registration of Overseas Citizen of India Cardholder.—

(1) The Central Government may, subject to such conditions, restrictions and manner as may be prescribed, on an application made in this behalf, register as an Overseas Citizen of India Cardholder—

(a) any person of full age and capacity,— (i) who is a citizen of another country, but was a citizen of India at the time of, or at any time after the commencement of the Constitution; or (ii) who is a citizen of another country, but was eligible to become a citizen of India at the time of the commencement of the Constitution; or (iii) who is a citizen of another country, but belonged to a territory that became part of India after the 15th day of August, 1947; or (iv) who is a child or a grandchild or a great grandchild of such a citizen; or

(b) a person, who is a minor child of a person mentioned in clause (a); or

(c) a person, who is a minor child, and whose both parents are citizens of India or one of the parents is a citizen of India; or

(d) spouse of foreign origin of a citizen of India or spouse of foreign origin of an Overseas Citizen of India Cardholder registered under section 7A and whose marriage has been registered and subsisted for a continuous period of not less than two years immediately preceding the presentation of the application under this section:

Provided that for the eligibility for registration as an Overseas Citizen of India Cardholder, such spouse shall be subjected to prior security clearance by a competent authority in India:

Provided further that no person, who or either of whose parents or grand-parents or great grand-parents is or had been a citizen of Pakistan, Bangladesh or such other country as the Central Government may, by notification in the Official Gazette, specify, shall be eligible for registration as an Overseas Citizen of India Cardholder under this sub-section.

(2) The Central Government may, by notification in the Official Gazette, specify the date from which the existing persons of Indian Origin Cardholders shall be deemed to be Overseas Citizens of India Cardholders.

Explanation.—For the purposes of this sub-section, "Persons of Indian Origin Cardholders" means the persons registered as such under notification number 26011/4/98 F.I., dated the 19th August, 2002, issued by the Central Government in this regard.

(3) Notwithstanding anything contained in sub-section (1), the Central Government may, if it is satisfied that special circumstances exist, after recording the circumstances in writing, register a person as an Overseas Citizen of India Cardholder.

7B. Conferment of rights on Overseas Citizen of India Cardholder.—

(1) Notwithstanding anything contained in any other law for the time being in force, an Overseas Citizen of India Cardholder shall be entitled to such rights, other than the rights specified under sub-section (2), as the Central Government may, by notification in the Official Gazette, specify in this behalf.

(2) An Overseas Citizen of India Cardholder shall not be entitled to the rights conferred on a citizen of India—

(a) under article 16 of the Constitution with regard to equality of opportunity in matters of public employment;

(b) under article 58 of the Constitution for election as President;

(c) under article 66 of the Constitution for election as Vice-President;

(d) under article 124 of the Constitution for appointment as a Judge of the Supreme Court;

(e) under article 217 of the Constitution for appointment as a Judge of the High Court;

(f) under section 16 of the Representation of the People Act, 1950 (43 of 1950) in regard to registration as a voter;

(g) under sections 3 and 4 of the Representation of the People Act, 1951 (43 of 1951) with regard to the eligibility for being a member of the House of the People or of the Council of States, as the case may be;

(h) under sections 5, 5A and section 6 of the Representation of the People Act, 1951 (43 of 1951) with regard to the eligibility for being a member of the Legislative Assembly or the Legislative Council, as the case may be, of a State;

(i) for appointment to public services and posts in connection with affairs of the Union or of any State except for appointment in such services and posts as the Central Government may, by special order in that behalf, specify.

(3) Every notification issued under sub-section (1) shall be laid before each House of Parliament.

7C. Renunciation of Overseas Citizen of India Card.—

(1) If any Overseas Citizen of India Cardholder of full age and capacity makes in prescribed manner a declaration renouncing the Card registering him as an Overseas Citizen of India Cardholder, the declaration shall be registered by the Central Government, and upon such registration, that person shall cease to be an Overseas Citizen of India Cardholder.

(2) Where a person ceases to be an Overseas Citizen of India Cardholder under sub-section (1), the spouse of foreign origin of that person, who has obtained Overseas Citizen of India Card under clause (d) of sub-section (1) of section 7A, and every minor child of that person registered as an Overseas Citizen of India Cardholder shall thereupon cease to be an Overseas Citizen of India Cardholder.

7D. Cancellation of registration as Overseas Citizen of India Cardholder.—The Central Government may, by order, cancel the registration granted under sub-section (1) of section 7A, if it is satisfied that—

(a) the registration as an Overseas Citizen of India Cardholder was obtained by means of fraud, false representation or the concealment of any material fact; or

(b) the Overseas Citizen of India Cardholder has shown disaffection towards the Constitution, as by law established; or

(c) the Overseas Citizen of India Cardholder has, during any war in which India may be engaged, unlawfully traded or communicated with an enemy or been engaged in, or associated with, any business or commercial activity that was to his knowledge carried on in such manner as to assist an enemy in that war; or

(d) the Overseas Citizen of India Cardholder has, within five years after registration under sub-section (1) of section 7A, been sentenced to imprisonment for a term of not less than two years; or

(da) the Overseas Citizen of India Cardholder has violated any of the provisions of this Act or provisions of any other law for the time being in force as may be specified by the Central Government by notification published in the Official Gazette; or

(e) it is necessary so to do in the interests of the sovereignty and integrity of India, the security of India, friendly relations of India with any foreign country, or in the interests of the general public; or

(f) the marriage of an Overseas Citizen of India Cardholder, who has obtained such Card under clause (d) of sub-section (1) of section 7A,—

(i) has been dissolved by a competent court of law or otherwise; or

(ii) has not been dissolved but, during the subsistence of such marriage, he has solemnised marriage with any other person.

"Provided that no order under this section shall be passed unless the Overseas Citizen of India Cardholder has been given a reasonable opportunity of being heard."

TERMINATION OF CITIZENSHIP

8. Renunciation of citizenship.—

(1) If any citizen of India of full age and capacity, ***, makes in the prescribed manner a declaration renouncing his Indian Citizenship, the declaration shall be registered by the prescribed authority; and, upon such registration, that person shall cease to be a citizen of India:

Provided that if any such declaration is made during any war in which India may be engaged, registration thereof shall be withheld until the Central Government otherwise directs.

(2) Where [a person] ceases to be a citizen of India under sub-section (1), every minor child of that person shall thereupon cease to be a citizen of India:

Provided that any such child may, within one year after attaining full age, make a declaration [in the prescribed form and manner] that he wishes to resume Indian citizenship and shall thereupon again become a citizen of India. * * * * *

9. Termination of citizenship.—

(1) Any citizen of India who by naturalisation, registration otherwise voluntarily acquires, or has at any time between the 26th January, 1950 and the commencement of this Act, voluntarily acquired, the citizenship of another country shall, upon such acquisition or, as the case may be, such commencement, cease to be a citizen of India:

Provided that nothing in this sub-section shall apply to a citizen of India who, during any war in which India may be engaged, voluntarily acquires the citizenship of another country, until the Central Government otherwise directs.

(2) If any question arises as to whether, when or how any [citizen of India] has acquired the citizenship of another country, it shall be determined by such authority, in such manner, and having regard to such rules of evidence, as may be prescribed in this behalf.

10. Deprivation of citizenship.—

(1) A citizen of India who is such by naturalisation or by virtue only of clause (c) of article 5 of the Constitution or by registration otherwise than under clause (b)(ii) of article 6 of the Constitution or clause (a) of sub-section (1) of section 5 of this Act, shall cease to be a citizen of India, if he is deprived of that citizenship by an order of the Central Government under this section.

(2) Subject to the provisions of this section, the Central Government may, by order, deprive any such citizen of Indian citizenship, if it is satisfied that—

(a) the registration or certificate of naturalisation was obtained by means of fraud, false representation or the concealment of any material fact; or

(b) that citizen has shown himself by act or speech to be disloyal or disaffected towards the Constitution of India as by law established; or

(c) that citizen has, during any war in which India may be engaged, unlawfully traded or communicated with an enemy or been engaged in, or associated with, any business that was to his knowledge carried on in such manner as to assist an enemy in that war; or

(d) that citizen has, within five years after registration or naturalisation, been sentenced in any country to imprisonment for a term of not less than two years; or

(e) that citizen has been ordinarily resident out of India for a continuous period of seven years, and during that period, has neither been at any time a student of any educational institution in a country outside India or in the service of a Government in India or of an international organisation of which India is a member, not registered annually in the prescribed manner at an Indian consulate his intention to retain his citizenship of India.

(3) The Central Government shall not deprive a person of citizenship under this section unless it is satisfied that it is not conducive to the public good that person should continue to be a citizen of India.

(4) Before making an order under this section, the Central Government shall give the person against whom the order is proposed to be made notice in writing informing him of the ground on which it is proposed to be made and, if the order is proposed to be made on any of the grounds specified in sub-section (2) other than clause (e) thereof, of his right, upon making application therefore in the prescribed manner, to have his case referred to a committee of inquiry under this section.

(5) If the order is proposed to be made against a person on any of the grounds specified in sub-section (2) other than clause (e) thereof and that person so applies in the prescribed manner, the Central Government shall, and in any other case it may, refer the case to a Committee of Inquiry consisting of a chairman (being a person who has for at least ten years held a judicial office) and two other members appointed by the Central Government in this behalf.

(6) The Committee of Inquiry shall, on such reference, hold the inquiry in such manner as may be prescribed and submit its report to the Central Government; and the Central Government shall ordinarily be guided by such report in making an order under this section.

11. Commonwealth citizenship. Omitted by The Citizenship (Amendment) Act, 2003 (6 of 2004), s. 10 (w.e.f. 3-12-2004).

12. Power to confer rights of Indian citizen or citizens of certain country. Omitted by The Citizenship (Amendment) Act, 2003 (6 of 2004), s. 10 (w.e.f. 3-12-2004)
13. Certificate of Citizenship in case of doubt.—The Central Government may, in such cases as it thinks fit, certify that a person with respect to whose citizenship of India a doubt exists, is a citizen of India; and a certificate issued under this section shall, unless it is proved that it was obtained by means of fraud, false representation or concealment of any material fact, be conclusive evidence that person was such a citizen on the date thereof, but without prejudice to any evidence that he was such a citizen at an earlier date.
14. Disposal of application under sections 5, 6 and 7A.—
    (1) The prescribed authority or the Central Government may, in its discretion, grant or refuse an application under sections 5, 6 and 7A and shall not be required to assign any reasons for such grant or refusal.
    (2) Subject to the provisions of section 15 the decision of the prescribed authority or the Central Government on any such application as aforesaid shall be final and shall not be called in question in any court.

14A. Issue of national identity cards.—
    (1) The Central Government may compulsorily register every citizen of India and issue national identity card to him.
    (2) The Central Government may maintain a National Register of Indian Citizens and for that purpose establish a National Registration Authority.
    (3) On and from the date of commencement of the Citizenship (Amendment) Act, 2003 (6 of 2004), the Registrar General, India, appointed under sub-section (1) of section 3 of the Registration of Births and Deaths Act, 1969 (18 of 1969) shall act as the National Registration Authority and he shall function as the Registrar General of Citizen Registration.
    (4) The Central Government may appoint such other officers and staff as may be required to assist the Registrar General of Citizen Registration in discharging his functions and responsibilities.
    (5) The procedure to be followed in compulsory registration of the citizens of India shall be such as may be prescribed.

15. Revision.—
    (1) Any person aggrieved by an order made under this Act by the

prescribed authority or any officer or other authority (other than the Central Government) may, within a period of thirty days from the date of the order, make an application to the Central Government for a revision of that order:

Provided that the Central Government may entertain the application after the expiry of the said period of thirty days, if it is satisfied that the applicant was prevented by sufficient cause from making the application in time.

(2) On receipt of any such application under sub-section (1), the Central Government shall, after considering the application of the aggrieved person and any report thereon which the officer or authority making the order may submit, make such order in relation to the application as it deems fit, and the decision of the Central Government shall be final.

Annexure C

The Citizenship (Amendment) Act, 2019 (No. 47 of 2019) [12th December, 2019]

1 (1) This Act may be called the Citizenship (Amendment) Act, 2019.

(2) It shall come into force on such date as the Central Government may, by notification in the Official Gazette, appoint.

2. In the Citizenship Act, 1955 (hereinafter referred to as the principal Act), in section 2, in sub-section (1), in clause (b), the following proviso shall be inserted, namely:— "Provided that any person belonging to Hindu, Sikh, Buddhist, Jain, Parsi or Christian community from Afghanistan, Bangladesh or Pakistan, who entered into India on or before the 31st day of December, 2014 and who has been exempted by the Central Government by or under clause (c) of sub-section (2) of section 3 of the Passport (Entry into India) Act, 1920 or from the application of the provisions of the Foreigners Act, 1946 or any rule or order made thereunder, shall not be treated as illegal migrant for the purposes of this Act;".

3. After section 6A of the principal Act, the following section shall be inserted, namely:—

'6B.(1) The Central Government or an authority specified by it in this behalf may, subject to such conditions, restrictions and manner as may be prescribed, on an application made in this behalf, grant a certificate of registration or certificate of naturalisation to a person referred to in the proviso to clause (b) of sub-section (1) of section 2.

(2) Subject to fulfilment of the conditions specified in section 5 or the qualifications for naturalisation under the provisions of the Third Schedule, a person granted the certificate of registration or certificate of naturalisation under sub-section (1) shall be

deemed to be a citizen of India from the date of his entry into India.

(3) On and from the date of commencement of the Citizenship (Amendment) Act, 2019, any proceeding pending against a person under this section in respect of illegal migration or citizenship shall stand abated on conferment of citizenship to him:

Provided that such person shall not be disqualified for making application for citizenship under this section on the ground that the proceeding is pending against him and the Central Government or authority specified by it in this behalf shall not reject his application on that ground if he is otherwise found qualified for grant of citizenship under this section:

Provided further that the person who makes the application for citizenship under this section shall not be deprived of his rights and privileges to which he was entitled on the date of receipt of his application on the ground of making such application.

(4) Nothing in this section shall apply to tribal area of Assam, Meghalaya, Mizoram or Tripura as included in the Sixth Schedule to the Constitution and the area covered under "The Inner Line" notified under the Bengal Eastern Frontier Regulation, 1873.'.

4. In section 7D of the principal Act,—

(i) after clause (d), the following clause shall be inserted, namely:—

"(da) the Overseas Citizen of India Cardholder has violated any of the provisions of this Act or provisions of any other law for time being in force as may be specified by the Central Government in the notification published in the Official Gazette; or";

(ii) after clause (f), the following proviso shall be inserted, namely:—

"Provided that no order under this section shall be passed unless the Overseas Citizen of India Cardholder has been given a reasonable opportunity of being heard.".

5. In section 18 of the principal Act, in sub-section (2), after clause (ee), the following clause shall be inserted, namely:—

"(eei) the conditions, restrictions and manner for granting certificate of registration or certificate of naturalisation under sub-section (1) of section 6B;".

6. In the Third Schedule to the principal Act, in clause (d), the following proviso shall be inserted, namely:—
   'Provided that for the person belonging to Hindu, Sikh, Buddhist, Jain, Parsi or Christian community in Afghanistan, Bangladesh or Pakistan, the aggregate period of residence or service of Government in India as required under this clause shall be read as "not less than five years" in place of "not less than eleven years".'.

Annexure D
National Population Register-2020

- To be copied from HLO Schedule
  Census House Number
  Household number
  Household Status:
  Available - 1
  Locked - 2
  Moved Out - 3
  Not Available - 4
  New - 5
  House Number and Locality
  Number of Members

Q1. Name of the Person

Q1b. (Skip for new household) Else in case of
  Available - 1
  Died - 2
  Moved Out - 3
  New Member - 4

Q2. Relationship to Head
  Head/Self - 01
  Spouse - 02
  Daughter/Son - 03
  Granddaughter/Grandson - 04
  Mother/Father - 05
  Sister/Brother - 06
  Daughter - in Law/Son-in-law - 07
  Grandmother/Grandfather - 08
  Mother-in-law/Father-in-law - 09
  Other Related Person - 10

Domestic Servant - 11
Other Unrelated Person - 12

Q3. Sex
Male - 1
Female - 2
Third Gender - 3

Q4. Marital Status
Never Married - 1
Currently Married - 2
Widowed - 3
Separated - 4
Divorced - 5

Q5. Date of birth as per English calendar -
Day Month Year (DD-MM-YYYY)

Q6. Place of Birth if within India, write the name of the state and district if outside India, write the name of the country and put ' - ' for district

Q7. * (i) Nationality as declared
Indian - 1
Others - write name of the country.

Q8. Educational Qualification
Pre-Primary-00
Class (1-12)-0-12
ITI - 13
Polytechnic - 14
Nursing Diploma - 15
Teacher Training Diploma - 16
Certificate/Other Diploma - 17
Bachelor/Undergraduate - 18
PG Diploma - 19
Masters/Post graduate - 20
M.Phil - 21
Doctorate & amp; above - 22
Without formal education - 23
Illiterate - 99

Q9. Occupation/Activity
Cultivator - 1
Agricultural Laborer - 2
Daily Wages Earner (other than Agricultural Labourer) - 3
Single/Family Worker/Self -

Employed - 4
Employer - 5
Government Employee - 6
Private Employee (Other than Domestic Helper) -7
Domestic Helper - 8
Non-Worker - 9

Q.10. Permanent Residential Address (for member other than head of household if Permanent address is same as head of the household, Put - mark in the box below S.No. and no need to repeat the address)

Q11. Whether Staying at present place since birth (i) Yes/No, if No, fill 11(b) else skip.
(i) Duration of stay at present place in years
(ii) Place of Last residence

Q12. If enumerated in this household, write serial number of the father, mother and spouse in the box

Q12. (i) If father, mother and spouse are not enumerated in this household or not alive, write their names along with date of birth else write serial number

Q.12 (ii) Place of Birth of Father & Mother if within India, write the name of the state and district if outside India, Write the name of the country and put '-' for district

Q13. (If available)
(i) Aadhar Number
(ii) Mobile Number
(iii) Voter ID Card Number
(iv) PAN Number
(v) Driving License Number

Serial Number of Respondents
Signature/Thumb impression of Respondent with date
Signature of Enumerator with date
Signature of Supervisor with date

Bibliography

Government of India

Annual Report, Ministry of Home Affairs, Government of India, 1991-92.

Annual Report, Ministry of Home Affairs, Government of India, 1999-2000.

Annual Report, Ministry of Home Affairs, Government of India, 2003-04.

Annual Report, Ministry of Home Affairs, Government of India, 2006-07.

Annual Report, Ministry of Home Affairs, Government of India, 2009-10.

Annual Report, Ministry of Home Affairs, Government of India, 2013-14.

Annual Report, Ministry of Home Affairs, Government of India, 2019-20.

Annual Report, Ministry of Home Affairs, Government of India, 2020-21.

Annual Report, Ministry of Home Affairs, Government of India, 2021-22.

Census of Imdia, 1901, Vol. IV.

Census of India, 1931, Vol. III, Part I.

Census of India, 1951, Vol. XII, Part I-A.

Census of India, India Series 1, Provisional Population Totals, Paper 1 of 2011.

Census of India 2011, Language, Paper 1 of 2018.

Constituent Assembly Debates, Vol. III (from 28th April, 1947 to 2nd May, 1947), Constituent Assembly Secretariat, New Delhi, 1947.

Constituent Assembly Debates, Vol.VII (from 4th November, 1948 to 8th January, 1949), Constituent Assembly Secretariat, New Delhi, 1949.

Constituent Assembly Debates, Vol. IX (from 30th July, 1949 to 18th September, 1949) Constituent Assembly Secretariat, New Delhi, 1949.

Constituent Assembly Debates, Vol. XI (from 14th November, 1949 to 24th November, 1949), Constituent Assembly Secretariat, New Delhi, 1949.

Lok Sabha Debates, Vol. IX (21st November to 5th December, 1955).

Report of the States Reorganisation Commission, 1955.

Report of the National Commission for Religious and Linguistic Minorities, 2007.

Government of Assam, Line System Enquiry Report, Shillong, 1938.

Assam Secretariat Records, Confidential B, 1964, File No. C232/46.

Government of Assam, Home and Political Department, October 20, 2012, *White Paper on Foreigners' Issue.*

Rao, B. Shiva (ed), *The Framing of India's Constitution,* Volume II to Volume V, 1967-1968, New Delhi, The Indian Institute of Public Administration.

Books

Ahmed, Imtiaz (1996), "Refugees and Security: The Experience of Bangladesh", In *Refugees and Regional Security in South Asia,* ed. S.D. Mani and Lok Raj Baral, New Delhi, Konark Publishers.

Balakrishnan, Varna and Singh Navsharan (2021), "Gendered Exclusions of the NRC", In *This Land Is Mine, I Am Not of This Land* (ed.) Harsh Mander and Navsharan Singh, New Delhi, Speaking Tiger Books LLP.

Barkat, Abdul (2011), "Political Economy of Deprivation of Hindu Minority in Bangladesh: Living with the Vested Property Act", in Abhijit Dasgupta, Masahiko Togawa and Abdul Barkat (eds.), *Minorities and the State: Changing Social and Political Landscape of Bengal,* New Delhi: Sage.

Barua, Sandhya (1982), "Assam in National Context and Historical Perspective", in *Social tension in North East India*, J.B. Bhattacharjee (ed), Shillong, North East Council for Social Science Research.

Basu, Arabinda, Dasgupta, Biman K., and Sarkar Jayanta (eds.) (2004), *Anthropology for North-east India: A Reader,* Calcutta, Indian National Confederation and Academy of Anthropologists, Indian Anthropological Society and National Museum of Mankind.

Bhatia, Gautam (2021), "The Judicial Presumption of Non-Citizenship", In *This Land Is Mine, I Am Not of This Land* (ed.) Harsh Mander and Navsharan Singh, New Delhi, Speaking Tiger Books LLP.

Baruah, Sanjib (1999), *India against Itself: Assam and the Politics of Nationality*, New Delhi, Oxford University Press.

Bhasin, Avtar Singh (2003), *India-Bangladesh Relations*, Vol. 1, New Delhi: Geetika Publishers.

Bhattacharyya, Hiranya Kumar (2018), *Operation Lebensraum Illegal Migration from Bangladesh,* New Delhi, Bloomsbury.

Bhattacharjee, J.B. (1982), *Social Tension in North-East India* (ed.) Shillong, North-East India Council for Social Science Research.

Bhttacharjee, Tapodhan (1982), "Tension in North-East", in *Social Tension in North-East India* (ed.), J.B. Bhattaharjee, Shillong, North-East India Council for Social Science Research.

Bosniak, L., (2006), *The Citizen and the Alien: Dilemmas of Contemporary Membership*, New Jersey: Princeton University Press.

Chakraborty, Debesh, Gautam Gupta and Sabari Bandyopadhyay, (1997), "Migration from Bangladesh to India, 1971-91: Its magnitude and causes", In *State, development and political culture: Bangladesh and India*, (ed.) Barun De and Ranabir Samaddar, New Delhi, Har-Anand Publication.

Chanchani, Mihika and Balakrishnan, Varna (2021), "Citizenship in India and Assam", In *This Land Is Mine, I Am Not of This Land* (ed.) Harsh Mander and Navsharan Singh, New Delhi Speaking Tiger Books LLP.

Chatterjee, Sarajit Kumar (2010), *North-East India: Dispersion and Discontent,* New Delhi, Abhijeet Publications.

Chatterjee, Suniti Kumar (1982), "Linguistic Survey of India: Languages and Scripts", In *The Cultural Heritage of India,* Vol. I, (Reprint), Calcutta, The Ramakrishna Mission Institute of Culture.

Das, B.M. (1984), "Some Aspects of Physical Anthropology of the Tribes of North-east India", In *The Tribes of North East India* (ed.) S. Karotemprel, Calcutta Firma KLM Private Limited.

______ (2004), "North-east India and the People", In *Anthropology for North-east India: A Reader* (eds.) Arabinda Basu, Biman K. Dasgupta, and Jayanta Sarkar, Calcutta, Indian National Confederation and Academy of Anthropologists, Indian Anthropological Society and National Museum of Mankind.

Das, Pushpita (2016), *Illegal migration from Bangladesh Deportation, Border fencing and work permit*, IDSA, Monograph Series No. 56, December.

Dasgupta, Abhijit, Togawa, Masahiko and Barkat, Abdul (eds.) (2011), *Minorities and the State: Changing Social and Political Landscape of Bengal,* New Delhi: Sage.

De, Barun and Samaddar, Ranabir, (1997), *State, development and political culture: Bangladesh and India* (ed), New Delhi, Har-Anand Publication.

Fazal,Tanweer, (ed.) (2013), *Minority Nationalisms in South Asia*, *South Asian Culture and History*, New York: Routledge.

Guha, Amalendu (1977), *Planter-Raj to Swaraj: Freedom Struggle and Electoral Politics in Assam 1826-1947*, New Delhi, Indian Council of Historical Research.

Guha, Ramachandra (2007), *India After Gandhi*, Picador India.

Guhathakurta, Meghna (2013), "Amidst the Winds of Change: The Hindu Minority in Bangladesh", in Tanweer Fazal (ed.), *Minority Nationalisms in South Asia, South Asian Culture and History*, New York: Routledge.

Hutton, J.H. (1951), *Caste in India*, second edition, Bombay, Oxford University Press.

Jayal, Niraja Gopal (2013), *Citizenship and Its Discontents: An Indian History*, Cambridge, MA, Harvard University Press.

________ (2016), "Citizenship", In Sujit Choudhury, Madhav Khosla and Pratap Bhanu Mehta (eds.), *The Oxford Handbook of the Indian Constitution*, Oxford University Press.

________ (2021), "Faith-Based Citizenship", In *This Land Is Mine, I Am Not of This Land* (ed.) Harsh Mander and Navsharan Singh, New Delhi, Speaking Tiger Books LLP.

Kashyap Anirban (1988), *Communalism and Constitution*, New Delhi, Lancers Books.

Karotemprel, S. (ed.) (1984), *The Tribes of North East India*, Calcutta Firma KLM Private Limited.

Kumar, B.B. (ed.) (2006), *Illegal Migration from Bangladesh*, Delhi, Astha Bharati.

Macfoy, M.K., (2014), "Introduction: Who is a Citizen? Feminism, Multiculturalism and Immigration", In *Citizenship*, R. Bellamy and M.K. Macfoy (eds.), Vol. II, 2014, New York: Routledge.

Mander, Harsh (2021), "Introduction", In *This Land is Mine, I Am Not of This Land* (edited) Harsh Mander and Navsharan Singh, New Delhi, Speaking Tiger Books.

________ (2021), "The Dark Side of Humanity and Legality", In *This Land is Mine, I Am Not of This Land* (edited) Harsh Mander and Navsharan Singh, New Delhi, Speaking Tiger Books.

Mander, Harsh and Singh, Navsharan (eds.) (2021), *This Land is Mine, I Am Not of This Land,* New Delhi, Speaking Tiger Books.

Mani, S.D. and Baral, Lok Raj (1996), "Refugees and Security: The Experience of Bangladesh", In *Refugees and Regional Security in South Asia* (ed.), New Delhi, Konark Publishers.

Mitra, Debala, (1982), "Foreign Elements in Indian Population" in *The Cultural Heritage of India,* Vol. II, 1982 (Reprint), Calcutta, The Ramakrishna Mission Institute of Culture.

Moon, Pemdrel (ed.) (1977), *Wavell: Viceroy's Journal*, Delhi, Oxford University Press.

Nag, Sajal (1990), *Roots of Ethnic Conflict*, New Delhi, Manohar.

Nandy, Chandan (2005), "Illegal Migration from Bangladesh to India: The Emerging Conflicts", *Mellon–MIT Foundation on NGOs and Forced Migration,* November.

Nicholas, Munsergh and Moon, Pendrel (ed.) (1982), *The Transfer of Power, 1942-47*, Vol. III, Her Majesty's Stationery Office, London.

Pakem, B. (ed.) (1997), *Insurgency in North-east India*, New Delhi, Omsons Publications.

Philipose, Pamela (2021), "A Tool Kit for Hindu Rashtra?", In *This Land Is Mine, I Am Not of This Land* (ed.) Harsh Mander and Navsharan Singh, New Delhi, Speaking Tiger Books LLP.

Phukan, Girin (1997), "Politics of Secessionism in North-east India", In *Insurgency in North-east India*" (ed.) B. Pakem, New Delhi, Omsons Publications.

Pramanik, Bimal (2006), "Illegal Migration from Bangladesh: A Case Study", in B.B. Kumar (ed.), *Illegal Migration from Bangladesh*, Delhi, Astha Bharati.

Roy, Anupama (2010), *Mapping Citizenship in India*, New Delhi, Oxford University Press.

________(2021), "Citizenship Regimes, Law and Belonging", In *This Land Is Mine, I Am Not of This Land* (ed.) Harsh Mander and Navsharan Singh, New Delhi, Speaking Tiger Books LLP.

Samaddar, Ranabir (1999), *The Marginal Nation: Transborder Migration from Bangladesh to West Bengal,* New Delhi: Sage.

Sharma, Dr. Brijendra Nath (1972), *Social and Cultural History of Northern India c.1000 1200 A.D.,* New Delhi, Abhinava Publications.

Articles

Agarwal, Akshat (2022), "An injured voice", *The Telegraph*, June 3.

Ahmed, Syed Zubair (1992), "Operation Pushback Grinds to Abrupt Halt", *The Times of India*, November 3.

Ahujs. Namrata Bui (2016), "Census and consensus", *The Week*, June 26.

________ (2021), "Due procedure followed in cases against activists". *The Week*, April 25.

Banerjee Paula, Hazarika Sanjoy, Hussain Monirul and Samaddar Ranabir (1999), "Indo-Bangladesh Cross-Border Migration and Trade", *Economic and Political Weekly,* September 4.

Bannerjee, Rabi (2019), "Grouse goes global", *The Week,* August 4.

Banerjee, Satrujit (2008), "Welcome to a new home", *The Telegraph*, April 9.

Basu, Deepankar, Das Debarshi (2020), "Assam's politics and the NRC", *Economic and Political Weekly*, Vol. LV, No. 5, February 1.

Beltran, Gonzalo Aguirre (1979), *Regions of Refuge*, Washington, The Society for Applied Anthropology Monograph Series, Monograph Number 12.

Bhat, M., Mohsin Alam (2019), "The Constituioanl Case against the Citizenship Amendmetn Bill", *Economic & Political Weekly,* Vol. LIV, No. 3, January 19, 2019, pp.12-14.

Bhatia, Gautam (2019), "The judicial presumption of non-citizenship", *The Hindu*, July 23.

Bhattacharje, Govind (2018), "Citizenship tangle", *The Statesman*, May 6.

Bhattacharya, Rakhee (2019), "NRC-CAA may derail NE growth", *The Statesman*, December 30.

Bhattacharjee, Sudipta and Pal, Sudeshna (2019), "NRC Anarchy", *The Telegraph*, August 25.

________ (2019), "Designating the 'other'", *The Statesman*, December 16.

________(2020), "Questions of Indigeneity", *The Statesman*, October 5.

Bhaumik Subir (2015), "Looking towards new prosperity", *The Telegraph*, September 1.

________ (2019), "It's Playing Risky Games", *The Times of India*, January 14.

Biswas, Prasenjit and Gogoi, Suraj (2016), "State & the stateless", *The Statesman*, November 7.

Biswas, Prasenjit (2017), "Murkier and murkier", *The Statesman*, September 25.

________(2017), "Bizarre goings-on in Asssam", *The Statesman*, October 9.

________ (2018), "Insiders, outsiders & improper legalese", *The Statesman*, January 15.

________(2018), "Unheard-of measures in Assam", *The Statesman,* March 26.

________ (2018), "On a slippery slope", *The Statesman,* June 4.

________ (2019), "Statelessness in Assam", *The Statesman*, May 20.

________ (2020), "Questions of Indigeneity", *The Statesman*, October 5.

Burki, Shahid Javed, and Swamy, Subramanian (1987), "South Asian Migration to United States; Demand and Supply Factors", *Economic and Political Weekly*, Vol. XXII, No. 12, March 21.

Chakravarty, Nikhil (1992), "Neighbouring on Inhospitality", *The Telegraph*, October 19.

Chatterjee, S.K. (1996), "Identity Issue in the Indian Context", *Journal of Human & Environmental Sciences,*Vol. 1, No. 1, Spring 1996, pp. 32-40.

Chaudhuri, Kalyan (1992), "Influx inbound: problems on the Indo-Bangladesh border", *Frontline*, November 6.

Kundu, Amitava, Mohanan, P.C., (2020), "Citizenship (Amendment) Act How Do We Move Forward?", *Economic & Political Weekly*, Vol. IV, No. 12, March 21.

Lama, J.B. (2010), "Infiltration row and its implications", *The Statesman*, August 23.

________ (2014), "Caught up in red tape as alien's' influx continues", *The Statesman*, September 10.

Lin, Sharat G. and Madan C. Paul (1995), "Bangladeshi migrants in Delhi: Social insecurity, state power, and captive vote banks", *Bulletin of Concerned Asian Scholars*, 27, No. 1.

Majumdar, Diptosh (1998), "I-card tabs on personal details", *The Telegraph*, May 8.

Mala Jay (2020), "Contrary to top BJP leaders' claims, anti-CAA-NCR protests are spreading, not losing momentum", *The National Herald*, January 23.

Mander, Harsh (2019), "A flawed process". *The Hindu*, September 2.

Marjit, Sugata (2020), "Aam Admi are terror-stricken, its bad effect on economy", *Ei Samay*, January 21.

Momin, Sajeda (2020), "Why NRC doesn't worry Gujarat", *The Telegraph,* March 9.

Mukherji, Deb (2020), "Shaheen soars as women raise flag", *The Telegraph*, March 5.

Murayama, Mayumi (2006), "Borders. Migration and Sub-Regional Cooperation in Eastern South Asia", *Economic and Political Weekly,* April 8.

Mishra, Soni (2020), "Broom for manoeuvre", *The Week*, March 8.

Mukherji, Shantanu (2016), "Hasina must do more for the Hindus", *The Statesman*, October 13.

Myrboh, Batskhem (2020), "The politics of Inner Line Permit Extension to Manipur", *Economic & Political Weekly*, Vol. LV, No. 5, February 1.

Nanda, Prakash (2003), "Immigration Imbroglio", *The Statesman*, February 23.

Narayanan, M.K. (2020), "Delhi's shame is India's shame", *The Hindu*, March 13.

Nilekani, Nandan and Kudva, Roopa (2020), "Aadhar at 10: taking stock – The unfinished work lies with the most vulnerable sections of society", *The Times of India,* January 7.

Patnaik, Prabhat (2019), "Matter of principle", *The Telegraph*, August 9.

Patricia, Mukhim (2018), "Far-reaching implications", *The Statesman*, January 8.

Poser, Jonathan (2007), "New thinking on immigration", *The Statesman,* September 21.

Pradhan, Dharmendra (2020), "Passing the Morality Test". *The Times of India*, January 8.

Pramanik, Bimal (2008), "Infiltration from Bangladesh: A Critical Analysis", *Dialogue*, Vol. 10, No. 2.

Prasad, Jayant (2015), "Breakthrough in India-Bangladesh ties", *The Hindu*, May 11.

Prashad, Vijay (2019), "A World of Migrants", *Economic & Political Weekly*, June 1, Vol. LIV, No. 22.

Rajappa, Sam (2020), "Third Pan-Indian Stir", *The Statesman,* March 8.

Rajeswar, T.V. (1990), "Serious influx from Bangladesh", *The Statesman*, April 6-7.

Ramachandran, Sujata (1999), "Of Boundaries and Border Crossings", *Interventions,* Vol.1 (2).

________ (2003), "Operation Pushback: Sangh Parivar, State, Slums and Surreptitious Bangladeshis in New Delhi", *Economic and Political Weekly*, February 15.

Ray, Tapas (1992), "A new mantra: Infiltration, BJP's electoral plank", *Frontline,* November 6.

Rohini, Mohan (2019), "Prove Your Grandfather Is Indian". *The Times of India*, August 2.

Rao, M. Maheswara, (1994), "Technique for foolproof ID cards", *The Hindu*, November 9, 1994, p. 11.

Roy Utpal and Mondal, Soumen (2016), "Shifting residencies from Bangladesh to India and its impacts on regional sustainability: an empirical study on Gaighata Block, North 24 Parganas, W.B." in the *Abstract Volume on International Conference on Urbanisation and Regional Sustainability*, Regional Science Association, India, Department of Geography, University of Calcutta.

Salve, Harish (2020), "CAA is necessary", *The Times of India,* March 5.

Samaddar, Ranabir (2019), "Migrants, NRC, and the paradox of protection and power", *The Wire*, April 12.

Sarker, Suvo Prosun (2015), "How humanitarian is this?" *The Statesman,* October 6.

Sharma, Manmohan (1990), "Bharat mein Bangladesh se ek karod bina bulaye mehmanon ki ghuspaith" (The infiltration of one million unwanted guests from Bangladesh into India), *The Punjab Kesari,* February 26.

Sharma, Saba (2018), "A national concern", *The Statesman*, July 23.

Shekhar, Shailesh (1993), "Bangla deportees flocking back to Delhi", *Pioneer*, July 23.

Shibil, Abdullah (2016), "How Bangladesh pipped its bigger neighbours", *The Statesman*, January 18.

Shourie, Arun (1993)."How countries kill themselves", *Observer of Business and Politics*, April 30.

Shukla, Rajiv (1995), "The unwanted guests: isn't it time that we sorted out the illegal Bangladeshi immigrants issue", *The Sunday*, February 12-18.

Sibal, Kapil (2020), "A tragic pattern of inaction", *The Hindu*, March 3.

Siddique, Nazimuddin (2019), "Discourse of Doubt", *Economic & Political Weekly*, March 9, Vol. LIV, No.10.

Singh, Aditi and Sunawala, Nergish (2020), "Chipko to Shaheen Bagh: Why mom-driven movements work", *The Times of India*, March 8.

Sinha, Sagarneel (2018), "Ripple effect", *The Statesman*, September 10.

Sinha, Lt. Gen. S.K. (2016), "Tackling illegal migration issue in Assam", *The Assam Tribune*, June 3.

Som, Nirupom (2012), "Dying for a language", *The Statesman*, April 1.

Thakur, Sankarshan (2020), "World of tomorrow", *The Telegraph*, March 4.

Thakuria, Nava (2017), "Uncertain future", *The Statesman*, September 11.

________ (2020), "Who is an Asomuya?", *The Statesman*, August 17.

________ (2022), "Exclusion & protection", *The Statesman,* May 30.

Verghese, Leah and Naik, Shruti (2020), "Flawed Foreigners' Tribunal", *The Hindu*, October 21.

Vinayak, M., (1992), "Infiltration, a growing threat", *The Hindu*, August 18.

Wankhede Harish (2020), "Waiting for Citizenship", *Economic and Political Weekly,* Vol. LV, No. 13, March 26.

Weiner, Myron, (1983), "The Political Demography of Assam's Anti-immigrant Movement", *Population and Development Review*, Vol. 9, No. 2, June.

________ (1993), "Rejected Peoples and Unwanted Migrants in South Asia", *Economic and Political Weekly,* August 21.

Editorials

Editorial titled "Send them back", *The Hindustan Times*, September 30, 1992.

Editorial titled "Aliens and Identity", *The Statesman*, November 28,1993.

Editorial titled "Stopping the flow", *The Hindu*, May 28, 1994.

Editorial titled "Passage to India", *The Times of India,* October 18, 2013.

Editorial titled "NRC Quagmire", *The Times of India*, July 19, 2019.

Editorial titled "Inclusion over exclusion", *The Hindu*, July 20, 2019.
Editorial titled "Numbing numbers" in *The Hindu,* August 1, 2019.
Editorial titled "Quandary of National Register of Citizens", *Economic & Political Weekly,* September 14, 2019, Vol. LIV, No. 37.
Editorial titled "Mission Impossible", *The Times of India*, October 21, 2019.
Editorial titled "NRC Fallout", *The Times of India,* November 7, 2019.
Editorial titled "Tread Carefully", *The Times of India,* November 21, 2019.
Editorial titled "Ignoble tryst", *The Telegraph,* December 13, 2019.
Editorial titled "Allow Peaceful Stir", in *The Times of India,* December 17, 2019.
Editorial titled "Firefighting Time", *The Times of India*, December 20, 2019.
Editorial titled "Hear the roar", in *The Telegraph*, December 20, 2019.
Editorial titled "Strike CAA Down", *The Times of India,* January 24, 2020.
Editorial titled "Delhi Riots, Again", *The Times of India,* February 26, 2020.
Editorial titled "Correct Course", in *The Times of India,* February 29, 2020.
Editorial titled "Politics of Communal Violence in Delhi", in *Economic & Political Weekly,* Vol. LV, No. 9, February 29, 2020.
Editorial titled "Aadhar as a hurdle", *The Hindu*, March 19, 2021.

Web sites

Citizenship Law Won't Impact Gaons With Portuguese Passports, www.ndtv.com › All India
Over 2 lakh Gaons, enjoying dual citizenship, will have to make a choice between India and Portugal economictimes.indiatimes.com " ..." Politics and Nation *thewire.in* "government" home-ministry-reconstitutes-...
censusindia.gov.in "2011-Common" IntroductionToNpr
It's time for India to adopt dual citizenship – The Print *theprint.in* Opinion
https://www.facebook.com/*...hindu...bangladesh...hindu.../24959253516...*
Remittances to India – Wikipedia *en.wikipedia.org* "wiki" Remittances_to_Inda for the years 2012-13 to 2017-18.
https://en.wikipedia.org/wiki/National_Register_of_Citizens_of_India
www.nationalheraldindia.com "NEWS" India

Newspapers

The Hindu, 2013-2022.
The Statesman, 2013-2022.
The Telegraph, 2013-2022.
The Times of India, 2013-2022.
Anandabazar Patrika, 2013-2022.
Ei Samay, 2013-2022.

Index